Java and Eclipse For Computer Science

By

Sean D. Liming and John R. Malin

Annabooks™

Java and Eclipse for Computer Science

Published in the United States by

Annabooks, LLC.
6432 Glendale Dr.
Yorba Linda, CA 92128 USA
www.annabooks.com

ISBN-13: 978-0-9911887-3-4

Dedication

To our family, friends, and future computer scientists

Table of Contents

Preface

"Tell me and I'll forget; show me and I may remember; involve me and I'll understand."
-Chinese Proverb

Near the end of a 4-week business trip, my mom called to tell me that my old high school needed help. The Computer Science teacher moved to another state, and they needed a teacher to take over the class to get students prepared to take the AP® test. Not an easy position to fill with a few months before the test, and she thought I could help out.

Flash back 28 years earlier. My freshman class was the first in my high school to have a computer course. The course was a computer literacy course that combined three topics: learning what a computer is; knowing how to use a word processor, WordStar; and programming with GWBasic. The computer for the class was the original IBM PC. The IBM PC had two floppy drives, no hard drive, keyboard, no mouse, an option ROM with GWBasic built in, a monochrome monitor, and the system booted to MS-DOS from one of the floppy drives. The book for the class was easy to read, and I was reading through it well before the class started. The use of the word processor application and learning how to make the computer follow instructions opened up a world of creativity for me. Once I had my own PC compatible computer, I was creating computer games, had the computer playing music, and was creating basic database solutions. There were no AP Computer Science or advanced programming languages courses back then. Fast forward a bit. Electronics was my big interest, so my college degree was in Electrical Engineering with a special focus on Computer Engineering. I took classes in Pascal and C to learn some high-level programming. Over the years, I self-taught myself programming languages like VB.NET and C#, and published a few programs for embedded systems. My background was good enough to handle something like a basic course in programming.

Flash forward to my mother's call. I was told that the APCS class was a single class with 13 students. There were a couple of books, tests already developed, and a slide deck. Since I was going to spend the next few months updating another book, I thought it might be interesting to go back to see how things have changed. How hard can this be?

Going back to teach at my old high school was a surreal experience. Memories of what high school was like came back in bits and pieces. One thing I do remember was how substitute teachers were treated. The first thing I did was put together a PowerPoint presentation for the students on my background and all the work I have done in the embedded/IoT market. I described my role as a computer consultant helping companies integrate the Windows operating systems into many different devices such as industrial controls, ATM Machines, Point-of-Sale systems, gaming systems, medical devices, and security systems. The only question from the students was why teach the class. A good question, and my response was to look back and see what schools are teaching now to see if it matches industry needs. From that point on, the students were very attentive; and much to my surprise, much better behaved than I remembered when I was in high school.

The first week was spent reviewing material to see where the students were at in there AP Computer Science preparation, and it quickly was apparent that they were really behind. With the material that was left to cover, school scheduling, and the date for the AP® test coming up, there was little time to do anything but present the material that was available and cover homework assignments. The first new topic to teach was on recursion. How does one teach such a challenging topic to students, many of whom had done almost no programming? The books and other class materials were dry, and nothing I found online was any better nor would hold my interest, much less that of the students. Then I came up with the idea to use a movie that had a parallel concept. You can read the recursion chapter to see how it was presented. The students remembered the movie and got the concept right away, and I also demonstrated a recursion implementation from one of my commercial computer programs. Since this approach to a topic worked, I brought in other programs I had written, robots that I developed, and I shared stories of my real work in industry to keep the class interesting.

As the days progressed, the answer to the question: "How hard could it be?" began to answer itself. The previous teacher chose to use a very simple Java editor that had no debugger. There is no debugger or editor when one takes the final AP® test. So, the chosen editor made sense, but a debugger will help visual learners see what is going on under-the-hood as a program is running. After one student made it known that a friend in another school was using Eclipse in their AP Computer Science course, I quickly scrambled to put a document together and move the class to use the Eclipse development environment. I continued to present course material, but there was something that was missing that wasn't obvious. The student interest in programming wasn't strong. I first thought it was a generational issue, but when I did the old test the students on the reading assignment, no one raised their hand to answer the questions. One day, I asked the class if they were doing the reading assignments from the textbook and without hesitation, one student said "No!" All eyes were on me, and a few nodded their heads in agreement with their fellow classmates. At that moment, the "something missing" became very clear. The main textbook for the class was ineffective.

The previous teacher had other textbooks on the back shelf, and after going through them it was clear that the learn-by-doing element was missing. Computer Science and Computer Programing are considered two separate paths, but in actuality, they are the same thing. A programmer has to have an understanding of the computer science concepts to pick the right solution for the application. Learning computer programming is an individual effort. Everyone's mind works a little differently. In industry, teams of programmers work together to write computer programs, but these teams are made up of individuals that have learned the basics. I was able to self-teach myself different programming languages from books that provided hands-on exercises. There are online programs and videos that provide good information but sitting down and writing code for several hours is how one learns to be a programmer. Hence, the idea of writing this book was born, and I discussed the idea with John who has many more years of programming experience than I.

We first released a small book based on my Eclipse write-up. It was a test to see if it helped others with their APCS studies, and the feedback was positive. Then we laid out what we wanted to accomplish for this book:

- Textbook/ Workbook combination – The National Training Laboratory developed the learning pyramid. The pyramid diagram shows a student's attention rate based on the style of teaching. Lecture and reading were near the bottom, but practice doing (or learn by doing) was at the top. We learned from a few IEEE journals that there is a movement to create a Blended and Flipped Class, giving the students more latitude to explore their interests. This book's style models some of the books we have written for industry. The final result, the basic material for computer science is covered, but intermixed are computer activities to keep the reader active, involved, and above all, programming.

- Logical and creative cognitive process or left brain versus the right brain – Computer programing requires not only the left logical side of the brain, but it also needs the right creative side of the brain to solve programming problems. Using a movie to introduce a computer science topic changed the way to look at a complex topic. We lead off all our chapters with a quote or a saying that gives a theme to the chapter. The idea is to get the creative thoughts flowing.
- Flow from Algebra – The chapter topic order has been put in place so as to follow the normal high school curriculum. AP Computer Science is usually taught at the senior level with students already past Algebra 2. We ease into the computer science by covering math and variables topics well before diving into objects.
- Eclipse IDE – As both of us have worked in industry for some time, we want to see students coming out of school ready to take on job opportunities. It is import to learn the tools of the trade. Chapter 2 covers the reasons why we choose Eclipse IDE over others. The book covers the different features of Eclipse at different points throughout the book. The student will have a good understanding of at least one professional development tool, and they will be able to adapt to other development tools in the future.
- Variety of projects – Rather than focus on one big programming project, we have written up several smaller projects for computer activities and programming homework. Many of these programs will have more features added to them in later chapters. This gives a natural way to review earlier work and further reinforce those principles.
- AP® Computer Science Test – The AP® Computer Science Test is a collaborative effort by many instructors around the country. Every question on the test is a different problem to solve. With the different problems in mind, we put in a variety of computer projects so the student has different types of problems to solve while learning the material.
- Beyond Computer Science material – Chapter 1-10 cover the material that will be on the AP® Computer Science test. Chapters 11-14 introduce other topics that could be used to help those who have to do end-of-the-school-year programming projects.
- The Internet – There is no escaping that the Internet is a powerful learning tool. There are solutions for the common and popular computer science projects and homework assignments on the Internet. Since many programmers rely on the Internet to find solutions, we embrace using the Internet with several activities and homework assignments.

- Our Insights – With many years of working in the industry, we sprinkled in our own experiences and programming techniques. Even with our experience, we can still remember what it was like when we knew nothing about computers and programming, so we tried to incorporate activities that would share some of the ah-ha's we got during the start of our careers.

The basic Computer Science concepts are in the public domain in some form or other, and we spent several years researching, writing, and re-writing to nail down the details and tell the story very differently. Our goal with this book is to provide a logical flow that builds up the students' knowledge as they go from one chapter to the next and provide a learn-by-doing experience along the way. The book is intended to be read from beginning to end. We hope that you find this book a useful tool. It is important to note that every instructor has his or her own method of teaching a class. If you get 10 teachers in a room and ask them how to teach a subject, you will probably get 20 answers. We expect that not everyone will agree with our approach, but we hope it is only a few. Even with all of our efforts to make a more effective book, we are not perfect. Being in the industry for a long time, we can take for granted how we write programs, which makes it challenging when teaching others. There were many little details that had to be covered to meet the curriculum requirements. In the end, mistakes can seep through are there may be areas that could use some polishing, so we encourage you to send us any feedback: http://www.annabooks.com/Contact.html. Any textbook is really a work in progress, so we welcome suggestions for improvement that we can incorporate in future editions.

-Sean Liming
May 2018

When Sean talked to me about producing a much-needed high school level Advanced Placement Computer Science textbook, it made me think about my start in the world of computers and programming. When I was an undergraduate, there was no computer science department or courses. There were no personal computers, cell phones, nor even any pocket calculators. We did computer programming on large mainframe computers as a tool for numerical analysis classes or to boil down experimental data using a Univac 1107 and then 1108. The programming languages we used were FORTRAN and ALGOL 60 on the Univac and Dartmouth BASIC. We programmed with punch-cards and printing terminals, teletype machines, no CRT or LCD displays in those days. Our Univac mainframe system on campus was managed as an open system; so, instead of submitting a deck of cards and coming back later for the printout and cards deck, we could actually put our decks into the card readers ourselves and wait for the printouts. The computer ran 24/7 with certain hours for certain classes, other hours for the profs' and grad students' research, and then there were times in the wee hours that were open to anyone. I spent many an hour during those wee hours getting my programs to run. I remember that there was one program we had to write for a numerical analysis class that was a root finding program that had the sneaky problem built in to wake us up to the precision of the variables we were using. If you programmed the equations in a straightforward manner, you would get intermediate calculations that would overrange the size of the variables that we were using. When we starting getting overrange errors during our calculations, the instructor wanted us to figure out that we would have to reorder the calculations so that the math was still correct, but that the intermediate calculations would not overrange the variables. I, on the other hand, figured out how to tell the computer how to use double-precision variables. I got an A for my ingenuity.

When I graduated with my MS in Physics, I almost immediately started using computers as design and analysis tools. The computers ranged from programmable calculators, like the HP-35, and the HP 98xx series of desktop computers, to Univac and IBM mainframes. I used the programmable devices of the day to solve complex differential equations by modeling the physical devices that I was working with, like grinding and polishing equipment, to determine their horsepower requirements, when I worked in the specialty glass industry.

When I was doing CRT design is when I got my first "personal computer". It was a DEC PDP-11/34 minicomputer. It also was my first embedded system. Through the use of interface cards and the software that I wrote, the PDP-11/34 was able to control all the subsystems for the CRT and not only do specialty testing but also produce custom display sequences. At this time, I had chosen to move away from the more traditional programming languages, like FORTRAN, Algol, and Pascal, and became interested in C. This was a programming language that gave you the low-level bit control of assembly language in a more structured programming language. I had UNIX installed on my PDP-11/34 with a C compiler, which allowed me to control and sequence bit patterns to the CRT control systems.

Shortly after this, the IBM-PC was launched, and anyone who was doing programming was all over it. I helped design and write several commercial products for the IBM-PC shortly after its introduction. The understanding I gained about both the IBM-PC hardware, as well as, its operating system, led me to more embedded system work, which was essentially putting MS-DOS into control systems with specialized software. The first of these was a network communications controller. These network controllers were always pushing the state of technology to get the maximum speed and throughput. These controllers were the frontrunners of what eventually would be the backbone of the Internet. Because of the speed and response requirements, I was exposed to and learned real-time programming on one of the first real-time kernels to be put on Intel x86 microprocessors, VRTX. This gave me a unique set of programming tools which took me down the path of embedded systems. I've worked with commercial and specialty real-time operating systems, wrote device drivers, and application and control software using many of the popular programming languages: C, C++, C#, Visual Basic, and now Java.

When I took my first programming class in college, I had no idea that computer programming would be such a big part of my career. Today, it is almost mandatory to interact with and program computers at some level. Many K-through-12 school systems are adding "coding" as mandatory classes, now. Learning how to program is as important as any other class in school, so I was more than interested in helping the next generation learn the core basics. Even if you never write code professionally, it helps to understand the structure and logic of the code that controls all the software-driven devices that we interact with, now, on a daily basis. We have tried to share a lot of the experience we have learned over the years directly through the exercises in this book, but we have also left some things to be discovered along the way, as well. We hope you enjoy the content and format of this book and that it stimulates your ingenuity.

-John R. Malin
May 2018

Acknowledgements

It has taken a long time to develop this book, and we have had lots of encouragement and recommendations from many people we know. The book would not have been possible without the aid of several individuals and companies. Our apologies if we forgot anyone.

Firstly, we have to thank Elaine Liming, Tanya Katnic, and others who recommended Sean as a substitute instructor. Of course, thanks go to the 13 students of Mater Dei High School's (Santa Ana, CA) AP® Computer Science class of 2011-2012 who triggered the idea and need for a different presentation of the material, practical examples, and insights from industry.

Special thanks to Almas Baimagambetov who allowed us to use his basic Frogger JavaFX game example as one of the JavaFX game projects. After several months of looking into different Java game engine possibilities, his JavaFX game examples were a perfect fit for the size and scope of the chapter.

Another special thanks goes out to the Eclipse foundation for the use of their logo on the cover and to Cindy Hickson & Mark Schreier of Oracle Corporation who help us secure permission to use the "Components of Oracle's Java SE 8" figure.

Finally, we would like to thank the people who helped put the finishing touches on the book, Becky Hayes and Tanya Katnic.

Annabooks

Annabooks provides a unique approach to embedded system services with multiple support levels. Our different offerings include books, articles, training, and project consulting. Our publications and courses focus on embedded PC architecture and Windows Embedded/IoT, which reach a wide audience from Fortune 500 companies to small organizations. We continue to expand our future services into new technologies and unique topics.

Books and eBooks

Starter Guide for Windows 10 IoT Enterprise
Professional's Guide to POS for .NET
Real-Time Development from Theory to Practice
The PC Handbook

Training Courses

Windows® 10 IoT Enterprise Training Course
Windows® 10 IoT Core Pro Training Course

Web: www.annabooks.com

1 The Future Starts Now

"Do. Or do not. There is no try."
- Yoda, from the movie: *The Empire Strikes Back,* A Lucasfilm Limited Production (1980)

July 29th, 9:15 PM Paris, France
A customer at a local bistro signals the waiter to bring the check and pays the bill. The waiter grabs the remote pin pad to process the chip card. He enters the final bill total, inserts the card, and waits for the connection. The card is processed in a few seconds.

July 28th, 9:00 AM New York City
A bike mail courier knows the morning traffic is going to be its typical congestion. He puts on the earbuds connected to the smartphone on the bicycle's handlebars, starts the music player, and launches the GPS mapping application. After several stops and the frequent honking of horns, he arrives at the drop-off location.

July 28th, 8:00 AM Chicago
A stock trader gets into the office and starts up her computer and all three monitors came to life. After she logs in, the system immediately launches the trade ticker program on one screen, business news feed on another, and company database program on the third screen, just in time to take her first client online meeting.

July 28th, 5:00 AM Pacific Ocean, 80 Nautical Miles from San Francisco
A bulk cargo ship is closing in on its destination after a 15-day crossing from Port of Kaohsiung, Taiwan. The captain gazes across the latest advanced technology in the bridge. Technology has made it easier to navigate and pilot ships and the bridge looks more like the console of a

spacecraft than it does to the basic analog controls and dials of 20 years ago. A call is received from the port to indicate the final correct heading, so a tug can help with the final docking. The captain gives directions to the pilot who enters the course into the computer console.

August 1st, 2:00 PM Grand Taipei Hotel, Taiwan
The check-in receptionist has called over the next guest in line. After greetings are exchanged, the guest provides the reservation information. The receptionist enters the information and form of payment into the computer. The computer presents several floor and room options, which she discusses with the guest. Once the guest selects the room, she creates two RFID keys, which she gives to the guest.

August 2nd, 3:00 PM Atlanta
The CAD designer takes her laptop to the meeting room to go over the new milling work with the machine operator. After covering the changes to the design and how the milling machine will be set up, the machine operator heads out to the factory floor. He goes to the milling machine's CNC interface and pulls down the new design from the company server. While he inspects the water and hydraulic lines, another worker loads the aluminum block onto the table. After the checkout is completed, the machine operator goes back to the CNC interface and clicks a button to start the milling process.

1.1 Our Connected World

All around the world, technology has been integrated into daily life. Whether the job is a waiter, broker, lawyer, doctor, ship captain, movie director, shop clerk, or mechanic, in today's world, every job interacts with computers in some way. The CEO of General Electric, Jeff Immelt, wrote in Linkedin's *Big ideas & Innovation* series in August 2016: "If you are joining the company in your 20s, unlike when I joined, you're going to learn to code. It doesn't matter whether you are in sales, finance or operations. You may not end up being a programmer, but you will know how to code. We are also changing the plumbing inside the company to connect everyone and make the culture change possible. This is existential and we're committed to this."

There are many computer devices of all shapes and sizes, such as ATM machines, thermostats, slot machines, point-of-sale systems, cloud servers, and projection systems. All of them need to be designed, built, and programmed. With the Internet of Things, Big Data, artificial intelligence, and billions of devices connecting to the Internet, more programmers are needed to fill the programming jobs required to implement these solutions.

1.2 Computer Activity 1.1: Computing Ideas Spread Throughout Human History

Getting a device that fits in the palm of the hand, that allows you to place phone calls, and that connects you to a world of information didn't happen overnight. Just the leap from a handheld calculator to the smartphone took 40 years; but the basic computing concepts go back centuries and come from different cultures, political situations, and a whole cast of characters that helped create our digital age. There is a lot of history and background to cover, but rather than dive into a whole history of computing and the drivers of the technology, we will let you use this digital technology to follow your curiosity and fill in the blanks. This is the first of several computer activities that are in the book. Instead of a lot of reading, we want to keep you active and engaged. Like the quote from Yoda, doing is important. As a programmer, you will find that using the Internet is a helpful tool in programming.

In this computer activity, you will find a list of names and terms below. Fill in the blanks with the names and terms that match the description. Using the Internet, you can search for each name and term that is not familiar to you and see the relevance each has contributed to the computing devices we have today.

Abacus
Ada Lovelace
Antikythera mechanism
Alan Turing
Altair 8800
ARPANET
Baghdad
Blaise Pascal
Bug
Charles Babbage
Charles Francis Jenkins
Dorothy Vaughan
Douglas Engelbart

George Boole
Grace Hopper
Guglielmo Marconi
Harwell CADET
Hedy Lamarr
Henry Edward Roberts
India
James E. West
John Bardeen
John von Neumann
Joseph Marie Jacquard
Katherine Johnson
Leonardo Bonacci "Fibonacci"

Martin Cooper
Nikola Tesla
Philo Farnsworth
Punch cards
QWERTY
Samuel Morse
Short Code
TCP/IP
Tim Berners-Lee
Walter Brattain
William Shockley
Xerox PARC

1. Developed approximately 4500 years ago, it was the first device used for counting:____________
2. Discovered in an ancient shipwreck in 1901, this ancient Greek device has been dated to 205 BCE and is believed to be the oldest analog computer:____________________
3. The number or digit 0 "zero" was invented in this country between the 5th to 7th centuries AD:_____________
4. The Arabic numerals 1,2,3,4,5,6,7,8,9 was developed by Arab mathematicians in the city of _____________ around 700, and was popularized in the Europe by Italian mathematician _____________ in 1202.
5. Invented the first working mechanical calculator in 1642: ____________________
6. In 1801, _______________ invented a mechanical loom that could be programmed to weave different textile patterns by using _______________. The loom is known as the first programmable machine.
7. Invented the telegraph for long distance communications in 1830s:_____________________
8. The inventor of the Analytical Engine in 1837 is known as the father of computing:_______________
9. This person is known as the world's first programmer: ________________________
10. This author wrote the book *The Mathematical Analysis of Logic* in 1847 that introduce Boolean algebra: _____________________
11. The typewriter was invented in 1860. In 1873, Christopher Latham Sholes created this keyboard layout that is still used today: _____________
12. This person is credited with inventing the radio in 1897:__________________; and this person made the first transatlantic wireless connection in 1901:_________________
13. These are the two inventors who demonstrated television in the late 1920's:

____
14. This actress invented "spread spectrum radio", which is used in cellular technology today: _______________

15. He wrote the paper "On Computable Numbers, With An Application to the Entscheidungsproblem", which led to the invention of software and our modern computer: ____________________
16. In 1947, these three individuals invented the transistor:______________________________
17. It is considered one of the first high-level computer language developed in 1949:_________________
18. The Zuse Z1, Atanasoff–Berry Computer, Colossus and ENIAC were computers that used electromechanical relays and vacuum tubes; this computer in 1955 is the first to only use transistors: ___________________
19. A mathematician who calculated the orbit trajectory for John Glenn's space flight and worked with another mathematician and computer scientist that gave NASA confidence in using digital computers. Who were they: ____________________ _____________
20. The developer of the first software compiler:____________, and urban legend has been associated with a moth in a computer for the term used in computers today:_________________
21. Invented the foil electret microphone, the same microphone that is used in cell phone and computers today:_________________
22. Invented the first computer mouse in 1968:____________________
23. The original project name for the Internet developed in1969:__________
24. ____________ invented the handheld cellular mobile phone in 1973 while working at Motorola.
25. The personal computer was first developed by ____________________ in 1975 and the computer was called the ________________
26. The first graphical user interface (GUI) was demonstrated at _____________ in 1975
27. This protocol was introduced in 1982 as a standard networking protocol for the ARPANET: _______________
28. The World Wide Web and the first web browser were invented by _____________ in 1989.

1.3 The 1s and 0s that make Computers Work

The human race has come a long way from using stones, sticks, and fingers for counting. The transistor led to integrated circuits and the microprocessor, which were the key technologies developed in the 20th century that made the digital age happen. We will leave it to physics, chemistry, and electrical engineering to discuss the details of the inner workings of a transistor, but the simplest description is that a transistor acts like a switch.

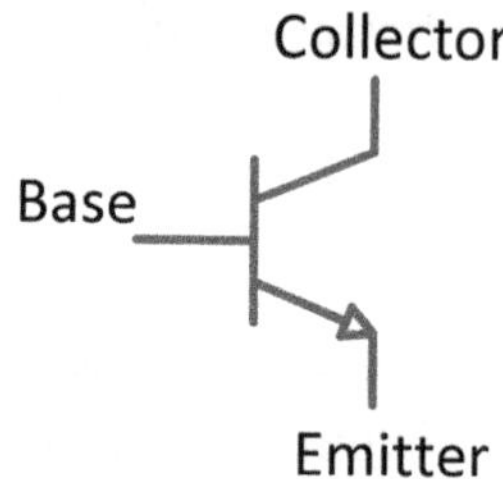

Figure 1.1 NPN Transistor

When the switch is on, this is the 1 state; and when it is an off, it is in the 0 state, thus a transistor is a binary or 2-state device. Computers do nothing more than perform operations on the binary values of 1 and 0, thus computers only know of a base 2 numbering system. The 1s and 0s can be combined together to represent numbers and letters. The table below shows the binary values of 0 through 15. Over the years, programmers have developed terminology for groups of 1s and 0s:

Bits – single digit that is either a 1 or 0, another way to look at is 1^2.
Nibble – 4 bits or 2^2
Byte – 8 bits or 2^3
Word – two bytes, 16 bits, or 2^4
Double Word – 4 bytes, 32 bits, or 2^5
Kilobytes (KB) – 1024 bytes, 8192 bits, 2^{10}
Megabytes (MB) – 1,048,576 bytes, 8,388,608 bits, or 2^{20}
Gigabyte (GB) – 1,073,741,824 bytes, 8,589,934,592 bits, or 2^{30}

Having to manage many 1s and 0s is easy for computers, but a bit cumbersome for humans, thus new base number systems are used to help make more sense for humans. Table 1.1 below lists Binary (Base 2), Octal (base 8), and Hexadecimal (base 16) for the Decimal values 0 through 15.

Decimal Base 10	Binary (BIN) Base 2	Octal (Oct) Base 8	Hexadecimal (Hex) Base 16
0	0000	0	0
1	0001	1	1
2	0010	2	2
3	0011	3	3
4	0100	4	4
5	0101	5	5
6	0110	6	6
7	0111	7	7
8	1000	10	8
9	1001	11	9
10	1010	12	A
11	1011	13	B
12	1100	14	C
13	1101	15	D
14	1110	16	E
15	1111	17	F

Table 1.1 Base Number Systems

Computers perform math and logical operations in binary. For example

1001 + 11 = 1100
or in decimal: 9 + 3 = 12

If you ever wondered what the Programmer mode was for your PC'S calculator is for, now you know.

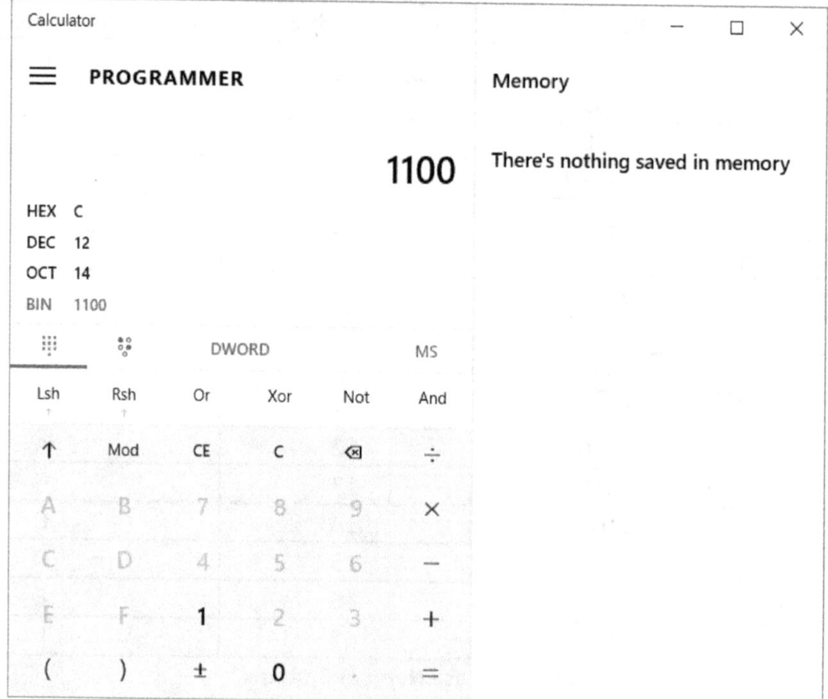

Figure 1.2 - Microsoft Calculator in Programmer Mode

Letters and special characters can also be represented in 1s and 0s. The ASCII (American Standard Code for Information Interchange) and Unicode are industry standards for numerical values that represent characters, encoding characters as binary numbers. ASCII and Unicode tables or converters can be found on the web.

1.4 Computer Architecture

Before there were digital computers, analog computers were the computation devices. Modern analog computers were developed in the early 20th century; but by the end of the century, digital computers dominated. So why did digital computers come to take over most computing tasks, why do they speak binary, and how do 1's and 0's both control these computers and manage the storing and manipulation of data? After all, analog computers existed long before digital computers. Complex mechanical analog computers have been found that date back to between 150 and 100 BC, with the Antikythera mechanism being probably the oldest known analog computer. One of the first modern analog computers was not electronic. It was the slide rule, which was arguably one of the first handheld computers. Even after the birth of digital computers, analog computers were still used in applications where the digital computers of the time just didn't have the compact size, speed, and power to manage the job. Automobiles up through the 1970's, and even beyond, relied heavily on analog computers for the control of their subsystems. These analog computers were largely non-electronic, even non-electric. These computers were mechanical, hydraulic, and pneumatic. Even after the microprocessor was being commercially used, analog computers still dominated in automobiles. The temperature and mechanical environment of an automobile is very challenging for electronics, so much of what was in the engine compartment was handled with non-electronic analog computers until extended temperature range electronics with the ability to handle the g-forces in a car were designed and manufactured at a relatively low price. Advancements in technology allowed microprocessors to have a wide temperature range, a small size, and a cheap price, thus most cars today have digital computers controlling the engine, transmission, braking, suspension, and dashboard functions.

Digital computers use 1's and 0's because it is very easy to make devices out of switches. A simple switch can either be on or off, providing the 1's and 0's of the binary number system. With the invention of transistor switches, it was easy to have transistors create and reliably sense the binary signals without having to provide a great deal of power supply regulation and signal noise cancellation. It is also easy to create a lot of transistor switches in a very small area, and hence the development of digital microelectronics allows us to put a computer in your pocket that would have taken rooms to accommodate when digital devices were first imagined. Binary arithmetic is quite easy to do with binary logic devices, so basic computing devices are simple to design and manufacture.

OK, so we have digital devices that we can make very small, so how do we harness them to do what we want? What is needed is a digital computer that will take instructions, encoded in binary, which will tell the computer what we want it to do and act on data, also encoded in binary. These encoded instructions are stored sequentially in memory and are separate from data, which is also stored in memory. Such a digital computer goes back to the Analytical Engine. Today's reprogrammable computer was first conceived by Alan Turing and made practical by John von Neumann whose paper *First Draft of Report on the EDVAC* led to the creation of the ENIAC computer. Von Neumann architecture, Figure 1.3, describes a digital computer's internal architecture. It is divided into several components:

1. Central Processing Unit (CPU)
    a. Arithmetic Logic Unit (ALU) that performs the mathematics
    b. Control Unit that has the instruction register and program counter
2. Memory to store data and instructions
3. Input mechanisms
4. Output mechanisms

Note: Most of today's modern microprocessors fall into 8-bit, 16-bit, 32-bit, or 64-bit classification. This classification is based on the width of the memory bus, the word size, and the ALU's ability to handle adding and subtracting of n-bits. An 8-bit processor can typically only access 8 bits of memory in one read or write cycle and add or subtract numbers up to 8 bits in size. A 16-bit processor can typically only access 16 bits of memory in one read or write cycle and add or subtract numbers up to 16 bits in size, and so forth.

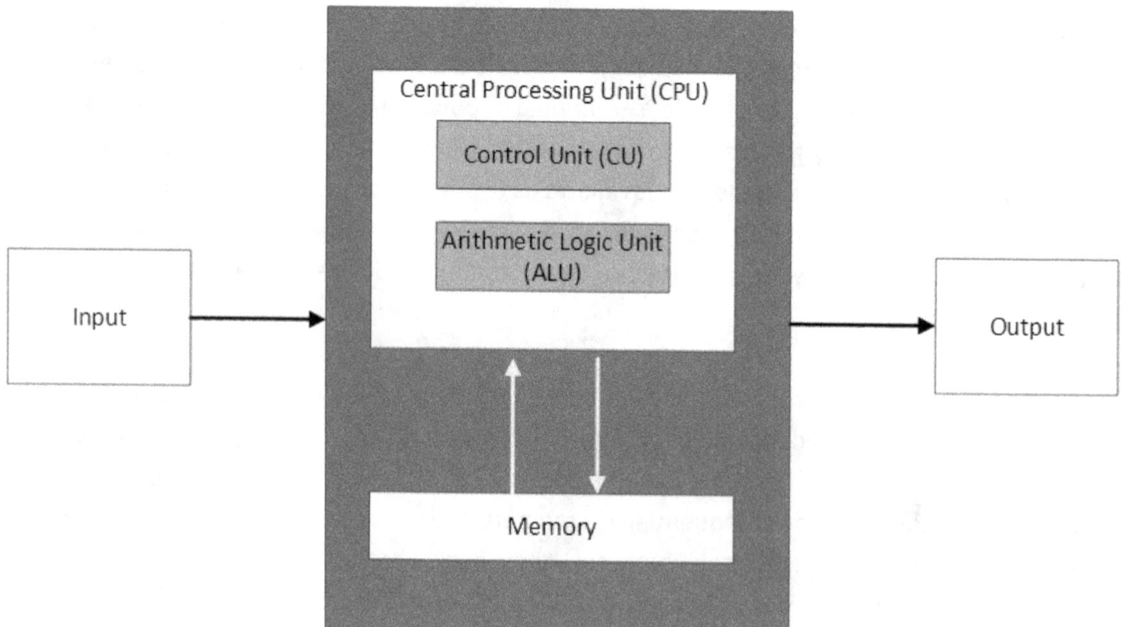

Figure 1.3 - Von Neumann Architecture Scheme

We can see that a computer's CPU has access to the memory of the computer. The CPU also has a Control Unit which is used to read memory locations and interpret what the contents of these memory locations mean. The Control Unit has a program counter, which is used to generate the address of the next instruction's memory location to read. A clock drives the Control Unit, which governs the pace at which the CPU reads its way through the instruction memory. As an instruction memory location is read, the program counter is incremented to point to the next location to read. The instruction that was read is analyzed by the CU's internal logic to determine what to do. Of the many operations that can be encoded in the CPU's instruction memory, the instruction may direct that additional successive memory locations be read and stored into internal CPU registers to then be acted upon, it may direct that the program counter be modified to jump to a new location in instruction memory and start executing code there, or it may direct the Arithmetic Logic Unit to perform an arithmetic operation on some data. These are just examples of some of the many operations that could be specified.

Back in the 1940s and 1950s, computers filled large rooms. The input devices where switches and punch cards (remember the loom), and the output was a printer. Now, whether it is the cell phone or a PC, most of today's modern computers still follow the von Neumann architecture, but the input and output peripherals have made computers friendlier to human interaction.

Figure 1.4 - Modern Computer

In today's computers, Figure 1.4, there is the microprocessor or microcontroller that contains the ALU, control unit, internal busses, and external bus interfaces. RAM and a firmware flash are external to the microprocessor. Input and output devices, as well as, storage devices both inside and outside the device connect to the external buses. To make computers reprogrammable, an operating system stored in an internal drive is launched into memory and provides the ability to load and run multiple applications. With all these elements, every general-purpose computer system follows a basic startup process:

1. Upon startup, the microprocessor points to a starting address in memory where the first instruction is fetched. The instruction is part of the firmware that is stored on a flash device.
2. The firmware initializes the various registers in the microprocessor and any external chipsets and input/output devices. If you have ever made changes to a computer's BIOS settings, these settings get initialized on startup.
3. The firmware brings the computer to a stable point to launch the operating system. To do this, the firmware looks for a boot device, which will have the operating system stored on it and a bootloader to load and run the operating system. The firmware will load and execute the bootloader code; which in turn, will load and execute the operating system. Once the firmware loads and turns over control to the bootloader, it is no longer needed.
4. As the operating system launches, device drivers will be loaded to take over control of the different hardware devices that are either resident in the microcontroller or connected to the microcontroller's external bus system.
5. Once the operating system has loaded and completely taken over control of all internal and external systems, the operating system will put itself in a state where it is looking for user input. At this point, the user can log in.

1.5 The Evolution of Computer Programming

As computers have evolved so has the way they are programmed. Gone are the days of flipping switches, paper tape, and punch cards. As more complex tasks were being demanded of the computer, focusing on 1s and 0s was too complex. Assembly language was too low-level and direct to the machine, but there was a need for a better way to write programs that address some of the repetitive code. In the late 1950's and through the 60's, higher-level programming languages and compilers were developed to allow programmers to write programs more fluently. Some of the first computer programming languages were ALGOL, FORTRAN, LISP, COBOL, and

BASIC. Programmers would write the program in the programming language and then run a compiler program that would take the program code and translate the program into machine code to create an executable program.

Until the 1970s, most programs were procedural or linear style programming. As programs got bigger and more complex, structured programming languages like C and Pascal were developed to help better organize programs into blocks of code (aka functions and subroutines). Eventually, this led to blocks of code or objects that could be reused for different programs, which led to the creation of C++. For a long time, C/C++ was the programming language of choice since it combined simple programming syntax for both high-level and low-level programming. In the 1990s, tools from Microsoft and Borland combined editors and debuggers, making development a little easier. Memory management became a challenge if programs were to support different processor architectures. Another limitation was that compiled applications had to be recompiled to run on different hardware platforms. This led to the development of portable programming languages like Java.

1.6 A Very Brief History of Java

In the late 70's and early 80's, the concept of write once and run on many systems was being explored at the University of San Diego with a version of Pascal called p-code. This early version of a managed code engine was popular on the first Apple computers, but the IBM PC with MS-DOS dominated the market. The idea that drove p-code was pushed aside.

In the early 1990's, developers at SUN Microsystems (now owned by Oracle) started the new wave of managed code languages called Java. The goal was to create Object-Oriented Programs (OOP) that could run on any platform with the help of a virtual machine. The virtual machine would handle any of the memory management clean-up. The growth of embedded systems (dedicated computers) was a natural target because of the breadth of operating systems and microprocessor used in the industry. The first device to use Java was an entertainment controller for cable television, but it didn't catch on. Java could have died at this point, but like anything that finds success, timing is everything. The Internet was in its infancy, and Internet developers saw the advantages of Java to write web applications that can run on any computer. Java quickly became the language for the Internet.

Today, Java is the top programming language used in the industry just ahead of C/C++. Java not only dominates the Internet, but it is used in many devices that we use every day. It is because of its popularity that Java was the programming language chosen to be on the AP® Computer Science exam.

1.7 Compiler versus Interpreter

A compiler and interpreter help to take the code we write in a higher language and convert it to something the computer can actually run. Today's compilers take the code and run it through multiple passes to turn it into something that the computer can run. Interpreted programming languages, like BASIC or Python, are compiled when the program is first executed. There are tradeoffs between the approaches when it comes to development and performance. It is a matter of the application that will decide which language that you are going to use.

For languages like Java, a compiler is used to translate the program into machine independent byte-code. A Java virtual machine is used to run the final byte-code, which handles the final translation to machine code. Even though the Java language is machine-independent, a Java virtual machine needs to be ported to a target platform. In the next chapter, you will see different Java virtual machine downloads available for different operating systems.

1.8 Computer Science

The opening line of the chapter is poignant to the start of any journey. Like any job or skill, you have to start somewhere to be a programmer. There are many different types of computer programs: firmware, ASIC programming, graphical interface applications, device drivers, security, and cloud computing, just to name a few. The world of programming has grown up so much that a whole scientific study has evolved around programming. Scattered throughout the book are various definitions, which brings us to the first term, Computer Science:

Definition: *Computer Science* – Simple definition: The study of automating algorithmic processes that scale.

The definition may seem abstract and short, but there are many different fields in computer science that range from the theoretical to the practical.

The first Computer Science degree program was formed at University of Cambridge Computer Laboratory in 1953, and the first program in the United States was established at Purdue University in 1962 as more computers became available. Today, there are about 258 universities with Computer Science programs in the United States. The computer science field will continue to grow and scale as cloud, artificial intelligence, and quantum computing takes shape over the next 50 years.

If you continue in a degree program in computer science, future courses will cover data structures, algorithms, computer architecture, operating systems, assembly language programming, C++ programming, database design, security, parallel processing, and artificial intelligence. Learning Java means you will be learning structured programming. There are different types of programming such as linear and event-driven programming. Other courses will cover these programming styles. If you would rather dive deeper into the design of computer hardware or integrated circuits, you will want to look into degrees in Electrical or Computer Engineering. If you decide that the world programming is not for you, we hope that we have provided some insight and appreciation for what programmers do.

1.9 AP® Computer Science Exam and About this Book

The AP® Computer Science test is developed by the College Board (www.collegebaord.org). The AP programs provide students the ability to take college-level courses in high school and to get college credit based on the results of taking an AP® exam associated with the course. The AP® Computer Science course is focused on the introduction to Computer Science that provides the fundamentals of problem solving, structured programming, use and implementation of commonly used algorithms, basic understandings of design, the ability to write and test Java programs based on the standard Java class library, and the ability to read and understand computer programs.

The AP® Computer Science Exam is broken into two parts. The first part of the exam consists of 40 multiple choice questions. You will have 1 hour and 30 minutes to answer all the questions. If you do the math, you have 2.25 minutes for each question. The second part of the exam is a free response section (written response) which has 4 questions with the same time constraint of 1 hour and 30 minutes. The math comes out to 22.5 minutes for each question. There are many computer science books, videos, and websites to help you prepare for the test. All of which are good to look into as they provide different teaching approaches to the subject matter. The goal of this book is to provide you with the fundamentals of computer science while learning a computer language and to get you familiar with real-world development tools. Chapters 2 through 10 of this book provide the basic subject matter that will be covered in the class and the exam. The later chapters bring all the topics together to create bigger programs. We do recommend that you get the study guides that come with sample tests. These tests will help give you insight and approaches on how to take the exam.

When it comes to computer programming, the best way to learn is to sit down at the computer and write programs. In the spirit of Yoda, the learn-by-doing approach is the best way to become a proficient programmer and will help you with the exam. There are a number of computer activities and programming assignments in the book to help you get a hands-on experience.

Note: *AP® is a trademark registered by the College Board, which was not involved in the production of, and does not endorse, this product.*

1.10 Summary and Homework Assignments

The long road to putting a computer in everyone's hand all around the world started centuries ago. As technology continues to change, the world of programming and Computer Science will continue to grow and evolve. Learning how to program can open up a whole big world of opportunity. This book is intended to help you with those first steps into programming. The next chapter will get you set up with the tools needed to write programs, but before we get there, here are a few final exercises questions:

1.10.1 Questions

1. Computing concepts aside, humanity has been creating tools to help improve society. Historians have found that the Ancient Greeks created other machines besides the Antikythera mechanism. List 3 of these ancient machines.
2. What is a modern analog computer that is small enough to be worn and is still in use today?
3. What company invented the first microprocessor? What was the first product that used this microprocessor?
4. Why was the transistor developed? What problem did it solve?
5. What is the hexadecimal value for the decimal number 20?

6. What is the ASCII binary value for the letter A?
7. What computer systems use the Octal number base? Why?
8. Name a popular computer architecture besides the von Neumann architecture.
9. What is the von Neumann bottleneck?
10. How does an ALU do subtraction? For example: 5 - 2?
11. What is the sum of the hexadecimal values 4F and 2A in hexadecimal and in decimal?

2 Eclipse and Objects

"The best things in life are free. The second-best things are very, very expensive."
– Coco Chanel

The founder of the iconic fashion brand didn't have computers in mind when she made this quote. As computer technologies go in and out of fashion, the push for free open-source software is becoming very pervasive. GNU Linux is what most people think about when it comes to free open software. Because of its economics and the technical ability to scale devices, Linux is by far the most widely used kernel. Think of all the Linux devices out there: smartphones, wireless routers, Blu-Ray players, and LCD TVs. There is something about "free" that seems to be working.

Programming tools have come a long way, too. We have gone from physical switches to punch cards to terminal editors to integrated development environments (IDE). The IDEs are one of the greatest achievements for programming. The combination of editor and debugger helps improve development time. There are many IDEs available for different programming languages. For Java, one of the most popular IDE's is Eclipse.

2.1 *Why Eclipse*

As there are many fashion brands available, there are many IDEs available for Java development. NetBeans, JCreator, BlueJ, and IntelliJ are just a few of the editors available. Every developer has his or her reason for choosing one IDE over another. It comes down to taste and style. Even though we, as authors, are familiar with Visual Studio, there are several reasons why we chose to write about Eclipse over the other Java IDEs.

Eclipse has a long history and has been backed by several major companies. VisualAge development tools were originally created by Object Technology International (OTI). IBM purchased OTI in 1996, and they create Eclipse based on VisualAge as the new Java-based IDE replacement. In 2001, IBM, Borland, QNX Software Systems, Red Hat, SuSE, and three other companies formed a consortium around Eclipse, which later became the Eclipse Foundation. The power of the Eclipse IDE is the ability to expand the base framework with plugins to add new tools and capabilities. The original consortium companies developed plugins for Eclipse, which saved them time from developing their own IDE tools. When Google set out to create their Android software development kit (SDK), they chose Eclipse for the development tools. Google has since moved on to create their own IDE for Android. Many other companies have created plugins for Eclipse, and because of the large support, the consortium has created a marketplace for free and pay for features. Because of this long history, Eclipse is synonymous with Java development. Best of all, Eclipse is free, which brings us back to the chapter introductory quote.

Some instructors choose simpler IDEs with no debugger to force students to think about what they are doing. There is nothing wrong with this approach, since you only have your brain when you take a test. Keep in mind for a course with tests, it is important to try problems out on paper first. The ability to see the program running in a debugger provides the visual feedback for what is really going on. Most programmers learn through using the debugger or what we like to refer to as "learn-by-doing".

We not only want you to learn the basic computer science concepts and a programming language, but we want to also teach you how to use development tools. Potential employers want to see that you have experience with development tools. With this foundation, you will be able to build up your programming experience, and you can later move to other tools and programming languages that you find appealing.

Disclaimer: Eclipse is an expansive tool. The Eclipse marketplace has over a thousand plugins that can be added to aid with program development. As we introduce different Eclipse features, we will also introduce third-party products that are related to the chapter topic. Some of these products are free and some have to be paid for. We are only introducing these plugins as examples of how to expand the use of Eclipse. These plugins were chosen at random or for specific examples and are not being endorsed by the authors or publisher.

With our answer to the question, let's get your development system set up.

2.2 Computer Activity 2.1: JDK and Eclipse Download and Installation

The Java SE JDK (Java Development Kit) and the *Eclipse IDE for Java Developers* are the basic tools needed for this book. Both are free downloads. Initial writing for this book was several Eclipse versions ago, which started with Juno. Java and Eclipse are constantly evolving, so the versions we talk about in this book are guaranteed to be older than the latest releases that you will find online. The steps listed here should stay consistent, but the pictures may change slightly with newer versions. You may have to make some adjustments, but the basic sequence should be the same.

The Eclipse IDE is written mostly in Java; so, it needs the Java runtime environment, JRE, to be able to run. To develop code using the Java programming language with Eclipse, not only is the Java runtime environment, JRE, needed; but also, the Java compilers and development tools, which are added in the Java Development Kit, JDK. The Java JRE is a subset of the Java JDK. When you install the JDK, the JRE is installed, as well as the Java compilers and development tools. Therefore, to develop code in Java using Eclipse, you must install the JDK and Eclipse for Java development. For a graphic outline of the Java environment for the Standard Edition 8, see Figure 2.1, below:

Java Language	Java Language
Tools & Tool APIs	java, javac, javadoc, jar, javap, jdeps, Scripting
	Security, Monitoring, JConsole, VisualVM, JMC, JFR
	JPDA, JVM TI, IDL, RMI, Java DB, Deployment
	Internationalization, Web Services, Troubleshooting
Deployment	Java Web Start, Applet / Java Plug-in
	JavaFX
User Interface Toolkits	Swing, Java 2D, AWT, Accessibility
	Drag and Drop, Input Methods, Image I/O, Print Service, Sound
Integration Libraries	IDL, JDBC, JNDI, RMI, RMI-IIOP, Scripting
Other Base Libraries	Beans, Security, Serialization, Extension Mechanism
	JMX, XML JAXP, Networking, Override Mechanism
	JNI, Date and Time, Input/Output, Internationalization
	lang and util
lang and util Base Libraries	Math, Collections, Ref Objects, Regular Expressions
	Logging, Management, Instrumentation, Concurrency Utilities
	Reflection, Versioning, Preferences API, JAR, Zip
Java Virtual Machine	Java HotSpot Client and Server VM

JDK
JRE
Compact Profiles
Java SE API

Figure 2.1 Components of Oracle's Java SE 8

When you are choosing which version of Eclipse and Java JDK, if you are developing on Windows or Linux, you must also decide which bit-width versions to choose. Windows and Linux can be either 32-bit or 64-bit, but Mac OS is 64-bit, only. Eclipse is available in 32-bit and 64-bit versions for Windows and Linux, also. When you install Eclipse, the Java environment bit-width has to match the bit-width of the version of Eclipse that you will install after it. Therefore, for a 32-bit installation of Eclipse, the 32-bit version of the Java JDK must be installed, first. Similarly, for a 64-bit installation of Eclipse, the 64-bit version of the Java JDK must be installed first. Because the Eclipse and JDK bit-widths must match, the libraries that are available to Eclipse are of the same bit-width as Eclipse, itself; so, the executables that are developed in the Eclipse IDE will be of the same bit-width as Eclipse. Currently, there is no way that a 32-bit Eclipse installation can generate a 64-bit executable image, for example. The compiler and libraries are provided by the Java environment, the Java environment bit-width has to match the bit-width of Eclipse or it will not install; so, to create 32-bit executables, you have to install 32-bit Eclipse and Java JDK, and to create 64-bit executables, you have to install 64-bit Eclipse and Java JDK.

2.2.1 Java JDK

The Java JDK contains the Java runtime environment, the compilers, packaging, and debugging tools that Eclipse requires.

1. Open a web browser and go to the Java download site: http://www.oracle.com/technetwork/java/javase/downloads/index.html
2. The link will take you to the Java SE Downloads tab (SE means standard edition). Java is constantly being updated. At the time of this writing, the latest working release is Java 9. Java 8 is now at the end of its development and is static. If you want to work with a version that is not being continually updated, we recommend that you start with Java 8. Scroll down to Java SE 8, Figure 2.2, and select the JDK Download button.

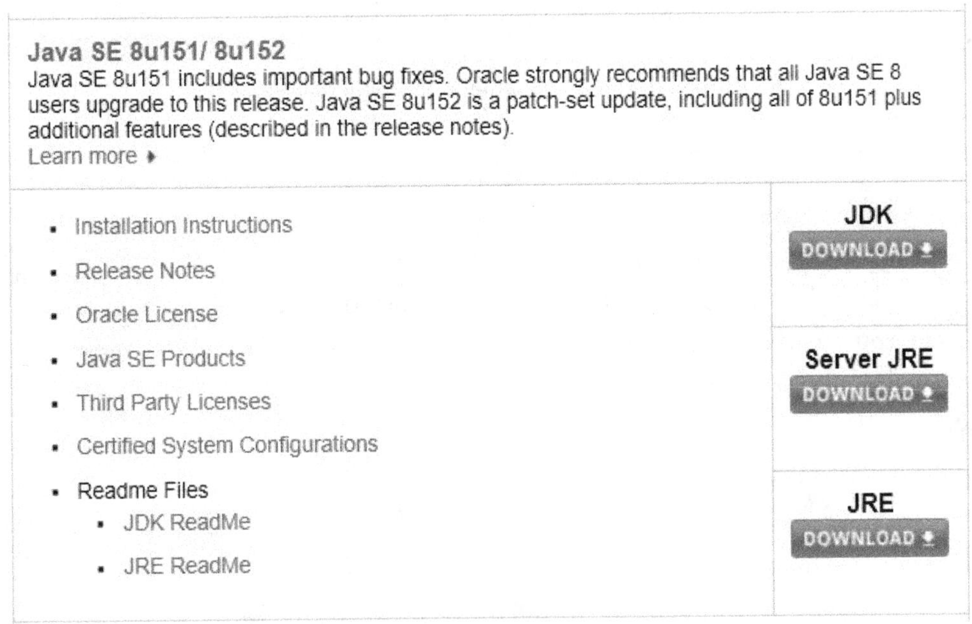

Figure 2.2 Java SE Download Link

3. When you select to download the JDK, you will be presented with a list of different JDK versions to download, Figure 2.3. If you are installing to Windows or Linux, select the bit-width version that matches your operating system and bit-width of Eclipse you intend to install for your development system.

Java SE Development Kit 8u151

You must accept the Oracle Binary Code License Agreement for Java SE to download this software.

○ Accept License Agreement ○ Decline License Agreement

Product / File Description	File Size	Download
Linux ARM 32 Hard Float ABI	77.9 MB	jdk-8u151-linux-arm32-vfp-hflt.tar.gz
Linux ARM 64 Hard Float ABI	74.85 MB	jdk-8u151-linux-arm64-vfp-hflt.tar.gz
Linux x86	168.95 MB	jdk-8u151-linux-i586.rpm
Linux x86	183.73 MB	jdk-8u151-linux-i586.tar.gz
Linux x64	166.1 MB	jdk-8u151-linux-x64.rpm
Linux x64	180.95 MB	jdk-8u151-linux-x64.tar.gz
macOS	247.06 MB	jdk-8u151-macosx-x64.dmg
Solaris SPARC 64-bit	140.06 MB	jdk-8u151-solaris-sparcv9.tar.Z
Solaris SPARC 64-bit	99.32 MB	jdk-8u151-solaris-sparcv9.tar.gz
Solaris x64	140.65 MB	jdk-8u151-solaris-x64.tar.Z
Solaris x64	97 MB	jdk-8u151-solaris-x64.tar.gz
Windows x86	198.04 MB	jdk-8u151-windows-i586.exe
Windows x64	205.95 MB	jdk-8u151-windows-x64.exe

Figure 2.3 Java SE Development Kit Download Versions

4. Install the JDK after it has been downloaded.

2.2.2 Eclipse IDE for Java Developers

Eclipse comes in different base packages. You can download any of the packages and run them side-by-side. You can have the Java IDE and the C/C++ IDE on the system at the same time. Figure 2.4 shows a comparison chart that depicts the different levels of support available for each package.

	Java	Java EE	C/C++	Committers 4.4.1	PHP	Java/Report	Java/DSL	Modeling Tools	Parallel Application	Testers	Automotive	RCP/RAP	Scout
Select packages to compare	☐	☐	☐	☐	☐	☐	☐	☐	☐	☐	☐	☐	☐
BIRT Framework						✓							
C/C++ Development Tools			✓						✓		✓		
Data Tools Platform		✓				✓							
Git Team Provider	✓	✓	✓	✓	✓		✓	✓	✓			✓	✓
Java Development Tools	✓	✓		✓		✓	✓	✓			✓	✓	✓
Java EE Developer Tools		✓				✓							
JavaScript Development Tools		✓				✓							
Jubula Functional Testing										✓			
Maven Integration for Eclipse	✓	✓					✓					✓	
Mylyn Task List	✓	✓	✓		✓	✓		✓	✓	✓		✓	✓
PHP Development					✓								

Figure 2.4 Support Level Comparison Chart

We will use the basic package for this book. You are more than welcome to try the other packages later. The instructions below are for a Windows system. In earlier versions of Eclipse, the install was basically a download of the compressed set of files for Eclipse; extract those files, find the Eclipse executable, and run it. Eclipse now has an installer that does all this for you and will create shortcuts for you.

1. Open a web browser and go to the www.eclipse.org/home/ website, Figure 2.5.

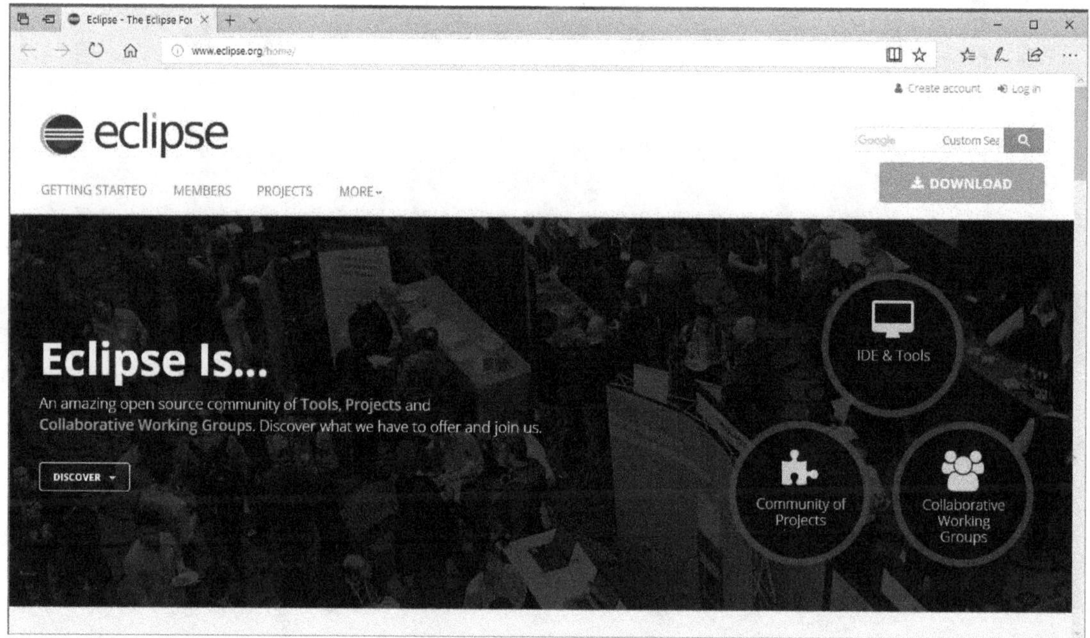

Figure 2.5 Eclipse Website

2. In the upper right, click on **DOWNLOAD**.
3. The Eclipse download website, Figure 2.6, will determine the OS you are running and the bit-width of your system; and in the bottom left will show its recommended default selection for download and install. You may click on the default **DOWNLOAD** button; or below the button, click on **Download Packages** to get to the installer and have the option to choose other versions.

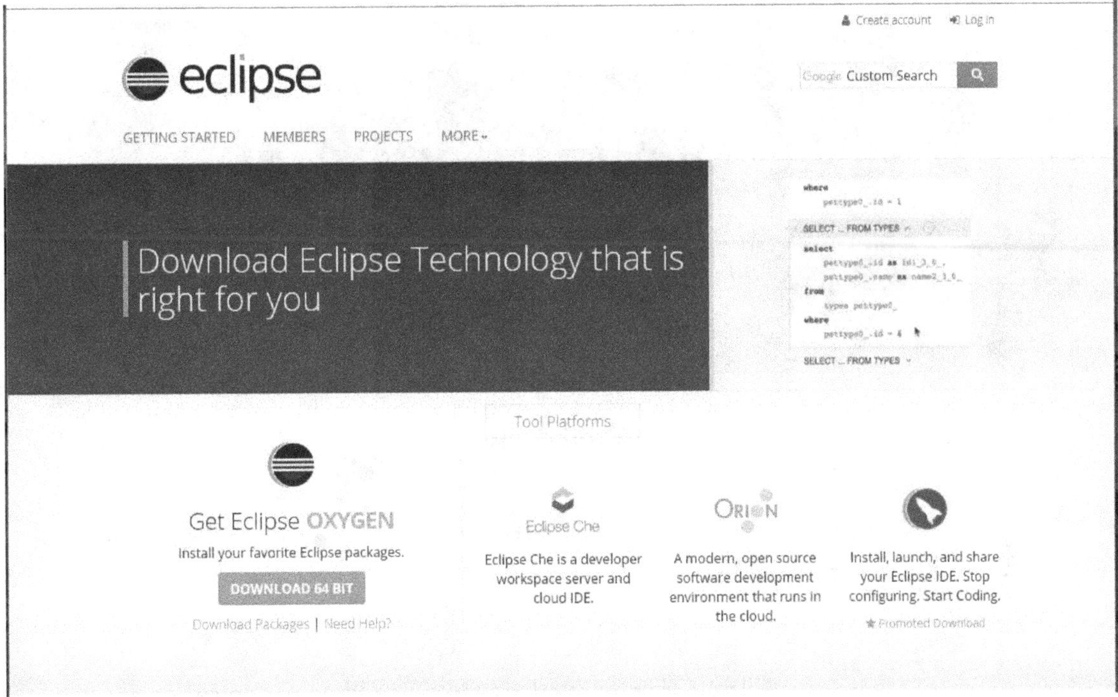

Figure 2.6 Eclipse Download

4. Eclipse now has an installer available for each supported OS, Windows, Figure 2.7, Linux, Figure 2.8, and Mac, Figure 2.9, that makes putting Eclipse on your system very easy.

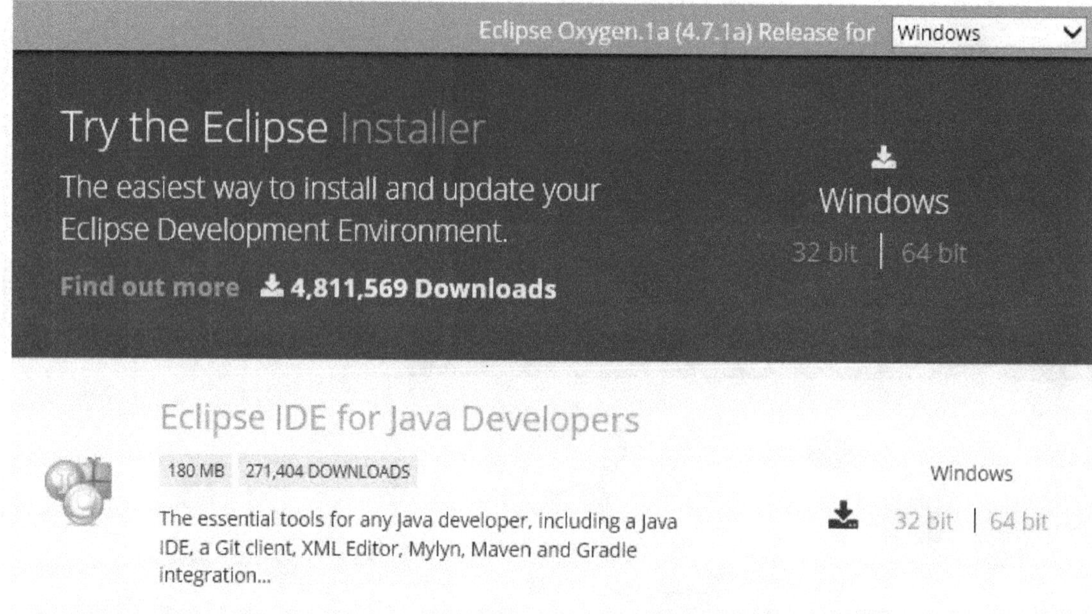

Figure 2.7 Eclipse for Windows Download

Figure 2.8 Eclipse for Linux Download

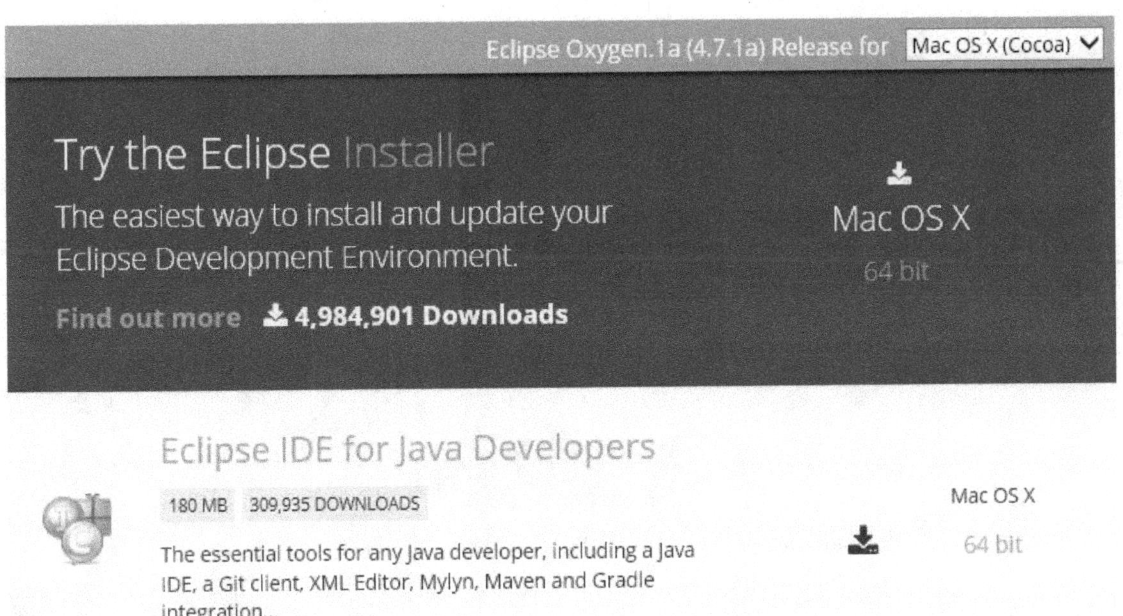

Figure 2.9 Eclipse for Mac Download

5. In the Try the Eclipse Installer box, under the OS you are running, click on the bit-width that matches the Java environment bit-width that you previously installed. The location that the download is coming from and the name of the installer file are shown under the DOWNLOAD button, Figure 2.10.

GETTING STARTED MEMBERS PROJECTS MORE

HOME / DOWNLOADS / ECLIPSE DOWNLOADS - SELECT A MIRROR

All downloads are provided under the terms and conditions of the **Eclipse Foundation Software User Agreement** unless otherwise specified.

Download from: United States - Princeton University Mathematics (http)

File: eclipse-inst-win64.exe SHA-512

>> Select Another Mirror

Figure 2.10 Eclipse Installer Download

6. Click the **DOWNLOAD** button. Save the installer in a convenient folder, such as, PC>Downloads>Eclipse.
7. After the installer is downloaded, go to the folder you downloaded it to and run it.
8. The Eclipse installer will launch with a selection screen of the various packages that can be selected, Figure 2.11. Click on **Eclipse IDE for Java Developers**.

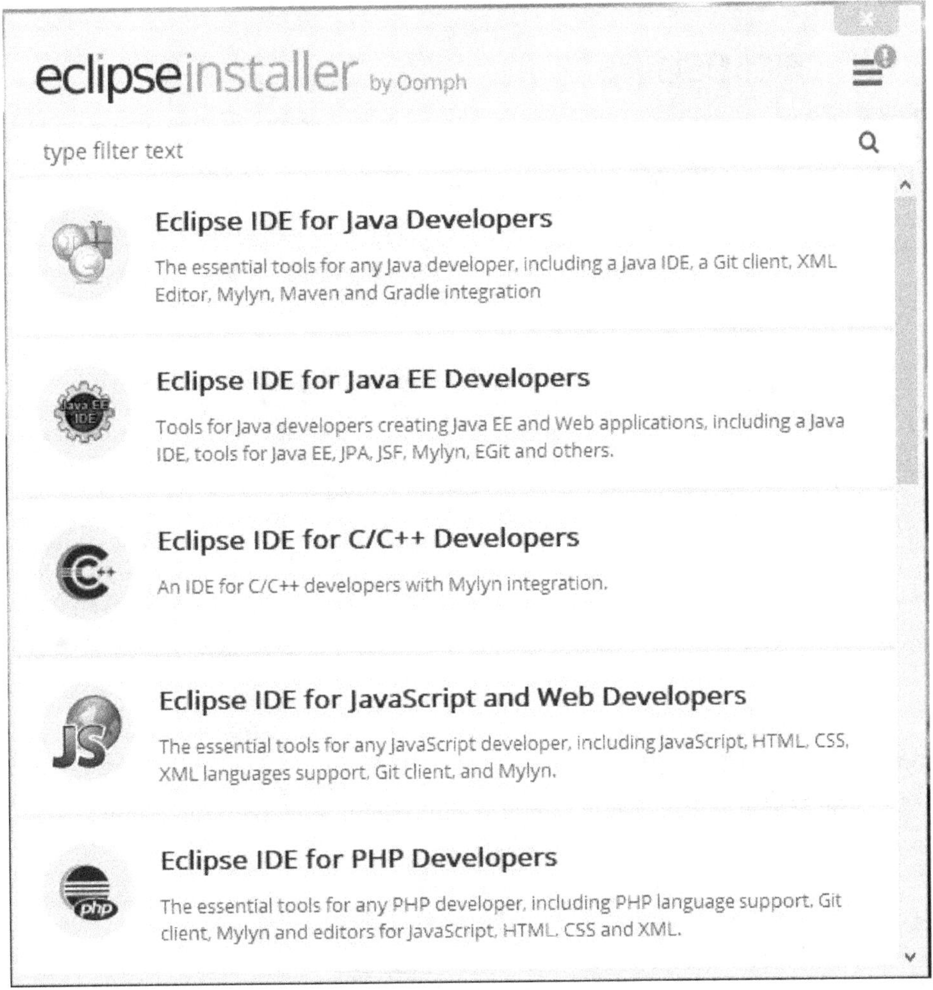

Figure 2.11 Installer Package Selection

9. The Eclipse installer will prompt you for the installation folder and to create shortcuts, Figure 2.12. Keep the defaults and click **INSTALL**.

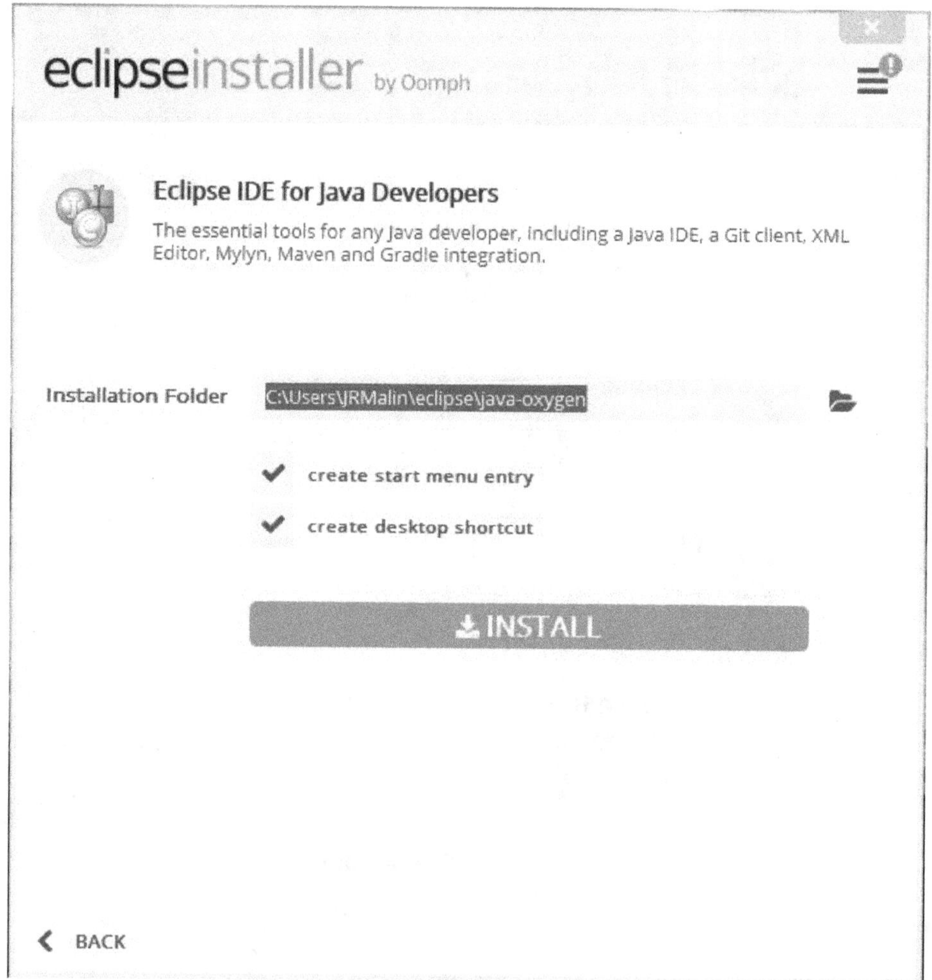

Figure 2.12 Eclipse Install Options

10. The installer will prompt you to accept the software user agreement. Review and then Click **Accept Now** and complete the installation. Do not be concerned about status indicating download taking longer than usual. Just wait for the installation to complete.
11. When the installation has completed successfully, Figure 2.13, click on **LAUNCH**.

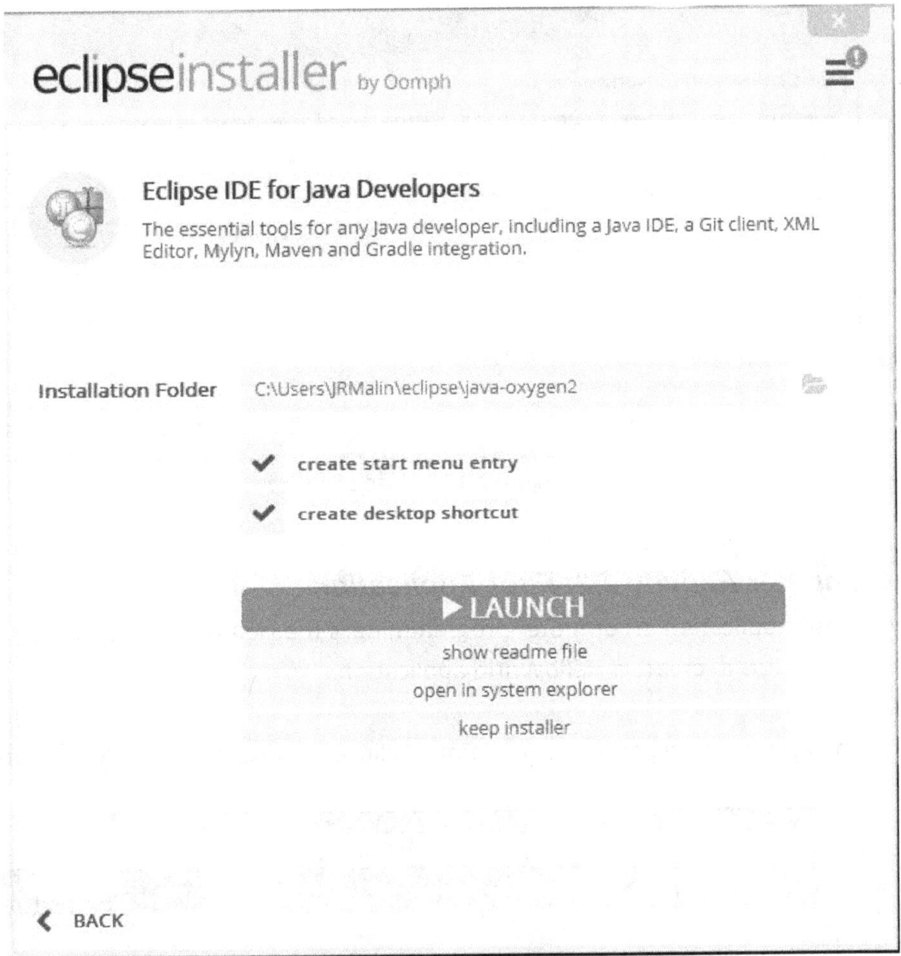

Figure 2.13 Eclipse Installation Completed Successfully

12. You will then be asked for the location of the workspace, Figure 2.14. The workspace is the location where you store your programs. You can always create new workspaces in different locations. For this exercise, keep the default location and click **Launch**. You are now ready to create the first application.

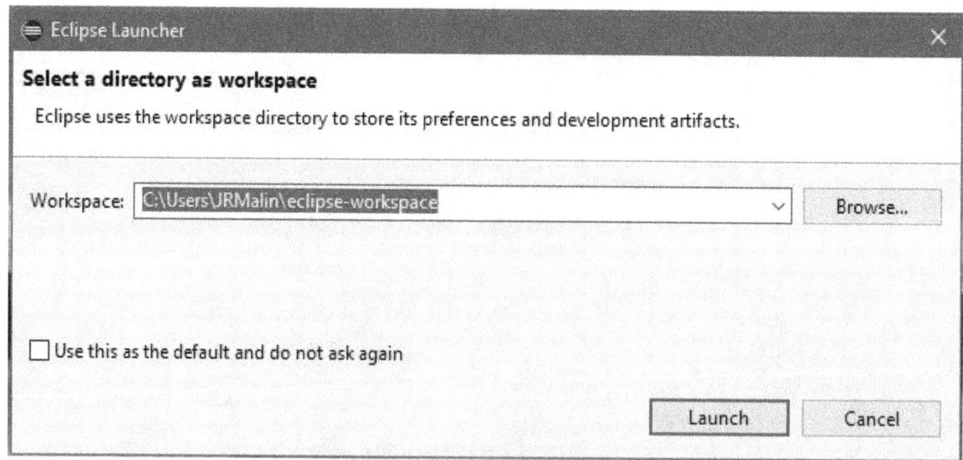

Figure 2.14 Eclipse Launcher

2.3 Computer Activity 2.2: First Application

The most basic application in computer programming is the HelloWorld application. We will start with the basic steps to create a HelloWorld application.

1. When you start Eclipse for the first time, Eclipse will display the Welcome tab, Figure 2.15.

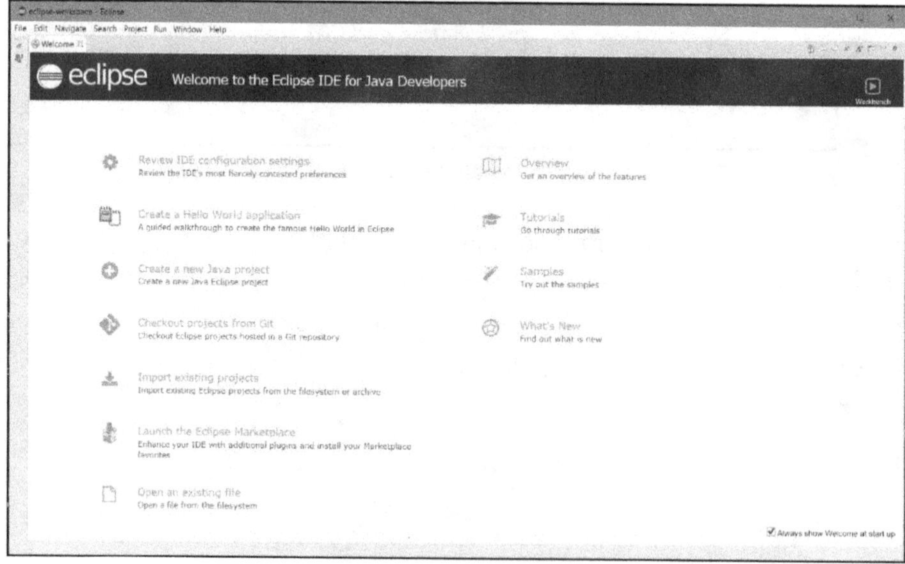

Figure 2.15 Eclipse Welcome Tab

The Welcome tab, Figure 2.15, has a lot of selections that will help you become familiar with using Eclipse to create and manage projects using Java.

2. If you look at the second selection on the left in the Welcome tab, you will see the Create a Hello World application topic that will guide you through the creation of the Hello World application. The Welcome tab will display by default every time Eclipse is launched unless you uncheck the **Always show Welcome at startup** checkbox at the bottom right of the Welcome tab. Click on the **Create a Hello World application**.
3. The Eclipse workspace will be displayed with a Cheat Sheets tab on the right-hand side, Figure 2.16.

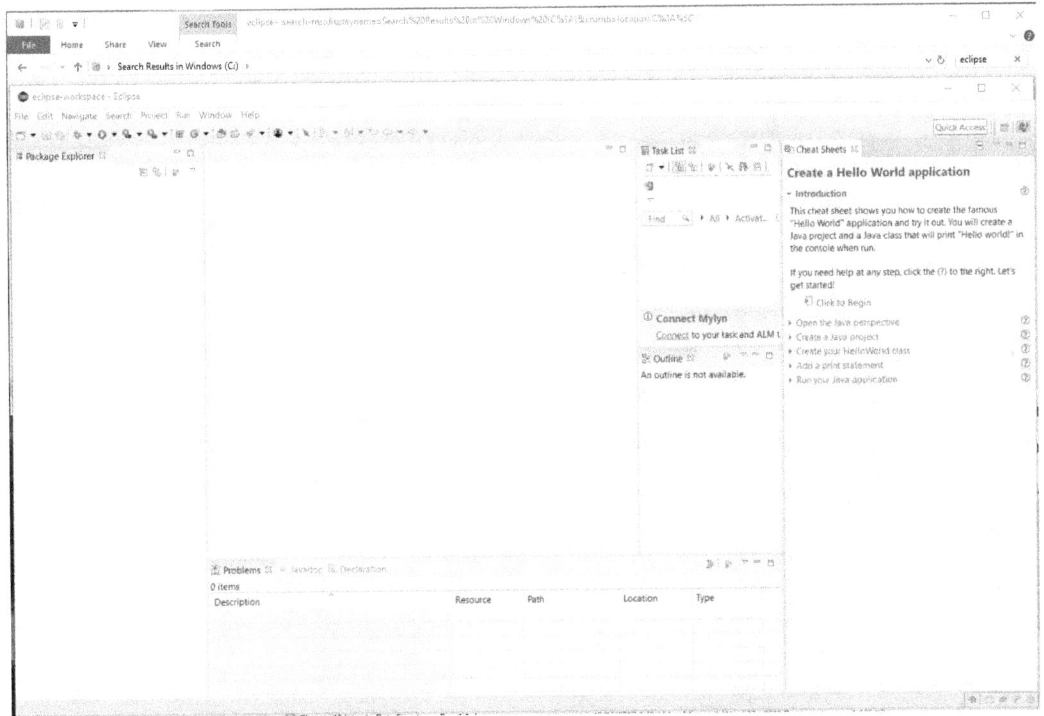

Figure 2.16 Eclipse IDE with Cheat Sheets Tab Showing

4. The Cheat Sheets tab will give you step-by-step directions for creating the Hello World program. Click on **Click to Begin**.
5. For each step, you can follow the directions and do the activity manually, which we recommend; or, you can click the **Click to perform** selection and it will be done for you. Follow the directions to ensure that you are in the Java perspective. Then click on **Click when complete**.

6. Before we can create anything, we need a project to put it all in. Either from the menu, select File->New->Java project, or as described in the Cheat Sheets, click on **New->Java Project**.
7. The New Java Project dialog appears, Figure 2.17. In the Project Name text box, enter "CH2CA2.1-HelloWorld".

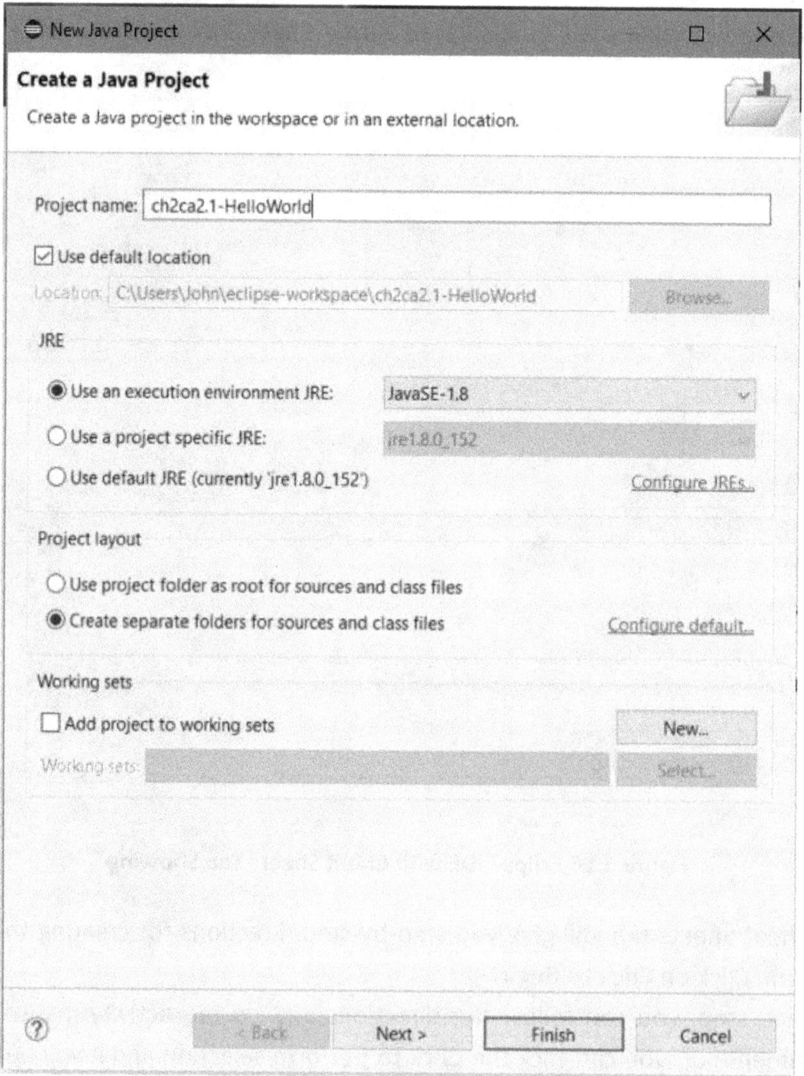

Figure 2.17 New Java Project Dialog

8. There are options to set the JRE environment and project layout. Keep the defaults and click **Finish**, and click **Click when complete** in the Cheat Sheets tab.

Figure 2.18 Package Explorer

9. Hello World will appear in Package Explorer, Figure 2.18, with any other packages that have been created. If this is your first project, it will be the only package displayed.
10. Expand the Hello World project so that you see the SRC folder and the JRE libraries, Figure 2.18.
11. Now we need to create a new class. Either follow the directions in the Cheat Sheets tab, or right-click on the **src** folder, and select **New->Class** from the context menu, Figure 2.19.

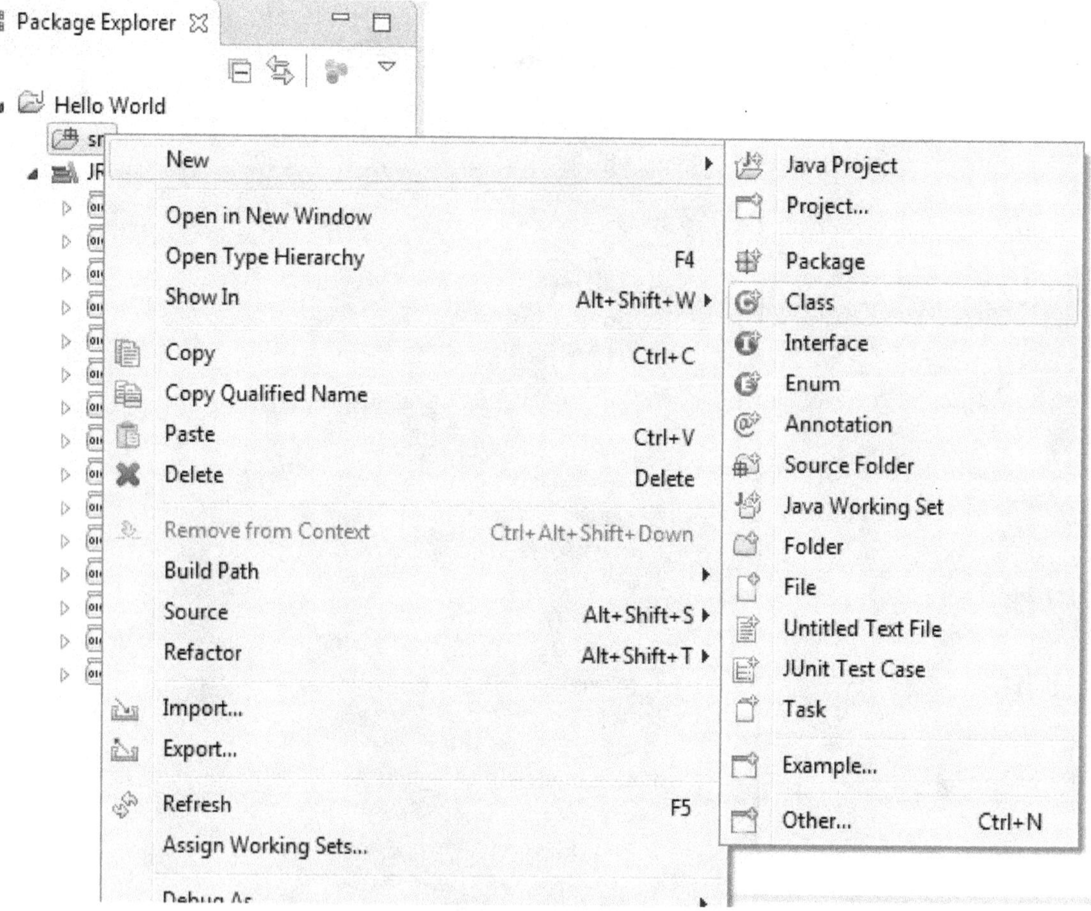

Figure 2.19 Create A New Java Class

12. A New Java Class dialog appears, Figure 2.20. Enter a package name in the Package text box: **helloworld**.
13. Next enter a Name for the new class: **HelloWorld**
14. Finally, select the method stub: **public static void main(String[] args).** This will create the main method for the application.

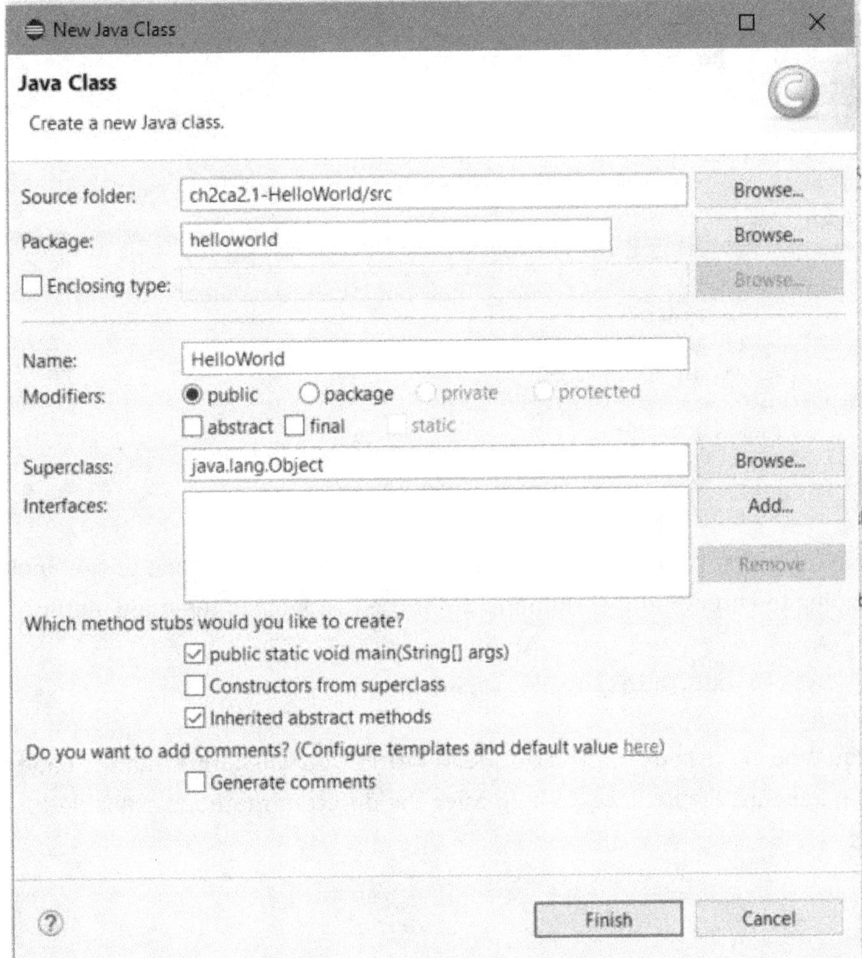

Figure 2.20 New Java Class Dialog

15. Click **Finish**, and the class gets generated along with the main method, Figure 2.21. Click **Click when Complete** in the Cheat Sheets tab.

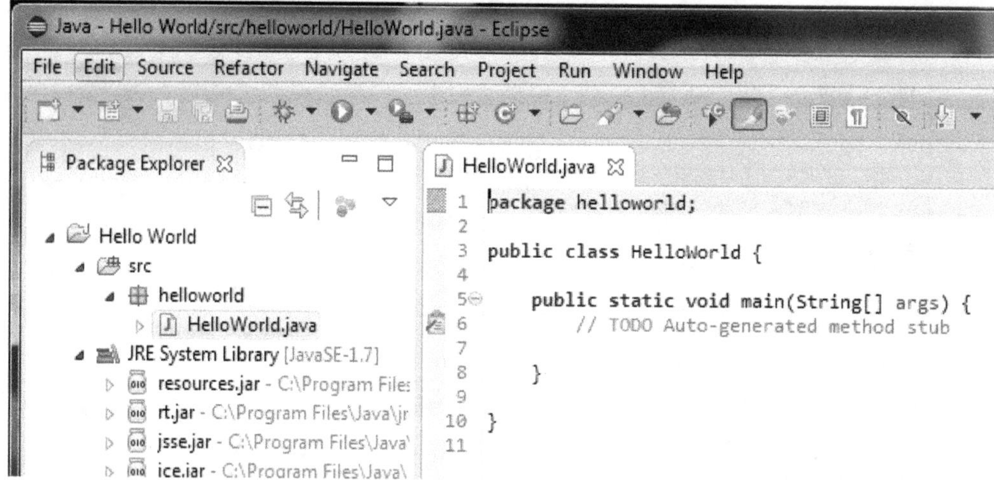

Figure 2.21 Newly Created Java Class

16. The middle view is the main editor, and it shows the source code to the application. We are going to enter a print statement. Enter the following in the main method:

```
System.out.println("Hello World");
```

As you type in the code to print out Hello World, you will notice that the code completion dialog appears, Figure 2.22, to help offer the different methods available for the System class.

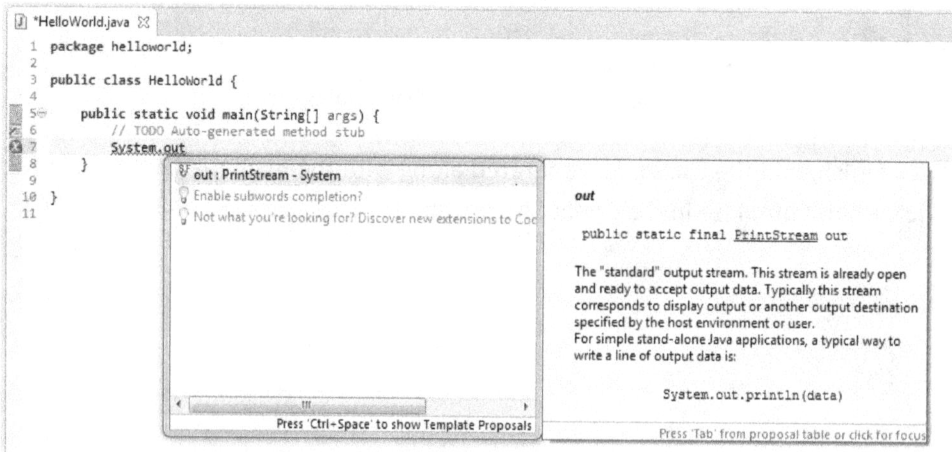

Figure 2.22 Code Completion Dialog

Code completion is a nice addition to help look up methods faster while you develop.

17. Save the project, and click **Click when complete** in the Cheat Sheets tab.
18. From the menu, select Run->Run or hit CTRL+F11 to run the application, or use the method outlined in the Cheat Sheets tab. The application is quickly compiled and output is shown in the bottom view under the console tab, Figure 2.23.

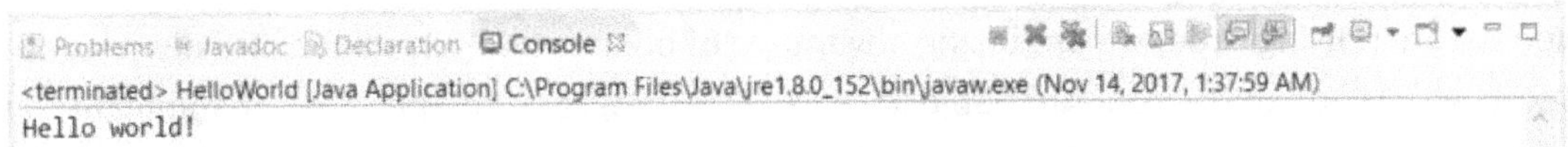

Figure 2.23 Output Dialog

2.4 *Structured Programming and Object-Oriented Programming (OOP) Brief Introduction*

If you have never programmed before, you might be thinking that the last exercise was a long way to just print "Hello World". Obviously, we need to explain this program before we can move forward; but first, let's look at the same program written in a different programming language called BASIC:

```
10 print "Hello World"
99 end
```

If you compare BASIC code to the Java code with a package, class, main, etc., you may think that BASIC is the better language from which to learn. BASIC was a popular programming language in the 1960s, 1970s, and 1980s. The first IBM PC came with the BASIC language support built in. BASIC went out of fashion because it was too difficult to maintain when programs became excessively large, memory limits were reached, and applications became more graphical. Programming languages like C, C++, and PASCAL offer structure and modularity, which allows a program to be broken down into specific parts. The holy grail of programming is reusable and extensible code, which has been achieved through Object-Oriented Programming (OOP). Most programmers use modern programming languages like Java, C++, C#, and VB.NET because of the expansive libraries and application programming interface (API) support available. Java was designed as a pure Object-Oriented (OO) language, so reusable code is at the heart of Java. The challenge to teach structured programming is to put the cart before the horse. You need a little

more programming before we can really see OOP in action. Explaining the structure for the Hello World application is important for moving forward, so we have to introduce OOP first.
In OOP, the key word is "Object".

Definition: *Object* – An object is an instance of a Class. Objects are an abstraction that has data and mechanisms to manipulate data.

When we are reusing code, we are taking advantage of objects that have been already created or objects we create ourselves. An "Object" is a little program snippet that manipulates and communicates information and manages data. Objects contain "Fields" and "Methods". The Fields (sometimes called properties) of a particular Object are data values that describe the attributes of the thing the Object represents. The Methods of a particular Object are the actions (subroutines or functions) that are responsible for the behavior of the Object.

The classic example of an object is to think of a file on a storage device. A file can have properties such as date created, size, name, author, the file data itself, etc. You can perform actions on a file such as move, create, delete, read, write, save, etc. In a program, you can have a file object that has fields that hold the properties of the file and methods that perform the actions that can act on any file; and you can re-use this code many times in an application.

When you created the Hello World project, the project was created in the workspace (aka directory) you defined when you first ran Eclipse. The project contains an src (source) folder and JRE System Library with JAR files. The JAR files are known as Java ARchive files. The JAR files contain the various Objects that we use when writing our programs, and these are automatically linked to the project. The JAR files are the reusable code that others have already developed; and best of all, the JAR files come free with Java.

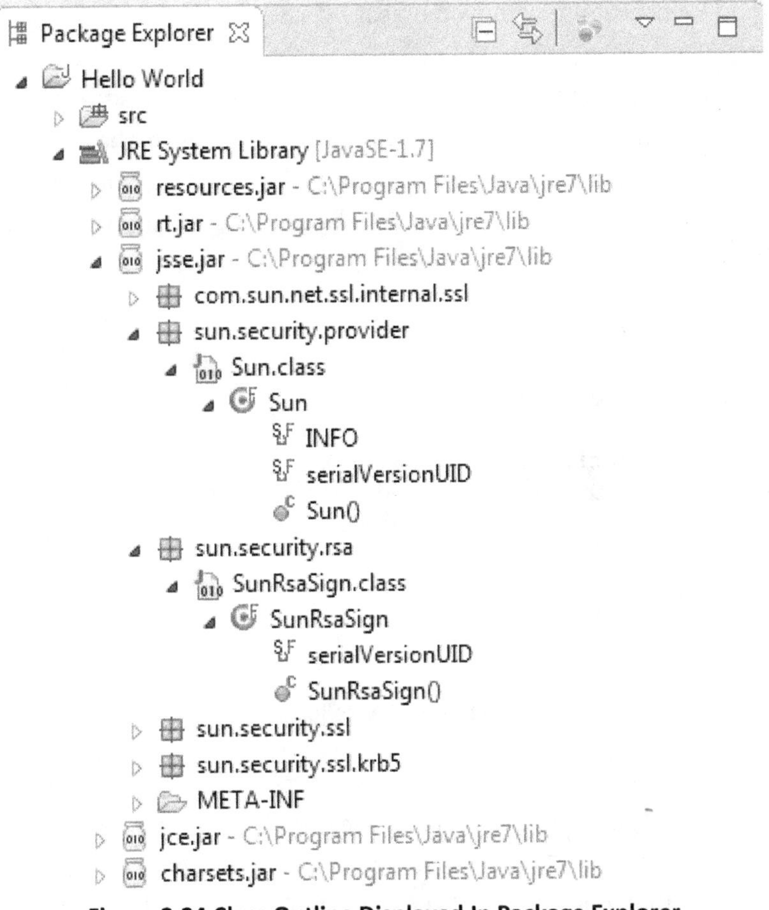

Figure 2.24 Class Outline Displayed In Package Explorer

The next step was to create the Class, which will contain the code. A "Class" is an object's definition.

Definition: *Class* – a class is the definition of the object.

Classes and objects are symbiotic. An object is an instance or a copy of a class. You created a class called HelloWorld. The HelloWorld class contains the main() method. The Java library contains many classes for use with your programs, and we will explore many of these classes throughout this book. You also defined a Package name. A "Package" is a convenient way to group multiple classes under a specific namespace. As you were creating the class, you clicked on a checkbox to add the main() method. The main() method is going to do the action.

Definition: *Method* – a procedure within an object / class.

The main() method is a special method that the Java runtime knows is the start of execution for the application. Without the main() method, the Java runtime doesn't have an entry point to run the code. If you try to run the application without a main() method, you will get an error. Once the skeleton of the project was created, you added the code statement to print the message Hello World, see Code Listing 2.1.

```
package  helloworld;

public class HelloWorld {

      public static void main(String[] args) {
           // TODO Auto-generated method stub
           System.out.println("Hello World");


      }

}
```

Code Listing 2.1 Hello World

The System.out.println() statement syntax is referred to as the "dot notation" because of the periods (dots). C#, VB.NET, and other OOP languages use this notation. System.out is the object or class, and println() is the method within this class that does the work. The main() method is calling another method that is in a different class. Just typing println("Hello World") is not enough, since the method is not defined anywhere in the local class. Entering System.out.println() tells the compiler to look for the println() method in the System.outclass. In this case, the System.out class is defined in one of the libraries included as part of the project. The println() method itself takes as input the message in quotations (""), which is called a string. We call this passing a string to the println() method. The println method knows how to communicate with the system's print device and outputs the string that was passed to it to the printer in a format that the printer understands and can print.

When you ran the application, Java.exe was called with the parameters to locate the main() method in the HelloWorld class. Hello World was then printed to the Console output at the bottom. You could also run the application at the command line using the following:

```
java.exe -Dfile.encoding=Cp1252 -classpath "<path to workspace>\Hello
World\bin" helloworld.HelloWorld
```

The -DFile.encoding=CP1252 option is the character encoding for English. You can omit this command line option and the program will still run.
The BASIC version of the program looks very simple compared to the Java version. At this point, it may not be clear why we need all of this structure, but it will make more sense as we move through the next few chapters and write some more code.

2.5 *Java Virtual Machine (JVM), a High-Level Description*

Throughout this book, you will create and run many different programs. How the program actually runs is not something one thinks about. This ignorance goes away when code needs to be optimized or a program runs on one machine but fails to run on another. The installation of the Java JRE included the installation of the Java Virtual Machine. The JVM acts as the layer between your application and the operating system/hardware platform it is running on, Figure 2.25.

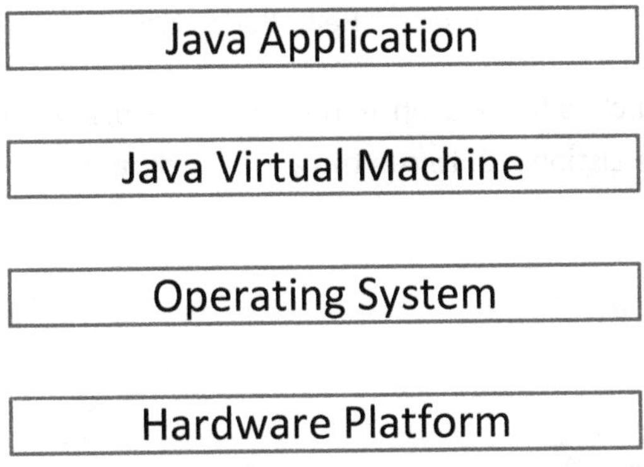

Figure 2.25 The Layers of the Java Virtual Machine

The JVM is designed to be portable so it can run on different operating system and hardware platform combinations such as Windows/x86, Android/ARM, etc. This portability allows you to write one application that can run on multiple platforms. The Oracle website supports different operating systems such as Linux, Mac OS X, Solaris, and Windows. Other companies have developed JVM solutions for their own platforms. A popular example is Google's Android. The JVM is a virtual machine that runs in memory and sets up the environment to run the application. Some of the items to get set up are a stack, registers, execution environment, garbage collector, and instruction set.

When you created the HelloWorld class, the HelloWorld.java file was created, Figure 2.26.

Figure 2.26 HelloWorld.java

When the program ran, it was first compiled to bytecode, which generates the HelloWorld.class file, Figure 2.27.

Figure 2.27 HelloWorld.class

If you open the HelloWorld.class file in Eclipse, the editor will display the bytecode. The JVM uses this information, Code Listing 2.2, to run the actual program.

```
// Compiled from HelloWorld.java (version 1.7 : 51.0, super bit)
public class helloworld.HelloWorld {

  // Method descriptor #6 ()V
  // Stack: 1, Locals: 1
  public HelloWorld();
    0  aload_0 [this]
    1  invokespecial java.lang.Object() [8]
    4  return
      Line numbers:
        [pc: 0, line: 3]
      Local variable table:
        [pc: 0, pc: 5] local: this index: 0 type: helloworld.HelloWorld

  // Method descriptor #15 ([Ljava/lang/String;)V
  // Stack: 2, Locals: 1
  public static void main(java.lang.String[] args);
    0  getstatic java.lang.System.out : java.io.PrintStream [16]
    3  ldc <String "Hello World"> [22]
    5  invokevirtual java.io.PrintStream.println(java.lang.String) : void [24]
    8  return
      Line numbers:
        [pc: 0, line: 7]
        [pc: 8, line: 10]
      Local variable table:
        [pc: 0, pc: 9] local: args index: 0 type: java.lang.String[]
}
```

Code Listing 2.2 HelloWorld.class File Contents

When the program runs, the bytecode is compiled to machine code by the execution engine, Figure 2.28. This is called just-in-time compilation (JIT). The compiler optimizes the code and executes the application.

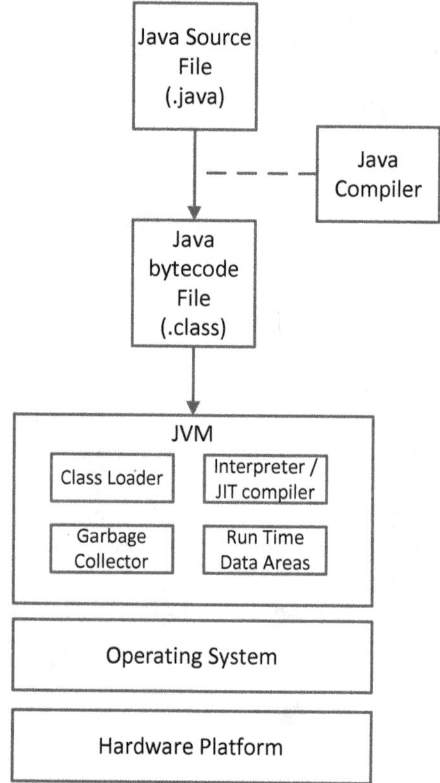

Figure 2.28 Java Executable Code Generation

Higher level interpreted languages like Java have an advantage of portability and memory management and is handled by the JVM. The disadvantage of higher level interpreted languages like Java is that they are slower in performance than lower level languages like C and assembly. The performance of the Java application is dependent on the JVM. Optimizing code for best performance may involve disassembly, but these optimization efforts are more for the extreme cases. There are Java-to-native-code compilers that look to optimize for best performance. We will look at some optimization techniques in a later chapter as an interesting aside.

2.6 Eclipse Feature: Searching

We will introduce different Eclipse features at various points in this book. Many computer applications have some built-in search capability. With an extensive library, Eclipse includes flexible search capability to search the local program files and the Java library, Figure 2.29.

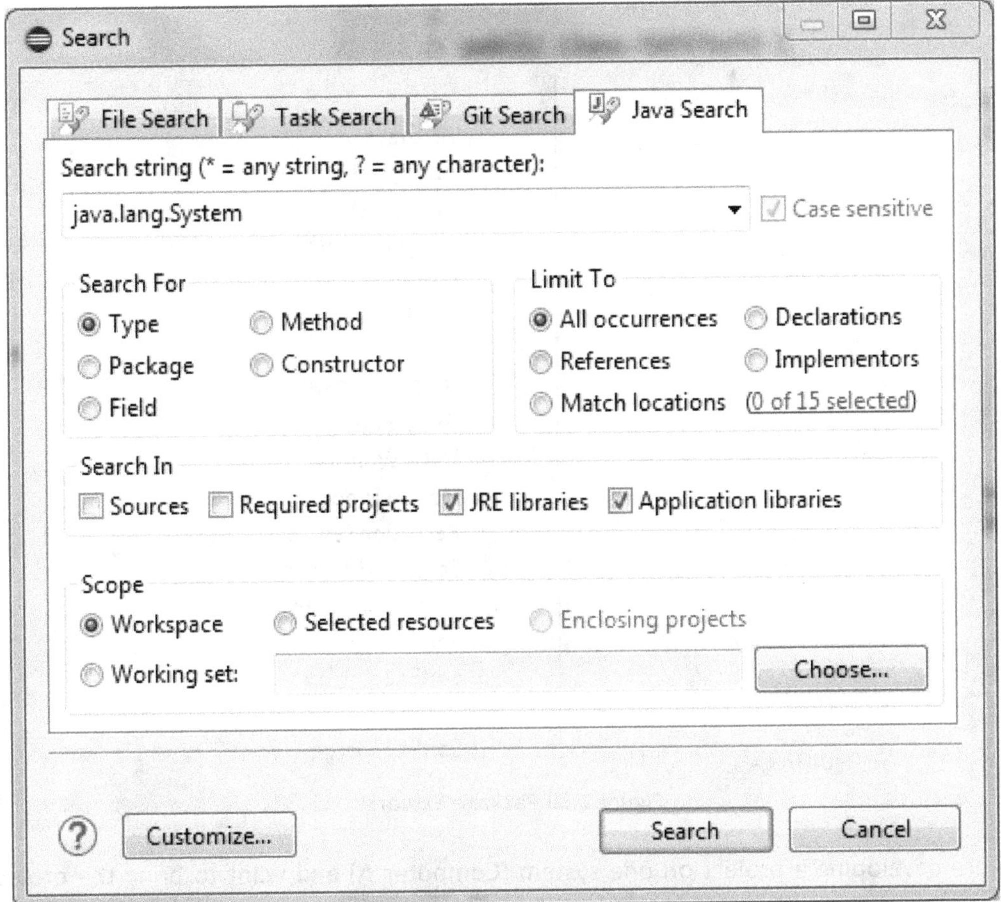

Figure 2.29 Eclipse Java Search

2.7 *Eclipse Feature: Moving Project from One System to Another*

You will most likely develop applications on one computer and have to transfer them to another computer. Turning in a programming assignment is one example. Eclipse projects are stored in a workspace folder. You can set and change the workspace to any folder on your system. Eclipse manages the project via the Package Explorer. The picture below shows the project folders in File Explorer and the same projects are visible in Package Explorer, Figure 2.30.

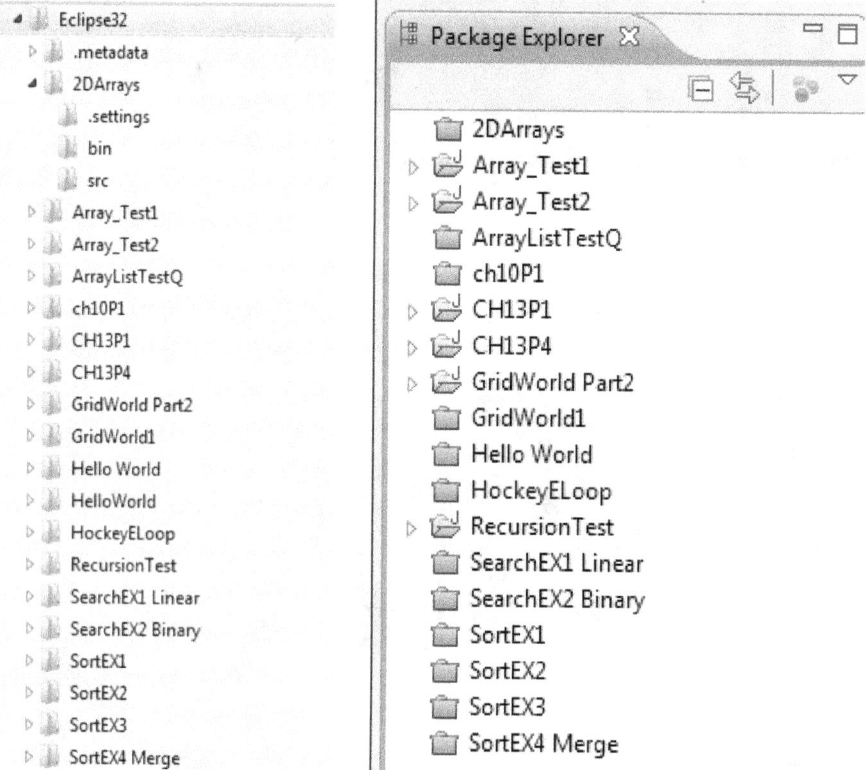

Figure 2.30 Package Explorer

If you are developing a project on one system (Computer A) and want to bring the project to another system (Computer B), you can simply copy the project folder over and import it into the Computer B's Eclipse workspace. Here are the basic steps:

1. In File Explorer of Computer A, copy the project folder to a flash disk. For our example, we will have a project called System A. Alternatively, you could also ZIP the folder up and e-mail it to yourself or copy it to a network drive. Just remember to unzip the folder on the new system.
2. Safely eject the flash disk when the copy is completed.
3. Remove the flash disk from Computer A.
4. Put the flash disk into Computer B.
5. Copy the project folder to the Eclipse workspace folder in Computer B.
6. Just because you copied the project to the workspace folder does not mean that the project will be viewable in Eclipse's Package Explorer. The project needs to be imported first. From the menu select File->Import.

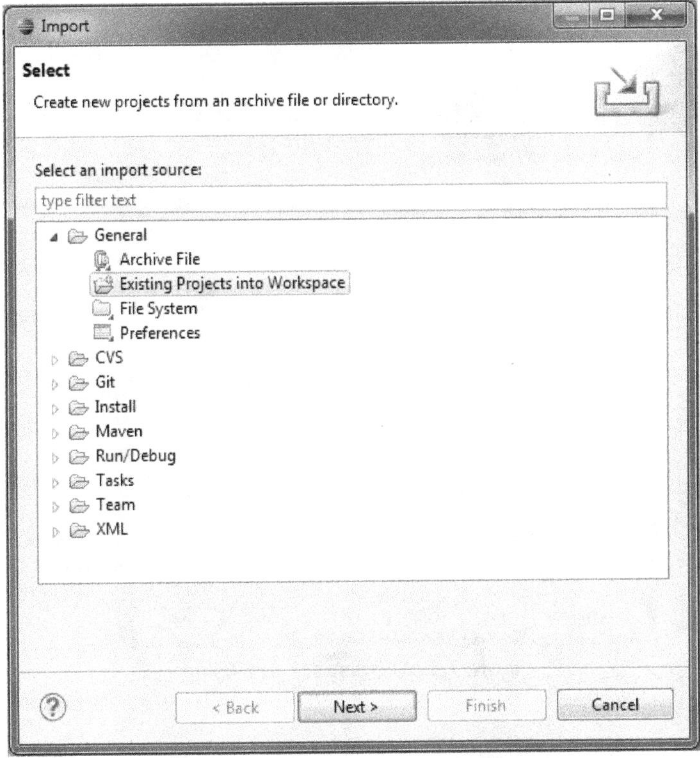

Figure 2.31 Workspace Import Dialog

7. The import dialog appears, Figure 2.31. Under General, select Existing Projects into Workspace.
8. Click **Next**.
9. In the next dialog, click the **Browse** button and select the workspace folder. The figure below, Figure 2.32, shows Eclipse32 as the workspace folder.

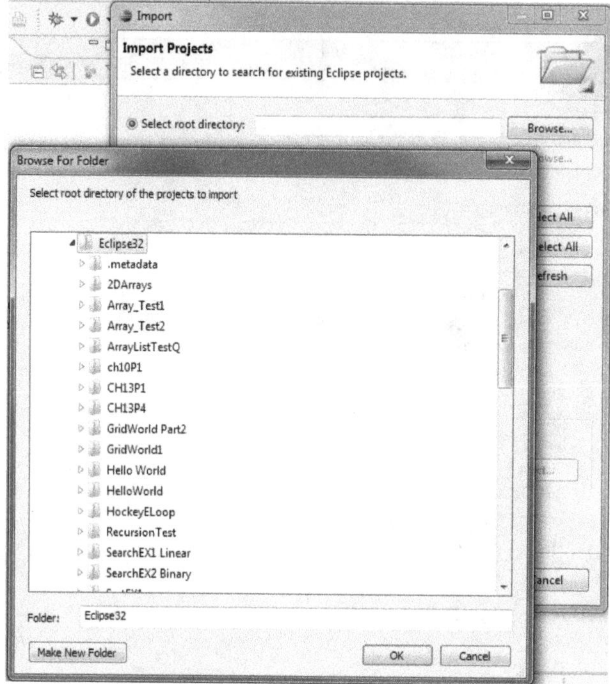

Figure 2.32 Workspace Browsing

10. Click **Ok.**
11. The Project's scroll box will be updated with the imported project found in the folder. Any project that is in the workspace already will be greyed out. Any projects that are not already part of the workspace will be visible and checked, Figure 2.33. Click **Finish**.

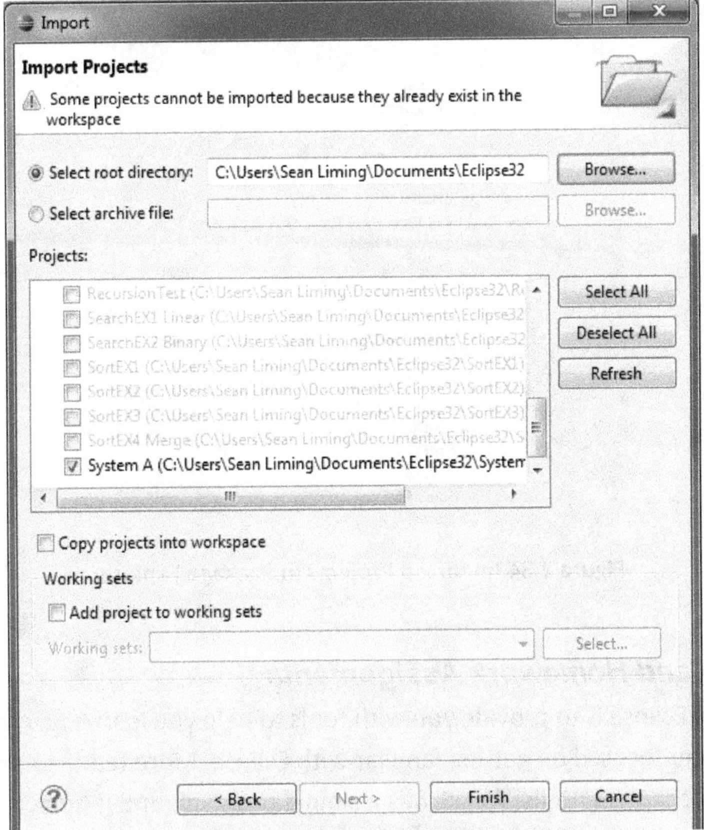

Figure 2.33 Updated Project Listing

You will see that the System A project has been successfully imported into Computer B, Figure 2.34. The simple copy and import process is much shorter than re-creating the whole project from scratch.

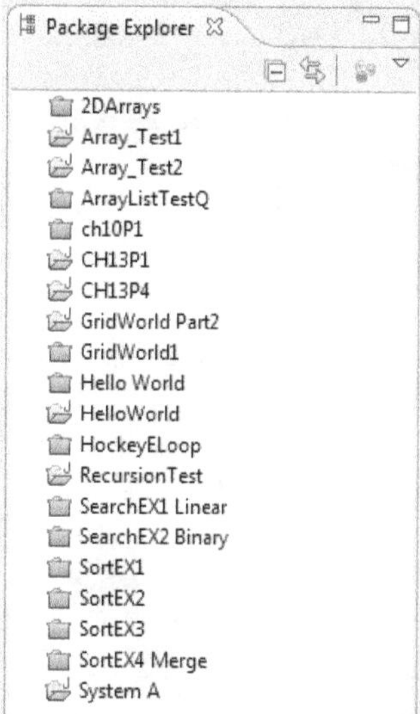

Figure 2.34 Imported Projects in Package Explorer

2.8 Summary and Homework Assignments

Our goal with using Eclipse is to provide you with tools to help you learn and give you a start with a career. This chapter focused on getting familiar with Eclipse. More features and capabilities will be covered in later chapters. Hello World was a simple program, and it helped introduce objects and structured programming that we will build upon starting in the next chapter. Java was designed to be a pure object-oriented language, thus everything you will be using comes from libraries that others have already created. Sometimes the best things in life are free. Before we move on to implement some of these libraries, here are a few questions.

2.8.1 Questions

1. Besides the IDEs listed in Section 2.1, name 2 more IDEs available for Java programming.
2. Right-click on the Hello World project and select close project. Create a new Java project in Eclipse called "NotRun". Create a class called **NoHello** with a package called **nohello**, and uncheck the box to include the main() method. What is the output from Eclipse when you try to run the program?

3. Given the following words for transportation, what do each of the words fall under: class, method, or field?

   Car
   Truck
   Forward
   Color
   Model
   Reverse
   Stop
   Seats
   Train
   Doors
   Bus
   Vehicle

4. What do Java EE and Java ME stand for?
5. What other programming languages does Eclipse support?
6. Eclipse was designed to compete against another popular IDE. The name Eclipse was chosen for the IDE as the intended purpose to eclipse this other IDE. What is the IDE and who is the manufacturer?
7. What are the version names and numbers of the different Eclipse releases?

3 Math and Strings

"This is it. That moment they told us about in high school where one day, algebra would save our lives."

– Gallagher, from the movie: *Red Planet*, Warner Bros. 2000

In the movie, *Red Planet*, astronauts and scientists have to use their skills to survive a crash landing on Mars. The line from the movie goes hand-in-hand with a question that students ask all the time: "Why do we have to learn algebra?" Seeing how algebra is applied in the real world is difficult to show when you are first learning it. You get a glimpse of applying algebra in chemistry and physics courses, but it is computer science and programming where you get to see practical uses of algebra. In this chapter, we will see how to perform basic math in Java, and then we will cover the use of strings to make the output more informative and to get information from the user.

3.1 Data Types and Math Operators

One of the first lessons in algebra covered different number sets such as natural numbers, whole numbers, integers, real numbers, and complex numbers. The reason why you needed to learn number sets might not have been clear, until now. Computers process 1s and 0s. Writing code with 1s and 0s can be done, but it is not practical. Java and other high-level languages turn lines of source code and data into 1s and 0s for the computer to process. You need to define the type of data in the source code, so the proper encoding to 1s and 0s takes place. Java defines 8 primitive data types, Table 3.1.

Data Type	Description	Usage
byte	8-bit signed two's complement integer. Minimum value -128, maximum value 127	byte a = 10
short	16-bit signed two's complement integer. Minimum value -32768, maximum value 32767	short x = 1000
int	32-bit signed two's complement integer. Minimum value -2^31, maximum value is 2^31 -1	int y = 56789
long	64-bit signed two's complement integer. Minimum value -2^63, maximum value is 2^63 -1	long b = 512346L
float	Single-precision 32-bit IEEE 754 floating point - typically used for large arrays of floating point numbers	float c = 54.7f
double	Double-precision 64-bit IEEE 754 floating point - typically used for decimal values	double h1 = 23.45
boolean	Single bit of information either true (1) or false (0)	boolean test = true
char	16-bit Unicode character	char c = 'A'

Table 3.1 Data Types

Other programming languages use similar data types, but the syntax will not be exactly the same as Java defines them. For example, C# defines a byte as a value from 0 to 255 and an sbyte as -128 to 127, whereas Java only has a byte which is defined as -128 to 127. As you can see from the list, there are several different versions of integers. The larger the maximum value of the integer type, the more bits are needed, and the more memory is used for the data storage. Float and double are used for very large numbers. Notice that the usage for larger numbers doesn't use a comma (,) as part of the internal storage. If you need/want commas, they need to be explicitly coded into the formatting of the string representation of the data or they need to be added when displayed or printed out.

Now that we can define data, we can perform some operations with the data. In algebra classes, you learned about the order of operation (PEMDAS). Computer languages follow the same math rules. Here are the basic operators including one extra that you might not have seen before, Table 3.2.

Operator	Description
()	Parentheses
*	Multiplication
/	Division
%	Modulus / Remainder
+	Addition
-	Subtraction

Table 3.2 Data Operators

The modulus operator yields the remainder of an integer division operation. For example, if 7 and 3 are integers, 7 % 3 is 1, because 7 / 3 = 2 with a remainder of 1. Because programs can become very large with lots of typing, programmers like to use shortcuts whenever possible. In addition to these basic math operators, Java includes a set of increment, decrement, and math-assignment operators, Table 3.3.

Operator	Description	Usage	Equivalent
++	Pre or post Increment	Pre: ++x Post: x++	x++ is the same as x = x + 1
--	Pre or post decrement	Pre: --x Post: x--	y++ is the same as y = y - 1
*=	Multiplication assignment	x*= value	z *= 5 is the same as z = z * 5
/=	Division assignment	y /= value	j /= 5 is the same as j = j / 5
%=	Modulus assignment	i %= value	k %= 5 is the same as k = k % 5
+=	Addition assignment	j += value	w += 5 is the same as w = w + 5
-=	Subtraction assignment	k -= value	i -= 5 is the same as i = i - 5

Table 3.3 Assignment Operators

The increment and decrement operators increment or decrement the numeric value by 1. For example:

```
int x = 5;
x++;
```

The equal sign (=) is known as the assignment. The statement int x = 5 means that x is assigned the value of 5. After x++ runs, the value of x is now 6. The increment can also be viewed as int x = x + 1. The pre- and post- operations are important. For example:

```
int x =10;
int y = 5;
int j = ++x - 2;
int k = y-- + 3
int z = x * y;
```

The x variable is incremented before the subtraction operation; thus, j equals the value 9. The y variable is decremented after the addition operation; thus, k equals the value 8. Both x and y have new values because of the increment and decrement operations in the previous statements, thus z equals the value 44 (11 * 4). The shorthand will become useful when we talk about iteration in the next chapter. The math assignment operators are similar. For example:

```
int y = 7;
y += 4;
```

The assignment can be viewed as y = y + 4. The value of y is 11. Now let's use Eclipse to test data types and the math operators.

3.1.1 Computer Activity 3.1: Data Type Test

Create a new Java project in Eclipse called "CH3CA3.1-Data Types". Create a new class in the project called "DataTypes" with a main() method and a package name "datatypes". In the main() method enter the code in Code Listing 3.1:

```
int x = 5;
double y = 2.5;
boolean test = false;
char c = 'g';

System.out.println(x);
System.out.println(y);
System.out.println(test);
System.out.println(c);
```

Code Listing 3.1 Data Type Test

What is the output when you run the program?

3.1.2 Computer Activity 3.2: Testing Math

Create a new Java project in Eclipse called "CH3CA3.2-Math Test". Create a new class in the project called "MathTest1" with a main() method and a package name "mathtest1". Code Listing 3.2 shows the whole program. Enter the contents of the main() method. Before you run the program, try to figure out the results of x, y, i, and j.

```
1. package mathtest1;
2.
3. public class mathTest1 {
4.
5.      public static void main(String[] args) {
6.          // TODO Auto-generated method stub
7.
8.          int x = 9;
9.          int y = 2;
10.         int i = 100;
11.         double j = 1.5;
12.
13.         x += y;
14.         j++;
15.         y = 5 + x * 3;
16.         i %= y;
17.         j += i--;
18.         y -= j;
19.         System.out.println(x);
20.         System.out.println(y);
21.         System.out.println(i);
22.         System.out.println(j);
23.
24.     }
25.
26. }
```

Code Listing 3.2 Math Test

After you have tried to figure out the values, run the program. Did you get the same results? In the last exercise, notice that j is a double. You need to be careful when mixing data types. The result from the program at line 17 was correct, since j can take the result from an integer operation. Because of the type mismatch in line 18, y -= j, since y is an integer and J is a double, y will be promoted to a double before the subtraction is done, and then the result will be converted to integer when the result of the subtraction is stored back in y. Note the value of y, and now use the cast (data type) operator to change the data type of j to an integer before the subtraction is done. In line 18 above substitute the following:

```
y -= (int) j;
```

Run the program and you will notice that the result of y is different from the result you obtained when you did not cast J to an integer. Either way, the result of y is an integer, but the end value of that integer is determined by the variable types that are in effect at the time of the mathematical operation; in this case, the subtraction. The cast operation (int) tells the Java runtime to temporarily treat the double as an integer when this line is executed. The data type of j does not change. When a double is cast to int, anything after the decimal is dropped. It is not rounded to an integer. It is truncated to an integer. Another area to watch out for is integer division. Code Listing 3.3 for example:

```
int y =11;
int z = 2;
int k = 4;
int w = (y + z) / k;
System.out.println(w);
```

Code Listing 3.3 Integer Division

The real value of w is a decimal value of 3.25. Since w is an integer data type, 3 is printed to the console and the .25 value is dropped. Remember: computers do what they are told, and if you accidentally mix types you might run into unexpected results. The proper solution, if the fractional part of the division is significant and needs to be stored and printed out, is to make w a double and to cast y, z, and k as double, Code Listing 3.4:

```
double w = ((double) y + (double) z) / (double) k;
```

Code Listing 3.4 Managing Type Mismatches

3.2 Math Methods

Complex operations such as square roots, exponent, powers, and trigonometry functions are already available as methods in the Java library. The Math class can be found in the rt.jar library under java.lang package. Table 3.4 is a short list of some of the available methods available in the Math class.

Math Method	Description
abs(double or int x)	Get the absolute value of x. Returns value of double or int
ceil(double x)	Rounds up to the next integer. Returns value of double
cos(double x)	Gets the cosine of x. Returns radians as double.
exp(double x)	Returns e^x as double
floor(double x)	Rounds down to the next integer. Returns value of double
log(double x)	Returns log base 10 of x. Returns value of double
max(double or int x, double or int y)	Returns the larger of the two values
min(double or int x, double or int y)	Returns the smaller of the two values
pow(double x, double y)	Returns the value of x^y Return value of double.
random()	Returns a decimal number greater than 0.0 and less than 1.0
round(double x)	Rounds the value of x up to the next integer if >= x.5. Rounds the value down if < x.5. Returns value is a long
sin(double x)	Returns the sine of y. Returns radians as double
sqrt(double x)	Returns the square root of x. Returns a double
tan(double x)	Returns the tangent of x. Returns radians as double

Table 3.4 Math Methods

You can view all the methods in Package Explorer or in the Java documents on the Oracle website. Most of the methods return double as the data type, so be careful when assigning values.

3.2.1 Computer Activity 3.3: Math Test 2

Let's do a simple test in Eclipse to see these methods in action. Create a new Java project called "CH3CA3.3-Math Test2". Create a new class in the project called "MathTest2" that has a main() method and "mathtest2" as the package name. Enter the following code in the main() method as shown in Code Listing 3.5.

```java
package mathtest2;

import java.util.Random;

public class MathTest2 {

    public static void main(String[] args) {
        // TODO Auto-generated method stub

        double x = 2.6;
        int y = -7;

        int j = Math.abs(y);
        System.out.println(j);

        double k = Math.ceil(x);
        System.out.println(k);

        double t = Math.floor(x);
        System.out.println(t);

        double maxvalue = Math.max(x, y);
        System.out.println(maxvalue);

        double minvalue = Math.min(x, y);
        System.out.println(minvalue);

        double z = Math.round(x);
        System.out.println(z);

        double r = Math.random();
        System.out.println(r);
    }
}
```

Code Listing 3.5 Math Test 2

Run the program. The values x and y are passed to the different methods. Notice that the Round() method rounds the value up to 3. Change x to 2.4 and run the program again. Notice that result is now 2. What is the result when you change x = 2.5? Does the result from Floor() or Ceil() change when you change the value of x? You can combine these math methods and the basic math operators from the last section to turn algebraic equations into Java program statements. For example, the following

$$y = \left(x + \frac{\sqrt{b}}{5}\right)^3$$

becomes the following statement in a Java program:

```
double y = Math.pow((x+(Math.sqrt(b)/5)), 3);
```

It takes some practice to see and write equations as single line statements in a program. A typical error occurs if a bracket is missed. If you miss a bracket, Eclipse will let you know immediately. If you are taking a written test, be sure to double check the brackets. One approach to the bracket problem is to start from the innermost pair and work your way out. There should be an equal pair. The other approach is to count the open brackets and compare to the count of closed brackets. The count of open brackets should be the same as the count of closed brackets. Based on what we know about the order of operation, do we need the () around `Math.sqrt(b)/5`?

3.3 *Variables and Constants*

To this point, we have used single letters as variables such as x, y, j, etc. These variables are known as local variables as they are declared within the {} of the method and exist only in that method. Java defines several variable types that we will cover in later chapters. Variables can also be words like 'counter', 'volume', or 'led1'. It is common practice for variables to start with a lower case. There are some reserved keywords in Java that you cannot use as variables, such as int, public, static, while, for, import, etc. These reserved words are used as directives for the programming language. Eclipse will warn or generate errors if you use these keywords. Sometimes you might be writing an algorithm for an equation that has a constant value. For example:

$$e = mc^2$$

The value for c is the speed of light in a vacuum or 299,792,458 meters per second. Having to enter the value each and every time would be a bit cumbersome. You could assign the value to 'c' like we have done in the previous exercise and examples, but the value of 'c' could change or get reassigned if you forget that it is a constant. The keyword 'final' is used to prevent the value from changing:

```
final double c = 299792458;
double e = m * c * c;
```

The final declaration means the value cannot change anywhere in the program. Eclipse will flag an error if 'c' is assigned another value or changed in the program. In this case, 'c' was lower case, but in practice, it is common practice to capitalize constant values so they stand out from variables that can change. For example:

```
final double MAXHEIGHT = 42;
```

3.4 Random Number Generator

The Math class includes a random() method that generated a random decimal number between 0.0 and 1.0. A random number generator is a fun, useful feature that can be used where random events or values are needed, such as the rolling of the dice or dealing a deck of cards. Quality assurance and test software programs take full advantage of a random number generator to simulate user input, sensor data, traffic flow, weather, etc. Because random events play an important role in different types of programs, Java comes with an extensive set of random number methods under the Random class. The Random class is in the rt.jar under the java.util package. Here are a few of the methods in the Random class shown in Table 3.5:

Random Method	Description
setSeed(long x)	Sets the seed of the random generator
next(int)	Returns a random integer
nextBoolean()	Returns true or false
nextInt(int n)	Returns a random integer value from 0 to n -1
nextDouble()	Returns a random decimal value from 0.0 up to and not including 1.0
nextLong()	Returns a random long value

Table 3.5 Random Number Generator Method

We can create some interesting programs using the random number generator, but first, let's use Eclipse to see the output from some of the methods.

3.4.1 Computer Activity 3.4: Random Number Test

In Eclipse, create a new Java project called "CH3CA3.4-Random Test". Create a new class called "RandomTest" with a main() method under the package called "randomtest", Code Listing 3.6.

```
1. package randomtest;
2.
3. import java.util.Random;
4.
5. public class RandomTest {
6.
7.     public static void main(String[] args) {
8.         // TODO Auto-generated method stub
9.
10.     }
11. }
```

Code Listing 3.6 RandomTest Class

Before you go further, we are going to do something a little different. Put the cursor in line 2 and hit Enter a couple of times to create a couple lines between line 2 and line3. Enter the following:

```
import java.util.Random;
```

Within the main() method enter the following:

```
Random gen = new Random();

int x = gen.nextInt(100);
System.out.println(x);

double y = gen.nextDouble();
System.out.println(y);

boolean z = gen.nextBoolean();
System.out.println(z);
```

The program should look similar to Code Listing 3.7:

```
1. package randomtest;
2.
3. import java.util.Random;
4.
5. public class RandomTest {
6.
7.     public static void main(String[] args) {
8.         // TODO Auto-generated method stub
9.
10.        Random gen = new Random();
11.
12.        int x = gen.nextInt(100);
13.        System.out.println(x);
14.
15.        double y = gen.nextDouble();
16.        System.out.println(y);
17.
18.        boolean z = gen.nextBoolean();
19.        System.out.println(z);
20.    }
21.}
```

Code Listing 3.7 Random Number Test

Run the program a few times, and you will see that the output appears to be different each time. If you think the random numbers are becoming too predictable, you can add the setSeed() method to reset the random number generator. We had to do something different in order to gain access to the Random methods. Line 3 was added to import the Random class. Also, line 10 creates a copy of the Random class type. These lines were not required when working with the Math class. Why are these classes being handled differently? The answer is in how the classes were originally created. As with the last chapter that introduced objects, we will explain the details in Chapter 6.

3.5 Strings

The output from the last few programs has been a little uninformative. Numbers without words or descriptors is not acceptable in the scientific community. The "Hello World" program in Chapter 2 demonstrated how to output text, or, in this case, a string. Strings are objects in Java. The String() class helps to define the string and offer methods to perform operations on the string. The class can be found in the rt.jar under java.lang. You can define a string in a couple of different ways:

```
String str1 = new String("Hello java");
String str2 = "Hello java";
```

The lines above do the exact same thing. Once the string has been created, it is considered immutable.

Definition: *Immutable* - means that the object is not able to be changed.

Even though the strings are immutable, you can perform some operations on them. The String class has about 42 methods available. Table 3.6 below lists some of the methods in the string class.

String Method	Description
charAt(int Index)	Returns the character at the specified index
compareTo(String)	Returns a 0 if the argument (String) is equal to the string. Returns a negative value if the string is lexicographically less than the (String) argument Returns a positive value if this string is lexicographically greater than the (String) argument
equals(String)	Returns the Boolean True if the string equals another string; otherwise, returns False
equalsIgnoreCase(String)	Returns the Boolean True if the string equals another string regardless of upper or lower case; otherwise, returns False
indexOf(String)	Returns the index as an integer of the first instance of the substring.
length()	Returns the length of the string as an integer
substring(int beginIndex)	Returns a string that starts at the beginIndex location until the end of the string.
substring(int beginIndex, int endIndex)	Returns a string that starts at the beginIndex location and ends up to the endIndex location
toLowerCase()	Returns the string with all lower case letters
toUpperCase()	Returns the string with all upper case letters
trim()	Returns the string with the leading and trailing spaces removed

Table 3.6 String Methods

In addition to the String methods, you can also join strings together in what is called concatenation.

Definition: *Concatenation* is an operation of connecting strings together.

For example, there are two strings

```
String str2 = "Today is ";
String str3 = "great day to learn Java";
```

You can combine these two strings using the addition symbol (+) into one string.

```
String str4 = str2 + str3;
```

The resulting string, str4, is "Today is a great day to learn Java". In this example the +, when used with string types, does not add numeric values, it concatenates the strings in the order listed in the code statement. We can use concatenation to provide better output in the println() method. Changing line 13 in the last activity, Code Listing 3.7, to the following will provide a more meaningful output:

```
System.out.println("The random number for nextInt is "+ x);
```

3.5.1 Computer Activity 3.5: Basic String Methods

In this program, we will apply the different methods to the string "Java is fun!" To better see the string and the index values, the following diagram in Table 3.7 shows the index number above each character in the string include the spaces. The index starts with 0.

0	1	2	3	4	5	6	7	8	9	10	11
J	a	v	a		i	s		f	u	n	!

Table 3.7 String Character Storage

When applying these methods to a string, it sometimes helps to draw a box or count the characters in the string. In Eclipse, create a new Java project called "CH3CA3.5-BasicStrings". Create a new class called "BasicStrings" with a main() method under the package called "basicstrings". Add the Code Listing 3.8 to the main method:

```
 String str1 = "Java is fun!";
 System.out.println("The length of the string is " + str1.length());
 System.out.println("The word fun starts at index " +
str1.indexOf("fun"));
 System.out.println("True or False, does the string equal the string
'Hello World' ? " + str1.equals("Hello World") );
 System.out.println("Here is the substring 'is fun!': " +
str1.substring(5));
 System.out.println("Here is another substring: " +
str1.substring(3,8));
 System.out.println("str1 is less than str2 " + str1.compareTo(str2));
 System.out.println("str2 is greater than str1 " +
str2.compareTo(str1));
 System.out.println("str3 and str1 are equal " + str3.compareTo(str1));
```

Code Listing 3.8 BasicString Class

Run the program. The length of the string is 12 and not 11. The index will start with 0, but there are 12 characters in the string. The index location of 'fun' starts at 8, which confirms the Table 3.7 index picture above. The first substring starts at index 5 until the end, thus "is fun!" is the result. The last substring gets the characters in the middle of the string. Notice that the letter 'f' is not part of this substring.

We have been using the println() method to provide output, but we could have used the print() method instead. The println() method will print the string and add a new line at the end so the next output to print can print on the next line. The print() method simply prints the string, but if you want to add a new line, you will have to add it. To do this, you can use what is called an escape sequence. For new line, the escape sequence is \n. When it comes to formatting the output of a string, there are several other escape sequence characters. Table 3.8 below lists the other escape sequences:

Escape Sequence	Description
\t	Inserts a tab
\b	Inserts a backspace
\n	Inserts a new line
\r	Inserts a carriage return
\f	Insert a form feed
\'	Insert a single quote character
\"	Insert a double quote character
\\	Insert a backslash character

Table 3.8 Character Escape Sequences

For example, here is a modified version of the first substring line using double quotes:

```
System.out.println("Here is the substring \"is fun!\": " +
str1.substring(5));
```

Note: Eclipse doesn't support \b or \r in the output console.

Also, notice that the String() class methods are being called from within the System.out.println method. The order of operation is also applied to dot notation similar to mathematical operations. The str1.substring() method is performed first. Once completed and the data returned, the System.out.println method will run using the results from str1.substring() call.

3.6 Getting User Input

To make console applications more interactive for the user, you will want the user to provide some input. Java supports three solutions for console application input. The first is to enter input from the command line. You will notice that the main method includes a string input: main(String[] args). Actually, this is a string array, which we will save for explanation in a later chapter. The next three solutions are for in-program user input. As there is a System.out, there is a System.in, which simply opens an input stream from the keyboard. Java is a language that continues to evolve and grow. Before the JDK 1.5 release, the first input program solution was to wrap System.in into a Buffered Reader. The following Code Listing 3.9 shows how this was done:

```
package inputtest;

import java.io.BufferedReader;
import java.io.InputStreamReader;
import java.io.IOException;

public class InputTest {

    public static void main(String[] args) {
        // TODO Auto-generated method stub

        System.out.println("Please enter a string and hit the \"Enter\" key :");

        try{
            BufferedReader bRead = new BufferedReader( new InputStreamReader(System.in));
            String str2 = bRead.readLine();
            System.out.println(str2);
            bRead.close();
        }
        catch(IOException e)
        {
            e.printStackTrace();
        }
    }
}
```

Code Listing 3.9 Input Test

This example introduces several concepts that we have yet to talk about, such as try-catch, error handling, and Class nesting. Several Java library imports are required to create the BufferedRead console input. The InputStreamReader defines where the input stream is coming from. In this case, it is the keyboard using System.in. The BufferedReader class has the readline() method to read a line from the console. A simpler solution came in Java v5. The Scanner class was added to simplify console input. Let's write a program using the Scanner class.

3.6.1 Computer Activity 3.6: Scanner Class for User Input

In Eclipse, create a new Java project called "CH3CA3.6-User Input2". Create a new class called "InputTest2" with a main() method under the package called "inputtest2". Add an input after the package and before the main() method:

```
import java.util.Scanner;
```

Add the following code to the main() method:

```
System.out.println("Please enter a string and hit the \"Enter\" key
:");
Scanner sRead = new Scanner(System.in);
String str3 = sRead.nextLine();
System.out.println(str3);
sRead.close();
```

Code Listing 3.10 shows what the program should look like

```
package jae.inputtest2;

import java.util.Scanner;

public class InputTest2 {

    public static void main(String[] args) {
        // TODO Auto-generated method stub

        System.out.println("Please enter a string and hit the
\"Enter\" key:");
        Scanner sRead = new Scanner(System.in);
        String str3 = sRead.nextLine();
        System.out.println(str3);
        sRead.close();

    }
}
```

Code Listing 3.10 Input Test 2

The application is much simpler to read. In both solutions, the close() method is called to close the input stream. It is good practice to close the stream or scanner after it has been used since you may want to re-open it later for other input. Run the application. You will have to place the cursor in the output window, enter some text, and then hit Enter. The string you entered should be re-printed to the screen. The Scanner class has several methods available. Table 3.9 contains a few of them:

Scanner Method	Description
close()	Closes the scanner
nextBoolean()	Converts user input to a Boolean and returns the Boolean value
nextInt()	Scans the user input and return the integer value
nextDouble()	Scans the user input and return the double value
nextLine()	Scans the user input and returns a string

Table 3.9 Utility Methods

The latest console input solution arrived in Java v6. The new java.io.console() class was added to provide formatted input and support for passwords. The object was provided with capabilities similar to the printf statement found in the C language. The Console class is more advanced than we want to cover here, thus for the console applications in this book, stick with the Scanner class. At some point, you may have to deal with strings or string input that has numbers that need to be treated as a numeric data type. Java comes with parsing methods to convert strings to numbers. The `Integer.parseInt(String)` converts the string to an Integer, and the `Double.parseDouble(String)` converts the string to a double. There are similar methods for long and float data types. Here is an application example in Code Listing 3.11:

```
String str4 = "42";
int myNum = Integer.parseInt(str4);
myNum++;
System.out.println("The number "+str4+" incremented by 1 is " + myNum);

String str5 = "3.45";
double myNum2 = Double.parseDouble(str5);
myNum2 += 2.10;
System.out.println("Adding 2.1 to " + str5 +" is " + myNum2 );
```

Code Listing 3.11 Number Data Types

3.7 Comments in Code

You may have to share your code with others, or go back to your code many years later. You might not remember what and why you wrote the code the way you did, so a good coding practice is to add comments in your code, especially if it is not obvious why the code was written the way it was. Adding comments that describe what your algorithm is doing helps the reader understand the code faster and provides the recall of that creative moment you were having years ago when you originally wrote the code. Comments are added two ways. The first is a single line comment that is preceded with two forward slashes //:

```
//This is a basic comment
```

You have seen this type of comment in every application so far:

```
// TODO Auto-generated method stub
```

Java treats the "//" and all text that follows until the end of the line as a comment and does not try to process it as code. In Eclipse and most editors, the single line comment is in the color green. If you need to write several lines of text, you can use the block comment that starts with /* and ends with */. In Eclipse as soon as you enter /*, you can write as many lines as you like. Eclipse will automatically add * for each line and */ for the end of the comment block.

```
/* This is a block
* comment that takes several lines
* to write
*/
```

If you are asked to add comments on a test, you can use either method; but if you use the block method, make sure you don't miss the * on each line or the end comment */. Only the /* at the beginning and the */ at the end of the comment block are required, but the *'s at the beginning of each line inside the block makes it easy to see the comment block at a glance. Note that you cannot nest block comments, i.e. you cannot have a comment block within a comment block. That will cause an error. You can nest single-line comments inside of a block comment, however.

3.8 Summary and Homework Assignments

You may never run into a life and death situation that requires your algebra skills, but algebra never goes away. You will see more uses of algebra in higher math and other sciences. We have seen in this chapter that computer science makes full use of algebra, which answers the question of why learning Algebra is important. The next chapter will then look at program flow, but here are a few questions and programming projects.

3.8.1 Questions

1. The movie *Red Planet* was released in 2000. There was another movie about a mission to Mars that came out that same year. What was the name of the movie?

2. Write a Java program statement for one root of the quadratic equation:

$$x = \frac{-b - \sqrt{b^2 - 4ac}}{2a}$$

3. Write a Java program statement for the Pythagorean equation

$$c = \sqrt{a^2 + b^2}$$

4. Write a Java program statement for the Arrhenius equation

$$k = Ae^{-E_a/(RT)}$$

5. Write a Java program statement for the Kepler's equation. You may substitute e for ε.

$$M = E - \epsilon \sin E$$

6. Given the following:

```
int x = 4;
int y = 7;
double z = 5.7;
String str1 = "3";
```

What are the results for each of these statements?

```
double j = x * y - z;
int t = x*y - (int) z;
int f = x * (int)(y - Math.round(z)) + Integer.parseInt(str1);
double c = Math.pow((double)x,Double.parseDouble(str1));
```

7. Are random generators really random? If not, what is the random number generator called?

8. What is the result of the following program?

```
package annabooks.mt3;

public class MathTest3 {

    public static void main(String[] args) {
        // TODO Auto-generated method stub

        double x = 3 + 6 * 5 - 3 / 2;

        System.out.println("The result for x is: " + x);
    }
}
```

9. For #8, what can be changed to obtain the correct result?

10. What is wrong with the following program? What happens when you run the program? What must be done to correct the program?

```
package annabooks.st;

public class StringTest {

    public static void main(String[] args) {
        // TODO Auto-generated method stub

        String str1 = "The quick brown fox jumped over the lazy dog.";

        System.out.println("The fox ran far away from the " + str1.substring(36,46) );

    }
}
```

11. What is the output of the following program? Does it work in Eclipse?

```
package annabooks.st;
public class StringTest {
    public static void main(String[] args) {
        // TODO Auto-generated method stub
        String str1 = "The quick brown fox jumped over the
lazy dog.";
        System.out.println("The fox ran far away from the " +
str1.substring(36,45) );
        String str2 = "Jerry has a very healthy appetite";
        String str3 = str2.substring(0, 1);
        String str4 = str2.substring(7, 8);
        String str5 = str2.substring(12, 13);
        String str6 = str2.substring(19, 20);
        String str7 = str2.substring(25);
        String str8 = str7.substring(0, 3);
        System.out.print(str3.substring(0, 1).toUpperCase() +
str4.substring(0,1)+ str5 + str6 + " " +
str8.substring(0,1).toUpperCase()+ str8.substring(1, 3)+"\n");
        String str9 = "any other name";
        System.out.print("\"A rose by the lake" +
"\b\b\b\b\b\b\b\b" + str9 + "\n");
    }
}
```

12. What is the output of the following program? Why? Hint: Check the Java String Class online.

```
1. package annabooks.st;
2.
3. public class StringCompare {
4.
5.     public static void main(String[] args) {
6.         // TODO Auto-generated method stub
7.
8.         String str1 = "Today is Sunday";
9.         String str2 = "Today is sunday";
10.
11.        System.out.println("The comparison result is " +
   str1.compareTo(str2));
12.        System.out.println("The comparison result is " +
   str2.compareTo(str1));
13.
14.    }
15. }
```

13. In #12, if you change the string in line 8 from "Today is Sunday" to "Today is monday", what is the result? Why?

14. What is the result if you change the string in line 8 to "Today is sunday"?

15. When the String compareTo method result is 0, what should be the output for String equals be?

3.8.2 Programming Projects

1. Write a program that asks a user to input a string, and then outputs to the user how many characters long the string is.

2. Create a simple calculator program that asks the user for two numbers and then outputs a user-friendly message with the sum of the two numbers.

3. Write a program that takes the following string, extracts the numbers, and outputs the product of the numbers as the answer to the question.

   "I am driving at a speed of 88 Km/h for 3.5 hours. How far have I traveled?"

4. Write a program that asks the user to guess a number between 0 and 10. When the user hits the enter key, the program uses the random number generator to generate the number between 0 and 10 and tells the user what number is.

5. When you pay cash at a grocery store, any change between 1 cent and 99 cents is dispensed using a coin dispenser. The coin dispenser dispenses quarters (.25), dimes (.10), nickels (.05), and pennies (.01). Assuming an infinite number of coins, create a program that accepts user input from 1 to 99 (cents) representing the change to be dispensed, and outputs the number of quarters, dimes, nickels, and pennies to be dispensed. The program should maximize the largest coins to the smallest. For example, an input value 68 (68 cents) would output:

   2 – Quarter(s)
   1 – Dime(s)
   1 – Nickle(s)
   3 – Penny(s)

4 Controlling the Program Flow and Iteration

"I honestly think you ought to sit down calmly, take a stress pill, and think things over."
– HAL 9000, from the movie *2001: A Space Odyssey*, Metro-Goldwyn-Mayer (MGM), 1968

"I am reliving the same day over and over."
-Phil Conners, from the movie *Groundhog Day*, Columbia Pictures Corporation, 1993

This is a chapter so important that it requires two movie quotes. Artificial Intelligence (AI) has come a long way since the 1960's. IBM's Watson has shown the ability to play chess and win on "Jeopardy!", but the IBM Watson is a very large computer that fills a room. Smaller AIs are coming in the form of Alexa, Cortana, and Siri for smart devices that require a constant connection to the Internet. We still have a few years to go before we have the level of interaction as HAL 9000 in the movie. Making decisions is an important part of programming. The programmer needs to provide the question and the possible solutions to the question. As the programmer, you are providing the thinking or the flow within the program. The goal of this chapter is to cover program flow control and the concept of iteration. As far as the second movie quote, no pun intended, but we will circle back to it later in the chapter.

4.1 Flowchart Diagram

Program flow/conditional branching statements are used to selectively steer the program execution based on the instantaneous state of the program. An old tool called a flow control diagram or flowchart can help draw a picture of the algorithm being developed. In English class, diagramming sentences was a visual aid to help better understand sentence structure. A flowchart provides a visual aid to see the program flow before the code is written. Applications like Microsoft's Visio were created to help generate flowcharts. Below are the basic elements of a program flowchart, Figure 4.1. We will use these elements to diagram the different flow control statements in this chapter.

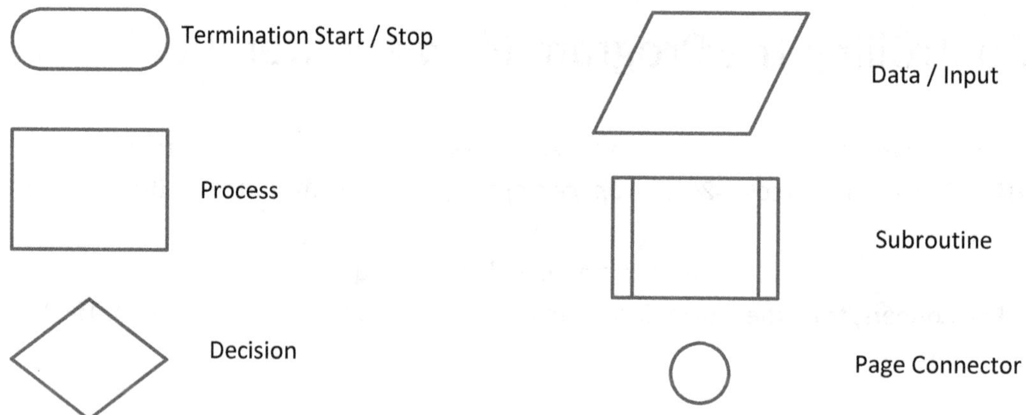

Figure 4.1 Flowchart Elements

Flowcharts are useful tools when you first start out programming. In practice, applications are getting more complex and multithreaded, and flowcharts are better used in team programming from a much higher level. Flowcharts will be used in this chapter as visual aids.

4.2 *If-Else Statement, Relational Operators, and Boolean Expressions*

After this long introduction, the big decision statement in Java is the 'if' statement.

If a condition is true, then perform this action.

The if-statement tests a condition for a Boolean result, which is either true or false. If you want to add some actions to perform when the condition is false, you can add the optional 'else' statement.

If a condition is true, then perform this action, else perform this other action.

Definition: *Condition* – A mathematical statement that resolves to a true or false.
Some languages call this the if-then-else statement, and the 'then'- is actually written in the code. The developers for Java removed the need for the extra text. Code Listing 4.1 is a simple program:

```
int w = 0;

if (w == 0)
{
      System.out.println("W is zero");
}
else
{
      System.out.println("W is not zero");
}
```

Code Listing 4.1 If-Then-Else Program

The program tests to see if w is equal to zero. If the condition is true, then "W is zero" is printed to the console. If the condition is false, then "W is not zero" is printed to the console. Notice that w = 0 and w == 0 are two different meanings. The single "=" is the assignment. The number 0 is assigned to w. The double "==" is the test to see if w equals 0. Many programmers make the basic mistake of confusing assignment with equals so watch out for this in your programs. Also, notice that there is no semicolon ';' after the if- and else- statements. This is because there is a block of code to follow. Figure 4.2 shows what the flowchart for the program looks like:

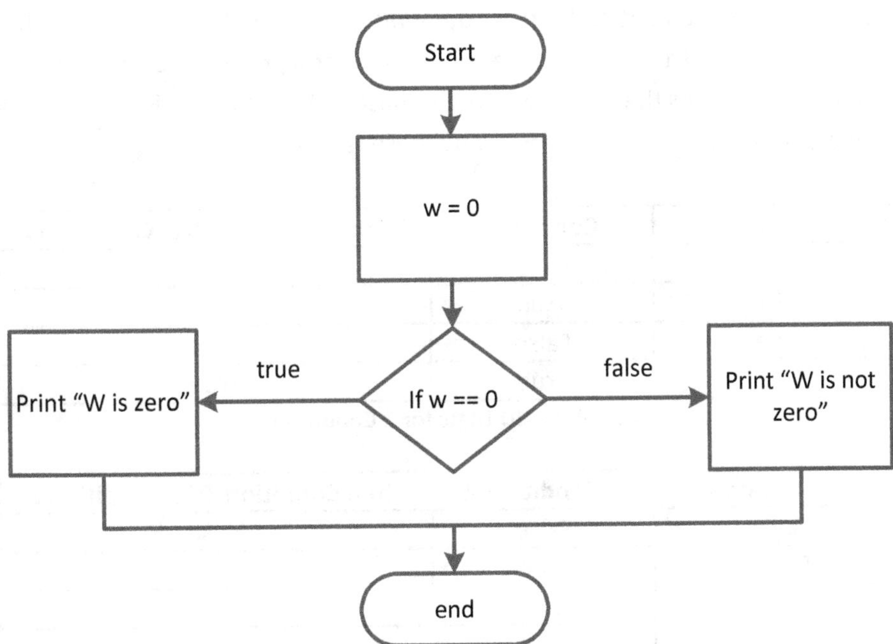

Figure 4.2 Zero Test Program Flowchart

Looking at the flowchart, the if-statement can take the program in two directions. The picture looks like an upside-down tree, thus programmers will say the if-statement creates a "branch". You will also hear programmers say the if-statement is a branch statement. The double equals '==' is a Relation Operator. The if-statement tests to see how two objects relate to each other. There are other Relational Operators such as less-than '<' and greater-than '>'. Table 4.1 below lists the other Relational Operators.

Relational Operator	Description
==	equal-to
<	less-than
>	greater-than
<=	less-than-or-equal-to
>=	greater-than-or-equal-to
!=	Not-equal

Table 4.1 Relational Operators

What if there are multiple conditions that need to be tested? You can handle these situations using three Boolean expressions: AND (&&), OR (| |), and NOT (!). For the AND (&&), all conditions must be true for the if-statement to be true; otherwise, the condition is false. For the OR (| |), only one condition must be true for the if-statement to be true; otherwise, the condition is false. The NOT (!) operator reverses the logic from true to false or false to true. For two conditions, the three Boolean expressions can be represented by these tables:

If Condition 1	If Condition 2	Then Condition 1 && Condition 2
False	False	False
False	True	False
True	False	False
True	True	True

Table 4.2 AND Logic for 2 Conditions

<table>
<tr><th>If Condition 1</th><th>If Condition 2</th><th>Then Condition 1 | | Condition 2</th></tr>
<tr><td>False</td><td>False</td><td>False</td></tr>
<tr><td>False</td><td>True</td><td>True</td></tr>
<tr><td>True</td><td>False</td><td>True</td></tr>
<tr><td>True</td><td>True</td><td>True</td></tr>
</table>

Table 4.3 OR Logic for 2 Conditions

Condition 1	! Condition1
True	False
False	True

Table 4.4 NOT Logic for 2 Conditions

Note that in Table 4.2 all conditions must be true for the AND result to be true, but in Table 4.3 all conditions must be false for the OR result to be false. Code Listing 4.2 shows a simple program that demonstrates the logic. Can you guess the output?

```
package iftest2;

public class IfTest2 {

    public static void main(String[] args) {
        // TODO Auto-generated method stub

        boolean x = true;
        boolean y = false;
        boolean z = true;

        if ( x == true && y == false )
        {
            System.out.println("The first condition is true");
        }
        else System.out.println("The first condition is false");

        if ( x == true || y == true)
        {
            System.out.println("The second condition is true");
        }
        else System.out.println("The first condition is false");

        if (!z)
        {
            System.out.println("The third condition is true");
        }
        else System.out.println("The third condition is false");

    }
}
```

Code Listing 4.2 Boolean Logic Demonstration Program

You will notice that we didn't use {} to create a block for the else-statements. When there is a single statement, a block is not needed, but it is recommended. The if-statements could have been written without the {}, but if you needed to add more code under the if and forget to put the brackets {} back in, the application will crash or not compile. Always using the {} to define the code block is good defensive programming practice. The result of the program is that the first two conditions are true and the last one is false. The program creates three Boolean variables. The first condition is true since x equals true and y equals false. Even though y equals false doesn't mean the condition fails. The condition that 'y equals false' is a true statement. By ANDing both true statements, the full condition is true. The second if-statement condition is also true. The condition that 'y equals true' is false. Since we are ORing the two conditions, the 'x equals true'is true, thus the full condition is true. The final if-statement demonstrates the NOT. The variable z is assigned true. The NOT changes the conditional test to false, and the result is false. Combinations of Boolean tests can be made using parenthesis (), which can make for some complex programming. For example, if we added another condition to the above program:

```
if (((x == true && !y == true) && (!y == z)) || (!x == z))
```

The result of this statement would be true. Chapter 3 discussed the order of operation, which also applies to Boolean logic. With complex Boolean expressions, you may want to optimize code for readability. One such solution is using a couple of transformation rules known as De Morgan's Laws:

```
!(x && y) is the same as !x || !y
!(x || y) is the same as !x && !y
```

The not (!) operator changes the AND to an OR and an OR to an AND. Also, the not operator changes Relational Operators. Greater-than becomes less-than and less-than becomes greater-than. Here is an example:

```
!(( x >= k) && !(x < y))
```

Transferring the not (!) through the expression

```
!(x >= k) || (x < y)
```

Doing one more transfer, the final expression is

(x < k) || (x < y)

4.2.1 Computer Activity 4.1 – Coin Flip

With conditional branching, we can combine the if-statement with the math and the strings from the previous chapters to develop some creative applications. For this project, you will create a simple coin flip game. The program will ask the user to enter "h" for heads and "t" for tails. The Boolean random generator will act as the coin flip to generate a true for heads or false for tails. The following logic table, Table 4.5, shows that there are 4 possible outcomes. Using the if-statement, the program will print the results.

User Input	Coin Toss	Result
Heads	Heads	Win
Heads	Tails	Loss
Tails	Heads	Loss
Tails	Tails	Win

Table 4.5 Coin Flip Outcomes

Create a new Java project in Eclipse called "CH4CA4.1-CoinFlip:" Create a new class called "CoinFlip" with a main() method and a new package called "coinflip". Below the package statement add the imports for the scanner and random generator:

```
import java.util.Scanner;
import java.util.Random;
```

In the main() method, first add the statements for the user input:

```
//Ask the user to choose heads or tails
System.out.println("Enter h for Heads or t for Tails :");
Scanner sRead = new Scanner(System.in);
String str1 = sRead.next();
sRead.close();
```

Next, create the Boolean generator:

```
//Generate the coin toss
Random gen = new Random();
boolean headstails = gen.nextBoolean();
```

Finally, add the if-statements to output the results:

```
//Print the results
if (str1.equals("h"))
{
    System.out.println("You chose heads");
}
else
{
    System.out.println("You chose tails");
}

if (headstails == true)
{
    System.out.println("The coin toss result is heads");
}
else
{
    System.out.println("The coin toss result is tails");
}
```

You can see that we are using the string equals() method to return the Boolean. A common mistake is to try to use == for String objects. The program should look like Code Listing 4.3:

```
package coinflip;

import java.util.Scanner;
import java.util.Random;

public class CoinFlip {

    public static void main(String[] args) {
        // TODO Auto-generated method stub

        //Ask the user to choose heads or tails
        System.out.println("Enter h for Heads or t for Tails :");
        Scanner sRead = new Scanner(System.in);
        String str1 = sRead.next();
        sRead.close();

```

```
        //Generate the coin toss
        Random gen = new Random();
        boolean headstails = gen.nextBoolean();

        //Print the results
        if (str1.equals("h"))
        {
            System.out.println("You chose heads");
        }
        else
        {
            System.out.println("You chose tails");
        }

        if (headstails == true)
        {
            System.out.println("The coin toss result is heads");
        }
        else
        {
            System.out.println("The coin toss result is tails");
        }

    }

}
```

Code Listing 4.3 Coin Flip Program

Run the program a few times and enter h and t to see the results. You have now created your first computer game. Create the flowchart for the program.

4.3 Nested If-Else

An if-else statement can be put into the block of another if-statement. This is called a nested if. Code Listing 4.4 is an example:

```
int g = 4;
int t = 7;
double n = 8.0;

if ( g < t )
{
        if (n < t)
        {
                System.out.println("n is less than t, and g is less then t");
        }
        else
        {
                System.out.println("t is less than n, and g is less then t");
        }
}
```

Code Listing 4.4 Nested If

If the first condition is true, the second condition is tested. If the first condition is false, n < t is never tested. Multiply nested if-statements can be confusing. It is important to indent your code so that others can follow the program flow. Figure 4.3 is the flowchart for the above Code Listing 4.4.

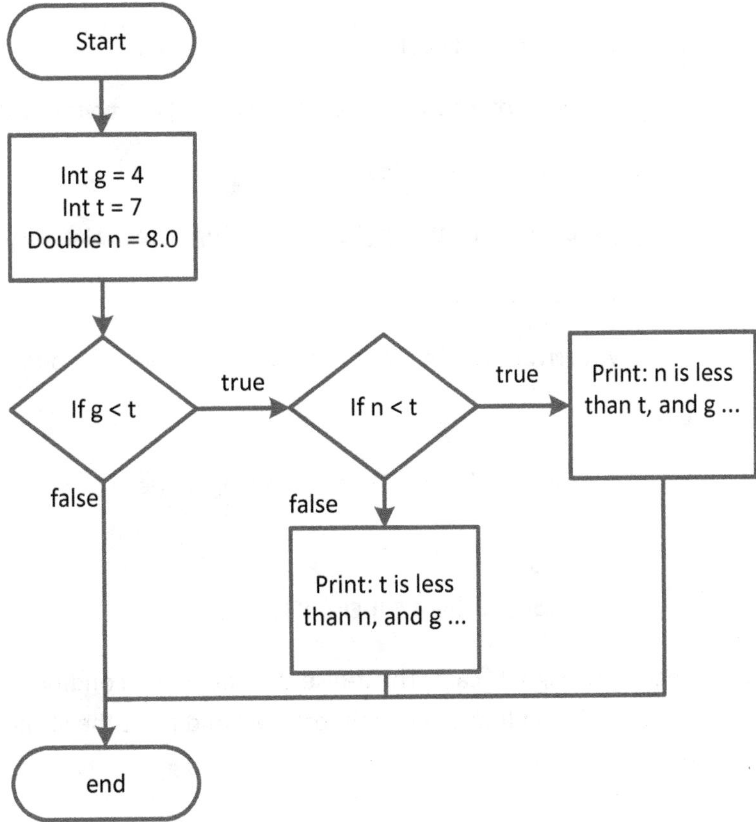

Figure 4.3 Nested If Flowchart

4.4 If-Else-If Ladder

For a series of conditions to test, you can use an if-else-if ladder. If the first condition is false, it tests the next condition. If the second condition is false, the next condition is tested, and so on. A final optional else-statement can be set up as the default condition. Code Listing 4.5 is an example of this construct.

```
package iftest3;

public class IfTest3 {

    public static void main(String[] args) {
        // TODO Auto-generated method stub

        String str = "car";
```

```

        if (str.equals("truck"))
        {
            System.out.println("I am taking the truck out today");
        }
        else if (str.equals("bike"))
        {
            System.out.println("I am taking the bike out today");
        }
        else if (str.equals("car"))
        {
            System.out.println("I am taking the car out today");
        }
        else
        {
            System.out.print("I am staying home");
        }
    }
}
```

Code Listing 4.5 If-Else-If Ladder

We defined a string object and assign it “car”. The if-else-if ladder has a condition to test what the value str matches. In this case, it will find the match for “car” and print the string. The flowchart for this looks like Figure 4.4:

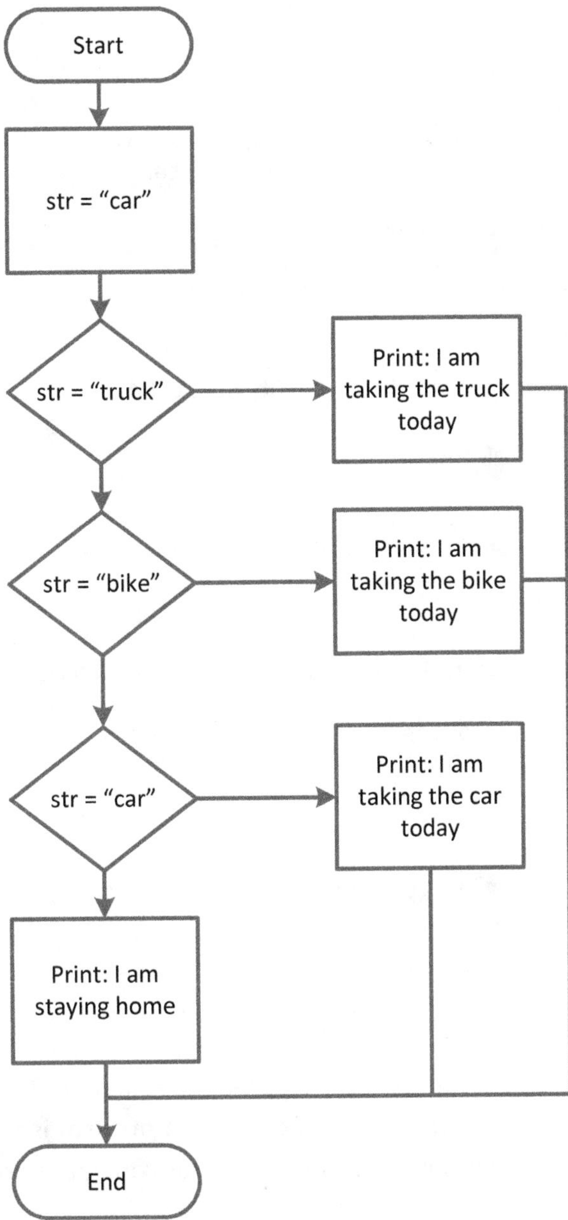

Figure 4.4 If-Else-If Ladder Flowchart

Each condition of the string doesn’t have to perform the same check. We can modify the ladder to add other conditions to test, Code Listing 4.6:

```
1. package iftest3;
2.
3. public class IfTest3 {
4.
5.     public static void main(String[] args) {
6.         // TODO Auto-generated method stub
7.
8.         String str = "car";
9.
10.        int NumberDay = 3; // 1 thru 7 is the number for Sunday
   through Saturday
11.
12.        if (str.equals("truck") && NumberDay == 2)
13.        {
14.            System.out.println("It is Monday. I am taking the truck
   out today");
15.        }
16.        else if (str.equals("bike"))
17.        {
18.            System.out.println("I am taking the bike out today");
19.        }
20.        else if (str.equals("car") && NumberDay == 3)
21.        {
22.            System.out.println("It is Tuesday. I am taking the car
   out today");
23.        }
24.        else
25.        {
26.            System.out.print("I am staying home");
27.        }
28.    }
29. }
```

Code Listing 4.6 Enhanced If-Else-If Ladder

For lines 12 and 20, both conditions must be true for the output to print. These different types of conditions are known as compound conditions. If either one of them is false, the condition is skipped to the next else if-statement. If none of the previous conditions are true, the final else will be executed.

4.4.1 Computer Activity 4.2 – Coin Flip Enhanced

Using the if-else-if ladder, let's modify the coin flip program to provide a different output response for the user. Comment out the original print results:

```
//Print the results
/*
if (str1.equals("h"))
{
    System.out.println("You chose heads");
}
else
{
    System.out.println("You chose tails");
}

if (headstails == true)
{
    System.out.println("The coin toss result is heads");
}
else
{
    System.out.println("The coin toss result is tails");
}
*/
```

After the commented out code, add the following it-else-if ladder:

```
if (headstails == true && str1.equals("h"))
{
    System.out.println("The coin is heads. You Win!");
}
else if (headstails == false && str1.equals("t"))
{
    System.out.println("The coin is tails. You Win!");
}
else if (headstails == true && str1.equals("t"))
{
    System.out.println("The coin is heads. Better luck next time.");
}
else if (headstails == false && str1.equals("h"))
{
    System.out.println("The coin is tails. Better luck next time.");
}
```

The new output provides the user with a different output experience. Run the program a few times to test the code. The if-else-if ladder uses two conditions per each rung to test the 4 possible outcomes. A final else-statement is not needed, since there can only be 4 results. Create a flowchart for the updated application.

4.5 Switch-Case

Besides the if-else statement, another decision/branching statement is the switch-case statement. The switch-case statement is a control statement that evaluates an expression against a number of possible values and executes a specific block of code depending on the matching value. It also provides for a default block of code that can be executed if none of the cases is satisfied. Notice that we used the word expression and not condition.

Definition: *Expression* – a combination of variables, constants, or functions that computes to produce another value.

Code Listing 4.7 is a simple example that checks an integer value.

```
package switchcasetest;

public class SwitchCaseTest {

    public static void main(String[] args) {
        // TODO Auto-generated method stub

        int planetnumber = 5;

        switch (planetnumber) {

            case 1:
                System.out.println("Mercury");
                break;
            case 2:
                System.out.println("Venus");
                break;
            case 3:
                System.out.println("Earth");
                break;
            case 4:
                System.out.println("Mars");
                break;
            case 5:
                System.out.println("Jupiter");
                break;
```

```
      case 6:
        System.out.println("Saturn");
        break;
      case 7:
        System.out.println("Uranus");
        break;
      case 8:
        System.out.println("Neptune");
        break;
      default:
        System.out.println("Not a planet");
    }
  }

}
```

Code Listing 4.7 Switch-Case

The switch statement checks the integer expression, “planetnumber”, against the 8 available integer values. If it finds a match, the program executes what is in the block. If there is no match, the default case will be executed. You may think that this is similar to the if-else-if ladder and that the flowchart diagram would look very similar. The difference is that the switch-case is checking for a single expression, and the if-else-if ladder can have more complex conditions to test. For switch-case, each case must match the same value type of the switch expression. The types supported by switch-case are String, char, int, byte, or short. You cannot mix types like strings and integers unless you do a caste or conversion ahead of time. The choice to use the if-else-if ladder versus switch-case is dependent on the problem to be solved. For example, a group of three radio buttons in a graphical application may be assigned the values 0, 1, and 2. A switch-case can be used to determine the next process when the user selects one of the three radio buttons.

The break-statement forces the program to jump out of the switch-case. If you forget the break statement, the program will continue to execute all the statements that follow. This is known as falling through. There might be situations where falling through can be exactly what you want. For example, several cases are to perform the same tasks. You can stack cases together and have a single block with a break statement. Here is a day of the week example:

```
case 1: //Sunday
case 7: //Saturday
    System.out.println("The weekend");
    break;
case 2: //Monday
case 3: //Tuesday
case 4: //Wednesday
case 5: //Thursday
case 6: //Friday
    System.out.println("Weekday");
    break;
```

The switch-case statement is a compact implementation of a series of the if-else-if ladder of Section 4.4. Code Listing 4.8 below shows how to express the planet identifier switch-case statement in Code Listing 4.7 above as an if-else-if ladder.

```
//If-else-if ladder version of the switch-case statement
if (planetnumber == 1) {
    System.out.println("Mercury");
}
else if (planetnumber == 2) {
    System.out.println("Venus");
}
else if (planetnumber == 3) {
    System.out.println("Earth");
}
else if (planetnumber == 4) {
    System.out.println("Mars");
}
else if (planetnumber == 5) {
    System.out.println("Jupiter");
}
else if (planetnumber == 6) {
    System.out.println("Saturn");
}
else if (planetnumber == 7) {
    System.out.println("Uranus");
}
else if (planetnumber == 8) {
    System.out.println("Neptune");
}
else {
    System.out.println("Not a planet");
}
```

Code Listing 4.8 If-Else-If Ladder Version of Switch-Case Statement

4.6 *Loops / Iteration*

The if-statement and switch statement provided conditional branching for our programs. The next construct is iteration and our second movie quote. In the movie *Groundhog Day*, the main character gets to relive the same day over and over until he finally figures out how to break the endless loop. In much the same way, iteration or loop statements repeat the execution of code until a condition is reached.

Definition: *Iteration* is a repetition of a process to achieve a desired result.

Loops can programmatically solve basic math sequences like factorial (n!). From a practical perspective, loops can be used to calculate compound interest for a savings account or a dividend payout for a stock over a given time period. This section will introduce the different loop statements that are available in Java.

4.6.1 While-Loop

The most basic loop is the while-loop. Here is the structure of the loop:

```
//While-loop
while(condition)
{
     //Repeated code block
}
```

The code is simply saying that: "While the conditional expression is true, run the block of code, and continue to run the block of code until the conditional expression is false." Hence, the while-loop executes a group of statements enclosed in {} until a specified expression evaluates to false. The while-loop is similar to the if-statement, except the code block is repeated. The conditional test in the while-statement is at the beginning of the loop, so the loop block will never execute if the test initially fails. Any variables to be part of the conditional expression must be declared before the while-loop to be in scope at the time of the conditional test. The variables declared inside the while-loop will only be created if the loop is executed. Code Listing 4.9 is an example:

```
package whiletest;

public class WhileTest {

    public static void main(String[] args) {
        // TODO Auto-generated method stub
        //Initialize the variable to test.
        int x = 0;

        //While-loop test
        while (x < 10) //test if x is less than 10
        {
            System.out.println("This is loop number " + x);
            x++; // increment x on each pass through the loop
        }
        System.out.println("x is now " + x);
    }
}
```

Code Listing 4.9 While-Loop

The variable x is an integer with a value assigned to 0. The while-loop tests to see if x is less than 10 and if the condition is true, then the code block is executed. The code block includes output to list the loop number, and the code block includes a statement to increment the value of x. The loop continues until x is no longer less than 10, which in this case is when x = 10. The value of x = 10 is tested in the while-loop and fails, the code block is not executed, and the program continues with the next statement after the while-loop. The final output displays the final value of x, which is now 10. A more complex condition with Boolean logic can be used with while-loops. The flowchart in Figure 4.5 is for this program.

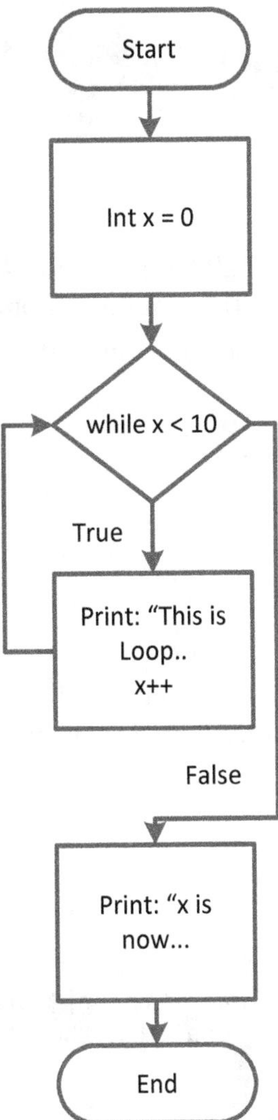

Figure 4.5 While-Loop Flowchart

A common error with programming loops is never terminating the loop. If the program fails to generate a false expression, the loop can go on forever. We call this an infinite loop

Definition: *Infinite-loop* is a loop for which there is no terminating condition.

There are some microcontrollers that require an infinite loop at the end of a program. The following while loop is a purposeful infinite loop:

```
//Infinite loop
while(true)
{
}
```

4.6.2 Do–While-Loop

The do-while-loop executes a group of statements enclosed in curly brackets "{}" repeatedly until a specified condition evaluates to false. The difference from the while-loop is that the statement or block of statements will execute at least one time before the expression is tested. Here is the basic structure:

```
//Do-while-loop
do
{
    //Repeated code block
}while(conditional);
```

The test, in the do-while, is at the end of the loop, not at the beginning like the while-loop; so the loop block will always execute at least once irrespective of the result of the test. Code Listing 4.10 is an example.

```
package dowhiletest;

public class DoWhileTest {

    public static void main(String[] args) {
        // TODO Auto-generated method stub

        int x = 10;
        do{
            System.out.println("This is loop number " + x);
            x++;
        }while (x < 10);

        System.out.println("x is now " + x);
    }

}
```

Code Listing 4.10 Do-While-Loop

The program looks very similar to the while-loop example, but this time x = 10. When the application runs, the code block is executed once and the loop is exited. The output doesn't make much sense to the user, but the do-while loop executed as expected. Change x = 0, and run the program. Now, you will have the same output as the while-loop example. The flowchart for the do-while loop looks like Figure 4.6.

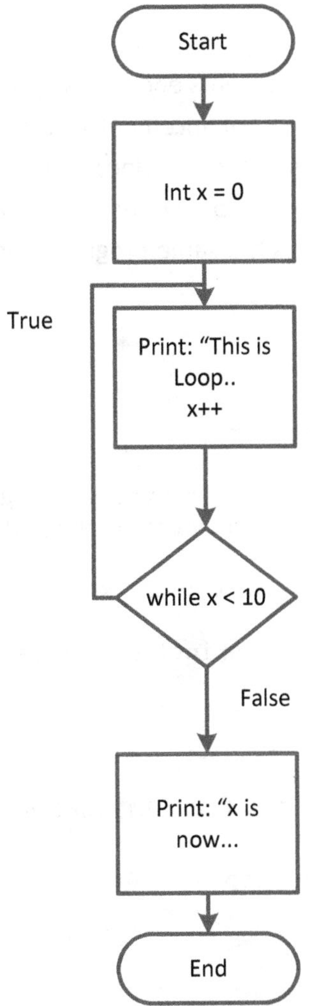

Figure 4.6 Do-While-Loop Flowchart

4.6.3 For-Loop

The most versatile loop is the for-loop. Here is the basic structure:

```
//For-loop
for(initialization, condition, iteration)
{
    //Repeated code block
}
```

The for-loop executes a group of statements enclosed in {} repeatedly until a specified condition evaluates to false. The for-loop is an enhancement to the while-loop. The for-loop provides a mechanism for initializing variables before the loop is begun and a mechanism for modifying variables after each pass through the loop. The test condition, like the while-loop, is performed at the beginning. Code Listing 4.11 is the same program from the while-loop, but implemented with a for-loop:

```
package forlooptest;

public class ForLoopTest {

    public static void main(String[] args) {
        // TODO Auto-generated method stub

        for (int x = 0; x < 10; x++)
        {
            System.out.println("This is loop number: " + x);
        }
        //System.out.println("x is now "+ x);    cannot be performed
    }
}
```

Code Listing 4.11 For-Loop

Figure 4.7 is the flowchart for the for-loop:

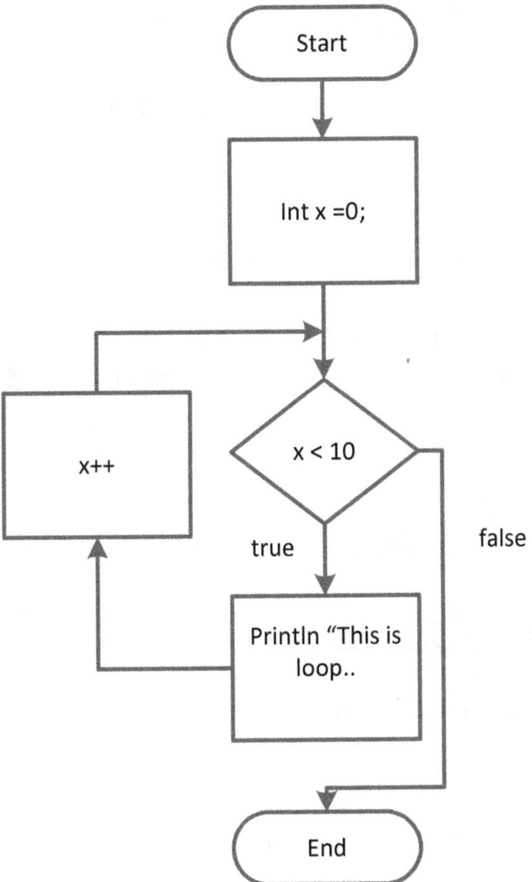

Figure 4.7 For-Loop Flowchart

The output will be the same as the while-loop, with one exception. The last output statement is commented out since it cannot run. Try uncommenting line 12 and see what happens when you run the application. The reason has to do with the "scope" of the variable x. The scope of variables will be discussed at a later time. To resolve the issue, we can make a change to move the declaration of x outside of the for-loop, Code Listing 4.12:

```
package forlooptest;

public class ForLoopTest {

    public static void main(String[] args) {
        // TODO Auto-generated method stub

```

```
        int x = 0;
        for ( ; x < 10; x++)
        {
            System.out.println("The value of x is " + x);
        }
        System.out.println("x is now "+ x);
    }
}
```

Code Listing 4.12 Modified For-Loop

The change leads to the same output as the while-loop. You don't have to define all 3 elements in the for-loop statement. The increment of x can be put into the loop code block.

```
int x = 0;
for ( ; x < 10; )
{
    System.out.println("The value of x is " + x);
    x++;
}
System.out.println("x is now "+ x);
```

The following would be the infinite loop using a for-loop:

```
for (;;) ;
```

4.6.4 Computer Activity 4.3 – Factorial

This activity will involve a for-loop and an if-statement to solve an algebra problem. The factorial of a positive integer n is denoted by n! which is a product of all positive integers less than or equal to n. For example, 4! is 24 = 4 * 3 * 2 * 1. The factorial function is defined as:

$$n! = \prod_{k=1}^{n} k$$

Another way to present the equation n! = n * (n-1)!, thus 5! = 5 * 4!, 4! = 4 * 3!, etc. Of course 0! = 1. In Eclipse, create a new Java project called "CH4CA4.3-FactorialLoop" and a new class with a main method called "FactorialLoop". Call the package "factloop". Modify and fill in the code, Code Listing 4.13, in the factorialloop.java file:

```
package factorialloop;

import java.util.Scanner;

public class FactorialLoop {

    public static void main(String[] args) {
        // TODO Auto-generated method stub

        //Ask the user for a value of n
        System.out.println("Enter a value for n:");
        Scanner sRead = new Scanner(System.in);
        int n = sRead.nextInt();
        sRead.close();

        //Set the initial factorial value
        int fact = 1;

        //Check for the condition of 1 or 0; if not true calculate the factorial
        if (!(n == 1 || n == 0))
        {
            for (int x = 1; x <= n ; x++)
            {
                Fact *= x;
            }
        }
        System.out.println("The factorial for " + n + " is " +fact);
    }
}
```

Code Listing 4.13 Factorial Calculator

Run the program and enter different values of n, but keep the value less than 10. You can use a calculator that supports “n!” to double check to see if the calculations are correct. The first part of the code asks the user for a value for n. An integer variable for the factorial is set to 1 since “1!” and “0!” equal 1. The if-statement checks for the case of 1 and 0. If n doesn’t equal 1 or 0, then the for-loop is executed to calculate the factorial. The variable x starts with 1 and is tested for the condition of less than or equal to n. The factorial value is simply the product of the variable fact multiplied by x. The product is calculated every iteration.

4.6.5 Enhanced For-Loop

The last loop is the enhanced for-loop. Also known as the for-each-loop in a programming language like C#, the enhanced for-loop is used to iterate through a collection to get the information about each of the items in the collection. The enhanced for-loop cannot be used to add or remove items from the source collection. If you need to add or remove items from the source collection, use a for-loop. A collection can be an array or an array list, and we will cover arrays, array lists, and enhanced for-loop examples in the next chapter.

4.6.6 Break and Continue

The main character in *Groundhog Day* tries every possible condition to break out of the infinite time loop that he is in. Sometimes you want to jump out of the middle of a loop or just skip some processing in a loop to continue with the next iteration. For example, a program might be searching through a group of records, and once it finds the record, it will stop searching. There are two statements that handle the situation. The first is the break-statement, which was covered in the switch-case statement. The break-statement simply breaks the code of execution and jumps out of the current block. The second is the continue-statement, which simply skips over any remaining statements to the next Boolean expression. Code Listing 4.14 is an example of the break-statement in action.

```
package breakcontinue;

public class BreakContinue {

    public static void main(String[] args) {
        // TODO Auto-generated method stub
        int x;

        for (x= 0; x <= 10; x++)
        {

            if (x ==6)
            {
                break;
            }

            System.out.println("this is loop number " + x);
        }
```

```
19.
20.         System.out.println("the final number is " + x);
21.     }
22. }
```

Code Listing 4.14 Break Statement

Here is the output:

```
this is loop number 0
this is loop number 1
this is loop number 2
this is loop number 3
this is loop number 4
this is loop number 5
the final number is 6
```

Line 12 checks to see if x equals 6, and if x equals 6, the program will break out of the loop. In this example, the loop never reaches the maximum value of 10. Code Listing 4.15 is the same program, but with the continue-statement:

```
1.  package breakcontinue;
2.
3.  public class BreakContinue {
4.
5.      public static void main(String[] args) {
6.          // TODO Auto-generated method stub
7.          int x;
8.
9.          for (x= 0; x <= 10; x++)
10.         {
11.
12.             if (x ==6)
13.             {
14.                 continue;
15.             }
16.
17.             System.out.println("this is loop number " + x);
18.         }
19.
20.         System.out.println("the final number is " + x);
21.     }
22. }
```

Code Listing 4.15 Continue Statement

Here is the output:

```
this is loop number 0
this is loop number 1
this is loop number 2
this is loop number 3
this is loop number 4
this is loop number 5
this is loop number 7
this is loop number 8
this is loop number 9
this is loop number 10
the final number is 11
```

When x equals 6, the rest of the code in the loop is skipped, and you move on to the next iteration. The output will show that loop 6 print line was skipped. The loop will continue until x equals 10.

4.6.7 Computer Activity 4.4 - Menu System with User input

Combining a switch-case with a loop provides a structure to have a menu system in a command line application. The user can make selections based on a numbered item and then enter further information into the program. In Eclipse, create a new Java project called "CH4CA4.4-MenuSystem" and a new class with a main method called "MenuSystem". Call the package "userinput". Modify and fill in the following code, Code Listing 4.16, in the MenuSystem.java file:

```
package userinput;
import java.util.Scanner;
public class MenuSystem {
    public static void main(String[] args) {
        // TODO Auto-generated method stub
        boolean closeprogram = false;
        Scanner sRead = new Scanner(System.in);
```

```
13.         do{
14.             System.out.println("Enter the number to selec the menu
   item");
15.             System.out.println("1. Enter a name");
16.             System.out.println("2. Enter an address ");
17.             System.out.println("3. Exit application");
18.
19.             int menuitem = sRead.nextInt();
20.
21.             switch(menuitem){
22.
23.                 case 1:
24.                     System.out.println("Enter a name");
25.                     //sRead.nextLine(); //Required since the
   nextInt() method doesn't consume carriage return
26.                     String sName = sRead.nextLine();
27.                     System.out.println("The name you entered is "
   +sName);
28.                     break;
29.
30.                 case 2:
31.                     System.out.println("Enter an address");
32.                     //sRead.nextLine();
33.                     String sAddress = sRead.nextLine();
34.                     System.out.println("The address you entered is "
   + sAddress);
35.                     break;
36.
37.                 case 3:
38.                     closeprogram = true;
39.                     break;
40.             }
41.
42.         }while(closeprogram == false);
43.
44.         System.out.println("Exiting program");
45.         sRead.close();
46.     }
47.}
```

Code Listing 4.16 Menu System

If you run the application, the application will continue to run until the user enters 3 to exit the application. Lines 25 and 32 read from the scanner and don't capture anything on the return. These two lines resolve a problem since the nextInt() method only consumes the number entered and not the carriage return. Comment out both lines and run the program. You will never be able to enter a name or address since the carriage return is sitting in the scanner input stream.

4.7 *Eclipse Feature: Flowchart Add-On*

What makes Eclipse a powerful IDE is the flexibility to allow companies to create companion software that plugs right in. The Eclipse marketplace can be accessed from the Eclipse IDE menu, Figure 4.8. You can browse a number of software tools to help with development. Some of the tools are free and some you have to pay for.

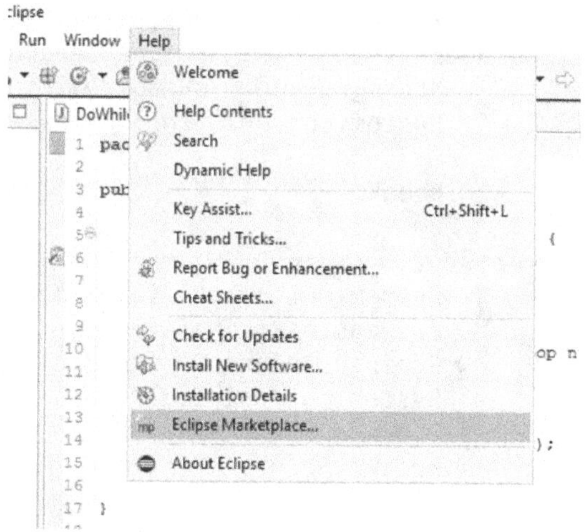

Figure 4.8 Accessing the Eclipse Marketplace

As we have been discussing flowcharts, there are several flowcharting tools available. If you do a search for flowchart in the Eclipse Market Place, you might come across a program called Code Rocket for Eclipse by Rapid Quality Systems, Figure 4.9. The program generates flowcharts based on your code, and it can generate code from a flowchart. The bottom of the page lists the critical information, such as the company that developed the software, supported operating systems, and what versions of Eclipse are supported.

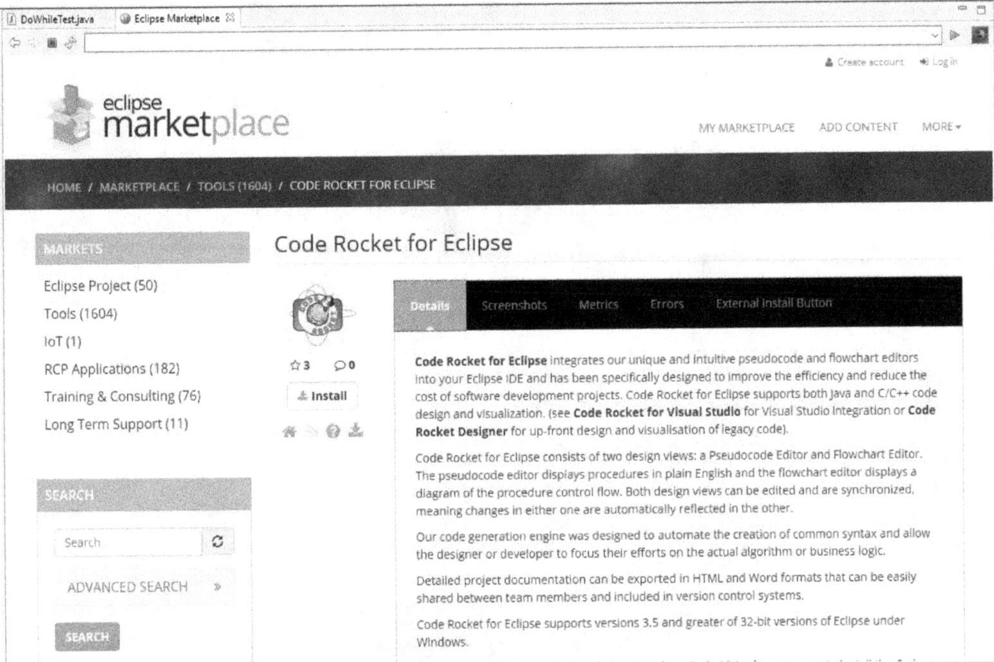

Figure 4.9 Code Rocket Listing in the Eclipse Marketplace

The software comes in two parts. There are the Eclipse plug-in and the actual tool that performs the flowchart generation. In this case, the software is available for purchase, but a trial version is available. Once both the plug-in and software are installed, a flowchart can be generated for your code by simply going to the menu: Window->Show View->Other... ->Code Rocket->Flowchart Editor, Figure 4.10.

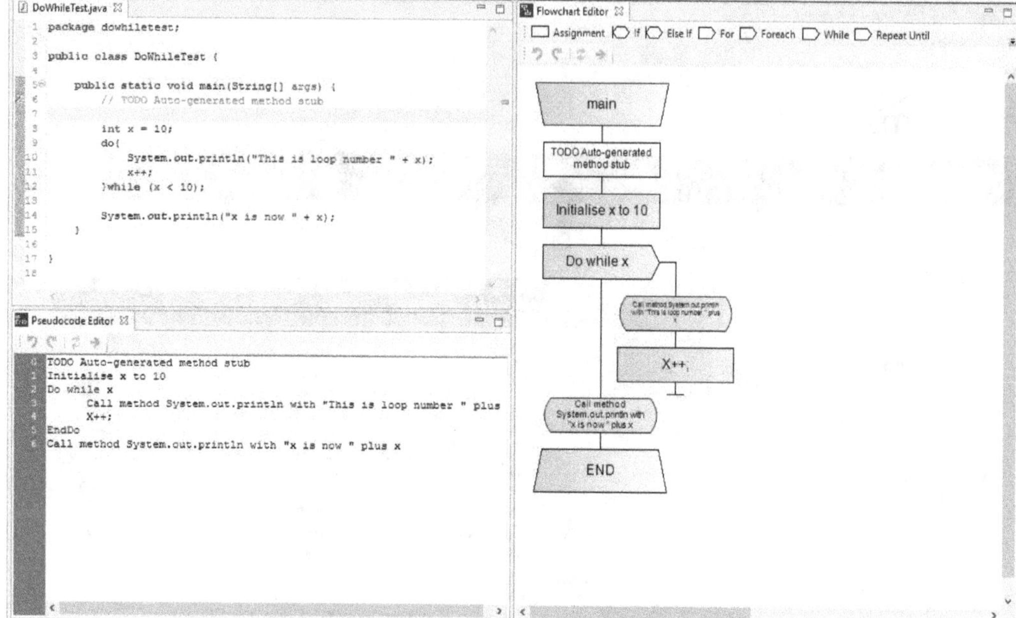

Figure 4.10 Code Rocket

4.8 Scope of Variables

The for-loop demonstrated that a variable defined within the for-loop is only available within the for-loop. This is known as the scope.

Definition: *Scope* is the lifespan of a variable. Where it is created, where it is available to the rest of the code, and where it is destroyed.

The curly brackets {} define a code block. If a variable is defined within the block, it is only available within the block and any nested blocks. The variable's scope is within the block. In the for-loop test example, we moved the initialization of x outside of the for-loop, which allowed the final print statement after the loop to use the value of x. We expanded the scope of x to be outside of the for-loop instead of being restricted to the for-loop code block. Code Listing 4.17 is a change of the earlier for-loop test:

```
1. package forlooptest;
2.
3. public class ForLoopTest {
4.
5.     public static void main(String[] args) {
6.         // TODO Auto-generated method stub
7.
8.         //int x = 0;
9.         for (int x = 0; x < 10; x++)
10.        {
11.            System.out.println("This is loop number: " + x);
12.            x++;
13.            if (x >= 9)
14.            {
15.                System.out.println("The value of x is " + x);
16.                break;
17.            }
18.        }
19.
20.        int x = 42;
21.        System.out.println("x is now " + x);
22.    }
23.}
```

Code Listing 4.17 Scope For-Loop Test Program

Line 8 was commented out. The variable x is defined in two locations: line 9 and line 20. The variable x defined in line 9 is only available for code within the for-loop and all nested blocks such as the if-statement. Line 20 defines a new x, and all code following within the block can use the new x. Without line 20, line 21 will be in error since x is undefined. The scope of a variable will be examined further when we talk about creating custom classes.

4.9 Eclipse Feature: Debugging

With the different branching, looping, and scope possibilities, programs can get more complex and error-prone. Errors are going to happen, but good coding practices and the right development tools will help to reduce the errors in code. There are three types of errors in a program: syntax errors, runtime errors, and logical errors. Syntax errors occur when you type something incorrectly in the editor. Most modern editors spot syntax errors fairly quickly. You probably have seen this as you have typed in some of the exercises in Eclipse. It is nice that the editor catches these, but when you take a test, you will be writing code by hand without the aid of an editor. Practice writing the program assignments by hand and then entering them into the editor to check what you wrote. Runtime errors occur when the program is running and cannot perform a statement. If you started the program in Eclipse, the program would stop with a red error in the output if a runtime error occurs. Logic errors are the most difficult to find. A program may have the correct syntax and never have a runtime error, but once in a while, an unexpected result occurs. Logic errors require the right tools to track down the root cause of the error, and this is where Eclipse's built-in debugger capability becomes helpful.

So far with Eclipse, you see the Package Explorer on the left, the editor in the middle, and other views on bottom and right. This is called the Java Perspective. Eclipse allows you to customize the views on the screen so that you can create your own perspectives to create and debug code. The top right corner contains the perspectives that you can switch to. Figure 4.11 shows the Java Perspective and the Debug Perspective options.

Figure 4.11 Eclipse Perspectives

4.9.1 Computer Activity 4.5 – Debugging an Application

This activity will walk you through the basics of debugging.

1. Create a new Java project called "CH4CA4.5-ForLoopDebug".
2. In the new project, create a new class with a main() method called FLDebug.
3. In the main method add the following code:

```
for (int x = 0; x < 5; x++)
{
    System.out.println("The current index is " +x);
}
```

4. Now, we need to set a breakpoint in the for-loop at the System.out.println call. Move the cursor to the left blue edge of the editor next to the line for the System.out.println. Double-click in the area to set a breakpoint. A dot will appear showing a breakpoint is available, Figure 4.12.

*FLDebug.java

```
public class FLDebug {

    public static void main(String[] args) {
        // TODO Auto-generated method stub
        for (int x = 0; x < 5; x++)
        {
            System.out.println("The current index is " +x);
        }
    }

}
```

Figure 4.12 Setting a Breakpoint

5. To debug the code, from the menu, select Run->Debug or hit F11. The perspective changes to the debug perspective, and the application starts to run until it hits the breakpoint, Figure 4.13.

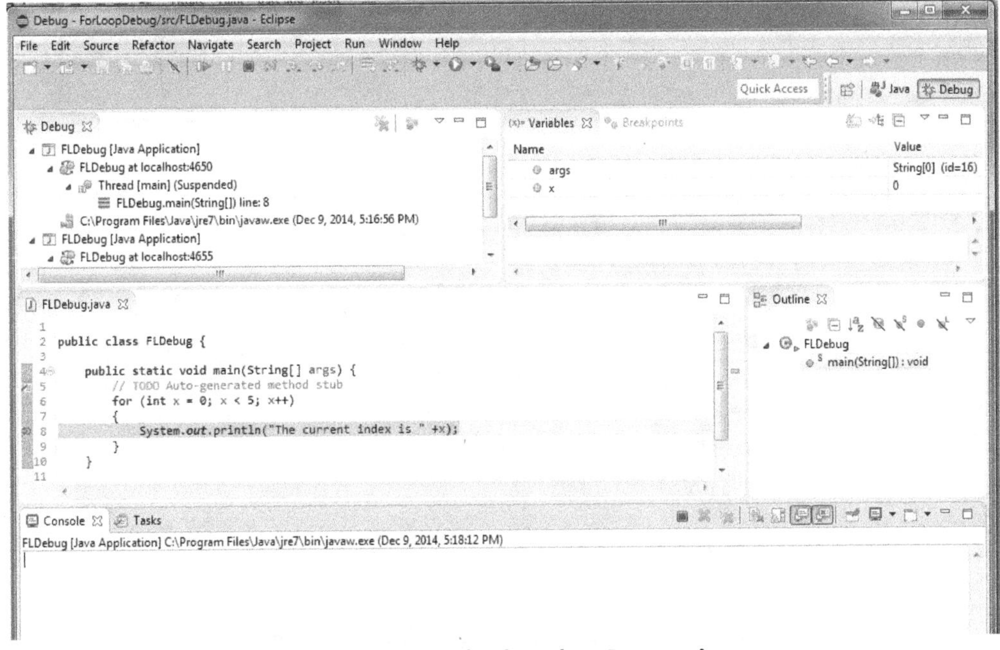

Figure 4.13 Running in Debug Perspective

6. You can now step through the code. Use the debug controls, Figure 4.14, or use the corresponding functions keys, Table 4.6. Click on the Step over or hit the F6 key a few times.

Figure 4.14 Debug Controls

Function Key	Debugger Action Taken
F5	Next Step into a program. Jumps into a method or function if these are the next steps.
F6	Step over a call. If the call is a method or function it will jump over and make these calls and move on to the next step.
F7	Goes to the calling code. You will return to the calling method or function.
F8	Run to the next breakpoint.

Table 4.6 Debug Function Keys

As you interate your way through the loop, you will see the x variable change values. The top right view shows the variables and the breakpoints set in the application, Figure 4.15.

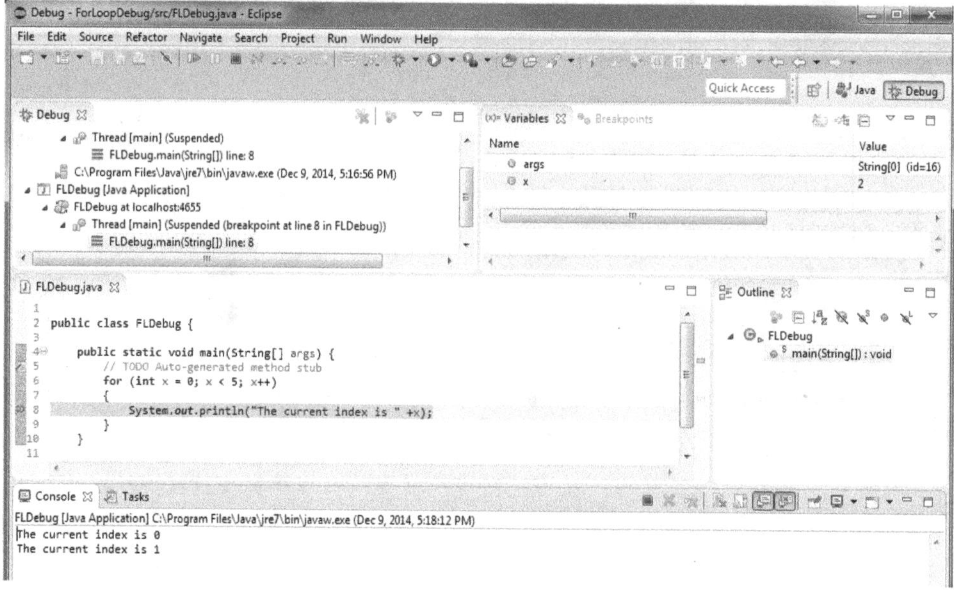

Figure 4.15 Monitoring Variables While Debugging

You can click continue or step through the code until it reaches the end. Eclipse will remain in the debug perspective, but you can make any changes in the editor that you wish. We will discuss other aspects of debugging in future chapters.

4.10 Summary and Homework Assignments

For the moment, computers cannot think like us, but we can mimic a decision-making process using the powerful if-statement. "If" the astronauts in *2001: A Space Odyssey* had asked HAL what the human error was rather than focus on the computer error, the movie would have gone in another direction. Phil Conners in *Groundhog Day* made different decisions in each day's iteration before finally breaking out of his infinite loop.

The chapter covered two very important topics: branching and iteration. Boolean expressions are used in both constructs to either branch the program into an alternate section of the code or break out of a loop. The program flow can get complex. Flowcharts provide one visual aid. The irony is that you almost have to think like the computer to avoid mistakes, which can be a challenge for large programs; but Eclipse's debugger can help step through the code to see what is going on. We will build on these constructs and exercises in this chapter throughout the rest of the book.

4.10.1 Questions

1. What does HAL stand for? What famous company do people think HAL infers?

2. What did Phil Conners in *Groundhog Day* have to do to break the loop?

3. In Computer Activity 4.3, we recommended 10 as the maximum value to enter in the factorial program. What can be changed to enter larger integer values?

4. Assuming x, y, and j are integers, for the following Boolean expression:

   (x < y) && (j >= x)

   If y = 12 and j = 10, what must x be for the Boolean expression to be true?

5. Assume x, y, and k are integers for the given the follow expression:

   (x >= y) && !((x == k) && (k < y))

   What guarantees the expression will be true?

   a. x < k must be false
   b. k < y must be true
   c. x > y and k > y must be true
   d. x == y must be true

6. Using De Morgan's Law, transform the following expressions:

   a. !(x * y < 30) && !((k <= x) || (y +1 > 7)
   b. !((Math.pow(y,x) > 5) || (!(x >= k) && (k > 10)))
   c. !((a != b) && (y >= 0))

7. Given the following program

```
1. package test;
2.
3. public class Test1{
4.
5.      public static void main(String[] args) {
6.           // TODO Auto-generated method stub
7.
8.           int x = 25;
9.
10.          do
11.          {
12.               System.out.println(x);
13.               --x;
14.          }while (x > 15);
15.     }
16.}
```

a. What is the output of the program?
b. What is the output if x = 11 on line 8?
c. Draw the flowchart for the program.

8. Given the following program:

```
package test;

public class Test1 {

    public static void main(String[] args) {
        // TODO Auto-generated method stub

        int x = 2;
        double y = 30;
        double j = 1.5;

        if (((double) (4 * x) < y))
        {

            j += y;

            if(j >= ((double)x))
            {
                y = Math.abs(j) * ((double)x);
            }

        }
        else
        {
            int k = 9;

            k *= Math.floor(j);

            y = k + x;
        }

    }
}
```

a. What is the value of y? What is the value of k?
b. What does the minimal integer value of x have to be for k = 18 and y = 26?
c. Draw the flowchart.

9. What are the final values of x, y, and j for the following program:

```
package test2;

public class Test2 {

    public static void main(String[] args) {
        // TODO Auto-generated method stub

        int x = 10;
        int y = 0;

        for(int j = 1; j <x; j += 2)
        {
            y = x % j;

            if (y == 0)
            {
                x -= 3;
            }
        }
    }
}
```

10. What are the final values of x, y, and str for the given program:

```
package test3;

public class Test3 {

    public static void main(String[] args) {
        // TODO Auto-generated method stub


        int x = 10;
        int y = 2;
        String str ="a";

```

```
    while (x > y)
    {
      switch(str)
      {

      case "a":
        x /= y;
        str = "b";
        break;
      case "b":
      case "c":
        y *= 2;
        str = "c";
        if (y == 4)
        {
          str = "a";
          x = 21;
        }
        break;
      default:
        y = 9;

      }
    }
  }
}
```

11. Take the following flowchart and write the code in Eclipse. What is the final value of x?

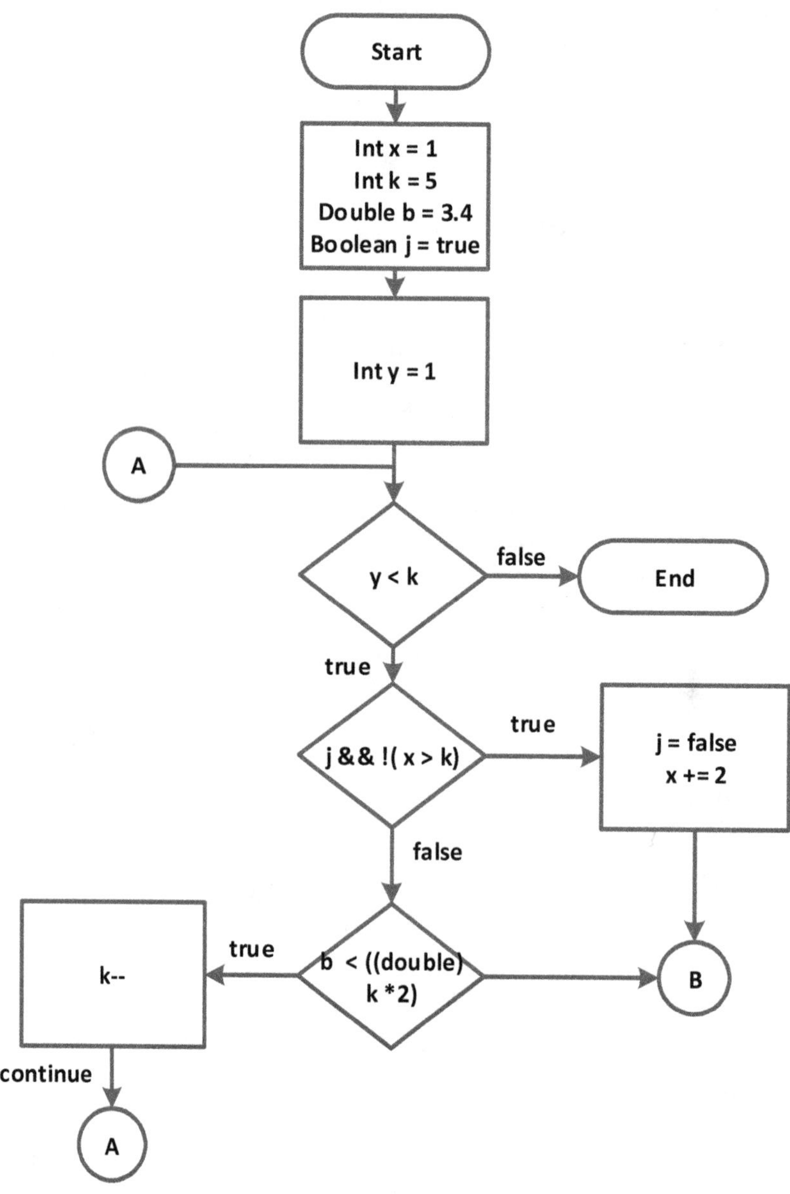

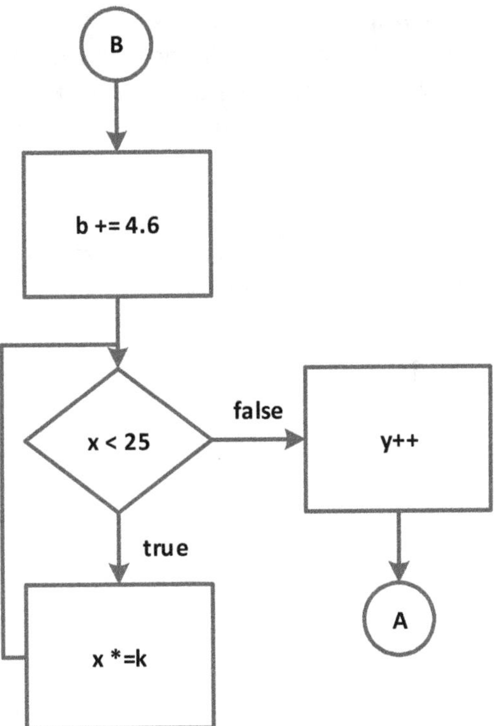

4.10.2 Programming Projects

1. Modify the coin flip program in Computer Activity 4.2 to ask the user if they want to play again with "y" for yes and "n" for no. If they select "y", the program will then ask for heads or tails. If they select "n", the program will just exit.

2. Create a program that will print out the following string object in reverse:

   ```
   String str1 = "Juno is headed to Jupiter";
   ```

   For example: retipuJ ot dedaeh si onuJ

3. The Magic 8-Ball is a popular novelty shop item. The Magic 8-Ball looks like a pool 8 ball that is filled with liquid and an icosahedron inside. A window lets you see the icosahedron.

Hold the Magic 8-Ball with the 8 facing up and the window facing down. As a yes/no question, and turn the ball over. The icosahedron rises to the window and provides an answer. Write a program that asks the user for a yes/no question, and then have the program randomly respond with 1 of the following 20 answers:

- It is certain
- It is decidedly so
- Without a doubt
- Yes - definitely
- You may rely on it
- As I see it, yes
- Most likely
- Outlook good
- Yes
- Signs point to yes
- Reply hazy, try again
- Ask again later
- Better not tell you now
- Cannot predict now
- Concentrate and ask again
- Don't count on it
- My reply is no
- My sources say no
- Outlook not so good
- Very doubtful

4. There are many companies that provide a dividend for people who own their stock. For example, Oracle (Ticker symbol: ORCL), the stewards for the Java language, pays a dividend every three months. At the time of writing this book, Oracle pays a dividend amount of 12 cents per share, and one share was priced at $41.00. Write a program that calculates the total dividend payout for a user who purchases shares of Oracle and holds the shares for several months. The program will ask how much they want to invest (greater than $100), the stock price, how many months they will hold on to those shares, and the quarterly dividend payment. The program will output how many shares and the total amount in dividends they received over the months they hold onto the shares. The program will then ask the user if they want to do another calculation. If the answer is yes, ask the same questions again. If the answer is no, end the program.

For example, the user spends $1000 to purchase 24.39 shares of Oracle stock. They will hold the stock for 24 months. With a dividend of 12 cents per share, he total dividend payout is $23.41 after 24 months

5. Yahtzee is a popular dice game from Hasbro. There are many variants of the game for phones and tablets in application stores. The players roll 5 dice and write down a score based on a certain combination. For example, the total number of 3s, or a straight sequence such as 2, 3, 4, 5 and 6. The player gets 3 rolls but can stop at any point to write down the score. For the first roll, all 5 dice are rolled. For the second and third roll, the player can keep dice they want to use for a score and roll the rest. The player must write down a score after the third roll.

   Write a program that uses the Random number generator (nextInt(int n)) to generate the 5 dice values 1 through 6. The program will roll the 5 dice. After the value of each die is displayed, the program will ask the user to roll again. If they want to roll again, the program should ask the user what dice that they want to keep, and then roll any dice they don't want to keep. If they don't want to roll again or it is the end of the third roll, the program should tell the user to write down the score. Hint: Use an INT variable to store each die value and a Boolean for each die to store roll again or not (next roll state).

6. Modify the Guess the Number program project in Chapter 3 to continuously ask the user for a number until they guess correctly. If the guess is too high, output that the number is lower. If the guess is too low, output that the number is higher. Output that they guessed correctly when the user finally guesses the number.

5 Arrays

"Stay between the lines; the lines are your friends."
-Isuzu Rodeo Commercial, August 1992

When you drive a car or truck around the city, you stay on the streets, follow the traffic signals, watch out for pedestrians, and watch the speed limit. Basically, you stay between the lines. If you were driving an off-road vehicle in the desert or field, there are no lines, traffic signals, or speed limits. Computer programs prefer to stay between the lines. Going out of bounds can make a program crash. The previous chapters have worked with single variables. This chapter dives into one of the areas of programming that stumps many students, grouping variables into a single data structure called an array. If you are new to programming, arrays can be a challenge, which is why the infectious line from the commercial is the quote for this chapter.

5.1 Arrays and the One-dimensional Arrays

An array is one of the first and simplest data structures (objects) used in computer programming.

Definition: *Array* (or Array Data Structure) is a collection of elements or variables of the same type. Each variable in the array is addressed by as many index values as the array has dimensions.

Arrays can be used to store data such as test scores, a list of daily temperatures, recipes, and addresses of contacts. The power of using arrays is the ability to manipulate and operate on them. The different loops discussed in the last chapter can be used to access individual elements in an array and walk through any or all of the elements of the array under program control. In Java, arrays are objects, thus they have properties and methods. The basic declaration format for one-dimensional arrays is as follows:

```
type[] <array name> = new type[ n as integer ];
```

Java has two ways to declare an array:

```
int[] scores = new int[5];

int scores[] = new int[5];
```

Both declarations perform the same operation: *new array of integers called "scores" that has 5 elements*. The first declaration is the preferred implementation for Java. The second declaration is supported to help those coming from other languages like C adapt to Java. When an array is declared, the value for each element is initialized to zero. To assign values to an individual element of an array, you use the array name with an integer index, for example:

```
scores[0] = 1;
scores[1] = 7;
scores[2] = 24;
scores[3] = 5;
scores[4] = 42;
```

The first index for an array is 0. The last index value is n-1, where n is the number of elements in the array. The first index for our "scores" array is 0, and the last index for our "scores" array is 4. The last index is not 5 since we start with 0. Many programmers have missed the 0 to n-1 indexing for arrays, so getting the length of an array is important, as well as not trying to index an array beyond its defined size. Since arrays are objects, the one property available is the "length" property, which returns the length of an array as an integer.

```
int scorelength = scores.length;
```

The length value can be used in loops that are iterating over the array. There are other methods available in arrays, but we will cover these methods in later chapters. For readability and simplicity, Java also allows array values to be set in the declaration known as an array literal:

```
int[] scores = {1,7,24,5,42};
```

Each element in the array is initialized with an integer value in the {}. The Java compiler turns the array literal into the code we discussed:

```
int[] scores = new int[5];
scores[0] = 1;
scores[1] = 7;
scores[2] = 24;
```

```
scores[3] = 5;
scores[4] = 42;
```

Besides integers, you can also declare arrays of different types such as char[], double[], Boolean[], float[], and String[]. Mentally picturing the contents of an array is important. You can think of each index as an address for the element, much like houses on a street. To visually represent an array, you could draw a box chart like Figure 5.1:

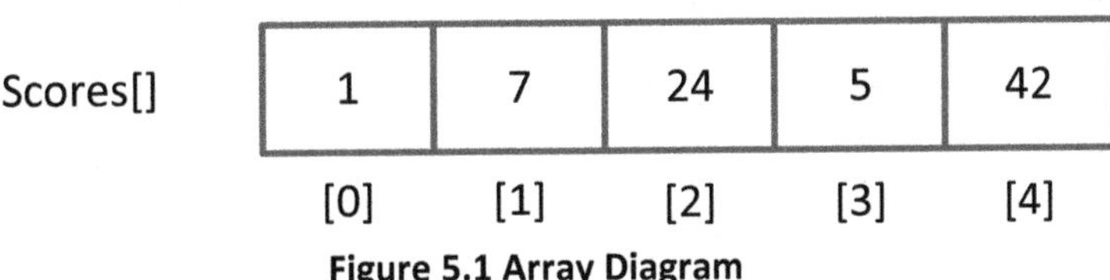

Figure 5.1 Array Diagram

When taking tests or doing a simple mental debugging exercise, a quickly drawn chart like Figure 5.2 might be better.

scores[]	Value
0	1
1	7
2	24
3	5
4	42

Figure 5.2 Debugging Array Chart

5.1.1 Computer Activity 5.1 – Basic Arrays and the Power of the Debugger

With this activity, we will create a simple array, fill in a few values, print the contents of the whole array, and use the debugger to step through the array handling. In Eclipse, create a new Java project called "CH5CA5.1-Array-Basic". Create a new class called "ArrayBasic" with a main() method and a new package called "arraybasic". In the main() method, add the following code:

```
int[] x = new int[10];

x[0] = 14;
x[1] = 17;
x[2] = 21;
x[3] = 3;
x[4] = 10;

for (int y = 0; y < x.length; y++ )
{
    System.out.println("Index " + y + " holds the following value: " +
x[y]);
}
```

The whole program should look like Code Listing 5.1:

```
1. package arraybasic;
2.
3. public class ArrayBasic {
4.
5.     public static void main(String[] args) {
6.         // TODO Auto-generated method stub
7.         int[] x = new int[10];
8.
9.         x[0] = 14;
10.        x[1] = 17;
11.        x[2] = 21;
12.        x[3] = 3;
13.        x[4] = 10;
14.
15.        for (int y = 0; y < x.length; y++ )
16.        {
17.            System.out.println("Index " + y + " holds the following
   value: " + x[y]);
18.        }
19.    }
20.}
```

Code Listing 5.1 Basic Array Program

The application fills in the first 5 elements and then prints all 10 elements in the array. Run the program to see the output. The values in indexes 5 through 9 hold the value zero because zero was assigned to each element when the array was declared in line 7. Now, set a breakpoint at line 7 and start debugging the application. The debugger will stop at line 7. Click on the menu icon to step over the line. You will notice that the Variables tab in the debug perspective adds the letter x for the array. Click on the arrow and you should see all the elements in the array filled with zeros, Figure 5.3.

(x)= Variables ☒ | Breakpoints

Name	Value
args	String[0] (id=16)
x	(id=19)
[0]	0
[1]	0
[2]	0
[3]	0
[4]	0
[5]	0
[6]	0
[7]	0
[8]	0
[9]	0

Figure 5.3 Debugger Display of Array x

Continue to step through the code and you will see the values change as the values are assigned in the code, Figure 5.4.

(x)= Variables ☒ | Breakpoints

Name	Value
args	String[0] (id=16)
x	(id=19)
[0]	14
[1]	17
[2]	21
[3]	0
[4]	0
[5]	0
[6]	0
[7]	0
[8]	0
[9]	0

Figure 5.4 Array X After 3 Iterations Through the Loop

Run the program to completion. Again, we see that the debugger helps to visually see what is going on when the code is running.

5.1.2 Computer Activity 5.2 - Out-of-Bounds

Now, we are going to see what happens when we try to increase the index beyond the array length. The program will generate the average high temperature for one week of temperature readings. In Eclipse, create a new Java project called "CH5CA5.2-Array-Temperature". Create a new class called "ArrayTemperature" with a main() method and a new package called "arraytemperature". In the main() method, add the following code:

```
double avgtemp = 0.0;
double[] temperature = {71.6, 74.0, 75.1, 75.1, 73.7, 73.6, 72.0};

for (int x = 0; x <= 7; x++){
    avgtemp += temperature[x];
}
avgtemp = (double)(Math.round((avgtemp /= 7 ) * 10)) / 10;

System.out.println("The average high temperature for the week is " +
avgtemp);
```

The final program should look like Code Listing 5.2:

```
package arraytemperature;

public class ArrayTemperature {

    public static void main(String[] args) {
        // TODO Auto-generated method stub

        double avgtemp = 0.0;
        double[] temperature = {71.6, 74.0, 75.1, 75.1, 73.7, 73.6, 72.0};

        for (int x = 0; x <= 7; x++){
            avgtemp += temperature[x];
        }

        avgtemp = (double)(Math.round((avgtemp /= 7 ) * 10)) / 10;

        System.out.println("The average high temperature for the week is " + avgtemp);
    }
}
```

Code Listing 5.2 Array Temperature Program

Note that avgtemp is used to first accumulate the sum of the temperatures before dividing that by the number of temperatures to get the average. This saves memory, having 1 less variable, saves on complexity, having one less variable assignment, and one can make the argument that by these reductions one also reduces the probability for code-induced errors. Run the program and you will get the following:

```
Exception in thread "main" java.lang.ArrayIndexOutOfBoundsException: 7
      at
arraytemperature.ArrayTemperature.main(ArrayTemperature.java:13)
```

Why did this happen? The temperature array is declared with the 7 high-temperature readings for each day of the week. We should have used the built-in field temperature.length instead of using the value 7 for 7 days, which sounds logical. If you step through the debugger, you will notice the for-loop trying to access temperature[7], which doesn't exist. Then Java throws an error, listing the index of 7 and the line number of the error: 13. The array indexes start with 0, thus the for-loop condition must end at n-1, which is 6 in this case. Modify line 11 so the condition is "x < temperature.length", and run the program. This time you get the correct output. Using fields like length, helps to prevent errors in the code. Index out of bounds is something that every programmer runs into at some point. This is where the quote about staying between the lines is an important one to follow. Going off-road in a program doesn't work.

5.1.3 Enhanced For-Loop (For Each)

The for-loop in the last exercise iterated over the whole array to sum up the temperature in preparation for calculating the average. Iterating over the whole array is a common occurrence in programming. Rather than using a variable as a counter to access each and every member of the whole array, the Enhanced for-loop uses a variable to iterate over a collection. The structure is as follows:

```
for (type variable : collection)
{
    // Body of the loop
}
```

The Enhanced for-loop basically says "for each variable in the collection, perform the following actions." The collection, in this case, is the array. The Enhanced for-loop is also known as the for-each loop. You will see other programming languages use a for-each statement. The variable type must match the type of the elements in the collection. If you try to iterate an integer variable over an array of doubles, Eclipse will notify you of a type mismatch. The advantage of the Enhanced for-loop is avoiding going out of bounds using indexing and counters. For the last activity, the for-loop could be changed to the following Enhanced for-loop:

```
for (double x : temperature)
{
    avgtemp += x;
}
```

As you can see, the other advantage is the readability of the code. You can still run the debugger and watch the Enhanced for-loop assign each value of the array to x from index 0 until the end of the array. Incrementing the loop index by 1 is handled automatically.

5.1.4 Computer Activity 5.3 – Enhanced For-Loop

Another common iteration over a whole array is performing a search. In this activity, you will write a program that counts the number of times an integer value is found in an array. In Eclipse, create a new Java project called "CH5CA5.3-Array-EFL". Create a new class called "ArrayEFL" with a main() method and a new package called "arrayefl". In the main() method, add the following code:

```
int z = 0;
int[] x = { 4, 5, 7, 8, 2, 3, 10, 7, 12,16, 4, 0, 1};

for (int y : x )
{
    if (y == 7)
    {
        z++;
    }
}

System.out.println("There were " + z + " instance(s) of 7 found.");
```

Run the program and you should get 2 instances of 7. The integer y iterates over each element in the array x. The integer z is incremented each time the value of 7 is found in the array. Let's search for the first instances of the value 7. Add the following code after the println statement above:

```
z = 0;
for (int y : x)
{
    if(y == 7)
    {
        break;
    }
    z++;
}
System.out.println("The value 7 was first found and index " + z);
```

The Enhanced for-loop will again iterate over the whole array, but when it finds a value it will break out of the loop and output the index value when the first 7 value was found. Like the loops in the previous chapter, the break statement is used to break out of the loop.

5.1.5 String Arrays

Chapter 3 introduced different data types including the String object. Like the other data types, you can create an array of Strings. Unlike numeric data types, the String array is not pre-populated with any content. To see a String array in action, an exercise in the last chapter had you reverse a string. Here is a similar project, but this one reverses the words.

```
String[] str1 = { "Juno", "is", "headed", "to", "Jupiter" };

for (int x = (str1.length - 1); x >= 0; x--)
{
    System.out.print(str1[x] + " ");
}
```

The first line declares the String array. Each word in the sentence is an individual element in the array. The for-loop lists the words in reverse order: "Jupiter to headed is Juno." Notice that for a String array, the string length is a property, not a method like it would be for a single String object.

5.1.6 Computer Activity 5.4 – Command Line Input

You may have noticed that the main() method contains a String array:

```
public static void main(String[] args)
```

The String array allows you to start the application with command line arguments. These arguments allow you to pass information into the program for processing. For this activity, we will create an application that takes in a single command line parameter and uses a switch-case to process the parameter. In Eclipse, create a new Java project called "CH5CA5.4-Array-CL". Create a new class called "ArrayCL" with a main() method and a new package called "arrayecl". In the main() method, add the following code:

```
switch(args[0]) {
case "a":
    System.out.println("The letter 'a' was entered");
    break;
case "b":
    System.out.println("The letter 'b' was entered");
    break;
```

```
case "c":
    System.out.println("The letter 'c' was entered");
    break;
default:
    System.out.println("Nothing was entered");
    break;
}
```

If you try to run the application, you will get an exception error. The program tried to access the empty args array.

```
Exception in thread "main" java.lang.ArrayIndexOutOfBoundsException: 0
        at arraycl.ArrayCL.main(ArrayCL.java:8)
```

This problem would also occur if the user didn't add any command line parameters. We can get around this exception error using a try-catch around the switch-case.

```
try{
    switch(args[0]) {
    case "a":
        System.out.println("The letter 'a' was entered");
        break;
    case "b":
        System.out.println("The letter 'b' was entered");
        break;
    case "c":
        System.out.println("The letter 'c' was entered");
        break;
    default:
        System.out.println("Nothing was entered");
        break;
    }
}
catch(Exception e){
    System.out.println("Nothing was entered");
}
```

Run the program with the added try-catch; instead of the exception, the program will output "Nothing was entered," as expected. That is because there are no command line arguments being passed to the program, which is the default condition for Eclipse. Chapter 8 will cover more details of Try-Catch exception handling. We can add command line arguments from within Eclipse, as if we had run the program from the command line. In the Package Explorer right-click on the ch5ca5.4-Array-CL package and select *Run As>Run Configurations...* The Run Configuration dialog box, Figure 5.5, will open.

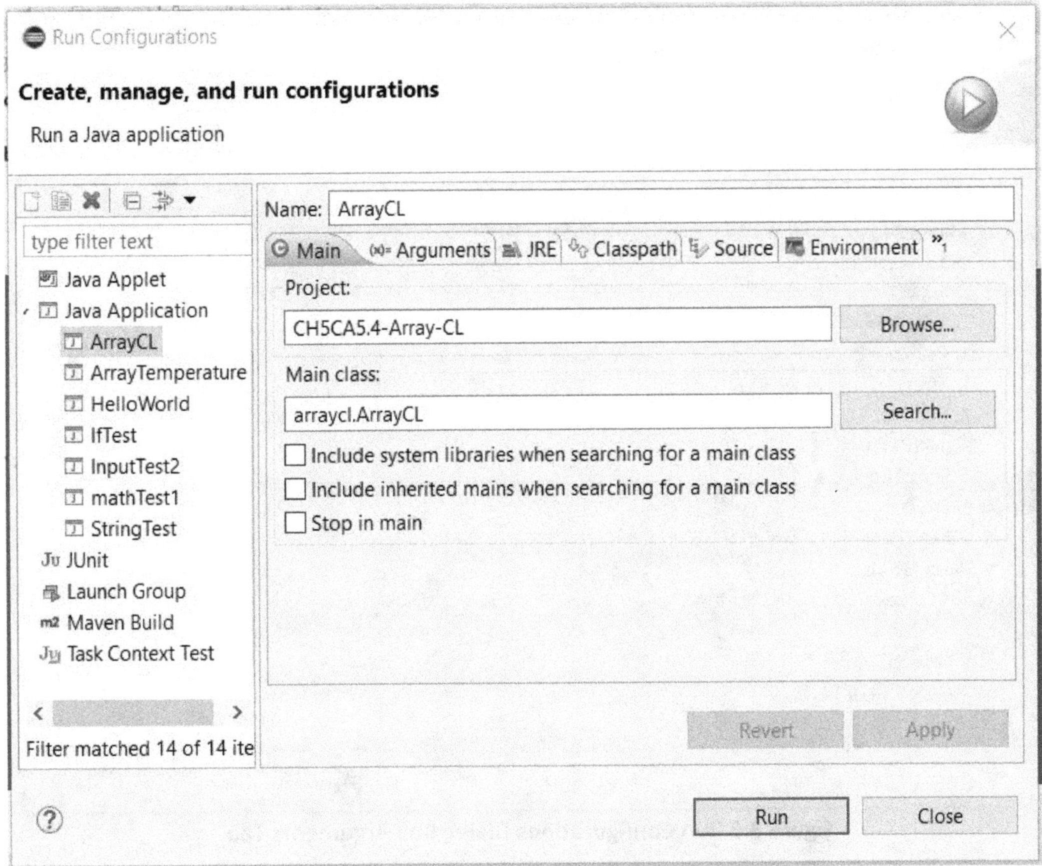

Figure 5.5 Run Configuration Dialog Box

Click on the Arguments tab, and in the Program arguments: box enter 'a' (without the single quotes). Click on the Apply button in the lower right; and, finally, click on Run to run the program with the command line argument of 'a', Figure 5.6.

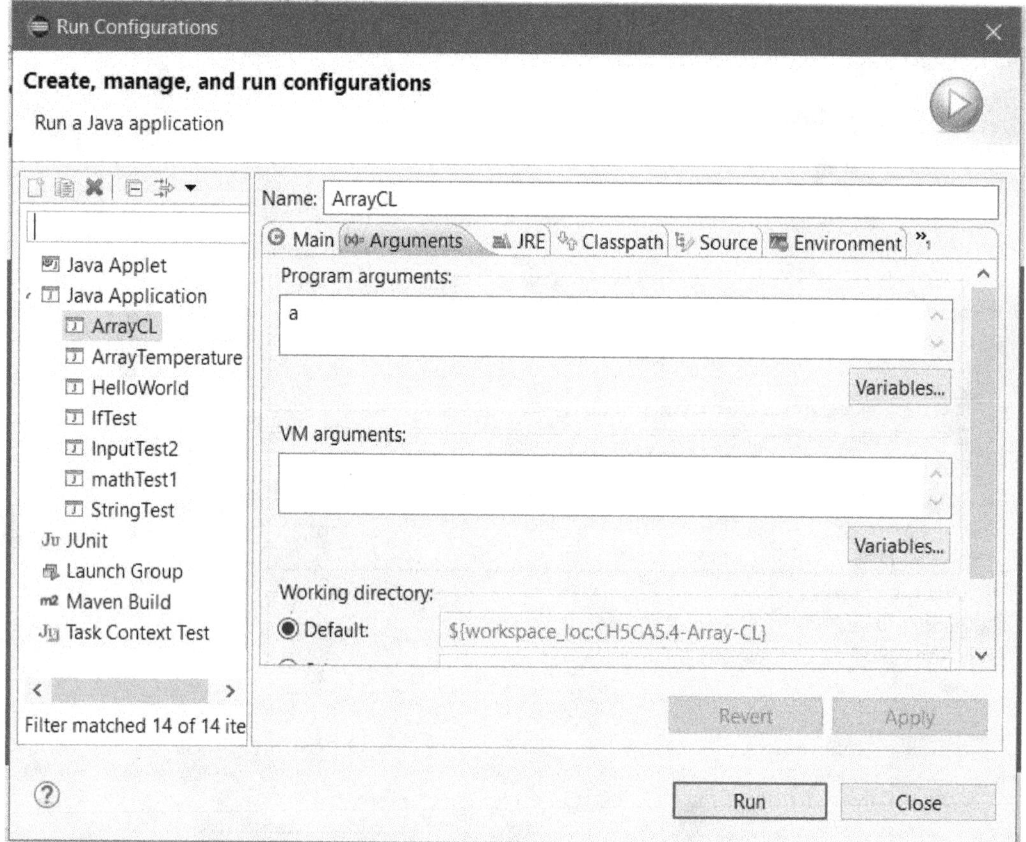

Figure 5.6 Run Configurations Dialog Box Arguments Tab

The program will output: "The letter 'a' was entered" to the console, as expected. Change the program arguments to other letters and observe the results. Try using a letter other than 'a', 'b', or 'c'. What does the program output? How would you change the program to handle this situation? This example demonstrated a single command line parameter, but the main() method's String array allows you to set up multiple command line parameters if needed.

You can also run the application and enter a value on the command line. Open a command window, and run the following (be sure to use the absolute path to the project directory):

```
java -classpath "<path to project>\Array-CL\bin" arraycl.ArrayCL a
```

You should get the same output.

5.2 Two-dimensional Arrays

So far, we have worked with one-dimensional arrays. Java supports two-, three-, or up to 255-dimensional arrays. Multidimensional arrays are known as arrays of arrays. A two-dimensional array is the simplest form of a multidimensional array. A two-dimensional array is declared as follows:

```
type[][]<array name> = new type[x index row][y index column]
```

Like the one-dimensional array, multidimensional arrays can be declared two ways:

```
int[][] scores = new int[4][5];

int scores[][] = new int[4][5];
```

The first method is the preferred method in Java. The latter is to help those coming from other languages, like C, adapt to Java. You can also declare an array with a literal using prepopulation data:

```
int [][] scores = {{1,6,7,8,9}, {5,10,4,13,6}, {6,8,2,1,4},
{23,4,1,7,17}};
```

Each grouping of numbers represents a row. The best way to visualize the two-dimensional array, scores[x][y], is to use a chart, Table 5.1.

Scores[][]	[][y = 0]	[][y = 1]	[][y = 2]	[][y = 3]	[][y = 4]
[x = 0][]	1	6	7	8	9
[x = 1][]	5	10	4	13	6
[x = 2][]	6	8	2	1	4
[x = 3][]	23	4	1	7	17

Table 5.1 Two-Dimensional Array Scores[][]

You can think of the two indices like the coordinates of a spreadsheet or address of a city block. One example of using a two-dimensional array is to store information like student tests scores. Each student is assigned a row and each column is a test. All the elements or cells will store the score for the test. Another example: a farmer wants to map crop production based on a land grid map. Each cell in the two-dimensional array represents an acre of land. Finally, think of all the games that use a grid: tic-tac-toe, reversi, chess, checkers, Battleship®, Connect Four™,

Minesweeper just to name a few. Each cell is used to store a game piece location. Drawing a chart when taking a test can help visualize where the data is being placed in the array.

5.2.1 Computer Activity 5.5 – Two-dimensional Array

For this activity, we will cover three concepts in one program. The first test will be the basic declaration and how to store the data for a two-dimensional array. We will also see how to get the length of rows and columns. The next two tests will do a search on a two-dimensional array, first using counters and the next using the enhanced for-loop. In Eclipse, create a new Java project called "CH5CA5.5-Array-2D". Create a new class called "Array2D" with a main() method and a new package called "arraye2d". The whole code listing is below, Code Listing 5.3, fill in the contents for the main() method:

```
package array2d;

public class Array2D {

    public static void main(String[] args) {
        // TODO Auto-generated method stub

        //Basic test
        int[][] test1 = new int[4][5];

        test1[0][0] = 5;
        test1[1][3] = 3;

        System.out.println("The row length is " + test1.length);
        System.out.println("The column length is " +
test1[0].length);

        //Search using counters
        int z = 0;
        int[][] test2 = {{3,2,6,5},{2,7,8,1},{4,2,7,2}};
        //int[][] test2 = {{3,2,6,5},{2,7},{4,2,7,2},{7,9,2,1,6,5}};

```

```
22.         //Counter search
23.         for(int x = 0; x < test2.length; x++)
24.         {
25.             for(int y = 0; y < test2[x].length; y++)
26.             {
27.                 if(test2[x][y] == 2)
28.                 {
29.                     z++;
30.                 }
31.             }
32.         }
33.
34.         System.out.println("The number 2 was found " + z + "
   times");
35.
36.
37.         //Enhanced for-loop search
38.         z = 0;
39.         for (int x[] : test2)
40.         {
41.             for(int y : x)
42.             {
43.                 if(y == 7)
44.                 {
45.                     z++;
46.                 }
47.             }
48.         }
49.         System.out.println("The number 7 was found " + z + "
   times");
50.     }
51. }
```

Code Listing 5.3 Two-Dimensional Array Test

Set a breakpoint at line 9 and run the debugger. As you step through the code, expand the test1 array, Figure 5.7. You will notice that the test1 array has an array under each array. That is why we say multi-dimensional arrays are an array of arrays. The array was populated with zeros. Lines 11 and 12 fill in some values.

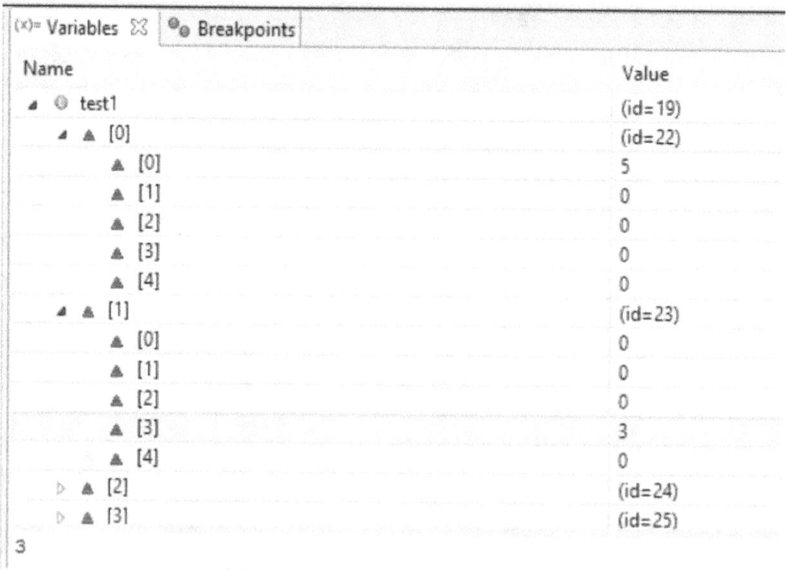

(x)= Variables ⊠ | ●● Breakpoints

Name	Value
test1	(id=19)
[0]	(id=22)
[0]	5
[1]	0
[2]	0
[3]	0
[4]	0
[1]	(id=23)
[0]	0
[1]	0
[2]	0
[3]	3
[4]	0
[2]	(id=24)
[3]	(id=25)

3

Figure 5.7 Two-Dimensional Array Contents

Lines 14 and 15 output the length of the row and the column for the array. Notice that to get the column length we used the first index 0. Since all of the rows have the same number of columns, we don't have to get the column length for each row. This might not always be the case, as we will see in the next section. As a test, stop the debugger and change the 0 to 1, 2, or 3. Re-run the debugger and you should get the same result.

Run the program without the debugger and see the full results. Line 19 introduces a new two-dimensional array. Lines 22 through 33, do a search for the number 2 using a nested for-loop sequence. The outer loop goes row-by-row, while the inner loop searches each cell in the row. If 2 is found, the integer 'z' is incremented by one. Once the outer loop is completed, the results are printed to the screen. Notice that the row length is used for the outer loop, and for the inner loop, test2[x].length is used to search each cell in the row. The program got the length of each row based on the value of x. As a test, change test2 array to eliminate the last value of the second row

```
int[][] test2 = {{3,2,6,5},{2,7,8},{4,2,7,2}};
```

Change test2[x].length to test2[0].length, and run the program. What happens to the program? Change test2[0].length back to test2[x].length and re-run the program. What happens to the program now? Originally, we could have used test2[0].length since the length is the same for all

rows, but there might be situations where this might not be the case. Using test2[x].length guarantees that we get the correct length of each row.
Add the value back to the original array

```
int[][] test2 = {{3,2,6,5},{2,7,8,1},{4,2,7,2}};
```

Run the program again. Lines 37 through 49, do a search of the array for the number 7; but this time, Enhanced for-loops are used to perform the search for both inner and outer loops. Line 39 uses an array to search over the collection of arrays, since a two-dimensional array is an array of arrays. The outer loop needs to search by array or row of arrays, thus "int x[]": is the item to search through. The inner loop needs to search each cell within the row, thus "int y" is used to search over the collection. Change contents of the array to the following (see comment line 20):

```
int[][] test2 = {{3,2,6,5},{2,7},{4,2,7,2},{7,9,2,1,6,5}};
```

Run the program again, and both searches shouldn't have any trouble searching the array. Again, the advantage of the Enhanced for-loop is not having to deal with counters and lengths.

Note: the values 2 and 7 are called Magic Numbers. There are a few definitions for Magic Numbers, but in this case, we are using a constant value as a literal. Proper coding would have been to use a constant name and assign it the value. This way if the value is used in other locations you can just use the symbolic name. If you use a Magic Number in several locations and then decide to change it, you have to be sure to change the Magic Number in every location that it is used. If you use a constant, you only have to change the one location where the constant is defined, and you won't have to worry about failing to update all of them. For example, here is the proper code technique that removes the magic number 2.

```
//Counter search
final int VALUECHECK1 = 2;
for(int x = 0; x < test2.length; x++)
{
    for(int y = 0; y < test2[x].length; y++)
    {
        if(test2[x][y] == VALUECHECK1)
        {
            z++;
        }
    }
}
```

5.2.2 Irregular arrays

The last example showed that it is possible for a multidimensional array to have columns of different length. This is known as an irregular or jagged array. For example, you want to track the attendance of an amusement park show. The show runs 2 times a day Monday through Thursday, 4 times on Friday, and 5 times on the weekends. The declaration of the irregular array would be as follows, assuming Sunday is the first row:

```
int[][] attendance = new int[7][];
attendance[0] = new int[5];
attendance[1] = new int[2];
attendance[2] = new int[2];
attendance[3] = new int[2];
attendance[4] = new int[2];
attendance[5] = new int[4];
attendance[6] = new int[5];
```

Java needs the initial declaration value for the number of rows. The number of columns can be declared individually. The diagram of the array would look like Table 5.2:

Attendence[][]	[y = 0]	[y = 1]	[y = 2]	[y = 3]	[y = 4]
[x = 0]					
[x = 1]					
[x = 2]					
[x = 3]					
[x = 4]					
[x = 5]					
[x = 6]					

Table 5.2 Irregular Array

5.3 The ArrayList

Arrays are a simple primitive data structure, but for something more complex or large, something else is needed. Think of the contact list in your smartphone. You can add, remove, and update contact information over time. Another example is finding the Isuzu commercial in a video database that is constantly changing. A data structure to hold data that can grow and change over time is required for a contact list or a video database. Arrays have a fixed length, and as you have seen in the previous exercises, they're challenging to add and remove data. If you continue to study computer science, you will run into a course on data structures, which will explore different data structures and algorithms to store and manage data within a program. Java comes with a Collections Framework. A collection is a grouping of objects into a single object, where you can perform operations like add, remove, and update. The Collections Framework contains different data structures and algorithms to support the different ways to manage data. The simplest structure from the Collections Framework that ties in well to the array is an ArrayList.

Definition: *ArrayList* is a collection of objects. Each object variable in the ArrayList is addressed by a single index value.

The differences between an array and an ArrayList is that an ArrayList can grow and shrink, and the ArrayList has methods such as add, remove, change, and retrieve items. The declaration for an ArrayList is as follows:

```
ArrayList <object> <arraylist name> = new ArrayList <object>();
```

The ArrayList is not part of the default library, so you will have to add an import to the program as follows:

```
import java.util.ArrayList;
```

Once the library import is added, the ArrayList and associated methods become available. Table 5.3 lists some of the methods.

ArrayList Method	Description
add(e)	Appends the ArrayList with the element e
add(int index, e)	Inserts an element e and a specific index location
get(int index)	Returns the element at the specific index
indexof(Object o)	Returns the index of the first occurrence of the specific element in the ArrayList; Returns -1 if the element doesn't exist
remove(int index)	Removes the element at the specific index
set(int index, e)	Replaces the element at a specific index with the element e
size()	Returns the number of elements in the ArrayList

Table 5.3 ArrayList Methods

5.3.1 Computer Activity 5.6 – Array List of Strings

In this activity, we will demonstrate using the ArrayList and its methods. In Eclipse, create a new Java project called "CH5CA5.6-ArrayList-Test". Create a new class called "ArrayListTest" with a main() method and a new package called "arraylisttest". The whole code listing is shown in Code Listing 5.4. Add the library import and fill in the contents of the main() method:

```
package arraylisttest;

import java.util.ArrayList;

public class ArrayListTest {

```

```
    public static void main(String[] args) {
        // TODO Auto-generated method stub

        ArrayList <String> fruit = new ArrayList<String>();

        fruit.add("apple");
        fruit.add("banana");
        fruit.add("orange");

        System.out.println("List Items:");
        for( int x = 0; x < fruit.size(); x++ )
        {
            System.out.println("Item #" + x + " is " + fruit.get(x));
        }

        System.out.println("");
        System.out.println("Add Item:");

        fruit.add(1,"lemon");

        for( String z : fruit)
        {
            System.out.println("Item #" + fruit.indexOf(z)  + " is " + z);
        }

        System.out.println("");
        System.out.println("Remove Item:");

        fruit.remove(3);

        for( String z : fruit)
        {
            System.out.println("Item #" + fruit.indexOf(z)  + " is " + z);
        }

        System.out.println("");
        System.out.println("Change Item:");

        fruit.set(0, "pear");

```

```
47.         for( String z : fruit)
48.         {
49.             System.out.println("Item #" + fruit.indexOf(z) + " is "
    + z);
50.         }
51.     }
52.}
```

Code Listing 5.4 Array List Test

Line 3 imports the library supporting ArrayList. Line 10 creates the String ArrayList with the following lines adding items to the list. The list is then printed out. The program then goes through inserting an item, removing an item, and then changing an item. Each time the ArrayList is printed out so you can visually see the changes to the ArrayList. Set a breakpoint at line 10, and run the debugger. Use the step-over button to step through the code. You will first see in the Variables tab the ArrayList being created, Figure 5.8.

(x)= Variables ☒ | Breakpoints

Name	Value
args	String[0] (id=16)
fruit	ArrayList<E> (id=19)
elementData	Object[0] (id=29)
modCount	0
size	0

Figure 5.8 ArrayList fruit Created

As you step through the code that adds items to the list, you will see the size value change and each item being added to the list, Figure 5.9.

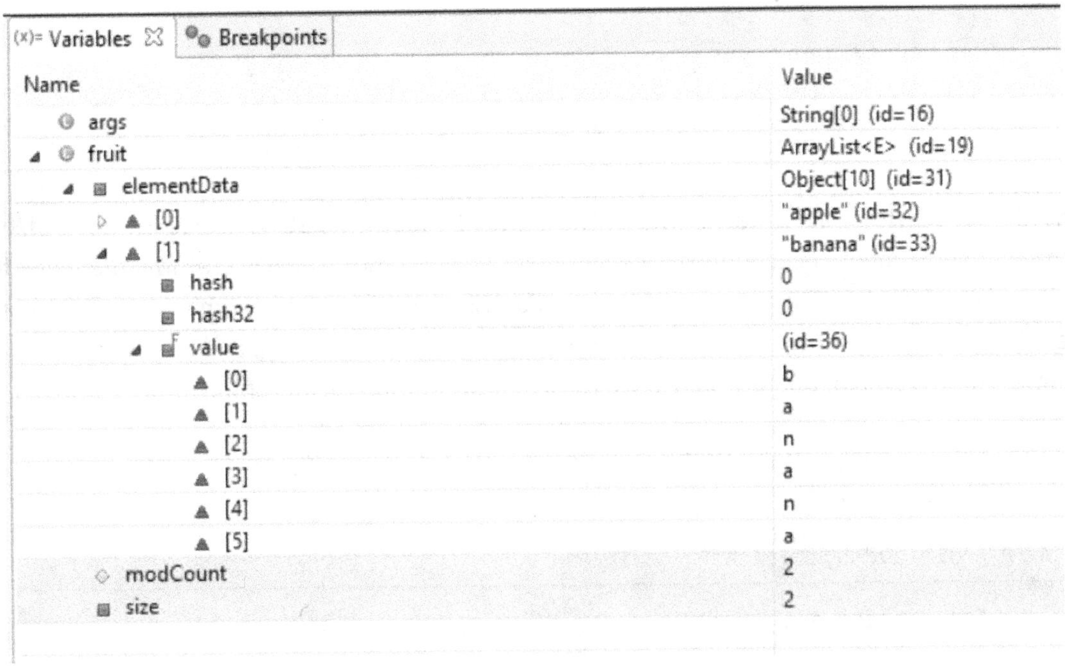

(x)= Variables | Breakpoints

Name	Value
args	String[0] (id=16)
fruit	ArrayList<E> (id=19)
elementData	Object[10] (id=31)
[0]	"apple" (id=32)
[1]	"banana" (id=33)
hash	0
hash32	0
value	(id=36)
[0]	b
[1]	a
[2]	n
[3]	a
[4]	n
[5]	a
modCount	2
size	2

Figure 5.9 Items Added to ArrayList

Each element is assigned an index value. If you expand an element value, you will see that the String is really a character array object. You cannot manipulate the character array since String objects are immutable. If you run the debugger on a String program from Chapter 3, you will see a character array being generated behind the scenes. The for-loop at line 17 demonstrates using two methods: size() and get(). The other printouts of the list use the enhanced for-loop and the indexOf() method to list the item number. Click on the resume button to let the program run to completion. Add the following to the end of the main() method:

```
System.out.println("");
System.out.println("Add Item:");

fruit.add("pear");

for( String z : fruit)
{
    System.out.println("Item #" + fruit.indexOf(z) + " is " + z);
}
```

Run the program and the final output listing should look like this:

```
Add Item:
Item #0 is pear
Item #1 is lemon
Item #2 is banana
Item #0 is pear
```

Why do we see Item #0 appears twice? The indexOf() method gets the first instance of the element. The element "pear" appears twice in the ArrayList, but indexOf() returns the index for the first "pear" found. The enhanced for-loop did print out the correct elements as the second "pear" in index 3. Replace the enhanced for-loop with a regular for-loop, and you should get the correct result. Now add the following code after line 50 and run the program.

```
System.out.println("");
System.out.println("Add Item:");

fruit.add(5, "peach");

for( String z : fruit)
{
    System.out.println("Item #" + fruit.indexOf(z) + " is " + z);
}
```

You should get a runtime error saying that the program has gone out of bounds.

```
Exception in thread "main" java.lang.IndexOutOfBoundsException: Index:
5, Size: 4
      at java.util.ArrayList.rangeCheckForAdd(Unknown Source)
      at java.util.ArrayList.add(Unknown Source)
      at arraylisttest.ArrayListTest.main(ArrayListTest.java:65)
```

There is no index 4, so inserting an item in index 5 is a logical error. Like Arrays, an ArrayList can run into out of bounds errors if you are not careful.

5.3.2 ArrayList of Numbers, Wrapper Classes, and Auto-boxing

We have seen that strings can be placed into an ArrayList, but what about numeric data types like int, double, long, etc.? ArrayList stores objects and not types, which means that the numbers need to be changed into an object to be stored into an ArrayList. To help store number types into an ArrayList, Java comes with equivalent wrapper classes to the different data types, Table 5.4.

Data Type	Wrapper Class
byte	Byte
short	Short
int	Integer
long	Long
float	Float
double	Double
boolean	Boolean
char	Character

Table 5.4 Java Wrapper Classes

The Wrapper Class wraps the type into an object. An object "x" that holds an integer can be created as follows:

```
Integer x = new Integer(12);
```

The best analogy is a birthday present. The present is put into a box and wrapped with paper, which later gets unwrapped. The act of wrapping and un-wrapping the value happens automatically. The term for wrapping and un-wrapping automatically is called auto-boxing. Here is an example of an ArrayList declaration for doubles and a couple of values added to the list:

```
ArrayList <Double> scores = new ArrayList<Double>();
scores.add(8.9);
scores.add(7.0);
```

The double values are automatically wrapped into objects stored into the ArrayList. When operations are performed, the objects are automatically unwrapped to double values.

```
y = scores.get(1)- 4;
```

5.3.3 Computer Activity 5.7 – Array List of Integers

We have seen an example of auto-boxing. Now, we will put the idea into practice. A softball team has played 4 games into the season. They have scored runs in each game:

Game 1 – 4 runs
Game 2 – 6 runs
Game 3 – 5 runs
Game 4 – 3 runs

Using an ArrayList, we will calculate the average runs-per-game so far. In Eclipse, create a new Java project called “CH5CA5.7-ArrayList-AutoBox”. Create a new class called “ArrayListAutoBox” with a main() method and a new package called “arraylistautobox”. The whole code listing is below in Code Listing 5.5. Add the library import and fill in the contents of the main() method:

```
1. package arraylistautobox;
2.
3. import java.util.ArrayList;
4.
5. public class ArrayListAutoBox {
6.
7.      public static void main(String[] args) {
8.           // TODO Auto-generated method stub
9.
10.          ArrayList <Integer> runs = new ArrayList<Integer>();
11.
12.          runs.add(4);
13.          runs.add(6);
14.          runs.add(5);
15.          runs.add(3);
16.
17.          double sum = 0.0;
18.          double avgruns = 0.0;
19.
20.          for (Integer x : runs)
21.          {
22.               sum += x;
23.          }
24.
25.          avgruns = sum/runs.size();
26.
27.          System.out.println("The average runs per game is " +
   avgruns);
28.     }
29. }
```

Code Listing 5.5 Auto-Boxing

Run the program and the average runs-per-game is 4.5. Lines 12-15 wrap the integer values into objects to be stored into the ArrayList. Line 22 unwraps the integer value and performs the addition. As you can see, no extra work has to be done. The Java libraries handle the auto-boxing internally. The only work that you have to do is to make sure that the ArrayList declaration uses the wrapper class and not the data type.

5.4 *Summary and Homework Assignments*

Arrays and ArrayLists provide a basic data structure to store and manage data. Remember, there is no off-roading with a computer program. As you develop programs, you need to be careful to not go out of bounds with arrays or Arraylists. The Enhanced for-loop was introduced as an alternative to keep the programs on the road. The computer activities have demonstrated that arrays can help with calculating sums, calculating averages, and performing searches, but there is much more to cover, which we will go into more detail in later chapters. The next two chapters will wrap what we learned in this and the last two chapters into custom classes; but before we dive in, here are a few questions and programming projects:

5.4.1 Questions

1. Given the following code segment

```
int x[], y;
int z = 0;

x = new int[3];
y = new int[2];

x[0] = 2;
x[1] = 3;
x[2] = 1;

y[0] = 8;
y[1] = 4;

for(int j =0; j < y.length; j++)
{
    for(int k = 0; k < x.length; k++)
    {
        z += (x[k]*2);
    }
    z-= y[j];
}

System.out.println("The final value is " + z);
```

a. What is wrong with the code?
b. If you correct the code, what is the final value?
c. Re-write the code using enhanced for-loops rather than counter for-loops.

2. What is wrong with the following code fragment, and how do you fix it:

```
int sum =0;
double[] scores = {1,6,7,8,3,2,7,8,9,10,6,4,3,2,7};
for(int counter = 0; counter <= 15; counter++ )
{
    sum += scores[counter];
}
```

3. What does the following code fragment do?

```
double x[] = {7,6.1,3,2,1.2,8.4,9,3,4,2};
double y[] = new double[x.length];
int k = 0;

for(int z = x.length-1; z >= 0; z-- )
{
    y[k] = x[z];
    k++;
}

for(int z = 0; z < x.length; z++)
{
    x[z] = y[z];
}

for(double z : x)
{
    System.out.print(z + " ");
}
```

4. The following program is missing 4 lines of code. Fill in the missing lines (11 and 12, and 17-18) so that the output is as follows:

```
Apple
Orange
Strawberry
Blueberry
Banana
```

```
Carrots
Onions
Squash
Cabbage
Sprouts
```

```java
package arrayhw3;

import java.util.ArrayList;

public class ArrayHW3 {

    public static void main(String[] args) {
        // TODO Auto-generated method stub

        ArrayList<String[]> produce = new ArrayList<String[]>();



        String[] fruit =
{"Apple", "Orange","Strawberry","Blueberry","Banana"};
        String[] vegetables =
{"Carrots","Onions","Squash","Cabbage","Sprouts"};





        for(String[] x: produce)
        {
            for(String y : x)
            {
                System.out.println(y);
            }
            System.out.println(" ");
        }

    }
}
```

5.4.2 Programming Projects

1. Write a program that stores ten (10) random Boolean values in an ArrayList. The program will then print out the count of "true" and "false" values in the ArrayList and print out the count for each true / false value.

2. Given the partially filled array:

```
double[] temperature = {65.7, 66.8, 67.8, 64.3, 0, 0, 0, 0};
```

Write a program that will insert the value of 64.5 at index 2 and move the others down the list. The 0 values can be discarded.

3. Given the array:

```
int[] scores = {5, 6, 2, 1, 7, 8, 3, 2, 2, 3, 4};
```

Write a program that will remove the fourth element in the list and move all other elements up. Fill in zeros for any empty indexes.

4. The vegetables ArrayList contains the following string values in this order: "carrots", "broccoli", "peas", "bananas", "turnips", "squash", "zucchini". Write a program that removes "bananas" from the list and then prints out the remaining list.

5. Write a program that asks a user to enter 5 positive integer values and outputs the average for all the values.

6. Write a program that fills in an integer array with 50 random integer values 0 through 100. The program will then output the array values and the minimum and maximum values in the array.

7. Consider the following code segment. The array sequence1 contains 4 integer values. What must the sequence1 values be so the output is 3 2 6 4? Hint: the values can be from 0 to 9.

```
int[] sequence1 = { ,  ,  ,  };
int[] sequence2 = new int[sequence1.length];
```

```
for( int x = 0 ; x < sequence1.length; x++)
{
    if((Math.pow(sequence1[x], 2) > 8) && (Math.pow(sequence1[x],
2)) != 1)
    {
        sequence1[x] = sequence1[x] - 2;

    }
}
int x = 0;

for(int y = sequence1.length -1; y >=0; y--)
{
    sequence2[x] = sequence1[y];
    x++;
}

for(int y: sequence2)
{
    System.out.print(y + " ");
}
```

8. The following is a 5x5 diagram having a letter in each cell. This can be represented as a two-dimensional array of chars. Using this array as test input, write a program that searches for each of the first 5 letters in the alphabet. As the program searches for each letter, it outputs the letter followed by "Found it n times!" if the letter was found at least once with 'n' being the number of times the letter was found, otherwise it outputs "Not found".

a	n	n	a	b
w	a	c	g	o
j	t	y	o	o
i	w	o	r	k
e	q	u	f	s

2-dimensional char array representing the diagram:

```
char[][] wordsearch2 = {
    {‘a’,’n’,’n’,’a’,’b’},
    {‘w’,’a’,’c’,’g’,’o’},
    {‘j’,’t’,’y’,’o’,’o’},
    {‘i’,’w’,’o’,’r’,’k’},
    {‘e’,’q’,’u’,’f’,’s’}
};
```

9. The game BINGO was formalized in 1930, and it is popular with non-profit organizations. Each player gets a 5x5 BINGO card with a random set of values. A caller draws a ping-pong ball from a hopper, and the caller announces the value on the ball. The values can be one of 5 groups of 15 numbers for a total of 75 possible values. The 5 groupings of values are as follows: B 1 through B 15, I 16 through I 30, N 31 through N 45, G 46 through G 60, and O 61 through O 75. When the caller draws a ball with N 34 from the hopper, they shout out “N 34” to the audience. The caller will throw a switch, and the BINGO board will light up with the value called. The typical BINGO board looks like the following:

B	1	2	3	4	5	6	7	8	9	10	11	12	13	14	15
I	16	17	18	19	20	21	22	23	24	25	26	27	28	29	30
N	31	32	33	34	35	36	37	38	39	40	41	42	43	44	45
G	46	47	48	49	50	51	52	53	54	55	56	57	58	59	60
O	61	62	63	64	65	66	67	68	69	70	71	72	73	74	75

No value can be called twice, so the caller puts the ball in a bin for storage for the next round. If the player’s game card has a match to the value called, the player marks the spot on their game card. Depending on the game, if a player gets 5 in a row on their card, the player yells: “BINGO!” to alert that they might have a winner. The caller and officials will double check for accuracy before declaring the winner. The balls are then put back into the hopper.

Write a program that will randomly generate the BINGO values. The program will ask the user (caller) to draw the value by typing the letter “d” and hitting enter, or type the letter “e” and hit enter to exit the program and end the game. If the user enters “d” again, the value will be printed on the screen, and the user will be asked to either enter “d” for a new draw or an “e” to exit the game. Each time a value is drawn, the whole list of values drawn during the game will be printed. No value can be called twice, so use array(s) to track the values.

10. Egg-hunt game. Write a program that creates a two-dimensional 5x5 array. At the start of the game, a 5 x 5 printout of "O"s will be displayed as the game board:

    OOOOO
    OOOOO
    OOOOO
    OOOOO
    OOOOO

    The program will randomly pick one x (row)- y (column) coordinate of the 25 cells with the top left coordinate being 0, 0. This cell is where the egg is located. The program will ask the user to enter the x (row: 0 through 4) and y (column: 0 through 4) coordinates of where they think the egg is hidden. If the x-y coordinate guessed by the user doesn't contain the egg, a counter is incremented by one and the board is reprinted with an "X" replacing the "O" in the location chosen. If the x-y coordinate guessed by the user contains the egg, the program outputs: "You found the egg!", reprints the game board with the letter "E" for where the egg was located, and the number of tries the user attempted.

11. Golf Handicap. Since every golf course is different, the US Golf Association (USGA) developed a rating system to help golfers compare their capabilities. This rating is called the "handicap". The handicap calculation is a bit complex, which makes it ideal for a computer program. Each golf course in the USA is given two rating numbers: a slope rating and a course rating. The two ratings and the player's total strokes are used to calculate the handicap differential for a single round of golf:

    Handicap Differential = (strokes - course rating) * 113 / slope rating

    If a golfer plays 20 rounds of golf, only the lower 10 handicap differential values are used to calculate the handicap. The lower 10 handicap differential values are averaged. The average is then multiplied by 0.96. The product is truncated to remove all decimal values to produce the final handicap for the golfer.

    A golfer plays 20 rounds of golf at the same golf course. The following array contains the best 10 scores out of the 20 rounds:

```
int[] strokes = {76,88,77,79,84,90,75,92,88,83};
```

The slope rating for the course is 125 and the course rating is 68.8. Write a program that calculates the player's handicap.

12. Update the Yahtzee dice from the Chapter 4 exercises. This time use a two-dimensional array to hold the dice in the first row and next roll state in the second row. Use loops to roll the dice, display dice rolls, and ask to keep dice.

6 Methods, Classes, and Packages

"Everything should be made as simple as possible, but not simpler."
-attributed to Albert Einstein

In chapter 2, we discussed object-oriented programming (OOP), and the main objective of OOP was to create reusable code. The hello world program was used as an example to introduce objects, classes, properties, and methods as well as the Java Archive library. The chapter provided a simple introduction as to act as a starting point to learn programming. OOP has many concepts to cover. Rather than diving into these concepts, the preceding three chapters have covered the basic programming concepts and constructs of data types, math, string objects, decisions, iteration, and basic data structures. Along the way, we used different objects, classes, methods like Math, String, ArrayList, and System; and we even had to import libraries like the Random and Scanner methods. Java is a pure object-oriented language so there is no escaping using objects. With the basic programming concepts covered, we can now discuss the OOP concepts with practical examples. The focus of this chapter is to cover class and method creation and architecture. The chapter will also cover how Eclipse helps to manage classes and to take advantage of some built-in features. OOP has several concepts and terminology, but through examples, we will try to make learning OOP as simple and interesting as possible.

6.1 Creating Methods

All the programs so far have been using only the main() method. You can have multiple methods in a project. Methods perform the actions or work within the program. When a method is called, the calling method is suspended and put on the stack to be retrieved when the method that is called completes its work, returns something, or simply returns. It is also important to architect methods properly. First, decide what the method will do. Second, for methods to be useful, we need to provide them the data to do the work. The data to be provided needs to go hand-in-hand with the work that needs to be performed. Third, the method should have the ability to return data or status, if necessary, when the work is completed.

So far, we have been working with local variables, those that exist between the {} in the method. When dealing with variables outside of the method or variables being passed to the method, Java has many different variable types. In this chapter, we will cover the rest of the variable types and their characteristics.

- Parameter Variables
- Instance Variables also known as field variables or class fields
- Class/static Variables

6.1.1 Passing Data Types and Objects

The different Math class methods discussed in Chapter 3 allowed you to pass a value into the method when you made a call to the method. This is known as "passing parameters". The method would perform whatever action or calculation it was designed to do, and then return either a result or void. Variables and objects can be passed to methods. The following diagram shows an example of a temperature conversion method, Figure 6.1.

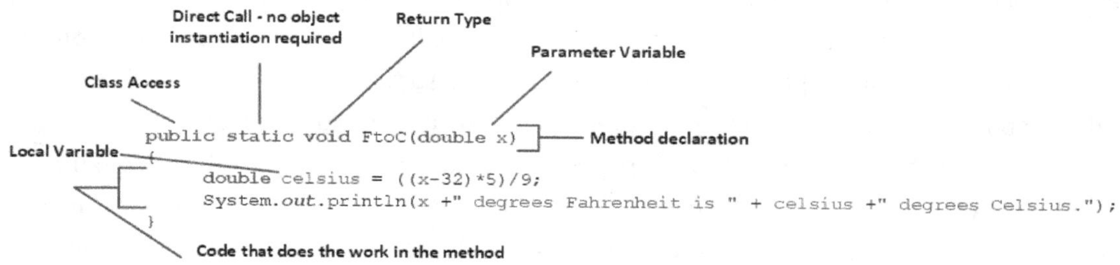

Figure 6.1 Temperature Conversion Method Example

The parameter to be passed to the method is typed double. The method declaration includes some keywords and the name of the method. The body of the method has a local variable that performs the conversions, and the second line displays the results. There is no return value since "void" was declared as the return type. Let's see the method in action.

6.1.2 Computer Activity 6.1 - Passing a Data Type

For this activity, we will create a program that contains two methods for temperature conversion (Fahrenheit to Celsius and Celsius to Fahrenheit). In Eclipse, create a new Java project called "CH6CA6.1-TempConv" and a new class with a main method called "TempConv". Call the package "jae.temptest". Modify and fill in the following code in the TempConv.java file, Code Listing 6.1.

```
package jae.temptest;

public class TempConv {

    public static void main(String[] args) {
        // TODO Auto-generated method stub

        double f = 75.3;
        double c = 32.9;
        TempConv.FtoC(f);
        TempConv.CtoF(c);
    }

    public static void FtoC(double x)
    {
        double celsius = ((x-32)*5)/9;
        System.out.println(x + " degrees Fahrenheit is " +  celsius
 +
 " degrees Celsius.");
    }

    public static void CtoF(double y)
    {
        double fahrenheit = (y*9/5)+32;
        System.out.println(y + " degrees Celsius is " + fahrenheit +
 " degrees Fahrenheit");
    }
}
```

Code Listing 6.1 Temperature Conversion Test Program

If you run the application, you will see the output for converting 75.3°F to °C and then 22.9 °C to °F. The two conversion methods have simple names. In the two temperature conversion method declarations, "public", "static", and "void" keywords are used just like you see in the main method. We will cover these keywords as we go through the chapter. Both methods take in "double" data type parameters. When you are typing the code to call the methods, Eclipse pops up a code complete dialog showing the data types to be entered, Figure 6.2.

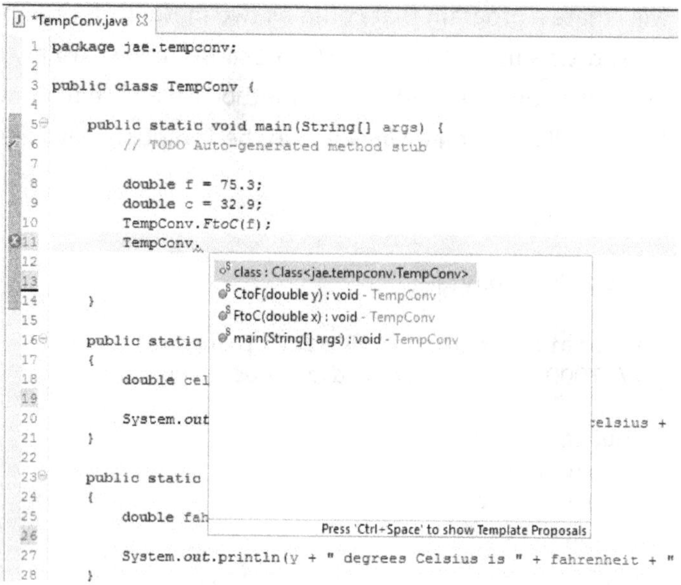

```
*TempConv.java
package jae.tempconv;

public class TempConv {

    public static void main(String[] args) {
        // TODO Auto-generated method stub

        double f = 75.3;
        double c = 32.9;
        TempConv.FtoC(f);
        TempConv.
                    class : Class<jae.tempconv.TempConv>
                    CtoF(double y) : void - TempConv
    }               FtoC(double x) : void - TempConv
                    main(String[] args) : void - TempConv
    public static
    {
        double cel

        System.out                                          celsius +
    }

    public static
    {
        double fah
                    Press 'Ctrl+Space' to show Template Proposals

        System.out.println(y + " degrees Celsius is " + fahrenheit + "
    }
```

Figure 6.2 Eclipse Code Completion Assistance

The menu shows the parameters that must be filled in when calling the methods. Once the call is made to the class, the values passed to the method are used to perform the conversion and the resulting output is displayed. After each call is complete, the next line in the main() method is run until the program completes.

6.1.3 Pass by Value versus Pass by Reference

Passing by value is just what you would expect. It is the passing of the value of a variable outside of a method to a local variable inside of a method. Only the value is transferred and used within the method. The original value of the variable outside of the method is unchanged. Passing by reference is the passing of the address of a variable outside of a method to a local variable inside of the method that can access the variable outside of the method by its address. Remember that any variable has a value, a storage size, and a storage address. A variable that contains an address is called a pointer in the C language. When methods have pointers to variables, they can change the values of the original variables. This can create some complex coding mechanisms and side effects. The designers of the Java language wanted to remove pointers and the ability to do pointer arithmetic from the language; but they couldn't get rid of all traces of pointers. When it comes to passing variables to a method, the value is passed to the method and can be used locally within the method's scope. The original variable value is not changed. In contrast, arrays are passed to a method by reference since they are objects. When the array is passed to a method, the address of the array is passed, not a copy of the values of each of the members of the array, and any changes made to the array locally in the method are made to the actual array object program-wide. The following program, Code Listing 6.2, demonstrates that concept.

```
package jae.vr;

public class ValueVsReference {

    public static void main(String[] args) {
        // TODO Auto-generated method stub
        int i = 2;
        int[] j = {4,5};
        System.out.println("i= " +i);
        System.out.println("j[0]= " +j[0]);
        System.out.println("j[1]= " +j[1]);

        //Pass value i  and reference j[]
        test1(j,i);

        //we see that j[1] gets changed and there is no return call
        System.out.println(" ");
        System.out.println("i= " +i);
        System.out.println("j[0]= " +j[0]);
        System.out.println("j[1]= " +j[1]);

        //Create a copy of j
        int[] h = test2(j,i);

        //h[] and j[] are pointing to the same object
        System.out.println(" ");
        System.out.println("i= " +i);
        System.out.println("j[0]= " +j[0]);
        System.out.println("j[1]= " +j[1]);
        System.out.println("h[0]= " +h[0]);
        System.out.println("h[1]= " +h[1]);

        test3(h,i);

        //h[] is passed to method. j[] is not passed, but j[] is also changed.
        //The original i value never changes
        System.out.println(" ");
        System.out.println("i= " +i);
        System.out.println("j[0]= " +j[0]);
```

```
40.             System.out.println("j[1]= " +j[1]);
41.             System.out.println("h[0]= " +h[0]);
42.             System.out.println("h[1]= " +h[1]);
43.
44.     }
45.
46.     public static void test1(int[] k, int x){
47.
48.             x++;
49.             k[1] = 7;
50.     }
51.
52.     public static int[] test2(int[] y, int p){
53.
54.             p--;
55.             y[0] = 9;
56.             return y; //returns the array, the original j[] is changed
57.     }
58.
59.     public static void test3(int[] k, int x){
60.
61.             x++;
62.             k[1] = 3;
63.     }
64. }
```

Code Listing 6.2 Pass By Value and Pass By Reference

Lines 7 and 8 create an integer variable, i, and an integer array, j[]; and the values are then printed to the screen.

```
i= 2
j[0]= 4
j[1]= 5
```

In line 14, the test1() method is called that passes both the variable, i, and the array, j[], to the method. The variable, i, is passed by value and the array, j[], is passed by reference. The method increments the variable and changes the second element in the array. The method has no return; but after the method executes, the values of i, and j[] are printed out again. The array has been changed and the variable has not.

```
i= 2
j[0]= 4
j[1]= 7
```

This is because i was passed by value. The value of i was copied to the integer, x, of the method. When x is incremented, i is not modified; in fact, the method has no access to i other than to copy its value when the method first executes. The array, j[], on the other hand, was passed by reference. The address of the k[] array of the method is set to the address of j[]. Therefore, j[] and k[] are pointing to, and addressing, the same object. When k[1] is modified, j[1] is modified, because they are both addressing the same object in memory.

In line 23, there is a call to the test2() method. The test2 method decrements its integer variable, p; and changes the first element of its array, y. This time an array is returned by the method to create another array. The array that is returned is the method's y array. After the method executes, the values of i and j[] are printed out again. Along with the new array, h[], which was created to accept the return of the method.

```
i= 2
j[0]= 9
j[1]= 7
h[0]= 9
h[1]= 7
```

In fact, j[] and h[] are not separate arrays; not only is the array, j[], passed to the method by reference, but the method returns its array, y[], by reference. The y[] array's address is set to the address of the j[] array when the method first executes. The method returns the address of the y[] array as it completes execution, and the newly created h[] array's address is set to the address of the y[] array. Therefore, both j[] and h[] point to, address, the same object.

Line 33 makes a call to the test3() method passing the h[] array and i variable to the method. The method increments the variable, x, which has the value of i copied to it, because i was passed by value. The method changes the second element in the array, k[], which is pointing to, addressing, the h[] array object; because h[] was passed by reference. After the method completes execution, the resulting printout of i, j[], and k[] shows that j[] and h[] have the same values since they actually point to the same object. The j[], h[], and k[] array objects are different references to the same array object. Though there are 3 array references, there is only 1 array.

```
i= 2
j[0]= 9
j[1]= 3
h[0]= 9
h[1]= 3
```

In the debugger, you can see that j[] and h[] have the same id value assigned proving that they are pointing to the same object, Figure 6.3.

Name	Value
args	String[0] (id=16)
i	2
j	(id=19)
[0]	9
[1]	7
h	(id=19)
[0]	9
[1]	7

Figure 6.3 Debugger Active Variable Listing

Pass by reference is very important since we need the ability to change, search, and sort data in a database. The pass by value versus pass by reference is an interesting topic of discussion on many discussion boards. In the end, the only way the developers of Java could have gotten completely away with the concept of pointers, would have been to pass the values of all the members of a complex object as the method call mechanism, and also have a mechanism to return the values of all the members of complex objects. Doing copies of large data structures each time a method is called, and having to replicate all that memory space, provides a heavy performance burden, as well as a system resource burden. It would also add to the complexity of how we deal with methods that we actually want to modify the objects that are being passed, especially if we are dealing with multiple objects. In the end, the developers of Java did keep the most important capability of pointers and provided for pointer management to be done behind the scenes.

6.1.4 Static Methods and Variables

The keyword "static" has been used for the main() method declaration, and we see it being used in the two temperature conversion methods.

Definition: *Static* – access a method or variable without the need to create an object.

Declaring static for main() is important since the JVM directly calls the main() method to run the program. The Math class is an example of static methods. All the methods in the Math class are static, and we simply referenced class name Math and the dot notation to the method that was to be called. For example:

```
double y = Math.pow((x+(Math.sqrt(b)/5)), 3);
```

Static methods are also called class methods, since the class name is used. In the temperature conversion program, TempConv.FtoC() was used. It is tempting to use static everywhere, but this would defeat the purpose of OOP. Static should be used for simple calculations like we see in the Math class or in the temperature conversion in the last activity. There are some rules about using static:

1. Static methods can directly call only other static methods. The exception is the main() method, which can access instance methods.
2. Static methods can only access static data.

Eclipse will warn you if you violate these rules by placing error and lightbulb symbols in the line numbers on the left.

6.1.5 Computer Activity 6.2 - Passing Objects

Methods are not limited to data type parameters or just a single parameter. Objects can also be passed to methods as well, and you can have more than one parameter. If you remember, Strings are objects, and in this computer activity, we are going to pass Strings to a couple of methods. In Eclipse, create a new Java project called "CH6CA6.2-StringFun" and a new class with a main method called "StringFun". Call the package "jae.stringfun". Modify and fill in the following code in the StringFun.java file, Code Listing 6.3.

```
package jae.stringfun;

public class StringFun {

    public static void main(String[] args) {
        // TODO Auto-generated method stub
        String str1 = "Demonstration of passing objects";
        System.out.println(str1);

        StringFun.removevowels(str1);
        StringFun.charactercount(str1, "t");
    }

```

```
    public static void removevowels(String str1)
    {
        String str2 = "";

        for(int x = 0; x < str1.length();x++)
        {

            if(str1.substring(x,x+1).equals("a") ||
  str1.substring(x,x+1).equals("e") ||
  str1.substring(x,x+1).equals("i") ||
  str1.substring(x,x+1).equals("o") ||
  str1.substring(x,x+1).equals("u") )
            {
                str2 +=" ";
            }
            else
            {
                str2 += str1.substring(x,x+1);
            }
        }
        System.out.println(str2);

    }

    public static void charactercount(String str1, String str2){

        int y = 0;

        for(int x = 0; x < str1.length(); x++)
        {
            if(str1.substring(x, x+1).equals(str2))
            {
                y++;
            }
        }
        System.out.println("The string contained " + y + " "+
             str2 +"(s).");

    }

}
```

Code Listing 6.3 Passing String Objects

If you run the program, you will see the two outputs from the two methods. The first method takes in a string and removes all vowels. The second method takes two strings and counts the number of times a letter is used in the string. Notice that the original string that gets passed to the methods never changes. Why is this, since the original string is passed by reference?

6.1.6 Return Data Types and Objects

Returning data after the method has completed the work is an important concept for breaking a program down into smaller pieces. Just as methods can take in data types or objects as parameters, data types or objects can be returned. A method can take in as many parameters as you desire, but only one data type or object can be returned. The last two computer activities did not provide any returns. The methods use the keyword "void" in the declaration, which says that no value is returned. There is nothing wrong with return nothing, but the temperature conversions and string fun methods are poorly implemented methods. The System.out.println should not be in the methods. The methods should only perform the action and return the results so that the method that receives the data or object can then perform further actions. When designing methods and classes, you need to take into account that others, including yourself, might want to re-use the methods in a different program. For example, the temperature conversion methods would return values that could be used in further calculations that did not want the results of the conversion to be printed out at the time of conversion.

6.1.7 Computer Activity 6.3 - Returning Data Types

Modify TempConv program in Computer Activity 6.1 as follows:

- Replace the calls to the methods in lines 10 and 11 with System.out.println calls that contain embedded calls to the temperature conversion methods to display the results.
- Comment out the System.out.println in the methods at lines 19 and 26.
- Change the temperature conversion methods' declarations to define each of them as returning a double.
- Add the return for the data type or object to each of the temperature conversion methods.

Here is the updated TempConv program in Code Listing 6.4:

```
package jae.temptest;

public class TempConv {

    public static void main(String[] args) {
        // TODO Auto-generated method stub

        double f = 75.3;
        double c = 32.9;
        System.out.println(f + " degrees Fahrenheit is " +
TempConv.FtoC(f) + " degrees Celsius.");
        System.out.println(c + " degrees Celsius is " +
TempConv.CtoF(c) + " degrees Fahrenheit");

    }

    public static double FtoC(double x)
    {
        double celsius = ((x-32)*5)/9;
        return celsius;
        //System.out.println(x + " degrees Fahrenheit is " +
celsius +
" degrees Celsius.");
    }

    public static double CtoF(double y)
    {
        double fahrenheit = (y*9/5)+32;
        return fahrenheit;
        //System.out.println(y + " degrees Celsius is " + fahrenheit
+
" degrees Fahrenheit");
    }
}
```

Code Listing 6.4 Returning Data Types

The two methods are now broken into their simplest implementation, and the two methods now return the type double. When the calculation in the method is completed, the values are returned so the class can choose what it wants to do with the results. In this case, it prints the results. Designing the methods to do specific work and return results, if any, is the proper architecture, which leads to better code reusability. You could also define methods that perform the output, but they should be limited to just performing the output, and they should provide some needed output formatting that the println methods don't provide.

6.2 Creating and Using Classes: Encapsulation and Instantiation

The programs created so far use a class based on the name of the project and a main() method. The main() method contains the whole program, which is fine for small programs. As programs become larger and more complex, having everything in the main() method is not practical. In the spirit of Einstein's famous quote, breaking a program down into smaller reusable components is at the heart of OOP, and we can break down the program using classes and methods. In Chapter 1, we talked about the different styles of code, and structured programming is what is going to be covered in this text. The idea is that breaking the program into small code snippets or modules will help make the program easier to manage. Back in chapter 2, we said the keyword in OOP is "Object". Classes are a definition of an object, classes contain variables and methods, and these are what are going to help us break down the programs. The best place to start is with an example.

6.2.1 Circle Class Example

The following program calculates the circumference of a circle. The program is broken into two separate .Java files. The first file is called CircleTest.java, Code Listing 6.5:

```
package jae.circle;

public class CircleTest {

    public static void main(String[] args) {
        // TODO Auto-generated method stub

        Circle mycircle = new Circle();
        System.out.println("The Circumgerence of a cicle with a
radius of 5cm is " + mycircle.circumference(5)+ "cm.");
    }

}
```

Code Listing 6.5 Program Entry Point

The second file is called Circle.java, Code Listing 6.6.

```
package jae.circle;

public class Circle {

    private final double PI = 3.14;

    double circumference(int radius)
    {
        return 2*PI*radius;
    }

}
```

Code Listing 6.6 Class File

So far, the programs we have created have existed in a single .Java file. In practice, classes should be placed in separate .Java files, thus keeping with the spirit of breaking things down as simple as possible. We will cover the reason behind why creating more .Java files actually simplifies the solution later in the chapter. In the CircleTest.java file, we see the usual class and main() from previous programs, but the Circle class is new. The Circle class represents a new code block {} and is not part of the CircleTest class code block. Both classes are part of the same package, which allows CircleTest to access Circle. The Circle class contains a constant and a method. The method performs the circumference calculation. When the main method runs, it creates a copy or an instance of the Circle class, and then calls the instance of the circumference() method with a value of 5. The circumference() method takes the value of 5 and returns the result of the circumference calculation. The main() method prints out the message and the calculation result. With a very simple example, there are many different OOP concepts on display. The biggest is called Encapsulation, Figure 6.4.

Definition: *Encapsulation* – the packaging of methods and variables into a single class object.

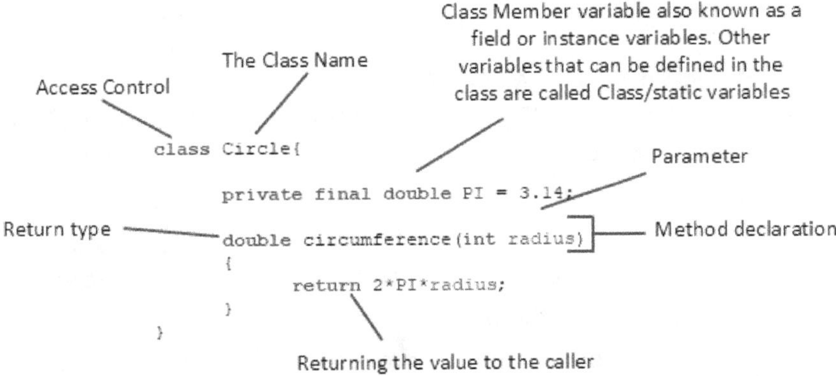

Figure 6.4 Class Object Encapsulation

In any of our previous programs, we would have just called the formula 2*PI*radius. Now, we have encapsulated the formula into a method, and the method into its own class. The Circle class contains two members: a constant variable and a method. The variable constant "PI" is also called a "field" or in other programming languages, it can be called a property. A method declaration consists of a method name, return type, and any parameters. The parameter is "radius", and using the full word allows others using your class to easily figure out what value needs to be passed in. It is good practice to have descriptive and concise parameter names, but you will find many computer science tests and examples in this book that use parameters with a single letter name in order to test and teach concepts. In order to get access to the class in the main() method, we must create a copy of the class in memory. Using the "new" operator to assign a class to a variable is known as instantiation.

```
Circle mycircle = new Circle();
```

Definition: *Instantiation* – Declare a real copy or an instance of an object.

From Chapter 2, we stated that classes and objects have a symbiotic relationship. The class is a concept. Only when the instance has been created is the actual object available. Once the object is available, you can access all the available class members using the dot notation just like you have been doing in previous programs. Since mycircle is an instance of a class, mycircle.circumference is called an instance method. If there were any declared variables in the class, these would be called instance variables. The constant value PI is not accessible to anything outside the class. Once the object has been destroyed, the instance of the method is also destroyed.

6.2.2 Architecting Classes – Class Members

Whether you are a building a medical device, a robot, a building, or writing a program, architecture is an important concept to understand. Stepping back from a project and working through a design before implementation will help create a better product in the end. The developers of Java looked at the various problems from other programming languages in an effort to create a language that is portable and reusable. Over the years, others have expanded the Java API and made improvements where the original version fell short. With all the changes, Java's success can be attributed to lots of debates, compromises, and careful architecting.

Because the Java library is expansive, you need to carefully architect your classes. First, make sure that there is nothing out there that is similar to what you are developing. In our Circle class, we have a constant for PI, but the Math class already has this constant available. Second, do your best to choose a class name that doesn't conflict with any other classes. Third, when creating a class, make sure that all members in the class are a logical fit. Adding a method to calculate the area of a rectangle to the Circle class would not make any sense. A better class name would be called "GeometricMath". The class would logically contain geometric math calculation methods. Reusable code is why OOP languages exist. Other developers using your code will expect to see a properly designed class.

6.2.3 Computer Activity 6.4 - The Call Stack and Eclipse Debugging

Let's see how debugging works with a separate class. For this activity, we will return to the Factorial example used in Chapter 4. A For-loop was used to calculate the factorial for a given value of n. We will place the loop in a method in a separate class. The first step is to come up with a name for the class. Factorial is part of a family of Mathematical Integer Sequences. There is an entire online list of all the know integer sequences (http://oeis.org/A046968). We will name the class IntSequences. This way we can add other sequences to the class in the future.

In Eclipse, create a new Java project called "CH6CA6.4-IntegerSequences". Create a new class with a main method called "IntSequensesTest". Call the package jae.intsequences, Code Listing 6.7. Create a second class called IntSequences with no main() method under the same jae.intsequences package, Code Listing 6.8. Eclipse will provide several warnings as items might not be available until you type them in. Create the IntSequences class first after the program has been created.

IntSequenceTest.java:

```java
package jae.intsequences;

import java.util.Scanner;

public class IntSequenceTest {

    public static void main(String[] args) {
        // TODO Auto-generated method stub
        IntSequences mysequences = new IntSequences();

        //Ask the user for a value of n
        System.out.println("Enter a value for n:");
        Scanner sRead = new Scanner(System.in);
        int n = sRead.nextInt();
        sRead.close();
        System.out.println("The factorial for " + n + " is " + mysequences.factorialloop(n));
    }
}
```

Code Listing 6.7 IntSequenceTest Main Entry Point

IntSequences.java:

```java
package jae.intsequences;

public class IntSequences {

    private int fact = 1;

    public int factorialloop(int n)
    {
        if(!(n==1|| n==0))
        {
            for (int x = 1; x <=n; x++)
            {
                fact*=x;
            }
        }
        return fact;
    }
}
```

Code Listing 6.8 IntSequences Class

If you look at the project in Package Explorer, Figure 6.5, you will see the FactorialLoop2.java file has two files and a class in each file.

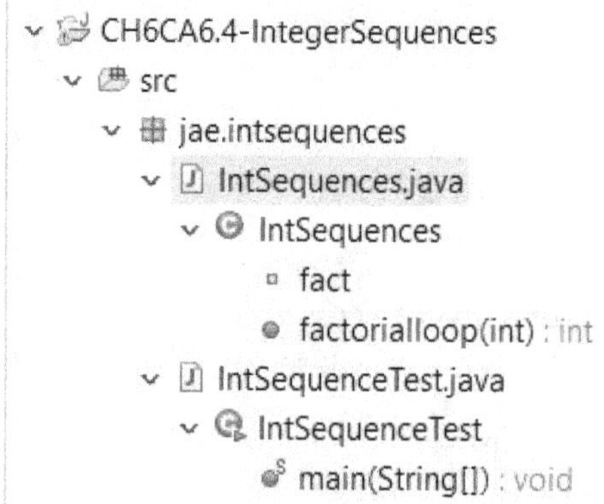

Figure 6.5 Package Explorer IntegerSequences

If you run the application, the result is the same as the previous factorial program. The difference is the actual work of the program has been broken up. The factorial calculation is encapsulated in a separate class in a separate file. In IntSequenceTest.java, line 9 created an instance of the class so we can call the method to perform the calculation. Place a breakpoint at line 16 in IntSequenceTest.java, and run the debugger. Enter the value 7 and hit enter. The debugger will reach the breakpoint. This time do a Step Into or hit F5. The debugger will jump to the class. Upper left pane of the Debug perspective shows the call stack, Figure 6.6. When a program starts, a call stack is created. A call stack is used to store information about the active methods.

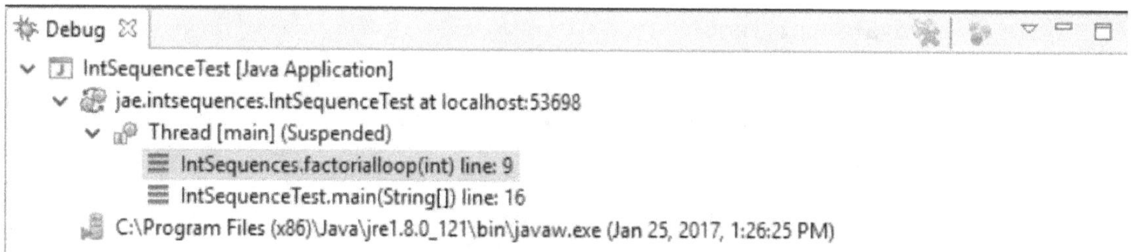

Figure 6.6 Call Stack

The call stack shows that when the debugger jumped into the factorialloop() method the main() method was suspended and put on the memory stack. The call stack allows you to see the exact program state. The class and method are shown together using dot notation. The line number shows where the debugger is with respect to the code listing. In the case of the main method, the line number shows where the jump to the factorialloop() method was made, line: 16. You can click on the FactorialLoop2.main(String[]) line: 16 and see the variables that are in the main method's scope, Figure 6.7.

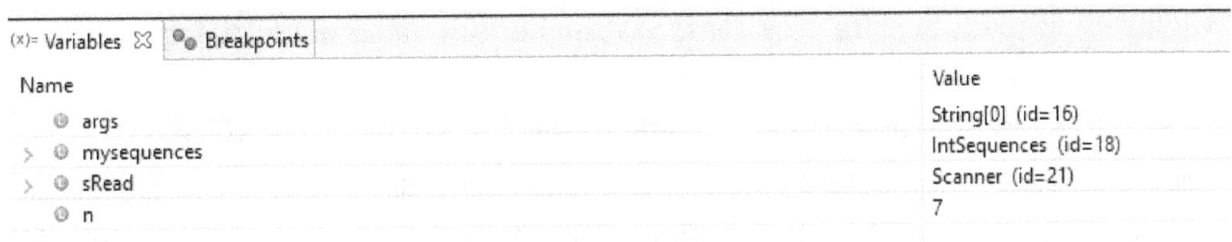

Figure 6.7 Main Method's Variables

Notice that mysequences is referenced the IntSequences object. What is not visible is that mysequences is referencing the memory location of the constructed IntSequences object. Click on the IntSequences.factorialloop(int) line 9, and you can continue debugging. You can Step Over or hit F6 to walk the debugger through the code. Once the return value is sent back, the IntSequences.factorialloop disappears and the main() method comes off the stack and is ready for more debugging, Figure 6.8. The call stack provides the ability to make the return to the calling method or thread and continue where the method left off.

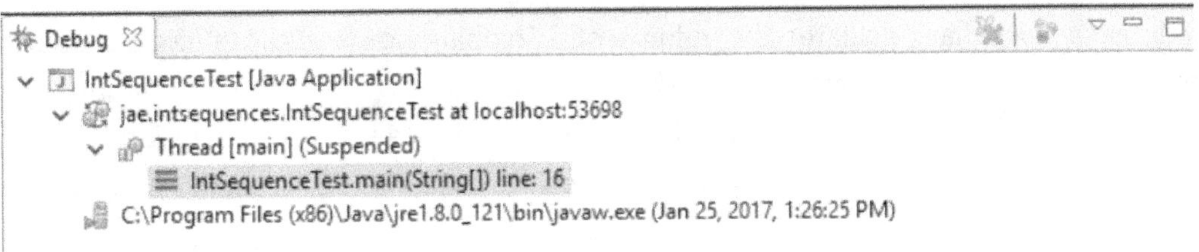

Figure 6.8 Call Stack Returned

If you had an application that had a method calling a method2 calling a method3, you would see the stack listing all three methods in the call stack. Memory is finite and so is the call stack. Too many nested method calls could cause the program to run out of memory.

6.2.4 Class Access Controls: Public, Private, and Protected

The ability to create your own reusable classes is a powerful tool. There will be times when you want to limit what is accessible from outside the class. The circle and IntSequence classes contain the "public" keyword that has been used in all of our programs so far. These two examples also introduce a new keyword: "private". Public, private, and protected are class access modifiers.

When a class member, method or variable are declared "public," anything outside the class can access the class member. The main() method is always declared "public" since it is the start of the program. If there is no declaration, then the default is public. When "private" is used in the declaration, only other class members within the class have access. In the factorial example, the "fact" variable was made private. The reason is simple: this value never changes, and nothing outside the class should be permitted to change the value. Only the internal class members have access, and in this case the factorialloop() method uses the variable to produce the result. If the variable was allowed to be changed from the outside, it could change the factorial result, which would be an error. The protected class modifier is used when inheritance is involved, which we will cover in the next chapter.

6.2.5 Special Class Methods: Constructor, Accessor, Mutator, and Finalize

There are four special methods used in classes. The Constructor is used in the creation of a class object, and Finalize is used for garbage collection in a class object. The other two methods are for access and changing (mutating) instance variables in a class object. The best way to cover these special methods is in a working example.

6.2.6 Computer Activity 6.5 - Special Class Methods

We will use a class that calculates the volume of a shipping box. In Eclipse, create a new Java project called "CH6CA6.5-SpecialMethods" and a new class with a main method called "ShippingBoxTest". Call the package "jae.shippingbox". Create a second class called ShippingBox under the same package. Modify and fill in the following code in the ShippingBoxTest.java file.

ShippingBoxTest.java, Code Listing 6.9:

```
package jae.shippingbox;

public class ShippingBoxTest {

    public static void main(String[] args) {
        // TODO Auto-generated method stub
        ShippingBox mybox = new ShippingBox();
        mybox.height = 10;
        mybox.length = 8;
        mybox.width = 5;
```

```
        System.out.println("The volume of the box is " +
mybox.boxVolume() + " cubic inches");
    }
}
```

Code Listing 6.9 ShippingBoxTest

ShippingBox.java, Code Listing 6.10:

```
package jae.shippingbox;

public class ShippingBox{

    public int length;
    public int width;
    public int height;

    public int boxVolume()
    {
        return length * width * height;
    }
}
```

Code Listing 6.10 ShippingBox Class

The ShippingBox class has the three fields for length, width, and height as well as the method to calculate the volume. The ShippingBoxTest main() method tests the class by first creating the object, setting the fields, and then outputting the volume result. In Eclipse, the code complete dialog shows the fields and the boxVolume() method, Figure 6.9.

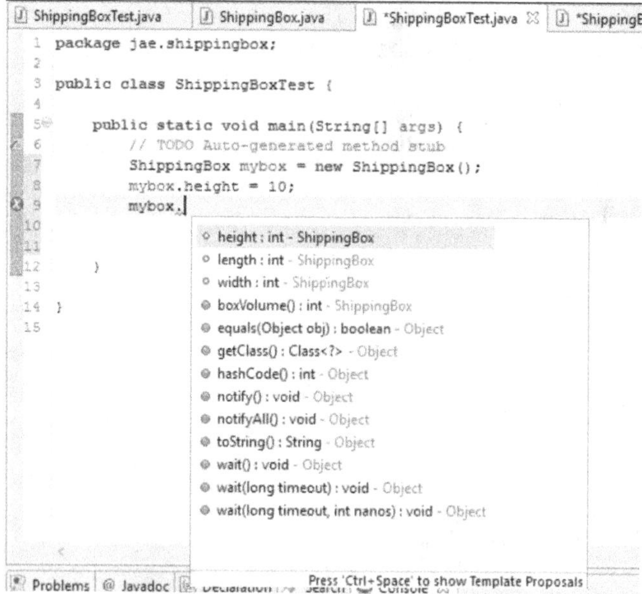

Figure 6.9 Code Complete Dialog

The problem with this code is that if you forget to fill in a field, the result will be in error. The solution to this is to use what is called a "constructor" to set up the fields during instantiation of the class.

Definition: *Constructor Method* – a special method used in Instantiation to set values in a class's fields. The constructor method has the same name as the class and doesn't return any value

Let's change the code and add what is called the constructor. In ShippingBoxTest.java, we will remove the 3 lines (8, 9, and 10) for initializing the variables. In ShippingBox.java, add the constructor method after the boxVolume() method, and put the values to be passed to the constructor method in the instantiation in line 7.

ShippingBoxTest.java, Code Listing 6.11:

```
1. package jae.shippingbox;
2.
3. public class ShippingBoxTest {
4.
5.     public static void main(String[] args) {
6.         // TODO Auto-generated method stub
7.         ShippingBox mybox = new ShippingBox(10, 8, 5);
```

```
        System.out.println("The volume of the box is " +
 mybox.boxVolume() + " cubic inches");
    }
}
```

Code Listing 6.11 Using ShippingBox Class Constructor

ShippingBox.java, Code Listing 6.12:

```
package jae.shippingbox;

public class ShippingBox {

    private int length;
    private int width;
    private int height;

    public int boxVolume()
    {
        return length * width * height;
    }

    //This is the constructor for the class
    public ShippingBox(int boxlength, int boxwidth, int boxheight) {
        length = boxlength;
        width = boxwidth;
        height = boxheight;
    }
}
```

Code Listing 6.12 ShippingBox Class with Constructor Added

Rather than having the three lines in the main() method after ShippingBox class instantiation setting the length, width, and height of the box, the values are passed during ShippingBox class instantiation. The Constructor method takes the values and fills in the fields. Now, a programmer can use the class to create objects for different box sizes without having to enter several lines of code for each new dimension. The original class still has another problem. Having all the fields publically available could also lead to problems. Someone could accidentally set a field for a dimension, which, in turn, miscalculates the volume. Using the "private" access control we can hide the fields from anyone outside of the class accidentally setting them. If we change the fields to private, this will make them instance variables. The constructor method can still set the fields since it is within the class. In Eclipse, the context menu only shows the boxVolume() method. The fields are not visible, and the constructor is not a selectable method, Figure 6.10.

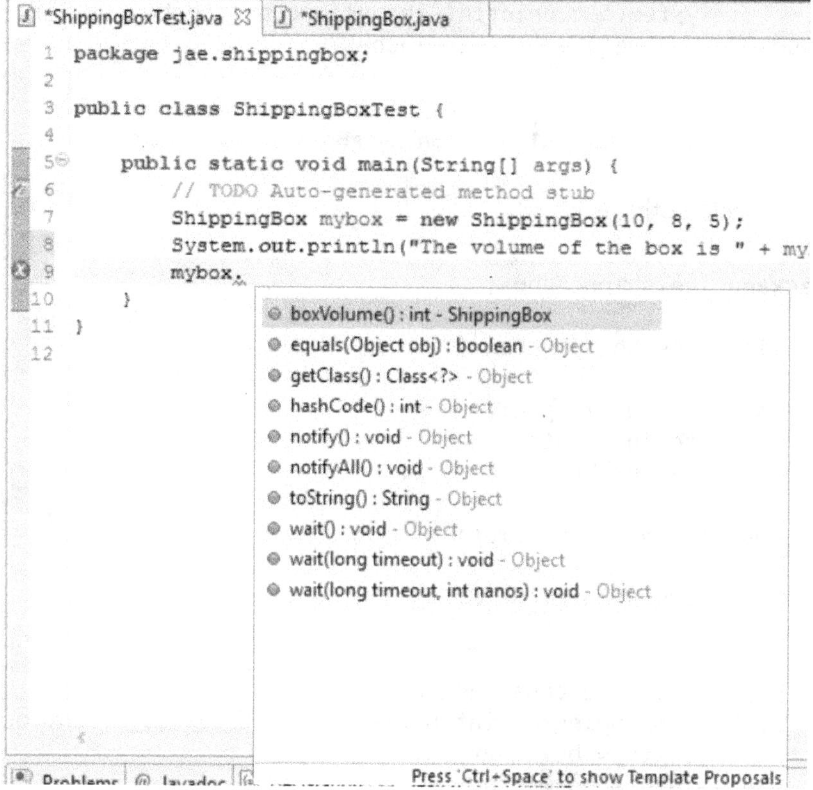

Figure 6.10 Code Complete Dialog Not Showing Private Fields or Constructor

What if a program needs to access the dimensions to calculate how many boxes can fit into a shipping container? Or maybe a box has an adjustable height. If the variables are "private", how can you access or change the field data? Accessor and mutator methods help to provide a back-door access to the fields.

Definition: *Accessor Method* – a method that returns a field value.

Definition: *Mutator Method* – a method that changes a field value

In some programming languages, the accessor method is called a "get" and a mutator is called a "set". In practice, the method names should start with get or set. The following shows the changes to add three accessor methods to get each dimension and mutator method to change the box height. The main() method adds lines(8-12) to test these methods.

ShippingBoxTest.java, Code Listing 6.13:

```
package jae.shippingbox;

public class ShippingBoxTest {

    public static void main(String[] args) {
        // TODO Auto-generated method stub
        ShippingBox mybox = new ShippingBox(10, 8, 5);
        System.out.println("The dimensions are " +
mybox.getBoxLength() + "in x" + mybox.getBoxWidth() +"in x" +
mybox.getBoxHeight()+ "in");
        System.out.println("The volume of the box is " +
mybox.boxVolume() + " cubic inches");
        mybox.setBoxHeight(3);
        System.out.println("The dimensions are " +
mybox.getBoxLength() + "in x" + mybox.getBoxWidth() +"in x" +
mybox.getBoxHeight()+ "in");
        System.out.println("The volume of the box is " +
mybox.boxVolume() + " cubic inches");

    }
}
```

Code Listing 6.13 ShippingBoxTest Using Accessor and Mutator Methods

ShippingBox.java, Code Listing 6.14:

```
package jae.shippingbox;

public class ShippingBox {

    private int length;
    private int width;
    private int height;

    public int boxVolume()
    {
        return length*width*height;
    }
    //This is the constructor for the class
    public ShippingBox(int boxlength, int boxwidth, int boxheight) {

        length = boxlength;
        width = boxwidth;
        height = boxheight;
```

```
    }
    //Mutator method to change box height
    public void setBoxHeight(int h){
        height = h;
    }
    //Accessor method to get height
    public int getBoxHeight(){
        return height;
    }
    //Accessor method to get length
    public int getBoxLength(){
        return length;
    }
    //Accessor method to get width
    public int getBoxWidth(){
        return width;
    }
}
```

Code Listing 6.14 ShippingBox Class with Accessor and Mutator Methods

When the program runs, the accessor methods are called to get the individual measurement values. The mutator method is called to change the height, and the new box size information is displayed. The last special class method is called finalize() method.

Definition: *Finalize Method* – called by the garbage collector to perform any cleanup activities before an object is destroyed

When a class object is created, objects are dynamically allocated a free pool of memory. There is a finite amount of memory in a computer, so at some point, memory will have to be freed up to prevent a program crash. A programming language like C++ makes you manually free memory once the object is no longer in use. Managed code languages like Java, VB.NET, and C# use a garbage collector to free up memory. The garbage collector automatically runs quietly in the background at some random interval of time. As objects are no longer being used, when the garbage collector runs, the object is removed and memory is recycled back to the free memory pool. Since there is no way to predict when the garbage collector will run, the garbage collector will call the finalize method to clean up anything the object was using before the object is destroyed. For our example, the program is so short that it terminates well before the garbage collector will run, thus a finalize() method is not needed. In practice, the finalize() should only be used for special cases when cleaning up the object is needed. For example, if a method had opened a file, the finalize method would be a clean way to close the file before the object is destroyed.

6.2.7 Classes in Separate Java Files

We stated earlier that in practice, classes should be in their own separate .java file. If there was a second class in a file and you tried to add a "public" keyword in front of the class definition, Eclipse will throw an error stating that the class must be in its own file. As programs get very large, having the program broken down into separate .java class files makes it easier to debug and manage. Various study guides and textbooks will show the class with main() and other classes one after another. Just know that these classes are really in separate files in the same package. Eclipse will let you include multiple classes in a single .java file, but be aware that access controls cannot be used in defining the class. Moving forward, the chapter exercises will have you write the computer activities with a single project containing multiple Java files.

6.2.8 Eclipse Feature: Quickly add Accessor / Mutator Methods and Introducing the "This" Keyword

Creating accessor and mutator methods in Java is a common occurrence. Eclipse has a built-in capability to generate accessor and mutator methods. Once the class variables have been written in code, you can go to the menu and select Source->Generate Getters and Setters... Using the last activity as an example, the following dialog appears with options for length, width, and height, Figure 6.11. You can select the methods to implement and Eclipse will add the methods to the class.

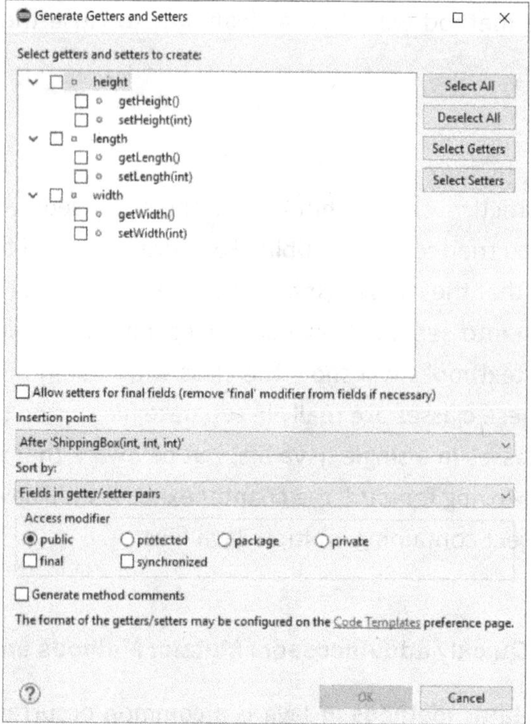

Figure 6.11 Eclipse Accessor/Mutator Auto-Generation

Checking all the boxes and clicking the OK button, Eclipse will generate the following code;

```
public int getLength() {
    return length;
}
public void setLength(int length) {
    this.length = length;
}
public int getWidth() {
    return width;
}
public void setWidth(int width) {
    this.width = width;
}
public int getHeight() {
    return height;
}
public void setHeight(int height) {
    this.height = height;
}
```

The code looks different than the original version from the activity. Both are correct and will function correctly. The code generated by Eclipse uses the field variable name along with get or set for the accessor and mutator methods. The name of the field variable is also used as the parameter that gets passed in, which may sound like a conflict with the field variable. What happens is that the method parameter is a local variable to the method. The field variable exists outside of the method, and the method variable exists inside the method, so the two variables with the same name do not collide. To access the field variable within the method, the "this" keyword is used to call out the field variable in "this" class instance. In the setLength() method, the "length" field variable is processed with the "this" in dot notation, "this.length" and assigned the "length" method parameter. This source code generation is a nice feature, but be very careful since what gets generated might not do exactly what you intended. Always inspect the auto-generated code carefully; and if need be, step through the code in the debugger to verify its operation.

6.2.9 Computer Activity 6.6 - Classes and Static Variables

The value of a static variable is the same in all instances of an object. The static variable can be considered a global. In this example, we will demonstrate using a static variable for interest rate in a bank account class. In Eclipse, create a new Java project called "CH6CA6.6-Bank" and a new class with a main method called "InterestTest". Call the package "jae.interest". Create a second class called BankAccount with no main() method and use the same package. Modify and fill in the following code.

InterestTest.java, Code Listing 6.15:

```
package jae.interest;

public class InterestTest {

    public static void main(String[] args) {
        // TODO Auto-generated method stub
        BankAccount customer1 = new BankAccount(1000);
        BankAccount customer2 = new BankAccount(500);
        customer1.setInterestrate(.005);
        System.out.println("Customer1 has a starting savings of " +
customer1.getSavingsAmount()+" and will get " +
customer1.MonthlyInterest() + " monthly interests with interest rate
of "+ customer1.getInterestrate()+"%");
```

```
        System.out.println("Customer2 has a starting savings of " +
    customer2.getSavingsAmount()+" and will get " +
    customer2.MonthlyInterest() + " monthly interests with interest rate
    of "+ customer2.getInterestrate()+"%");
        BankAccount.interstrate = .0025;
        System.out.println("Customer1 has a starting savings of " +
    customer1.getSavingsAmount()+" and will get " +
    customer1.MonthlyInterest() + " monthly interests with interest rate
    of "+ customer1.getInterestrate()+"%");
        System.out.println("Customer2 has a starting savings of " +
    customer2.getSavingsAmount()+" and will get " +
    customer2.MonthlyInterest() + " monthly interests with interest rate
    of "+ customer2.getInterestrate()+"%");

    }
}
```

Code Listing 6.15 InterestTest

BankAccount.java, Code Listing 6.16:

```
package jae.interest;

class BankAccount{

    private double savings;
    static double interstrate = .001;

    BankAccount(double deposit){

        savings = deposit;
    }
    public double MonthlyInterest(){

        return (savings*interstrate);
    }
```

```
    public void setInterestrate(double rate){
        interstrate = rate;
    }
    public double getInterestrate(){
        return interstrate;
    }
    public double getSavingsAmount()
    {
        return savings;
    }
}
```

Code Listing 6.16 BankAccount Class

The BankAccount class has two variables. The first is an instance variable that will hold the savings for the account. The second is a class field that is used to calculate the monthly interest on the account. An initial percentage rate of .001 is assigned to the static variable to avoid an error. A constructor method sets up the accounts. Two accessor methods get the field values. A mutator method allows for changing the "interstrate" value. Finally, there is a method to calculate the monthly interest based on the amount in savings.

The main() method sets up two accounts (customer1 and customer2) by creating two objects. Each account is set up with a different savings amounts. To demonstrate, the static "interstrate" variable is global; the value is changed by way of a variable using the customer1 instance in line 9. In lines 10 and 11, the output shows that both accounts have the same interest rate. In line 12, the interest rate is changed using the simple class variable call. The output from lines 13 and 14 shows the new interest rate has been applied to both accounts.

6.2.10 Computer Activity 6.7 - An Array of Objects – Custom Data Structure

The previous chapter covered Arraylists, which is a collection of objects. Now that we know how to create our own custom object, we can use an Arraylist to create a basic inventory program. In this activity, we will create an inventory program with an OfficeSupply class that stores an item name and the quantity. An arraylist will be used to store OfficeSupply objects. In Eclipse, create a new Java project called "CH6CA6.7-OfficeInventory," and a new class with a main method called "OfficeInventory". Call the package "jae.inventory". Create a second class called OfficeSupply. Modify and fill in the following code. OfficeInventory.java, Code Listing 6.17:

```java
package jae.inventory;

import java.util.ArrayList;

public class OfficeInventory {

    public static void main(String[] args) {
        // TODO Auto-generated method stub
        ArrayList <OfficeSupply> mySupplies = new
ArrayList<OfficeSupply>();
        mySupplies.add(new OfficeSupply("Penciles",50));
        mySupplies.add(new OfficeSupply("Pens",73));
        mySupplies.add(new OfficeSupply("Pads of Paper",85));
        mySupplies.add(new OfficeSupply("paperclips",400));
        mySupplies.add(new OfficeSupply("staples",500));

        for (OfficeSupply x : mySupplies)
        {
            System.out.println("There are "+ x.getQuantity() +" "+
x.getItem());
        }
    }
}
```

Code Listing 6.17 Office Inventory

OfficeSupply.java, Code Listing 6.18:

```java
package jae.inventory;

class OfficeSupply {

    private String item;
    private int quantity;
    public String getItem() {
        return item;
    }
    public void setItem(String item) {
        this.item = item;
    }
    public int getQuantity() {
        return quantity;
    }
    public void setQuantity(int quantity) {
        this.quantity = quantity;
    }
```

```
    public OfficeSupply(String item, int quantity) {
        this.item = item;
        this.quantity = quantity;
    }
}
```

Code Listing 6.18 OfficeSupply Class

The OfficeSupply class stores two items: the name of the item and the quantity. The constructor fills in both field variables on a creation of a new object. The accessor and mutator methods get and set the field variables. The main() method creates an arraylist of OfficeSupply objects. In order to add the objects to the arraylist, a "new" OfficeSupply object is created using the OfficeSupply constructor and values for the two parameters. In the last chapter, there were a couple of examples of string arraylists. Adding the item "`new OfficeSupply("staples",500)`" to the OfficeSupply arraylist is like adding "apple" to the String arraylist. The enhanced For-loop prints out all the items in the collection by using the accessor methods. If you want to change the quantity of an item, it is a simple matter of getting the index and using the mutator method to change the quantity.

```
mySupplies.get(2).setQuantity(165);
```

6.3 Eclipse Reference Icons

As we are starting to dig deeper into the computer science topics, you probably notice that Eclipse has icons next to every little item. From folders to boxes, triangles and dots, and green circles with "C"s in them, the icons act as a visual aid next to the element seen on the screen, Table 6.1. As programs get bigger, the icons sometimes help debug what it going on in the program, such as making something static when it shouldn't be.

ICON	Description
	compilation unit (*.java file)
	source folder
	class (public)
	package visible class
	public field
	default method (package visible)
	public field
	JAR file without attached source
	stack frame
	debug target

Table 6.1 Eclipse Reference Icons

The whole list of icons can be found in the Eclipse help documentation: http://help.eclipse.org/oxygen/index.jsp?topic=/org.eclipse.jdt.doc.user/reference/ref-icons.htm. Each release of Eclipse may have subtle changes or additions to the list. It is important to check out the update list for the release that you are using.

6.4 Packages and Jar Files

The Java API is extensive and growing. Thousands of developers have put many hours into developing the Java API that millions of developers use. Today, it is reported that there are more than 4000 classes in the Java 8 library. To keep everything in order, an organizational structure had to be developed. This is where packages come in.

Definition: *Package* – A technique for organizing classes into namespaces. A Package is also known as a library.

Packages allow classes to exist in the same namespace. Different .java files with different classes can be in the same package or namespace. Being in the same namespace allows all the classes to reside in the same scope and access each other's class members. We touched on packages back in Chapter 2 in the HelloWorld project, and we have been a little bit liberal on package names until this chapter. Packages are an important part of managing and grouping like classes into a single manageable item. Package Explorer on the left side in Eclipse is appropriately named, since it allows you to explore the different packages. The package name can be used in the dot notation in a program. There are 217 packages in the Java 8 library. Here are a few of the popular Java packages, Table 6.2:

Package	Description
java.lang	Contains the basic classes that are automatically imported into every project
java.util	Basic data structure classes
java.io	Read and write I/O operations
java.net	Contains classes for writing network programs
javax.swing	Classes for creating GUI applications

Table 6.2 Popular Java Packages

These 217+ packages are stored in Java Archive (JAR) files.

Definition: *Java Archive (JAR) File* – A file that contains one or more packages.

When you installed the Java runtime back in Chapter 2, the JAR files containing all packages and the class were also installed. There are approximately 14 JAR files that come with the Java runtime. These numbers don't account for all the available third-party libraries developed by different companies and individuals. The encapsulation within encapsulation in big packages sounds like a Russian matryoshka doll, but when trying to manage a large number of APIs, the implementation provides the best architecture, Figure 6.12.

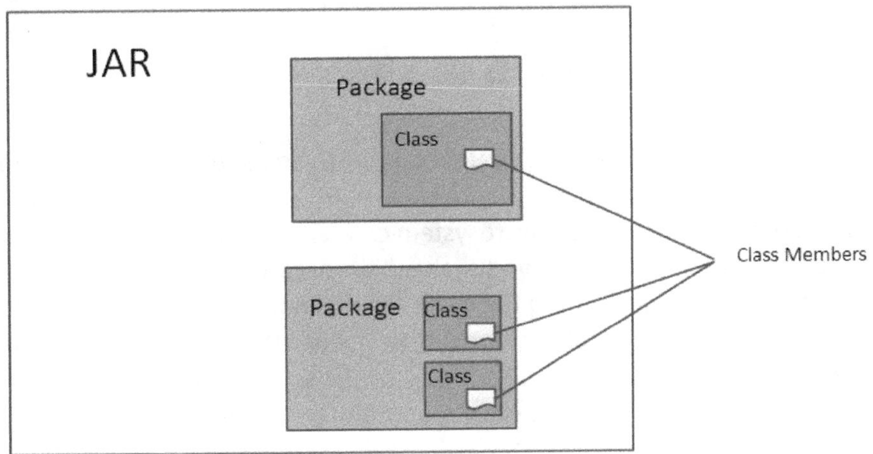

Figure 6.12 Java Archive Architecture

As we saw with the HelloWorld program, when a new project is created, the Java libraries are attached to the project automatically, Figure 6.13.

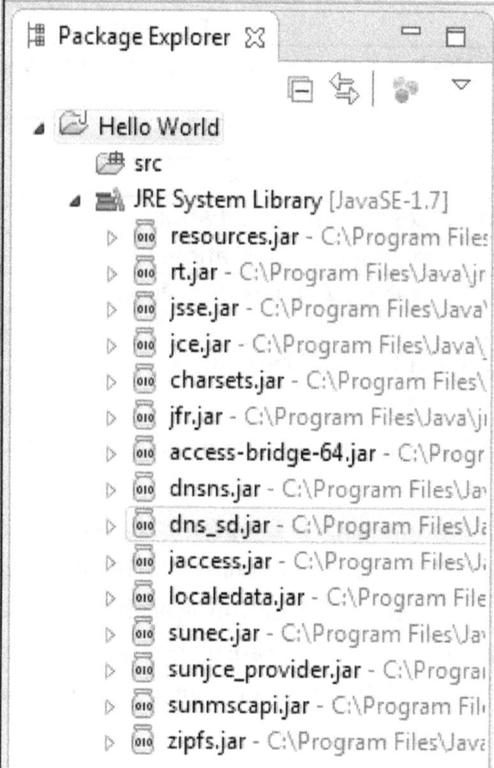

Figure 6.13 Java Libraries in a Package

There are some guidelines and rules when naming and creating packages:

- The name starts with a lower-case letter; and for the most part, all other letters are also lower case.
- The name must be unique. Sun Microsystem created some of the first libraries, and they took their Internet domain name and changed the order: com.sun. When Oracle acquired Sun Microsystems, they also used the same convention, com.oracle. It doesn't have to be a domain name, but it has to be unique. We have been using "jae." for "Java and Eclipse".
- Members of the package should be a logical fit. A package that has classes for chemistry calculations would not include classes for accounting, for example.

6.4.1 Computer Activity 6.8 Creating Custom Libraries

Breaking a program into smaller pieces of code, encapsulating them into Classes, and packaging them so others can re-use the code is at the heart of OOP. JAR files provide the mechanism to share your code. In this computer activity, we will create a new project that has a package with three classes containing math equations. Using Eclipse, the package will be exported to a JAR file and tested using a different project. Since there are a few details to be covered with Eclipse menu items and dialogs, we will go through the activity step-by-step.

Step 1 – Create the project and three classes

The first step is to create 3 classes in three .java files.

1. Create a new Java Project in Eclipse called "CH6CA6.8-Custom Library".
2. Right-click on the src folder and select New->Class from the context menu.
3. In the Java Class dialog, set the package name to jae.mathib.
4. The name of the class will be called BasicMath.
5. DO NOT CHECK THE "public static void main(String[] args)". The box must be unchecked. The class will not have a main method. Click Finish.
6. This class will have very simple static methods to perform basic math on two integer values. Enter the following in the BasicMath.java file, Code Listing 6.19:

```
package jae.mathlib;

public class BasicMath {

    //Add two numbers: A + B
    public static int Add(int A, int B)
    {
        int C = A + B;
        return C;
    }
    //Subtract two numbers: A - B
    public static int Subtract(int A, int B)
    {
        int C = A - B;
        return C;
    }
```

```
    //Multiply two numbers: A * B
    public static int Multiply(int A, int B)
    {
        int C = A * B;
        return C;
    }
    //Divide two numbers: A / B
    public static int Divide(int A, int B)
    {
        int C = A / B;
        return C;
    }
    //Produce the Modulus between to numbers: A % B
    public static int Modulus(int A, int B)
    {
        int C = A % B;
        return C;
    }
}
```

Code Listing 6.19 Basic Math Library Module

7. Save the project.
8. In Package Explorer, under the CustomLibrary project, right-click on the jae.mathlib package. Select New->Class from the context menu.
9. Since you right-clicked on the package to generate the class, this time the package name is already filled in. The name of the class will be called GeomerticMath and click Finish.
10. DO NOT CHECK the "public static void main(String[] args)". The box must be unchecked. The class will not have a main method. Click Finish.
11. The class will contain methods of geometric shape equations. Enter the following in the GeomerticMath.java file, Code Listing 6.20:

```
package jae.mathlib;

public class GeometricMath {
    private double PI = 3.14;

    //Circumference of a circle
    public double circumference(int r)
    {
        return 2 * PI * r;
    }
```

```
    //Area of a circle
    public double circlearea(int r)
    {
        return PI * r * r;
    }
    //Area of a rectangle
    public double rectanglearea(int l, int w)
    {
        return l * w;
    }
    //Area of a triangle
    public double trianglearea(int base, int height)
    {
        return (base * height) / 2;
    }
}
```

Code Listing 6.20 Geometric Math Library Module

12. Save the project.
13. In Package Explorer, under the CustomLibrary project, right-click on the jae.mathlib package. Select New->Class from the context menu.
14. Since you right-click on the package to generate the class, this time the package name is already filled in. The name of the class will be called FamousEquations and click Finish.
15. DO NOT CHECK the "public static void main(String[] args)". The box must be unchecked. The class will not have a main method. Click Finish.
16. The class will contain two methods for two famous equations: $E=mc^2$ and F=ma. Enter the following in the FamousEquations.java file, Code Listing 6.21:

```
package jae.mathlib;

public class FamousEquations {

    private double c = 299792458;

    //E=mc2 Energy Mass Conversion
    public double Emc2(double mass)
    {
        return mass * c * c;
    }

    //F=ma - Newton's 2nd Law
    public double Fma(double mass, double acceleration)
    {
        return mass * acceleration;
    }
}
```

Code Listing 6.21 Famous Math Equations Library Module

17. Save the project.

We made all the BasicMath class methods static methods, and the methods in the other two classes are non-static. This was done for demonstration purposes. Notice that the icons for the static methods have an S with the green dot, Figure 6.14. The fields for PI and speed of light constants have been made private so they will not be accidentally changed.

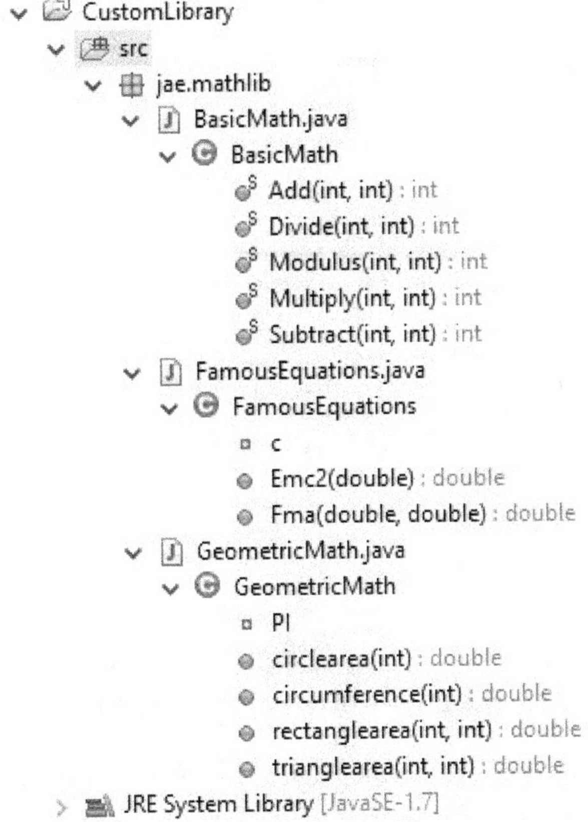

Figure 6.14 Math Library in Package Explorer

At this point, you could add a fourth class with a main() method to use as a test from within the project. Importing libraries is not required since all the classes would be in the same package. The separate test class would allow you to debug and locate any issues with your classes before sharing them. You can instantiate the classes in the test application even though the classes are in separate .java file because they are all in the same package namespace. The following picture shows what the project would look like with the test class, Figure 6.15. Notice the green class icon has a green arrow implying that this is a runnable class.

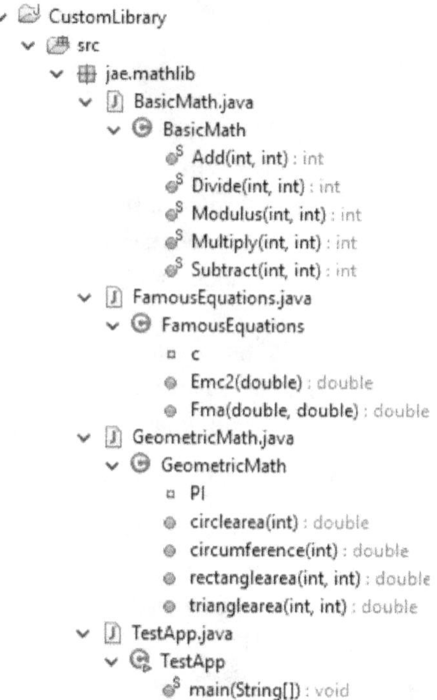

Figure 6.15 Math Library with TestApp Added

At some point, you will also have to use the library in a different project. We will skip creating a test class and export the library for testing.

Step 2 – Export the JAR file

With the project saved, the package can be exported to a JAR file

1. Double check that there are no warnings or errors in any of the project files.
1. Right-click on the jae.mathlib package.
2. Select Export from the context menu.
3. In the Export dialog, select Java->JAR File, Figure 6.16.

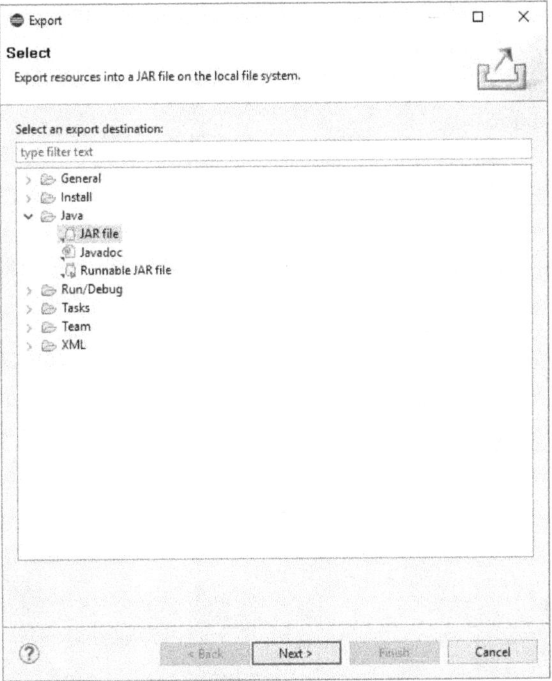

Figure 6.16 Export the JAR File

4. The JAR Export dialog appears. The correct package containing our class has been selected. Select a path to be in the CustomLibrary project folder and name the JAR file jae.mathlib.jar, Figure 6.17.

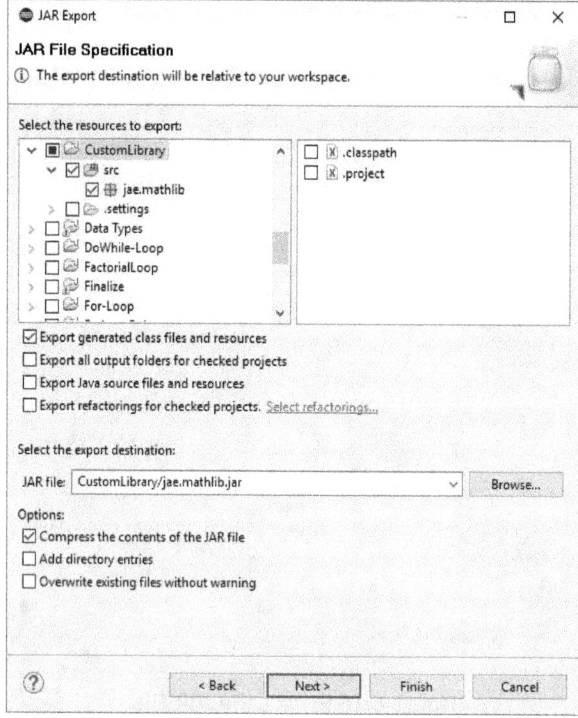

Figure 6.17 Set JAR Export File Specification

5. Click Next.
6. Keep the defaults in the JAR Packaging options and click Next.
7. In the JAR manifest dialog, click on the Details button next to the Seal some packages, Figure 6.18.

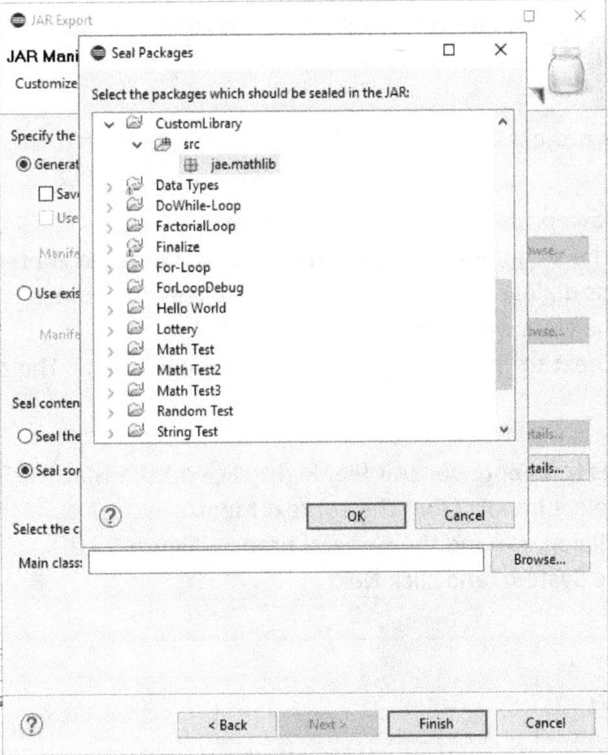

Figure 6.18 Seal Packages

8. Select the jae.mathlib that is in the CustomLibrary project folder. Click OK.
9. Click Finish and the JAR file will be created, Figure 6.19.

Name	Date modified	Type	Size
.settings	7/7/2016 12:27 PM	File folder	
bin	7/7/2016 12:29 PM	File folder	
src	7/7/2016 12:29 PM	File folder	
.classpath	7/7/2016 12:27 PM	CLASSPATH File	1 KB
.project	7/7/2016 12:27 PM	PROJECT File	1 KB
jae.mathlib.jar	7/7/2016 3:44 PM	Executable Jar File	2 KB

Figure 6.19 Custom Library Created

If there are problems when you exported the JAR file, you can check the Problems tab at the bottom of the editor.

Step 3 – Test the Library

Let's create a new Java project that will test the newly created library.

1. Create a new Java project called CH6CA6.8-MathLibTest.
2. Right-click on the src folder and select New-> Class from the context menu.
3. In the Java Class dialog, set the package name to jae.mathibtest.
4. The name of the class will be called MathLibTest.
5. Check the box next to "public static void main(String[] args)". The class will have a main() method.
6. Click Finish.
7. The next step is to import our JAR file. Right-click on the MathLibTest project in Package Explorer and select Import from the context menu.
8. In the Import dialog, expand the General branch, Figure 6.20.
9. Click on the File System, and click Next.

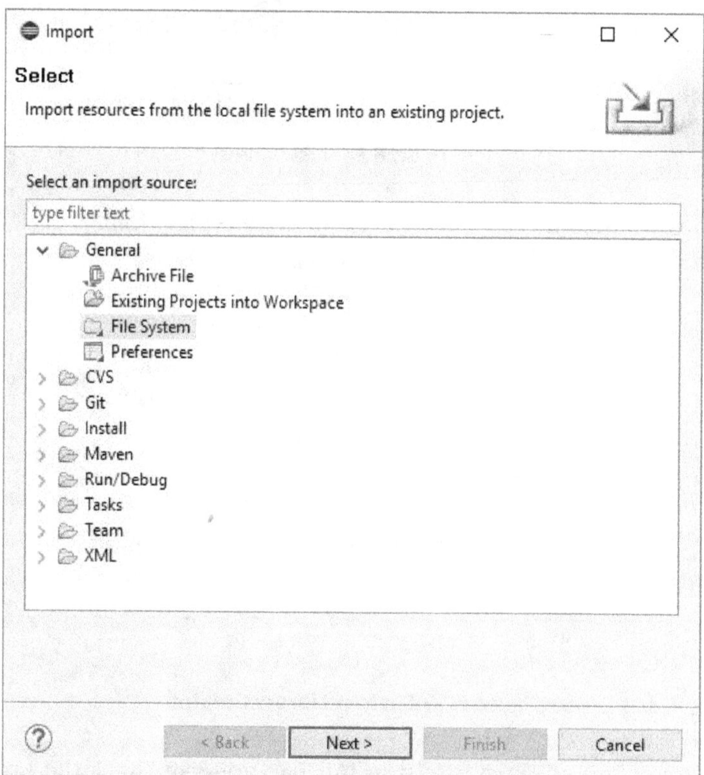

Figure 6.20 Import Custom Library

10. In the File System dialog, click on browse and open the directory that contains the jae.mathlib.jar file.
11. The jae.mathlib.jar file will appear in the selection box on the right. Check the jae.mathlib.jar and click Finish, Figure 6.21.

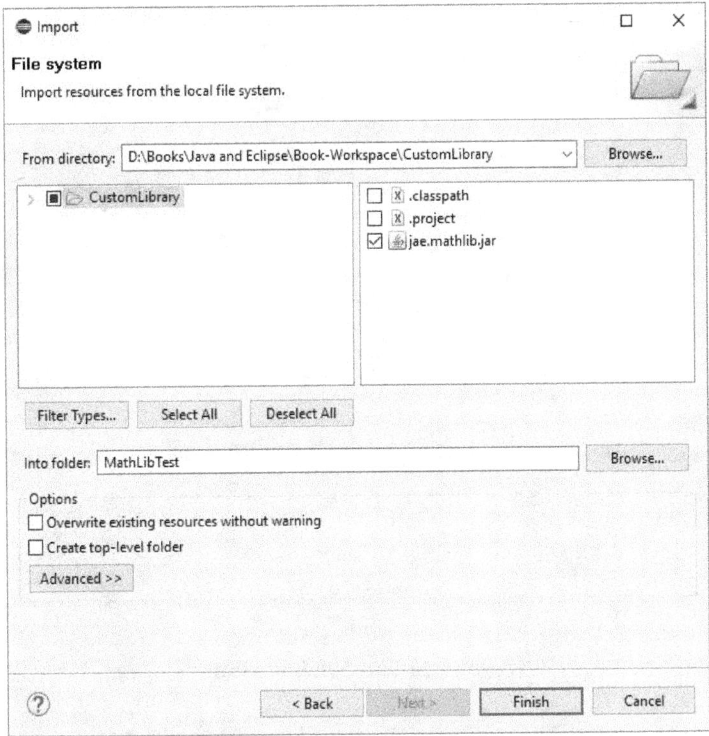

Figure 6.21 Selecting Library to Import

The jae.mathlib.jar is added to the project, Figure 6.22. The next step is to ensure that the library is part of the build.

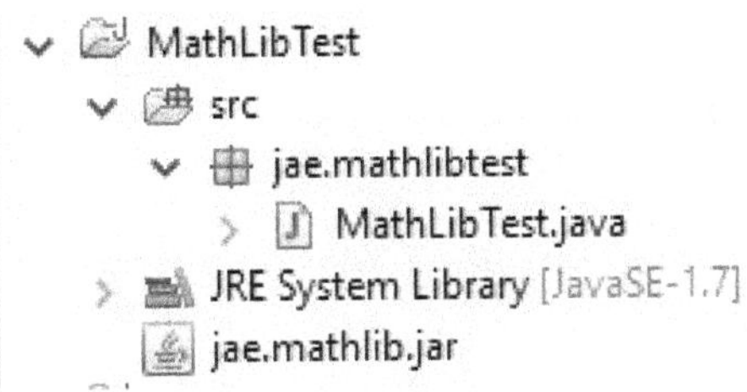

Figure 6.22 Library Added to Project

12. Right-click on the MathLibTest project in Package Explorer and select Properties from the context menu.
13. On the left-hand side, click on Java Build Path.
14. In the middle, click on the Libraries tab.
15. Click on the Add JARs... button and open the jae.mathlib.jar file, Figure 6.23.

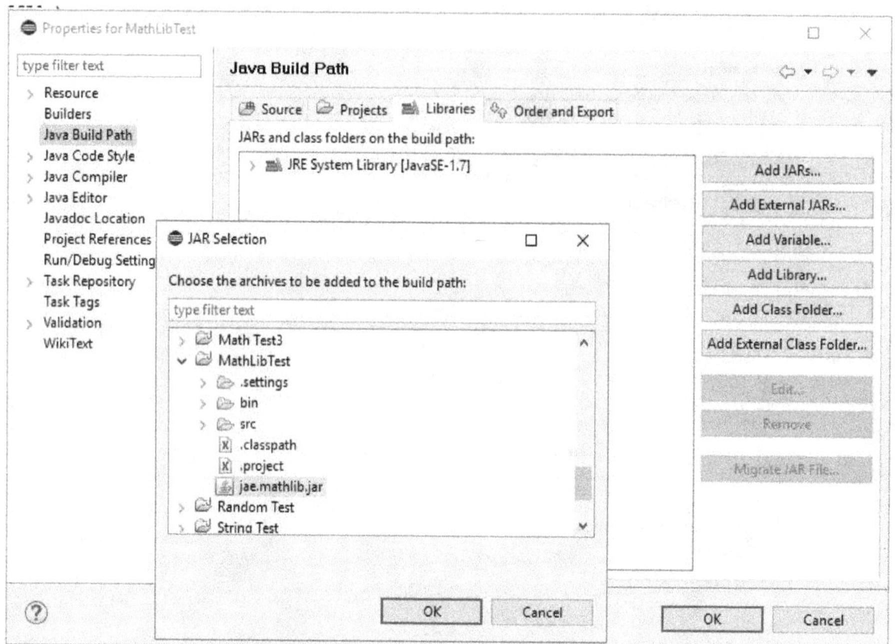

Figure 6.23 Set Java Build Path

16. The jae.mathlin.jar file will appear in the list of Libraries in the build path. Click OK to close the project properties dialog.
17. In the code editor, add an import statement for the jae.mathlib library. As you type in the name and once you hit the period (dot), Eclipse will present the two packages available, Figure 6.24. If you hit enter on jae.mathlib name in the pop-up window the code will enter the default to include all classes:

```
import jae.mathlib.*;
```

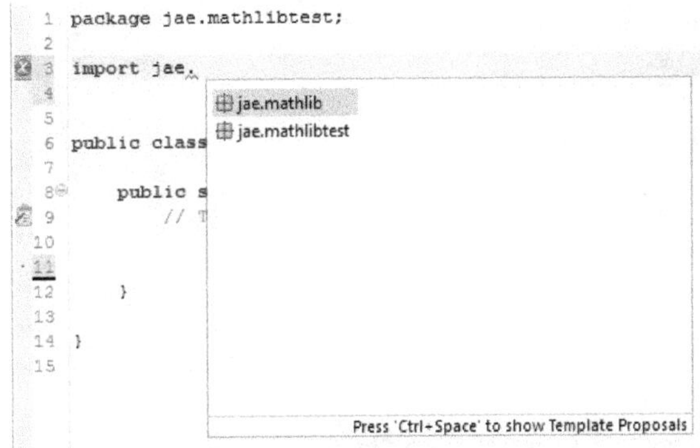

Figure 6.24 Adding Import Statement in Eclipse Code Editor

Alternatively, if you continue typing the name beyond the period (dot), you could add imports for individual classes, Figure 6.25.

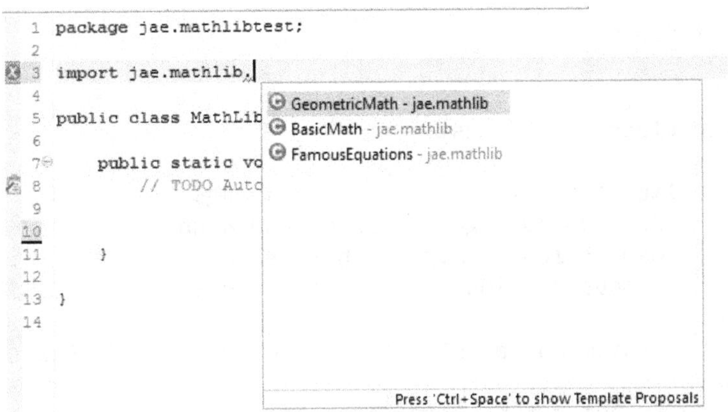

Figure 6.25 Importing Individual Classes in Eclipse Code Editor

For now, just use the jae.mathlib.*, Figure 6.26.

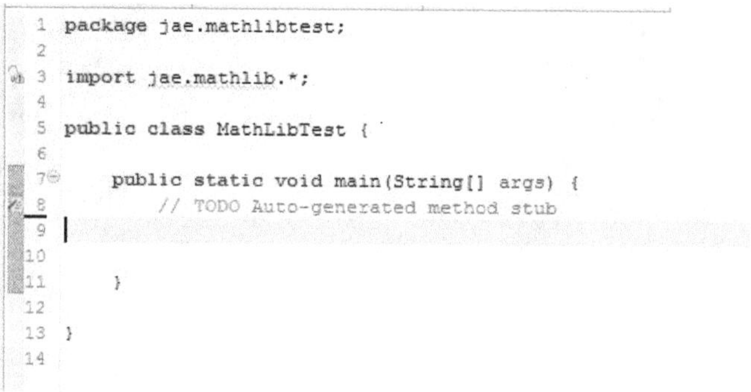

```
package jae.mathlibtest;

import jae.mathlib.*;

public class MathLibTest {

    public static void main(String[] args) {
        // TODO Auto-generated method stub


    }

}
```

Figure 6.26 Importing All Classes in Eclipse Code Editor

18. Here is the whole source code to the project, Code Listing 6.22. Finish the test application by entering lines 10 through 15.

```
1. package jae.mathlibtest;
2.
3. import jae.mathlib.*;
4.
5.
6. public class MathLibTest {
7.
8.     public static void main(String[] args) {
9.         // TODO Auto-generated method stub
10.        GeometricMath mygeomath = new GeometricMath();
11.        FamousEquations myequations = new FamousEquations();
12.
13.        System.out.println("Addition 10 + 3 = "+ BasicMath.Add(10, 3));
14.        System.out.println("Area of a circle with radius 5 cm is " +
   mygeomath.circlearea(5) + "  square cm");
15.        System.out.println("The force that it takes to get a 1587.3 Kg car accelearting at 9.8 m/s is " + myequations.Fma(1587.3, 9.8)+ " N force");
16.    }
17. }
```

Code Listing 6.22 Custom Library Test Application

The application tests all three classes. Line 13 calls the static method Add() to add two integers. Since Add() is a static method, an object wasn't required. Lines 10 and 11 create objects for the other two classes, and lines 14 and 15 test a method from each of the remaining two classes using the objects.

19. Set a breakpoint on 13.
20. Run the debugger.
21. Once the breakpoint is reached, click on the Step Into (or F5) key. The debugger will report that the source is not found, Figure 6.27 During the export process, there was a check box for exploring all the source code and resources. We didn't export the source into the JAR, thus the source to the class is hidden.

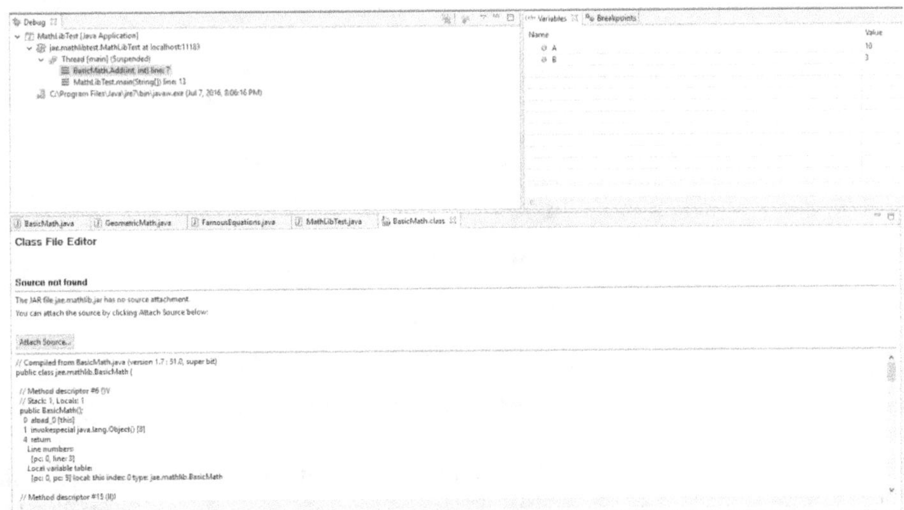

Figure 6.27 Debugging MathLibTest

22. Stop the debugger, and switch back to the Java perspective.

If you want to go back and export the JAR file again, you can select to include the source. It is recommended to have a different JAR file name. Putting a "–source" in the name will let you and everyone else know that the source is available, Figure 6.28. Having two JAR files with and without source is up to the developer. Sometimes hiding the code is required to protect intellectual property. Having the source code available allows you to debug any issues with your classes.

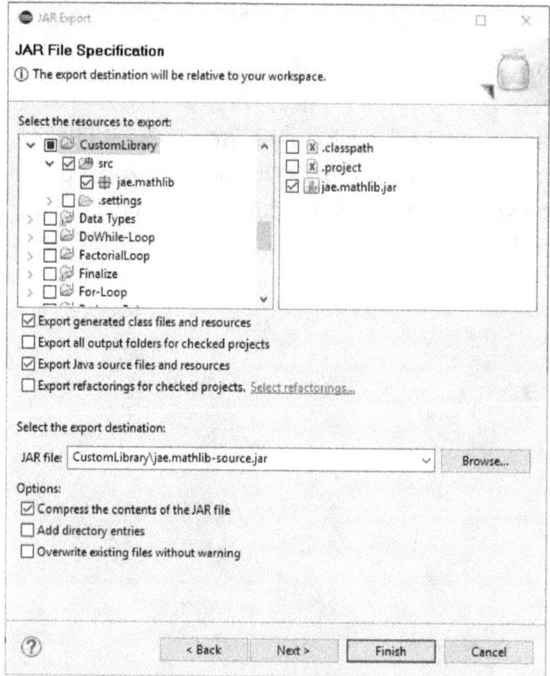

Figure 6.28 Exporting Library Source Code

If you import the source code version of the JAR file in the MathLibTest program, you will be able to run the debugger and jump into the class and continue debugging through the class code, Figure 6.29.

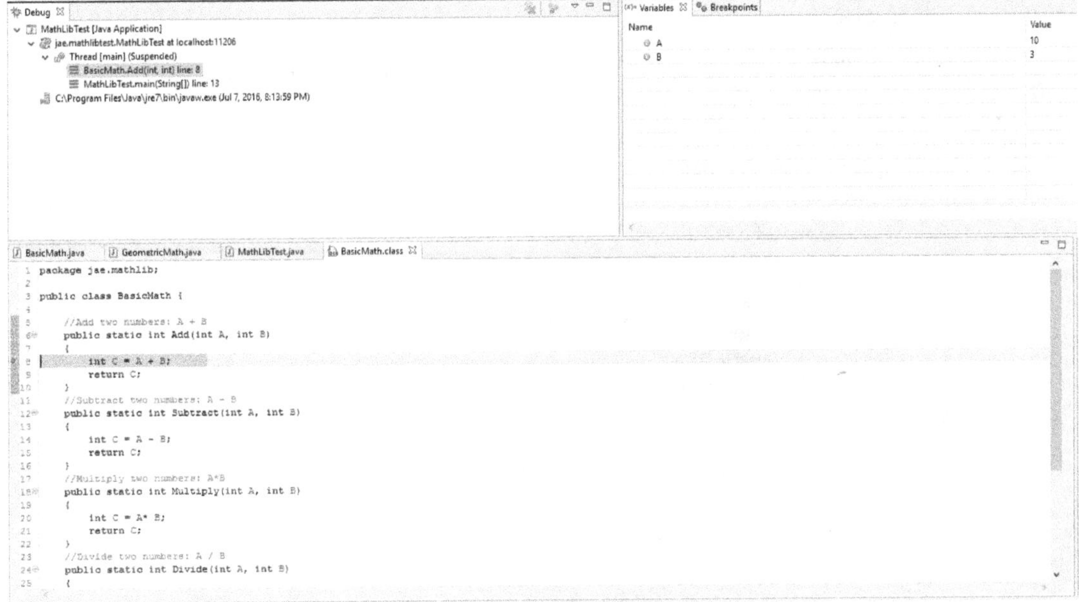

Figure 6.29 Debugging Into the Library

6.5 *Javadoc and Eclipse*

Whether you supply source code with the JAR file or not is up to you. Developers will want to know how to use your library, so documenting your library is the next step. With over 4000 classes developed over a couple of decades, the developers of Java realized this issue early on and developed a utility called Javadoc.exe. The utility can export the class information to HTML files.

6.5.1 Computer Activity 6.9 - Generating Documentation for Custom Packages

Using the CustomLibrary project, we will generate documentation for the library.

1. Right-click on the jae.mathlib package.
2. Select Export from the context menu.
3. Click on Javadoc, and click Next, Figure 6.30.

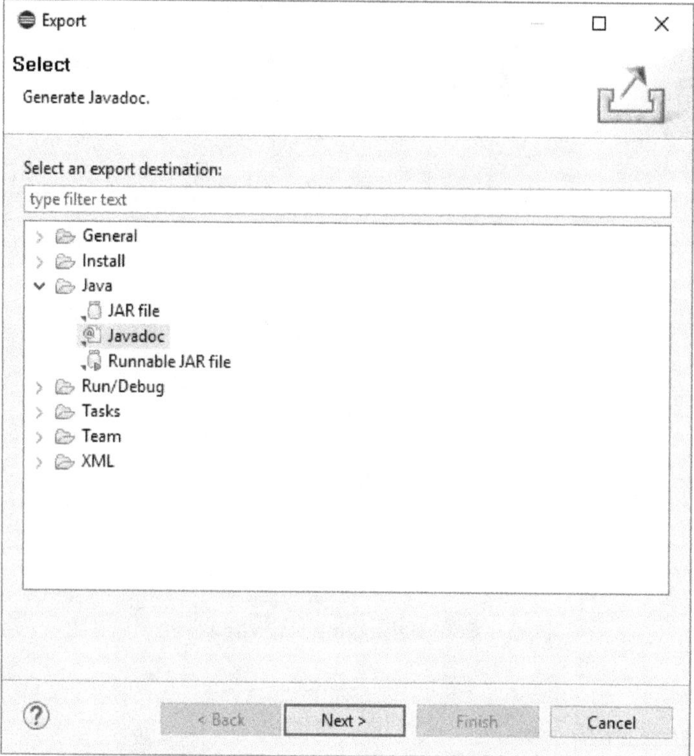

Figure 6.30 Selecting Documentation Export

4. The Javadoc Generation dialog appears, Figure 6.31. Click on Configure and open the location of the Javadoc.exe file that was installed with the Java runtime.

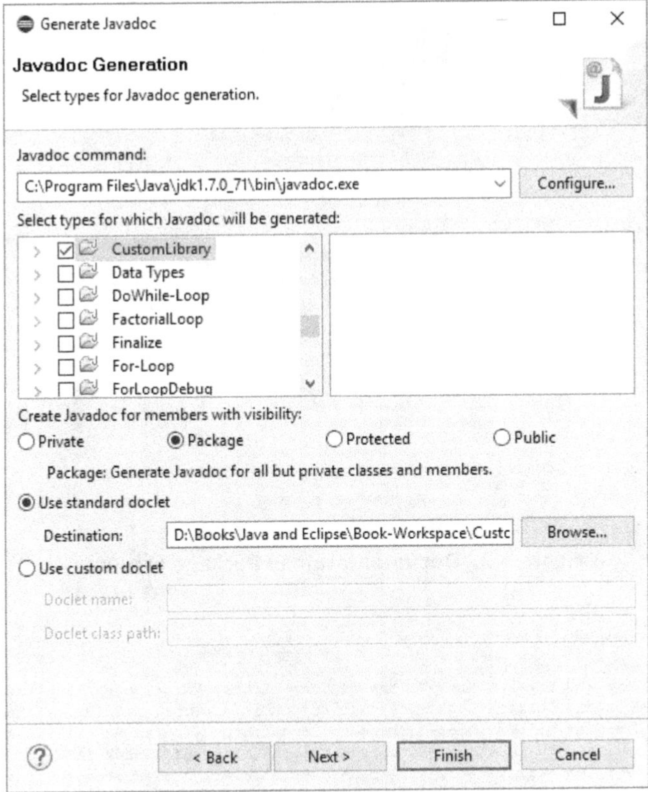

Figure 6.31 Javadoc Generation Dialog

5. Make sure that the CustomLibrary project is selected.
6. You can control what Javadoc will export to documentation. If you want to output everything, you can select Private. If you want to only have public class members visible, just select public. If you want to export everything but the private members, select Package. For this example, select Package.
7. Click on the Browse... and make sure the target folder is called doc under the CustomLibrary folder.
8. Click Finish, and the documents will be generated, Figure 6.32 and Figure 6.33.

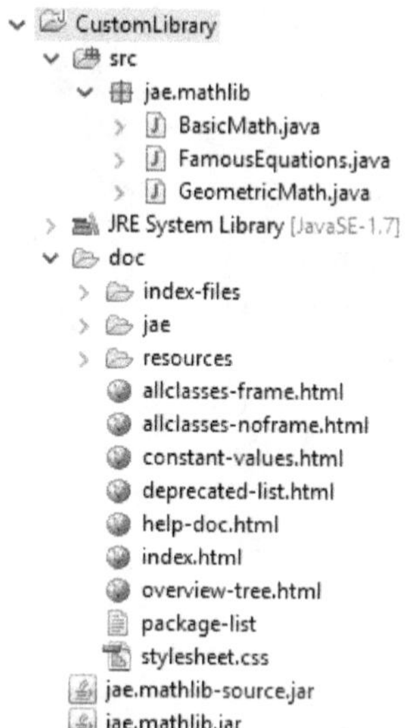

Figure 6.32 Documentation in Package Explorer

Problems | @ Javadoc | Declaration | Search | Console

<terminated> Javadoc Generation

```
Generating D:\Books\Java and Eclipse\Book-Workspace\CustomLibrary\doc\index-files\index-9.html...
Generating D:\Books\Java and Eclipse\Book-Workspace\CustomLibrary\doc\index-files\index-10.html...
Generating D:\Books\Java and Eclipse\Book-Workspace\CustomLibrary\doc\index-files\index-11.html...
Generating D:\Books\Java and Eclipse\Book-Workspace\CustomLibrary\doc\index-files\index-12.html...
Generating D:\Books\Java and Eclipse\Book-Workspace\CustomLibrary\doc\deprecated-list.html...
Building index for all classes...
Generating D:\Books\Java and Eclipse\Book-Workspace\CustomLibrary\doc\allclasses-frame.html...
Generating D:\Books\Java and Eclipse\Book-Workspace\CustomLibrary\doc\allclasses-noframe.html...
Generating D:\Books\Java and Eclipse\Book-Workspace\CustomLibrary\doc\index.html...
Generating D:\Books\Java and Eclipse\Book-Workspace\CustomLibrary\doc\help-doc.html...
```

Figure 6.33 Javadoc Generation

In Package Explorer, you can open up the doc folder and double-click on the index.html, Figure 6.34. The classes that were included in the project are listed on the index page. Click on the class, and a new page appears showing the details of the methods available in the class. If you had selected Private to include all the members, you would have seen the constant fields as well. As you can see, the Javadoc utility makes documenting the classes a breeze, but it is important to note that creating the Javadoc doesn't get one out of putting comments in the code.

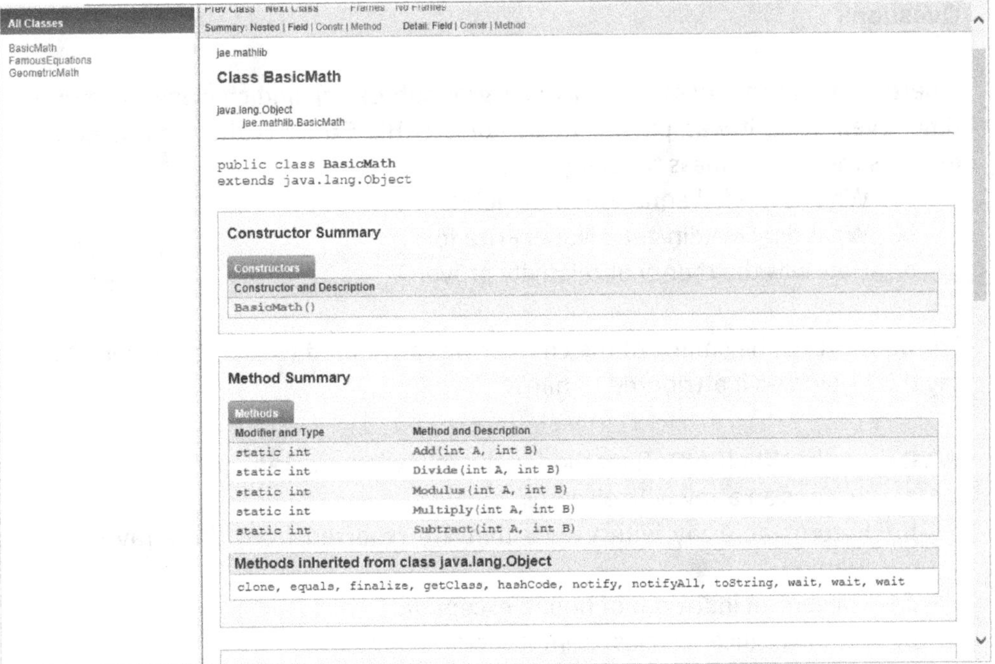

Figure 6.34 Javadoc Index.html

6.6 Summary and Homework Assignments

Creating reusable code is the heart and soul of Object-Oriented Programming (OOP). If you put everything into a single class, your application could be thousands of lines long. The analog to Einstein's quote is breaking the code into smaller classes. Debugging large programs can be tedious; but if the code is broken into smaller pieces, debugging the whole application becomes simpler and easier. This chapter took an inward to outward approach in discussing the Java library structure. Methods help create a structure to break the actions of the program into smaller pieces. Classes helped group like fields and methods into a single object. Packages group classes into a single namespace. Finally taking these packages, Eclipse can be used to export a JAR file so that we can share our code with others. The library structure is only the start of our discussion on OOP, and it was the simplest topic to cover. The more complex topics are in the next few chapters, but first here are a few questions and programming projects.

6.6.1 Questions

1. Albert Einstein's theory of relativity was groundbreaking and challenging to prove at the time. Eventually, it was proven to be correct. His $E=mc^2$ is the famous equation that explains the ratio of mass to energy.
   a. What is the full equation to $E=mc^2$?
   b. What did Einstein get a Nobel Prize for?
   c. How was the theory of relativity proven?

2. The quote at the beginning of the chapter was attributed to Albert Einstein. Did he really say this? How was it attributed to him?

3. What does the WhatDoIDo() method in the following program do?
   a. Returns an array with all zeros
   b. Returns an array with values that are reversed from the array passed to the method
   c. Triggers an index out of bound exception
   d. Nothing since the class is improperly instantiated
   e. Swaps the first and last elements of an array passed to the method and returns a new array

```
package jae.class1;

public class mytestclass1 {

    public static void main(String[] args) {
        // TODO Auto-generated method stub
        myclass mytest = new myclass();

        int[] x = {54,67,3,1,9};

        for(int i = 0; i < x.length; i++)
        {
            System.out.print(x[i] +" ");
        }
        System.out.println(" ");

        int[] j = mytest.WhatDoIDo(x);
```

```
        for(int i = 0; i < j.length; i++)
        {
            System.out.print(j[i] +" ");
        }
    }
}

public class myclass {

    public int[] WhatDoIDo(int[] x)
    {
        int z = 0;
        int[] y = new int[x.length];

        for(int i=x.length-1; i >= 0; i--,z++)
        {
            y[z] = x[i];
        }
        return y;
    }
}
```

4. What is wrong with the following program?

```
package sun.util;

public class SkipTest {

    public static void main(String[] args) {
        // TODO Auto-generated method stub

        SkipEven myskiparray = new SkipEven();
        int[] x = {6,5,7,2,8,9,4};
        for(int i = 0; i < x.length; i++){
            System.out.print(x[i] + " ");
        }
        System.out.println("");

        myskiparray.FilterEvenElements(x);
    }
}
```

```
public class SkipEven {

    public void FilterEvenElements(int[] x)
    {

        for(int i = 1; i < x.length; i+=2)
        {
            System.out.print(x[i]+" ");
        }
    }
}
```

5. Write the StringInfo class that goes with the following program:

```
package jae.class3;

public class StringInfoTest {

    public static void main(String[] args) {
        // TODO Auto-generated method stub
        StringInfo mystr = new StringInfo("The quick brown fox jumps
over the lazy dog");
        System.out.println("The number of words in the string is " +
mystr.wordcount);
        System.out.println("The number of characters in the string is
" +
mystr.charcount);
        System.out.println("The number of spaces in the string is " +
mystr.spacecount);
    }
}
```

6. Given the following program

```
package jae.class4;

public class MileagestatsTest {

    public static void main(String[] args) {
        // TODO Auto-generated method stub

        Mileagestats mytruck = new Mileagestats(18.9, 36);
        System.out.println("My trucks possible mileage range is " +
mytruck.getVehiclerange()+ " miles.");
```

```
    }
}

public class Mileagestats {

    private double mpg;
    private double tankgallons;
    private static double vehiclerange;

   /* Constructor goes here */

    public double getTankgallons() {
        return tankgallons;
    }

    public double getVehiclerange() {
        return vehiclerange;
    }

}
```

What must the constructor be to fill in the variables?

A.

```
Mileagestats(double milespergallon, double totalfuelcapacity)
{
    mpg = milespergallon;
    tankgallons = totalfuelcapacity;
    vehiclerange = mpg * tankgallons;
}
```

B.

```
 public void Mileagestats(double milespergallon, double
totalfuelcapacity)
 {
     mpg = milespergallon;
     tankgallons = totalfuelcapacity;
     vehiclerange = mpg * tankgallons;
 }
```

C.

```
Mileagestats(double mpg, double tankgallons)
{
    this.mpg = mpg;
    this.tankgallons = tankgallons;
    vehiclerange = mpg * tankgallons;
}
```

D.

```
Mileagestats(double mpg, double tankgallons)
{
    vehiclerange = mpg * tankgallons;
}
```

E.

None of the above since static variables cannot be accessed in constructors.

F.

A and C

G.

B and D

7. Given the last program, which of the following accessor methods should be used to return the mpg value:

A.

```
public static double getMpg() {
    return mpg;
}
```

B.

```
public double getMpg() {
    return mpg;
}
```

C.

```
private double getMpg() {
    return mpg;
}
```

D.

```
public double getMpg() {
    return vehiclerange / tankgallons;
}
```

8. Given the following program:

```
package jae.class5;

import java.util.ArrayList;

public class ListModifiersTest {

    public static void main(String[] args) {
        // TODO Auto-generated method stub

        ListModifiers mystrchange = new ListModifiers();

        ArrayList<String> fruit = new ArrayList<String>();

        fruit.add("apple");
        fruit.add("banana");
        fruit.add("orange");
        fruit.add("lemon");
        fruit.add("pear");
        fruit.add("peach");

        for(String x : fruit)
        {
            System.out.print(x + " ");
        }
        System.out.println(" ");

        ArrayList<String> fruit2 = new ArrayList<String>();

        fruit2 = mystrchange.RemoveEven(fruit);

        for(String y : fruit2)
        {
            System.out.print(y + " ");
        }
    }
}
```

Create the ListModifiers class so that fruit2 will print out the following items:

```
apple orange pear
```

Hint: Think about what needs to be returned from the `mystrchange.RemoveEven(fruit)` call.

9. Is it possible to use the "this" keyword for static fields? Why or Why Not?

10. For Computer Activity 6.4, in the IntSequenceTest.java file, if line 9 is commented out, and line 16 is changed to the following:

```
System.out.println("The factorial for " + n + " is " +
new IntSequences().factorialloop(n));
```

Will the application still run correctly? Why or why not?

6.6.2 Programming Projects

1. Create a Java project called Random. The project will have two classes under the jae.random package. The first class will be called RandomGen, and in this class write a RandomGen25 method that returns an array of 25 random integers that range from 0 to 100. The second class will be called RandomTest that has a main() method that will first call RandomGen25 and then print out each array element on the same line separated by a space. Hint: The two classes are in two separate .java files.

2. Expanding on the Random project. Add a new method called RandomGen50 to the RandomGen class. Create a new class under the jae.random package called RandomSearch. Create a method in RandomSearch called ValueFinder(int[] x, int j) that returns a Boolean. Add to the RandomTest class's main() method a call to ValueFinder(x,j), where x is the array of 50 random integers and j = 7, and print out if the 7 was found or not found in the array. Could the RandomGen methods in these last two exercises have been made "static"?

3. Given the following list of conversion methods to include:

   - inches to centimeters
   - centimeters to inches
   - meters to yards

- yards to meters
- kilometers to miles
- miles to kilometers
- liters to gallons
- gallons to liters
- milliliters to fluid ounces
- fluid ounces to milliliters
- grams to ounces
- ounces to grams
- kilograms to pounds
- pounds to kilograms
- Celsius to Fahrenheit
- Fahrenheit to Celsius

design a Metric/English library that breaks these methods into separate classes based on measurement type: distance, volume, weight, and temperature. Use jae.metricenglish as the package name.

4. In the Egg Hunt game in Chapter 5, write a new program that breaks the program into two classes. One class has the main() method that will create the 2-dimensional array and create and an instance of the second class. It will then make two calls from the second class to generate the game board and play the game. The second class will handle the printing of the game board, tracking of the turns, generating the random egg location, taking in user input, and checking to see if the user found the egg.

5. Create a new coin flip application called CoinFlip2. There will be two classes: CoinFlip and CoinFlipGame. Both classes will be under the jae.coinflip package.

   The CoinFlipGame class will have the following:

   - A main() method
   - Will ask the user for h for heads and t for tails
   - Will call the method to flip the coin
   - Will print the result on one line
   - Will print wins and losses on another line
   - Will ask the user if they want to play again – y for yes and n for no. If y, ask h for heads and t for tails. If no, list the final score and end the program.

The CoinFlip class will have the following:

- A method that will take in the user input
- The method will use a Boolean to generate true for heads or false for tails
- Will match the user input with the result, set a value if the user won or another value if the user lost, and return a string "Heads" for true or "Tails" for false.

6. Chapter 4 introduced a dividend calculator exercise for purchasing a company's stock. Create a new dividend calculator project that a user can use for any stock. Some stocks pay a dividend each month, some pay every three months, and some only once a year. The dividend calculator method should be in its own class and take the following information from the user: stock price, how much money they are going to spend on the stock, dividend rate for the stock, the dividend payment period (monthly, quarterly, or yearly), and the period (in months) the stock will be held. The program should be able to access the class to get the amount of stock purchased and the total dividend received over the period the user will hold the stock. After the dividend calculation and the amount of stock purchase has been displayed, the program will ask if the user wants to do another calculation.

7. In exercise 11 in Chapter 5, had you write a golf handicapping program. A golfer plays at several different golf courses. Create a new Java project with a class that can calculate the handicap for different courses. Here are the different courses and 10 best rounds out of 20 the player had on each course.

   - Course 1 – Course Rating 65.4 / Slope Rating 114, Strokes = {90, 91,86}
   - Course 2 – Course Rating 70.3 / Slope Rating 126, Strokes = {103, 94, 92, 89}
   - Course 3 – Course Rating 69.2 / Slope Rating 126, Strokes = {106, 93, 88}

8. The Yahtzee game project was introduced in Chapter 4 Exercises and updated with arrays to track dice and next role state in Chapter 5. For this exercise, write a new Yahtzee program that keeps the score for a single player. The standard Yahtzee score sheet can be found on the Internet or look at one of the free variants for a phone or tablet. The program should be broken into different classes: one for the main() method, a second for dice, and a third for scoring. The player will be able to manually enter the score using a menu system.

9. Re-create the Bingo program in chapter 5 and move the drawing of the bingo number to a different class, leaving the user interaction in the main() method.

10. Based on the Computer Activity 6.7 Office Supply program, create an address book program that stores contact name, address, phone number, and e-mail address. The program will be menu- driven:

    1 - Print the contact list stored in the ArrayList with all the information on a single line.
    2 - Add a contact to the list.
    3 - Remove a contact from the list.
    4 - Edit individual contact information – name, address, phone, and e-mail.
    5 – Exit the program.

    Use the scanner class to capture user input. Hint: there is a little-known issue with the scanner class, the netInt() method doesn't consume the last newline character.

7 Inheritance and Polymorphism

"We used the complete DNA of a frog to fill in the holes and complete the code."
-Mr. DNA, from the movie *Jurassic Park*, Universal Pictures 1993

We inherit our DNA from our parents. Our parents inherited their DNA from their parents. Our grandparents inherited their DNA from their parents, and so on. Our DNA has been built upon what has been passed down to us. The last chapter focused on the basics of methods and classes. The chapter also discussed how classes are put into packages that make up the whole Java library. Many developers have worked on creating the Java library, which gets passed to us to expand upon for use in our programs. Going back to the idea of reusable code, we not only want to be able to reuse code, but we want to expand upon the libraries that have been provided. This chapter will look at the core OOP concepts of inheritance and polymorphism that help us build on the Java library.

7.1 Inheritance

In the Shipping Box example in the last chapter, we skipped over a key item. When you started to enter the mybox instance to access the boxVolume() method, a context window appears showing all of the available properties and methods to select from. The boxVolume() method is in the list as expected, but there are several other methods in the list, Figure 7.1. Where did these come from?

```
package jae.shippingbox;

public class ShippingBoxTest {

    public static void main(String[] args) {
        // TODO Auto-generated method stub
        ShippingBox mybox = new ShippingBox();
        mybox.

    }

}
class ShippingB

    private int
    private int
    private int

    public int
    {
        return
    }

}
```

```
boxVolume() : int - ShippingBox
equals(Object arg0) : boolean - Object
getClass() : Class<?> - Object
hashCode() : int - Object
notify() : void - Object
notifyAll() : void - Object
toString() : String - Object
wait() : void - Object
wait(long arg0) : void - Object
wait(long arg0, int arg1) : void - Object
Press 'Ctrl+Space' to show Template Proposals
```

Figure 7.1 mybox Context Menu

These methods didn't appear by accident. These methods were inherited from another class. Inheritance is another one of the tenets of OOP.

Definition: *Inheritance* – a class object is based on another class object or superclass that will either extend or change the superclass.

What happened was that the ShippingBox class inherited methods from another class. If the Java library is the DNA of Java programming, inheritance allows users to add to the DNA. What is this class and where did this class come from? Before we go further let's demonstrate the basics of inheritance.

7.1.1 Computer Activity 7.1 - Basic Inheritance Example

In Eclipse, create a new Java project called "CH7CA7.1-BasicInheritance". Create a new package called "jae.basicinheritance". Now create new Java class with a main() method under the package called "TestInheritance", Code Listing 7.3. Create two new java classes under the package with no main method called "TestA", Code Listing 7.1, and "TestB", Code Listing 7.2. Modify and fill in the code for each class. Start with the Test two classes before filling in the TestInheritance main() method.

```
package jae.basicinheritance;

public class TestA {

    String A = "This is TestA class";
    public void TestAOutput()
    {
        System.out.println(A);
    }
}
```

Code Listing 7.1 TestA.java

```
package jae.basicinheritance;

public class TestB extends TestA {

    String B = "This is TestB class";
    public void TestBOutput() {
        System.out.println(B);
    }
}
```

Code Listing 7.2 TestB.java

```
1. package jae.basicinheritance;
2.
3. public class TestInheritance {
4.
5.     public static void main(String[] args) {
6.         // TODO Auto-generated method stub
7.         TestB myclass = new TestB();
8.         myclass.TestAOutput();
9.         myclass.TestBOutput();
10.    }
11. }
```

Code Listing 7.3 TestInheritance.java

Here is the output if you run the application:

```
This is TestA class
This is TestB class
```

In the main() method, we created an instance of the TestB class in line 7, and we were able to call the TestAOutput() method that is in TestA class in line 8. With the “extends” keyword, TestB inherits the publicly available encapsulated items in the TestA class, thus the TestAOutput() method could be called with an instance of the TestB class. There are terms for the relationship between the two classes. TestA is known as the "Superclass" and TestB is the "Subclass". The superclass knows nothing about subclasses, and a superclass cannot call or access any encapsulated items in a subclass. A Superclass can have multiple subclasses. Multiple class inheritance is not supported in Java. so subclasses can only inherit or extend a single class.

7.2 *The Object Class*

As you were typing in the main method to call the two methods, you should have noticed the context menu appear showing all the methods and objects available, Figure 7.2.

```
package jae.basicinheritance;

public class TestInheritance {

    public static void main(String[] args) {
        // TODO Auto-generated method stub

        TestB myclass = new TestB();

        myclass.





    }

}

class TestA
{
    String A = "T

    public void T
    {
        System.ou
    }
}

class TestB extends TestA
```

```
A : String - TestA
B : String - TestB
equals(Object obj) : boolean - Object
getClass() : Class<?> - Object
hashCode() : int - Object
notify() : void - Object
notifyAll() : void - Object
TestAOutput() : void - TestA
TestBOutput() : void - TestB
toString() : String - Object
wait() : void - Object
wait(long timeout) : void - Object
wait(long timeout, int nanos) : void - Object
Press 'Ctrl+Space' to show Template Proposals
```

Figure 7.2 myclass Context Menu

For the instance of TestB class, we see the two strings and two methods from both classes, and we see other methods available. These methods come from a special class call "Object". The Object class is the superclass to all other objects. Every class in the Java library can be traced back to inheriting the Object class. Although TestA class doesn't have "extends" for the Object class, it is created by default when TestA was created. When TestB class inherits from TestA, TestB also inherits from the Object class, Figure 7.3.

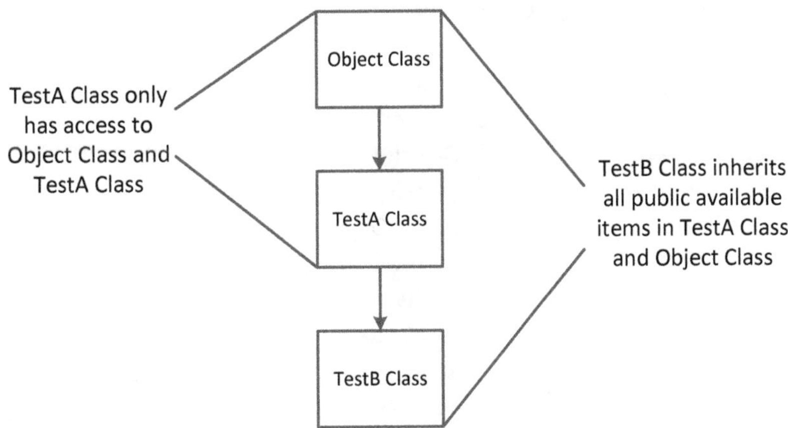
Object Class
TestA Class
TestB Class
TestA Class only has access to Object Class and TestA Class
TestB Class inherits all public available items in TestA Class and Object Class

Figure 7.3 Inheritance Chart

The Object class defines several public available methods and two protected methods, Table 7.1.

Object class methods	Description
boolean equals(Object o);	Compares two objects
Class getClass();	Provides information about the class at runtime
int hashCode();	Return the hash code associated with the object
void notify();	Resume execution of a thread waiting on the object
void notifyAll();	Resume execution of all threads waiting on the object
String toString();	Converts the object to a String and returns the string

void wait();
void wait(long timeout);
void wait(long timeout, int nanos);
	Waits on another thread of execution. There are options to set a timeout.

protected Object clone() throws CloneNotSupportedException;	Creates and returns a copy of the object
protected void finalize() throws Throwable;	Called by the garbage collector when there are no more references to the object

Table 7.1 Object Class Methods

The Object class can be found in rt.jar file under java.lang, Figure 7.4.

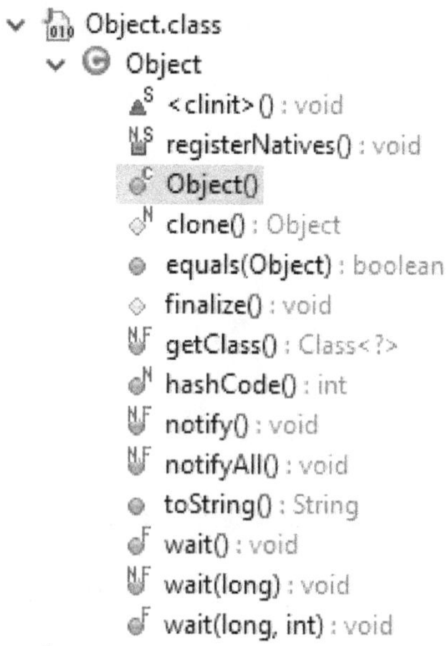

Object.class
Object
<clinit>() : void
registerNatives() : void
Object()
clone() : Object
equals(Object) : boolean
finalize() : void
getClass() : Class<?>
hashCode() : int
notify() : void
notifyAll() : void
toString() : String
wait() : void
wait(long) : void
wait(long, int) : void

Figure 7.4 Object Class

```
/**
 * Class {@code Object} is the root of the class hierarchy.
 * Every class has {@code Object} as a superclass. All objects,
 * including arrays, implement the methods of this class.
 *
 * @author  unascribed
 * @see     java.lang.Class
 * @since   JDK1.0
 */
public class Object {
```

When you create a new java class, you may have noticed that a Superclass is called out: java.lang.Object, Figure 7.5. This is how TestA class was able to access the Object superclass. You could change the supper class to something else. For example, when you created TestB class you could have changed java.lang.Object to jae.basicinheritance.TestA. The “extends TestA” would have been automatically added to the TestB class.

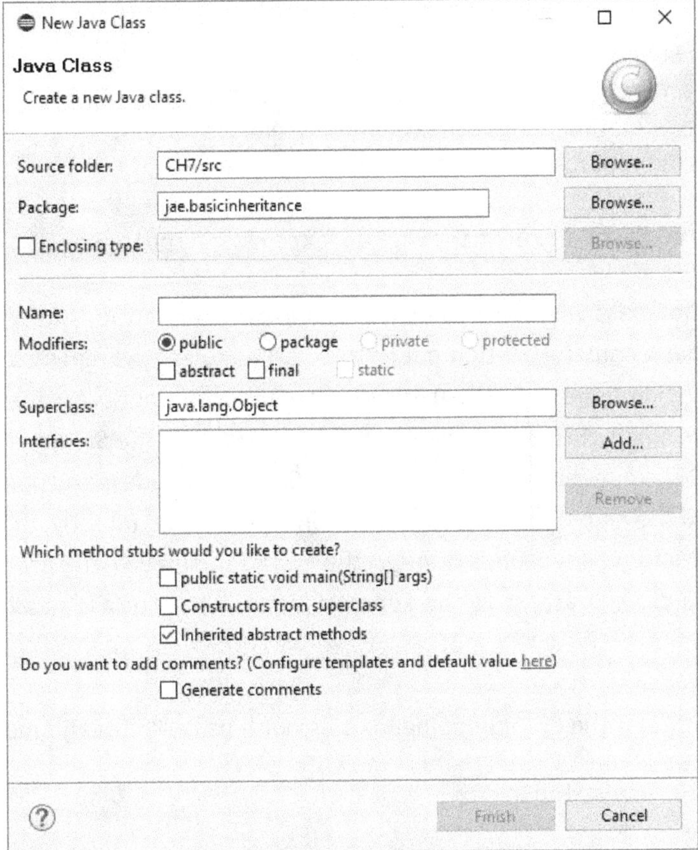

Figure 7.5 Create New Java Class

7.3 *Inheritance with Constructors and Class Access*

We learned about constructors and class access in the last chapter. The same access rules apply when it comes to inheritance. The combination of constructors, class access, and inheritance makes class library development a little more interesting and complex. Let's take a look at an example.

7.3.1 Computer Activity 7.2 - ColorShippingBox Class Inherits from ShippingBox Class

For this activity, we will build on the ShippingBox activity from the last chapter. In the ShippingBox class, we ended up with a constructor and several accessor and mutator methods. We will create a ColorShippingBox class that inherits the ShippingBox class and extends its functionality.

1. Expand the ShippingBox project in Package Explorer
2. Right-click on the jae.shippingbox package and select Class
3. Create a new ColorShippingBox class with no main() method.
4. In the class definition add the works extends ShippingBox:

```
public class ColorShippingBox extends ShippingBox
```

The ColorShippingBox class will add a color value to the box dimensions in the constructor. The ShippingBox class has a constructor that needs to be called to set the dimensions of the box. The new ColorShippingBox requires a constructor that will take arguments for the box color and the dimensions for the ShippingBox class. The problem is how to call the ShippingBox constructor to set the dimensions. The dimensions are private in the ShippingBox class and not directly accessible to the subclass, and the ShippingBox constructor cannot be called directly. In order to make the ShippingBox constructor call, which is done in the ColorShippingBox constructor, Java uses the keyword "super" to provide access to the superclass from the subclass so all class initialization stays in one object.

5. Code Listing 7.4 is the ColorShippingBox class with its variables and methods.

```
package jae.shippingbox;

public class ColorShippingBox extends ShippingBox{
    private String color;

    //Constructor
    ColorShippingBox(String c, int boxlength, int boxwidth, int boxheight )
    {
        super(boxlength, boxwidth, boxheight );
        color = c;
    }

    //Mutator
    public void setBoxColor(String c)
    {
        color =c;
    }

```

```
    //Accessor
    public String getBoxColor()
    {
        return color;
    }
}
```

Code Listing 7.4 ColorShippingBox Class

When the constructor to the ColorShippingBox is called, the super() keyword is called to call the ShippingBox constructor to pass through the dimensions.

6. In the main() method in the ShippingBoxTest class, add the following

```
ColorShippingBox myColorBox = new ColorShippingBox("white", 11,10,12);
System.out.println("The color for my shipping box is " +
myColorBox.getBoxColor());
System.out.println("The dimensions are " + myColorBox.getLength() + "in
x" +
myColorBox.getWidth() +"in x" + myColorBox.getHeight()+ "in");
System.out.println("The volume of the box is " + myColorBox.boxVolume()
+
" cubic inches");
```

The myColorBox is an instance of the ColorShippingBox class, and when the instance is created the arguments are passed to the ColorShippingBox constructor. The color, dimensions, and volume are called through the accessors since the parameters are private. When you run the application, the following is the output:

```
The dimensions are 10in x8in x5in
The volume of the box is 400 cubic inches
The dimensions are 10in x8in x3in
The volume of the box is 240 cubic inches
The color for my shipping box is white
The dimensions are 11in x10in x12in
The volume of the box is 1320 cubic inches
```

If you set a breakpoint on the line with the creation of the myColorBox instance and run the debugger and step through the code, you will see that ShippingBox class is accessed as the ColorShippingBox instance in the Debugger, Figure 7.6.

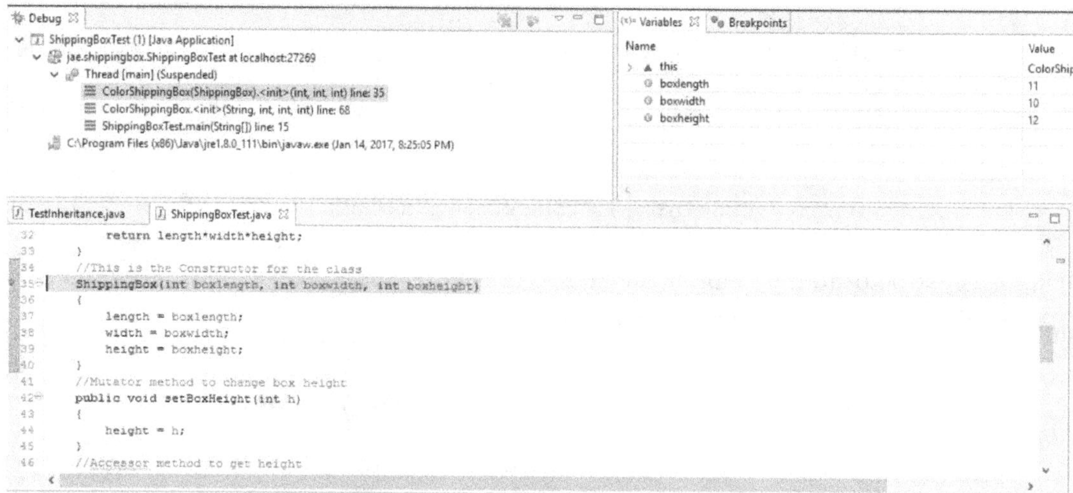

Figure 7.6 ShippingBoxTest Class Access

7.3.2 Computer Activity 7.3 - Subclass Accessing Superclass Using Super Key Word

Super is not limited to the constructor. The subclass uses the super keyword to access superclass' publicly available encapsulated items as if they are static. As a little demonstration, let's modify the TestInheritance project from Computer Activity 7.1.

1. In the TestInheritance.java, comment out line 8 that calls myclass.TestAOutput():

```
//      myclass.TestAOutput();
```

2. In the TestBOutput() method, add the following two lines after System.out.println(B):

```
super.TestAOutput();
System.out.println(super.A);
```

3. Here is the output when you run the application:

```
This is TestB class
This is TestA class
This is TestA class
```

In this case, the super keyword allows access to the superclass method and string object. Creating a new instance of the TestA class just to access the encapsulated items would have been extra code that complicates the project. The super keyword makes it easier for a subclass to take advantage of the features in the superclass.

7.3.3 Protected Access

In the last chapter, we talked about class access controls. We focused on public and private, but there is one more class access control called protected. Protected variables and methods can be accessed within the class by classes in the same packages and subclasses. Here we have a project with two packages and several classes defined, Figure 7.7.

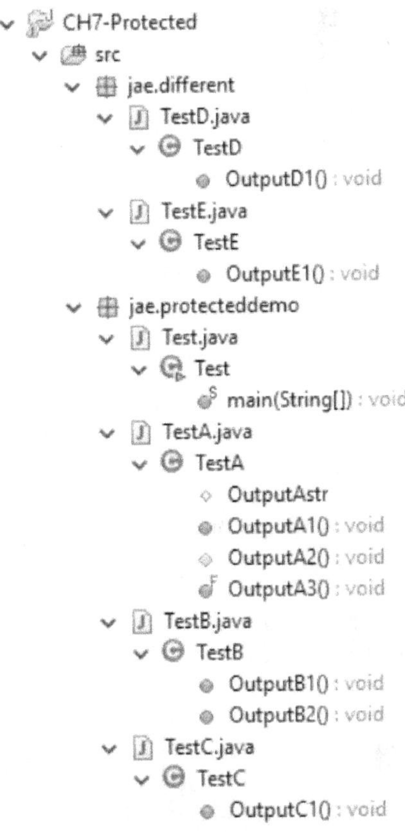

Figure 7.7 Protect Access Sample Project

Here is the code for each class:

```
package jae.protecteddemo;

public class Test {

    public static void main(String[] args) {
        // TODO Auto-generated method stub

        TestA myTestA = new TestA();
        TestB myTestB = new TestB();

        myTestA.OutputA1();
        myTestA.OutputA2();
        myTestB.OutputA2();
        myTestB.OutputB1();
        myTestB.OutputA3();
    }
}
```

```
package jae.protecteddemo;

public class TestA {

    protected String OutputAstr = "This is TestA Class";

    public void OutputA1(){

        System.out.println("Output A1");
    }

    protected void OutputA2(){
        System.out.println("Output A2");
    }

    public void OutputA3(){

        System.out.println(OutputAstr);
    }
}
```

```
package jae.protecteddemo;

public class TestB extends TestA {
```

```
    public void OutputB1(){

        super.OutputA2();
    }
    public void OutputB2(){
        System.out.println(super.OutputAstr);
    }
}
```

```
package jae.protecteddemo;

public class TestC {

    public void OutputC1(){

        TestA myTestA = new TestA();
        myTestA.OutputA2();
    }
}
```

```
package jae.different;

import jae.protecteddemo.*;

public class TestD {

    public void OutputD1(){
        TestA myTestA = new TestA();
        myTestA.OutputA1(); //Cannot access protected members in TestA
    }
}
```

```
package jae.different;

import jae.protecteddemo.TestA;

public class TestE extends TestA {

   public void OutputE1(){

        super.OutputA2();
    }
}
```

TestA class has a protected variable and method. The TestB inherits from TestA, and TestC, which is in the same package, creates an instance of TestA. Both TestB and TestC classes can access the protected members in TestA. TestD is not in the same package and doesn't inherit from TestA, thus TestD cannot access either protected members. The protected members will not show up in autocomplete, Figure 7.8.

Test.java | TestA.java | TestB.java | TestC.java | *TestD.java

```
package jae.different;

import jae.protecteddemo.*;

public class TestD {



    public void OutputD1(){
        TestA myTestA = new TestA();

        myTestA.

    }

}
```

equals(Object obj) : boolean - Object
getClass() : Class<?> - Object
hashCode() : int - Object
notify() : void - Object
notifyAll() : void - Object
OutputA1() : void - TestA
OutputA3() : void - TestA
toString() : String - Object
wait() : void - Object
wait(long timeout) : void - Object
wait(long timeout, int nanos) : void - Object

Press 'Ctrl+Space' to show Template Proposals

Figure 7.8 Autocomplete Showing Available Methods

TestE class is also in a different package, but it inherits from TestA. TestE can access the protected members in TestA class because of inheritance. Protected is primarily used for libraries to protect internal library members so that they can share resources in the library and be protected from the outside world. In the Object class, there are two protected methods, Clone() and Finalize(). As expected, these methods don't show up in the context menu in the class instance.

7.4 Eclipse Feature: Quickly Creating Constructors

Constructors are used so much that Eclipse includes several options to quickly create them. The first is when you create the class itself. There is a checkbox option under "Which method stubs would you like to create?" called Constructors from the superclass, Figure 7.9.

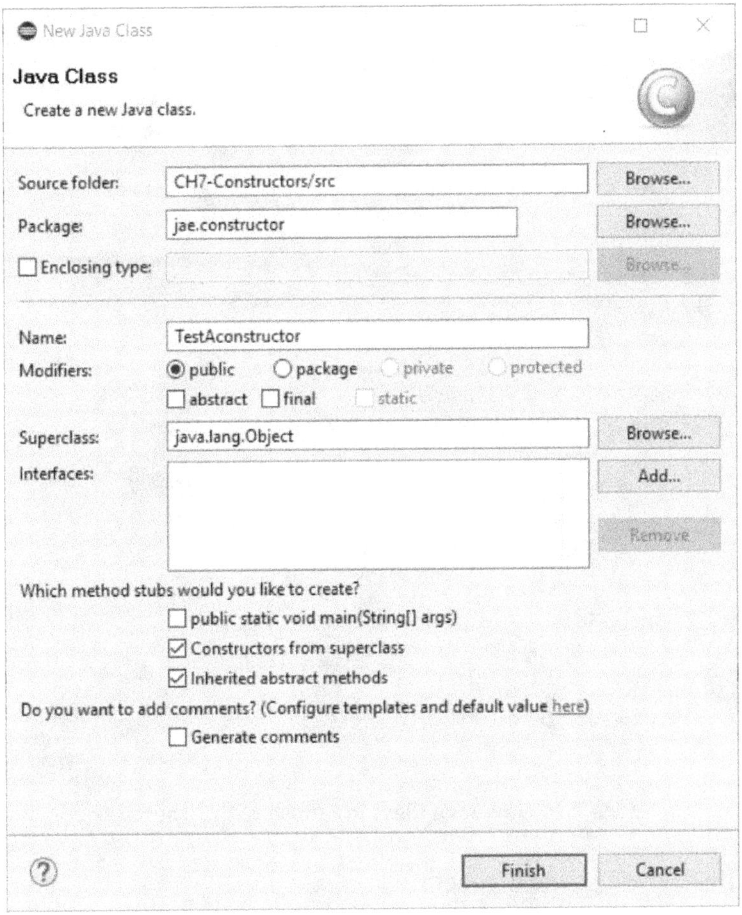

Figure 7.9 New Java Class Options in Eclipse

When you click Finish, Eclipse will generate a constructor.

```
package jae.constructor;

public class TestAconstructor {

    public TestAconstructor() {
        // TODO Auto-generated constructor stub
    }

}
```

Since the Object class was the constructor, there is not much to see, but if we change java.lang.Object to a class with a constructor, jae.constructor.TestAconstructor, Figure 7.10:

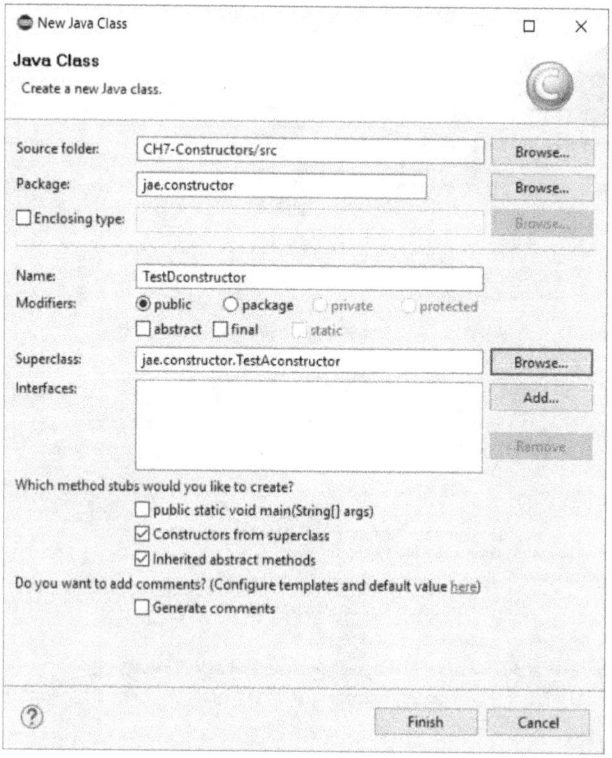

Figure 7.10 New Java Class in Eclipse with Superclass

Click Finish, and the following code is generated:

```
package jae.constructor;

public class TestDconstructor extends TestAconstructor {

    public TestDconstructor() {
        // TODO Auto-generated constructor stub
    }

}
```

What is missing is the call to super() since the TestAconstructor superclass has a constructor. Again, Eclipse is not perfect. The second option is when you have entered a few fields and want to generate a constructor based on these fields. For example, here is a class with a couple of fields.

```
package jae.constructor;

public class TestBconstructor {

    int i;
    int[] j = new int[5];


}
```

From the menu, select Source->Generate Constructor using Fields..., Figure 7.11:

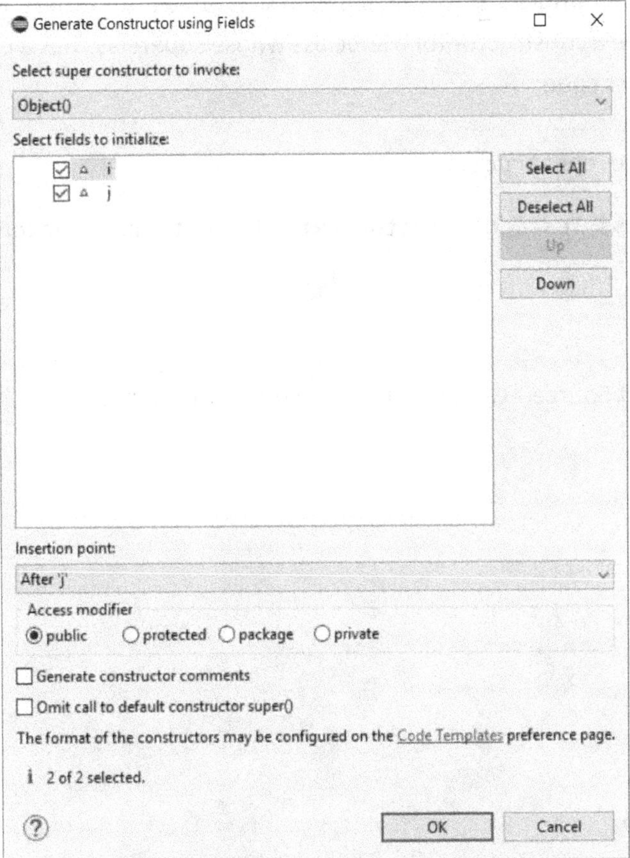

Figure 7.11 Generate Class Constructor Using Eclipse

After selecting the fields and clicking OK, the constructor with the fields will be generated:

```
package jae.constructor;

public class TestBconstructor {

    int i;
    int[] j = new int[5];
    public TestBconstructor(int i, int[] j) {
        super();
        this.i = i;
        this.j = j;
    }
}
```

The super() call can be removed since the superclass is Object and there is no constructor. The final option is to create a constructor for a subclass whose superclass has a constructor. Let's start with the following class code:

```
package jae.constructor;

public class TestCconstructor extends TestAconstructor {


}
```

From the menu, select Source->Generate Constructor from a Superclass, Figure 7.12:

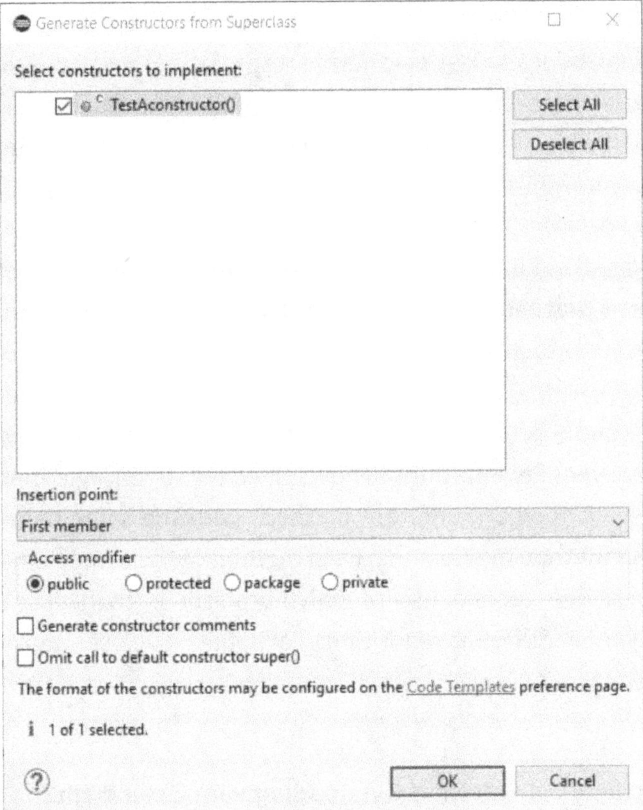

Figure 7.12 Generate Class Constructor Using Eclipse

Click OK, and the resulting code is just like creating the class, but it includes the super() keyword.

```
package jae.constructor;

public class TestCconstructor extends TestAconstructor {

    public TestCconstructor() {
        super();
        // TODO Auto-generated constructor stub
    }

}
```

7.5 Polymorphism

The previous chapter introduced class creation (encapsulation) and how to put the classes into libraries. We can re-use these libraries for different programs. Inheritance allows us to create subclasses that extend the classes we have created previously. Now, we come to a very interesting OOP feature called polymorphism.

Definition: *Polymorphism* – In Greek, the term means "many forms". For computer science, we are talking about objects that can take on many forms, or more specifically one interface that can handle multiple types.

Polymorphism has a couple of usages in OOP. First, rather than having to create a different method for every data type, Polymorphism allows us to create a single method that can handle multiple data types. We can create different methods with the same name that have different arguments. We call this method overloading. Each method of the same name must have different input parameter types. The second use of polymorphism is to have a subclass override a superclass method with a different algorithm. Let's take a closer look at overloading and overriding.

7.5.1 Computer Activity 7.4 - Method Overloading with BasicMath2

The custom library in the last chapter contained the BasicMath class. The BasicMath class contained several static methods for performing basic math operations on two integer values. What if a value was a double and you want a double math result? The BasicMath class is not going to work unless we make some changes.

1. Open the BasicMath.java from the last chapter in Eclipse.
2. Edit the file and add the double type equivalent math operations shown in Code Listing 7.5:

```
public class BasicMath {

    //Add two numbers: A + B
    public static int Add(int A, int B)
    {
        int C = A + B;
        return C;
    }
```

```
    public static double Add(double A, double B)
    {
        double C = A + B;
        return C;
    }
    //Subtract two numbers: A - B
    public static int Subtract(int A, int B)
    {
        int C = A - B;
        return C;
    }
    public static double Subtract(double A, double B)
    {
        double C = A - B;
        return C;
    }
    //Multiply two numbers: A*B
    public static int Multiply(int A, int B)
    {
        int C = A* B;
        return C;
    }
    public static double Multiply(double A, double B)
    {
        double C = A* B;
        return C;
    }
    //Divide two numbers: A / B
    public static int Divide(int A, int B)
    {
        int C = A / B;
        return C;
    }
    public static double Divide(double A, double B)
    {
        double C = A / B;
        return C;
    }
    //Produce the Modulus between to numbers: A % B
    public static int Modulus(int A, int B)
    {
        int C = A % B;
        return C;
    }
```

```
    public static double Modulus(double A, double B)
    {
        double C = A % B;
        return C;
    }
}
```

Code Listing 7.5 Overloading Math Methods

3. Save the file.
4. Since there has been an update to our library, we need to export the jae.mathlib.jar file again. Follow the same steps in the last chapter to export the jae.mathlib.jar file. You will be warned about overwriting the current jar file. Just click the "Yes" button.
5. Open the MathLibTest.java file that you created in the last chapter.
6. Import the newly created jae.mathlib.jar file into the project.
7. In the MathLibTest main() method, clear out the contents and enter the following

```
 int i = 5;
 int j = 2;

 System.out.println("The result of 5 + 2 is " + BasicMath.Add(i, j));
 System.out.println("The    result    of    5/2    +    2    is    "    +
BasicMath.Add((double) i/j, j));
```

As you type in the BasicMath with the dot, you will get a list of all the available methods, Figure 7.13:

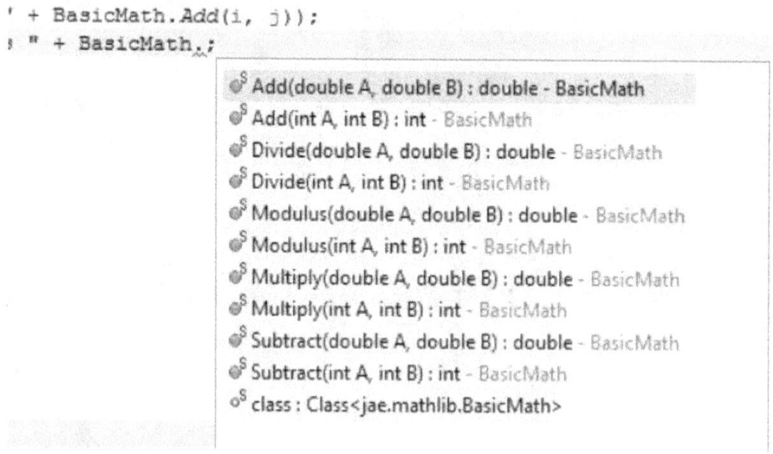

```
" + BasicMath.Add(i, j));
; " + BasicMath.;
```

Add(double A, double B) : double - BasicMath
Add(int A, int B) : int - BasicMath
Divide(double A, double B) : double - BasicMath
Divide(int A, int B) : int - BasicMath
Modulus(double A, double B) : double - BasicMath
Modulus(int A, int B) : int - BasicMath
Multiply(double A, double B) : double - BasicMath
Multiply(int A, int B) : int - BasicMath
Subtract(double A, double B) : double - BasicMath
Subtract(int A, int B) : int - BasicMath
class : Class<jae.mathlib.BasicMath>

Figure 7.13 BasicMath Class Methods Shown by Eclipse

Notice that the Object class methods are not available when you call a class's static methods. If you created an instance of the BasicMath class, the inherited Object class methods would appear.

8. For the first addition, select the integer Add method. For the second addition, choose the double Add method.
9. Set a breakpoint on the first println, and run the debugger.
10. Step into the first println, you will see the debugger marker jump to the int Add method.
11. Step over and step into the second println, and the debug marker will be at the double Add method.

Polymorphism allows us to overload with any arguments so Add(String s1, String s2) can be created as a valid overload of the Add method.

7.5.2 Computer Activity 7.5 - Constructor Overloading with ColorShippingBox

Constructors can also be overloaded, which will give you different options when first generating an object. For this activity, we will add a new constructor to the ColorShippingBox class that sets up standard box sizes for small, medium, or larger.

1. Open the ShippingBoxTest.java file in Eclipse.
2. In the ShippingBox class, add two mutator methods to change the dimensions of length and width.
3. In the ColorShippingBox Class, add the following new constructor method after the original constructor:

```
 ColorShippingBox(String standardbox)
 {
     super(1,1,1); //required since the Superclass constructor gets
called
     first
     if (standardbox.equals("small"))
     {
         super.setHeight(11);
         super.setLength(9);
         super.setWidth(1);
         color = "brown";
     }
     if (standardbox.equals("medium"))
     {
         super.setHeight(11);
```

```
            super.setLength(11);
            super.setWidth(5);
            color = "brown";
        }
        if (standardbox.equals("large"))
        {
            super.setHeight(15);
            super.setLength(15);
            super.setWidth(15);
            color = "brown";
        }

}
```

4. In the ShippingBoxTest class main() method, add the following code to the end of the code that is already there:

```
 ColorShippingBox myColorBox2 = new ColorShippingBox("medium");
 System.out.println("The  color  for  my  shipping  box  is  "  +
  myColorBox2.getBoxColor());
 System.out.println("The dimensions are " + myColorBox2.getLength()
+
"in x" +   myColorBox2.getWidth() +"in x" + myColorBox2.getHeight()+
"in");
 System.out.println("The     volume    of     the     box     is     "    +
myColorBox2.boxVolume() +
  " cubic inches");
```

5. Run the application and you should get the following output:

```
The dimensions are 10in x8in x5in
The volume of the box is 400 cubic inches
The dimensions are 10in x8in x3in
The volume of the box is 240 cubic inches
The color for my shipping box is white
The dimensions are 11in x10in x12in
The volume of the box is 1320 cubic inches
The color for my shipping box is brown
The dimensions are 11in x5in x11in
The volume of the box is 605 cubic inches
```

The new constructor takes in a string argument. Based on the string value, the dimensions and color parameters are set to standard values for a small, medium, or large box. Since the

ColorShippingBox is a subclass to the ShippingBox, the superclass constructor must be called first. Java will always call the superclass constructor first before calling the rest of the subclass. The call to super(args) must be the first line in the subclass constructor. In this example, the call to super(1,1,1) is a placeholder to create the object, and the mutator methods are then used to set the actual values.

Let's say we have 3 classes, A, B, C. Class A has a constructor. B is a subclass of A. C is a subclass of B. If you create an instance of C and call the constructor, class A's constructor is called first, then class B, and finally class C.

7.5.3 Computer Activity 7.6 - Inheritance, Polymorphism, and Overriding Methods

Another interesting feature of polymorphism is the ability for a subclass to override a superclass's methods. This allows you to use the same method interface to run a different algorithm. Let's go back to the BasicInheritance project.

1. Open TestInheritance.java, and TestB.java in Eclipse
2. Add the following TestAOutput() method to the TestB class:

```
public void TestAOutput() {
    System.out.println("The TestAOuput has been overridden");
}
```

3. In TestInheritance main() method, uncomment out line 8 for myclass.TestAOutput().
4. Run the project and the output should be as follows:

```
The TestAOuput has been overridden
This is TestB class
This is TestA class
This is TestA class
```

The TestAOuput() method in TestB class has overridden the method of the same in the TestA class. When the program runs, Java will use the method in TestB to run the call myclass.TestAOutput(). The super keyword still calls the TestAouput() method in TestA class. If you want to prevent something from being overridden, using the "final" keyword in the declaration will prevent the subclass from overriding.

```
public final void TestAOutput()
```

7.6 *Eclipse Feature: Quickly Adding Overrides*

Like creating constructors quickly, Eclipse also an automated solution to generate overrides. In the last activity with TestB.java selected, you could have simply gone to the menu and selected Source->Override/Implement Methods. The following dialog will appear, Figure 7.14:

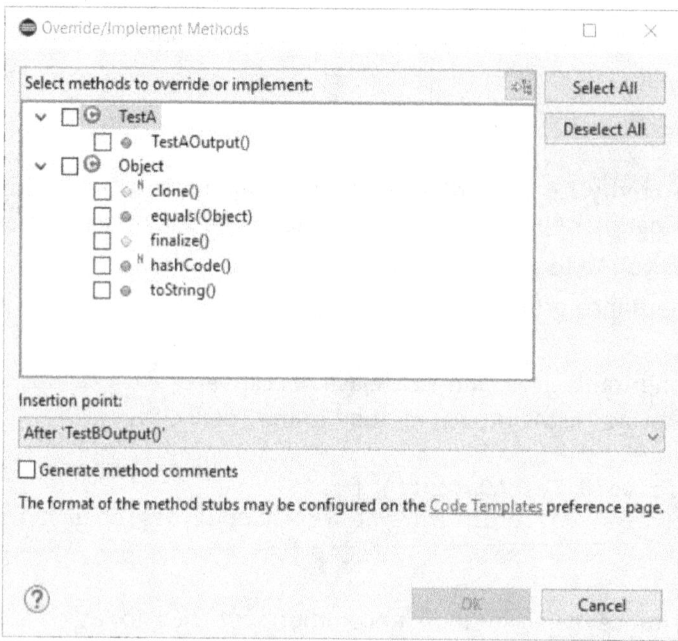

Figure 7.14 Generating Override Method with Eclipse

Simply select TestAOutput() and click Ok. The following code is generated:

```
@Override
public void TestAOutput() {
    // TODO Auto-generated method stub
    super.TestAOutput();
}
```

The super.TestAOutput() method call is not needed and can be removed. The quick override generation feature comes in handy when you have to keep track of all of the items that need to be implemented.

7.7 Architecting A Library: Abstract Class and Interface Type

The power of OOP allows you to expand the library with your own custom classes. The last chapter discussed architecting individual classes. Inheritance and polymorphism show how your class can fit into a larger library. It is not only important to architect your classes, but good architectural practices are important when building a whole library. It is not only important to group the classes into a single library family, but leaving room for future expansion plays a key role in the design of a library. Different classes can have similar interfaces, but with a different implementation. For example, cars, trains, and airplanes all fit under the transportation family. Each has similar features like passengers, steering, wheels, breaking, and engine, but the implementation of all three is different. For example, cars have a steering wheel, planes have a control stick or yoke, and trains don't have internal steering at all. There are two features that help address generic implementations and help create a class hierarchy: abstract class and interface type.

7.7.1 Computer Activity 7.7 - Abstract Class Example

Let's take a look at an abstract class first.

Definition: *Abstract Class* – a generic class that encapsulates fields and default methods. If there are methods that subclasses will override, these methods can be declared as abstract and have no implementation or algorithm. The abstract class cannot be instantiated.

Abstract classes are the superclass for a group of subclasses. The abstract class encapsulates fields, constants, constructors and methods that are to be used by the subclasses. If a method is going to be overridden by the subclasses, the method can be declared as an abstract method. The abstract method only needs to be declared, but not implemented. Abstract methods can only be declared in abstract classes. Once a subclass inherits the abstract class, all abstract methods must be implemented in the subclass.

In this computer activity we will create a library of 3D shapes for a rectangular prism, cone, and sphere, Figure 7.15. We will create an accessor class that encapsulates items used in all subclasses. Each subclass for each shape class will have a constructor and private fields for the dimensions. The classes that will provide information on volume and surface are based on the dimensions of each shape.

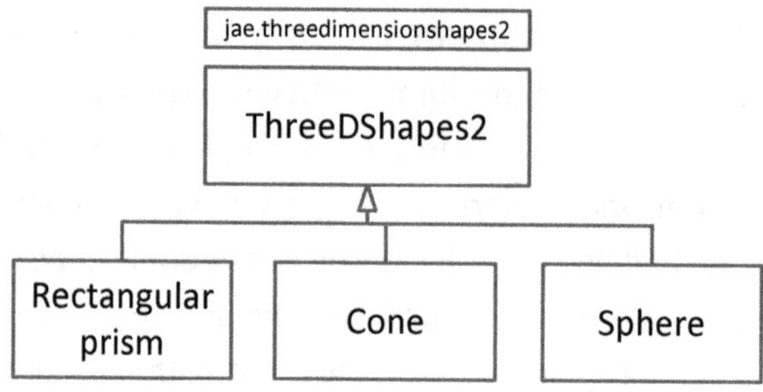

Figure 7.15 3D Shape Class Hierarchy

In Eclipse, create a new Java project called "CH7CA7.7-ThreeDShapes". Create a new package called"jae.threedimensiondshapes". Create a new Java class with a main() method under the package called "Test3DShapes".

1. Now we will create an abstract class. Create a new class called "ThreeDShapes" and select the abstract modifier checkbox, Figure 7.16.

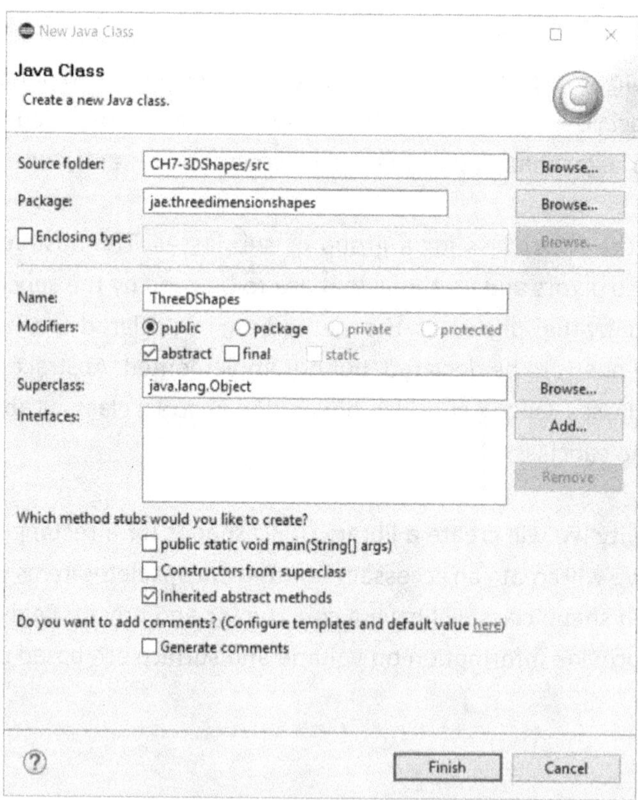

Figure 7.16 Creating an Abstract Class with Eclipse

2. Click Finish and the code generated should look like this:

```
package jae.threedimensionshapes;

public abstract class ThreeDShapes {


}
```

The "abstract" modifier is used to declare an abstract class. If you look in Package Explorer, the class symbol has an 'A' in it to denote an abstract class.

3. Fill in the following code in the TreeDShapes class, Code Listing 7.6:

```
package jae.threedimensionshapes;

public abstract class ThreeDShapes {

    final double PI = 3.14159;
    String color;

    public String getColor()
    {
        return color;
    }
    abstract double volume();
    abstract double surfacearea();
}
```

Code Listing 7.6 TreeDShapes Class

The abstract class encapsulates the common items that all the classes will share. The class has a constant, a String field, an accessor method to be used by all classes, and two abstract methods. If you remember the keyword "final" from chapter 3, the "final" keyword is used to declare that the constant PI cannot be overridden by any subclass. Final can also be used in method declarations to prevent methods from being overridden. The getColor() method is used by all classes to return the String value. The two abstract methods for volume and surface are made abstract since the formula to calculate each shape is implemented differently.

4. Create a new class called RectPrism with the superclass set to jae.threedimensionshapes.ThreeDShapes. Make sure the "Inherited abstract methods" and the "Constructors from superclass" checkboxes are checked, Figure 7.17.

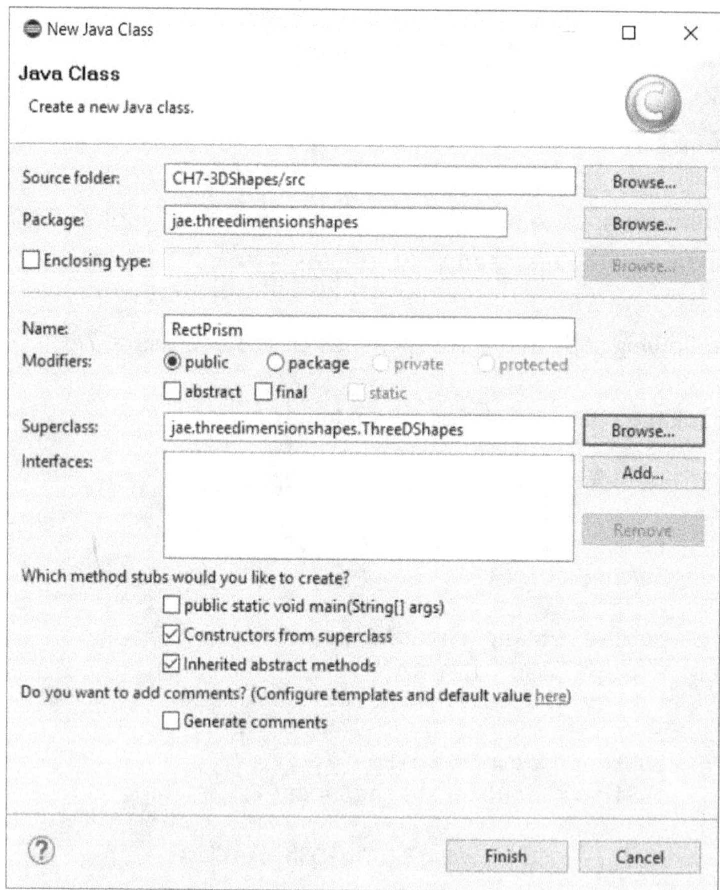

Figure 7.17 Creating a Subclass for an Abstract Class in Eclipse

5. Click Finish and the following code will be generated:

```
package jae.threedimensionshapes;

public class RectPrism extends ThreeDShapes {

    public RectPrism() {
        // TODO Auto-generated constructor stub
    }
```

```
    @Override
    double volume() {
        // TODO Auto-generated method stub
        return 0;
    }

    @Override
    double surfacearea() {
        // TODO Auto-generated method stub
        return 0;
    }
}
```

The class is an extension of the ThreeDShapes abstract class. Eclipse automatically fills in the abstract methods to be overridden and implemented in the class. The constructor is also added.

6. Create three private fields for length, height, and width. You can use the Source code generation features in Eclipse to generate the get and set methods. Set the accessors and mutators to be listed after the three private fields, Figure 7.1:

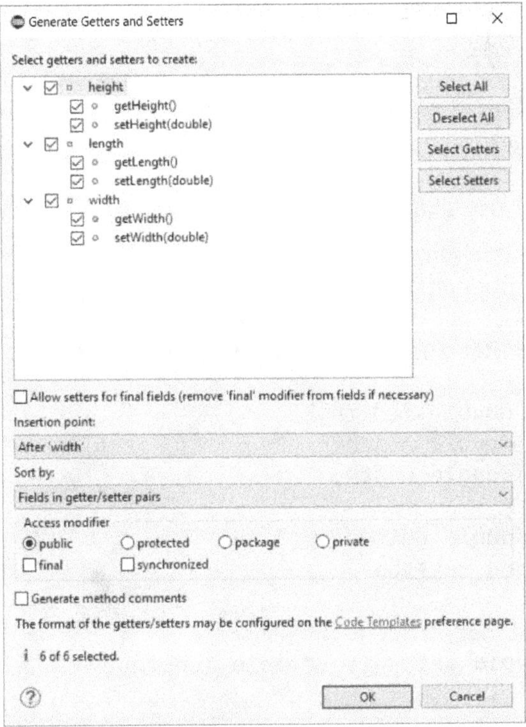

Figure 7.18 Generate Class Fields with Eclipse

7. Add the code for the constructor

```
public RectPrism(double length, double height, double width, String
color) {
    // TODO Auto-generated constructor stub
    this.length = length;
    this.height = height;
    this.width = width;
    super.color = color;
}
```

8. Fill in the override methods

```
@Override
double volume() {
    // TODO Auto-generated method stub
    return length*height*width;
}

@Override
double surfacearea() {
    // TODO Auto-generated method stub
    return                  (2.0*length*height)                  +
(2.0*height*width)+(2.0*length*width);
}
```

The final class code should look like the following, Code Listing 7.7:

```
package jae.threedimensionshapes;

public class RectPrism extends ThreeDShapes {

    private double length;
    private double height;
    private double width;

    public double getLength() {
        return length;
    }

    public void setLength(double length) {
        this.length = length;
    }

```

```
    public double getHeight() {
        return height;
    }

    public void setHeight(double height) {
        this.height = height;
    }

    public double getWidth() {
        return width;
    }

    public void setWidth(double width) {
        this.width = width;
    }

    public RectPrism(double length, double height, double width, String color) {
        // TODO Auto-generated constructor stub
        this.length = length;
        this.height = height;
        this.width = width;
        super.color = color;
    }

    @Override
    double volume() {
        // TODO Auto-generated method stub
        return length*height*width;
    }

    @Override
    double surfacearea() {
        // TODO Auto-generated method stub
        return (2.0*length*height) + (2.0*height*width)+(2.0*length*width);
    }
}
```

Code Listing 7.7 Class RectPrism

Repeat the steps to create classes for the cone and sphere. Use the Math class methods for some of the formulas. Also, remember what we learned in Chapter 3. Formulas with constant numbers require a decimal zero to return double. Fill in the Test3DShapes main() method with the following, to test our code:

```
Cone mycone = new Cone(5,7, "blue");
RectPrism myprism = new RectPrism(7,3,5,"yellow");
Sphere mysphere = new Sphere(11,"brown");

System.out.println("The " + mycone.getColor()+ " cone has a volume of "
+
mycone.volume()+" cubic inches and a surface area of " +
mycone.surfacearea()+
" square inches");

System.out.println("The " + myprism.getColor()+ " rectagular prism has a
volume of " + myprism.volume()+" cubic inches and a surface area of " +
myprism.surfacearea()+" square inches");

System.out.println("The " + mysphere.getColor()+ " sphere has a volume of
" + mysphere.volume() +" cubic inches and a surface area of "
+mysphere.surfacearea()+" square inches");
```

When you run the application, you will get the color, volume, and surface area results for all the shapes. The super keyword was used to access the constant PI value. If you wanted to export the library to a jar file, you should first delete the Test3DShapes.java file, since it is not needed in the final library. Eclipse provides a class hierarchy view.

1. In Package Explorer, click on jae.threedimensionshapes
2. Hit the F4 key or right-click on jae.threedimensionshapes and select "Open Type Hierarchy". A new tab will appear listing all the class names and showing the subclasses under the abstract ThreeDShapes class, Figure 7.19.

Figure 7.19 Type Hierarchy View in Eclipse

7.7.2 Computer Activity 7.8 - Interface Type Example

An Abstract class encapsulating common items to be used by subclasses is a typical construct, but classes are limited to inheriting only one superclass. Interface types were introduced to get around this limitation.

Definition: *Interface Type* – A generic type that only encapsulates abstract methods, final constants, and final static fields. An Interface is used to specify a behavior that subclasses must implement.

An Interface type gets around the limitation that classes may only inherit one superclass, and allows classes to implement more than one interface, which means more abstract methods. Let's say you and a team are creating a multiplayer online game. The game includes characters like wizards, witches, elves, ogres, dragons, etc. Each character will be a class unto itself and would exist under a "character" abstract class. The characters will have movement and sounds, but each character will move and sound differently. An interface type called "movement" would contain methods like run, walk, and jump, and there would be an interface type for sounds that would contain talking, yelling, screaming, movement sounds, laughing, etc. The different character classes would inherit the character abstract class and implement both interfaces. The character classes would fill in the method details for all abstracted classes. Interface types also allow for some flexibility to create individual behaviors that individual classes in a group of classes can use.

Some characters could have an angry attack feature and others might not. The AngryAttack interface can be implemented by some characters, but not by all.

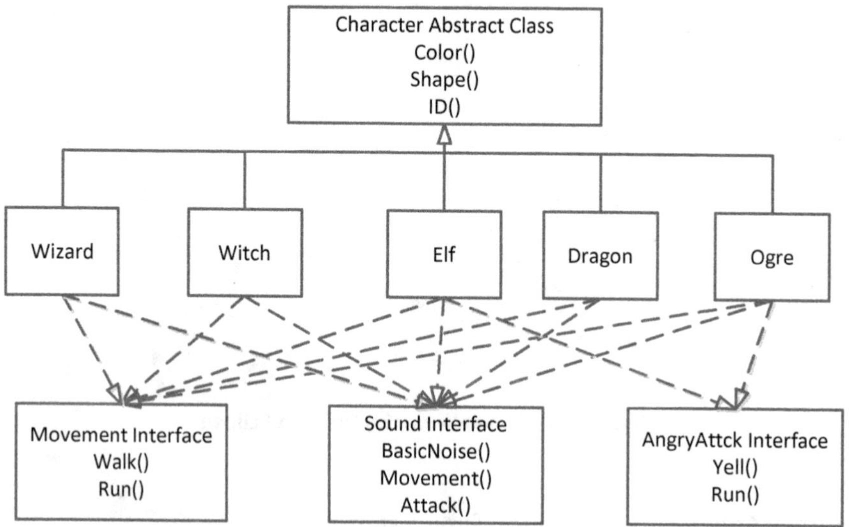

As a demonstration of this computer activity, we will add to the 3DShapes project and use an Interface type instead of an Abstract class. We will recreate the three classes for rectangular prism2, sphere2, and cone2. Under the "ThreeDShapes" project, create a new package called "jae.threedimensiondshapes2". Create a new Java class with a main() method under the package called "Test3DShapes2", Figure 7.20.

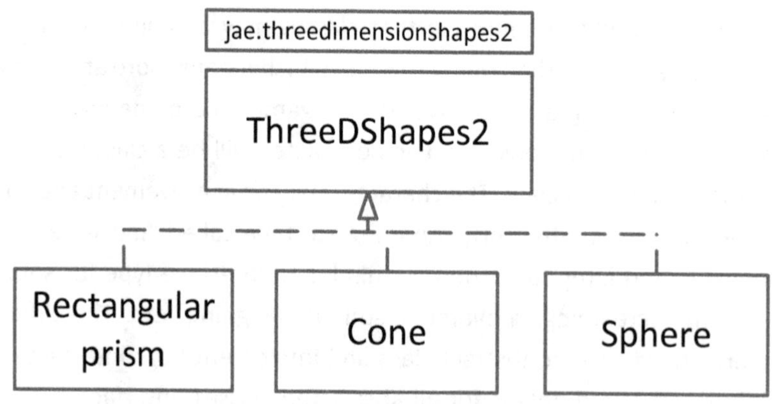

Figure 7.20 3D Shape 2 Class Hierarchy

1. Now we will create an Interface class. Right-click on jae.threedimensiondshapes2 package and select New->Interface from the context menu. Since an Interface is a type and not a class, Eclipse provides a different option to create an interface, Figure 7.21.

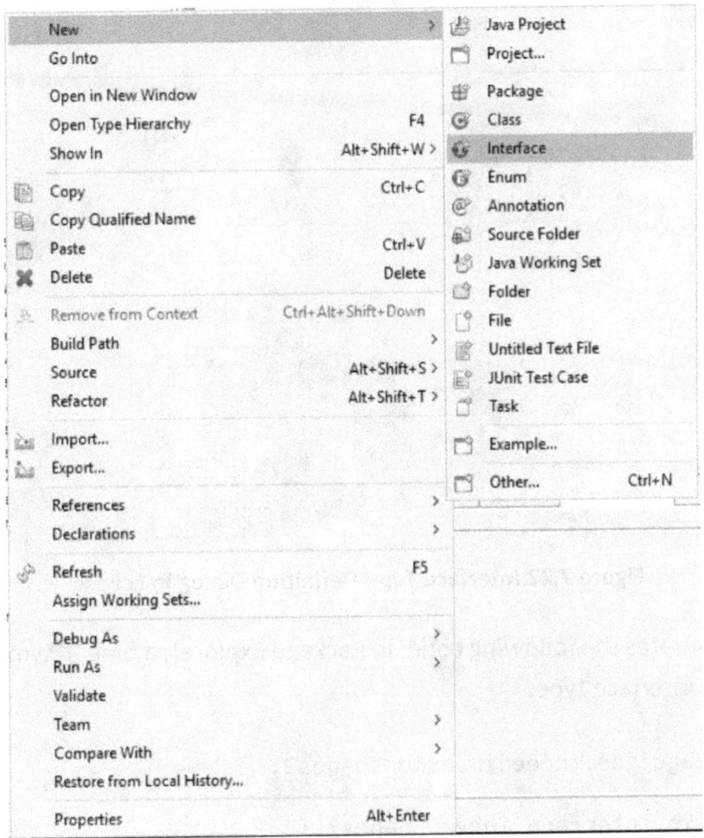

Figure 7.21 Creating an Interface Type in Eclipse

2. A dialog appears, Figure 7.22. Enter the name of the interface as ThreeDShapes2 and click Finish.

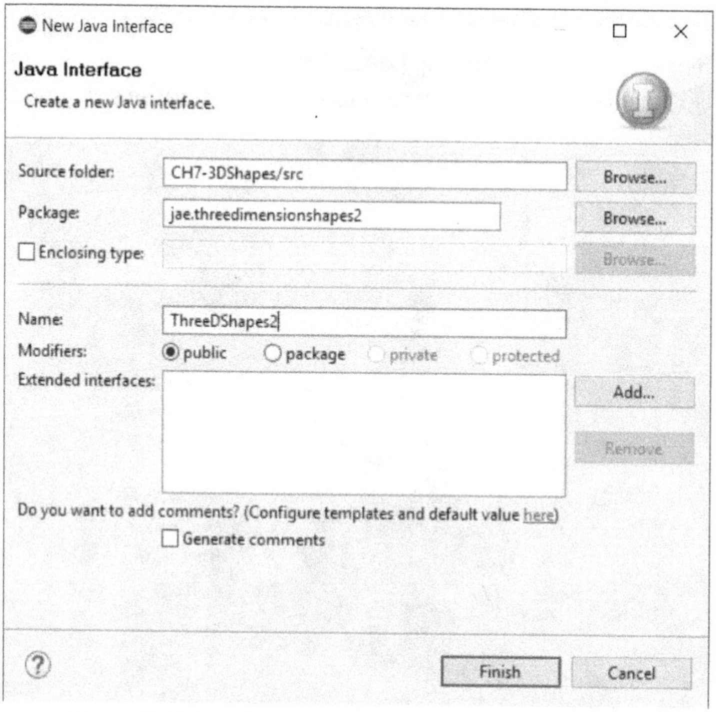

Figure 7.22 Interface Type Definition Dialog in Eclipse

Eclipse generates the following code. In Package Explorer, a blue 'I' symbol designates the code as an Interface type.

```
package jae.threedimensionshapes2;

public interface ThreeDShapes2 {
}
```

Notice that the word "class" is not used in the declaration, but the word "interface" is used. Again, an interface is a type, not a class.

3. Now we can fill in the code

```
package jae.threedimensionshapes2;

public interface ThreeDShapes2 {
    double PI = 3.14159;
    double volume();
    double surfacearea();
}
```

The constant PI is in italics. Constants can be in an interface, but they are final and cannot be changed. The color field and getColor() method have been removed and will be encapsulated in each shape class.

4. Now, create the Sphere2 class. This time you don't need to specify a superclass, but you do need to add an Interface. In the Java Class dialog, click the Add... button next to the Interfaces: box.
5. Another dialog will appear, Figure 7.23. Start to type "ThreeDShapes2" into the Choose interfaces box, and the ThreeDShapes2 will show in the Matching items. Click on the ThreeDShapes2 interface item in the Matching items. Then click the Ok button to close the dialog.

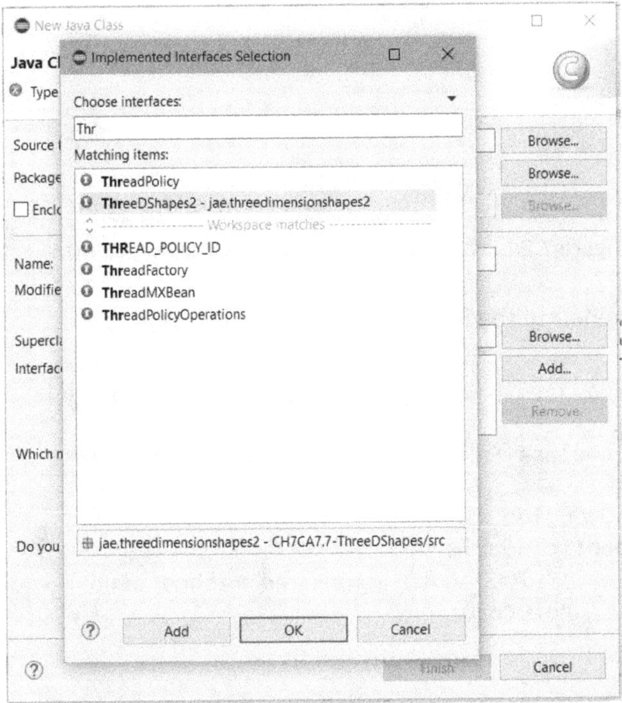

Figure 7.23 Adding an Interface Type to a Class in Eclipse

6. The Interface will be put into the list, Figure 7.24. A class can inherit more than one interface. Click Finish.

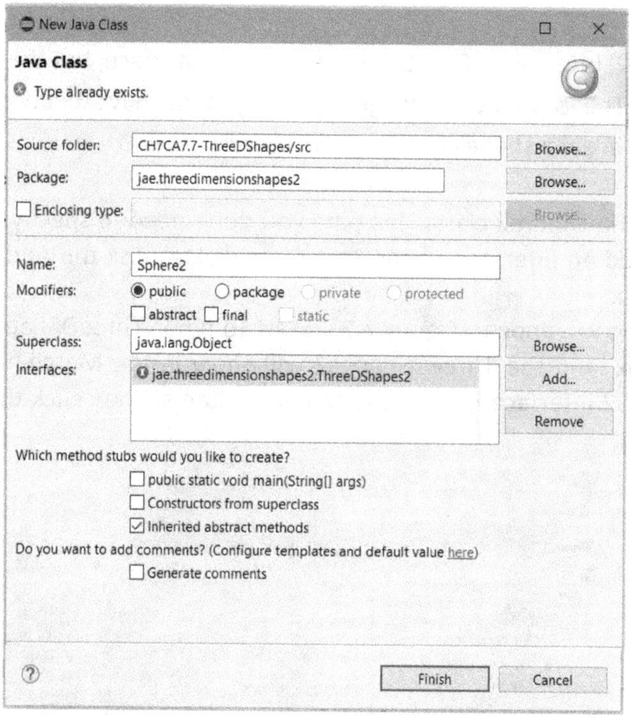

New Java Class

Java Class

Type already exists.

Source folder: CH7CA7.7-ThreeDShapes/src Browse...

Package: jae.threedimensionshapes2 Browse...

Enclosing type: Browse...

Name: Sphere2

Modifiers: public package private protected

abstract final static

Superclass: java.lang.Object Browse...

Interfaces: jae.threedimensionshapes2.ThreeDShapes2 Add... Remove

Which method stubs would you like to create?

public static void main(String[] args)

Constructors from superclass

Inherited abstract methods

Do you want to add comments? (Configure templates and default value here)

Generate comments

Finish Cancel

Figure 7.24 Sphere2 Class Created from Interface using Eclipse

Eclipse will generate the following code:

```
package jae.threedimensionshapes2;

public class Sphere2 implements ThreeDShapes2 {

    @Override
    public double volume() {
        // TODO Auto-generated method stub
        return 0;
    }

    @Override
    public double surfacearea() {
        // TODO Auto-generated method stub
        return 0;
    }
}
```

The code includes the classes defined in the Interface. Fill in the rest of the code that includes the constructor, dimensions, accessor methods, and mutator methods. Also, include a String for color and a method to return the color value. Here is the final code for the class, Code Listing 7.8:

```
package jae.threedimensionshapes2;

public class Sphere2 implements ThreeDShapes2 {

    private double radius;
    private String color;

    public double getRadius() {
        return radius;
    }

    public void setRadius(double radius) {
        this.radius = radius;
    }

    public String getColor(){
        return color;
    }

    public Sphere2(double radius, String color) {
        // TODO Auto-generated constructor stub
        this.radius = radius;
        this.color = color;
    }

    @Override
    public double volume() {
        // TODO Auto-generated method stub
        return (4.0/3.0)*PI*Math.pow(radius, 3);
    }

    @Override
    public double surfacearea() {
        // TODO Auto-generated method stub
        return 4.0*PI*radius*radius;
    }
}
```

Code Listing 7.8 Sphere2 Class with Interfaces

Notice that the PI (italicized) is used in the formulas. The PI is a static value that comes from the interface. Repeat the same steps for RectPrism2 and Cone2 classes. Fill in the following code in the Test3DShapes2 main() method:

```
Cone2 mycone = new Cone2(5,7, "blue");
RectPrism2 myprism = new RectPrism2(7,3,5,"yellow");
Sphere2 mysphere = new Sphere2(11,"brown");

System.out.println("The " + mycone.getColor()+ " cone has a volume of " + mycone.volume() + " cubic inches and a surface area of " + mycone.surfacearea() + " square inches");

System.out.println("The " + myprism.getColor()+ " rectagular prism has a volume of " + myprism.volume() + " cubic inches and a surface area of " + myprism.surfacearea()+" square inches");

System.out.println("The " + mysphere.getColor() + " sphere has a volume of " + mysphere.volume() + " cubic inches and a surface area of " + mysphere.surfacearea() + " square inches");
```

Run the program, and it will produce the same results as before. How do you choose between Abstract class and interface type? The answer is not so simple. If you are going to create a hierarchy with some generic implemented methods that are to be used by all subclasses, the Abstract class is the best. If there are no generic implemented methods to be shared by all classes, an Interface is best. In the 3DShapes project, we showed how both an Abstract class and Interface type can be implemented. The Abstract class would be better in this case since the color field and getColor() method are shared by all.

Once the Abstract class and Interface types are in the library, others can use them to add to the library and create their own classes. It is important to take the time to architect your class libraries and determine how they will be organized. What methods need to be implemented by all classes and what behaviors can be separated out will determine what goes into the classes, abstract classes, and interface types.

7.8 Java Library Subset for AP® Computer Science and the List Interfaces

With over 4000 classes in the standard class library, you will not be expected to know all of them for the AP® Computer Science test. The College Board has posted a subset of the Java library to be covered. Here are the top-level Java classes. There are only a few methods that will be covered on the test from each class. The College Board website has documentation on the methods that will be covered. Please be aware that the list is adjusted over time.

- class java.lang.Object
- class java.lang.Integer
- class java.lang.Double
- class java.lang.String
- class java.lang.Math
- interface java.util.List<E>
- class java.util.ArrayList<E>

We have covered the details for most of these classes, but the List interface class was only indirectly covered. The ArrayList discussed in chapter 5 implements the List interface class. The following is the ArrayList declaration:

```
public class ArrayList<E> extends AbstractList<E> implements List<E>,
RandomAccess, Cloneable, java.io.Serializable
```

The code details can be found online at sites like grepcode.com and www.docjar.com. You can see that the ArrayList implements several interfaces including List. The List class can be found in the Library, Figure 7.25.

List.class
List<E>
add(E) : boolean
add(int, E) : void
addAll(int, Collection<? extends E>) : boolean
addAll(Collection<? extends E>) : boolean
clear() : void
contains(Object) : boolean
containsAll(Collection<?>) : boolean
equals(Object) : boolean
get(int) : E
hashCode() : int
indexOf(Object) : int
isEmpty() : boolean
iterator() : Iterator<E>
lastIndexOf(Object) : int
listIterator() : ListIterator<E>
listIterator(int) : ListIterator<E>
remove(int) : E
remove(Object) : boolean
removeAll(Collection<?>) : boolean
replaceAll(UnaryOperator<E>) : void
retainAll(Collection<?>) : boolean
set(int, E) : E
size() : int
sort(Comparator<? super E>) : void
spliterator() : Spliterator<E>
subList(int, int) : List<E>
toArray() : Object[]
toArray(T[]) <T> : T[]

Figure 7.25 List Class

We have used a few of these methods already. The ArrayList has many more methods included because of the other interface and the abstract classes. Even though the List class is an interface class, you can create a new List object by the following, since ArrayList is a List:

```
List<String> myStr = new ArrayList<String>();
```

7.9 Documenting the Library with Unified Modeling Language (UML) – Class Diagrams

In chapter 3, we introduced how to enter comments into your code. In chapter 4, flowcharts were introduced as a way to have a picture of how an algorithm is going to function. The last chapter discussed how to use Javadoc to generate documentation for your classes. Documentation is an important part of programming. When an application is developed by a 50-plus member team, being able to communicate what code is supposed to do is very important. If the application has a large number of classes, a big picture diagram is needed. In the mid-1990's, Unified Modeling Language (UML) was developed as a way to visualize big software projects. In 2005, UML was approved by the International Organization of Standardizations as an approved ISO standard. There are different types of UML diagrams, but the one most used is the class diagram. The class diagram provides the basic high-level information of the class such as class name, variables, and methods, Figure 7.26.

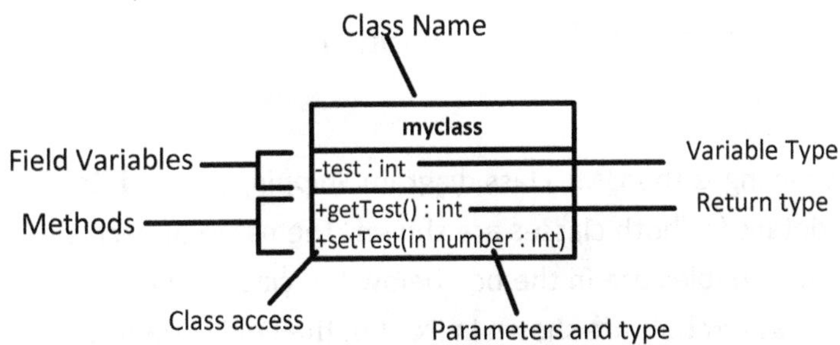

Figure 7.26 UML Class Diagram

Each item in the class diagram shows the class access such as public, private, and protects using some basic symbols:

+	Public
-	Private
#	Protected
/	Derived
~	Package

Other elements for the class show if a method is static, the class is abstract, and any constants:

Bold	Class Name
Underline	static
Italic	abstract
All caps	constants

When it comes to linking the classes together, there are several line styles that show the type of link being made between the classes, such as inheritance in implementation:

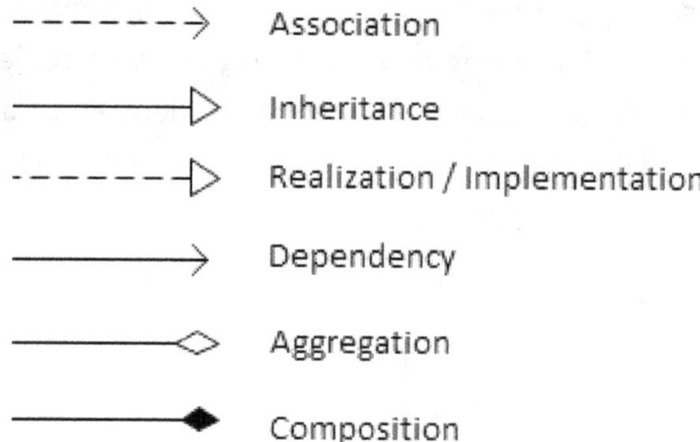

For example, the following is the UML class diagram ShippingBox and ColorShippingBox classes, Figure 7.27. All the details for both classes are shown. The name of each class is clearly shown in bold. The private field variables are in the box below the class name, and all methods are in the last box. The class access symbols are shown in front of the field variables and methods. The value for each variable is displayed after the colon ":". The return value for the method is similarly shown after the colon ":". The methods also show the parameters and type. The arrow with solid line shows that ColorShippingBox inherits from ShippingBox.

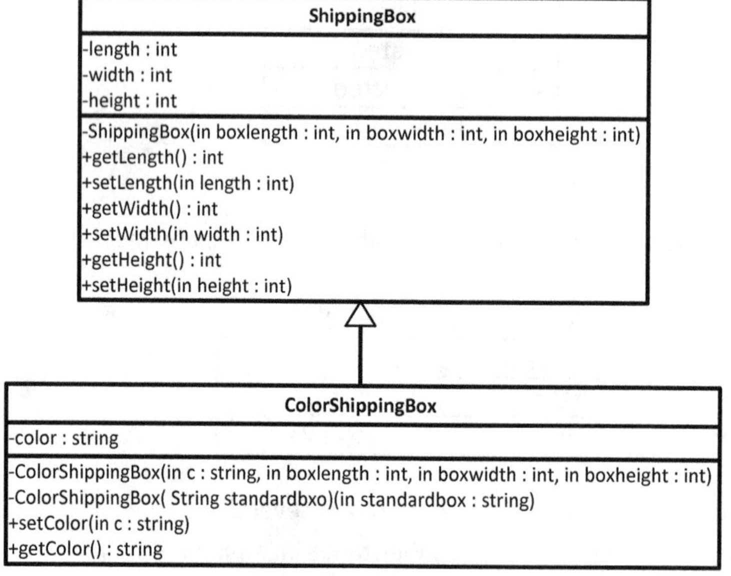

Figure 7.27 ShippingBox and ColorShippinggBox UML Class Diagrams

7.10 Eclipse Feature: UML Add-Ons

You will not have to draw the class by hand since there are UML software tools available. There are tools that are free and tools that you have to pay for. There are three types of UML tools. First, there are standalone UML editors. Second, there are UML editors that plug into Eclipse, and these allow you to draw the UML diagram and fill in the code behind the class. Finally, there are Java-to-UML tools that generate a UML diagram. Table 7.2 below has an example of each, which are currently free:

UML Tool	**Web Address**	**Description**
Violet UML Editor	http://alexdp.free.fr/violetumleditor/page.php	A free GPL licensed UML editor for students first learning UML.
Papyrus	https://www.eclipse.org/papyrus/	A full Eclipse development environment that includes a professional UML modeling solution. You can generate code from UML and UML from code.
ObjectAid	http://www.objectaid.com/home	An Eclipse add-on that creates UML diagrams from Java source code.

Table 7.2 UML Add-Ons

There are other UML tools in the Eclipse marketplace. If we had you downloaded Papyrus in Chapter 2 rather than a basic Eclipse environment, working with Eclipse would have been very confusing without the information in these last two chapters. Whole classes and books could be made by simply using UML and Papyrus, so we will not go into it in too much detail. If you want to move to Papyrus, you are more than welcome to, but this book will continue to focus on the basic Eclipse development environment. If you want to see a UML diagram for some of your programs, go to http://www.objectaid.com/installation and follow the step-by-step installation directions to install ObjectAid into Eclipse. Once ObjectAid has been installed, you can generate a UML diagram for the 3Dshapes projects:

1. Open the 3Dshapes project.
2. Right-click on the jae.threedimensionshapes package and select New-> other from the context menu.
3. ObjectAid UML Diagram will appear in the list. Expand the item and select ObjectAid Class Diagram, and click Next.
4. In the Create a new UML Class Diagram, Figure 7.28, Give the UML Class Diagram a name, "3DShapesUML", and click Finish.

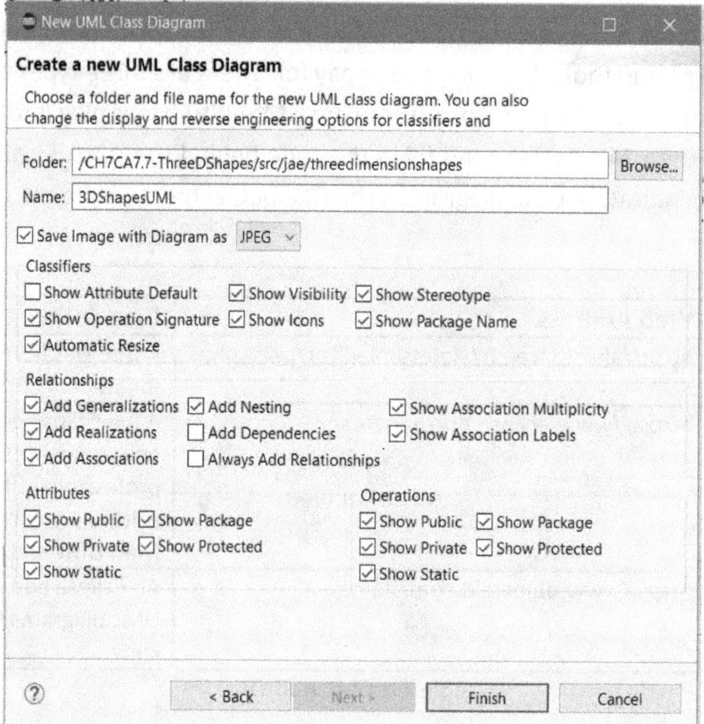

Figure 7.28 ObjectAid Create a new UML Class Diagram Dialog

5. A tab with the 3DShapesUML name and blank contents appears in the Eclipse editor window. Select all the .Java files under the package and drag them to the blank space. The class diagram will be generated, Figure 7.29.

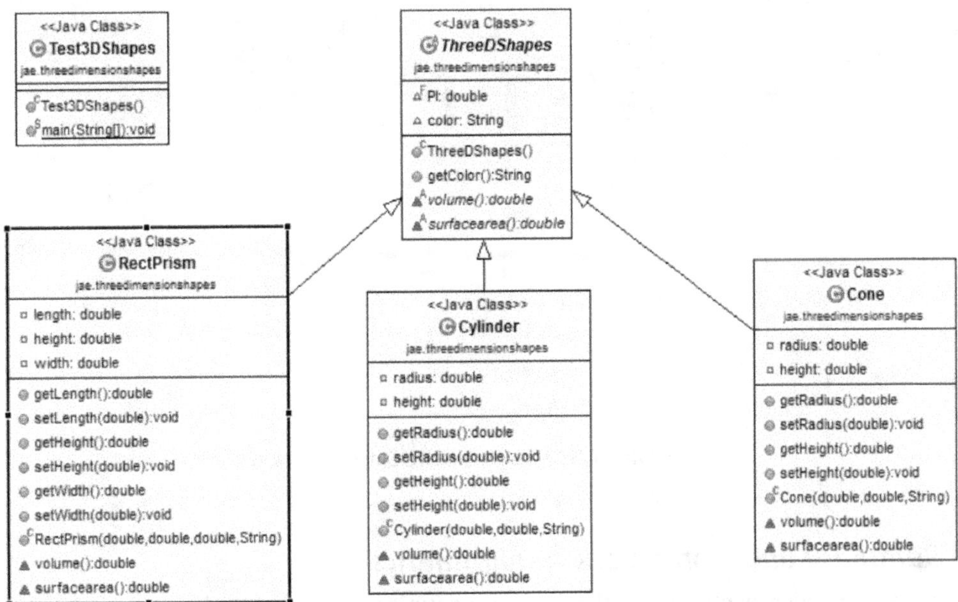

Figure 7.29 – ObjectAid UML Class Diagram

ObjectAid follows the generic UML implementation. The ThreeDShapes class name is in italics since it is an abstract class. The three shape classes are shown inheriting from the ThreeDShapes class. The details of the classes use the Eclipse symbols rather than the generic UML symbols. The Test3DShapes class is not associated with any of the other classes, and the main() method has an underline since it is static. If you double-click on any item in the boxes, the code for the class will appear and highlight the item you double- clicked on. Below is the same class diagram from Papyrus, Figure 7.30.

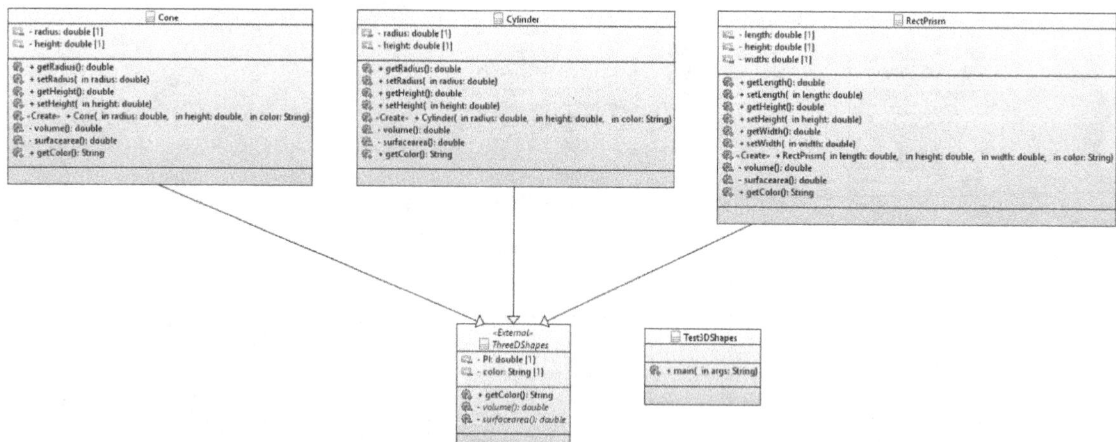

Figure 7.30 Papyrus UML Class Diagram

7.11 Summary and Homework Assignments

Inheritance and polymorphism are the keys to grouping our custom classes into a larger library, and also allowing you to share and re-use code for different purposes. If you go through the Java library, you can trace the relationships of the different classes to abstract classes and interface types. The Java Library is the DNA from which to build your programs. Because of OOP, we can add and expand the Java library with our own custom class implementations. In short, we are adding our own custom DNA, but unlike the movie *Jurassic Park*, hopefully, your programs will not grow up to attack and eat everyone.

With the ability to create our own classes and use inheritance and polymorphism to build up libraries, writing and testing programs are going to get a little more complicated. The Eclipse editor and debugger can guide us through program execution so we can identify the basic errors. There are always the runtime errors that can be tricky to track down. The next chapter covers best coding and error handling practices to help us write better code. Before we go on, here are some questions and programming projects on inheritance and polymorphism.

7.11.1 Questions

1. These last two chapters have covered the details of creating classes and custom libraries. What are the three tenets of object-oriented programming?

2. Building on Computer Activity 7.6, add the following to the TestInheritance main() method:

```
TestA myclass2 = new TestB();
myclass2.TestAOutput();
```

   a) Which TestAOuput() method will run? The method in the TestA class or the override method in TestB class? Why does it run that TestAOuput() method from that class?
   b) Why is there no option for myclass2.TestBOutput()?
   c) Is it possible to create myclass3 object as follows:

```
TestB myclass3 = new TestA();
```

3. What happens when you put the following code into the ThreeDShapes2 interface? Why?

```
public String getColor(){
    return color;
}
```

4. A Superclass has the following field declared.

```
private static double k = 4.3;
```

   How can the value of k be changed in the subclass?

   a. super.k = <new value>;

   b. The Superclass has the following mutator:

```
public static void setK(double k) {
    Calc1.k = k;
}
```

   c. The Superclass has the following mutator:

```
public static void setK(double k) {
    this.k = k;
}
```

d. None of the above, since it is a static field in a Superclass

5. An interface has the following field

```
static double pTest = 10.5;
```

How can the value of pTest be changed in the subclass?

a. `pTest = new value;`

b. Through a Superclass mutator:

```
public static void setpTest(double pTest) {
    this.pTest = pTest;
}
```

c. The value cannot be modified since all fields are final and static in an Interface.

6. Is the following possible? Why or Why not?

```
List<String> myStr = new List<String>();
```

7. A CarRental Class has the following superclass constructors:

```
public CarRental() {
    // TODO Auto-generated constructor stub
    this.Carclass = "Economy";
    this.price = 49.95;
    this.passagers = 4;
}

public CarRental(String Carclass, double price, int passangers)
{
    this.Carclass = Carclass;
    this.price = price;
    this.passagers = passangers;
}
```

The CarRentalCustomer class is a subclass of the CarRental superclass, and it has the following two fields

```
private String CustomerName;
private String CustomerNumber;
```

What is the constructor(s) for the CarRentalCustomer subclass that includes the customer name and customer number as parameters in the constructor call?

8. Given the following interface:

```
public interface StatFormulas {

    double function1(int AB, int hits);
    double function2(double innings, int runs);
    double function3(double innings, int errors);
    void StatResults();

}
```

What is wrong with the following class that implements the interface?

```
public class StatVarient1 implements StatFormulas {

    @Override
    public double function1(int AB, int hits) {
        // TODO Auto-generated method stub
        return hits/AB;
    }
    @Override
    public double function2(double innings, int runs) {
        // TODO Auto-generated method stub
        return runs/innings;
    }
    @Override
    public void StatResults() {
        // TODO Auto-generated method stub
        System.out.println("The batting average for 10 hits in 24 at
bats
        is " + this.function1(24, 10));
        System.out.println("The ERA for 5 runs on 30.3 innings is "
+
        this.function2(30.3, 5));
```

```
    }
}
```

9. What is wrong with the following:

```
public class DNAChem {

    public int Seq1 = 5;
    public int Seq2 = 10;
    public double Totalstig = 33.5;

    public double DNAChem3(int DNAdie, double RunTime)
    {
        double Process = DNAdie/Seq1 + RunTime;
        return Totalstig + Process;

    }

    abstract double DNAChem5(int DNAdie, double RunTime);

    public double DNAChem7(int DNAdie, double RunTime)
    {
        double Process = DNAdie/Seq2 + RunTime*2;
        return Totalstig + Process;

    }
}
```

10. The following method is declared in a superclass. How can it be called by the subclass?

```
public FinalPrice(double price) {

    System.out.println("The total price is "+ price);
}
```

11. Draw the UML class diagram for the classes in the Protected example in Section 7.3.3. Include all classes.

The following program is for the next two questions. The program consists of 4 classes with the last class having the main() method.

```java
package jae.superclass;

public class MYCLASS1 {

    public int a;
    private int b;
    public MYCLASS1(int a, int b) {
        super();
        this.a = a;
        this.b = b;
    }

    public int sumnumbers(){
        return a + b;
    }
}
```

```java
package jae.superclass;

public class MYCLASS2 extends MYCLASS1 {

    public int a;
    public int d;

    public MYCLASS2(int a, int b) {
        super(a, b);
        // TODO Auto-generated constructor stub
    }

    public MYCLASS2(int a, int b, int a2, int d) {
        super(a, b);
        this.a = a2;
        this.d = d;
    }

    public int multiple(){

        return d = a * super.sumnumbers();
    }
}
```

```java
package jae.superclass;

public class MYCLASS3 extends MYCLASS2 {

    public int e;
```

```
    public int f;

    public MYCLASS3(int a, int b) {
        super(a, b);
        // TODO Auto-generated constructor stub
    }

    public MYCLASS3(int a, int b, int a2, int c) {
        super(a, b, a2, c);
        // TODO Auto-generated constructor stub
    }

    public MYCLASS3(int a, int b, int a2, int c, int e, int f) {
        super(a, b, a2, c);
        this.e = e;
        this.f = f;
    }

    public int modulus(){

        e*= f;
        return e %= super.d;
    }
}
```

```
package jae.superclass;

public class TestClasses {

    public static void main(String[] args) {
        // TODO Auto-generated method stub

        MYCLASS2 MyClass2Instance = new MYCLASS2(2, 5, 8, 7);
        MYCLASS3 MyClass3Instance = new MYCLASS3(2, 8, 4, 10, 4, 2);

        System.out.println(MyClass2Instance.d);
        System.out.println(MyClass3Instance.modulus());
        System.out.println(MyClass3Instance.e);
        System.out.println(MyClass2Instance.multiple());
        System.out.println(MyClass2Instance.d);
        System.out.println(MyClass3Instance.sumnumbers());
    }
}
```

12. What is the output of the program?

13. If the second constructor for MYCLASS2 is changed to the following, what is the output? Why? What does this say about variable names and the 'this' operator?

```
public MYCLASS2(int a, int b, int a2, int d) {
    super(a, b);
    a = a2;
    this.d = d;
}
```

7.11.2 Programming Projects

1. Add a cylinder and a rectangular pyramid class to the 3DShapes project.

2. Expand the Egg Hunt game from Chapter 6 by adding a head-to-head game between two players. Create a player class that has the player name (String) and final turns score (int) as field variables. The program will first ask the name of each player. Each player will get his or her own game board and will take turns guessing the coordinates to find the egg. Each player must find the egg on his or her game board; and once both players have found the egg, the final number of turns for each player is reported. The player with the lowest turns wins.

3. Building on the expanded Egg Hunt game in the last exercise, track the total number of turns for three rounds of the game between two players. The total number of turns will be added up for the 3 rounds, and the player with the lowest number of turns wins.

4. Expand the coin flip game from chapter 6. Create a player class that has the player's name (String) and final turns score (int) as field variables. The program will ask for the player's name and track the score for each player. Two players flip the coin 5 times. The one that guesses the coin flip correctly the most number of times wins the game.

5. Expand the Yahtzee game to track the score for two players. The program will ask for the player's name. Each player will take turns rolling the dice and entering a score. The player with the highest score wins.

8 Software Development, Exception Handling, and Other Debug Techniques

"To err is human..."

-Alexander Pope from his poem *An Essay on Criticism, Part II*, 1711

The last two chapters discussed breaking programs down into smaller pieces and how to best organize the smaller pieces into a larger library of constructs. No matter how hard programmers try to simplify things, there is no escaping software bugs. User input errors, calculation errors, boundary errors, memory leaks, infinite loops, and just plain logic errors can slow development down. Hopefully using IDEs like Eclipse can cut down on the most common errors that were routinely being made before IDEs were available: syntax errors.

We could have drawn from a quote about humans making mistakes from a wide range of movies and TV shows. It doesn't matter the genre since a story without some human error is not much of story. The opening chapter quote is simple and to the point. The full line from the poem reads *'"To err is human, to forgive, divine'"*. Computers follow the direction provided. When there is a bug in a computer program, the computer can be unforgiving. Working in teams to develop large software programs requires processes and tools to make sure everything comes together. This chapter covers the techniques and approaches to software design and provides help to avoid programming errors.

8.1 Software Design Process and Regulations

Whether you are working by yourself or with a team, good software design practices lead to better code with fewer errors. Writing the code is only a part of the whole software design process. There are several steps to a project, and every company has a different approach. Here are the generic steps:

- Specification –The specification details what the program is supposed to do. The specification is written in plain language and may have some high-level descriptions of features and functions to be implemented. Everyone in the company including management, sales, marketing, quality assurance, and the software team have input in a specification. Depending on the project, the end customer might have input as well.

- Design/Outline – Once the specification has been approved, the next step is to do the high-level design. This entails developing flowcharts, UML diagrams, or even pseudo code. At this step, individual developers are assigned specific tasks.

Definition: *Pseudocode* – is a mix of readable language and code to help further define a specific software function.

- Implementation - Pseudocode can make for a nice transition to final code if implemented properly, but most developers prefer the visual tools and jumping to writing code, which brings us to this step which is writing the code. The objective is to take the design and turn it into code.

- Testing/Code Review – Bringing all the code pieces together and testing is the fourth step. Implementation and testing are ongoing processes. If testing finds errors, then fixes have to be implemented until the program is working correctly. Some companies do code reviews at this point to make sure that all standards are being met.

- Documentation – The final step is to document the design. If all the other steps have been completed, putting the final design documentation together should be a simple step.

Every company has some variation of the software development process, and there are outside regulatory compliances that must also be met. Up until the 1980's, software development processes were not well defined. The US government had several software projects with cost overruns. To help pick the best contractors to do software work, the US government created the Capability Maturity Model (CMM). The CMM is used to best describe the software processes and practices an organization has in place. Depending on the industry, there are other code and process standards to follow, such as FDA for medical devices and PCI compliance for point of sale systems. With software development processes and compliance standards for outside regulations, being a software developer is more than just writing code.

8.2 Code Standards – "Defensive Coding"

What these regulations want to see is an effective coding standard. Every organization and private contractor has a coding standard. The details of the coding standard can vary, but the goal is to create a standard that everyone will follow, so the code files can easily be debugged and changes tracked. The code of any software developer in the company or contracted by the company should be easily understood by any other software developer in or contracted by the company. The basic coding standards deal with formatting:

- File Header – Each code file has a commented header that lists the name of the file, date, author, and what the program is about. Any changes to the file are listed by date and what was changed.

- Method headers – The code might not be obvious to the reader so this commented section describes what the method performs.

- Code Blocks – The code standard will define proper indentations, brackets, proper method names, and other standard practices that are in effect.

Defensive coding was mentioned in other chapters as an approach to preventing errors. A good coding standard helps to implement good defensive coding practices. For example, it is perfectly fine to write an if-else statement as follows:

```
if (w == 0)
   System.out.println("w is zero");

else
    System.out.println("w is not zero");
```

The problem with the implementation is that if you want to enter more lines of code to either the "if" code block, the "else" code block, or both and you forget to add the brackets {} to the modified code block, the code will not work as intended. This:

```
if (w == 0)
   System.out.println("w is zero");

else
   System.out.println("w is not zero");
   System.out.println("this will only print if w is not zero");
```

Is not the same as this:

```
if (w == 0)
   System.out.println("w is zero");

else
{
    System.out.println("w is not zero");
    System.out.println("this will only print if w is not zero");
}
```

A good editor like the one in Eclipse may do some automated indentation, which will alert you to add the brackets, but a coding standard would require you to add the brackets automatically. The proper defensive code would look as follows:

```
if (w == 0)
{
    System.out.println("w is zero");
}
else
{
    System.out.println("w is not zero");
}
```

Even if there is only 1 line in each of the code blocks when originally written, bracketed code blocks are good defensive programming. This protects you against making mistakes if you modify the code in the future, and it also makes it more readable.

8.3 Eclipse Feature: Code Refactoring

Sometimes a code review will yield requests to make changes to the code without changing functionality. The reasons could vary, such as renaming a variable, breaking up a large method, breaking out some code to be put into a method for others to use, or compacting code to a single line. These code changes are known as Code Refactoring.

Definition: *Code Refactoring* - Restructures existing code without changing the behavior.

Most modern IDE's have some code refactoring operations. Eclipse has an extensive set of code refactoring operations under the Refactoring menu. The following computer activity demonstrates a couple of refactoring operations.

8.3.1 Computer Activity 8.1 - Rename a Variable and Inline Refactoring

In Eclipse, create a new Java project called "CH8CA8.1-RefactoringTests". Created a new package called "jae.refactortests". Now create a new Java class with a main() method under the package called "Refact1", and add the Code Listing 8.1:

```
package jae.refactortests;

public class Refact1 {

    public static void main(String[] args) {
        // TODO Auto-generated method stub
        double Savings = 1500.75;
        double interestRate = .002;

        Savings = AddInterest(Savings, interestRate);

        System.out.println("The new savings totals is " + Savings);
    }

    public static double AddInterest(double s, double i) {
        double newSavingsTotal = (double)Math.round((s + (s * i)) *
100) / 100;
        return newSavingsTotal;
    }
}
```

Code Listing 8.1 Refactoring Test

The variables "s" and "i" are okay, but not very descriptive for someone re-using the method. Let's rename each variable. Use the mouse to highlight one of the "s" variables and then go to the menu and select Refactor->Rename. A tag will appear asking you to enter the new name and hit Enter, Figure 8.1.

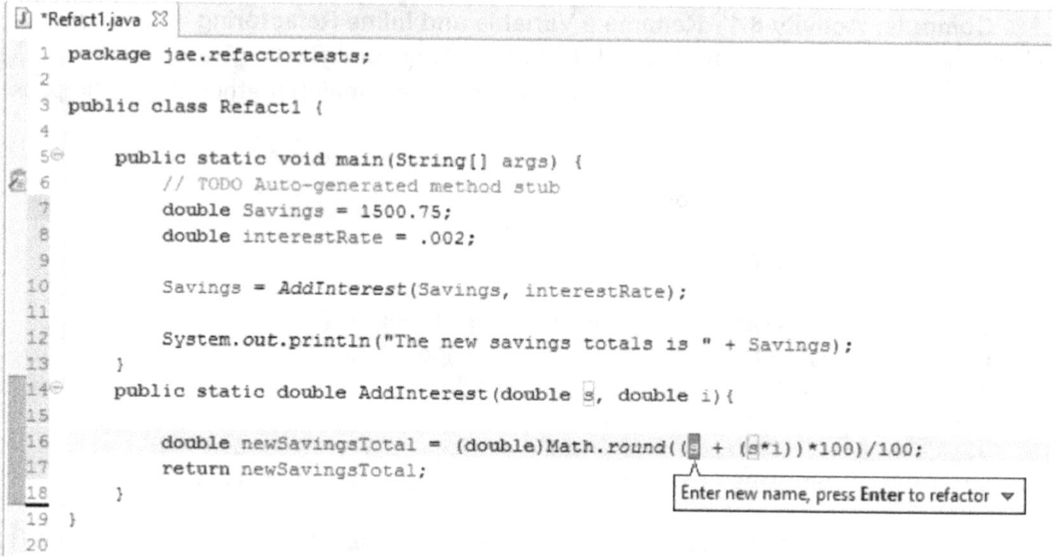

*Refact1.java

```
package jae.refactortests;

public class Refact1 {

    public static void main(String[] args) {
        // TODO Auto-generated method stub
        double Savings = 1500.75;
        double interestRate = .002;

        Savings = AddInterest(Savings, interestRate);

        System.out.println("The new savings totals is " + Savings);
    }
    public static double AddInterest(double s, double i){

        double newSavingsTotal = (double)Math.round((s + (s*i))*100)/100;
        return newSavingsTotal;
    }
}
```

Enter new name, press **Enter** to refactor

Figure 8.1 Using Refactoring to Change Variable Name

Make the name "savings" and hit Enter. When you do all the "s" variable references in the local method it will be changed to "savings". Repeat the same steps to change the name for the "i" variable to "interestrate". The code should look as follows.

```
public static double AddInterest(double savings, double interestrate) {
    double newSavingsTotal = (double)Math.round((savings + (savings *
interestrate)) * 100) / 100;
    return newSavingsTotal;
}
```

Even though there were a few instances of the variable letters, changing them individually is not a good practice. If there were many more instances of the variables in the local method, you might miss one, or misspell one or more of them. Refactoring the variables in this way is a good defensive coding technique. The next refactoring technique is to reduce the lines of code by doing an Inline refactoring. The AddInterest() method uses a temporary variable to store the new savings amount. The variable is not really needed. Use the cursor to highlight the "newSavingsTotal" variable and select Reactor->Inline... from the menu. A dialog appears, Figure 8.2, noting the occurrence of the variable.

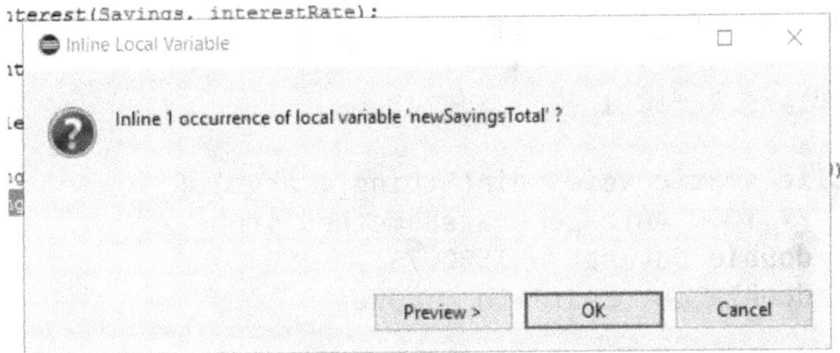

Figure 8.2 Inline Refactoring

Click the Ok button, and the code will be changed to the following:

```
 public static double AddInterest(double savings, double interestrate)
{
     return (double)Math.round((savings + (savings * interestrate)) *
100) / 100;
 }
```

If for some reason the method is not needed at all, the AddInterest method is only used once inside the class and never used outside of the class. For example, the method can be refactored using inline refactoring. Use the cursor to highlight the AddInterest method name and select Reactor->Inline... from the menu. A dialog appears, Figure 8.3, asking if you want to remove the method altogether. Keep the box checked and click Ok.

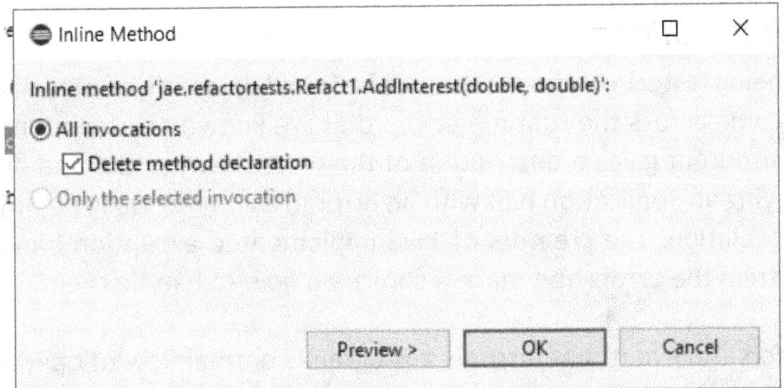

Figure 8.3 Inline Refactoring a Method

The declaration is removed, inline code is substituted for the method call, and the code now looks like Code Listing 8.2:

```
1. package jae.refactortests;
2.
3. public class Refact1 {
4.
5.      public static void main(String[] args) {
6.           // TODO Auto-generated method stub
7.           double Savings = 1500.75;
8.           double interestRate = .002;
9.
10.          Savings = (double)Math.round((Savings + (Savings *
   interestRate)) * 100) / 100;
11.
12.          System.out.println("The new savings totals is " + Savings);
13.     }
14. }
```

Code Listing 8.2 Refactored Code after Method In-lining

The use of inline refactoring also optimizes the code execution by removing the overhead of a call to and return from a method, especially when the method was only used once, in this example. You could have unchecked the box and kept the method declaration. Line 10 would still have changed to include the calculation, but the method declaration would still be available for other places in the program. Also note that when you invoke the refactoring operation, you also have the option to preview what the result would be. You can compare the current code with the refactored code, side-by-side, before actually modifying the code.

8.4 Exception Handling

As the program is being tested, runtime errors will be found. In our discussion about arrays, loops, and iteration, we came across the runtime errors that are known as exceptions. The application halts, and the error output gives a description of the error down to the line number where the error occurred. Having an application halt with an error in a commercially deployed application is not an acceptable solution. The creators of Java implemented exception handling; so you, the developer, can address the errors and make a choice on how to handle them.

Definition: *Exception* - An event that disrupts a program's normal flow of operation.

When an error occurs, the Java VM will throw an exception object. The "throwable" exception objects are in the Java library under the Java.lang.throwable, Figure 8.4.

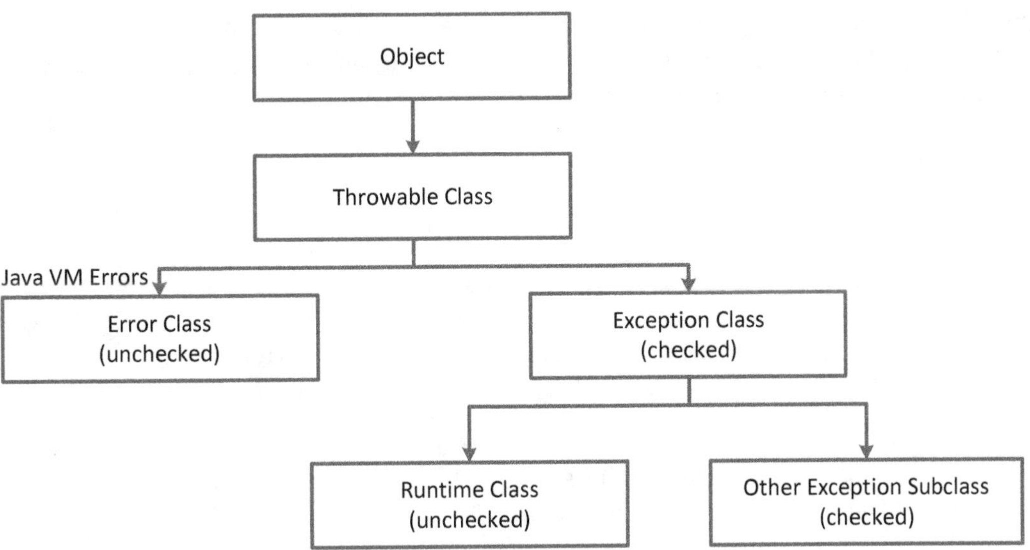

Figure 8.4 Throwable Exception Objects

Once the exception is thrown, the Java VM analyzes the call stack looking for a handler to address the exception. If none is found the program terminates, which we have already seen. Java uses the exception handler "Try-Catch-Finally" statement mechanism to provide the exception handler. A Try-Catch example was shown in Chapter 3 for reading user input. Let's take a closer look at a user input example.

8.4.1 An Example of the Exception Handler: Try-Catch-Finally

All the code standards and features in Eclipse that help you write a program cannot protect against the biggest of human error, the end user. Chapter 3 introduced the Scanner methods to allow users to provide input to the application. In Chapter 4, the Scanner methods were used in the Factorial and Menu System computer activities. Both of these applications ask the user to enter an integer. If the end user accidentally entered a letter, the program would crash with a runtime error, Figure 8.5.

```
Enter a value for n:
a
Exception in thread "main" java.util.InputMismatchException
	at java.util.Scanner.throwFor(Unknown Source)
	at java.util.Scanner.next(Unknown Source)
	at java.util.Scanner.nextInt(Unknown Source)
	at java.util.Scanner.nextInt(Unknown Source)
	at factorialloop.FactorialLoop.main(FactorialLoop.java:15)
```

Figure 8.5 Input Caused Runtime Error

Rather than having the program crash completely, the exception handling statement "try, catch, and finally" can be used to address the error, deal with it, and allow the program to continue execution. The statement structure is as follows:

```
try
{
    //Code block that could possibly throw an exception.
}
catch (exception type)
{
    //If the exception is triggered, this code block runs
}
finally
{
    //Code block always runs regardless of the exception or no
exception
}
```

The "try" code block attempts to execute the code contained in the block. If there is a failure, the "catch" block then executes to handle the exception. The optional "finally" block allows actions to be performed regardless if there is an exception or not. Code Listing 8.3 is a modified version of the factorial program with try-catch-finally added:

```
package factorialloop;

import java.util.Scanner;

public class FactorialLoop {

    public static void main(String[] args) {
        // TODO Auto-generated method stub

        //Ask the user for a value of n
        System.out.println("Enter a value for n:");

        int n = 0;
        Scanner sRead = new Scanner(System.in);
        try
        {
            n = sRead.nextInt();
        }
```

```
        catch (Exception e)
        {
            System.out.println("Error: Please enter a numeric value");
            sRead.close();
            System.exit(0);
        }
        finally
        {
            sRead.close();
        }

        //Set the initial factorial value
        double fact = 1;

        //Check for the condition of 1 and 0; if not true calculate the factorial
        if (!(n == 1 || n == 0))
        {
            for (int x = 1; x <= n ; x++)
            {
                fact *= x;
            }
        }
        System.out.println("The factorial for " + n + " is " + fact);
    }
}
```

Code Listing 8.3 Input Testing with Try/Catch/Finally

Since the "try" block creates a new code block, the initialization of "n" has to take place outside the try-statement. The try-statement checks the input for the read of an integer. If the value is not an integer, the code in the "catch" block will run, display an error statement, and exit the program. We want the program to exit so that it doesn't compute the factorial based on bad input. If the value is an integer, the catch code block is skipped, the "finally" block, which always runs, runs to close the input stream, and the code continues as before to calculate and display the factorial. In this case, the exception handler, try-catch-finally, provides a graceful method for handling the error and letting the user know that something failed.

8.4.2 Checked and Unchecked Exceptions

The generic "Exception" class type was used in the previous program, but there are various subclass types available. The classes are broken into two different groups: checked and unchecked (runtime) exceptions.

Definition: *Unchecked Exceptions* – These are exceptions that are not caught by the compiler and are the runtime exceptions you are familiar with already, see Table 8.1. The input scanner example in the last section is an example of an unchecked exception. The compiler doesn't see that an error is possible, and the program compiles without error.

Definition: *Checked Exceptions* – These exceptions are caught by the Java compiler and your code must address them with a try-catch statement, see Table 8.2. The table doesn't list all the Check Exceptions. For example, an error opening a file must be addressed with a try-catch statement or the compiler will throw an error.

The following tables list some of the Unchecked and Checked Exception types.

Unchecked Exception Type	Description
ArithmeticException	Arithmetic error, such as divide-by-zero.
ArrayIndexOutOfBoundsException	Array index is out-of-bounds.
ArrayStoreException	Assignment to an array element of an incompatible type.
ClassCastException	Invalid cast.
EnumConstantNotPresentException	An attempt is made to use an undefined enumeration value.
IllegalArgumentException	Illegal argument used to invoke a method.
IllegalMonitorStateException	Illegal monitor operation, such as waiting on an unlocked thread.
IllegalStateException	Environment or application is in an incorrect state.
IllegalThreadStateException	Requested operation not compatible with current thread state.
IndexOutOfBoundsException	Some type of index is out-of-bounds.
NegativeArraySizeException	Array created with a negative size.
NullPointerException	Invalid use of a null reference.
NumberFormatException	Invalid conversion of a string to a numeric format.
SecurityException	Attempt to violate security.
StringIndexOutOfBounds	Attempt to index outside the bounds of a string.
TypeNotPresentException	Type not found.
UnsupportedOperationException	An unsupported operation was encountered.

Table 8.1 Unchecked Exception Types

Checked Exception Type	Description
ClassNotFoundException	Class not found.
CloneNotSupportedException	Attempt to clone an object that does not implement the Cloneable interface.
IllegalAccessException	Access to a class is denied.
InstantiationException	Attempt to create an object of an abstract class or interface.
InterruptedException	One thread has been interrupted by another thread.
NoSuchFieldException	A requested field does not exist.
NoSuchMethodException	A requested method does not exist.
ReflectiveOperationException	Superclass of reflection-related exceptions.

Table 8.2 Checked Exception Types

In the last example, we could have been a little more specific with the "catch" statement if we include:

```
import java.util.InputMismatchException;
```

The catch statement could use: **catch** (InputMismatchException e) instead of **catch** (Exception e), and the modified factorial code would look like Code Listing 8.4.

```
package factorialloop;

import java.util.Scanner;
import java.util.InputMismatchException;

public class FactorialLoop {

    public static void main(String[] args) {
        // TODO Auto-generated method stub

        //Ask the user for a value of n
        System.out.println("Enter a value for n:");

        int n = 0;
        Scanner sRead = new Scanner(System.in);
        try
        {
            n = sRead.nextInt();
        }
        catch (InputMismatchException e)
        {
            System.out.println("Error: Please enter a numeric value");
            e.printStackTrace();
            sRead.close();
            System.exit(0);
        }
        finally
        {
            sRead.close();
        }

        //Set the initial factorial value
        double fact = 1;

        //Check for the condition of 1 and 0; if not true calculate the factorial
```

```
        if (!(n == 1 || n == 0))
        {
            for (int x = 1; x <= n ; x++)
            {
                fact *= x;
            }
        }
        System.out.println("The factorial for " + n + " is " + fact);
    }
}
```

Code Listing 8.4 Input Testing with Catch InputMismatchException Error

The ability to specify exception type means you can have multiple catches to address different exception types for a single try-statement.

```
try
{
    //Code block that could possibly throw an exception.
}
catch (exception type1 )
{
    //If the exception is triggered, this code block runs
}
catch (exception type2 )
{
    //If the exception is triggered, this code block runs
}
```

8.4.3 Exception Methods

The catch-statement defines the object "e" as Exception class object. There are a number of methods associated with the Exception object. For example, the PrintStackTrace() method prints out the standard stack trace that you have seen before:

```
catch (InputMismatchException e)
{
    System.out.println("Error: Please enter a numeric value");
    e.printStackTrace();
    sRead.close();
    System.exit(0);
}
```

```
java.util.InputMismatchException
	at java.util.Scanner.throwFor(Unknown Source)
	at java.util.Scanner.next(Unknown Source)
	at java.util.Scanner.nextInt(Unknown Source)
	at java.util.Scanner.nextInt(Unknown Source)
	at factorialloop.FactorialLoop.main(FactorialLoop.java:18)
```

The error output is still useful. Developers and companies that perform life cycle and regression testing log the information to separate files for later review. The information can be used to determine if additional error handling code to protect from the logged errors is required.

8.4.4 Computer Activity 8.2 - Throwing an Exception

An exception can be manually thrown if you know there is the possibility of an error. In this computer activity, we will create a division class and method that checks for a divide by zero scenario. Open Eclipse and create a new project called "CH8CA8.2-ThrowExample". Create a package called "jae.throwexample", and two class files called "TestThrow" that will have a main() method and "MathDivide". In the "MathDivide" class, add Code Listing 8.5:

```
package jae.throwexample;

public class MathDivide {

    public static double myDiv(double x, double y, int index)
    {

        try{
            if (y == 0){
                throw new ArithmeticException("index " + index + "
has a
zero");
            }
        }
        catch (ArithmeticException e){
            System.out.println("Divide by zero caught: "+
e.getLocalizedMessage());
        }
        return x/y;
    }
}
```

Code Listing 8.5 MathDivide Class

In the "TestThrow" class, add Code Listing 8.6:

```
package jae.throwexample;

public class TestThrow {

    public static void main(String[] args) {
        // TODO Auto-generated method stub

        double[] i = {2.5, 15.0,3.0,0.0,50.0,65.0};
        double j = 100.00;
        double[] z = new double[i.length] ;

        for (int k = 0; k < i.length; k++){

            z[k] = MathDivide.myDiv(j, i[k], k);
        }
        System.out.println(" ");
        System.out.println("The final array values: ");
        for (int y = 0 ; y < z.length; y++){
            System.out.println("Index " + y + " is " + z[y]);
        }
    }
}
```

Code Listing 8.6 TestThrow Class

The application sends a factor and an array of divisors to the myDiv() method. The myDiv() method has an event handler built in, checking to see if the divisor is zero. If the divisor is equal to zero, the throw-statement throws an ArithemeticException. The ArithemeticException creates a local message for the index location of the error in the array. The catch displays an error message and the local message. The "new" operator had to be used since the throw-statement throws an object and not a type; thus, we are throwing a new object. In this case, the program continues on and finishes the calculation. Here is the output when you run the program:

```
Divide by zero caught: index 3 has a zero

The final array values:
Index 0 is 40.0
Index 1 is 6.666666666666667
Index 2 is 33.333333333333336
Index 3 is Infinity
Index 4 is 2.0
Index 5 is 1.5384615384615385
```

A divide by zero error would have been caught regardless of the event handler in the code. For this example, the event handler provided some detailed information that can help track down the problem.

8.4.5 Computer Activity 8.3 - Forcing the Handling of a Possible Exception

If you don't want to directly handle a possible exception in your class, but you want to make sure the developer who is using your class will implement an exception handler, you can use the throws statement. In this computer activity, we will create the start of a menu-driven program and have a MainMenu() method that requires an exception handler implementation. Open Eclipse and create a new project called "CH8CA8.3-ThrowsExample". Create a package called "jae.throwsexample", and two class files called "TestThrows" that will have a main() method and "ThrowsDemo". In the "ThrowsDemo" class, add Code Listing 8.7:

```
package jae.throwsexample;

import java.util.Scanner;

public class ThrowsDemo {

    public static int mainMenu() throws Exception {

        int i = 0;
        System.out.println("Please select an item");
        System.out.println("1 New Record");
        System.out.println("2 Edit Record");
        System.out.println("3 Save Record");
        System.out.println("4 Delete Record");

        Scanner iRead = new Scanner(System.in);
        i  = iRead.nextInt();
        iRead.close();
        return i;
    }
}
```

Code Listing 8.7 ThrowsDemo

In the "TestThrows" class, add Code Listing 8.8:

```
package jae.throwsexample;

public class TestThrows {

    public static void main(String[] args) {
        // TODO Auto-generated method stub

        int MenuItem = 0;

        try{
            MenuItem = ThrowsDemo.mainMenu();
        }
        catch(Exception e)
        {
            System.out.println("Error: You need to enter an item number: " + e.toString());
        }
        System.out.println("The menu item select is " + MenuItem);
    }
}
```

Code Listing 8.8 TestThrows

The mainMenu() method declaration includes the throws-statement setting up an Exception. Since Exception is a checked exception, the main() method in the "TestThrows" class must implement an exception handler. If an exception handler is not implemented, the code line will be flagged, Figure 8.6.

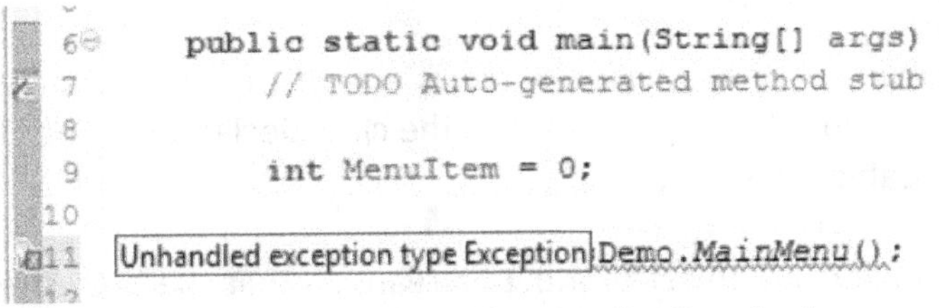

```
public static void main(String[] args) {
    // TODO Auto-generated method stub

    int MenuItem = 0;

Unhandled exception type Exception Demo.MainMenu();
```

Figure 8.6 Exception Handler Required

If we had chosen to use RuntimeException instead of Exception, there will be no warning that an exception handler is required, since RuntimeException is an unchecked exception. Also, there would be no need to add `throws RuntimeException` to the mainMenu() declaration. To satisfy the need for a checked exception handler, the main() method includes the exception handler and makes the call to the mainMenu() method within the try-statement. If a number is entered, the number value is returned; anything else pops an exception. There are many debates on whether to implement checked versus unchecked exceptions. Forcing a checked exception means that the developers have to have many event handlers in their code. Many developers choose the unchecked exceptions to provide flexibility for other developers.

8.4.6 Computer Activity 8.4 - Create Your Own Exception Subclass

The last computer activity has one glaring issue. There are only 4 menu times, but the user can enter any numeric value. One could force the developer to do a check or create a custom exception subclass that provides specific details, but with so many built-in exception classes, you have to ask yourself a few questions:

- Is there an exception type already available?
- Does a custom exception help to differentiate from other canned exceptions?
- Does the code throw more than one related exception?
- Do you want the package you are creating to be self-contained?

For our menu example, an exception class doesn't exist that addresses the menu item number error. A custom exception subclass would help. In this computer activity, we will build on the last activity to add a custom exception handler class for our menu system. Under the ThrowsExample project, create a new class called "MenuSelectionException" that inherits abstract methods from java.lang.Exception superclass. Add the following code:

```
package jae.throwsexample;

public class MenuSelectionException extends Exception {

}
```

Using the word "Exception" in the subclass name is a best practice to show that this is an exception class. A warning indicator appears next to the class declaration. The Throwable class is part of the java.io.Serializable class.

Definition: *Serialize* – Convert an object to a byte stream so that the byte stream can be later turned back into an object or deserialized.

The ID is needed as a check to make sure that the correct object was deserialized. Move the mouse over the class declaration and you will get options on how to add the ID, Figure 8.7.

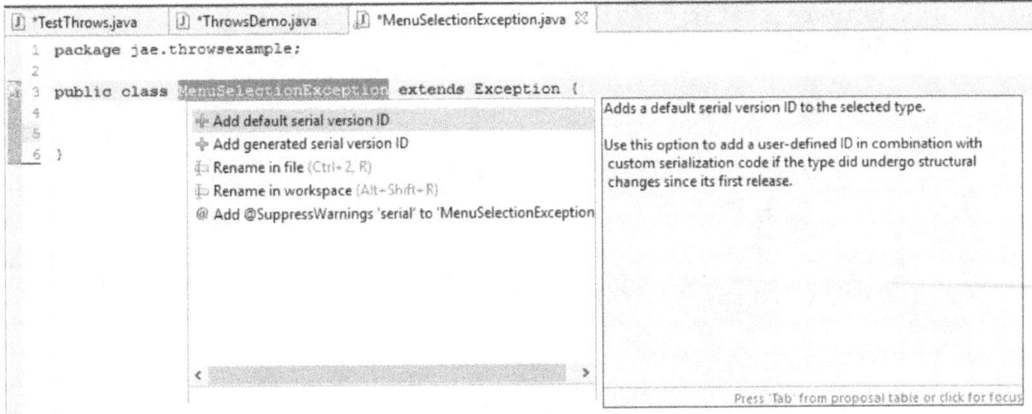

Figure 8.7 Serialization ID Generation in Eclipse

Select "add generated serial version ID" and click OK in the dialog. The ID will be added to the code, Code Listing 8.9.

```
package jae.throwsexample;

public class MenuSelectionException extends Exception {

    /**
     *
     */
    private static final long serialVersionUID = 3118046998686962000L;

}
```

Code Listing 8.9 Serialization Generated by Eclipse

Since the custom exception inherits from the Exception class, which inherits from the Throwable class, all of the methods in the upper class are available to the new MenuSelectionException class. There is nothing more that is required to be added to the custom exception, but it is good practice to have the event handler provide some useful information to the developer or user when an exception is thrown. Therefore, add a constructor method and override the toString() method. The resulting code is shown in Code Listing 8.10.

```
package jae.throwsexample;

public class MenuSelectionException extends Exception {

    /**
     *
     */
```

```
    private static final long serialVersionUID = 3118046998686962000L;

    int menuitem;

    MenuSelectionException(int mi){
        menuitem = mi;
    }

    public String toString(){
        return "Invalid Menu Selection " + menuitem;
    }
}
```

Code Listing 8.10 Custom Exception Handler with Enhanced Feedback

In the MainMenu() method, insert the following code at line 19 before the return call:

```
if(i < 1 || i > 4){
    throw new MenuSelectionException(i);
}
```

The full ThrowsDemo code becomes Code Listing 8.11.

```
1. package jae.throwsexample;
2.
3. import java.util.Scanner;
4.
5. public class ThrowsDemo {
6.
7.     public static int mainMenu() throws Exception {
8.
9.         int i = 0;
10.        System.out.println("Please select an item");
11.        System.out.println("1 New Record");
12.        System.out.println("2 Edit Record");
13.        System.out.println("3 Save Record");
14.        System.out.println("4 Delete Record");
15.
16.        Scanner iRead = new Scanner(System.in);
17.        i  = iRead.nextInt();
18.        iRead.close();
```

```
        if(i < 1 || i > 4){
            throw new MenuSelectionException(i);
        }
        return i;
    }
}
```

Code Listing 8.11 ThrowsDemo with Custom Exception

Run the program and enter a menu item. Try entering letters and other numeric values that are not 1 through 4. You should catch the exception when you enter anything other than the 1 through 4.

```
Please select an item
1 New Record
2 Edit Record
3 Save Record
4 Delete Record
0
Error: You need to enter an item number: Invalid Menu Selection 0
The menu item select is 0
```

8.4.7 The Final Piece to Creating Class Libraries

The event handler and the ability to create custom event handlers are the last pieces to creating the class library. When designing your classes, you should address how others will use the classes and defend against possible errors ahead of time.

8.5 Assertions

An old debug technique often used during software testing is to simply print out location and key data information at certain points in the code. In Java, this can be done with calls to call System.out.println. Another technique is to use the assert keyword. An assert evaluates a condition. If true, the code continues. If false, the code throws an AssertionError object. There are two syntax implementations:

```
assert condition;
```

```
assert condition: expr;
```

The latter can pass an expression, expr, which is a value or string to the AssertionError constructor. The expression is converted to a string to be displayed when the assertion fails. You would only want asserts to be active in test code and to remove them from final production code. The nice thing about asserts is that they are designed to be conditionally active. The default compile condition for asserts is for asserts to be off. If you place an assert in your code, run it, and the assert condition fails, no AssertionError object will be thrown. You must turn asserts on for them to be actively compiled into the executable object. This is done by going to the Eclipse menu and selecting Run->Run Configuration. Then in the Run Configurations dialog click on the Arguments tab. In the VM arguments box type in "-ea", which is the switch for the Java Virtual Machine to turn on asserts, Figure 8.8. Then either select Apply or Run, and the asserts will now be active until you remove the "-ea" switch from the Run Configurations.

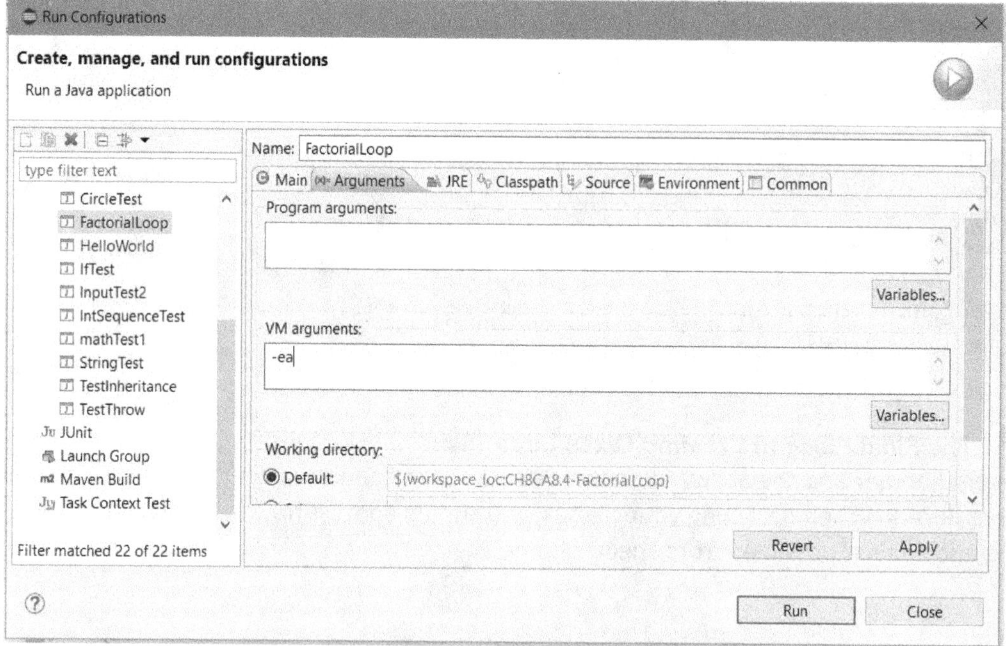

Figure 8.8 Enabling Asserts in the Eclipse Run Configuration

The nice thing about the assert architecture is that when you have completely tested and debugged your code, you don't have to chase down all the assert statements in all the code modules and delete them from the production version. You only need to turn asserts off, which is the default configuration.

8.6 Eclipse Feature: VisualVM Add-on

Code reviews and software testing can reveal problems with the code. For the most part, the Eclipse IDE and debugger can help to resolve most issues; but sometimes finding the source of a problem requires a developer to dig a little deeper. The VisualVM tool provides a visual representation of the Java VM and monitoring of the application running in real time.

- Provides a summary of the Java VM version being used, libraries/JAR files imported, process ID of the application, and other system information.
- Real-time monitoring of CPU and memory usage.
- Monitoring of actively running threads.
- Monitoring of memory allocation to find memory leaks.
- Application profiling.
- Garbage collector monitoring.

The VisualVM tool has plug-ins available, so it can be expanded to add more features. For this computer activity, VisualVM will be set up and tested with the Factorial program.

8.6.1 Computer Activity 8.5 - VisualVM and FactorialLoop

VisualVM is located on Github (https://visualvm.github.io). There are two downloads: VisualVM application and the Eclipse plug-in. Download both plug-ins and unzip the contents.

Eclipse Plug-in - https://visualvm.github.io/idesupport.html
VisualVM - https://visualvm.github.io/download.html

First, install the Eclipse plug in.

1. Open Eclipse and select Help->Install New Software... from the menu.
2. The Install dialog appears, click the add button.
3. The Add Repository dialog appears, Figure 8.9, click the local button and open the root of the Eclipse Plugin folder.

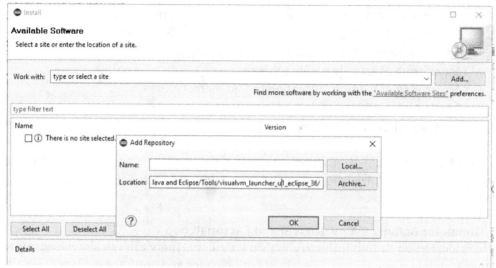

Figure 8.9 Install VisualVM Eclipse Plugin

4. Expand the branches and check the box next to "VisualVM Launcher Feature", Figure 8.10.

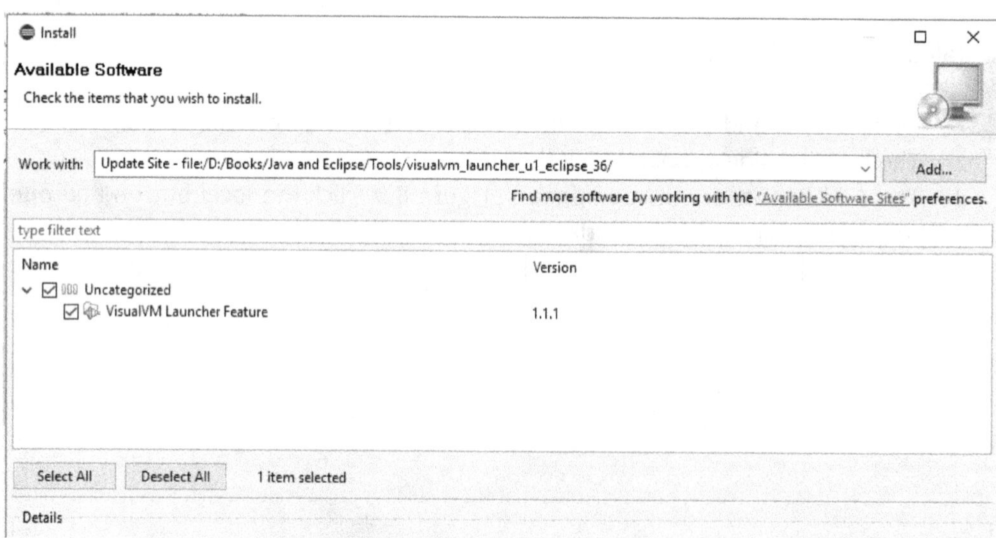

Figure 8.10 Selecting VisualVM Launcher Feature

5. Click Next, read and accept the license agreement; click Next, and then click Finish to start the installation. The installation will take some time. Once completed, Eclipse will restart.

The next step is to point to the VisualVM software.

1. Open Eclipse, if it is not already open.
2. From the menu, select Window-Preferences.
3. Expand the tree on the left, under Run/Debug->Launching.
4. Click on VisualVM Configuration.
5. Set the VisualVM Executable to point to the VisualVM.exe application you downloaded and unzipped, Figure 8.11.
6. Set the JDK location to the root path of the JDK, Figure 8.11.

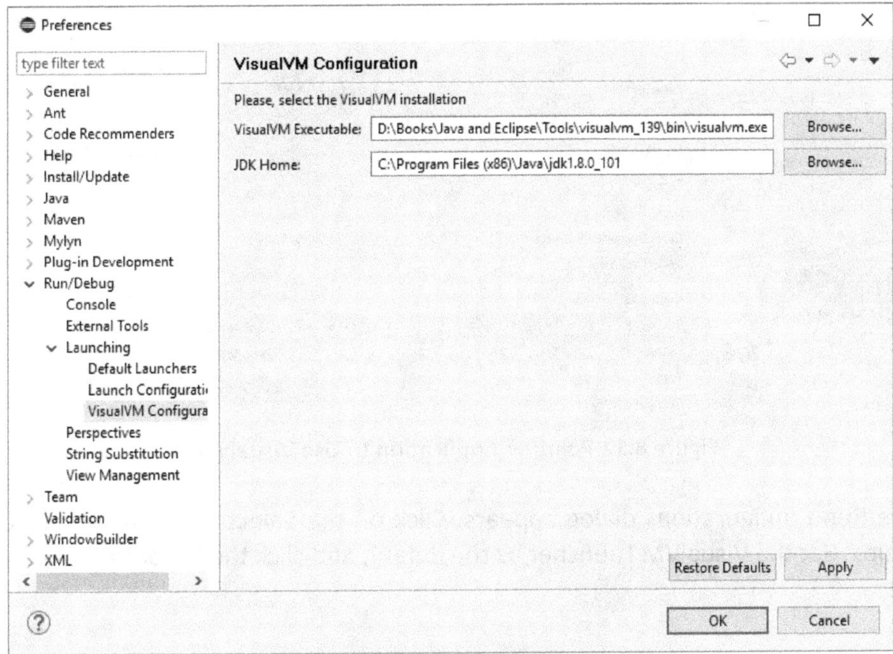

Figure 8.11 Point to VisualVM Software

7. Click the OK button to accept changes.

The final step is to point the application to use the VisualVM with a specific argument.

1. Open the FactorialLoop application created in Chapter 4.
2. In Package Explorer, right-click on the title of the application.
3. From the context menu, select Run As->Run Configurations..., Figure 8.12.

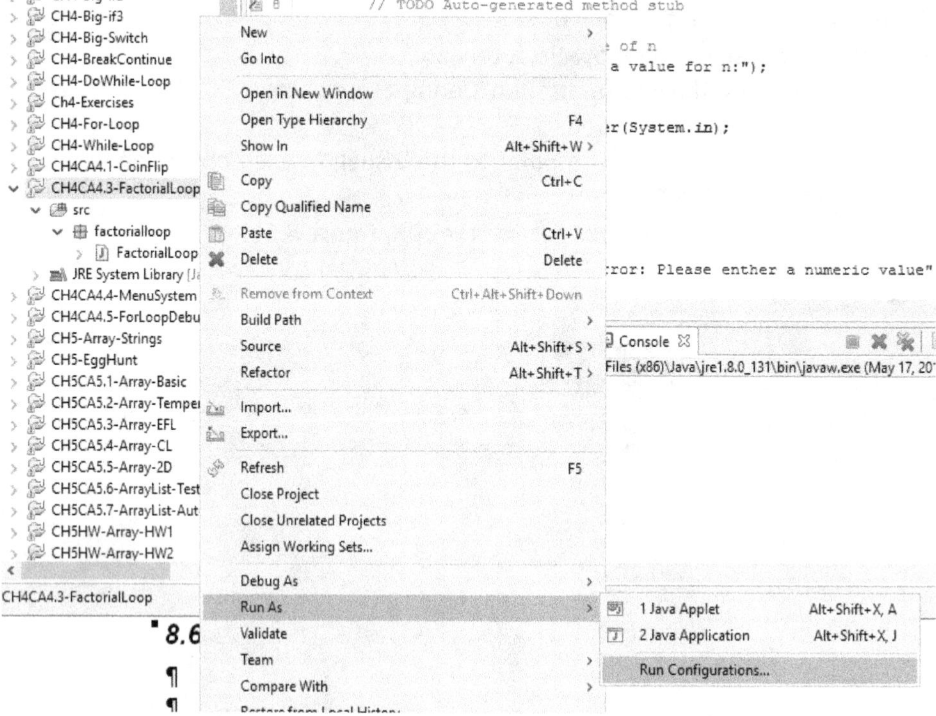

Figure 8.12 Pointing Application to Use VisualVM

4. The Run Configurations dialog appears. Click on the Select other at the bottom of the dialog. Set the VisualVM Launcher as the default and click the OK button, Figure 8.13.

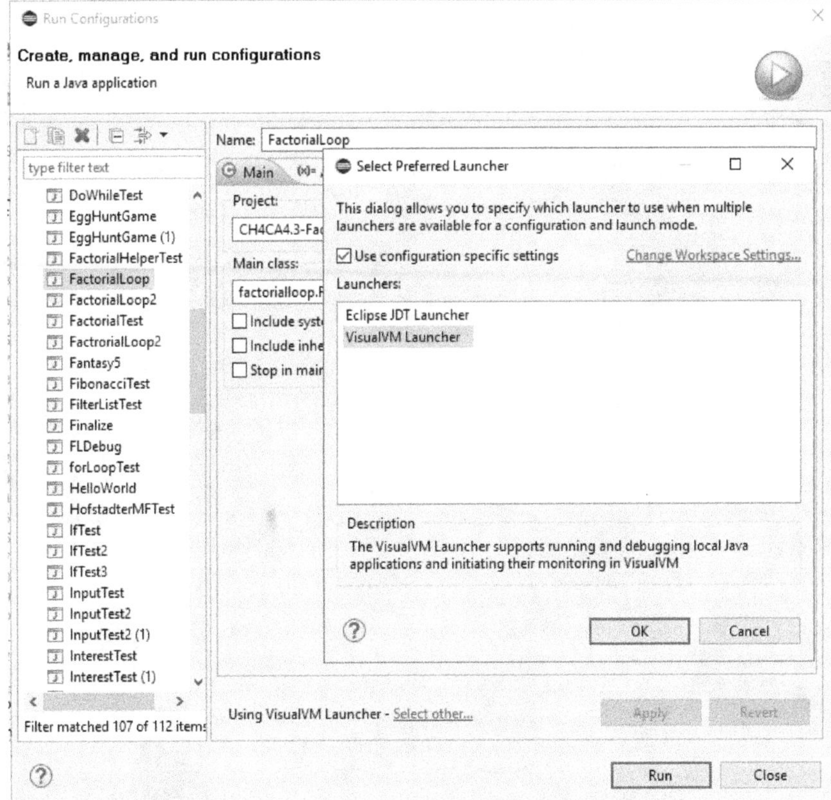

Figure 8.13 Select VisualVM Launcher for the Application

5. Click on the Arguments tab and add the following argument "-Xverify:none" under VM Arguments, Figure 8.14. Click Apply button and then click the Close button.

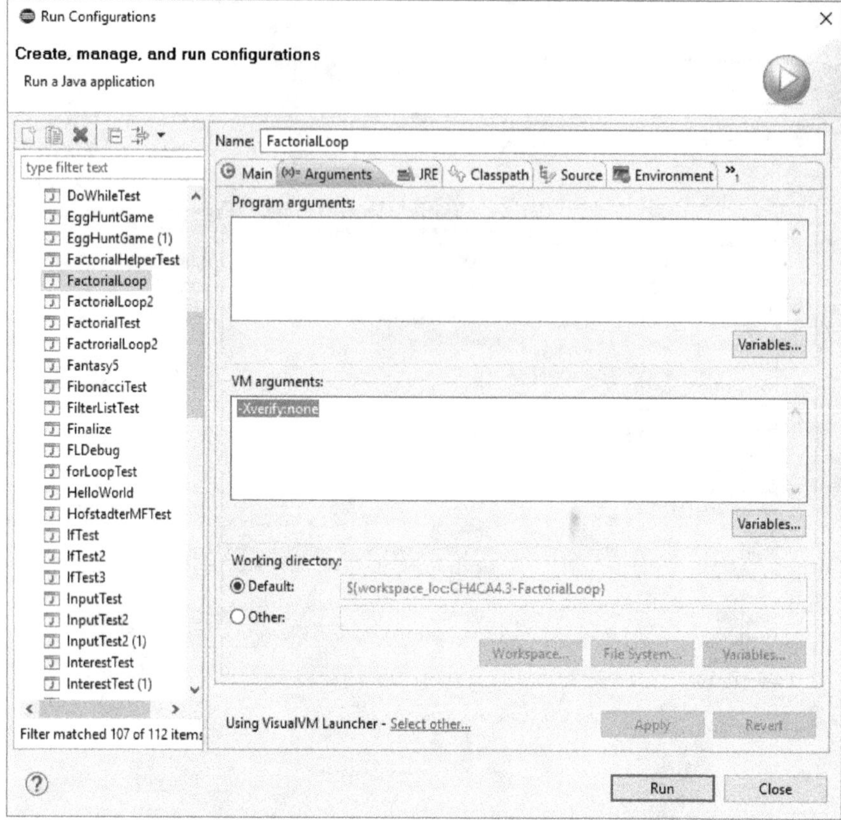

Figure 8.14 Set VisualVM Launcher VM Argument

6. In the FactorialLoop.java file, put a breakpoint at the user input line (`n = sRead.nextInt();`).
7. Run the debugger, VisualVM will start, Figure 8.15, and the debugger will stop at the breakpoint.

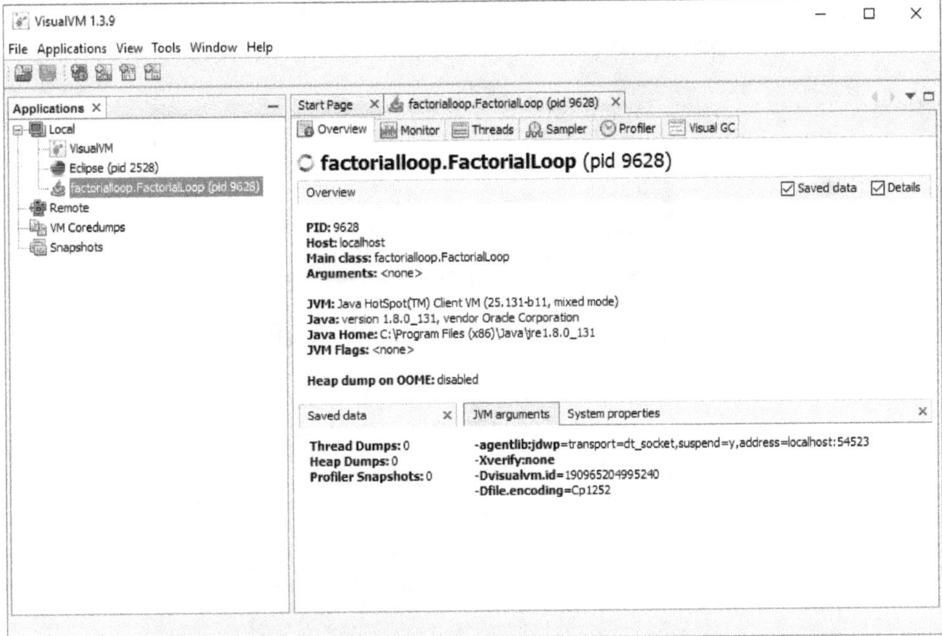

Figure 8.15 VisualVM Launches in Debug Mode

The running application along with the assigned ID is listed on the left. VisualVM offers different tabs to monitor running CPU and memory usage, all the running threads, and profile the application, Figure 8.16.

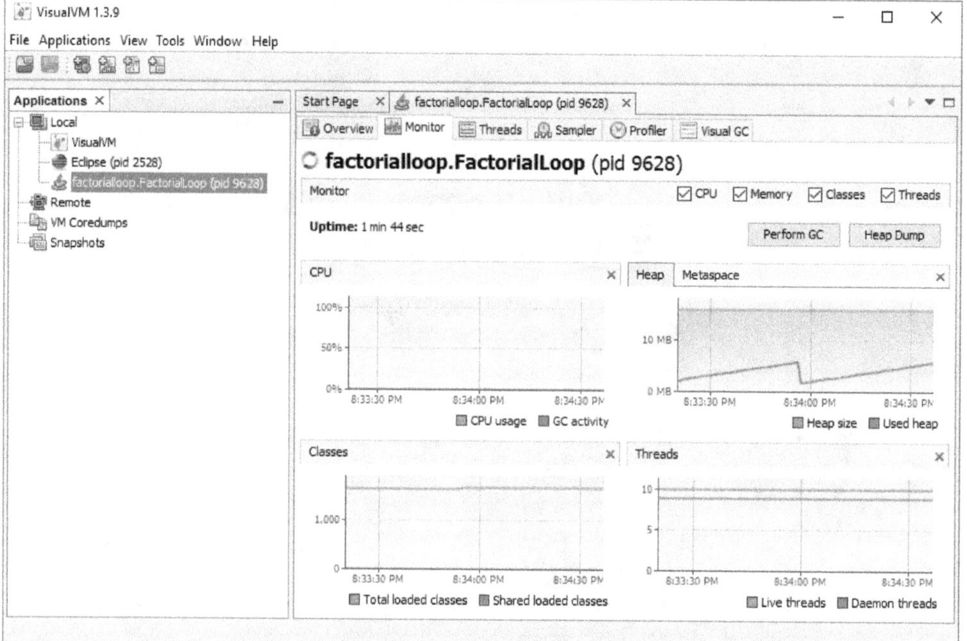

Figure 8.16 VisualVM Tabs

8. Click on the Profiler tab and then click the CPU button to start the profile, Figure 8.17. In Eclipse, enter a value for n and hit Enter. Then click on the Run button to continue the debugging.

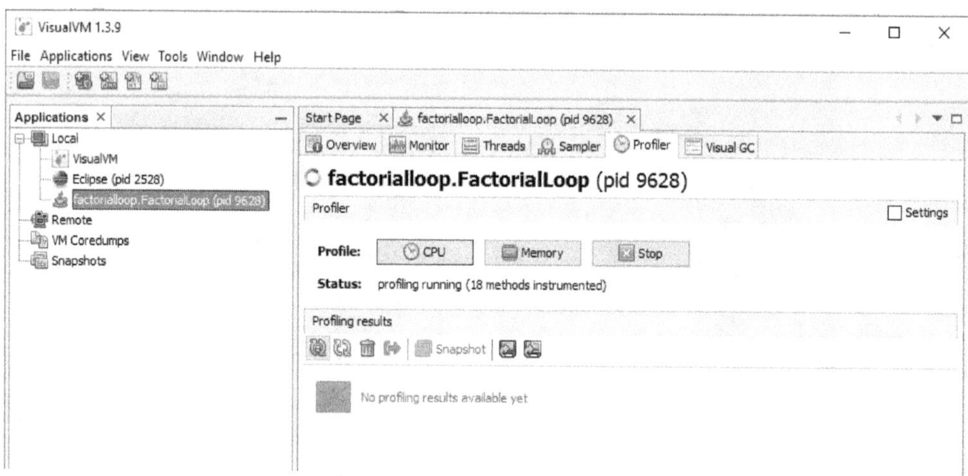

Figure 8.17 VisualVM Profiler

9. The application will terminate and VisualVM will ask you to save the snapshot. Click OK to save the snapshot, Figure 8.18.

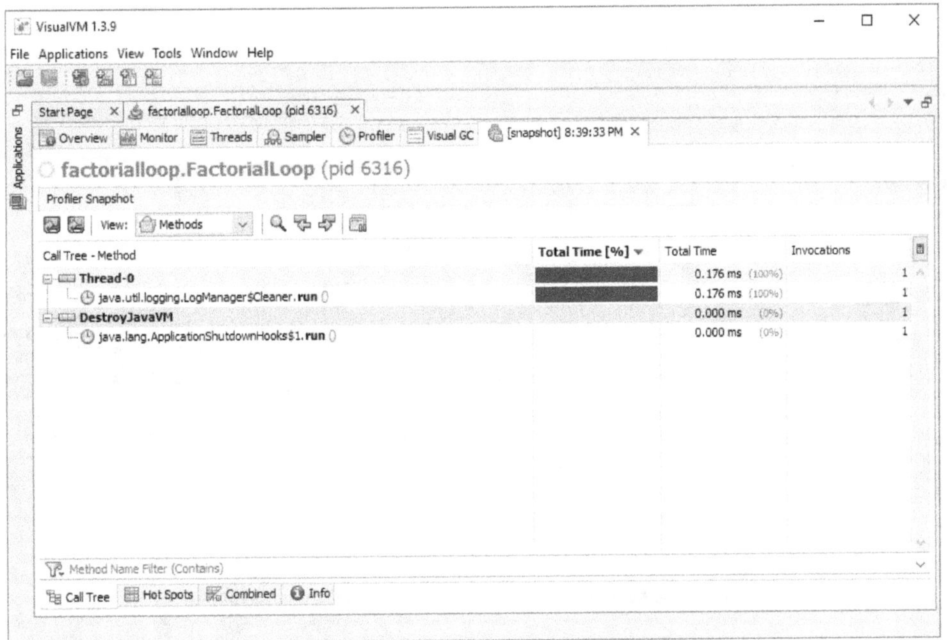

Figure 8.18 VisualVM Profiler Snapshot

The profiler snapshot provides CPU runtime information. Profilers are nice tools, but they should be used as guides since they can impact code performance. The Factorial is a simple application so there is not much here to see, but we will revisit the profiler capability in a later chapter. You can also add plugins to see more features.

10. From the VisualVM menu, select Tools->Plugins.
11. Click on the Available Plugins tab.
12. Select the VisualGC plugin on the left side, Figure 8.19.

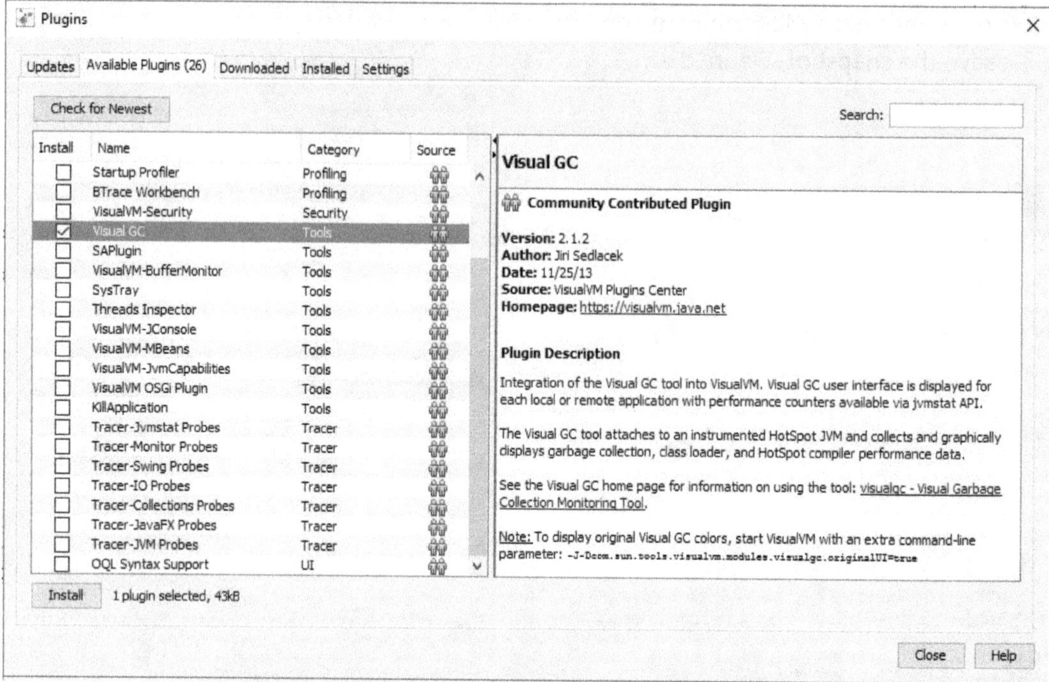

Figure 8.19 Selecting the Visual GC Plugin for VisualVM

13. Click the Install button and follow the rest of the dialogs to install the plugin.
14. A new Visual GC tab will appear, Figure 8.20. Visual GC is for advanced developers working on applications that are sensitive to system timing issues. The applications in this book are simple enough to not need to go to this level, but as your programs become more sophisticated, garbage collection impact on runtime often becomes an important issue.

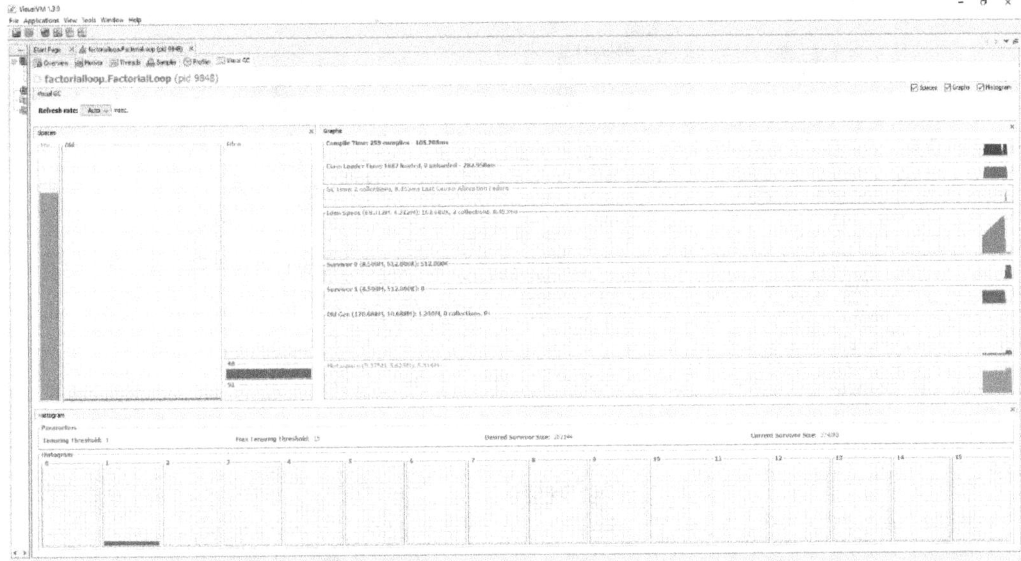

Figure 8.20 Visual GC Tab is Added to VisualVM

Note: Once the VisualVM plugin is installed, each application that runs will ask which debugger launcher you want to start, Figure 8.21.

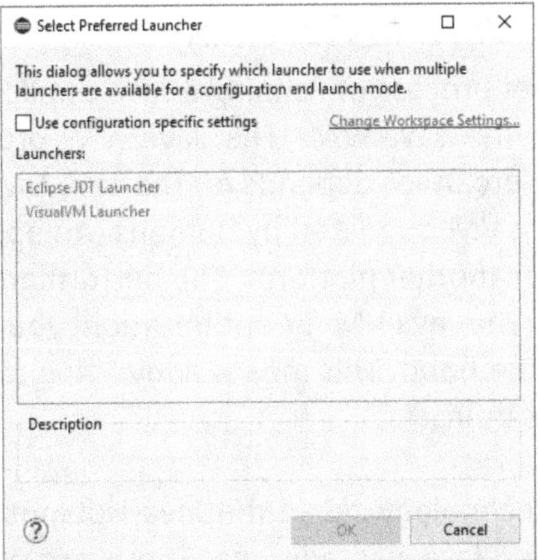

Figure 8.21 Debugger Launcher Selection

You can set up the default launcher for the workspace, by click on the "Change Workspace Settings...", and then setting the preferences, Figure 8.22. Individual applications can be set up using the Run As steps above.

Figure 8.22 Launcher Preferences

8.7 The Very Deep End: Java-to-Assembly

Chapter 2 covered the high-level process of running a Java application. The main component to running a Java application is the Java VM. The Java VM provides memory management, optimization, JIT, class loaders, etc. A lot depends on the Java VM to run the Java program. It is important to know that the Java VM is created by humans. An application that runs well on one platform might not work well on another platform. The performance can depend on the Java VM port. Rather than depending on the Java VM for optimization, you may have to dig a little deeper to see what is going on under the hood. This means converting Java code to assembly language to see what the Java compiler is doing.

Internally, the Java VM has a technology called the Java Hotspot Performance Engine, which is available on desktop and server Java VM editions. There are a number of Hotspot compiler options that print out compiler operations, optimization, and assembly: -XX:+PrintCompilation, -XX:+PrintInlining, and -XX:+PrintAssembly. It takes some deep understanding to grasp the output so that you can better optimize the code. Making optimization changes to the code leads back the different code refactoring features we discussed earlier. We only introduce the Java-to-Assembly concept as something to keep in mind as you become more proficient in complex Java programming and increase your understanding of the CPU hardware that your software runs on.

Any practical example is beyond the scope of this book; but as you continue to learn more as a developer, optional techniques like this can be very helpful.

8.8 *Summary and Homework Assignments*

Making errors is not only human but part of software development. A company or personal coding standard, good defensive development practices, and a repeatable design process can go a long way towards preventing many errors from happening. If errors do happen, there are tools and techniques to help determine the cause of an error so a resolution can be implemented. Errors in the code are not the only issue since users interact with the programs. To help gracefully address possible runtime errors, exception handling is the last piece for architecting class libraries. The next chapter covers another computer science technique before putting it all together to analyze algorithms. Before we go further, here are some questions and programming projects:

8.8.1 Questions

1. What are the 5 CMM levels?

2. Different companies can have different software processes in place. For different companies to work on the same contract, what has replaced the CMM model?

3. Should custom exception subclass be made public or private in a class library?

4. Given the following program:

```java
package jae.ch8hw1;

public class SomeProgram {

    public static void main(String[] args) {
        // TODO Auto-generated method stub

        int x = 2;
        int y = 3;
        int k = foobar(x,y);
        System.out.println("The final result is " + k);
    }

```

```
14.     public static int foobar(int i, int j){
15.
16.         int p = i;
17.         j *= Math.pow(j, i);
18.         p+= (j * 9);
19.         return p;
20.     }
21. }
```

a. What would lines 8 through 11 look like if "k" was inline refactored?
b. Is it possible to inline "p" reducing lines 16-18 to one line? If not, what would inline refactoring p look like?
c. Is it possible to inline refactor "j"?

5. What is wrong with the code fragment?

```
.
.
.
try{
    ch = chInput();
}
System.out.println("You pressed " + ch);
.
.
.
```

6. What is wrong with the following program, and what needs to be fixed?

```
package jae.ch8hw3;

import java.io.*;
import java.util.Scanner;

public class FooBar5 {

    public static void main(String[] args) {
        // TODO Auto-generated method stub

        System.out.println("Enter a number");
        try{
            int k = SelectionInput();
        }
```

```
        catch(IOException ex){
            System.out.println("Not a number");
        }
        System.out.println("Your number is " + k);
    }

    public static int SelectionInput() throw IOException{

        Scanner sRead = new Scanner(System.in);
        int n = sRead.nextInt();
        sRead.close();
        return n;
    }
}
```

7. What error is thrown by the following code fragment? Write the event handler to catch the error.

```
package jae.ch8hw4;

public class FooBar4 {

    public static void main(String[] args) {
        // TODO Auto-generated method stub

        int[] k = {5,9,2,5,3,7,8,9,1,0,8};

        for (int i = 1; i < k.length-1; i++){
            k[(++i)*2] -= (k[i]+i);
            System.out.println("k["+i+"] is " + k[i]);
        }
    }
}
```

8. What would the following code look like when if you chose to refactor the code to extract a method called avgScoreCalc() out of lines 10 through 14?

```
1. package jae.ch8hw5;
2.
3. public class AverageScores {
4.
5.     public static void main(String[] args) {
6.
7.         int sum =0;
```

```
        double avg = 0;
        double[] scores = {1,6,7,8,3,2,7,8,9,10,6,4,3,2,7};
        for(int counter = 0; counter < scores.length; counter++)
        {
            sum += scores[counter];
        }
        avg = (double)sum/(double)scores.length;
        System.out.println("The average is " + avg);
    }
}
```

8.8.2 Programming Projects

1. Add an exception handler to the BasicMath library created in Chapter 6 to address divide-by-0 for Divide() and Modulus() methods.

2. Modify the CoinFlip2 game from Chapter 6 by adding a custom exception class that catches any input values that are not “h”, “t”, “y”, or “n”. Allow the user try again if there is an error.

3. Modify the Address program created in Chapter 6 by adding a try-catch to catch non-numeric input values.

4. Modify the Egg Hunt game from Chapters 6 (or the modified versions in Chapter 7) by adding an event handler to catch non-numeric input values and custom exception class values that are greater than 4.

9 Recursion

"Dream Within a Dream"
– Song title from the movie: *Inception,* Warner Bros. 2010

In the movie *Inception*, the characters use a device to share a dream state with one another. To get out of the dream state, a kick such as falling, water contact, or possible physical harm wakes the dreamer out of the dream state. The device also allows the characters to create a dream within another dream, thus two kicks are needed to wake up from two dream levels. If they continue to enter more dreams without a kick, they could end up in limbo. The movie *Inception* parallels a programming concept in computer science called Recursion.

Definition: *Recursion* is a method to solve a problem using smaller instances of the same problem, or more simply have a method call itself.

In the spirit of the movie, recursion is a method calling a method, and to return from a method the kick is called the base case or termination condition. The best way to see recursion in action is to look at a simple exercise.

9.1 Computer Activity 9.1 - Factorial Recursion Style

Back in Chapter 4, we covered the Factorial. A factorial is a positive integer n, denoted by "n!", that is a product of all positive integers less than or equal to n. For example, 4! would be 24 = 4 * 3 * 2 * 1. The factorial function is defined as:

$$n! = \prod_{k=1}^{n} k$$

Another way to present the equation n! = n * (n-1)!, thus 5! = 5 * 4!, 4! = 4 * 3!, etc. Of course 0! = 1. In Chapter 4 we use an If-condition and a For-loop to find a factorial. Recursion is also an iterative loop that has a method that calls itself. We will discuss loops versus recursion a little later. Let's see what the solution looks like using recursion. In Eclipse, create a new Java project called "CH9CA9.1-FactorialRecursion" and a new class called FactorialTest. Call the package jae.intsequences. Modify and fill in Code Listing 9.1 in the FactorialTest.java file:

```
1. package jae.intsequences;
2.
3. import java.util.Scanner;
4.
5. public class FactorialTest {
6.
7.     public static void main(String[] args) {
8.         // TODO Auto-generated method stub
9.         Scanner userInput = new Scanner(System.in);
10.        System.out.println("Enter n:");
11.        int n = userInput.nextInt();
12.        System.out.println(n + "! is " + fact(n));
13.        userInput.close();
14.    }
15.
16.
17.    public static int fact(int n){
18.        if (n == 1 || n == 0) //Base case 1
19.            return 1;
20.        else
21.            return n * fact(n - 1); //Method calls itself
22.    }
23.}
```

Code Listing 9.1 FactorialTest

The main() function allows the user to enter a number for n, and then print the result of the recursive call to fact() in Line 12. Within the fact() method, we first check for the base case (again in the spirit of the movie this would be the kick), which is 1! or 0!. If n is > 1, then in Line 21, fact() is called again. fact() will continuously be called until n == 1, which is the base case. Run the application and enter 5 in the console, and you should see that 120 is the answer, Figure 9.1.

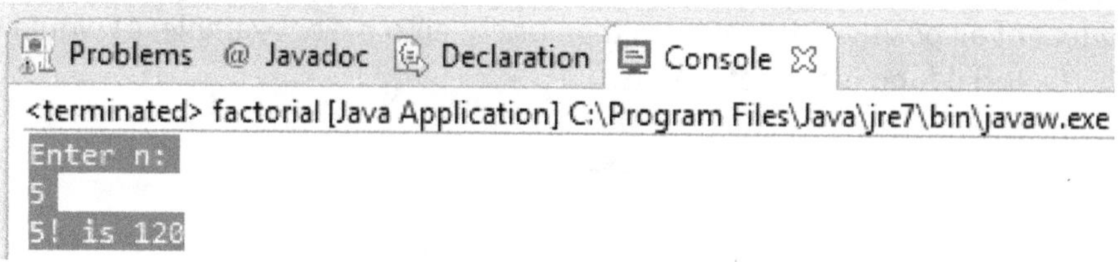

Figure 9.1 - Factorial Output

What happens if there is no base case or the wrong termination condition is entered? Comment out lines 18, 19, and 20. Run the program again and enter 5 for the factorial. The result will be is a stack overflow error, as shown in Figure 9.2. Every time the method calls itself, the calling method is placed on the stack. When there is no base case, there is no return and the program continues until it runs out of memory for the application and terminates with an error. This type of programming error is known as Infinite Recursion. In the movie, it would be going into limbo.

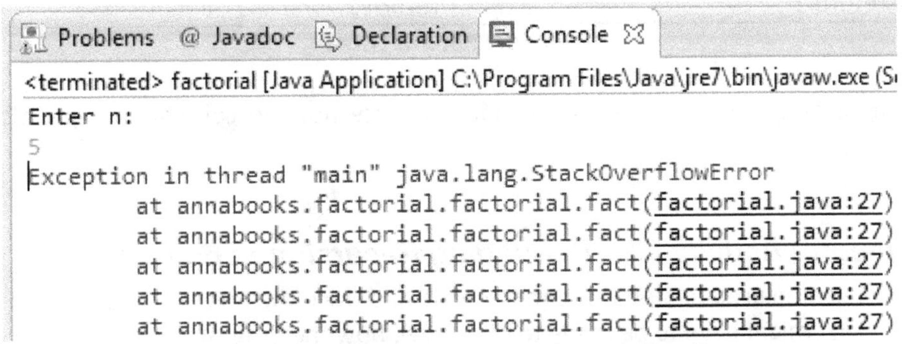

```
Problems  @ Javadoc  Declaration  Console
<terminated> factorial [Java Application] C:\Program Files\Java\jre7\bin\javaw.exe (S
Enter n:
5
Exception in thread "main" java.lang.StackOverflowError
        at annabooks.factorial.factorial.fact(factorial.java:27)
        at annabooks.factorial.factorial.fact(factorial.java:27)
        at annabooks.factorial.factorial.fact(factorial.java:27)
        at annabooks.factorial.factorial.fact(factorial.java:27)
        at annabooks.factorial.factorial.fact(factorial.java:27)
```

Figure 9.2 - Infinite Recursion - Result Stack Overflow

Definition: *Infinite recursion* is the result of an error in a program where the base case was not entered correctly. The error will result in the program stopping with a stack overflow.

Recursion is a challenging programming concept. Always remember, the computer follows the instructions that are provided, thus a return from a method is just like any other return from a computer's point of view. For programmers, recursive calls can be difficult to track because the same variables are being used, but the variables are really in a new scope each time. The challenge is to track the scope of each method call. As we did with loops and arrays, you can use a table to write out each step, but rather than trace variables, you will trace methods for recursive calls. First, write out all of the calls made down to the base case:

n = 5, which is greater than 1, thus fact is called:

Call Stack	Return
fact(5) = 5 * fact(5 - 1)	
fact(4) = 4 * fact(4 - 1)	
fact(3) = 3 * fact(3 - 1)	
fact(2) = 2 * fact(2 - 1)	
fact(1) = return 1	

Table 9.1 Calls Listed

Next, starting from the bottom, write all the returns and walk back up the stack:

Call Stack	Return
fact(5) = 5 * fact(5 - 1)	5 * 24 = 120 – Final result
fact(4) = 4 * fact(4 - 1)	4 * 6 = 24
fact(3) = 3 * fact(3 - 1)	3 * 2 = 6
fact(2) = 2 * fact(2 - 1)	2 * 1 = 2
fact(1) = return 1	return 1, which is the base case

Table 9.2 Returns Listed

When taking a test, you might not have time to write out the call stack so practice will be important.

9.2 Computer Activity 9.2 - Debugging Recursion in Eclipse

The debugger can be used to step through the code and trace the recursive calls. There are some adjustments that might have to be made to clearly see how the program is working. Using the last exercise, uncomment lines 18, 19, and 20. Set a breakpoint at line 18, which is within the recursion call. Hit F11 or start the debugger, and Eclipse will switch to the Debug perspective. Enter the value of 5 on the Console and hit Enter. The program will run until it hits the breakpoint. If you step over or hit F6 continuously, you will step through the code and see the recursive calls being made. The Debug tab shows the call stack increasing with each recursive call, Figure 9.3.

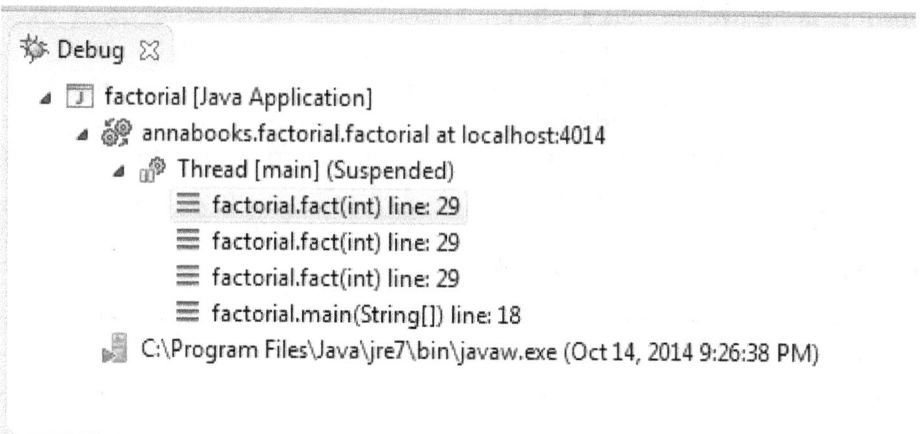

Figure 9.3 Debugger Call Stack

Unfortunately, the variable n goes down in value and the goes back up once the base case is reached. You never see the product result of n x (n-1)! on the returns from the recursive calls. A slight modification is needed to be made to the program. Edit fact() method to add a temporary variable to store and return the product result, Code Listing 9.2.

```
public static int fact(int n)
{
    int temp = 0;
    if (n==1 || n ==0) //Base case 1
        return 1;
    else
    {
        temp = n * fact( n - 1); //Method calls itself
        return temp;
    }
}
```

Code Listing 9.2 Factorial Method with Temporary Variable Added

Start the debugger again, enter 5, and step through the code again. Once the base case has been reached, you will notice that the return value 'temp' shows the product result for n. You will also notice that temp is 0 upon each return before the multiplication occurs. Again, we see the concept of programming scope in action. The temp variable was set to 0 prior to making the call within that instance of the method. Once the return has been made, Figure 9.4, the program is back into the calling method that had temp = 0.

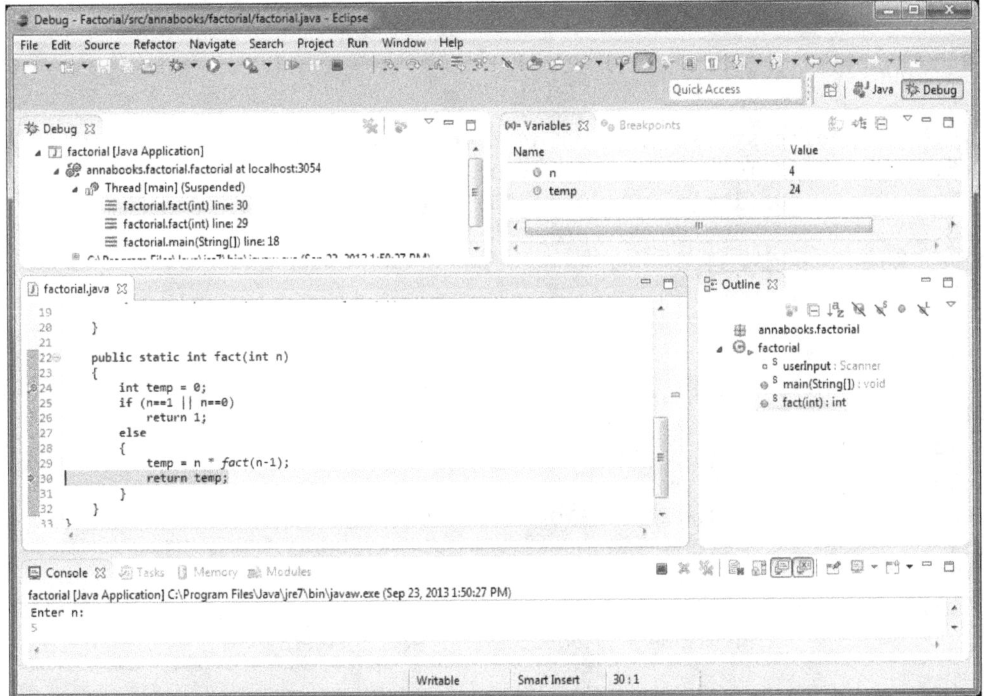

Figure 9.4 Using a Temporary Variable to Aid Recursive Debugging

Adding a temporary variable helps to better see the recursive calls being made, but once the debugging is completed, the temporary variables should be removed.

9.3 Computer Activity 9.3 - Iteration versus Recursion

Recursion is an elegant and clean way to solve certain types of problems that require iterative operations, but there are times when recursion can be inefficient. Each time a method calls a method, it is placed on the stack when the call is made, which in a deeply recursive call can take up valuable computer resources. For this next example, we will use the Fibonacci sequence, Figure 9.5:

$$f_1 = 1, f_2 = 1, f_n = f_{n-1} + f_{n-2}$$

Figure 9.5 Fibonacci Sequence Calculation

The sequence gets the sum of the first prior two numbers in the sequence: 1, 1, 2, 3, 5, 8... In Eclipse, create a new Java project called "CH9CA9.3-Fibonacci" and a new class called "FibonacciTest". Call the package "jae.intsequences". Modify and fill in Code Listing 9.3 in the FactorialTest.java file:

```
package jae.intsequences;

public class FibonacciTest {

    public static void main(String[] args) {
        // TODO Auto-generated method stub
        for(int n = 1; n <= 45; n++){
            System.out.print("Fibonacci("+n+") result is "+fibonacci(n));
        }
    }

    public static long fibonacci(int n)
    {
        if(n <= 2) return 1;
        else
            //Two recursion calls to the same method
            return fibonacci(n - 1)+ fibonacci(n - 2);
    }
}
```

Code Listing 9.3 Fibonacci Series Recursive Program

Rather than having the user enter a number for n, the For-loop will enter the values 1 through 45 for n. Line 8 makes the call to the recursive method and will output the result for each value of n. Run the application, and you should get the following results:

```
Fibonacci(1) result is 1
Fibonacci(2) result is 1
Fibonacci(3) result is 2
Fibonacci(4) result is 3
Fibonacci(5) result is 5
Fibonacci(6) result is 8
:
:
:
Fibonacci(43) result is 433494437
Fibonacci(44) result is 701408733
Fibonacci(45) result is 1134903170
```

The output for each value of n starts out really fast, but as the value of n gets larger the output slows down. Create a new method called "fibonacci2()" that uses a for-loop, and change the main() method to call this method in place of the recursive method, Code Listing 9.4.

```
1. package jae.intsequences;
2.
3. public class FibonacciTest {
4.
5.      public static void main(String[] args) {
6.           // TODO Auto-generated method stub
7.           for(int n = 1; n <= 45; n++){
8.                System.out.print("Fibonacci("+n+") result is
   "+fibonacci2(n));
9.           }
10.     }
11.
12.     public static long fibonacci(int n)
13.     {
14.          if(n <= 2) return 1;
15.          else
16.               //Two recursion calls to the same method
17.               return fibonacci(n - 1)+ fibonacci(n - 2);
18.     }
```

```

    public static long fibonacci2(int n)
    {
        if (n<=2) return 1;
        else
        {
            long fn = 0;
            long fn1 = 1;
            long fn2 = 1;
            for (int x = 3; x <=n;x++)
            {
                fn = fn1+fn2;
                fn2 = fn1;
                fn1 = fn;
            }
            return fn;
        }
    }
}
```

Code Listing 9.4 Fibonacci Series Iterative Optional Solution

The same base case of n <= 2 is addressed. The For-loop starts the iteration at 3 since n > 2. The equation is used to add the two previous values in the sequence, and two variables hold the previous two values to be used in the next iteration. Run the application and you will notice that output is much faster. Why is the recursive solution slower? We need to map the recursive calls to get a better understanding of what the program execution looks like. Let's look at the case when n = 5, Figure 9.6. There are two recursive calls, we will map the recursive calls to the base case of n <= 2 for clarity.

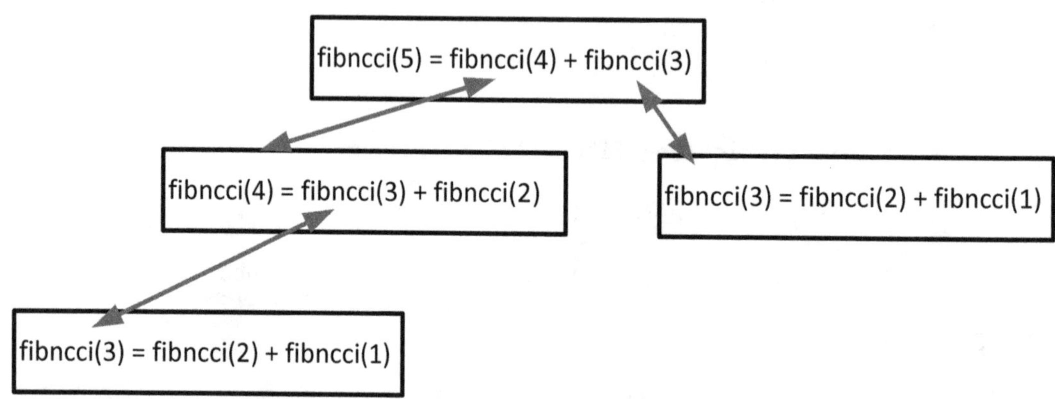

Figure 9.6 Map of Recursive Fibonacci Series Calculation for n = 5

What you see is that multiple calls are being made to the recursive method with the same value, i.e., fibncci(3) is called twice and fibncci(2) is called three times. The greater the values of n, the more repetitions like these are occurring. From a programming perspective, the problem with the Fibonacci sequence is the two recursive calls fanning out into more recursive calls. For the Fibonacci sequence, the iterative solution is the better solution from a programming perspective. We will talk more about algorithm efficiency in the next chapter.

9.4 Computer Activity 9.4 - Mutual Recursion

The last two examples show a single integer sequence or data set. What if there are two data sets that are dependent on each other?

Definition: *Mutual Recursion* is a form of recursion where two functions call each other. Each call is reduced to a simpler set until a base case is reached.

The most popular mutual recursion example on the Internet is odd and even numbers.

Odd = 1, 3, 5, 7, 9....
Even = 2, 4, 6, 8, 10...

In Eclipse, create a new Java project called "CH9CA9.4-OddEven" and a new class called "OddEvenTest". Call the package "jae.mutualrecursion". Modify and fill in Code Listing 9.5 in the OddEvenTest.java file:

```
package jae.mutualrecursion;

import java.util.Scanner;

public class OddEvenTest {

    public static void main(String[] args) {
        // TODO Auto-generated method stub
        Scanner userInput = new Scanner(System.in);
        System.out.println("Enter a number:");
        int n = userInput.nextInt();
        System.out.println("The number "+n+ " is "+ check_even(n));
        userInput.close();
    }
    public static String check_even(int n)
    {
        if(n==0){
            return "Even";
        }
```

```
        else{
            //call the mutual method
            return check_odd(n-1);
        }
    }
    public static String check_odd(int n)
    {
        if(n==0){
            return "Odd";
        }
        else{
            //call the mutual method
            return check_even(n-1);
        }
    }
}
```

Code Listing 9.5 Mutual Recursion

The main() function accepts user input for a number, and then check_even is called. The base case of n == 0 is checked. If the base case is not reached, the check_odd method is called with n decremented by 1. In the check_odd method, the base case is again checked. If the base case is not reached, the check_even method is called with n decremented by 1. The calls back and forth between the two methods continues until n == 0. Run the application and enter an odd number, Figure 9.7.

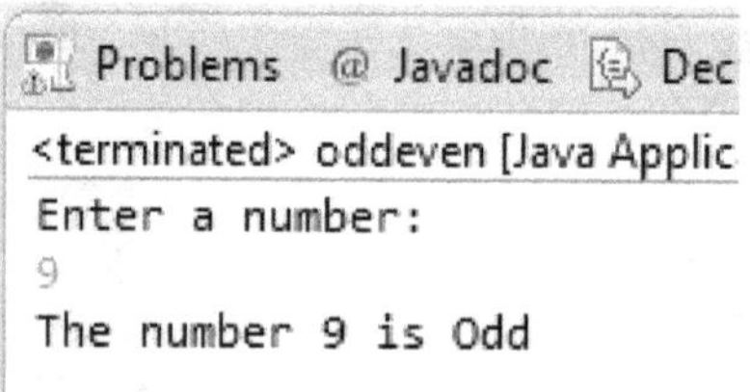

Figure 9.7 Test An Odd Number

Run the application again and enter an even number, Figure 9.8.

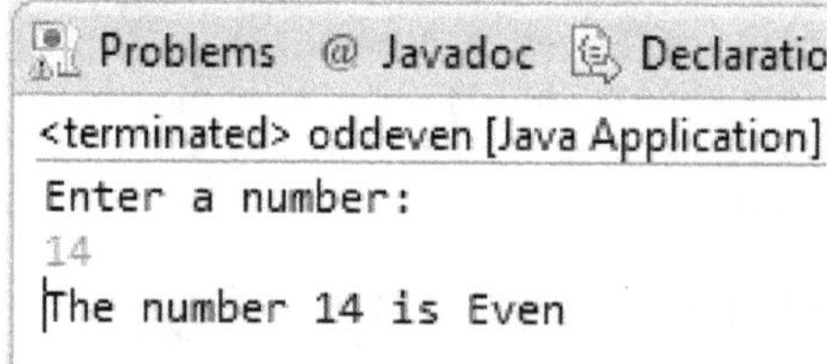

Figure 9.8 Test An Even Number

The debugger is a powerful tool to see mutual recursion in action. Since there are two functions, you need to set two breakpoints. Set the breakpoints at lines 18 and 27. Run the debugger and watch n decrease until the base case is reached and the odd or even determination is made. Upon the return of each call, n looks like it is increasing, but in fact, the value of n before the call is being restored from the stack.

9.5 Tail Recursion

Each recursive call saves the current information on the stack and then jumps to the next routine, which takes CPU cycle time and memory space. Deeply recursive calls take time and resources, and you run the risk of stack overflow. There is a technique that is used to optimize recursive calls.

Definition: *Tail Recursion* is when the final statement of the function/method is the recursive call into the same function/method.

Tail Recursion allows the compiler to optimize the recursive process. If the compiler recognizes the tail recursion condition, it can eliminate the call entirely, saving execution time and stack resources. Therefore, you, as the programmer, have some control over the efficiency of the resulting code execution, if tail recursion can be used in your particular recursive code. The factorial exercise is an example of Tail Recursion.

9.6 Computer Activity 9.5 - Private Recursive Helper Method

All the examples so far have a little flaw. The user can enter a value that is n < 0, which would create infinite recursion. As we learned in Chapter 8, try-catch could be used to catch exceptions, which is fine for our own code. If the factorial recursion solution was put in a Java library, anyone who uses it might not implement try-catch and could run into a problem. The solution is to create a method that addresses the error conditions and then calls the private recursive method. In a library, the error handling method would be made public and the recursive method made private.

Definition: *Private Recursive Help Method* is a coding technique that makes the program more reliable by hiding the recursive method behind the public method.

In Eclipse, create a new Java project called "CH9CA9.5-FactorialHelper" and a new class called "FactorialHelperTest". Call the package "jase.helpermethod". Create a second class called "FactorialLib" and put it in the same package. Modify and fill in Code Listing 9.6 for FactorialHelperTest.java file and Code Listing 9.7 for FactorialLib.java.

```
package jae.helpermethod;

import java.util.Scanner;

public class FactorialHelperTest {

    public static void main(String[] args) {
        // TODO Auto-generated method stub

        Scanner userInput = new Scanner(System.in);
        FactorialLib myfact = new FactorialLib();
        System.out.println("Enter a number (number > 0):");
        int n = userInput.nextInt();
        System.out.println(n + "! is " + myfact.factorialhelper(n));
        userInput.close();
    }
}
```

Code Listing 9.6 FactorialHelperTest

```
package jae.helpermethod;

public class FactorialLib {

    public int factorialhelper(int n)
    {
        if (n >= 0) //check to see if the value is correct
        {
            return fact(n); //call if the value is correct; otherwise throw an error
        }
        else
        {
            throw new IllegalArgumentException("Error: the number must be greater than 0");
        }
    }

    private int fact(int n)
    {
        if (n == 1 || n == 0 )
        {
            return 1;
        }
        else
        {
            return n * fact(n - 1);
        }
    }
}
```

Code Listing 9.7 FactorialLib

The helper and recursive methods are placed in a separate class to demonstrate what it would be like if they were in an actual library. Run the program, and enter a value greater than 0. You will see the program run correctly as before. Now re-run the program and enter a -1. The if-else statement in factorialhelper() method will catch the error and throw the exception, which provides better feedback than stack overflow. The helper method acts as a guard for the recursive call. Could the check for n < 0 been put into the fact() method? The answer is yes, but the code would have to do the check every recursive call. To paraphrase the Einstein quote from Chapter 6, it wouldn't be breaking the problem down to be as simple as possible. As was discussed in the three previous chapters, architecting your code is important. The recursive helper method is another technique to write better code.

9.7 A Real-World Example

At this point, you may ask the question: "Why use recursion if it takes up so many resources and ends up with a possible stack overflow?" Many programmers avoid recursion because of this concern. For the factorial and Fibonacci solution, iteration is the better approach. There are specific cases where recursion is the best option. Two examples are sorting and search algorithms, that we will talk about in the next chapter, and searching through a file system's trees.

Your authors ran into the file system tree search when we created a Windows application called *Component Helper*. The application was for use with an old Microsoft product call Windows® XP Embedded. The application took a before-and-after snapshot of a Windows system to spot changes when something was installed. The snapshot captured both registry and file data. The information was stored in files which were used to find the differences between the before and after snapshots. The output was two files that could be used with the Windows® XP Embedded development tools. The program was developed using VB.NET under .NET Framework 1.1 since VB.NET was a little more advanced than C# at that time. One of the main functions was traversing the whole file system to find each and every directory, subdirectory, and file. Recursion was used to solve that problem. Code Listing 9.8 shows the subroutine that performed the file capture.

```
'Subroutine: FLALL - File List ALL
'
'This sub is recursively calls itself to get a list of all the files in a drive.
'The function supports any drive. Application is limited to C drive only.
'A handle to the temp flie list (flist) is passed to the sub. Information is stored
'in the open file.
'
Private Sub FLALL(ByVal subdirs As String, ByVal fStreamWriter As StreamWriter)
    'This subroutine generates the file lists
    'It will call itself as it trasnverses the directory tree

    'Don't access the System Volume Information directory - Protected!
    If subdirs.EndsWith("\System Volume Information") Then
        Exit Sub
    End If

    'Check for the Abort flag
    If AbortFlag = "Abort" Then
        Exit Sub
    End If

    'Get the local files with the current directory
    Dim aFileN As String() = Directory.GetFiles(subdirs, "*")
    Dim aFile As String
    For Each aFile In aFileN
        fStreamWriter.WriteLine(aFile)
        fStreamWriter.WriteLine(File.GetCreationTime(aFile))
        fStreamWriter.WriteLine(File.GetLastWriteTime(aFile))
        lblSTS2.Text = aFile.ToString
        Update()
    Next

    'Find any subdiretories, and get those files too
    Dim subsubdirs As String() = Directory.GetDirectories(subdirs, "*")
    Dim ssdir As String
    For Each ssdir In subsubdirs
        fStreamWriter.WriteLine(ssdir)
        fStreamWriter.WriteLine(Directory.GetCreationTime(ssdir))
        fStreamWriter.WriteLine(Directory.GetLastWriteTime(ssdir))
        FLALL(ssdir, fStreamWriter) 'recursive call to this subroutine
    Next

End Sub
```

Code Listing 9.8 Real World Recursive Subroutine

The subroutine checks for a directory that cannot be accessed, and it looks for an abort signal from a user abort button on the application. The subroutine then captures information for each file in the current directory using a for-each loop and stores the information in a file. Then each subdirectory from the root is accessed, and their files are captured. The recursive call is made in line 40. After going down the branch, the routine then goes down sub-branches. The recursion will go up-and-down all the files system branches until the whole file system has been searched. The actual base case here is when there are no more branches or files to search. Although this is not the most efficient solution, the point here is that it doesn't matter what programming language you use, the basic concepts discussed in this book can be applied and are being applied in the real world, today.

9.8 *Summary and Homework Assignments*

Recursion is a powerful programming method and an asset to your programming skill set. The key point is to break the problem down to the base case, which will provide the kick to derive the result. Recursion is used in specific situations, such as sorting and searching where it becomes a little complex for iterative solutions. Look to create tail recursion solutions, because they provide the best performance. We will introduce a better use of recursion in the next chapter, but here are some homework questions and programming projects first.

9.8.1 Questions

1. If you have not seen the movie *Inception*, it is a good movie to watch to illustrate the recursion concept. How many dream levels did the characters go down in the climactic sequence?

2. In the OddEvenexercise, Code Listing 9.5, if you change line 12 from check_even(n) to check_odd(n), does this change the result of the program? If it does, why?

3. Section 9.6, a Private Recursive Helper Method demonstrated how a public method addressed the case for a user inputting n < 0. How would you address the case of someone entering a floating-point number, like 1.2 for n?

4. Consider the following method function1(n):

```
1. public static int function1(int n)
2. {
3.       if (n <= 0)
4.       {
5.            return 15;
6.       }
7.       else if (n == 5)
8.       {
9.            return 25;
10.      }
11.      else
12.      {
13.           return 2 * function1(n % 4 - 1);
14.      }
15. }
```

a. What is the result for n = 12?
b. What is the result for n = 6?
c. What is the result for n = 26?
d. What happens if you change line 3 from n <= 0 to n == 0 for n =12, n=6, and n = 26?

5. Consider the following method stars(n):

```
public static void stars(int n)
{
      if (n <= 5)
      {
           System.out.println("*");
      }
      else if (n == 10)
      {
           System.out.println("--");
      }
      else
      {
           System.out.println("+++");
           stars(n / 2);
      }
}
```

a. What is the output for n = 15?

b. What is the output for n = 10?
c. What is the output for n = 55?
d. What is the output for a, b, and c, if line 7 is changed from n == 10 to n >= 10?

6. Consider the following recursive method function2. What is the result for function2(27, 7)?

```
public static int function2(int n, int x)
{
      if( n <= 5 || x <= 5)
      {
            return (n - x) * 2;
      }
      else if (n <= x)
      {
            return 1;
      }
      else
      {
                  return function2(function2(n / 3, x / 2), x);
      }
}
```

9.8.2 Programming Projects

1. Write a recursion program that allows a user to input a number for 'n' for the following integer sequence:

   f(n)=$\sum_{n=0}^{\infty}(n^2+1)$

   f(0) = 1

   The first few numbers in the sequence are 1, 3, 8, 18...

2. The following is known as the Hofstadter Female and Male sequences. Write a program that uses mutual recursion and outputs the result for both sequences for a user who inputs any value for n. Implement a recursive helper method to check for n < 0.

   F(0) = 1
   M(0) = 0
   F(n) = n - M(F(n - 1)), for n > 0

M(n) = n - F(M(n - 1)), for n > 0

3. Write a program that uses recursion to take a user input string and outputs the string in reverse. For example, the user enters: "Java is Fun!". The output would be: "!nuF si avaJ".

4. Write a recursion program that finds the word 'cat' in the following sentence: "They spotted the cat in the tree." The result should return true that it found the word 'cat'. If the sentence is "The dog is in the yard", a search for the word cat should return false.

5. Create a new solution for Chapter 5, Proramming Project 8 that uses recursion to search for each of the first 5 letters of the alphabet in the 2-dimensional array. Create the same output for letters that are found and those letters that are not found.

6. The Towers of Hanoi is a popular recursion assignment. The background story revolves around Chinese monks, 64 disks, 3 posts, and the end of the world. There are various explanations for the story on the Internet. Each of the 64 disks is round with a hole in the middle, and they are all of a different size. The puzzle is that there are three posts. One post has all 64 disks stacked from the largest on the bottom to the smallest on top. The objective is to move all of the disks from one post to one of the other posts so they stack from the largest on the bottom to the smallest on top. There are some conditions:

   - Only one disk can be moved at a time.
   - Only the disk at the top of any stack can be moved.
   - Larger disks cannot be placed on smaller disks.
   - Any disk on any post can be moved to any other post as long as the disk that is moved is smaller than the disk it will be put on top of.

   a. Based on the legendary story, about how long would it take the monks to complete the project (how many moves)?
   b. Who was the originator of the legend?
   c. What is the minimum number of moves based on n number of disks?
   d. Write a program that uses the recursion method moveRings(int rings, String post1, String post2, String post3) to solve the problem based on user input for the number of rings. "n" is the number of rings, post1, post2, post3 are the posts, and post1 is the starting post. And post3 is the end. The output should show each ring move: "Ring 2 from Post1 to Post2".

10 Sort and Search with Introduction to Algorithm Analysis

"The world isn't run by weapons anymore, or energy, or money. It's run by little ones and zeroes, little bits of data. It's all just electrons."
– Cosmo from the movie: *Sneakers,* Universal Pictures 1992

A little-known movie at the dawn of the Internet age delivers a prophetic quote. It is all about the data. In 1992, no one could have really guessed how the Internet could integrate tightly into society. Suffice to say that big data is a hot topic, and the need to sort, search, and analyze large amounts of data is what many companies are working toward mastering. The Internet gives us access to large amounts of data, from text files, pictures, videos, and audio files. An Internet search in the 1990's involved typing something in a text box and getting back a bunch of data that for the most part didn't address what we were searching for. When we do an Internet search today, the search engine offers solutions to fill in the rest of your search question as you are typing (or speaking); and when you hit return, the results come pretty close to what we are looking for. The speed at which we access data today is a not only a tribute to more powerful computers, but to highly efficient algorithms that can search all the little bits of data, great and small.

Big data is not just about Internet searching. There are many tasks that require efficient algorithms to analyze data such as stock trading, DNA sequencing, advertising statistics, traffic analysis, and many more. There are many books and courses that deep dive into writing data management algorithms and working with data structures. This chapter introduces algorithm analysis to introduce common notations on growth rate and algorithm efficiency (also known as complexity analysis). All the work in the previous chapters from math, iteration, decision, arrays, and recursion leads us to analyze different sort and search algorithms in this chapter. Determining the growth rate will help us determine the efficiency of the algorithm.

10.1 Algorithm Analysis Introduction – Big-O Notation

The goal of any algorithm is to complete that task in the shortest time possible in whatever application it is used. The performance of any algorithm is not just determined by how efficiently it is coded, but also by the data sets on which it is being used. The more efficiently the algorithm can handle large amounts of data the better. Algorithm analysis studies the amount of resources in time and storage that an algorithm requires when running. For our introduction, we will focus on time resources and limit our examples to a single data set. The last chapter compared the performance for the different Fibonacci sequence algorithms and showed that the iteration algorithm was much faster than the recursion algorithm. The two Fibonacci algorithms show that there are two ways to solve the problem, but one is more efficient for a small dataset. What happens when the data set gets larger? How an algorithm's performance changes as the data set gets larger is referred to as how well the algorithm scales; that is to say, how long does the algorithm's runtime change with the size of the data set it is processing? Comparing algorithms specifically by absolute time measurement is not practical, since different computers and programming languages can change the raw speed of an algorithm. What can be determined is the relative growth rate. This type of analysis can show asymptotic upper and lower bounds, worst-case and best-case scaling for a given algorithm as the dataset gets larger. The asymptotic bounding methodologies are known as Big Omega-Ω, Big Theta –Θ, and Big – O.

We will use a few diagrams to describe Big-Ω (Big-Omega), Big–Θ (Big-Theta), and Big–O. The use of these methodologies is to provide a lower bound on the execution time of an algorithm, an upper bound on the execution time of an algorithm, or tight bounding of the execution time of an algorithm as the data set size varies in size. Big-O notation gives an asymptotic upper bound on execution time, Big-Ω notation provides an asymptotic lower bound on execution time, and Big–Θ provides asymptotic tight bounding (a hard upper and lower bound) on execution time. Let's examine each of these notation methodologies to see how they work.

The first diagram below, Figure 10.1, shows a complex function f(x), which could be an actual measurement of an algorithm's execution time versus the size of the data set being processed. Next to that function is a simpler function g(x) that has a similar growth rate, especially in the region where the data set being processed is large.

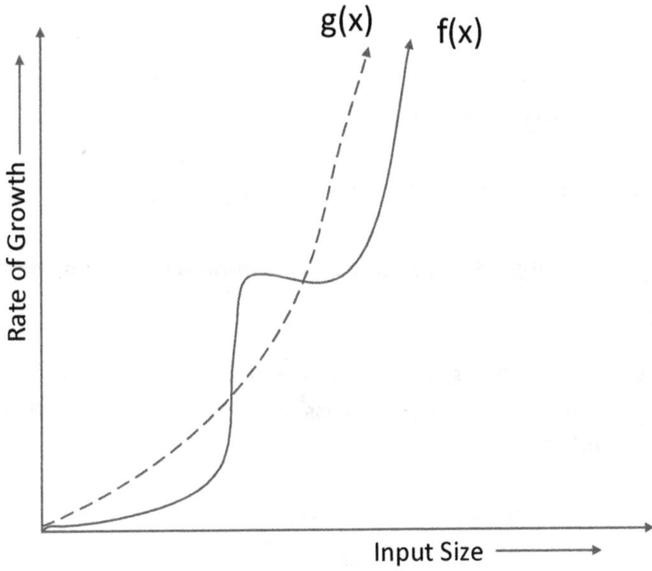

Figure 10.1 Complex and Simple Functions for Comparison

Since Big-Ω notation is a lower bound, Figure 10.2 shows that the appropriate constant multiplier, c_2, $c_2*g(x)$ can be chosen such that that f(x) will never cross below $c_2*g(x)$ after x_0. This would provide the Big-Ω notation lower bound for f(x).

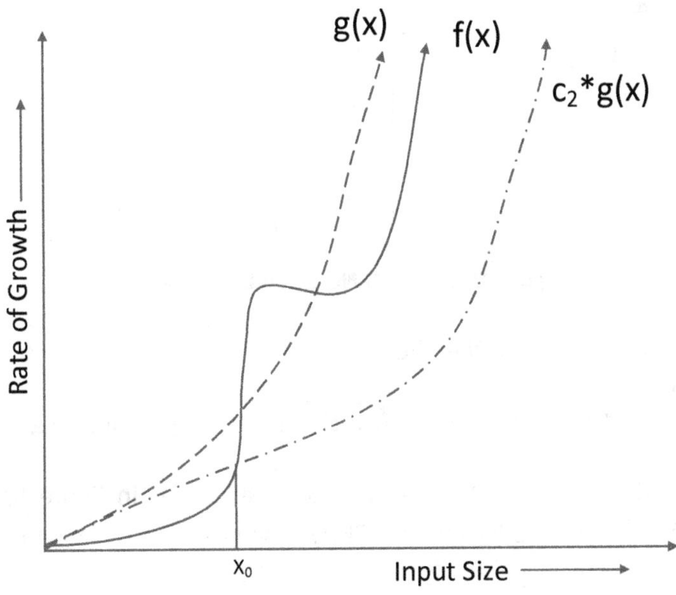

Figure 10.2 Big Omega-Ω Lower Bound

The formual Big-Ω definition would then be:

$$f(x) \in \Omega(g(x)) \text{ if } c_2, x_0 > 0 \text{ such that } f(x) \geq c_2*g(x) \text{ for all } x \geq x_0$$

Note: the ϵ symbol above means "is in", such as f(x) is in Big-Ω of g(x) if the following conditions are met.

Big-O notation is the upper bound. Figure 10.3 shows that for a different constant multiplier, c_1, $c_1*g(x)$ can be chosen such that f(x) will never cross above $c_1*g(x)$ after x_0. This would provide the Big-O notation lower bound for f(x).

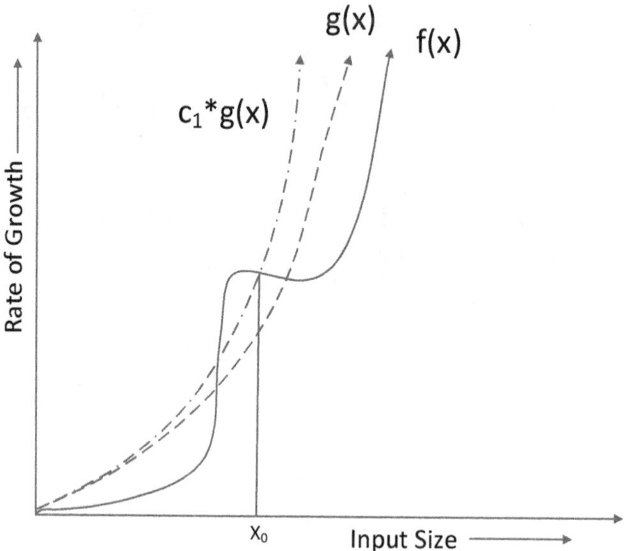

Figure 10.3 Big – O Notation Upper Bound

The formual Big-O definition would then be:

$$f(x) \in O(g(x)) \text{ if } c_1, x_0 > 0 \text{ such that } f(x) \leq c_1*g(x) \text{ for all } x \geq x_0$$

Big-Θ notation is the tight bounding by Big-Ω and Big-O as shown in Figure 10.4. Big- Θ is defined as two constants that f(x) never goes above $c_1*g(x)$ or below $c_2*g(x)$ for some point x_0 and after.

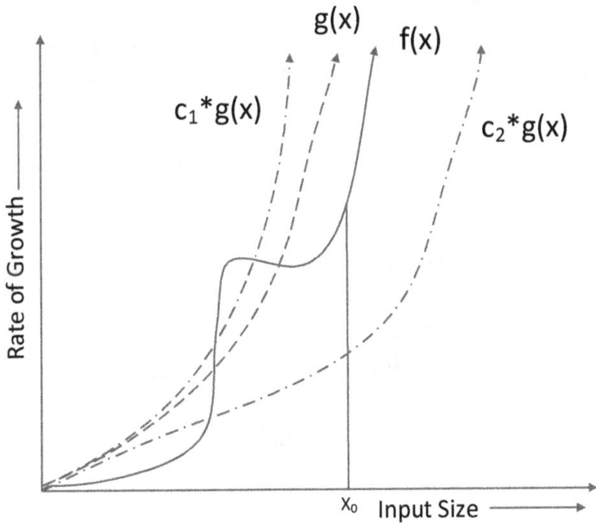

Figure 10.4 Big Theta – Θ Notation Bounded by Big Omega-Ω and Big-O

The formual Big - Θ definition becomes:

$$f(x) \in \Theta\ (g(x)) \text{ if } c_1, c_2, x_0 > 0 \text{ such that } c_1*g(x) \geq f(x) \geq c_1*g(x) \text{ for all } x \geq x_0$$

Out of the three, Big-O is the one that gets the most attention, since it is the upper bound and is the highest growth rate. You may have read on the Internet or heard from others that understanding Big-O notation involves complicated math, empirical tests, and voodoo. We can set your mind to rest that there is no voodoo required, but there are some high-level math concepts. Understanding the properties of linear, power series, exponential, logarithmic, and other types of functions is required, which are best left to a data structures and algorithms course; but through the rest of the chapter, we will cover the basic analysis approach for Big-O notation. In general, a strong foundation in mathematics will help to understand Big-O notation.

Note: If you are taking the AP® Computer Science A exam, Big-O notation is not covered. This may change over time. Please see the latest study guides and check with the College Board website. Even though it is not covered, the effort to understand Big-O notation will help you with analyzing algorithms.

10.1.1 A Simple Example

Throughout these examples, 'n' will represent an integer which is the size of the dataset that the algorithm is working on, thus "n" will be used for the Big-O notation. Let's say we have the following function:

$$f(n) = 79n^3+2n-1$$

For larger values n, or as n-> ∞, the contribution that 2n-1 makes to the value of f(n) is relatively small and can be dropped from the Big-O analysis. The $79n^3$ term has the greatest impact on the value of f(n), and hence the growth rate. The constant, 79, can be dropped since it has no bearing on growth rate, thus the Big-O notation for the example function is $O(n^3)$.

Note: In mathematics, "x" is designated for real numbers while "n" is for integers.

10.1.2 Code Example of O(1)

The first code example is of a constant output, Code Listing 10.1. The code below has a method called AddConstantToFirstElement(). No matter how many times the method is called, the time to calculate the result is the same, thus the Big-O notation for a constant is O(1).

```
package jae.basicbigo;

public class BasicBigO {

    public static void main(String[] args) {
        // TODO Auto-generated method stub

        int[] myarray = {6,7,8,2,3};

        AddConstantToFirstElement(myarray,3);

        for(int i = 0; i < myarray.length; i++)
        {
            System.out.print(myarray[i] + " ");
        }
    }

```

```
    public static void AddConstantToFirstElement(int[] IntArray, int x)
    {

        IntArray[0] += x;
    }
}
```

Code Listing 10.1 Big O Constant Added to First Array Element

10.1.3 Code Example of O(n)

In the code example below, Code Listing 10.2, a for-loop is used to add a constant value to all elements in the array.

```
1. package jae.basicbigo;
2.
3. public class BasicBigO {
4.
5.     public static void main(String[] args) {
6.         // TODO Auto-generated method stub
7.
8.         int[] myarray = {6,7,8,2,3};
9.
10.        AddConstant(myarray, 5);
11.
12.        for(int i = 0; i < myarray.length; i++)
13.        {
14.            System.out.print(myarray[i] + " ");
15.        }
16.    }
17.
18.    public static void AddConstant(int[] IntArray, int x ){
19.
20.        for(int i = 0; i < IntArray.length; i++)
21.        {
22.            IntArray[i] += x;
23.        }
24.    }
25. }
```

Code Listing 10.2 Big O Constant Added to Array Elements

If we pass larger and larger arrays to the AddConstant() method, the time to process the array goes up linearly. How do you figure the Big-O notation? Line 20 is the for-loop so we will have "n" elements from the array, and we will assign this line "n". Line 22 is constant, and we will assign it 'c'.

```
public static void AddConstant(int[] IntArray, int x ){

    for(int i = 0; i < IntArray.length; i++) //n
    {
        IntArray[i] += x; //c
    }
}
```

The total time is T(n) = c*n, thus the Big-O notation is O(n), since the constant does not contribute to the relative rate.

10.1.4 Code Example of O(n^2)

The final code example, Code Listing 10.3, has the method, ComplexChange(), that features nested for-loops.

```
package jae.basicbigo;

public class BasicBigO {

    public static void main(String[] args) {
        // TODO Auto-generated method stub

        int[] myarray = {6,7,8,2,3};

        ComplexChange(myarray,2);
        for(int i = 0; i < myarray.length; i++)
        {
            System.out.print(myarray[i] + " ");
        }
    }
    public static void ComplexChange(int[] IntArray, int x){

        for(int i = 0; i < IntArray.length; i++){ //n
            for(int j = 0; j < IntArray.length;  j++){ //n

                IntArray[j] = (IntArray[j] * x) - I; //c
            }
        }
    }
}
```

Code Listing 10.3 Big O Complex Constant Addition to Array Elements

Like the last example, we can assign 'n' to lines 18 and 19 for the two for-loops and a constant 'c' for line 21. The total time is $T(n) = c*n*n$ or $T(n) = c*n^2$, thus dropping the constant the Big-O notation is $O(n^2)$. If there were 3 nested for-loops, the Big-O notation would be $O(n^3)$, if there were 4 nested for-loops, the Big-O would be $O(n^4)$, and so on.

10.1.5 The Beginning of the Big Picture

Taking the three code examples, we draw the three growth rates on a single graph, Figure 10.5.

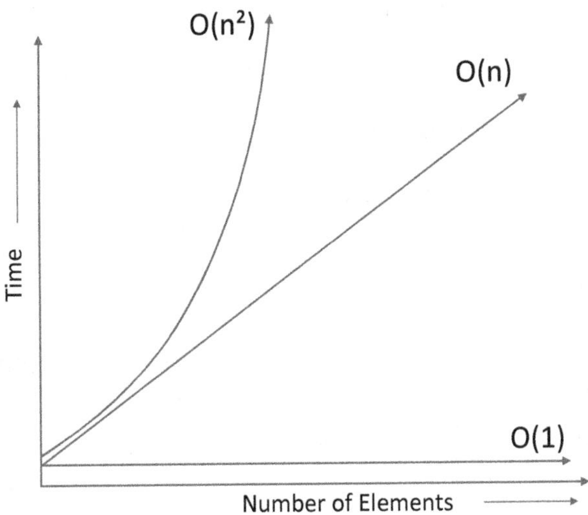

Figure 10.5 Big O Growth Rate Comparison Graph

Obviously, $O(n^2)$ has the worst efficiency as the dataset grows. O(n) increases linearly as the dataset grows, and O(1) has a constant time result irrespective of the data set size. Now that we have a basic notation to describe algorithm efficiency, let's dive into sorting and see how it applies.

10.2 Computer Activity 10.1 - Sorting Algorithms

There are many sorting algorithm solutions that have been developed over the years. In this section, we will implement four of the most popular sort algorithms that will help us see growth rates in action. First, we need to create a few classes to generate an integer array, print an array, and a test class to run the algorithms. Next, each search algorithm will be introduced in separate sections and added to the project. The last step will be to do a speed test on each algorithm for a relatively large dataset to demonstrate the different growth rates for each algorithm.

Create a project called "CH10CA10.1-SortAlgorithms". Create a class called "SortTest" with a main() method under a package called "jae.sort". Create a class under the jae.sort package called "PrintArrayOutput". Create another class under jae.sort package called "RandomIntegerDataSet". In the PrintArrayOutput class, add Code Listing 10.4:

```
package jae.sort;

public class PrintArrayOutput {

    public static void PrintArray(int[] aDS )
    {
        for(int i = 0; i < aDS.length ; i ++)
        {
            System.out.print(aDS[i] + " ");
        }
        System.out.println(" ");
    }
}
```

Code Listing 10.4 PrintArrayOutput Class with Integer Array Print Method

The method takes an array and prints out all values in the array. The method is made static so we can directly call the method when we want to test parts of our algorithm. In the RandomIntegerDataSet class, add Code Listing 10.5:

```
package jae.sort;

import java.util.Random;

public class RandomIntegerDataSet {

    private int[] rds;
    private int n;

    public int[] getRds() {
        return rds;
    }

```

```
    public int getN() {
        return n;
    }

    public RandomIntegerDataSet(int n) {
        //super();
        this.n = n;
        GenerateArray();
    }

    public void GenerateArray()
    {
        rds = new int[n];

        Random gen = new Random();

        for(int i = 0; i < n; i++)
        {
            rds[i] = gen.nextInt(100);
        }
    }
}
```

Code Listing 10.5 RandomIntegerDataSet Class

The constructor creates an array of size ‘n’ that is passed in and then randomly fills all array elements with integers between 0 and 99. The ability to change the size of the array will help us with the timing tests that we will cover later. In the SortTest class, add Code Listing 10.6 to the main() method:

```
1. package jae.sort;
2.
3. public class SortTest {
4.
5.     public static void main(String[] args) {
6.         // TODO Auto-generated method stub
7.         int n = 10;
8.         int[] raDS = new int[n];
9.
10.        RandomIntegerDataSet myDS = new RandomIntegerDataSet(n);
11.        PrintArrayOutput.PrintArray(myDS.getRds());
12.
13.        //Preserve the created array
14.        raDS = myDS.getRds().clone();
15.    }
16. }
```

Code Listing 10.6 SortTest Class

For our initial testing, we will keep the array size of 10 elements. Lines 8 and 10 create the array and populate it with random values. Line 11 then prints out each element in the array. Different sorting algorithms have different growth rates. We will compare all the algorithms' performance at the end of the activity. Since a reference to the array is passed to the methods, we don't want to change the values of the array. Line 14 creates a copy of the array that will be passed to each sort algorithm. When you run the program, you will get a list of 10 integer values printed to the output window.

10.2.1 Selection Sort

The first sort algorithm is the simplest. Selection Sort iterates through all elements in the array going from right to left. The algorithm looks for the smallest value and then swaps the values at the current index. For example, here is an array of values:

```
57 22 78 64 7 4 34 71 43 50
```

Let's say we want to sort from low to high. Starting at position 0, which holds the value of 57, the algorithm looks for the lowest value in the rest of the array:

4 22 78 64 7 **57** 34 71 43 50 //First iteration finds and swaps values 4 and 57
4 **7** 78 64 **22** 57 34 71 43 50 //Next the values of 7and 22 are swapped
4 7 22 64 78 57 34 71 43 50
4 7 22 34 78 57 64 71 43 50
4 7 22 34 43 57 64 71 78 50
4 7 22 34 43 50 64 71 78 57
4 7 22 34 43 50 57 71 78 64
4 7 22 34 43 50 57 64 78 71
4 7 22 34 43 50 57 64 **71** **78** //The last two values are swapped
4 7 22 34 43 50 57 64 71 78 //Even though everything is sorted there is one more iteration

Let's write the code for the Selection Sort. Create a class under the jae.sort package called "SelectionSort", and add Code Listing 10.7:

```
package jae.sort;

public class SelectionSort {

    //Data Set to sort gets passed in to the method
    //Put the values in ascending order
    public static void sort(int[] dstoSort)
    {
        for(int i = 0; i < dstoSort.length; i++)
        {
            //Find the smallest value in the array
            int smallest = dstoSort[i];
            int indexValue = i;

            for(int k = i + 1; k < dstoSort.length; k++)
            {
                if(dstoSort[k] < smallest)
                {
                    smallest = dstoSort[k];
                    indexValue = k;
                }
            }

```

```
24.                 //swap elements
25.                 int temp = dstoSort[indexValue];
26.                 dstoSort[indexValue] = dstoSort[i];
27.                 dstoSort[i] = temp;
28.             }
29.     }
30. }
```

Code Listing 10.7 Select Sort Algorithm

In the SortTest Class, add the following code after line 14:

```
//Selection Sort
System.out.println("\nSelection Sort:");
SelectionSort.sort(raDS);
PrintArrayOutput.PrintArray(raDS);
```

Running the application, an array of ten random integers is generated. The Selection Sort algorithm is called and sorts the array in ascending order.

```
        29 69 96 99 15 41 60 27 10 44

Selection Sort:
        10 15 27 29 41 44 60 69 96 99
```

There are two for-loops in the algorithm. The start of the first for-loop gets the first value at index 0, the second for-loop compares all the rest of the values in the array starting at index 1. Once the smallest value is found the second for-loop terminates and the lower and higher values have their positions swapped. The outer loop continues until all values have been processed. If you want to see each iteration change, add the following code to print out the arrays current state after line 27 in the SelectionSort class:

```
PrintArrayOutput.PrintArray(dstoSort);
```

Now, we look at the Big-O notation for Selection Sort. We see that we have nested for-loops, so it is a good guess that the Big-O notation is going to be O(n^2), but there is some math to prove this. The Selection Sort is a little more complex than the simple nest loop earlier. There are different paths to get the notation result. Since the inner loop is really (n-2) through the data set, the total time can be expressed as follows:

$$T(n) = c\sum_{i=0}^{n-1}\sum_{k=i}^{n-2}$$

This looks like $T(n) = cn^2$ that we saw earlier. Another way of looking at the total time is as follows:

$$T(n) = 1 + 2 + ... + (n-2) + (n-1)$$

This representation matches the Arithmetic Series which is defined as follows:

$$\sum_{i=1}^{n} i = 1 + 2 + \cdots + n = \frac{n(n+1)}{2}$$

Thus, the total time is:

$$T(n) = 1/2\,(n^2 + n)$$

which can be regressed to (n^2) by eliminating the +n term, which has a small contribution as n becomes large, and eliminating the constant. As we guessed, the Selection Sort Big-O notation is $O(n^2)$. Selection Sort works well for small data sets, but as the data set gets larger, the total time to process goes up as the square.

10.2.2 Insertion Sort

The Insertion Sort algorithm is another simple sort solution. For sorting values in ascending order, the concept is to go through each element and check the value with the values in the preceding position. If the value in the higher position is smaller than the value in the lower position, insert the value into the lower position. For example, let's say we have the following values in an array:

```
59 92 61 75 32 69 6 99 45 66
```

The first iteration checks the value at position 1 (92) with that of position 0 (59). Since 59 is smaller, there is no change.

`59 92 61 75 32 69 6 99 45 66` // 61 is next and is smaller than 92

`59 61 92 75 32 69 6 99 45 66` // values are swapped, and 75 is compared to 92

`59 61 75 92 32 69 6 99 45 66` // 75 is smaller and the values are swapped

`32 59 61 75 92 69 6 99 45 66` // 32 is next and the values are moved up so 32 is inserted into position 0.

`32 59 61 69 75 92 6 99 45 66` // Same for 6

`6 32 59 61 69 75 92 99 45 66`

`6 32 59 61 69 75 92 99 45 66` // no change for 99

`6 32 45 59 61 69 75 92 99 66` // 45 is inserted at position 2 and the values between 2 and 8 are moved up

`6 32 45 59 61 66 69 75 92 99` // 66 is the last and the algorithm concludes once each element has been sorted

Let's write the code for the Insertion Sort. Create a class under the jae.sort package called "InsertionSort", and add Code Listing 10.8:

```
package jae.sort;

public class InsertionSort {

    public static void sort(int[] dstoSort)
    {
        //Start are position 1 to compare with previous positions
        for(int i = 1; i < dstoSort.length; i++){

            int k = i - 1;
            int temp = dstoSort[i];
            //Check k value and if the temp value is less than the current value at position k
            while((k >= 0) && (dstoSort[k] > temp))
            {
                //Move the values up the array
                dstoSort[k + 1] = dstoSort[k];
                k--; //decrement to check the value in the next position down
            }
            //Perform the final swap of the value into the k+1 position
            dstoSort[k + 1] = temp;
        }
    }
}
```

Code Listing 10.8 Insertion Sort

In the SortTest Class, add the following code after the Selection Sort calls:

```
//reset temp array
raDS = myDS.getRds().clone();

//Insertion Sort
System.out.println("\nInsertion Sort:");
InsertionSort.sort(raDS);
PrintArrayOutput.PrintArray(raDS);
```

The first step has the original array copied back to the temp array. The temp array is then passed to the sorting algorithm. Running the application, an array of ten random integers is generated. The Selection Sort and Insertion Sort algorithms are called to sort the array in ascending order.

```
27 5 29 54 53 12 75 7 97 14
```

Selection Sort:

```
5 7 12 14 27 29 53 54 75 97
```

Insertion Sort:

```
5 7 12 14 27 29 53 54 75 97
```

Insertion Sort uses a nested while-loop inside of a for-loop combination to iterate through each element in the array. The outer for-loop starts with element 1 (i = 1) and sets up the inner while-loop to start at one position before with k = i - 1. The value at the "i" position is stored in a temp variable. The inner while-loop performs the comparison with each element before position "i". If temp is less than the value at the position "k", line 16 moves the lower value up a position, (k+1). If temp is greater than the value at the position, the while-loop is exited and the temp value is placed into position (k+1). If you want to see each iteration change, add the following code to print out the array's current state at line 21 in the InsertionSort class:

```
PrintArrayOutput.PrintArray(dstoSort);
```

The Big-O notation for an Insertion Sort follows the same math proof as the Selection Sort, thus Insertion Sort is also $O(n^2)$.

10.2.3 Merge Sort

We have implemented two sorting algorithms that work well for small datasets but perform poorly for larger datasets. The next sorting algorithm is Merge Sort, which implements a divide-and-conquer approach to sorting data. Using a recursion technique, an array is broken down into smaller arrays until there are two or one element arrays. Once the base case of the recursion call is reached, the smaller arrays are arranged with the values in ascending order. The smaller arrays are then merged and sorted together until the whole array is one and all values are in ascending order. For example, let's say we have the following values in an array:

```
92 47 93 73 4 31 19 63 62 88
```

The array is split into two halves (92 47 93 73 4) and (31 19 63 62 88). The two halves are then split into two halves and split again until an array with 1 or two elements is left. The arrays are merged and sorted back together as we come up the recursion. The following is a Merge Sort tree diagram.

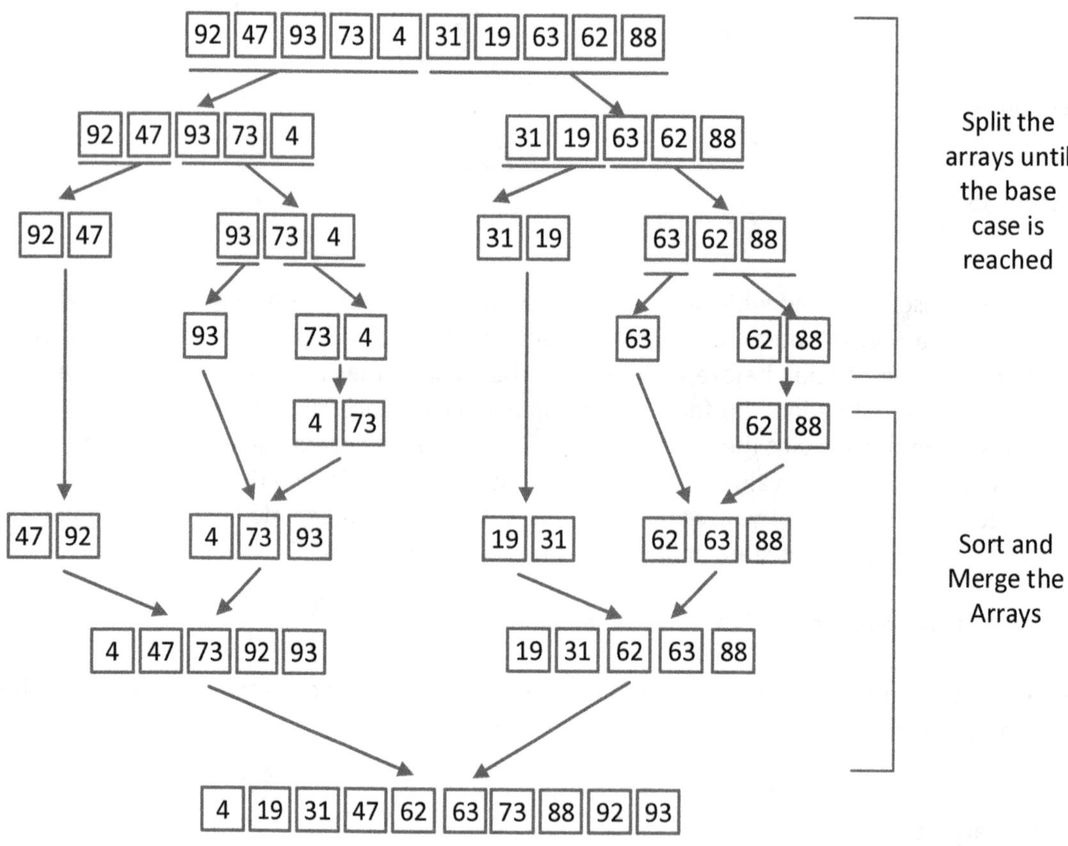

Let's write the code for the Merge Sort. Create a class under the jae.sort package called "MergeSort", and add Code Listing 10.9:

```
package jae.sort;

public class MergeSort {

    //Recursive helper method
    public static void sort(int[] dstoSort)
    {
        if(!(dstoSort.length <= 1)){
            mSort(dstoSort);
        }
    }

    private static void mSort(int[] dstoSort){

        if(dstoSort.length > 1){ //base case for recursion

            //Split the array in half
            int[] firstHalf = new int[dstoSort.length / 2];
            int[] secondHalf = new int[dstoSort.length - firstHalf.length];
            for(int i = 0; i < firstHalf.length; i++){
                firstHalf[i] = dstoSort[i];
            }
            for(int i = 0; i < secondHalf.length; i++){
                secondHalf[i] = dstoSort[firstHalf.length+i];
            }
            mSort(firstHalf);
            mSort(secondHalf);
            merge(dstoSort, firstHalf, secondHalf);
        }
    }

    private static void merge(int[] dstoSort, int[] firstHalf, int[] secondHalf)
    {
        int index = 0;
        int firstHalfIndex = 0;
        int secondHalfIndex = 0;

```

```
        //Do the sort of the two arrays
        while((firstHalfIndex < firstHalf.length) &&
    (secondHalfIndex < secondHalf.length))
        {
            if(  firstHalf[firstHalfIndex] <
    secondHalf[secondHalfIndex] )
            {
                dstoSort[index++] = firstHalf[firstHalfIndex++];
            }
            else
            {
                dstoSort[index++] = secondHalf[secondHalfIndex++];
            }
        }
        //Copy both halves together
        while(firstHalfIndex < firstHalf.length)
        {
            dstoSort[index++] = firstHalf[firstHalfIndex++];
        }
        while (secondHalfIndex < secondHalf.length)
        {
            dstoSort[index++] = secondHalf[secondHalfIndex++];
        }

    }
}
```

Code Listing 10.9 Merge Sort

In the SortTest Class, add the following code after Insertion Sort calls:

```
//reset temp array
raDS = myDS.getRds().clone();

//Merge Sort
System.out.println("\nMerge Sort:");
MergeSort.sort(raDS);
PrintArrayOutput.PrintArray(raDS);
```

Running the application, an array of ten random integers is generated. The three sort algorithms are called to sort the array in ascending order.

```
91 94 48 54 20 26 65 4 60 85

Selection Sort:
4 20 26 48 54 60 65 85 91 94

Insertion Sort:
4 20 26 48 54 60 65 85 91 94

Merge Sort:
4 20 26 48 54 60 65 85 91 94
```

If you want to see the merged arrays, add the following code to print out the arrays' current state at line 59 in the MergeSort class:

```
PrintArrayOutput.PrintArray(dstoSort);
```

The Merge Sort uses a recursive helper method to check to see if the array is empty or not. A call is then made to the mSort () method, which is the recursive method in the algorithm. The method splits the array in half and then calls itself to split the arrays again. When `dstoSort.length > 1` is reached, the second half of the original array is split in half until the base case is reached. Coming up out of each recursion call, the merge() method is called to sort and merge the arrays. Once the second half of the array has completed the merge and sort, the final merge and sort bring both halves back together. The Big-O analysis for a divide-and-conquer is a little bit more complex. For our purposes, we can take advantage of a solution that has been derived for most divide-and-conquer algorithms called Master Theorem. The proof for Master Theorem is beyond the scope of this book, but you can read more about it online at the Master Theorem Wikipedia page. We can use the generalized Master Theorem as it applies to the Merge Sort to determine the Big-O notation. The definition of Master Theorem uses the following formula:

$$T(n) = aT\left(\frac{n}{b}\right) + \theta(n^k log^p n)$$

Where 'a' ≥ 1, 'b' > 1, 'k' ≥ 0 and 'p' is a real number. Using this formula, there are three cases that can be used to figure out the Big-O notation for a divide-and-conquer algorithm:

Case 1: If 'a' > 'b^{k}'

$$T(n) = \theta(n^{\log_b a})$$

Case 2: If 'a' = 'b^{k}' and
If "p" > -1

$$T(n) = \theta(n^{\log_b a} \log^{p+1} n)$$

If 'p' = -1

$$T(n) = \theta(n^{\log_b a} \log\log n)$$

If 'p' < -1

$$T(n) = \theta(n^{\log_b a})$$

Case 3: If 'a' < 'b^{k}' and

If 'p' ≥ 0

$$T(n) = \theta(n^k \log^p n)$$

If 'p' < 0

$$T(n) = O(n^k)$$

For the case of Merge Sort, the algorithm divides the elements into two parts using recursion and there is an O(n) time for the merge() method; thus, total time is

$$T(n) = T\left(\frac{n}{2}\right)T\left(\frac{n}{2}\right) + cn$$

Or expressed as:

$$T(n) = 2T\left(\frac{n}{2}\right) + cn$$

Using Master Theorem case 2 where a = 2, b = 2, thus $\log_2 2 = 1$, and c is just a coefficient, k = 1, p = 0, the Big-O notation for Merge Sort is O(nlogn). The performance of Merge Sort is better than Selection Sort or Insertion Sort for larger values of n.

10.2.4 Quicksort

The final sorting algorithm is Quicksort, which is also another divide-and-conquer approach to sorting arrays. The algorithm selects 1 item from the array called a "pivot". The array is then searched from both low and high indexes to find values that are higher and lower than the value. When a higher value is found at a lower index and a lower value is found at a higher index, the values are swapped. The operation continues until the pivot value is moved into place. Once the pivot value has been moved into place, a new pivot value is calculated; and the process is repeated again until the whole array is sorted. For example, let's say we have the following values in an array:

```
27 33 11 9 70
```

The choice of a pivot value can be any of the values in the array, but we will choose the middle value 11. Starting at index 0, we look for any values that are greater than 11, and in this case, it is at index 0 (27). Next starting at the high index 4, we look for any values less than 11, and in this case, it is at index 3 (9). Two indexes have been found with values greater and lower than 11, and then a swap is performed

```
9 33 11 27 70
```

The process starts again. We look for values larger than 11 at the lower index values and smaller values than 11 at the upper indexes. Index 1 (33) and Index 2 (11) are then swapped.

```
9 11 33 27 70
```

Since the pivot has moved, a new pivot value must be calculated. Eventually, the value of 33 is calculated to be the pivot and the final values are swapped.

```
9 11 27 33 70
```

Let's write the code for the Quicksort. Create a class under the jae.sort package called "QuickSort", and add Code Listing 10.10:

```
package jae.sort;

public class QuickSort {

    //Recursive helper method
    public static void sort(int[] dstoSort){

        if(!(dstoSort.length <= 1)){
            qSort(dstoSort, 0, dstoSort.length - 1);
        }
    }

    private static void qSort(int[] dstoSort, int low, int high){

        //base case for recursion
        if( low >= high){
            return;
        }

        //Get high and low index and pivot value in the middle of the array
        int i = low;
        int j = high;
        int pivot = dstoSort[low+(high-low) / 2];

        //use the pivot to find higher values at the low index and low values at the high index
        while ( i <= j)
        {
            //Find the lower index
            while(dstoSort[i] < pivot){
                i++;
            }
            //Find the higher index
            while(dstoSort[j] > pivot){
                j--;
            }
            //Swap values if low index is equal or less than high index
            if(i <= j){
                swap(dstoSort, i++, j--);
            }
        }
```

```
            //Pivot moved into place, calculate new pivot
            if (low < j){
                qSort(dstoSort, low, j);
            }
            if(high > i){
                qSort(dstoSort, i, high);
            }
        }

        //swap values at low and high index
        private static void swap(int[] dstoSort, int i, int j){
            int temp = dstoSort[i];
            dstoSort[i] = dstoSort[j];
            dstoSort[j] = temp;
        }
}
```

Code Listing 10.10 Quick Sort

In the SortTest Class, add the following code after Merge Sort calls:

```
//reset temp array
raDS = myDS.getRds().clone();

//Quick Sort
System.out.println("\nQuick Sort:");
QuickSort.sort(raDS);
PrintArrayOutput.PrintArray(raDS);
```

Running the application, an array of ten random integers is generated. The four sort algorithms are called to sort the array in ascending order.

```
51 80 42 26 47 49 91 76 24 78

Selection Sort:
24 26 42 47 49 51 76 78 80 91

Insertion Sort:
24 26 42 47 49 51 76 78 80 91

Merge Sort:
24 26 42 47 49 51 76 78 80 91

Quick Sort:
24 26 42 47 49 51 76 78 80 91
```

If you want to see the iterations of the arrays, add the following code to print out the arrays' current state at line 40 in the QuickSort class:

```
PrintArrayOutput.PrintArray(dstoSort);
```

The Quicksort algorithm starts with a recursive helper function to check if the array has 1 or fewer items in it. A call is made to qSort() method and will then be called recursively. The low and high indexes are set up, and the pivot value is calculated to be at the mid-way point in the array. The nested while-loops do most of the work to find values larger and smaller than the pivot value. The swap method is called to move the values to the proper location on either side of the pivot value. Once the pivot value is itself moved into place, qSort() is recursively called to calculate new low and high indexes, as well as a new pivot value. The process continues again until all items are sorted.

Calculating the Big-O notation for quicksort is a little complex, and the proofs to calculate Big-O are best left to other, more advanced courses. The starting index choice of the pivot value affects the performance. If you start at index 0 or at the top index of the array, the sorting is unbalanced since the algorithm is working from either end and has to go through the whole array T(n) = 1 + 2 + 3 ...+ n-1, which results in Big-O notation of O(n^2). If the pivot is chosen to be in the middle of the array, like the code we implemented, the array is nearly evenly split, which makes the sort balanced. The resulting Big-O notation is (nlogn).

10.2.5 Timing Test and the Sort Solution in the Java library

We now have implemented four different sort algorithms, and we have covered the basic Big-O analysis for each. Now let's see the performance in action. We will modify the SortTest class to add a timer to test each sort algorithm for larger arrays.

1. In the SortTest class, comment out all lines with "PrintArrayOutput.PrintArray(raDS)". Since the arrays are going to get bigger, it will be impossible to print out very large arrays.
2. If you added any "PrintArrayOutput.PrintArray()" calls in any of the sort classes, comment these out as well.
3. In the SortTest class, add two long integers for start and stop time

```
int n = 10;
int[] raDS = new int[n];

long StartTime;
long StopTime;

RandomIntegerDataSet myDS = new RandomIntegerDataSet(n);
  //PrintArrayOutput.PrintArray(myDS.getRds());
```

```
//Preserve the created array
raDS = myDS.getRds().clone();
```

4. For each call to the different sort method, add timer calls around each sort method to get the start and stop time. Next, add a call to print out the total time, which is the stop time – start time. For example:

```
//Selection Sort
System.out.println("\nSelection Sort:");
StartTime = System.currentTimeMillis();
SelectionSort.sort(raDS);
StopTime = System.currentTimeMillis();
System.out.println(" Total time: " + (StopTime - StartTime));
//PrintArrayOutput.PrintArray(raDS);
```

5. Run the application and you should get an output as similar to the following:

```
Selection Sort:
 Total time: 0

Insertion Sort:
 Total time: 0

Merge Sort:
 Total time: 1

Quick Sort:
 Total time: 0
```

Now, we will test for larger values of n. In the SortTest class, change the value of n from 10 to 1000:

```
int n = 100000;
int[] raDS = new int[n];

long StartTime;
long StopTime;

RandomIntegerDataSet myDS = new RandomIntegerDataSet(n);
```

Run the application. The output will look similar to the following:

```
Selection Sort:
   Total time: 1

Insertion Sort:
   Total time: 1

Merge Sort:
   Total time: 1

Quick Sort:
   Total time: 1
```

In the SortTest class, change the value of n at line 7, Code Listing 10.6, to 1000, 2500, 5000, 10000, 25000, 50000, 100000, and 250000 and run the application for each value. Your times will vary. Table 10.1 below shows the time results for each increase in the value n. You will notice that the change in total time for each sort algorithm matches the Big-O notation for that algorithm. The Quicksort provides the fastest sorting algorithm where Selection and Insertion sort algorithms perform more slowly for larger values of n.

Value for n	Selection Sort (ms)	Insertion Sort (ms)	Merge Sort (ms)	Quicksort (ms)
1000	1	1	1	1
2500	5	3	1	1
5000	16	11	1	1
10000	61	36	3	1
25000	365	229	5	3
50000	1458	895	9	3
100000	5764	3540	17	6
250000	35874	22255	34	15

Table 10.1 Sort Times for Increasing n

If we run Visual VM (discussed in chapter 8) and run profiling, you can see that the Selection and Insertion sort CPU times are longer than the other two sorting algorithms, Figure 10.6. The QuickSort gets a little skewed with the profiler running.

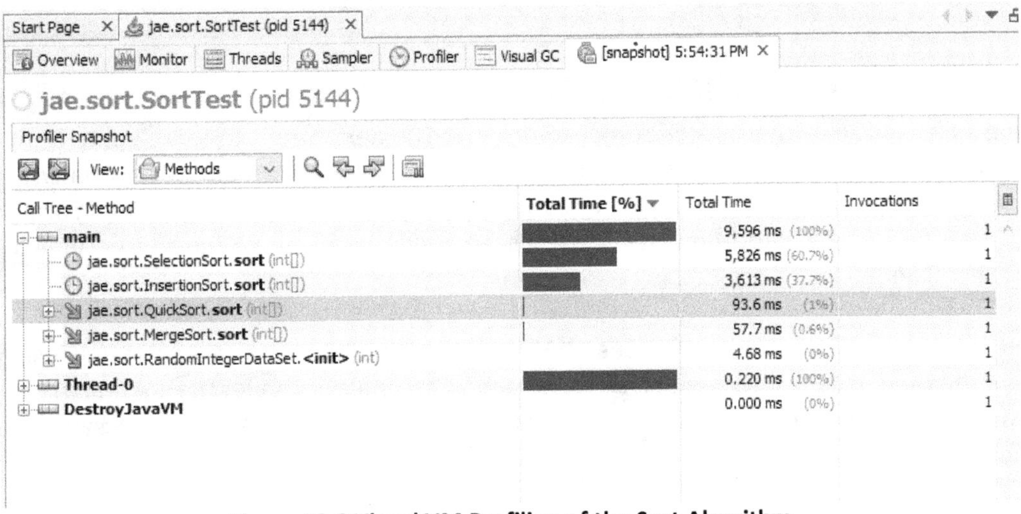

Figure 10.6 Visual VM Profiling of the Sort Algorithm

We can now add O(nlogn) to our earlier graph, Figure 10.7.

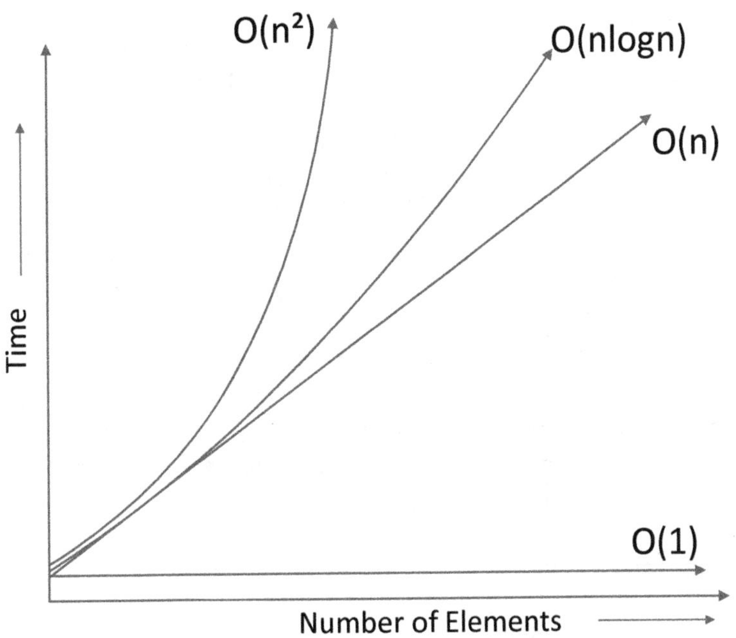

Figure 10.7 Big-O Growth Rate Comparison Graph

You don't have to implement your own quicksort algorithm into your code. The Java library already has the quicksort algorithm in the Array class (java.util.Arrays). There are different overriding sort() methods implemented in the class.

10.3 Computer Activity 10.2 - Searching Algorithms

Sorting an array is only one aspect of managing data. The next step is to search data to find an item we want to look for. In this computer activity, we will implement two popular search algorithms. First, we need to create a few classes to generate an integer array, print an array, and a test class to run the algorithms. Next, each search algorithm will be introduced in separate sections and added to the project.

Create a project called "CH10CA10.2-SearchAlgorithms". Create a class called "SearchTest" with a main() method under a package called "jae.search". Create a class under the jae.search package called "PrintArrayOutput". Create another class under jae.search package called "RandomIntegerDataSet".

In the PrintArrayOutput class, add Code Listing 10.11:

```
package jae.search;

public class PrintArrayOutput {

    public static void PrintArray(int[] aDS )
    {
        for(int i =0; i < aDS.length ; i ++)
        {
            System.out.print(aDS[i]+" ");
        }
        System.out.println(" ");
    }
}
```

Code Listing 10.11 PrintArrayOutput Class

The method takes an array and prints out all values in the array. The method is made static so that we can directly call the method when we want to test parts of our algorithm. In the RandomIntegerDataSet class, add Code Listing 10.12:

```
package jae.search;

import java.util.Random;

public class RandomIntegerDataSet {

    private int[] rds;
    private int n;
```

```

    public int[] getRds() {
        return rds;
    }

    public int getN() {
        return n;
    }

    public RandomIntegerDataSet(int n) {
        //super();
        this.n = n;
        GenerateArray();
    }

    public void GenerateArray()
    {
        rds = new int[n];

        Random gen = new Random();

        for(int i = 0; i < n; i++)
        {
            rds[i] = gen.nextInt(100);
        }
    }
}
```

Code Listing 10.12 RandomIntegerDataSet Class

The constructor creates an array of size 'n' that is passed in, and then randomly fills all array elements with integers between 0 and 99. In the SearchTest class, add Code Listing 10.13 to the main() method:

```
package jae.search;

import java.util.Arrays;

public class SearchTest {

    public static void main(String[] args) {
        // TODO Auto-generated method stub
        int n = 100;
        int[] raDS = new int[n];

        RandomIntegerDataSet myDS = new RandomIntegerDataSet(n);
```

```
13.         PrintArrayOutput.PrintArray(myDS.getRds());
14.
15.         //Preserve the created array
16.         raDS = myDS.getRds().clone();
17.     }
18. }
```

Code Listing 10.13 Search Test Class

The code generates an array size of 100 elements. Lines 12 and 13 create the array and then print out each element in an array. Lines 10 and 16 create a copy of the array so that we pass the copy of the array to each search algorithm. The import of the java.util.Arrays library will be used later. When you run the program, you will get a list of 100 integer values printed to the output window.

10.3.1 Linear / Sequential Search

The first search algorithm is called Linear Search (also called Sequential Search). As the name implies, the algorithm starts at index 0 and continues until a match is found. If a match is found, the index for the item found is returned. The worst case is that there is no match, which results in all items in the array being searched, thus the Big-O notation for Linear Search is O(n).

Let's write the code for the Linear Search. Create a class under the jae.search package called "LinearSearch", and add Code Listing 10.14:

```
package jae.search;

public class LinearSearch {

    public static int Search(int[] dstoSearch, int data){

        for(int j = 0; j < dstoSearch.length; j++)
        {
            if(dstoSearch[j] == data)
            {
                return j;
            }
        }
        return -1; //Data not found
    }
}
```

Code Listing 10.14 LinearSearch Class

In the SearchTest Class, add the following code after line 16:

```
//Linear / Sequential Search
//Unsorted array
System.out.println("\nLinear / Sequential Search:");
int k = LinearSearch.Search(raDS, 76);
if( k == -1){
    System.out.println("Data not found");
}
else
{
    System.out.println("Data found at index: " + k);
}
```

Running the application, an array of 100 random integers is generated. The code looks for the value 76. If the value is found, the LinearSearch() method will return the index location for the value 76 in the array. If a match is not found, the value "-1" is returned. Run the program a few times to see matches and no matches. The advantage of the Linear Search is that the array can remain random.

10.3.2 Binary Search

Searching for 1 item is simple and Linear Search is fast. There is even a faster search algorithm called Binary Search. A Binary Search requires that the array is sorted first. Then the array is split in half and the value is tested to see if the value is in the first or second half of the array. The array is divided again and again until the item is found or not found.

For example, the follow sorted array has 5 values. We want to find if the value 16 is in the array.

7	16	32	48	52
[0]	[1]	[2]	[3]	[4]

First, the low and high indexes are used to calculate the middle of the array. The middle index of the array is 2 with the value 32.

7	16	32	48	52
[0]	[1]	[2]	[3]	[4]

The value of 32 is greater than 16 so the 16 must be in the lower half of the array. The high index value is changed to 1, and the search continues

7	16	32	48	52
[0]	[1]	[2]	[3]	[4]

Since the array is an odd value the mid index is halved, the new midpoint is index 0. The value of 7 is less than the value of 16. The low index value is increased to 1.

7	16	32	48	52
[0]	[1]	[2]	[3]	[4]

The midpoint index is now 1, and since 16 is equal to 16, the index value 1 is returned. Let's write the code for the Binary Search. Create a class under the jae.search package called "BinarySearch", and add Code Listing 10.15:

```
package jae.search;

public class BinarySearch {

    public static int Search(int[] dstoSearch, int data){

        int low = 0;
        int high = dstoSearch.length - 1;
        while( low <= high)
        {
            //Find the middle index
            int mid = low + (high - low) / 2;
            //First check the data at the mid point, return if item found
            if(dstoSearch[mid] == data){
                return mid;
```

```
            }
            //else check if the mid value is less then the data
            //if true the value might be in the upper part of the array
            else if(dstoSearch[mid] < data){
                low = mid + 1;
            }
            //else if the data is greater, it is in the lower part of the array
            else{
                high = mid - 1;
            }
        }
        return -1;
    }
}
```

Code Listing 10.15 BinarySearch Class

In the SearchTest Class, add the following code after the calls to the Linear Search:

```
//binary Search
System.out.println("\nBinary Search:");
//Sort the array first
Arrays.sort(raDS);
PrintArrayOutput.PrintArray(myDS.getRds());
int j = BinarySearch.Search(raDS, 76);

if( j == -1){
    System.out.println("Data not found");
}
else
{
    System.out.println("Data found at index: " + j);
}
```

Running the application, an array of 100 random integers is generated. Both search algorithms run. In the case of the binary search, the array is first sorted using the Java library sort() method, and the sorted array is printed out. The code looks for the value 76. If the value is found, the BinarySearch() method will return the index location for the value 76 in the array. If a match is not found, the value "-1" is returned. The index return will be different than the Linear Search. Run the program a few times to see matches and no matches. Since the Binary Search is a divide-and-conquer algorithm, the Master Theorem is used again for determining the Big-O notation. The array of "n" is divided by two on each pass through the loop, and there is a constant time to process each value of n. The total time works out to be as follows:

$$T(n) = T\left(\frac{n}{2}\right) + 1$$

Where 'a' = 1, 'b' = 2, thus $\log_2 1 = 0$, and 'k' =0, and 'p' = 0. Using Master Theorem case 2, the Big-O notation for a Binary Search is O(log n).

10.3.3 Search in the Java library

Like sorting, you don't have to create your own search algorithm. The Array class (java.util.Arrays) contains support for the Binary Search. There are different overriding binarySearch() methods implemented in the class.

10.4 Algorithm Analysis – The Final Picture

Table 10.2 puts all the sort and search algorithms into a single table:

Algorithm	Big-O
Selection Sort	O(n2)
Insertion Sort	O(n2)
Merge Sort	O(nlogn)
Quicksort	O(nlogn)
Linear Search	O(n)
Binary Search	O (log n)

Table 10.2 Sort and Search Big-O Summary

There is a website (http://bigocheatsheet.com/) that provides the Big-O notation for many popular sort and search algorithms. The final graph for the Big-O notations covered in this chapters looks like Figure 10.8:

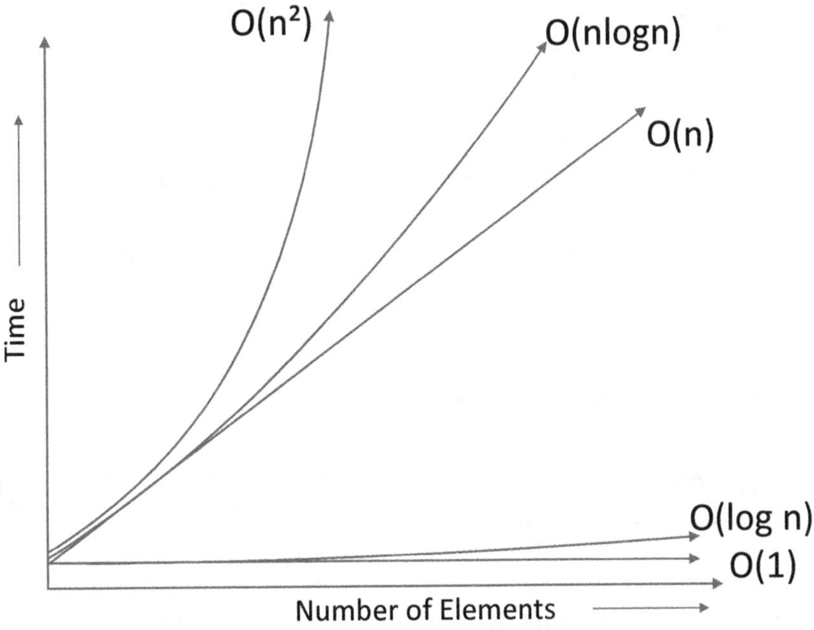

Figure 10.8 Big-O Growth Rate Comparison Graph

10.5 Summary and Homework Assignments

Today, we take Internet searching for granted, but there are some real mathematics and science behind the scenes. Even though the Java library already includes the most popular sort and search algorithms, the goal of this introduction to computer science class is for you to get familiar with analyzing algorithms. This chapter is a culmination of all the previous chapters. Creating these popular sort and search algorithms from scratch tests what we have learned from the previous chapters. More advanced computer science classes will dive deeper into different algorithm analysis techniques.

To get a good visual understanding of how these and other similar algorithms work, visit the site: AlgoRythmics (https://www.youtube.com/user/AlgoRythmics) that contains some very clever videos showing these algorithms in action.

We have covered the basic computer science concepts. The next few chapters help take this knowledge and build graphical programs and other interesting topics, but here are some homework questions and programming projects first.

10.5.1 Questions

1. In the 1992 movie *Sneakers*, the character Cosmo has another quote that is relevant today. What is it?

2. Who developed the Quick Sort Algorithm? And in what year was it developed?

3. Who developed the Merge Sort Algorithm? And in what year was it developed?

4. Why does sorting take longer than searching?

5. Draw the Merge Sort Tree for the following array of values:

6. The following integer array is passed into the Binary Search algorithm to find the value 22. Why does the result from the Binary Search algorithm say data is not found?

```
int[] myData = {2,5,7,13,15,26,22,35,78,89};
```

7. The Java library comes with a Quicksort method in the Array class (java.util.Arrays). What is the timing for an array with the following number of elements: 1000, 2500, 5000, 10000, 25000, 50000, 100000, and 250000? How does it compare to the Quicksort algorithm created from scratch? Faster, slower, or the same?

8. What is the Big-O notation for the following:

   a. $f(n) = n^n + n^4 + 3n$
   b. $f(n) = n^{0.5} + 1500n$
   c. $f(n) = 15n * 10n * n + n^2 + 17$
   d. $f(n) = e^n + n^4 + 20n$
   e. $f(n) = e^{n-5} + n! + 100n^2 + 14$

9. For the Big-O notation in question #8, redraw Figure 10.8 and add the growth rates for a, c, d, and e.

10. Would sorting an array before a Linear Search make the search go faster?

10.5.2 Programming Projects

1. Write a Binary Search Algorithm using recursion.

2. Write a Selection Sort algorithm that puts the array in descending order.

3. Write a Quicksort algorithm that puts the array in descending order.

4. The Internet allows programmers to share their code. The open source community has many websites and forums that allow programmers to help other programmers. For example: https://www.sanfoundry.com/java-program-implement-merge-sort/. Search the Internet for two different Mergesort examples. Add both Mergesort examples to the Sort Algorithm's Project by creating two classes, MergeSort2 and MergeSort3. What is the timing for each MergeSort for an array with the following number of elements: 1000, 2500, 5000, 10000, 25000, 50000, 100000, and 250000? How do they compare to the MergeSort implemented in Section 10.2.3? What does this say about freely available source code?

The following integer array will be used for program projects 5 and 6:

```
int[] myData = {26, 76, 30, 63, 69, 62, 91, 19, 74, 48, 28, 54, 65, 93,
55, 81, 32,  99, 36, 87, 42, 91, 1, 99, 0, 75, 81, 65, 27, 18, 72, 28,
58, 7, 84, 20, 38, 86, 35,49, 15, 33, 9, 84, 39, 86, 29, 29, 91, 70, 65,
11, 6, 74, 65, 17, 65, 54, 46, 14, 25, 9, 44, 51, 33, 87, 37, 44, 19,
34, 42, 80, 74, 63, 31, 3, 34, 56, 23, 92, 55, 9, 79, 48, 25, 87, 75,
38, 49, 73, 93, 48, 74, 58, 17, 94, 67, 5, 13, 86};
```

5. Write a program that searches for the value 48 in the array, counts the number of times the value 48 is found, and prints out the count result.

6. Write a program that sorts the array in ascending order, removes all duplicate values, backfills the remain indexes with 0, and prints the final array.

7. Write an program that sorts and outputs the following character array in alphabetical order:

```
char[] myLetters = {'h', 'j', 'r', 'c', 'u', 'o', 'a', 'n'};
```

8. Write a program that sorts the following array in ascending order and prints the sorted array.

```
String[] myFruit = {"Strawberry", "Orange", "Banana", "Apple",
"Blueberry",
"Lemon", "Grapefruit", "Grape"};
```

11 Introduction to GUI Programming with Swing and JavaFX

"It was one of those sort of apocalyptic moments. I remember within ten minutes of seeing the graphical user interface stuff, just knowing that every computer would work this way someday. It was so obvious once you saw it. It didn't require tremendous intellect. It was so clear."

-Steve Jobs

The development of the graphical user interface (GUI) took several decades and many individuals to develop all of the different elements: window, icon, menu, and pointing device. The mainframe systems of the 1960's started with dumb command line terminals all connected to a single mainframe. The first personal computers had a command line interface, which was okay for some. Programs like spreadsheets and word processors made a computer useful, but they were not true graphical user interfaces. They were still character-oriented displays. In the late-1980s and into the 1990s, true GUI interfaces made personal computers easier for the masses. Along with being able to print what-you-see-is-what-you-get (WYSIWYG) and the birth of the Internet, the computers were being brought to the masses. The advantage of a graphical user interface is in the simplicity of just point and click rather than memorizing a bunch of keyboard commands. GUI interfaces have evolved in the early 21st century to accommodate touch screens, where you can swipe and input other gestures by touching the display. Within 50 years, the computer terminals have moved from a dumb, character-oriented, CRT-based computer terminal, to high speed, high resolution, flat screen LCD touch screens on virtually every device from TVs, to automobile dashboards, to kitchen appliances, to smartphones that give us the ability to connect to the Internet universe.

All of the programs that we have developed so far are command line applications. Command line applications are great for testing functions and building utilities, but for end users, the best interface is a GUI interface. It is now time to create some applications with a GUI so that we can start making programs that will be part of the larger universe. This chapter covers creating GUI applications using the Swing and JavaFX library packages.

11.1 AWT and Swing

By the time Java was released in 1995, all personal computer operating systems were GUI based. Java came with the Abstract Window Toolkit (AWT). Like most early technologies, AWT had some issues. First, it had limited functionality. Second, commercial applications didn't have a consistent look and feel across different platforms, since AWT was tied to the native OS subroutines for displaying controls. The Java developers worked to fix the problems to make applications look more consistent across platforms and provide rich capability. Swing was introduced in 1997 as a portable GUI solution with a rich functionality and consistent look and feel across platforms. Swing was built on top of AWT, and Swing is totally written in Java so it doesn't depend on the OS subroutines. The AWT libraries (java.awt.*) and Swing libraries (javax.swing.*) are part of rt.jar, Figure 11.1.

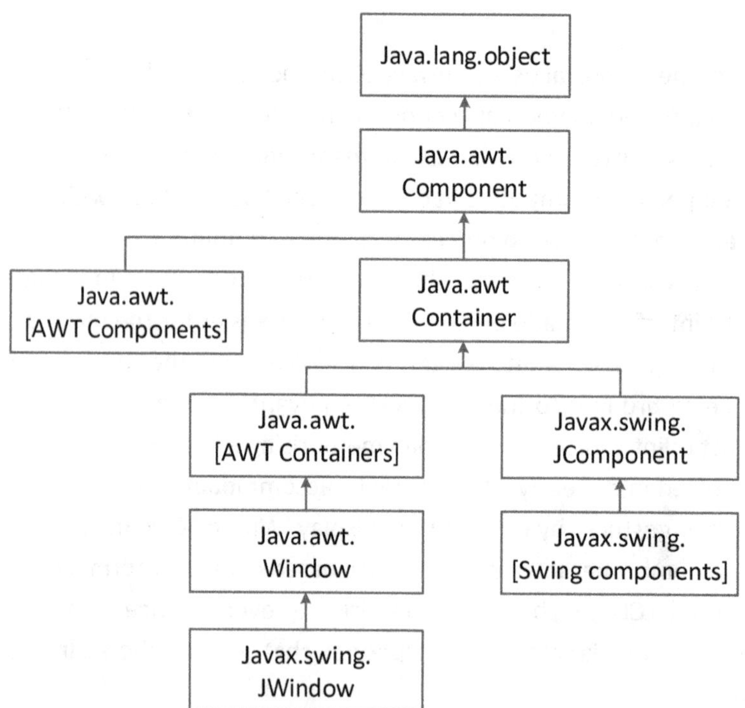

Figure 11.1 Java AWT and Swing Graphic Library Architecture

A Swing GUI application is comprised of several layers. The Window itself holds everything in specified dimensions and includes controls to shrink, expand, and close the window. The Frame is the base container for holding all the components. A container is a specialized Frame that can provide different panes to hold different layouts. A Layout provides the way components will be arranged in a specific Frame pane. Components are the different control items that the user will interact with, such as buttons, checkboxes, text boxes, etc. Figure 11.2 shows a typical Swing GUI structure.

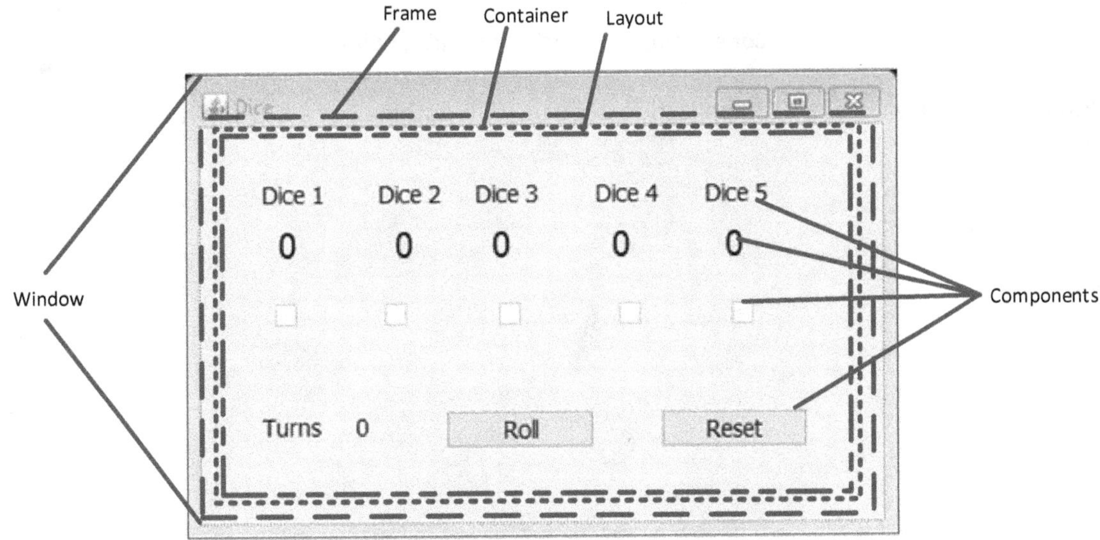

Figure 11.2 Swing GUI Structure

Note: The group at IBM that created Eclipse also created a GUI toolkit called the Standard Widget Toolkit (SWT). SWT is heavily dependent on the native OS subroutines like AWT. SWT has limitations since it is not easily portable, and there is limited OS support.

11.1.1 Computer Activity 11.1 - Basic Drawing with Swing/AWT

This computer activity will cover the basics of setting up the GUI application and drawing items in the application. Create a project called "CH11CA11.1-BasicShapes". Create a package called "jae.basicshapes". Create a class called "BasicDrawingTest" with a main() method under "jae.basicshapes". In the BasicDrawingTest Class, add Code Listing 11.1:

```
package jae.basicshapes;

import javax.swing.*;

```

```
5. public class BasicDrawingTest {
6.
7.     public static void main(String[] args) {
8.         // TODO Auto-generated method stub
9.         JFrame myWindow = new JFrame("BasicShapes");
10.        myWindow.setSize(500, 500);
11.        myWindow.setDefaultCloseOperation(JFrame.EXIT_ON_CLOSE);
12.        myWindow.setVisible(true);
13.    }
14. }
```

Code Listing 11.1 BasicDrawingTest Class

Run the application, and a GUI application appears with nothing but a title and window controls, Figure 11.3.

Figure 11.3 Basic Graphic Window with Title and Window Controls

A GUI application is set in a frame. Line 9 creates a new JFrame instance. JFrame class in Swing extends the Frame class in AWT, which extends awt.Window, which extends awt.Container. Line 10 sets the size of the frame. In this case, the frame is set up 500x500 pixels wide, where the top left coordinate is 0,0 and bottom right coordinate is 500,500. Line 11 set up the action, and when the instance of the frame is closed, it will close the applications. Line 12 makes the frame visible so that when you run the application the frame appears.

With the frame created, the next step is to put a component in the frame. You are probably familiar with some components like buttons, check boxes, scroll bars, etc. In this example, we will add a panel component with some drawings on the panel. Create a new class called

"BasicShapesPanel" under the "jae.basicshapes" that has javax.swing.JPanel as the superclass. A caution icon appears next to the class declaration. JPanel is a serializable class, thus a serial version UID is needed. Click on the caution icon, and then click on the "Add generated serial version ID" in the context window. To draw something in the panel, we will override the paintComponent() method that is inherited from one of the upper classes. Fill in Code Listing 11.2 for the BasicShapesPanel class:

```
package jae.basicshapes;

import javax.swing.JPanel;
import java.awt.*;

public class BasicShapesPanel extends JPanel {

    /**
     *
     */
    private static final long serialVersionUID =
6462471638279768474L;

    public void paintComponent(Graphics g){
        g.fillRect(50, 70, 50, 60);
        g.drawRect(150, 50, 80, 70);
        g.setColor(Color.blue);
        g.drawLine(300, 400, 450, 450);
        g.setColor(Color.GREEN);
        g.drawOval(250, 100, 100, 250);
        g.drawOval(300, 200, 50, 50);
        g.setColor(Color.ORANGE);
        g.draw3DRect(50, 400, 100, 25, true);
    }
}
```

Code Listing 11.2 BasicsShapesPanel Class

In the BasicDrawingTest class, between lines 11 and 12 in the main() method add the following code to add the panel to the frame:

```
BasicShapesPanel myShape = new BasicShapesPanel();
myWindow.add(myShape);
```

The first line creates a new BasicShapesPanel component instance, and the second line adds the component to the frame. If you run the application, the GUI application appears and the frame gets filled in with the panel covered in the shapes we drew, Figure 11.4.

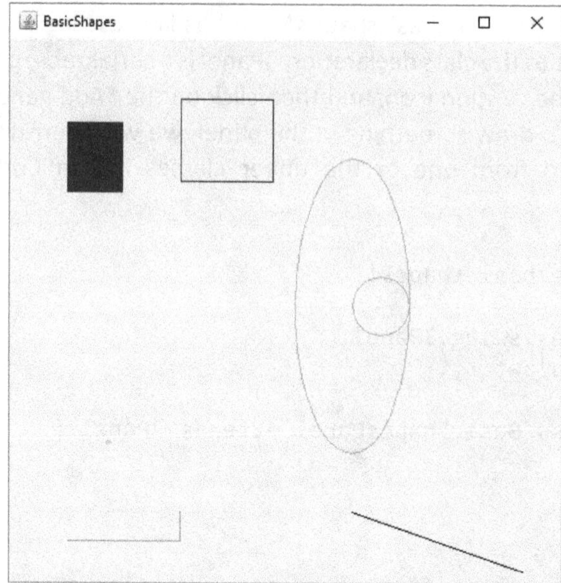

Figure 11.4 Basic Graphic Window with BasicsShapePaned Added

When the application runs, the Java windowing toolkit makes the call to the paintComponent() method and passes the Graphics parameters automatically. The Graphics class is an abstract class that allows you to draw on the component. There are several method calls to draw shapes for rectangles, ovals, and lines on the panel component. We can set the color before drawing the shape and use the built-in Color definitions in the java.awt library.

The JPanel class is one of many component classes in the javax.swing library. Here are the immediate subclasses to JComponent; some of these component subclasses have more subclasses:

AbstractButton, BasicInternalFrameTitlePane, Box, Box.Filler, JColorChooser, JComboBox, JFileChooser, JInternalFrame, JInternalFrame.JDesktopIcon, JLabel, JLayer, JLayeredPane, JList, JMenuBar, JOptionPane, JPanel, JPopupMenu, JProgressBar, JRootPane, JScrollBar, JScrollPane, JSeparator, JSlider, JSpinner, JSplitPane, JTabbedPane, JTable, JTableHeader, JTextComponent, JToolBar, JToolTip, JTree, JViewport

11.1.2 Event-Driven Programming

GUI applications that interact with the user are based on an event-driven programming paradigm. When a GUI application starts, the main loop waits or listens for external events such as a user clicking on a button control or touching a touchscreen. When an event is triggered, the event handler is called to perform some action. The event handler is also known as a callback routine. This next computer activity will demonstrate this basic concept.

11.1.3 Computer Activity 11.2 - Hello World, Again! With a Button Event.

In this computer activity, we will create an application with a Button component; when the button is clicked, a message is sent to the console.

Create a project called “CH11CA11.2-HelloWorldAgain”. Create a package called “jae.buttonexample”. Create a class called “ShowButton” with a main() method under “jae.buttonexample”. In the ShowButton Class, fill in Code Listing 11.3:

```
package jae.buttonexample;

import javax.swing.*;

public class ShowButton {

    public static void main(String[] args) {
        // TODO Auto-generated method stub
        JFrame myWindow = new JFrame("Button Example");
        myWindow.setSize(300,200);
        myWindow.setDefaultCloseOperation(JFrame.EXIT_ON_CLOSE);
        JButton helloButton = new JButton("Click for Message");
        myWindow.add(helloButton);


        myWindow.setVisible(true);
    }
}
```

Code Listing 11.3 ShowButton Class

Run the application, and you will get a GUI application with a button control that fills the frame, Figure 11.5. If you click on the button, the button will look like it is being pressed but nothing will happen.

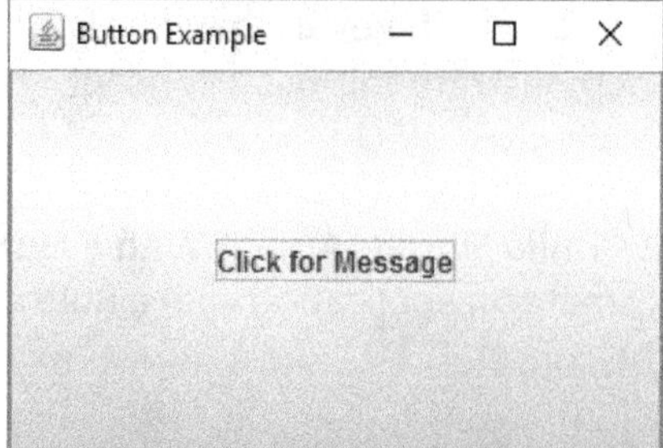

Figure 11.5 Full-Frame Button Control

Now let's add the code behind the click. Create a new class called "OnClickListener" under the "jae.buttonexample" package declaration. Add the line:

```
import java.awt.event.*;
```

Add to the class declaration: "implements ActionLister". A caution symbol will appear next to the class, requesting the method to be implemented, Figure 11.6. Click on the caution symbol, and select "Add unimplemented methods" from the context window, and fill in the rest of the code, Code Listing 11.4.

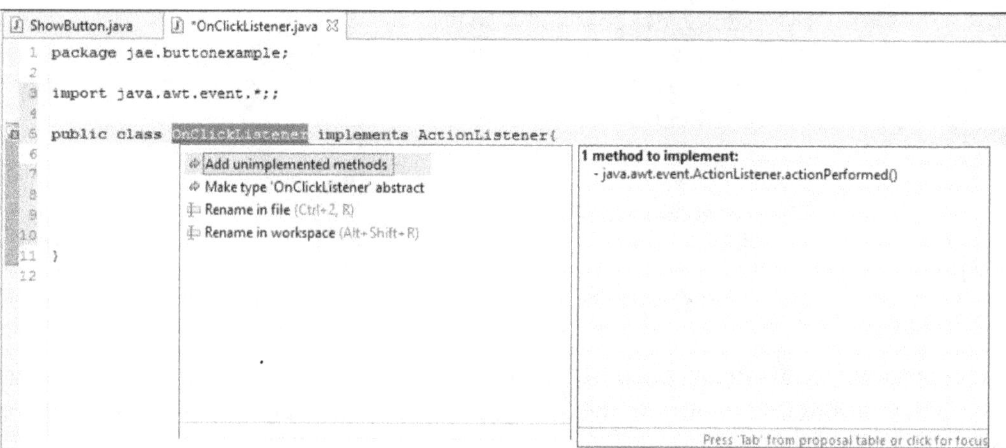

Figure 11.6 Method Implementation Requested in Eclipse

```
package jae.buttonexample;

import java.awt.event.*;

public class OnClickListener implements ActionListener{

    @Override
    public void actionPerformed(ActionEvent arg0) {
        // TODO Auto-generated method stub
        System.out.println("Hello World, Again!");
    }
}
```

Code Listing 11.4 OnClickListener Code Implementation

The actionPerformed() method will be called when the button is clicked. The ActionEvent that gets passed in contains information about the event, but none of the information is needed to perform the action. If there were multiple buttons using the same actionPerformed() method, an if-then decision could be added to figure out which button was pressed and perform the action for that button. The only action in this example is to print out a message at the console window. In the "ShowButton" class, fill in the code that adds the new listener and inks it to the button, Code Listing 11.5:

```
package jae.buttonexample;

import javax.swing.*;

public class ShowButton {

    public static void main(String[] args) {
        // TODO Auto-generated method stub
        JFrame myWindow = new JFrame("Button Example");
        myWindow.setSize(300, 200);
        myWindow.setDefaultCloseOperation(JFrame.EXIT_ON_CLOSE);
        JButton helloButton = new JButton("Click for Message");
        myWindow.add(helloButton);

        OnClickListener buttonListener = new OnClickListener();
        helloButton.addActionListener(buttonListener);

        myWindow.setVisible(true);
    }
}
```

Code Listing 11.5 Add OnClickListner to the ShowButton Class

Run the application again. Clicking on the button this time produces the action to be performed, Figure 11.7.

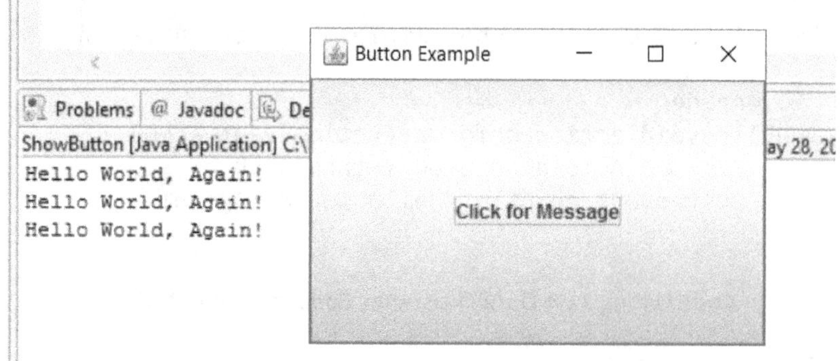

Figure 11.7 Button Click with Button Click Listener Implemented

Line 15 in the main() method adds the new OnClickListener, which implements the callback that prints out the message. Line 16 associates the action listener to the button. When you click on the button, the message appears, but the application never terminates. You can keep on clicking the button.

11.1.4 Computer Activity 11.3 - Swing Layout Management

So far, we have explored two GUI programs with a single component filling the Frame. The next step is to add multiple components to the frame. AWT comes with different layout management classes that create a structure for placing components on a pane. Layouts are added to the Frame/Container pane to allow for multiple components. There are 8 layout classes:

1. BorderLayout
2. BoxLayout
3. CardLayout
4. FlowLayout
5. GridBagLayout
6. GridLayout
7. GroupLayout
8. SpringLayout

The online Java documentation has demo examples for each layout. For this computer activity, the BoxLayout will be used to create a GUI application with a button on top of a text field. When the button is pressed a message appears in the text field. Create a project called CH11CA11.3-BoxLayout. Create a package called "jae.boxlayout". Create two classes. The first will be called

"ShowBoxLayout", and it will have the main() method. The other class will be called "CustomBoxLayout". In the CustomBoxLayout class add the following imports:

```
import javax.swing.*;
import java.awt.*;
```

In the class declaration, add the following

```
import java.awt.event.ActionEvent;
```

A caution symbol will appear next to the class, requesting that the method needs to be implemented. Click on the caution symbol and select "Add unimplemented methods" from the context window. Since the text field will be shared between two classes, add the following to the class to declare a JTextField:

```
public static JTextField myText;
```

Create a new public method called showGUI, and fill in the following code:

```
public void showGUI(){
    JFrame myFrame = new JFrame("BoxLayout");
    myFrame.setSize(300, 100);
    myFrame.setDefaultCloseOperation(JFrame.EXIT_ON_CLOSE);

    Container myPane = new Container();
    myPane.setLayout(new BoxLayout(myPane, BoxLayout.Y_AXIS));

    JButton myButton = new JButton("Click for Message");
    myButton.setAlignmentX(Component.CENTER_ALIGNMENT);
    myPane.add(myButton);
    myButton.addActionListener(this);

    myText = new JTextField();
    myText.setAlignmentX(Component.CENTER_ALIGNMENT);
    myPane.add(myText);

    myFrame.add(myPane);
    myFrame.setVisible(true);
}
```

In the actionPerformed method, fill in the following code:

```
// TODO Auto-generated method stub
myText.setEnabled(true);
myText.setText("Hello World, Again!");
```

Code Listing 11.6 is the full code listing for the class:

```
package jae.boxlayout;

import javax.swing.*;
import java.awt.*;
import java.awt.event.ActionEvent;
import java.awt.event.ActionListener;

public class CustomBoxLayout implements ActionListener{

    public static JTextField myText;

    @Override
    public void actionPerformed(ActionEvent e) {
        // TODO Auto-generated method stub
        myText.setEnabled(true);
        myText.setText("Hello World, Again!");
    }

    public void showGUI(){
        JFrame myFrame = new JFrame("BoxLayout");
        myFrame.setSize(300, 100);
        myFrame.setDefaultCloseOperation(JFrame.EXIT_ON_CLOSE);

        Container myPane = new Container();
        myPane.setLayout(new BoxLayout(myPane, BoxLayout.Y_AXIS));

        JButton myButton = new JButton("Click for Message");
        myButton.setAlignmentX(Component.CENTER_ALIGNMENT);
        myPane.add(myButton);
        myButton.addActionListener(this);

        myText = new JTextField();
        myText.setAlignmentX(Component.CENTER_ALIGNMENT);
        myPane.add(myText);

```

```
36.         myFrame.add(myPane);
37.         myFrame.setVisible(true);
38.     }
39. }
```

Code Listing 11.6 CustomBoxLayout Class

In the ShowBoxLayout class, fill in the following code:

```
package jae.boxlayout;

public class ShowBoxLayout {

    public static void main(String[] args) {
        // TODO Auto-generated method stub
        CustomBoxLayout showMyLayout = new CustomBoxLayout();
        showMyLayout.showGUI();
    }
}
```

Creating the JFrame was put into a separate class in order to access non-static methods. The showGUI() method sets up the frame as before. There is no call to a separate custom panel this time, and all panel and component setups are in the same method. Lines 24-25 of the CustomBoxLayout class create the container, and the BoxLayout is set up. Since the BoxLayout is a class, we instantiate the BoxLayout class object within the setLayout() method. The instance is never used again, so there is no need to break it out into a separate line. The layout is set up for components listed on the y-axis. Lines 27-30 set up the button. The button has a label, and the alignment is centered in the pane. The button is added to the pane, and the connection between the button and the ActionListerner method is made. Lines 32-34 add the JTextField. Like the button, the text field is centered in the pane. The actionPerformed method sets the text in the text field when the button is pushed. Run the application, and the button appears above the text field. Click the button and the message appears in the text field, Figure 11.8.

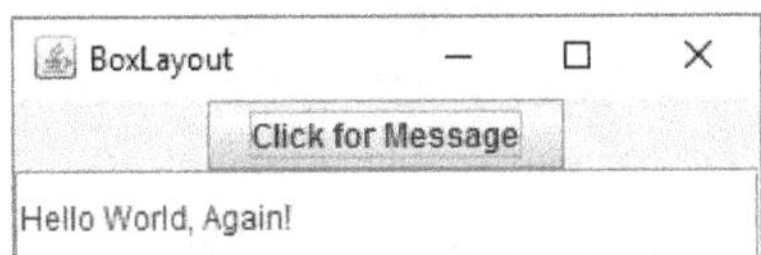

Figure 11.8 CustomBoxLayout Graphic Layout

11.1.5 GUI by Code versus GUI by Designers

Computer science wants to focus on the code and algorithms, but having to place the components into their proper location through code can be a bit tedious. In reality, programmers simply lay out the controls using a GUI designer tool, and then write the callback routines behind the controls. Eclipse comes with a GUI design tool called WindowBuilder, Figure 11.9. If it is not part of your Eclipse download, it can be added from the Eclipse marketplace. We will show you how to install WindowBuilder in Section 11.1.6. WindowBuilder makes it easy to lay out the controls visually.

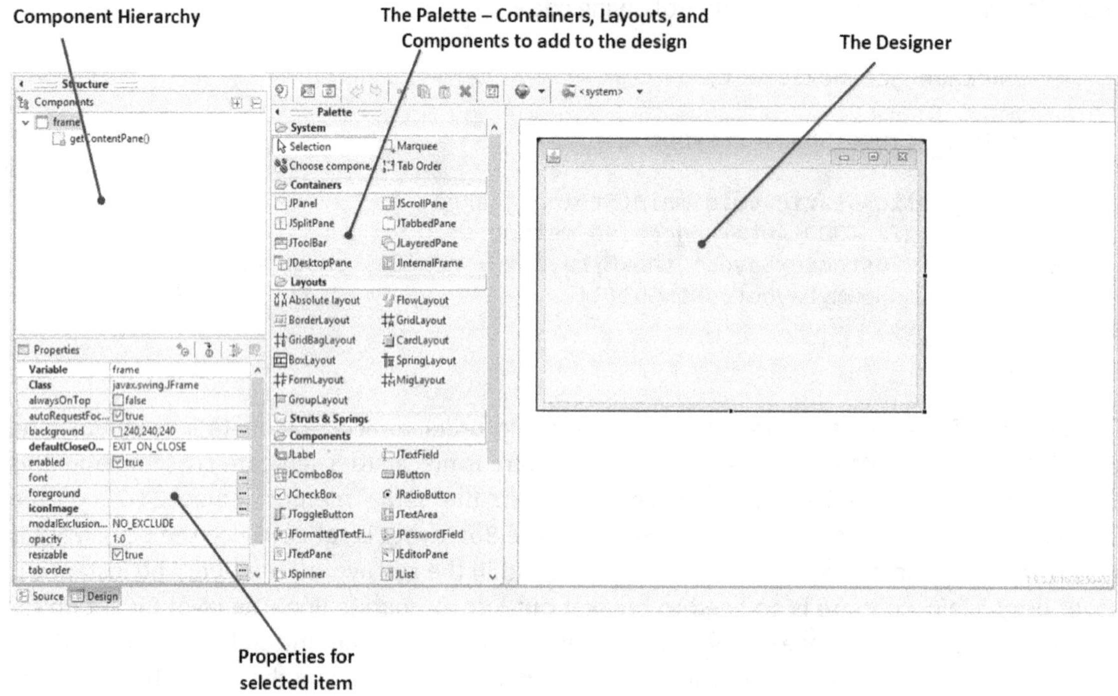

Figure 11.9 Eclipse WindowBuilder

WindowBuilder has all of the containers, layouts, components and other items available in a Palette. You simply click on an item and then click on the layout pane to place the item. The components will be added to the component list on the left side. Once the item has been placed, individual properties for the item can be changed in the lower left. Even though WindowBuilder makes it easy to set up a GUI interface, you still should be familiar with the underlying code.

11.1.6 Computer Activity 11.4 - GUI Coin Flip Game

The coin flip game was covered in earlier chapters. In this computer activity, we will use WindowBuilder to create a GUI version of the game that tracks a player's score, Figure 11.10.

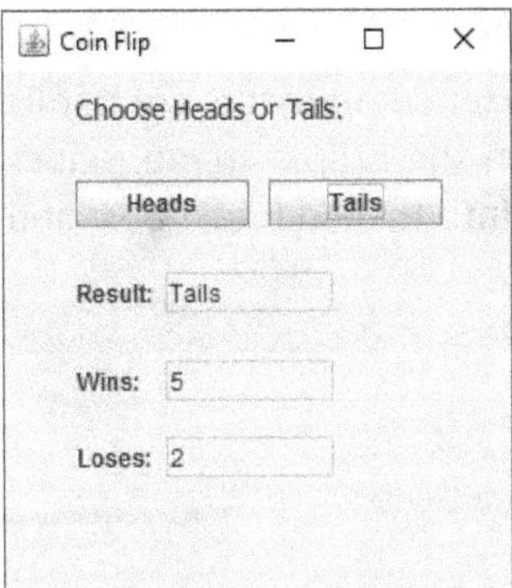

Figure 11.10 GUI Version of Coin Flip Game

First, make sure that WindowBuilder is installed. From the Eclipse menu, select Help->About Eclipse, Figure 11.11.

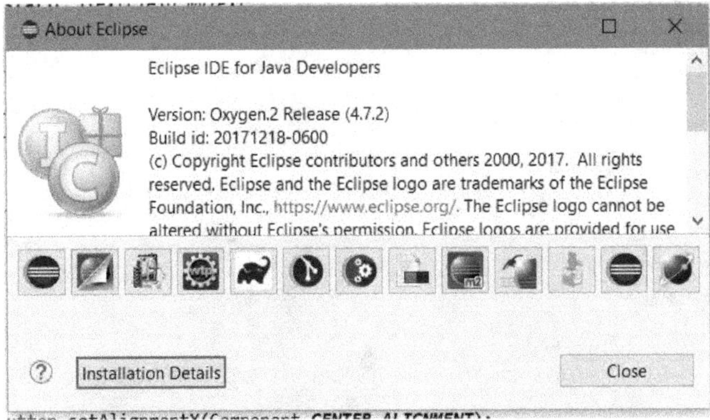

Figure 11.11 Help About Eclipse

Then click Installation Details, Figure 11.12

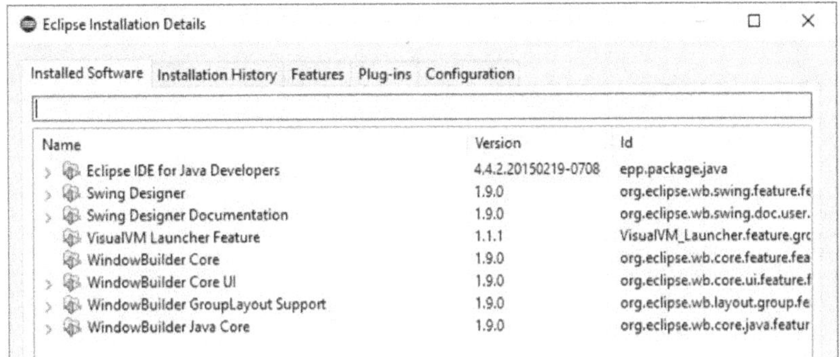

Figure 11.12 Eclipse Installation Details Showing WindowBuilder Installed

Scroll down, and if the WindowBuilder components are not listed, you can install WindowBuilder from the Eclipse Marketplace. From the Eclipse menu, select Help->Eclipse Marketplace. In the Search tab, type "WindowBuilder" into the Find: text box, and click Go, Figure 11.13.

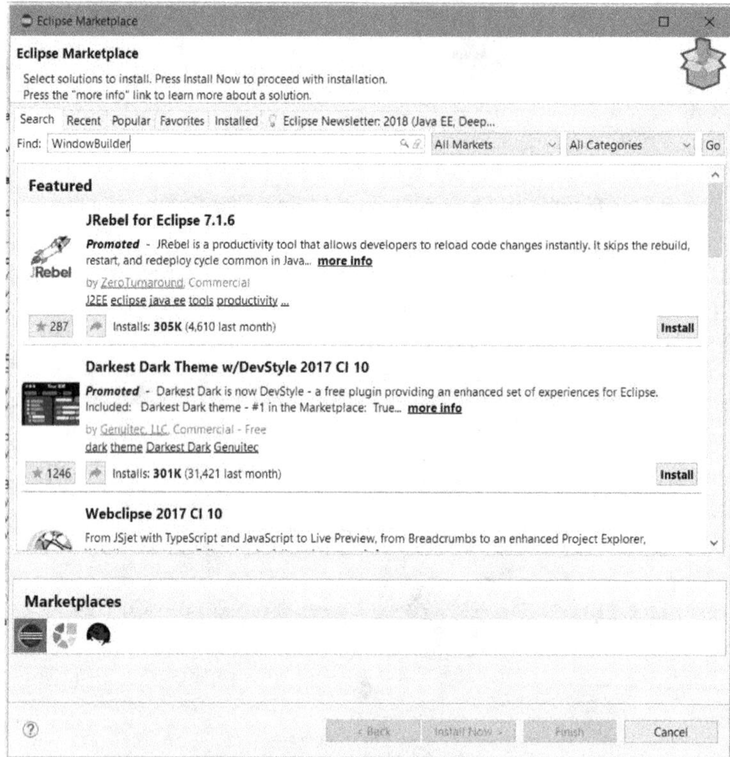

Figure 11.13 Eclipse Marketplace

WindowBuilder will be found and displayed, Figure 11.14. Click on the Install button for WindowBuilder.

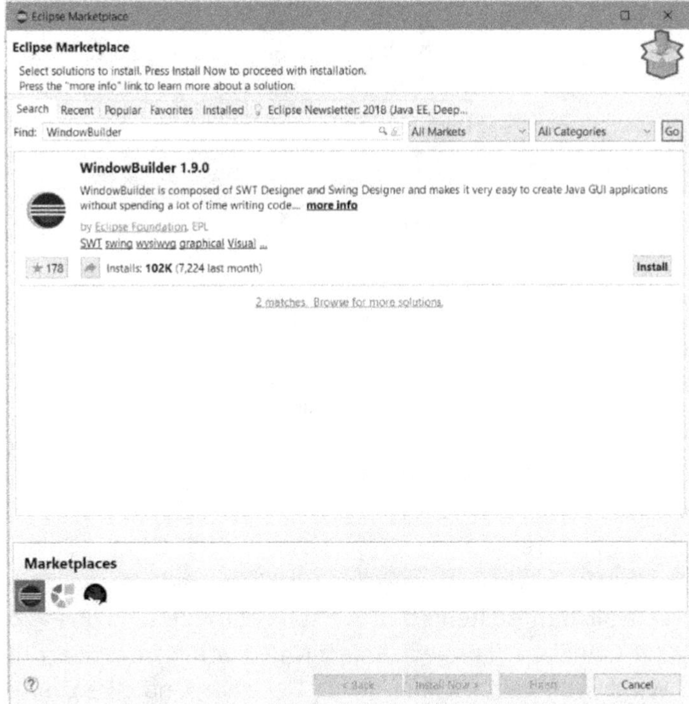

Figure 11.14 WindowBuilder Found in Eclipse Marketplace

Follow the installation dialog boxes. Install all the components, Figure 11.15:

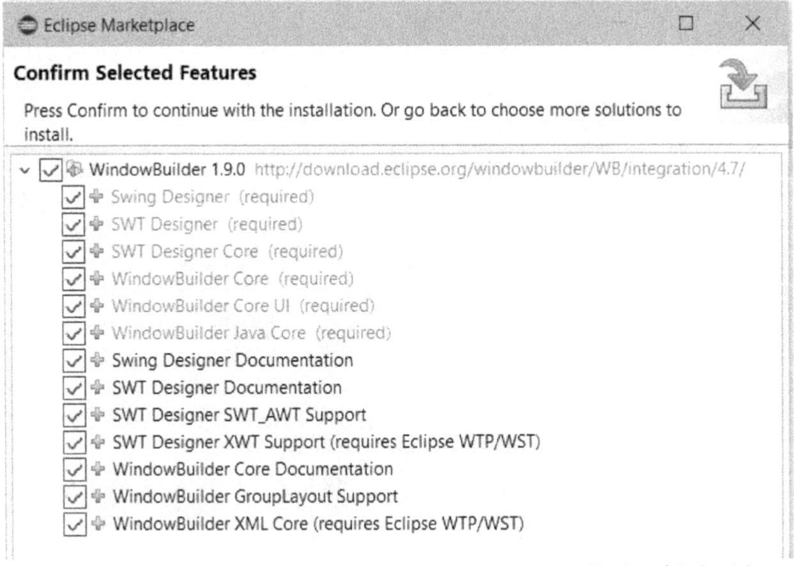

Figure 11.15 WindowBuilder Full Component Installation (default)

Review and Accept the license agreement. Then click Finish, and you will be prompted to restart Eclipse, Figure 11.16:

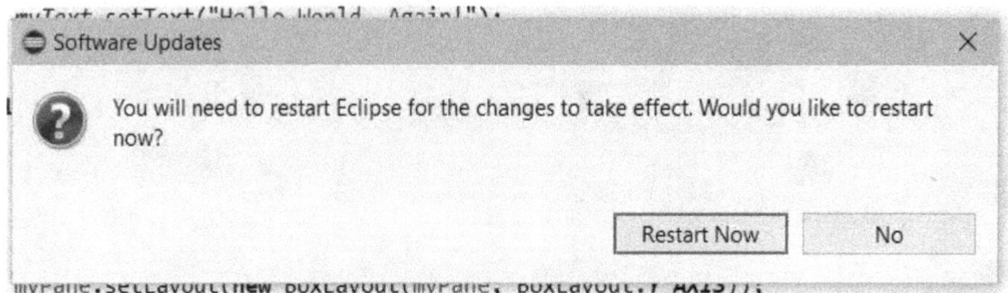

Figure 11.16 Eclipse Post-Installation Restart Prompt

Click Restart Now and Eclipse will restart with WindowBuilder now installed.

With WindowBuilder installed, create a new project called "CH11CA11.4-CoinFlipGUI". In previous projects, we would have you go through creating packages and classes. This time we will start WindowBuilder to create all of these items and the start of the JFrame. In Package Explorer, right-click on the CH11CA11.4-CoinFlipGUI project. Select New->Other from the context window. In the New dialog, expand WindowBuilder, expand Swing Designer, and click on Application Window. Click Next, Figure 11.17.

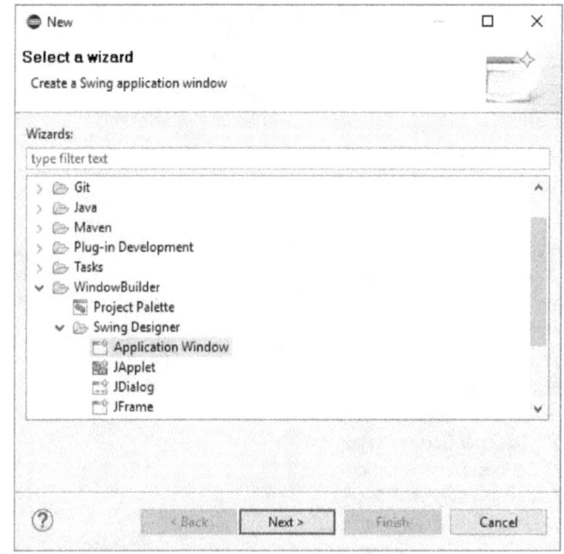

Figure 11.17 Creating an Application Window with WindowBuilder

In the New Swing Application dialog, enter the Package name "jae.coinflipgui" and the Name "CoinFlipGUI". Click Finish, Figure 11.18.

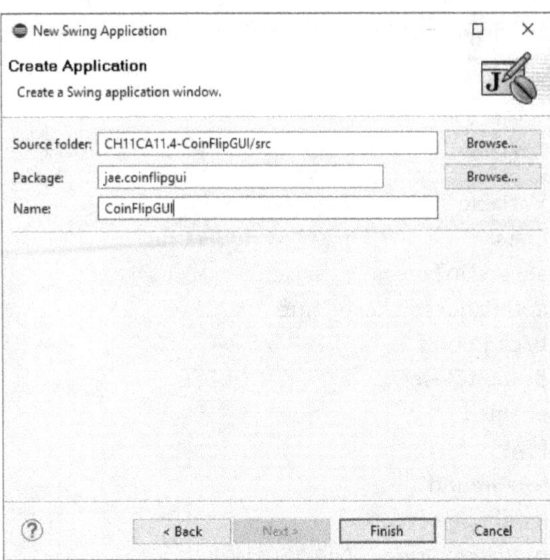

Figure 11.18 New Swing Application Information

The wizard will generate the CoinFlipGUI.java file with the CoinFlipGUI class. The wizard sets up the main() method to call the CoinFlipGUI() method. We did the same setup manually in Computer Activity 11.3, except with different class files. At the bottom of the Java source file window, there are tabs for Source and Design, Figure 11.19. Click on the Design tab.

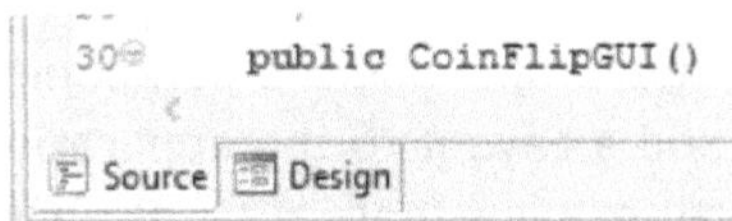

Figure 11.19 Source and Design Tabs in Eclipse

If you are using code that someone else has supplied, if you have updated Eclipse and restarted it, or if you are using GUI code that was written from scratch with WindowBuilder, the Design tab may not be available automatically. If the Design tab is not showing when you open the .java file or if you want to generate a design view for code written from scratch—WindowBuilder is one of few GUI designer tools that will parse the code and create a WindowBuilder design representation—right-click on the .java file in the Package Explorer and select Open With->WindowBuilder Editor; and the Design tab will be added to the editor window. When you select the Design tab, WindowBuilder will parse the code and verify the design components. It may take a minute to actually display all of the windows and information, so be patient.

After the Design tab is selected and WindowBuilder completes parsing any available code, the designer appears with a blank application on the right. Click on the empty application frame on the right (not in the layout area). The Properties pane will display all of the properties of the frame. In the Properties pane, scroll down until you see "title". In the blank box next to title enter "Coin Flip" and hit Enter.

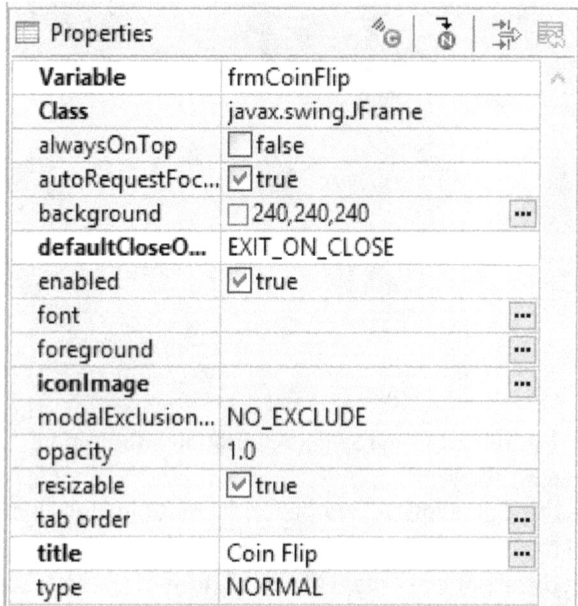

Figure 11.20 - CoinFlip Properties

The title will now appear in the empty frame and the Components will show the frame changes to frmCoinFlip. We are going to add a Layout to the application. The Palette pane lists all the Layouts discussed earlier, and there are a few more available in WindowBuilder. Click on Absolute layout. The selection will look depressed. Now, move the mouse over to the application in the empty area, and the frame turns green. Click on the application in the empty space. Nothing appears to have happened, but this layout allows you to place the components anywhere in the frame. Now, we will add the components to the application.

1. Click on JLabel:
   a. Click on the top right area of the application.
   b. Enter the following text: "Choose Heads or Tails:", and hit Enter.
   c. In the properties, select the "..." button next to font and change the font size to 14.
   d. Use the mouse to expand the label so that all of the text is shown.

2. Click on JButton:
    a. Click on area in the application below the first label and to the left in the pane.
    b. Change the text to say "Heads". In the properties, the variable name gets changed to btnHeads to distinguish this button from other possible buttons.
3. Click on JButton:
    a. Click on area in the application below the first label and to the right of the Heads button. As you move the mouse around in the pane before you click and establish the button's location, notice that when the new button is aligned vertically with the previous button, a thin blue line going through both buttons at the base of the button labels will show. If you move out of alignment with the previous button, the line will disappear. Let's align the two buttons, vertically, so pick a horizontal position to the right of the first button, and then move up or down until the blue alignment line is displayed and then click the mouse.
    b. Change the text to say "Tails".
4. Click on JLabel:
    a. Place the Label below Heads button. Use the horizontal alignment line to align the left side of the label with the left side of the Heads button.
    b. Change the text to "Result".
5. Click on JTextField:
    a. Place the text field to the right of Result label. Use the vertical alignment line to align the text field with the Result label.
    b. In the properties for the new text field, change the Variable name to "txtResult" and uncheck "editable".
6. Click on JLabel:
    a. Place the Label below Results label. Use the horizontal alignment line to align the left side of this new label with the left side of the Result label.
    b. Change the text to "Wins".
7. Click on JTextField:
    a. Place the Text filed to the right of Wins label and below the txtResult text field. Use the alignment lines to align the left edge with the left edge of the txtResult text field and the base with the base of the Wins label.
    b. In the properties for the new text field, change the Variable name to "txtWins" and uncheck "editable".
8. Click on JLabel:
    a. Place the Label below the Wins label. Use the alignment line to align the left edge to the left edges of the 2 previous labels above it.
    b. Change the text to "Losses".

9. Click on JTextField:
   a. Place the Text field to the right of the Losses label. Use the alignment lines to align the left edge to the left edges of the 2 previous text fields above it and the base with the base of the Losses label.
   b. In the properties for the new text field, change the Variable name to "txtLosses" and uncheck "editable".

Adjust the size of the application so that all of the components are framed in the center. It should look similar to Figure 11.21. Save the application.

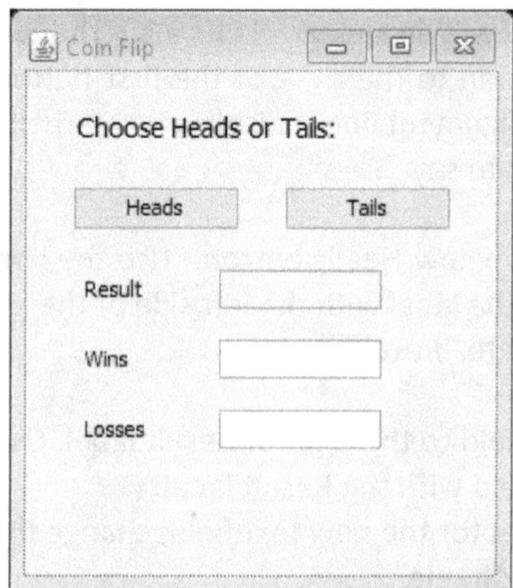

Figure 11.21 Coin Flip WindowBuilder Designer GUI

The final step is to add the code behind the controls. Click on the Source tab. The layout is set to null, and all of the controls are set in specific coordinates with the setBounds() method call. Add the import for the Random classes.

```
import java.util.Random;
```

In the CoinFlipGUI class, there are a number of private declarations for the frame and the text fields. Add the following below the private text fields for tracking the score and Random number generator instance.

```
private int wins = 0;
private int losses = 0;
private Random gen;
```

In the CoinFilpGui() method, before the initialize(), add the code to instantiate the random generator.

```
public CoinFlipGUI() {
    gen = new Random();
    initialize();
}
```

Click on the "Design" tab to go back to the design view. In the application, right-click on the Heads button, and select Add event handler->mouse->mouseClicked from the context window, Figure 11.22.

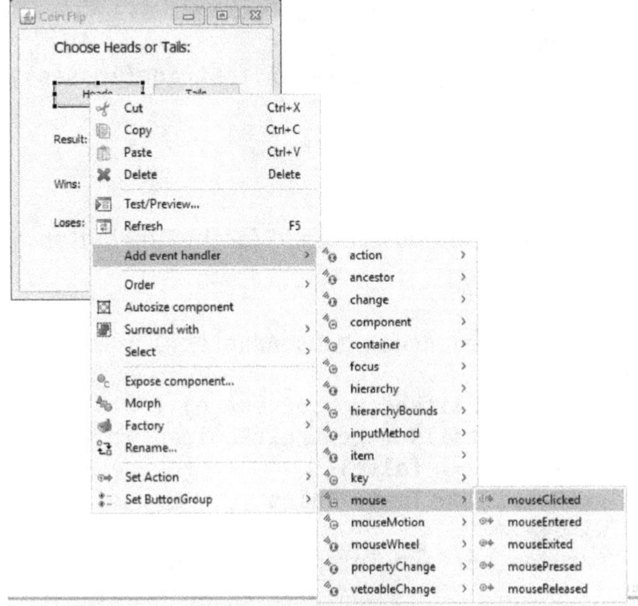

Figure 11.22 Adding Mouse Click Event Handler

In the initialize() method, an "addMouseListener" is added below the instantiation of the "Heads" button. In the mouseClicked() method, fill in the code to handle when the user clicks the heads button.

```
btnHeads.addMouseListener(new MouseAdapter() {
   @Override
   public void mouseClicked(MouseEvent arg0) {
       boolean headstails = gen.nextBoolean();
       if(headstails == true){
           txtResult.setText("Heads");
           wins++;
           txtWins.setText(Integer.toString(wins));
       }
       else
       {
           txtResult.setText("Tails");
           losses++;
           txtLosses.setText(Integer.toString(losses));
       }
   }
});
```

Repeat the steps to generate the "addMouseListener" for the Tails button, and fill in the following code:

```
btnTails.addMouseListener(new MouseAdapter() {
     @Override
     public void mouseClicked(MouseEvent e) {
         boolean headstails = gen.nextBoolean();
         if(headstails == false){
             txtResult.setText("Tails");
             wins++;
             txtWins.setText(Integer.toString(wins));
         }
         else{
             txtResult.setText("Heads");
             losses++;
             txtLosses.setText(Integer.toString(losses));
         }

     }
});
```

Save and run the application. Click on the buttons randomly and you should get wins and losses results. Most of the development work was creating the GUI itself. Once the GUI was created, adding the code that we have worked with in the past was simple. The main application's functionality is in the button click event handlers. A random Boolean value is generated and depending on the button click, either the user makes the right guess and gets a win, or guesses wrong and gets a loss. A command line game is now a GUI game. How the application starts up is a little different than what we have seen so far. The main() method is present and is called by the JVM when the application is started. The main() method contains some concepts not previously discussed:

```
public static void main(String[] args) {
     EventQueue.invokeLater(new Runnable() {
        public void run() {
              try {
                  CoinFlipGUI window = new CoinFlipGUI();
                  window.frmCoinFlip.setVisible(true);
              } catch (Exception e) {
                  e.printStackTrace();
              }
        }
     });
 }
```

The Runnable() class is used for running code in a separate thread. We mentioned threads when we talked about debugging but never fully defined it.

Definition: *Thread* – A thread of execution is the smallest piece of code that an operating scheduler can run.

When you run different applications, the operating system makes each application m run in different threads. Some applications are multithreaded and can spawn threads to have code run simultaneously. There is a lot more to creating a multithreaded application that we will not cover in this book. In this particular case, the wizard sets up the Swing application for the GUI to run in a separate thread. The Run() method is being overridden to launch the CoinFlipGUI() constructor method and then show the frame. An anonymous instantiation of the Runnable() class is passed to the EventQueue. The EventQueue is what handles different events from touchscreen, mouse, keyboard etc. The EventQueue is what kicks off the thread to launch the application. The event handler is there to catch any possible errors.

11.1.7 Computer Activity 11.5 – Explore Other Swing Controls

There are other controls besides labels, text fields, and buttons. In this computer activity, we will implement a Swing application that demonstrates checkboxes, radio buttons, toggle buttons, scroll bar, and a progress bar. Create a new Java project called "CH11CA11.5-OtherControls". In Package Explorer, right-click on the CH11CA11.5--OtherControls project. Select New->Other from the context window. In the New dialog, expand WindowBuilder and click on Application Window, and click Next. Enter "jae.othercontrols" for the package and OtherControls for the class name and click Finish. The program space will be created as before. Click on the design tab to open the designer. We will create a program that will look like Figure 11.23:

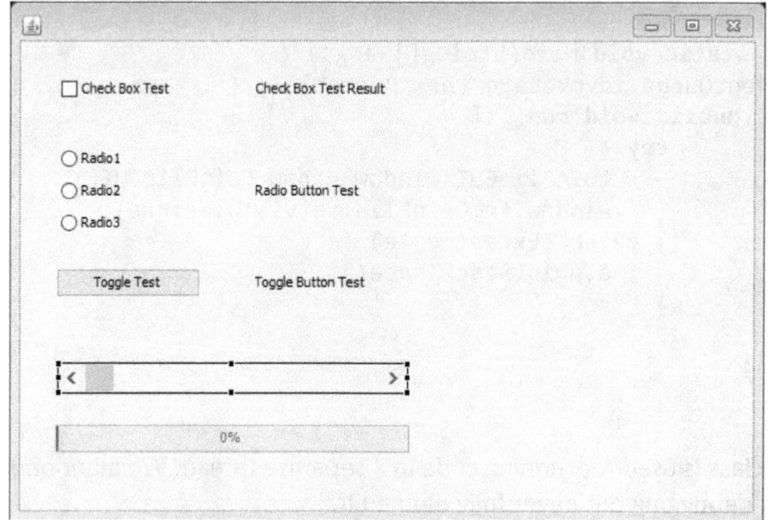

Figure 11.23 Other Swing Controls GUI

In the Layouts, click on Absolute layout and then click in the middle of the frame. Next, we will add the different controls (refer to Figure 11.23 for the control positioning):

1. Click on JLabel:
    a. Add JLabel to the panel.
    b. Change the name to lblCheckBox.
2. Click on JLabel:
    a. Add JLabel to the panel.
    b. Change the name to lblRadioButtonTest.
3. Click on JLabel:
    a. Add JLabel to the panel.
    b. Change the name to lblToggleButtonTest.
4. Click on JCheckBox:
    a. Add JCheckBox to the panel.
    b. Change the text to "Check Box Test".
    c. Change the variable to "chckbxCheckBoxTest".
5. Click on JRadioButton:
    a. Add JRadioButton to the panel.
    b. Change the text to "Radio1".
    c. Change the variable to "rbRadio1".

6. Click on JRadioButton:
    a. Add JRadioButton to the panel.
    b. Change the text to "Radio2".
    c. Change the variable to "rbRadio2".
7. Click on JRadioButton:
    a. Add JRadioButton to the panel.
    b. Change the text to "Radio3".
    c. Change the variable to "rbRadio3".
8. Click on JToggleButton:
    a. Add JToggleButton to the panel.
    b. Change the text to "Toggle Test".
    c. Change the variable to "tglbtnToggleTest".
9. Click on JProgressBar:
    a. Add JProgressBar to the panel.
    b. Change the variable to "progressBar".
    c. Set stringPainted to true.
10. Click on JScrollBar:
    a. Add JScrollBar to the panel.
    b. Change the variable to "scrollBar".
    c. Change orientation to HORIZONTAL.

Double-check that the controls are laid out per Figure 11.23 above. The next step is to group the radio buttons, so that selecting one radio button unchecks the other radio buttons. In the designer, right-click on Radio1, and select SetButtonGroup->New Standard from the context menu. This will add Radio1 button to a group. The component tree shows the new button groups with the added radio button. Change the variable name for the button group to "bgroup", Figure 11.24.

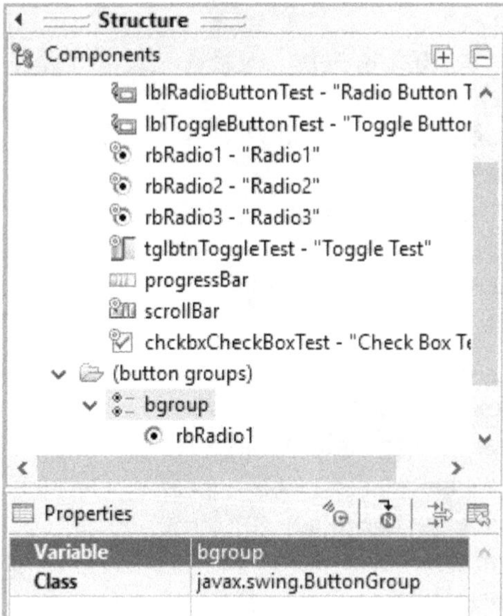

Figure 11.24 Assigning Button Groups

Repeat the actions to add a radio button to a group and add Radio2 and Radio3 buttons to the "bgroup" by right-clicking each button in either the component tree or the control layout window and selecting SetButtonGroup->bgroup. Save the file. Now we need to add events to each of the different controls. Before we do, we need to do some code cleanup. Click on the Source tab. Make sure that the three labels are listed before the controls. Add the keyword "final" before the declarations for lblCheckBox, lblRadioButtonTest, lblToggleButtonTest, rbRadio1, rbRadio2, rbRadio3, tglbtnToggleTest, progressBar, and new scrollbar. Adding "final" prohibits the control from being extended. Make sure to save the project.

Click on the Design tab. In the panel, right-click on the check box, and select Add event handler->item->itemStateChanged. This will add the event listener to the code. Fill in the following code:

```
chckbxCheckBoxTest.addItemListener(new ItemListener() {
    public void itemStateChanged(ItemEvent arg0) {

        if(chckbxCheckBoxTest.isSelected() == true){
           lblCheckBox.setText("Check box is checked");
        }
        if(chckbxCheckBoxTest.isSelected() == false){
            lblCheckBox.setText("Check box is unchecked");
        }
    }
});
```

When the checkbox is checked or unchecked, the text on the label will change. Right-click on the Radio1 control, and select Add event handler->item->itemStateChanged. This will add the event listener to the code. Fill in the following code:

```
rbRadio1.addItemListener(new ItemListener() {
    public void itemStateChanged(ItemEvent e) {
        if (rbRadio1.isSelected() == true){
            lblRadioButtonTest.setText("Radio1 is selected");
        }
    }
});
```

Right-click on the Radio2, and select Add event handler->item->itemStateChanged. This will add the event listener to the code. Fill in the following code:

```
rbRadio2.addItemListener(new ItemListener() {
    public void itemStateChanged(ItemEvent e) {
        if(rbRadio2.isSelected() == true){
            lblRadioButtonTest.setText("Radio2 is selected");
        }
    }
});
```

Right-click on the Radio3, and select Add event handler->item->itemStateChanged. This will add the event listener to the code. Fill in the following code:

```
rbRadio3.addItemListener(new ItemListener() {
    public void itemStateChanged(ItemEvent e) {
        if(rbRadio3.isSelected() == true){
            lblRadioButtonTest.setText("Radio3 is selected");
        }
    }
});
```

By grouping the 3 radio buttons into a single group, the group makes sure that one and only one radio button is selected at a time. When a radio button is selected, the label will change to tell you which button was selected. Right-click on the Toggle Button, and select Add event handler->item->itemStateChanged. This will add the event listener to the code. Fill in the following code:

```
tglbtnToggleTest.addItemListener(new ItemListener() {
    public void itemStateChanged(ItemEvent e) {
        if(tglbtnToggleTest.isSelected()== true){
            lblToggleButtonTest.setText("Toggle is checked");
        }
        if(tglbtnToggleTest.isSelected()== false){
            lblToggleButtonTest.setText("Toggle is unchecked");
        }
    }
});
```

Like the check box, the event handler will determine if the toggle button has been pressed or un-pressed. Right-click on the Scroll Bar, and select Add event handler->adjustment->adjustmentValueChanged. This will add the event listener to the code. Fill in the following code:

```
scrollBar.addAdjustmentListener(new AdjustmentListener() {
    public void adjustmentValueChanged(AdjustmentEvent arg0) {

        progressBar.setValue(scrollBar.getValue());
    }
});
```

As the user scrolls the scroll bar the value of the progress bar also changes. Save the project. Run the project and test the different controls. Do they do what you expect? If you are interested in seeing the event handlers in action, place a breakpoint in one or more of the event handlers, and step through the code to see the event handler get activated when you click on a control and watch it make the appropriate change to the associated control or label.

11.2 JavaFX

Swing has been the popular Java GUI solution for a long time, but as computer hardware became more mobile in the mid-2000s, the application programming paradigm started to shift. A new GUI program implementation combining web design and code was taking root. The idea is to have the GUI layout setup in a markup language (XML) and the code behind the GUI is written in Java, C#, etc... The Java solution to this new programming paradigm is called JavaFX. JavaFX was first released in 2008 as a scripting language to create web-based interfaces. After Oracle acquired Sun Microsystems, the focus for JavaFX was to become a GUI solution to replace Swing moving forward. In 2011, JavaFX 2.0 moved away from being a scripting language to a Java API set with rich UI controls, and FXML as the markup language. JavaFX 8 libraries (javafx.*) are now standard with the JRE/JDK v8 under jfxrt.jar. Swing/AWT will still be part of the Java library, but Oracle has announced that no further development will be made on Swing and JavaFX will be the GUI paradigm moving forward. JavaFX has some of the same concepts as Swing/AWT. There are buttons, text fields, layouts, etc. The GUI can be developed in code or using a GUI designer. There are some differences in terminology. For example, for Swing/AWT the GUI is created in a window/frame, and for JavaFX, the GUI is created in a Scene. Another example is components in Swing are called controls in JavaFX. The analogy is that JavaFX is like a theater where a stage and scene are set up. The next two computer activities provide the basic setup and coding examples.

The terminology for a JavaFX GUI application takes on a movie or play theme. The Window is called a Stage. Rather than Frame, there is a Scene, which holds all the controls the user will interact with. The Container provides different layouts to arrange the controls. The Controls are the buttons, check boxes, text boxes, etc. the user will interact with, Figure 11.25.

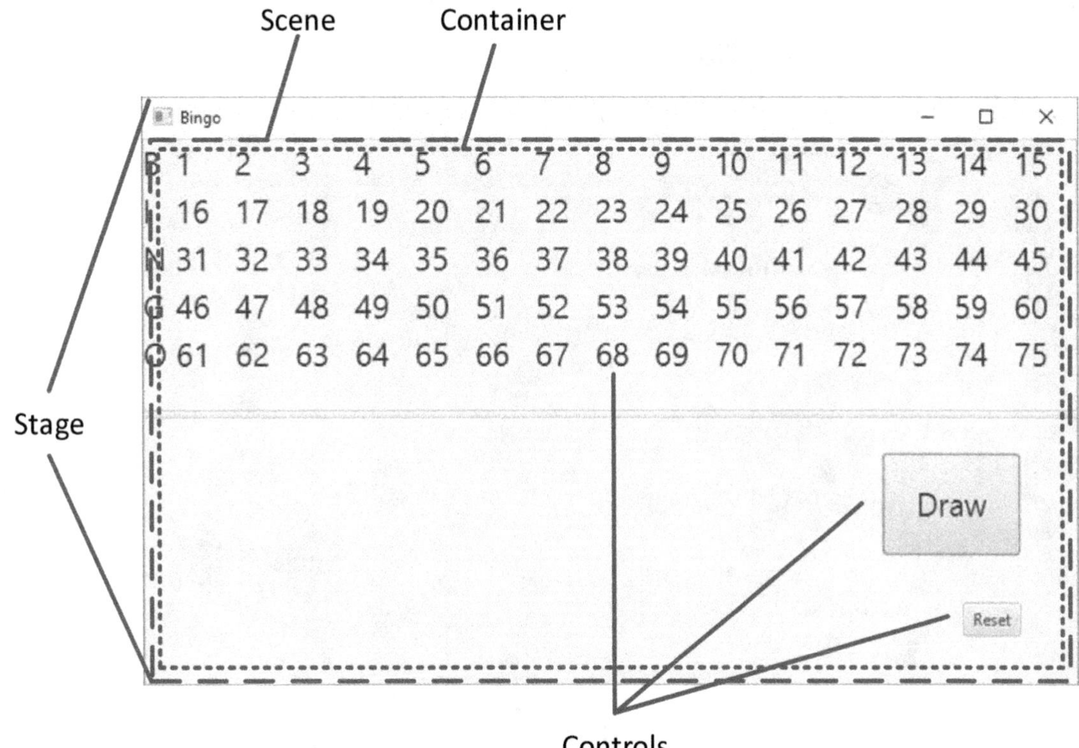

Figure 11.25 JavaFX GUI Metaphor

JavaFX implements a "Node" relationship between all the layouts and controls. Each control and layout added to the scene is considered a Node. There are parent and child nodes. For example, the layout node could have a button, text filed, and a radio button as child nodes. The nodes create a hierarchy, and all nodes lead back to the "root" node, which is the parent to all. The following computer activity looks at creating a JavaFX program via code only.

11.2.1 Computer Activity 11.6 - Eclipse Add-on: JavaFX e(fx)clipse

To build JavaFX applications, make sure that you have the latest version of Eclipse. To work with JavaFX and tools here, Eclipse Neon 4.6 is the minimum requirement. You can have more than one Eclipse version on your computer, but the workspaces have to be different.

The first step is to add the e(fx)clispe toolkit. The e(fx)clipse project adds tools for creating applications with JavaFX. As we did with WindowBuilder, we can go to the Eclipse Marketplace for e(fx)clipse. From the menu, select Help->Eclipse Marketplace... Type in "e(fx)clipse" in the find box, and click go, Figure 11.26.

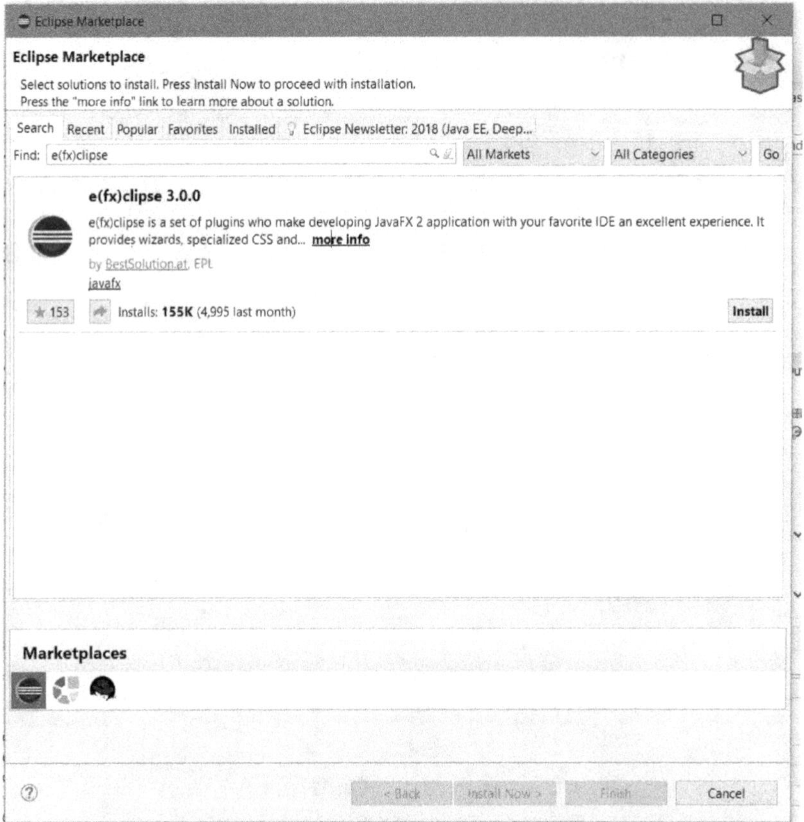

Figure 11.26 Searching Eclipse Marketplace for e(fx)clipse

If you click the more info link at the end of the e(fx)clipse description, you will be shown more detailed information about the e(fx)clipse plugin, Figure 11.27.

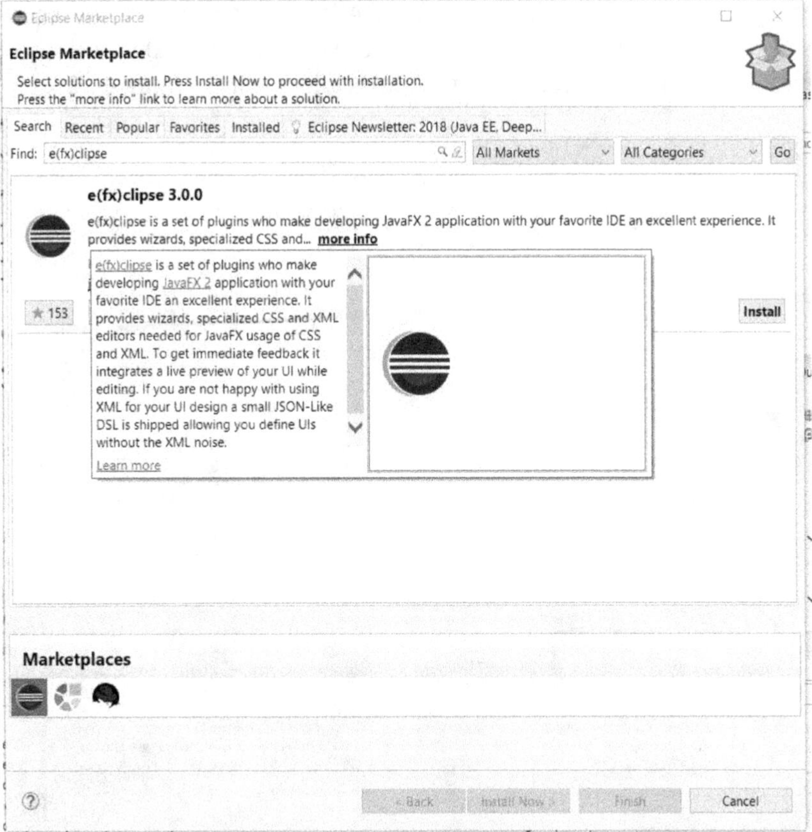

Figure 11.27 e(fx)clipse Plugin Detailed Information

Click the e(fx)clipse Install button. You will be presented with the license review dialog. Review and accept the license and click the Finish button. It will take a minute or so to install. You can see the progress at the bottom status bar of Eclipse. When the installation is complete, you will be prompted to restart Eclipse, Figure 11.28.

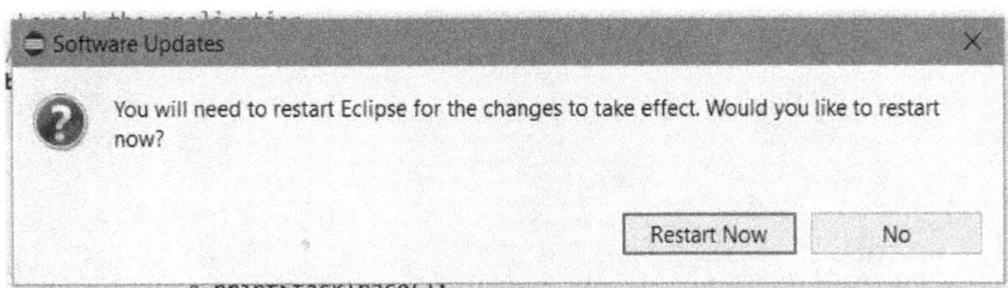

Figure 11.28 Eclipse Restart Prompt

Click the Restart Now button, and restart Eclipse. After Eclipse restarts, you can confirm that e(fx)clipse has been installed by clicking Help->About Eclipse and clicking the Installation Details button. In the Installed Software tab, you will see e(fx)clipse – IDE, Figure 11.29.

Figure 11.29 Eclipse Installation Details Showing e(fx)clipse Installed

Now, from the menu, select New->Other, Figure 11.30.

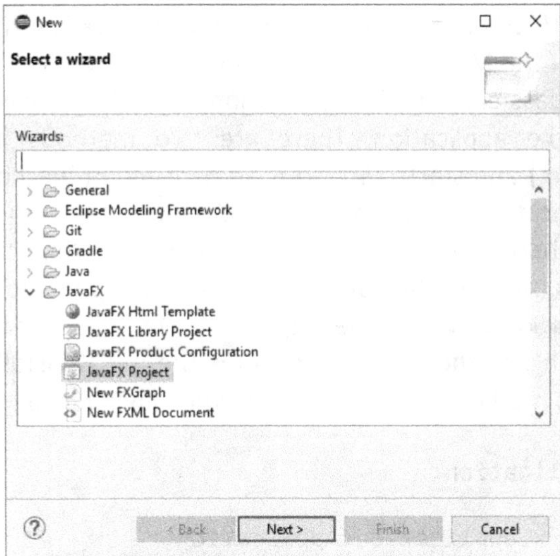

Figure 11.30 Create New JavaFX Project

Expand the tree, click on JavaFX Project, and click Next.

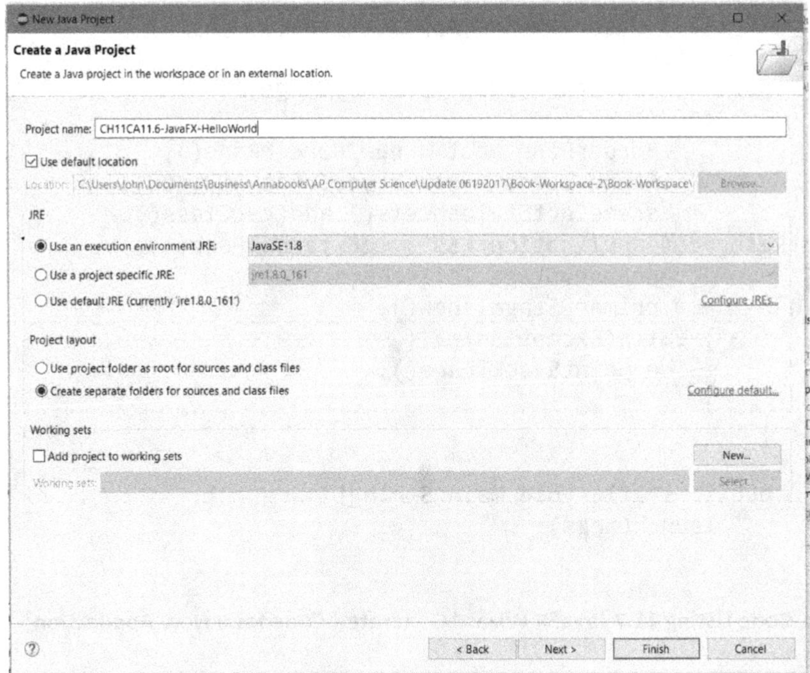

Figure 11.31 Name the JavaFX Project

Enter the project name "CH11CA11.6-JavaFX-HelloWorld and click Finish, Figure 11.31. The wizard creates a Main.java file for the Main class, Code Listing 11.7, as well as, an application.css. In the Main.java file, the Main class extends the Application Class. The Application class provides the entry point to launch the application. There are two methods in the Application class implemented here: launch() and start(). Start() is an overridden method that is the main entry point for all JavaFX applications. The Application class has two other methods that can be overridden: the init() method for application initialization when Application class is loaded, and the stop() method to help clean up the application when the app is closed. These two overrides can be added via the menu Source->Override/Implement Methods. The traditional main() method makes a call to the launch() method, which performs the initial installation and then calls the start() method. The start() method is what is used to run a JavaFX application.

```
package application;
import javafx.application.Application;
import javafx.stage.Stage;
import javafx.scene.Scene;
import javafx.scene.layout.BorderPane;
public class Main extends Application {
    @Override
    public void start(Stage primaryStage) {
        try {
            BorderPane root = new BorderPane();
            Scene scene = new Scene(root,400,400);
            scene.getStylesheets().add(getClass().
getResource("application.css").toExternalForm());
            primaryStage.setScene(scene);
            primaryStage.show();
        } catch(Exception e) {
            e.printStackTrace();
        }
    }
    public static void main(String[] args) {
        launch(args);
    }
}
```

Code Listing 11.7 JavaFX Wizard Generated Code for a New Application

The start() method creates a BorderPane and establishes a scene on the BorderPane to set up the GUI. The BorderPane is one of the available Layouts in JavaFX. The BorderPane is the equivalent of the BorderLayout in Swing. The application is set up to a size of 400x400. Now, we will create an application that is similar to the application created in Computer Activity 11.3. This time the button will toggle the message displayed on the text field on each click. Add the following imports:

```
import javafx.event.ActionEvent;
import javafx.event.EventHandler;
import javafx.geometry.Pos;
import javafx.scene.control.Button;
import javafx.scene.control.TextField;
import javafx.scene.layout.VBox;
```

Remove the BorderPane import. Between the Main class declaration and the start() method, add the following files that will be used to toggle the message:

```
public boolean toggle = true;
```

Create a new method in the Main class called “myFinalHello”, and fill in the following code:

```
public void myFinalHello(Stage primaryStage){

      VBox myBox = new VBox();
      Scene scene = new Scene(myBox,300,200);

scene.getStylesheets().add(getClass().getResource("application.css").
toExternalForm());
      Button btnHello = new Button();
      btnHello.setText("Click for Final Hello");
      TextField txtOutput = new TextField();
      txtOutput.setAlignment(Pos.CENTER);
      btnHello.setOnAction(new EventHandler<ActionEvent>() {
          public void handle(ActionEvent e){
              if(toggle == true){
                  txtOutput.setText("The Final Hello World");
                  toggle = false;
              }
              else
              {
                  txtOutput.setText("JavaFx is fun!!!");
                  toggle = true;
              }
          }
      });
      myBox.getChildren().addAll(btnHello,txtOutput);
      myBox.setAlignment(Pos.CENTER);
```

```
        primaryStage.setTitle("Final Hello World");
        primaryStage.setScene(scene);
        primaryStage.show();
    }
```

The VBox layout is used in place of the BoarderPane layout. All of the controls will be placed one after the other in a vertical stack. The button and text field controls are created. The text in the text field is set for center alignment. The action for the button uses the anonymous instantiation of the EventHandler class with the event handler displaying a message to the text box based on the current state of the toggle field. The controls are added to the VBox instance and centered in the scene. A title is added and the GUI is finally displayed. Modify the start() method to simply call the myFinalHello() method with the primaryStage parameter.

```
    public void start(Stage primaryStage) {
        try {
            myFinalHello(primaryStage);
        } catch(Exception e) {
            e.printStackTrace();
        }
    }
```

Save and run the application. Click on the button and the message should toggle between the two messages, Figure 11.32.

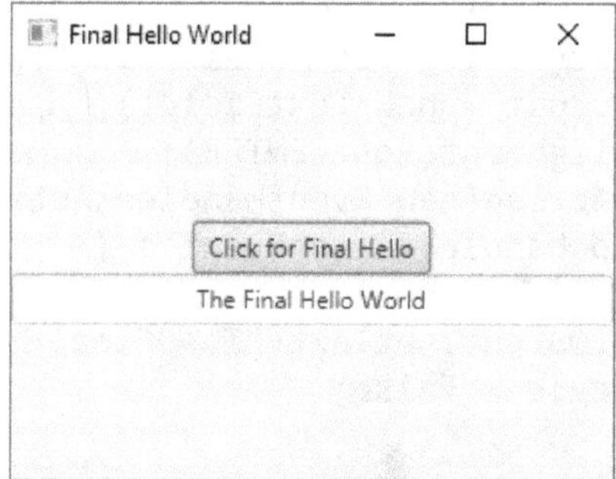

Figure 11.32 JavaFX-HelloWorld Application

11.2.2 Computer Activity 11.7 - JavaFX GUI Designer SceneBuilder

Like Swing, you can program JavaFX by code like we did in Computer Activity 11.6, or you can program with a GUI tool. For JavaFX, this means using SceneBuilder to create an FXML file. SceneBuilder is a separate tool developed by Oracle. It integrates with Eclipse but runs as a separate application, as opposed to being a plugin like WindowBuilder. Oracle developed the SceneBuilder and released it as open source, which Gluon has taken and built a release with an installer, which makes it easy to add to your development system. The JavaFX plugin installed in Computer Activity 11.6 has a place to point to the SceneBuilder executable so that once installed and registered, will be launched through Eclipse.

To install SceneBuilder, first, download the appropriate installation package from Gluon. The SceneBuilder download site is:

http://gluonhq.com/products/scene-builder/

Select the Scene Builder package that matches your development environment and click the Download button for that package. At the time of this writing, Windows Installer 64-bit for Java 8 was used, Figure 11.33.

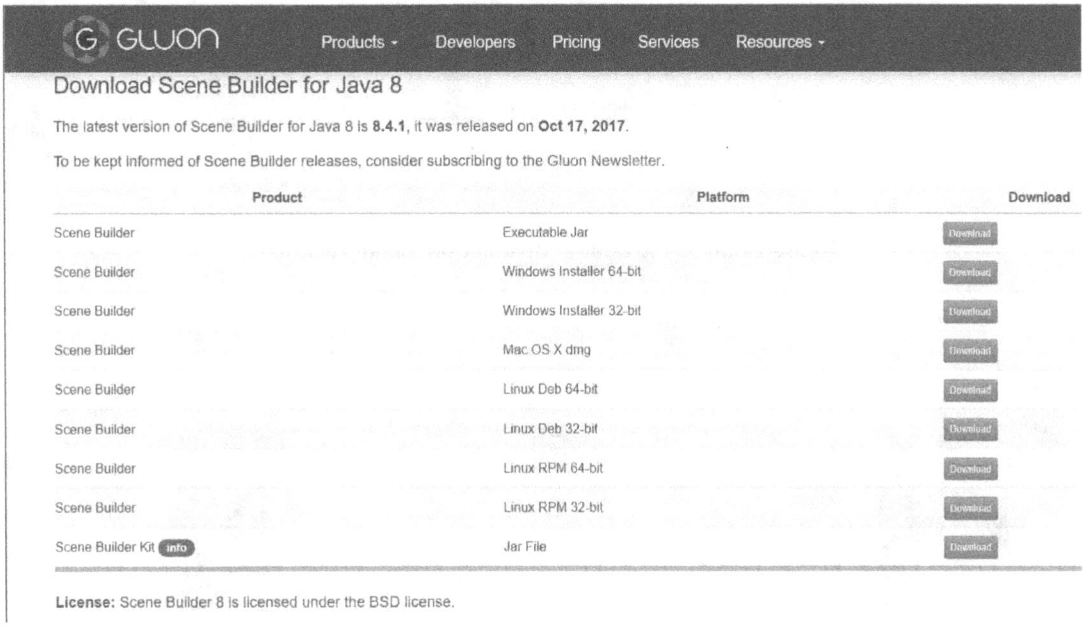

GLUON Products - Developers Pricing Services Resources -

Download Scene Builder for Java 8

The latest version of Scene Builder for Java 8 is **8.4.1**, it was released on **Oct 17, 2017**.

To be kept informed of Scene Builder releases, consider subscribing to the Gluon Newsletter.

Product	Platform	Download
Scene Builder	Executable Jar	Download
Scene Builder	Windows Installer 64-bit	Download
Scene Builder	Windows Installer 32-bit	Download
Scene Builder	Mac OS X dmg	Download
Scene Builder	Linux Deb 64-bit	Download
Scene Builder	Linux Deb 32-bit	Download
Scene Builder	Linux RPM 64-bit	Download
Scene Builder	Linux RPM 32-bit	Download
Scene Builder Kit info	Jar File	Download

License: Scene Builder 8 is licensed under the BSD license.

Figure 11.33 Gluon Download Site for Scene Builder

Select Save As and save the installer in a convenient folder. Go to that folder and run the SceneBuilder installer. The installer will run and present a License Agreement dialog box. Review and accept the license agreement and click Next. The installer will present you with a dialog to select the installation location, Figure 11.34. Accept the default or change it to the location you prefer, but make note of the installation path, we will use that to tell Eclipse where to find it when we want to run it from Eclipse. You can even copy the path text, at this point. Select next.

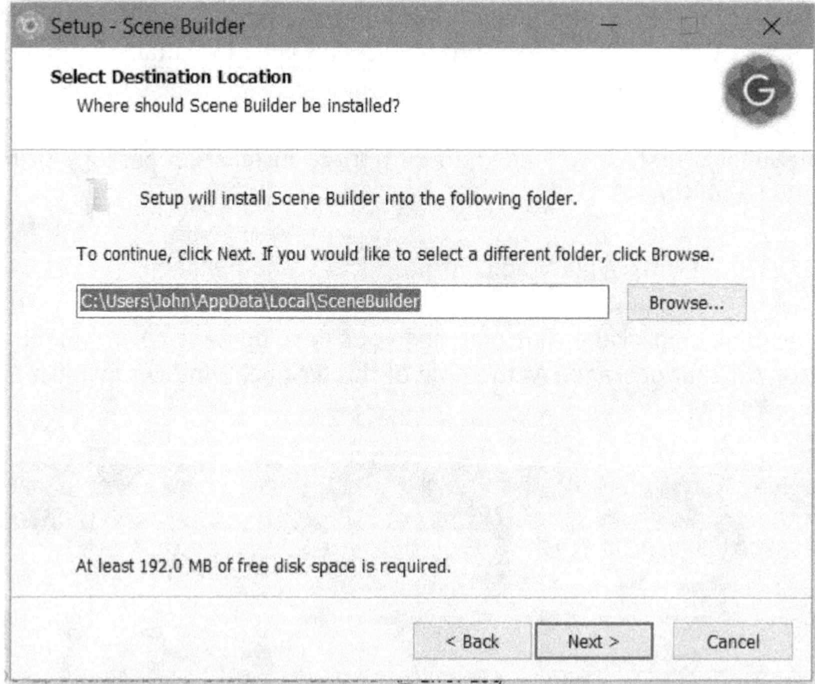

Figure 11.34 Scene Builder Installation Install Location

After installation, SceneBuilder will run, Figure 11.35:

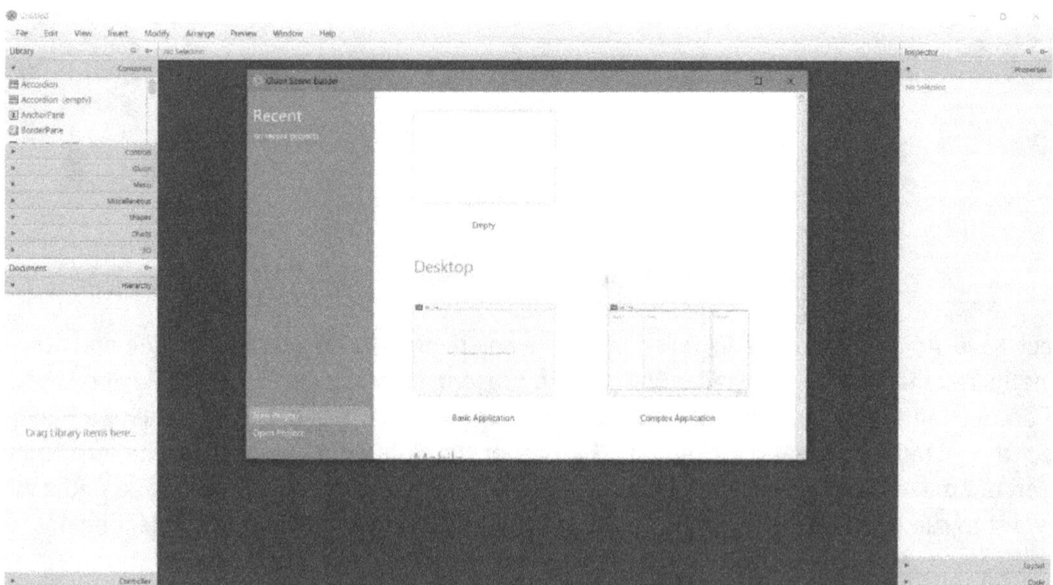

Figure 11.35 SceneBuilder Installation Complete

When you close the project history window for the first time, you will be prompted to register with Gluon for updates, Figure 11.36.

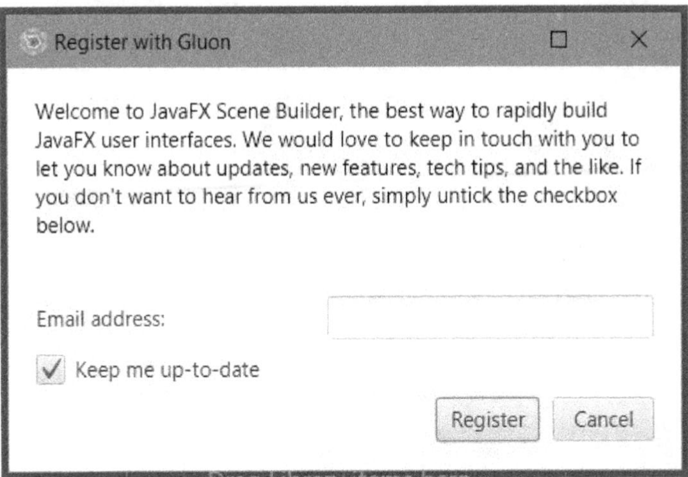

Figure 11.36 Post SceneBuilder Installation Gluon Registration

Gluon has a number of development tools, so you may find it beneficial to register. Now, we want to register SceneBuilder with Eclipse. This is where you will need the installation path. Open Eclipse and from the menu, select Window->Preferences. On the left-hand side, click on JavaFX. The pane on the right will have a text box to set the location for the SceneBuilder executable that was just installed, Figure 11.37. Either paste in the path, if you copied it during the installation process, or click Browse, and browse to the location of the installed SceneBuilder.exe file. Click the Apply and Close button when finished.

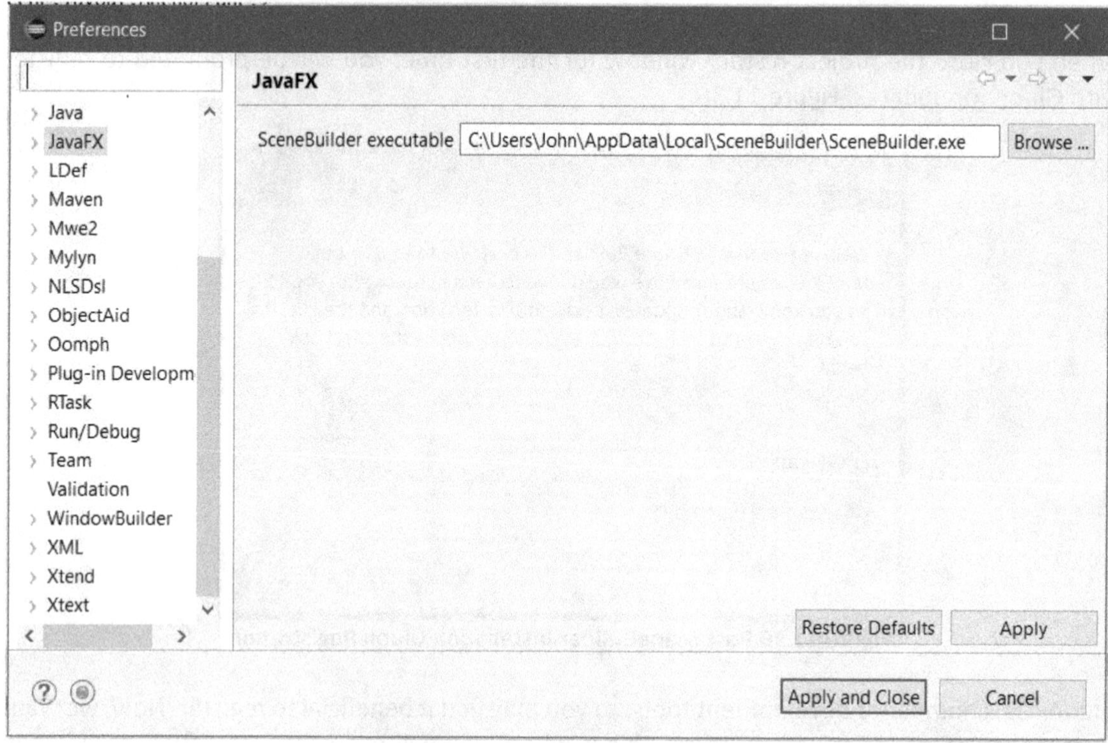

Figure 11.37 Register SceneBuilder with Eclipse

In this exercise, we will, now, create a JavaFX temperature conversion application using SceneBuilder that will look like Figure 11.38.

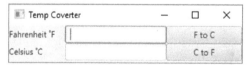

Figure 11.38 JavaFX Temperature Conversion Application using SceneBuilder

Create a new JavaFX project called "CH11CA11.7-JavaFXTempConv". Once the new project has been created, expand the project in Package Explorer. Right-click on "application" package, Figure 11.39, and select New->Other.

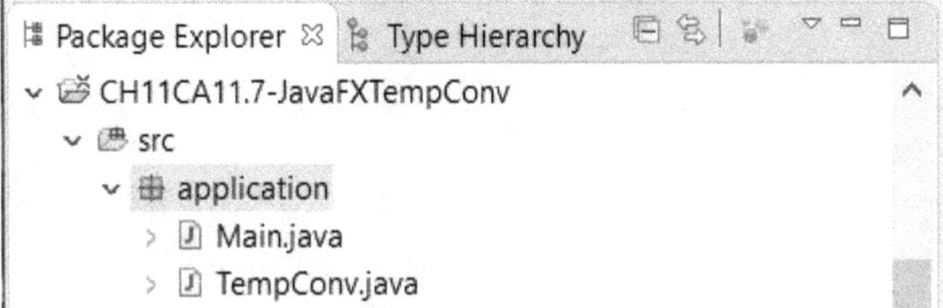

Figure 11.39 Right-Click application

Expand JavaFX and select New FXML Document, Figure 11.40. Click the Next button.

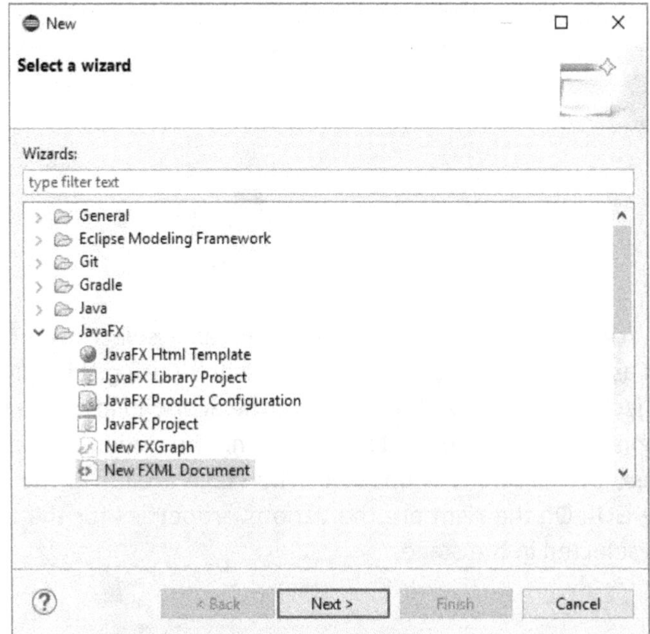

Figure 11.40 Create a new FXML Document

For the name of the file enter “TempGUI” and click the Finish button, Figure 11.41.

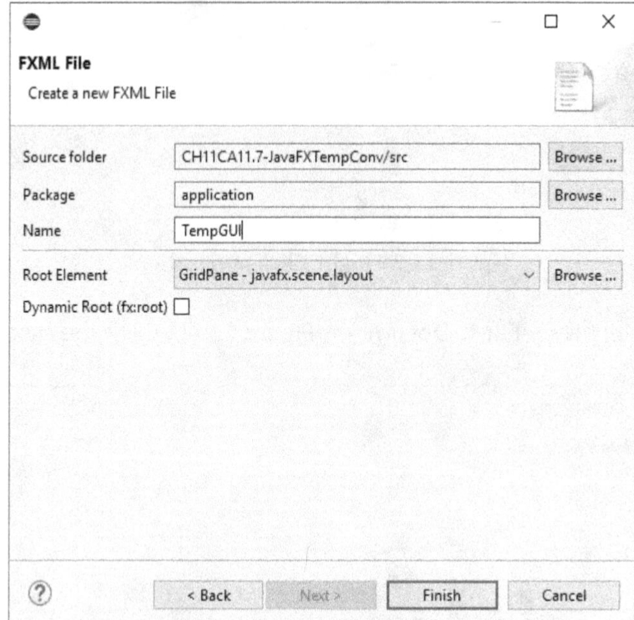

Figure 11.41 Name New FXML File

In Package Explorer, right-click on the TempGUI.fxml and select Open with SceneBuilder. SceneBuilder will run as a separate application, but it will be using the FXML file of the Eclipse JavaTXTempConv project, Figure 11.42. The layout of the SceneBuilder tool has elements to add to the stage on the upper left with a hierarchy containing the nodes on the lower left. As items are added to the stage, the hierarchy is updated. The stage area is in the middle. The stage is where you create the GUI. On the right are the various properties for the controls and layouts, depending on what is selected in the stage.

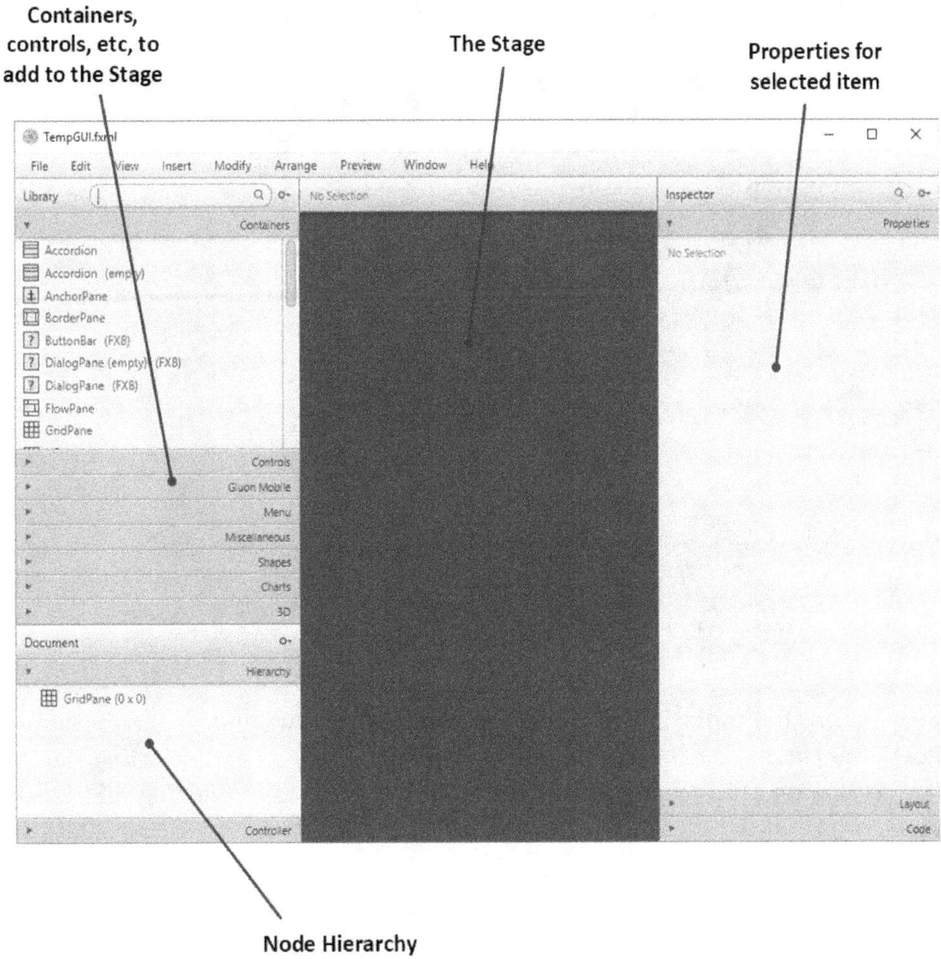

Figure 11.42 SceneBuilder Launched from Eclipse

Remove any container that is in the hierarchy by right-clicking it selecting Delete. Add a GridPane by expanding the Containers in the Library and dragging and dropping the GridPane container onto the Stage, Figure 11.43.

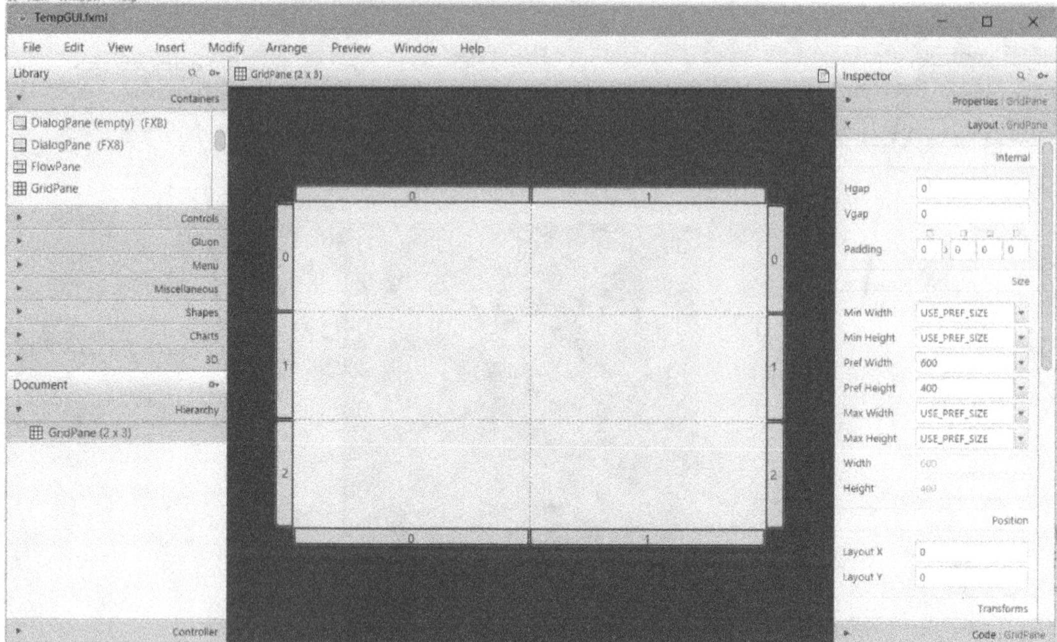

Figure 11.43 Add GridPane Container to the Stage

The GridPane aligns the controls in a grid layout. We need 2 rows and 3 columns for our GUI, so delete Row 2 by clicking on the Row 2 label, then right-clicking, and selecting Delete. Add a column by clicking on the Column 2 label, then right-clicking, and selecting Add Column After, Figure 11.44.

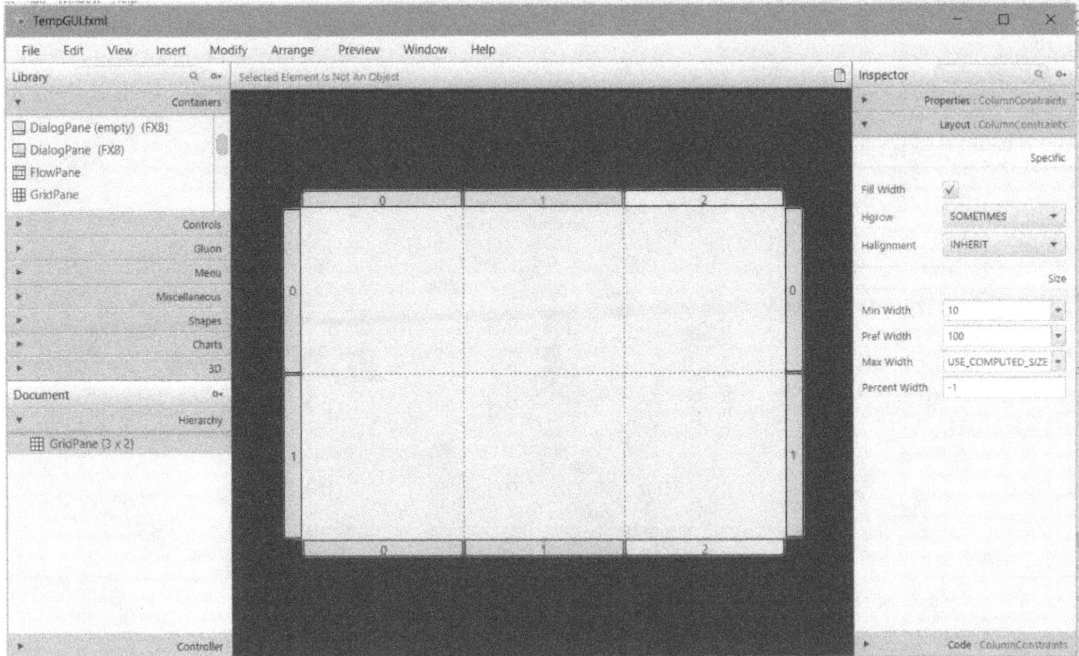

Figure 11.44 Remove 1 Row and Add 1 Column to the GridPane Container

Under Controls in the Library, drag and drop 2 Label controls onto the GridPane container, one in cell column 0, row 0, and the other in cell column 0 row 1. Next, from the Library, drag and drop 2 TextField control onto the GridPane container, one in cell column 1, row 0, and the other in column1, row 1. Finally, from the Library, drag and drop 2 Button controls onto the GridPane container, one in cell column 2, row 0, and the other in cell column 2, row 1, Figure 11.45.

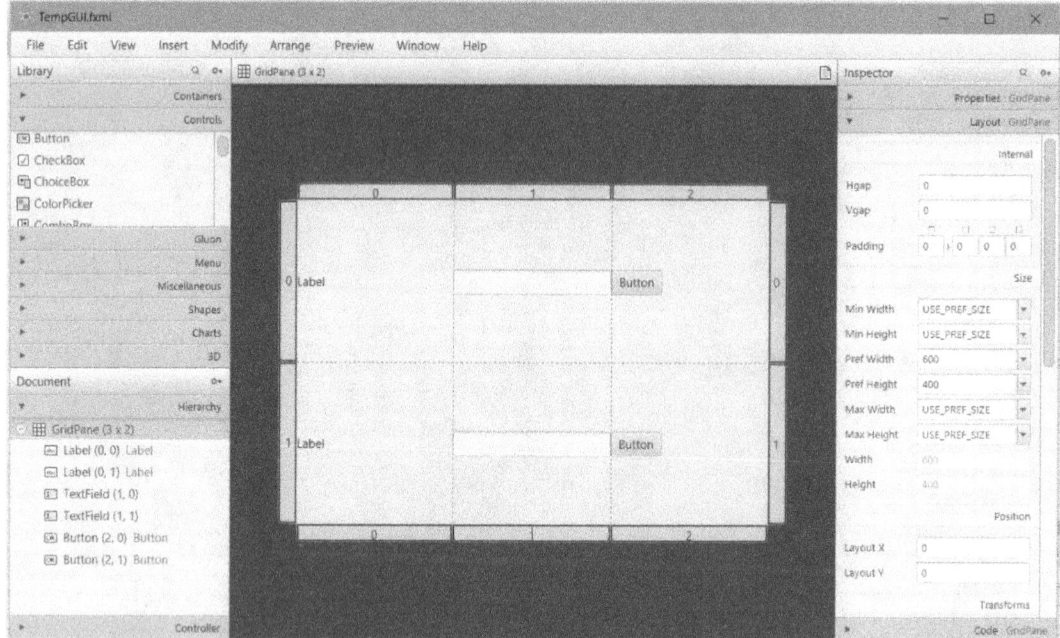

Figure 11.45 Controls Added to the GridPane Container

Click on the first label, column 0, row 0, and on the right side, Inspector, expand properties. In the text property enter "Fahrenheit", Figure 11.46. Repeat the same steps for the second label and enter "Celsius" for the text property.

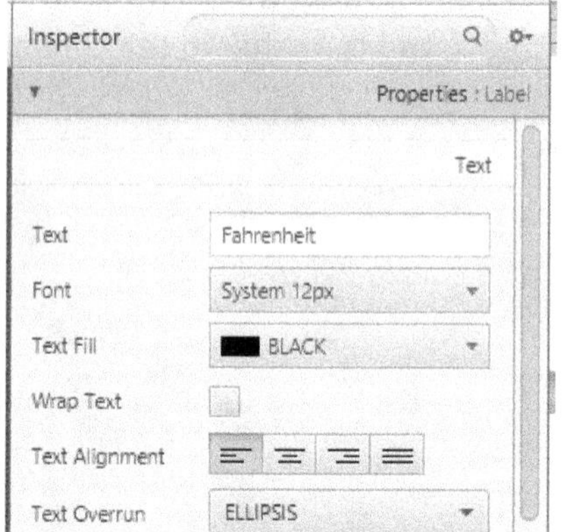

Figure 11.46 Set Label Control Text Property

Click on the TextField control next to the Fahrenheit label. Expand the Code properties on the right. For fx:id enter "txtF", Figure 11.47. The id will be used in the supporting code to read and write data to this control. Repeat the steps for the TextField control next to the Celsius label and enter txtC for the fx:id.

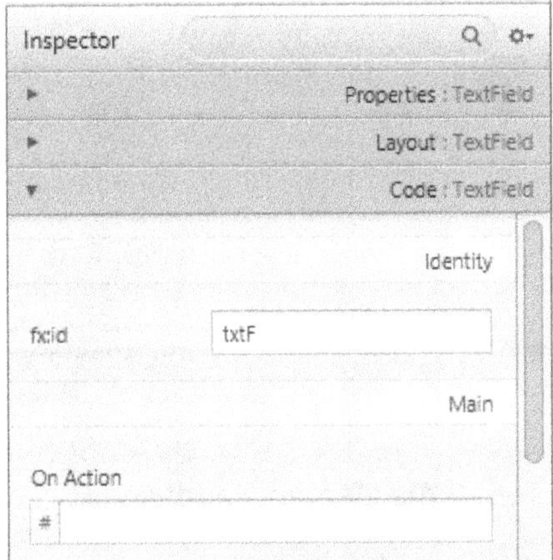

Figure 11.47 Set TextField Control ID

Click on the Button control that is in line with the Fahrenheit label. Under properties, change the text to “F to C”, and under Code set the fx:id to “btnFtoC”. Scroll down in the Code section and locate “On Mouse Clicked” from the Mouse group and enter “convFtoC”. Repeat these steps for the Button control that is in line with the Celsius label and set the text to “C to F”, the fx:id to “btnCtoF”, and the On Mouse Clicked to “convCtoF”, Figure 11.48.

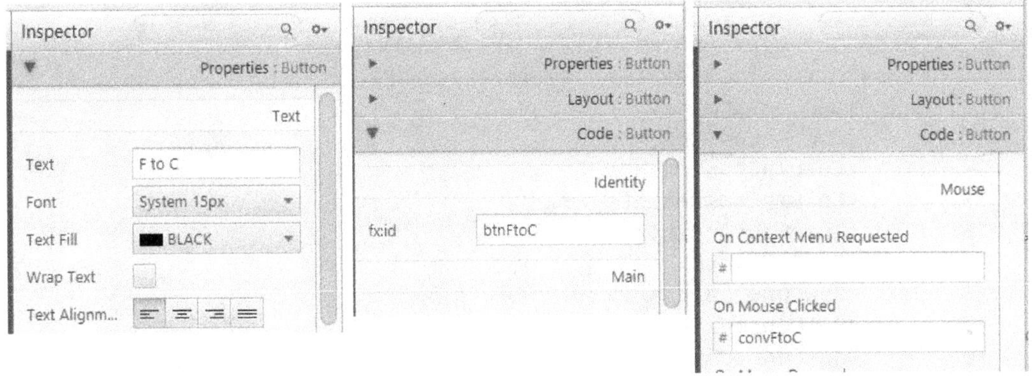

Figure 11.48 Configuring the Button Control

Finally, click on the GridPane in an area away from any of the controls, fly over the container’s lower right corner, click on the corner when the when the mouse cursor changes to the resize symbol, and drag the corner in along the diagonal to resize the overall GridPane so that it looks similar to Figure 11.38. Save the project. A preview of the application running can be run. From the menu, select Preview->Show Preview in Window, Figure 11.49.

Figure 11.49 TempGUI Scene Preview

Close the preview window when finished, and close SceneBuilder. You can open the TempGUI.fxml file in Eclipse to see all the elements added via SceneBuilder, Code Listing 11.8.

```
<?xml version="1.0" encoding="UTF-8"?>

<?import javafx.scene.control.Button?>
<?import javafx.scene.control.Label?>
<?import javafx.scene.control.TextField?>
<?import javafx.scene.layout.ColumnConstraints?>
<?import javafx.scene.layout.GridPane?>
<?import javafx.scene.layout.RowConstraints?>


<GridPane xmlns:fx="http://javafx.com/fxml/1"
xmlns="http://javafx.com/javafx/8.0.102">
    <columnConstraints>
        <ColumnConstraints />
        <ColumnConstraints />
        <ColumnConstraints />
    </columnConstraints>
    <rowConstraints>
        <RowConstraints />
        <RowConstraints />
        <RowConstraints />
    </rowConstraints>
    <children>
        <Label text="Fahrenheit" />
        <Label text="Label" GridPane.rowIndex="1" />
        <TextField fx:id="txtF" GridPane.columnIndex="1" />
        <TextField fx:id="txtC" GridPane.columnIndex="1"
GridPane.rowIndex="1" />
        <Button fx:id="btnFtoC" mnemonicParsing="false"
onMouseClicked="#convFtoC" text="F to C" GridPane.columnIndex="2" />
```

```
28.         <Button fx:id="btnCtoF" mnemonicParsing="false" onMouseClicked="#convCtoF" text="C to F" GridPane.columnIndex="2" GridPane.rowIndex="1" />
29.     </children>
30. </GridPane>
```

Code Listing 11.8 FXML Listing with SceneBuilder Additions

Even an FXML file refers to the Java library with imports. Line 11 defines the GridPane container. Lines 23-28 define the controls added to the GridPane.

Now, we need to add the code behind the controls. To do this we need to create a new class. In Eclipse, add a new class to the project and call it “TempConv”. This will create the TempConv.java file with the TempConv class shell. Add Code Listing 11.9 to the class and don’t forget to add the import statements, as well:

```
package application;

import javafx.scene.input.MouseEvent;
import javafx.fxml.FXML;
import javafx.scene.control.Button;
import javafx.scene.control.TextField;

public class TempConv{

    @FXML
    private Button btnFtoC;

    @FXML
    private Button btnCtoF;

    @FXML
    private TextField txtF;

    @FXML
    private TextField txtC;


    public void convFtoC(MouseEvent event){

        double Celsius = (Double.parseDouble(txtF.getText())-32)*5/9;
        txtC.setText(Double.toString(Celsius));
    }

```

```
29.     public void convCtoF(MouseEvent event){
30.
31.         double Fahrenheit =
    (Double.parseDouble(txtC.getText())*9/5)+32;
32.         txtF.setText(Double.toString(Fahrenheit));
33.     }
34. }
```

Code Listing 11.9 GUI Control Handlers

The TempConv class adds the declarations for the Button and TextField controls. The @FXML is an annotation to the control declaration. The annotations will help the FXMLLoader make the link between the FXML file and the class to finish the instantiation. In SceneBuilder, the actions for the button mouse click events were defined as convFtoC and convCtoF. The two methods that were added to the class at line 23 and line 29 perform the action when a button is clicked. If the "F to C" button is clicked, and the convFtoC method is run, which takes the value in the Fahrenheit text field, converts it from a string to a double. Then the resulting value is converted from Fahrenheit to Celsius and displayed as a string in the Celsius text field. The "C to F" button runs the convCtoF method, which performs a similar action, converting the string in the Celsius text field to the appropriate Fahrenheit string and displaying it in the Fahrenheit text field.

In the TempGUI.fxml file, add fx:controller="application.TempConv" to line 11 to link the FXML file to the TempConv class. Change:

```
 <GridPane xmlns:fx=http://javafx.com/fxml/1
xmlns="http://javafx.com/javafx/8.0.102">
```

To:

```
 <GridPane xmlns:fx=http://javafx.com/fxml/1
xmlns=http://javafx.com/javafx/8.0.102
fx:controller="application.TempConv">
```

In the Main.java file, remove the javafx.scene.layout.BorderPane import and add the javafx.fxml.FXMLLoader and the javafx.scene.Parent imports. Within the Main class, remove the creation of the BorderPane, Scene classes, and the call to the scene.getStylesheets().add(...) method. Replace them with a call to FXMLLoader.Load(...) with TempGUI.fxml file argument, a call to the primaryStage.setTitle(...) method, and modify the argument in the primaryStage.setScene as shown in Code Listing 11.10:

```
1. package application;
2.
3. import javafx.application.Application;
4. import javafx.fxml.FXMLLoader;
5. import javafx.stage.Stage;
6. import javafx.scene.Parent;
7. import javafx.scene.Scene;
8.
9.
10. public class Main extends Application {
11.     @Override
12.     public void start(Stage primaryStage) {
13.         try {
14.             Parent root = FXMLLoader.load(getClass()
15.                     .getResource("TempGUI.fxml"));
16.
17.             primaryStage.setTitle("Temp Coverter");
18.
19.             primaryStage.setScene(new Scene (root));
20.             primaryStage.show();
21.         } catch(Exception e) {
22.             e.printStackTrace();
23.         }
24.     }
25.
26.     public static void main(String[] args) {
27.         launch(args);
28.     }
29. }
```

Code Listing 11.10 JavaFXTempConv Main.java

The Parent class is the base class for the JavaFX Scene, and line 14 instantiates "root" with the FXMLLoader.load() method. Line 19 takes the root scene and creates a new scene and sets the new scene for the stage. When the show() method is called, the FXMLLoader loads the FXML file on to the window stage and finishes the instantiation of the controls between TempConv.java and TempGUI.fxml, Figure 11.50.

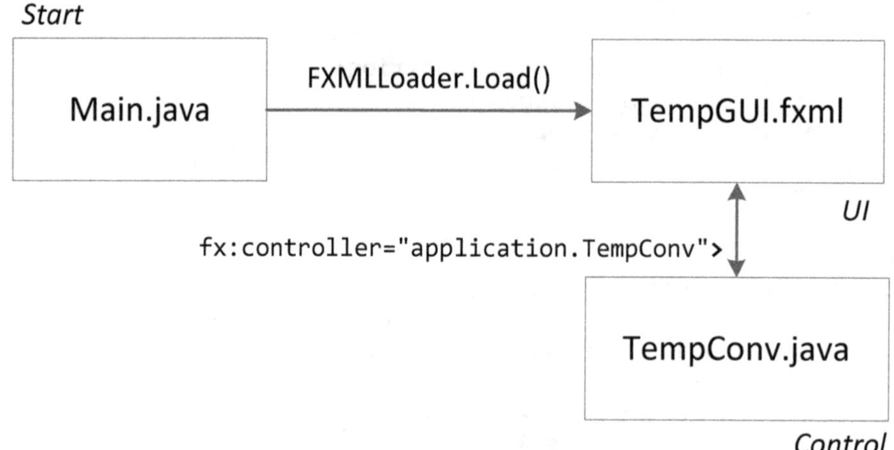

Figure 11.50 JavaFX Load Flowchart

Save all the files and run the application. Enter a number into one of the text fields and click the button next to the text field. The value in the other text field will show the conversion. Try converting 212° F to C and 0° C to F. Are the conversions correct?

11.2.3 JavaFX initialize() method

In the last chapter, the sort and search projects had an array filled with integers prior to performing the sort or search operation. For the coin flip game, we were able to instantiate "gen" in the CoinFlipGUI() method prior to initializing the GUI. If you look at the last JavaFX program, it might not appear on the surface that you can pre-run anything prior to GUI launched. JavaFX supports an initialize() method that gets automatically called when FXMLLoader loads the FXML file and calls the control class.

```
Public void initialize(){

    //Your code here

}
```

For the previous project, if there was anything to set up in the application, the above method could have been added to the TempConv class.

11.2.4 Computer Activity 11.8 - Explore Other JavaFX Controls

Like Swing, there are other controls besides buttons, labels, and text boxes. In this computer activity, we will implement a JavaFX application that demonstrates checkboxes, radio buttons, toggle buttons, scroll bar, and a progress bar, as per Figure 11.51.

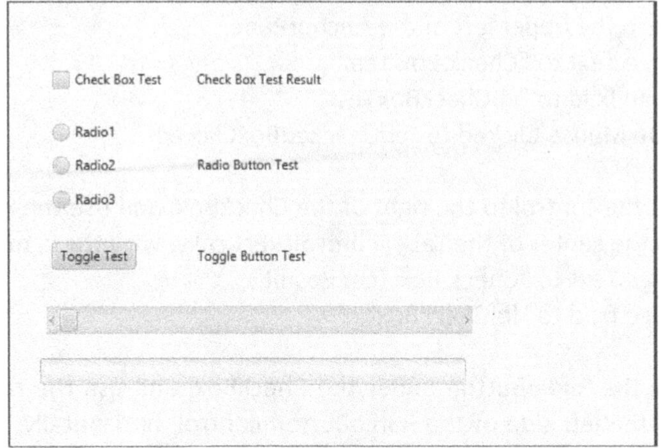

Figure 11.51 JavaFx GUI to Demonstrate Other JavaFX Controls

Create a new JavaFX Project called "CH11CA11.8-JavaFXOtherControls". Create a New FXML Document called "OtherControls", Figure 11.52.

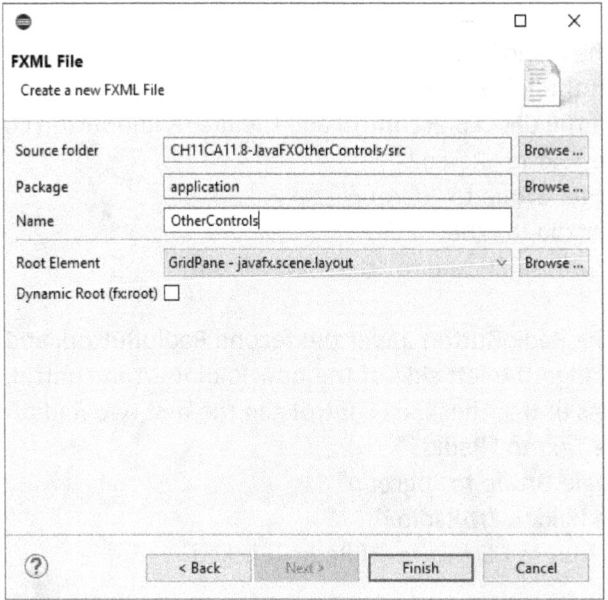

Figure 11.52 Create New FXML Document Named OtherControls

Open the OtherControls.fxml with SceneBuilder. Remove any nodes under the Document->Hierarchy. In Containers in the library, click and drag an AnchorPane container to the stage area. Select, drag, and drop the following controls onto the AnchorPane container:

1. CheckBox
    a. Place in the upper left of the AnchorPane
    b. Change Text to "Check Box Test"
    c. Change fx:id to "cbCheckBoxTest"
    d. Set On Mouse Clicked to "cbCheckedBoxClicked"
2. Label
    a. Place the control to the right of the CheckBox, and use the red alignment line to align the center of the Label control, vertically, with the center of the Checkbox.
    b. Change Text to "Check Box Test Result"
    c. Change fx:id to "lblCheckBox"
3. RadioButton
    a. Place the RadioButton under the CheckBox, and use the red alignment line to align the left side of the RadioButton control, horizontally, with the left side of the CheckBox control.
    b. Change Text to "Radio1"
    c. Set Toggle Group to "bgroup"
    d. Change fx:id to "rbRadio1"
    e. Set On Mouse Clicked to "rbRadio1Clicked"
4. RadioButton
    a. Place the RadioButton under the first RadioButton, and use the red alignment line to align the left side of the new RadioButton control, horizontally, with the left sides of the CheckBox control and the first RadioButton control.
    b. Change Text to "Radio2"
    c. Set Toggle Group to "bgroup"
    d. Change fx:id to "rbRadio2"
    e. Set On Mouse Clicked to "rbRadio2Clicked"
5. RadioButton
    a. Place the RadioButton under the second RadioButton, and use the red alignment line to align the left side of the new RadioButton control, horizontally, with the left sides of the CheckBox control and the first two RadioButton controls.
    b. Change Text to "Radio3"
    c. Set Toggle Group to "bgroup"
    d. Change fx:id to "rbRadio3"
    e. Set On Mouse Clicked to "rbRadio3Clicked"

6. Label
   a. Place the Label under the CheckBox Test Result Label and use both of the red alignment lines to align the left side of the new Label control, horizontally, with the left side of CheckBox Test Result Label; and align the center of the new Label control, vertically, with the Radio2 RadioButton control.
   b. Change Text to “Radio Button Test”
   c. Change fx:id to “lblRadioButtonTest”
7. ToggleButton
   a. Place the ToggleButton under the RadioButton controls and use the red alignment line to align the left side of the ToggleButton control, horizontally, with the left sides of the CheckBox and RadioButton controls.
   b. Change Text to “Toggle Test”
   c. Change fx:id to “tbToggleButtonTest”
   d. Set On Mouse Clicked to “tbToggleClicked”
8. Label
   a. Place the Label under the Radio Button Test Label and use both red alignment lines to align the left side of the new Label control, horizontally, with the left sides of the CheckBox Test Result and Radio Button Test Labels, and align the center of the new Label control, vertically, with the ToggleButton control.
   b. Change Text to “Toggle Button Test”
   c. Change fx:id to “lblToggleButtonTest”
9. ScrollBar (horizontal)
   a. Place the ScrollBar underneath all of the previous controls, and use the red alignment line to align the left side of the ScrollBar control, horizontally, with the left side of the CheckBox, RadioButton, and ToggleButton controls.
   b. Change fx:id to “sbScroll1”
   c. Set On Mouse Clicked to “sbScrollDetect”
   d. Set On Mouse Moved to “sbScrollDetect”
10. ProgressBar
   a. Place the ProgressBar underneath all of the previous controls, and use the red alignment line to align the left side of the ProgressBar control, horizontally, with the left side of the CheckBox, RadioButton, ToggleButton, and ScrollBar controls.
   b. Change fx:id to “pbProgress1”

Resize the AnchorPane, if necessary, so the GUI looks like Figure 11.51. Save the file. In Eclipse, under the project, create a new Java class called “Control”. Open the OtherControls.fxml file in Eclipse to view the FXML code. On the line with the <AnchorPane> tag add the following argument to the end of the declaration:

```
fx:controller="application.Controls"
```

Save the project. In SceneBuilder, from the menu, select View->Show Sample Controller Skeleton. A window will appear showing what the code in the Controls class should look like, Figure 11.53. Click on the Full checkbox in the bottom left corner. Click on Copy.

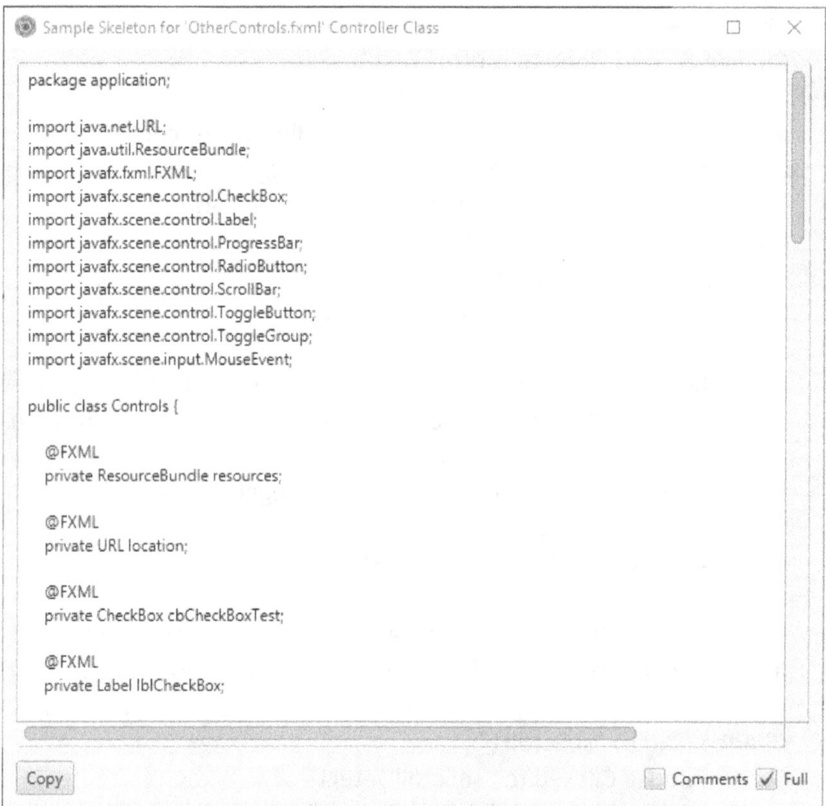

Figure 11.53 Sample Controller Skeleton

In Eclipse, select all of the code in the Controls.java file and paste the contents of the Sample Controller Skeleton that you just copied, replacing the Eclipse class code with the SceneBuilder generated code. Rather than enter each control and event handler separately, this step saves a little time, providing you with a skeleton of the imports, definitions, and methods that you will need for the controls. You will notice the initialize() method is included, and the code in it is a double-check that the controls are in the FXML file. Now that we have the skeleton, we can simply fill in the methods:

```
@FXML
void cbCheckedBoxClicked(MouseEvent event) {
    if(cbCheckBoxTest.isSelected() == true){
    lblCheckBox.setText("Check box is checked");
    }
    if(cbCheckBoxTest.isSelected() == false){
    lblCheckBox.setText("Check box is unchecked");
    }
}

@FXML
void rbRadio1Clicked(MouseEvent event) {
    lblRadioButtonTest.setText("Radio1 button checked");
}

@FXML
void rbRadio2Clicked(MouseEvent event) {
    lblRadioButtonTest.setText("Radio2 button checked");
}

@FXML
void rbRadio3Clicked(MouseEvent event) {
    lblRadioButtonTest.setText("Radio3 button checked");
}

@FXML
void sbScrollDetect(MouseEvent event) {
    pbProgress1.setProgress((sbScroll1.getValue() / 100));
}

@FXML
void tbToggleClicked(MouseEvent event) {
    if(tbToggleButtonTest.isSelected() == true){
    lblToggleButtonTest.setText("Toggle Button is checked");
    }
    if(tbToggleButtonTest.isSelected() == false ){
    lblToggleButtonTest.setText("Toggle Button is unchecked");
    }
}
```

Save the project. The code is similar to Swing. The only exception is the progress bar. Rather than integer values, the JavaFX progress bar goes from 0 = 0% to 1 = 100%, thus the value obtained from the scroll bar is divided by 100. The scroll bar has two events so that any user interaction with the scroll bar will move the progress bar. The issue is if only mouse click was implemented;

a user could swipe at the scroll bar and move the scroll bar, but not trigger an event. Finally, modify Main.java to load the fxml application per Code Listing 11.11:

```
package application;

import javafx.application.Application;
import javafx.stage.Stage;
import javafx.scene.Scene;
import javafx.scene.Parent;
import javafx.fxml.FXMLLoader;


public class Main extends Application {
    @Override
    public void start(Stage primaryStage) {
        try {

            Parent root = FXMLLoader.load(getClass().getResource("OtherControls.fxml"));

            primaryStage.setTitle("Other Controls");
            primaryStage.setScene(new Scene (root));
            primaryStage.show();


        } catch(Exception e) {
            e.printStackTrace();
        }
    }

    public static void main(String[] args) {
        launch(args);
    }
}
```

Code Listing 11.11 Final Main.java Code Listing

Run the application and you should be able to access all of the controls as before. As a test of the initialize() method discussed in the last section, we can set the checkbox to true as the default startup state. Add the following to the end of the initialize() method:

```
cbCheckBoxTest.setSelected(true);
```

Run the application again. This time the checkbox is already checked on startup, rather than the default of unchecked.

11.3 Summary and Homework Assignments

The user interface has come a long way since the terminals for mainframes of the 1960s. Where the previous chapters have dealt with the science behind computer programming, this chapter on GUI programming shows there is also some art. With multiple application stores with thousands of apps for mobile and PC systems, the ability to write GUI applications is an important part of computer programming. Virtual reality and virtual overlay are the next computer interfaces, and these new interfaces will require the ability to program in 3-dimensional space, which adds a new approach for interacting with the computer and the world around you. The computer terminal is more than a TV with a typewriter in front of it. Being able to write GUI applications opens up a universe of possibilities. We only touched on the basics of creating GUI applications. There is a lot more detail than we can cover in a single chapter. Now that we have the ability for users to interact with our applications, they will want to be able to save data, which brings us to the next chapter. Before we move on, here are some questions and programming projects.

11.3.1 Questions

1. Why was the GUI library named Swing?
2. What were the design goals behind Swing?
3. Who is credited with developing JavaFX?
4. Draw the MVC interaction diagram.

11.3.2 Programming Projects

1. Create a triangle-shaped class to draw an equilateral triangle.
2. Modify CH11CA11.3 BoxLayout of Computer Activity 11.3 by adding a second button between the other components that has the label "Java?" on the button. Use the same actionPerfomed for both buttons. The first button will still produce the same message, but the "Java?" button will show the message "Java GUI is fun!" Hint: you must use setActionCommand and getActionCommand.

3. Creating a Swing GUI program that takes text input from a user and with a click of a button, displays the sentence with the characters in reverse below the Reverse button, Figure 11.54.

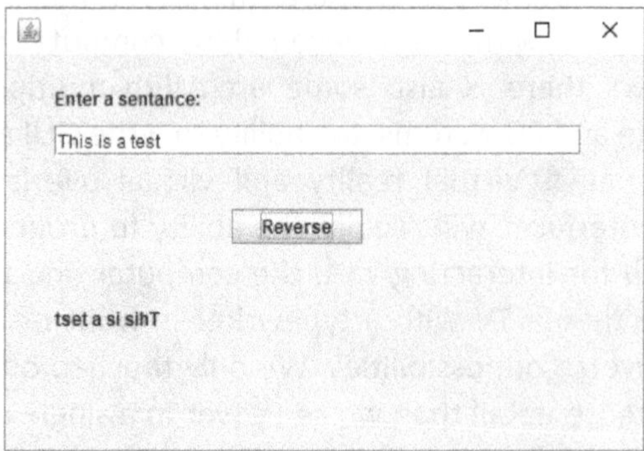

Figure 11.54 Text Reversal Application GUI

4. In Chapter 4, a programming project had you create a dividend calculator. Create a Swing GUI program for a dividend calculator.

5. In Chapter 4, a programming project had you create a Yahtzee dice program. Create a Swing GUI program that displays the integer values for 5 numbers representing the 5 dice. Use checkboxes so that the user can select which dice to hold for the next roll, each die that is checked is a don't roll, and each die that unchecked is a roll. The program must keep track of the number of rolls, and the maximum is 3. A reset would clear the values and clear the number of rolls so that the dice can be rolled again. Two buttons should be used for the "roll" and "reset" functions, Figure 11.55.

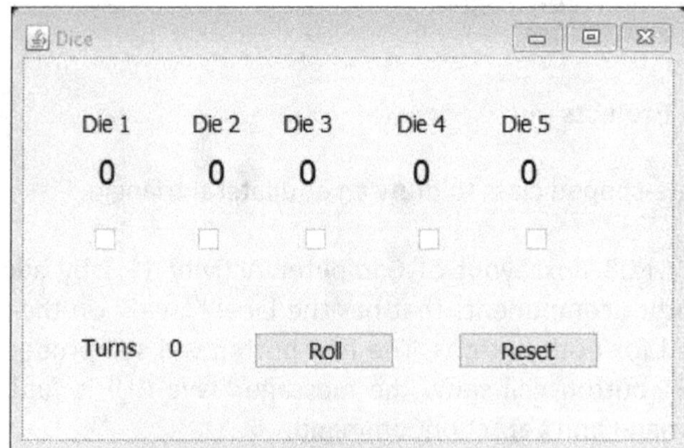

Figure 11.55 Swing GUI for Yahtzee

6. Building on the Yahtzee game in #5, to the Swing GUI, add a score sheet below the dice to keep score for 4 players, where users manually enter their scores. Have the program calculate the final score for each player.

7. In Chapter 5, a programming project had you create a BINGO application. Create a JavaFX GUI application for the BINGO game. Use label controls to display the numbers as they are drawn. Have a button for the draw and another button for a reset, Figure 11.56.

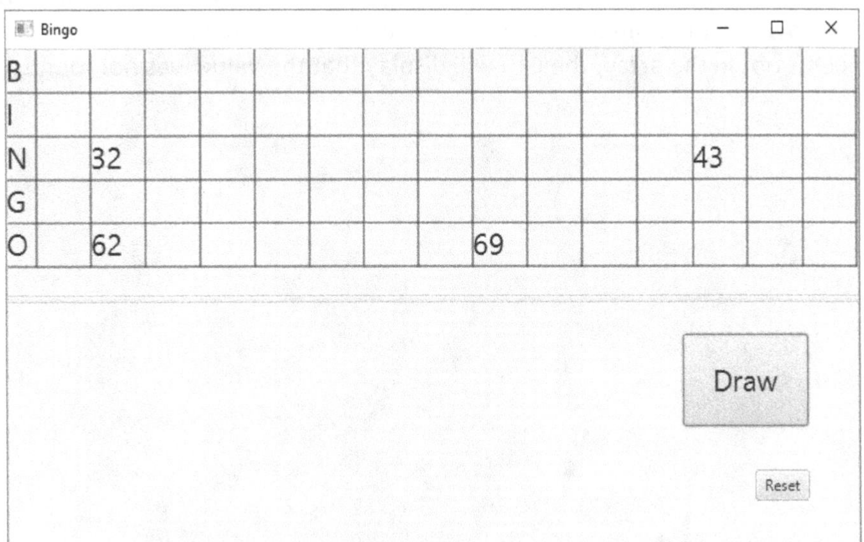

Figure 11.56 JavaFX GUI for the Bingo Game

8. In Chapter 5, a programming project had you create an Egg Hunt game. Create a JavaFX GUI application for the Egg Hunt game. Use buttons in place of "O"s to create a grid. After the user clicks on the button, the button is disabled. The number of tries printed as well as an indication that the egg has been found. A reset button allows the user to start a new game.

9. Create a simple JavaFX GUI calculator application that adds, subtracts, multiplies, and divides. You may use the custom library from Chapter 6 Computer Activity 6.8.

10. Create a JavaFX GUI application that takes an integer input by the user and calculates either a Fibonacci or factorial value based on the integer that the user enters into a text box.

11. Create a JavaFX GUI application that interacts with all the FamousEquations and GeometricMath methods in the custom library from Chapter 6 Computer Activity 6.8. Use a Tab Layout to split between the 2 classes.

12. Create a JavaFX GUI application that generates a random array of 100 integers between 0 and 99. The GUI interface will have a place for the user to enter a number and click on a search button to see if the number is in the array. If the number is in the array, the GUI will display that the number is in the array and how many times it is in the array. If the number is not in the array, the GUI will display that the value was not found.

12 File I/O using the Stream Classes

"Things are not always what they seem; the first appearance deceives many; the intelligence of a few perceives what has been carefully hidden."
Phaedrus (Roman Poet) c. 15 BC – c. 50 AD.

Most people don't think much about the details when saving photos, movie clips, music, or word documents to a storage device. Press the save button or the save menu item and the file is put on the storage device. From a programming point of view, saving a file is not so straightforward. So far, we have seen how to input data from a keyboard or GUI interface, sort and search data, and touched on datasets in Chapter 6 with the inventory Computer Activity. The problem with the inventory program was when the program closed, all data was lost. This chapter will look at the basics of storing data to files by looking at how to save different types of data using different Stream Io classes

12.1 Java's Stream I/O

Reading and writing files is an input and output (I/O) operation. Java I/O operations are performed using streams.

Definition: *Stream* – An abstraction that either inputs or outputs data.

We have been using the stream classes all along when our programs used the Scanner class to get user input and called System.out.println() to print to a console. Streams get attached to different devices such as a printer, the network, or a storage device, but the operations performed are the same. The input device is a "read-in" operation and the output device is a "write-out" operation. The streams send data sequentially in a first-in-first-out operation. The stream classes are defined in the java.io packages with a few extra stream classes in the java.nio package. The top-level classes are InputStream, OutputStream, Reader, and Writer, Figure 12.1.

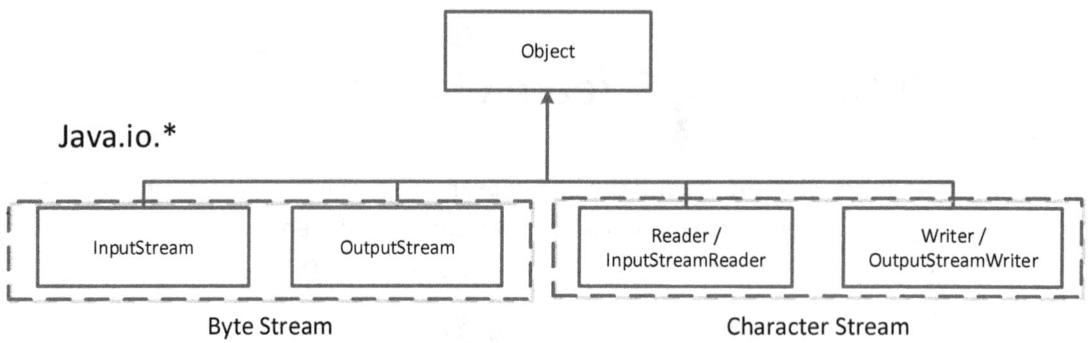

Figure 12.1 Java Stream I/O Top Level Classes

There are two types of streams in Java, byte and character; and there are several stream classes for each one. As the name implies, Byte stream handles the input and output of bytes. Byte stream is best used when working with binary data such as picture and sound files. Character streams are used for handling the input and output of characters. It is best to use a character stream when reading and writing to text files. There are 53 classes in the java.io package. The classes are split between input and output in most cases. The different computer activities in this chapter will look at a few of these classes, which are summarized in Table 12.1:

Type	**Byte Stream Classes**		**Character Stream Classes**	
	Input	**Output**	**Input**	**Output**
Basic	InputStream	OutputStream	Reader InputStreamReade r	Writer OuputStreamReade r
Buffere d	BufferedInputStrea m	BufferedOutputStrea m	BufferedReader	BufferedWriter
Data	DataInputStream	DataOutputStream		
Files	FileInputStream	FileOutputStream	FileReader	FileWriter
Objects	ObjectInputStream	ObjectOutputStream		

Table 12.1 Java Stream Classes

12.2 Reading and Writing with Byte Streams

First, we will look at the FileInputStream and FileOutputStream classes. The constructors for these classes are:

```
FileInputStream("file name")
FileOutputStream("file name")
FileOutputStream("file name", boolean append)
```

There are several constructors for the FileOutputStream. The second constructor listed above has the option to append the file. If set to true, all data written to the file is added to data that is already present. If false, all the data is overwritten. There are several methods that go with the FileInputStream class. Table 12.2 shows those methods we will be working with:

FileInputStream Method	Description
void close()	Closes the input stream. Any further attempts to read from the file will trigger an exception.
int read()	Returns either an integer on the byte read or -1 signaling an end of file (EOF).
int read(byte[] buffer)	Will read the bytes up to buffer.length, and puts the bytes into buffer[]. Returns the actual number of bytes read.

Table 12.2 File Input Class Methods Used in this Chapter

There are several methods that go with the FileOutputStream class. Table 12.3 lists those methods we will be working with:

FileOutputStream Method	Description
void close()	Closes the output stream. Any further attempts to write to the file will trigger an exception.
void write(int b)	Writes an integer to the output stream.
void write(byte[] buffer)	Writes a complete byte array to the output stream.

Table 12.3 File Output Class Methods Used in the Chapter

12.2.1 Computer Activity 12.1 - Reading and Writing Bytes to Binary File

FileInputStream and FileOutputStream will be used to create and write to a binary file and then open and read the binary file. Create a folder called "java" in the root of the C drive. In Eclipse, create a new Java project called "CH12CA12.1-ByteRW", create a new package in the project called "jae.byterw", and create a new class called "BasicByteRW" with a main() method. Fill in Code Listing 12.1 for the BasicByteRW.java file:

```java
package jae.byterw;

import java.io.*;

public class BasicByteRW {

    public static void main(String[] args) throws IOException {
        // TODO Auto-generated method stub

        byte[] i = {99, 32, 15, 29, 30, 48, 2, 127, 25};

        FileOutputStream fosFileOut = null;
        FileInputStream fisFileIn = null;

        //write the data to a file
        try{
            fosFileOut = new FileOutputStream("c:\\java\\test.bin");
            fosFileOut.write(i);
        }
        catch(IOException ex){
            System.out.println("Write IO error" + ex);
        }
        finally{
            fosFileOut.close();
        }


        //read the data from a file
        try{
            fisFileIn = new FileInputStream("c:\\java\\test.bin");
            byte[] rBuffer = new byte[100];
            int j = fisFileIn.read(rBuffer);
            for(int x = 0; x < j; x++){
                System.out.print(rBuffer[x] + " ");
            }
        }
        catch(IOException ex){
            System.out.println("Read IO error" + ex);
        }
        finally{
            fisFileIn.close();
        }
    }
}
```

Code Listing 12.1 BasicByteRW Class

Make sure you have a c:\java directory on your system, and then run the application. You should get the array of numbers listed in the output console and written to the test.bin file located in c:\Java directory. Line 3 imports the Java.io package, which includes the FileInputStream and FileOutputStream classes. Since the methods in these classes can throw an exception, line 7 adds a "throws" for the IOException class. Line 10 has the data that will be written to the file. As we discussed in Chapter 8, since there can be an exception thrown when accessing a file, a try-catch-finally must be used, and the instance variables are set up before the try-catch-finally code in lines 12 and 13. The first try-catch-finally opens the file and writes the whole byte array to the file. If there is an error, the catch will output the error. No matter if the write to the file is successful or not, the final code will run and close the output stream. Opening the test.bin file in a text editor like Notepad will only show garbage characters since the file is in binary format, Figure 12.1.

test.bin - Notepad

File Edit Format View Help

Figure 12.2 – Binary Contents of test.bin File in a Text Editor

The data is stored in binary (1's and 0's) in sequential order, Figure 12.3.

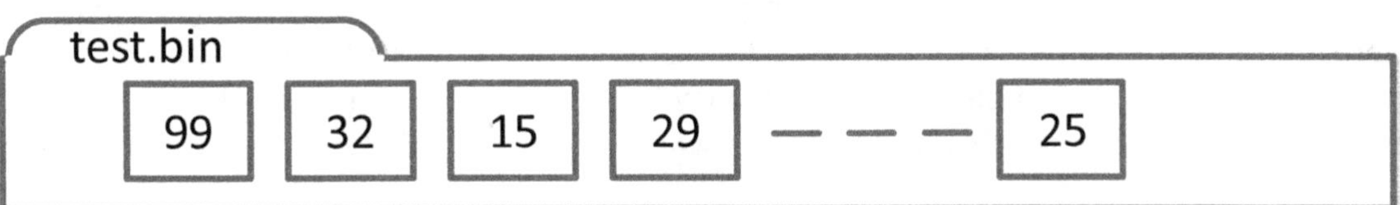

Figure 12.3 Binary File Storage Sequence

Line 29-42, open and read the file. The output is sent to the console. The file is read into a buffer with a pre-determined size. Setting the byte array to 100 was arbitrary. This works great if you know the size of the file, but this might not always be the case. A different implementation could be used with the read() method where a loop is used to read in each character until the end of file is found. Running the debugger and stepping through the code, the type of stream is listed in as the value for fosFileOut and fisFileIn, Figure 12.4. The append option is also listed for the FileOutputStream.

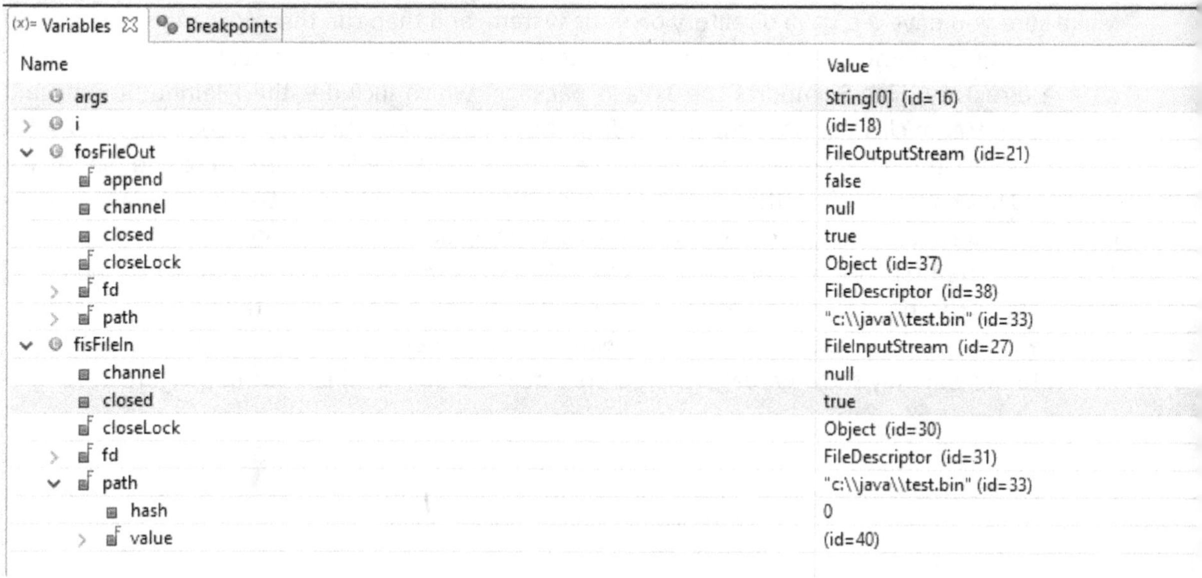

(x)= Variables ✕ | Breakpoints

Name	Value
args	String[0] (id=16)
> i	(id=18)
∨ fosFileOut	FileOutputStream (id=21)
append	false
channel	null
closed	true
closeLock	Object (id=37)
> fd	FileDescriptor (id=38)
> path	"c:\\java\\test.bin" (id=33)
∨ fisFileIn	FileInputStream (id=27)
channel	null
closed	true
closeLock	Object (id=30)
> fd	FileDescriptor (id=31)
∨ path	"c:\\java\\test.bin" (id=33)
hash	0
> value	(id=40)

Figure 12.4 Debugger Variable Listing

12.3 Auto File Close with Try-with-Resource

The close() method is used often with streams. Forgetting to close the stream can result in having lost data and a program crash; although Eclipse will provide a warning if you forget the close() method. To help programmers streamline the code, a new try-with-resource statement was added to JDK 7 to automatically close the stream when finished with the try-catch. For Computer Activity 12.1, the try-catch-finally statements would become the following try-with-resources statement:

```
 try(FileOutputStream fosFileOut = new
FileOutputStream("c:\\java\\test.bin")){
    fosFileOut.write(i);
 }
 catch(IOException ex){
    System.out.println("Write IO error" + ex);
 }
```

The instantiation of the FileOutputStream is the resource made in the try statement. No need to define the FileOutputStream variable outside the try-catch. The finally with the close() method is removed.

12.3.1 Computer Activity 12.2 – Byte Stream with Auto File Close and Integer Read/Write

In this Computer Activity, we will re-implement Computer Activity 12.1 using the try-with-resources statement and the integer read and write methods. In Eclipse, create a new Java project called "CH12CA12.2-ByteTryRes", create a new package in the project called "jae.bytetryres", and create a new class called "BasicByteTryRes" with a main() method. Fill in Code Listing 12.2 for the BasicByteTryRes.java file:

```
package jae.bytetryres;

import java.io.*;

public class BasicByteTryRes {

    public static void main(String[] args) throws IOException {
        // TODO Auto-generated method stub

        int[] i = {54, 12, 1, 7, 30, 248, 2, 127, 25};
        //write the data to a file
        try(FileOutputStream fosFileOut = new
  FileOutputStream("c:\\java\\test2.bin");   ){

            for(int x =0; x < i.length; x++){
                fosFileOut.write(i[x]);
            }
        }
        catch(IOException ex){
            System.out.println("Write IO error" + ex);
        }

        //read the data from a file
        try(FileInputStream fisFileIn = new
  FileInputStream("c:\\java\\test2.bin")){
            int j = 0;
            do{
                j = fisFileIn.read();
                System.out.print( j + " ");
            }while(j != -1);
        }
        catch(IOException ex){
            System.out.println("Read IO error" + ex);
        }
    }
}
```

Code Listing 12.2 BasicByteTryRes Class

Run the application, the output will list the array of values including the end-of-file flag (-1), and a new test2.bin file will be created. The try-with-resources statement simplifies the code. This time an integer array is saved to a file and read back to be outputted to the console. Line 14 has a for-loop that writes each byte to the file. Line 25 has a do-while-loop that reads in each byte until the end-of-file character is reached. This read implementation gets around guessing the buffer size needed for the file.

12.4 Saving Other Primitive Data Types using DataInputStream and DataOutputStream

Bytes are not the only data type to be saved to a file. Other primitive types such as Integers, Booleans, float, char, and doubles can also be written to and read from files using DataInputStream and DataOuputStream. The constructor for these two:

```
DataInputStream(InputStream in)
DataOutputStream(OutputStream out)
```

The inputstream and outputstream source can be any device: printer, file, scanner etc. To access a file, the FileInputStream and FileOutputstream are used:

```
DataInputStream(new FileInputStream("file name"))
DataOutputStream(new FileOutputStream("file name"))
```

There are several methods for different primitive types that go with the DataInputStream class. Table 12.4 shows those methods we will be working with:

DataInputStream Method	Description
void close()	Closes the input stream. Any further attempts to read from the stream will trigger an exception.
Boolean readBoolean()	Reads a Boolean value from the input stream.
Double readDouble()	Reads a double value from the input stream.
Int readInt()	Reads a int value from the input stream.

Table 12.4 Data Input Stream Methods

There are several methods for different primitive types that go with the DataOutputStream class. Table 12.5 shows those methods that we will be working with:

DataOutputStream Method	Description
void close()	Closes the output stream. Any further attempts to write to the stream will trigger an exception.
void writeBoolean(Boolean val)	Writes a Boolean value to the output stream.
void writeDouble(double val)	Writes a double value to the output stream.
void writeInt(int val)	Writes an int value to the output stream.

Table 12.5 Data Output Stream Methods

12.4.1 Computer Activity 12.3 - Reading and Writing Primitive Data Types using DataInputStream and DataOutputStream

This Computer Activity will save a group of Boolean, double, and int values to a file, read the data back from the file, and output the data to the console. In Eclipse, create a new Java project called "CH12CA12.3-DataIOStream". In the new project create a package called "jae.dataiostream" and create a class under the package called "DataIOStream" with a main() method. Fill in Code Listing 12.3 for the DataIOStream.java file.

```
package jae.dataiostream;

import java.util.Random;
import java.io.*;

public class DataIOStream {

    public static void main(String[] args) throws IOException{
        // TODO Auto-generated method stub
        Random gen = new Random();

        try(DataOutputStream dOut = new DataOutputStream(new FileOutputStream("c:\\java\\test3.bin"))){

            for(int x = 0; x < 3; x ++){
                dOut.writeInt(gen.nextInt(100));
                dOut.writeBoolean(gen.nextBoolean());
                dOut.writeDouble(gen.nextDouble());
            }
        }
        catch(IOException ex){
            System.out.println("Write IO error" + ex);
        }
```

```
23.
24.          try(DataInputStream dIn = new DataInputStream(new
    FileInputStream("c:\\java\\test3.bin"))){
25.
26.              for(int x = 0; x < 3; x ++){
27.                  System.out.println("" + dIn.readInt());
28.                  System.out.println("" + dIn.readBoolean());
29.                  System.out.println("" + dIn.readDouble());
30.              }
31.          }
32.          catch(IOException ex ){
33.              System.out.println("Read IO error" + ex);
34.          }
35.      }
36. }
```

Code Listing 12.3 DataIOStream Class

Run the application, and you will get 3 sets of the int, Boolean, and double in the output. Lines 12 and 24 implement the DataOutptuStream and DataInputStream, respectively, using the try-with-resources statement. Lines 14-17 generate and save the int, Boolean, and double values in a specific order. Lines 26-29 read the values from the file in the same order. The values are written to the file sequentially, which means the type order is set into the file: int, Boolean, double, see Figure 12.5.

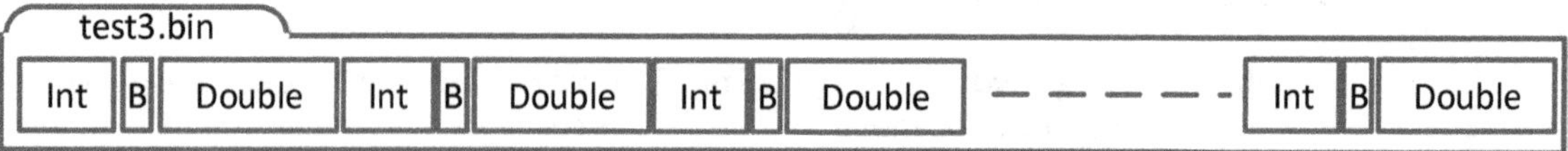

Figure 12.5 Output File Data Sequence

The values have to read from the file in the same type order. If lines 27-29 are re-arranged and not in alignment with the data type in the file, the output would be in error. Careful planning in structuring the data in a file is import to design up front. For example, a file for Inventory records would have a mix of strings and numbers. Reading and writing files would have to entail each record set and their location in the file. Class objects can be used to group different data types together and methods can be designed to make the proper read and write sequences.

12.5 Saving Objects

Not only can data types be saved to files, but objects can also be saved to files. The last stream classes to discuss are the ObjectInputStream and ObjectOutputStream. The constructors for these two classes are as follows:

```
ObjectInputStream(InputStream in)
ObjeRandAccessFilctOutputStream(OutputStream out)
```

The inputstream and outputstream can be any device: printer, file, scanner etc. To access a file, the FileInputStream and FileOutputstream are used:

```
ObjectInputStream(new FileInputStream("file name"))
ObjectOutputStream(new FileOutputStream("file name"))
```

There are several methods for different primitive types that go with the ObjectInputStream class. Table 12.6 shows a few of the methods we will be working with:

ObjectInputStream Method	Description
void close()	Closes the input stream. Any further attempts to read from the stream will trigger an exception.
Object readObject(Object obj)	Reads an object from the input stream.

Table 12.6 ObjectInputStream Class Methods

There are several methods for different primitive types that go with the ObjectOutputStream class. Table 12.7 shows a few of the methods we will be working with:

ObjectOutputStream Method	Description
void close()	Closes the output stream. Any further attempts to write to the stream will trigger an exception.
void writeObject(Object obj)	Writes a Boolean value to the output stream.

Table 12.7 ObjectOutputStream Class Methods

12.5.1 Computer Activity 12.4 - Saving Objects to Files

An EmployeeRecord class will be created and used to store a name and an employee number to a file. As we touched on in Chapter 8, in order to save the object to the stream, the object must be made serializable. We can then use the classes ObjectOutputStream and ObjectInputStream to serialize and de-serialize the object. In Eclipse, create a new Java project called "CH12CA12.4-EmployeeRecords" and create a new package under the new project called "jae.employeerecords". Create two classes under the new package. The first will be called "EmployeeRecordsIO" with a main() method, and the second will be called "EmployeeRecord". For the EmployeeRecord.java file, fill in the Code Listing 12.4, but Eclipse will ask you to fill in the serialVersionUID. You only need to click on warning next to the class declaration, and select add default serialVersionUID.

```
package jae.employeerecords;

import java.io.Serializable;

public class EmployeeRecord implements Serializable{


    /**
     *
     */
    private static final long serialVersionUID = 1L;
    public String employeename;
    public int employeenumber;

    EmployeeRecord(String name, int number){
        employeename = name;
        employeenumber = number;
    }
    EmployeeRecord(){

    }
}
```

Code Listing 12.4 EmployeeRecord Serializable Class

The class simply stores the employee name and employee number. The two constructors provide two different ways to instantiate a new instance of the class. The serialVersionUID is what allows the class to be sent via a stream to a file. The primitive data types and String objects implement the Serializable class; thus, they were already set up to use stream I/O classes. Create the EmployRecordsIO class with a main method, and fill in the EmployeeRecordsIO.java file with Code Listing 12.5:

```
package jae.employeerecords;

import java.io.*;

public class EmployRecordsIO {

    public static void main(String[] args) throws IOException{
        // TODO Auto-generated method stub

        EmployeeRecord emp =  new EmployeeRecord();
        EmployeeRecord emp1 = new EmployeeRecord("Sally", 1);
        EmployeeRecord emp2 = new EmployeeRecord("Bob", 2);
        EmployeeRecord emp3 = new EmployeeRecord("Sarah", 3);

```

```
15.         try(ObjectOutputStream oOut = new ObjectOutputStream(new
   FileOutputStream("c:\\java\\test4.ser"))){
16.             oOut.writeObject(emp1);
17.             oOut.writeObject(emp2);
18.             oOut.writeObject(emp3);
19.         }
20.         catch(IOException ex){
21.             System.out.println("Write IO error" + ex);
22.         }
23.
24.         try(ObjectInputStream oIn = new ObjectInputStream(new
   FileInputStream("c:\\java\\test4.ser"))){
25.
26.             for(int x = 0; x < 3; x++){
27.                 emp = (EmployeeRecord) oIn.readObject();
28.                 System.out.println("Employee Name: " +
   emp.employeename + " EmployeeNumber: " + emp.employeenumber);
29.             }
30.         }
31.         catch(IOException ex){
32.             System.out.println("Read IO error" + ex);
33.         }
34.         catch (ClassNotFoundException e) {
35.             // TODO Auto-generated catch block
36.             e.printStackTrace();
37.         }
38.     }
39. }
```

Code Listing 12.5 EmployRecordsIO Class

Run the application, and you will get a list of the 3 employee names with their employee numbers. In lines 10-13, create different instances of the EmployeeRecord class. The first instance will be used when reading from the file. The other 3 create employee records. Lines 15-22 simply save the records to the file. The file name extension ends with a ".res". This is a standard conversion in Java for a file with save objects in it. Each object has the data type included. The data sequence is shown in Figure 12.6:

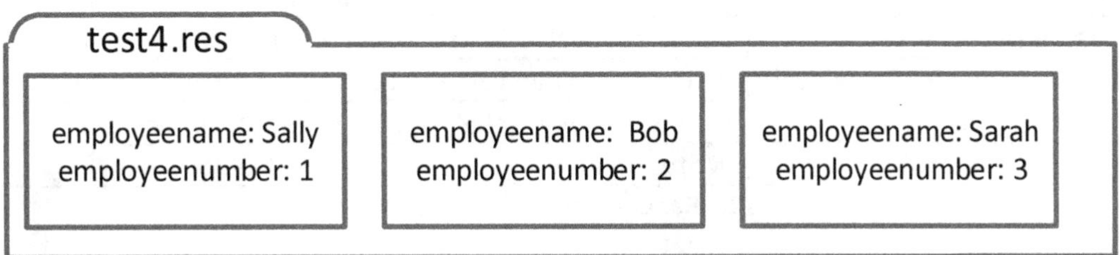

Figure 12.6 Output File Data Sequence

Lines 24-37 read the objects from the file and output them to a console. Because a return object could throw an exception if the object doesn't exist, the second catch must be implemented. When the object is read from the file in line 27, the "emp" instance variable gets the object and the dot notation can be used to access the different fields in the returned object.

12.6 Random Access File

All of the Computer Activities so far have written and read data to files in sequential order. If we want to read a data record that is in the middle of the file, we have to read each record until we get to the desired record. A value in the middle of a file cannot be changed unless you read the whole file, make the change at the single location, and then write back the complete modified file. Java also supports a different kind of file called a Random Access File. A Random Access File can be thought of as an array. A pointer can be set to a location where you want to read or write data. The data type being saved will dictate the pointer offset values. For example, if the data type is a double, then each value is on an 8-byte boundary. Access to the file data would be on multiples of 8. Random Access Files are implementations of the on DataInput and DataOutput interfaces, and not the stream classes. The constructor is as follows:

```
RandomAccessFile("file name", <"r" or "rw">)
```

Notice there isn't a separate input and output class. The file can be accessed with the optional 'r' for read-only or 'rw' for read/write access. There are several methods in the RandomAccessFile class. Table 12.8 shows a few of the most commonly used methods:

RandomAccessFile Method	Description
void close()	Closes the output stream. Any further attempts to write to the stream will trigger an exception.
void seek(long pos)	Sets the file pointer to the pos offset location from the beginning of the file.
long length()	Return the length of the file.
long getFilePointer()	Return the file pointer's current offset location.
Boolean readBoolean	Reads a Boolean value at the current offset location.
double readDouble()	Reads a double value at the current offset location.
int readInt()	Reads a int value at the current offset location.
void writeBoolean(Boolean val)	Writes a Boolean value to the current offset location.
void writeDouble(double val)	Writes a double value to the current offset location.
void writeInt(int val)	Writes an int value to the current offset location.

Table 12.8 RandomAccessFile Class Methods

12.6.1 Computer Activity 12.5 – Random Access File

This Computer Activity provides a basic demonstration of the file pointer in action. In Eclipse, create a new Java project called "CH12CA12.5-RandomAccess". Create a new package in the project called "jae.randomaccess", and create a new class called "RandomAccess" with a main(); method. Fill in Code Listing 12.6 for the RandomAccess.java file:

```
package jae.randomaccess;

import java.io.*;

public class RandomAccess {

    public static void main(String[] args) throws IOException {
        // TODO Auto-generated method stub

        int[] i = { 1, 2, 3, 4, 5, 6, 7, 8, 9};

        try(RandomAccessFile rafIO = new
  RandomAccessFile("c:\\java\\test5.dat", "rw")){

            for(int x = 0; x < i.length; x++){
                rafIO.writeInt(i[x]);
            }
        }
        catch(IOException ex){
            System.out.println("Random Access File IO error" + ex);
        }

        try(RandomAccessFile rafIO = new
  RandomAccessFile("c:\\java\\test5.dat", "r")){

            //In is 4 bytes in size
            rafIO.seek(8);
            System.out.println("The value is " + rafIO.readInt());
        }
        catch(IOException ex){
            System.out.println("Random Access File IO error" + ex);
        }

```

```
32.         try(RandomAccessFile rafIO = new
   RandomAccessFile("c:\\java\\test5.dat", "rw")){
33.
34.             //In is 20 bytes in size
35.             rafIO.seek(20);
36.             rafIO.writeInt(15);
37.             rafIO.seek(0);
38.             for(int x = 0; x < (rafIO.length() / 4) ; x++){
39.                 System.out.println("The value is at index offest" +
   x * 4 + " is " + rafIO.readInt());
40.             }
41.         }
42.         catch(IOException ex){
43.             System.out.println("Random Access File IO error" + ex);
44.         }
45.     }
46. }
```

Code Listing 12.6 RandomAccess Class

Line 10 defines an integer array that gets saved to a file in lines 12-20. The next try-catch block at line 22 opens the file for read-only access and sets the file pointer to an offset of 8 to read the third value in the file, which has a value of 3. Remember that the indexing of objects is similar to the indexing of an array. What would be the array index is now an offset multiplier, where the offset into the file is the size of the object in bytes multiplied by the offset multiplier. The object 1 in an array would be at index 0, so the offset multiplier is 0 for object 1. An integer is 4 bytes long, so the file offset for object 1 is (0 * 4) which equals 0. As expected, the offset into the file of the first object, object 1, is 0. The object 2 in an array would be at index 1, so the offset multiplier is 1 for object 2. Again, an integer is 4 bytes long, so the file offset for object 2 is (1 * 4) which equals 4. Object 2 is at file offset 4. Continuing this logic, the object 3 in an array would be at index 2, so the offset multiplier is 2 for object 3. An integer is 4 bytes long, so the file offset for object 3 is (2 * 4) which equals 8. Object 3 is at file offset 8. Clearly, if the object index is n, then the offset multiplier will be (n – 1), so the file offset for object n will be (n – 1) * 4, for an integer object. Refer to Figure 12.7:

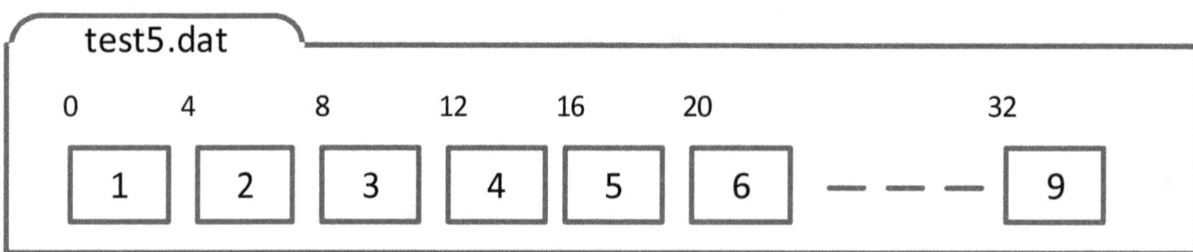

Figure 12.7 Output File Data Sequence

The last try-catch block at line 32 opens the file for read/write access, moves the pointer to object index 6, which has an offset multiplier of 5 (5 integers in) and a file offset of 20 which is (5 * 4), changes the value at index 6, resets the position in the file to the start of the file, and prints out all the values in the file. Line 38 uses the file size divided by the data type length to calculate the end of the loop. Run the file, and the output should be as follows:

```
The value is 3
The value is at index 0 is 1
The value is at index 4 is 2
The value is at index 8 is 3
The value is at index 12 is 4
The value is at index 16 is 5
The value is at index 20 is 15
The value is at index 24 is 7
The value is at index 28 is 8
The value is at index 32 is 9
```

12.7 Reading and Writing with Character Streams

Writing characters to a file is possible with the other stream classes, but character stream is the best solution if you want to work with Unicode text. The two-character stream classes are FileWriter and FileReader. FileWriter extends OutputStreamWriter, and FileReader extends InputStreamReader. Both character stream classes get the various read() and write() methods. The constructors are as follows:

```
FileReader("file name")
FileWriter("file name")
FileWriter("file name", boolean append)
```

The FileWriter has two different constructors. The append option for the second constructor either appends to the file when set to true or overwrites the file when set to false. The first constructor always overwrites. The FileWriter class has several methods. Table 12.9 shows a few of the most commonly used methods:

FileWriter Method	Description
void close()	Closes the output stream. Any further attempts to write to the file will trigger an exception.
void write(String str)	Writes a string to the output stream.
void write(char[] cBuf)	Writes a complete array of characters to the output stream.

Table 12.9 FileWriter Class Methods

The FileReader class has several methods. Table 12.10 shows a few of the most commonly used methods:

FileReader Method	Description
void close()	Closes the input stream. Any further attempts to read from the file will trigger an exception.
int read()	Reads a single character from the input stream or a -1, signaling an end of file (EOF).
int read(char[] cBuf)	Will read an array of characters from the input stream until an end-of-file is reached or an I/O error occurs. Returns the actual number of bytes read or -1 if the end-of-file is reached (EOF).

Table 12.10 FileReader Class Methods

12.7.1 Computer Activity 12.6 - Basic Reading and Writing of a Text File

This Computer Activity demonstrates a basic write and read from text file. In Eclipse, create a new Java project called “CH12CA12.6-BasicRWText”. Create a new package in the project called “jae.basicrwtext”, and create a new class called “BasicRWText” with a main(); method. Fill in Code Listing 12.7 for the BasicRWTex.java file:

```
package jae.basicrwtext;

import java.io.*;

public class BasicRWText {

    public static void main(String[] args) throws IOException {
        // TODO Auto-generated method stub

        String myString = "An example of a text file created in Java.";
        try(FileWriter fwOut = new FileWriter("c:\\java\\test6.txt")){
            fwOut.write(myString);
        }
        catch(IOException ex){
            System.out.println("Write IO error" + ex);
        }

```

```
18.         try(FileReader fwIn = new
    FileReader("c:\\java\\test6.txt")){
19.
20.             char[] myBuf = new char[100];
21.             int i = fwIn.read(myBuf);
22.
23.             for(int x = 0; x < (i - 1); x++){
24.                 System.out.print(myBuf[x]);
25.             }
26.         }
27.         catch(IOException ex){
28.             System.out.println("Read IO error" + ex);
29.         }
30.     }
31. }
```

Code Listing 12.7 BasicRWText Class

Run the program and this time a text file is created. Because it is a text file, the file can be open and read in any editor like Notepad, Figure 12.8.

test6.txt - Notepad

File Edit Format View Help

An example of a text file created in Java.

Figure 12.8 Basic Reading and Writing Output Text File

Line 10 has the string that will be saved to the file. The try-catch block at line 11 opens the new text file and writes the string to the file. The next try-catch block opens the file and reads the characters to a buffer. Line 21 gets the total number of characters read and uses that value in the for-loop to print out each character to the console. The problem with the buffer for a text file is that you might not know the size of the file and how large the buffer needs to be. There is a different solution to reading in individual characters using the BufferedReader class. The BufferedReader and BufferedWriter classes provide an efficient way to read and write whole lines of text from a file. The buffer size by default is 8192 characters, which is assumed to address most cases. The BufferedReader and BufferedWriter constructors are as follows:

```
BufferedReader(Reader in)
BufferedReader(Reader In, int buffersize)
BufferedWriter(Writer in)
BufferedWriter (Writer In, int buffersize)
```

The classes use other stream Reader and Writers as the I/O stream. The optional buffersize allows you to change the default buffer size. Table 12.11 show some of the most commonly used class methods:

BufferedReader Method	Description
void close()	Closes the input stream. Any further attempts to read from the file will trigger an exception.
int read()	Reads a single character from the input stream. Returns -1 signaling an end of file (EOF).
String readline()	Reads a line of text from the input stream and returns a string.

Table 12.11 BufferedReader Class FileReader Methods

Table 12.12 show some of the most commonly used class methods:

BufferedWriter Method	Description
void close()	Closes the output stream. Any further attempts to write to the file will trigger an exception.
void newline()	Writes a line separator.
void write(String str)	Writes a string to the output stream.

Table 12.12 BufferedWriter Class FileWriter Methods

Now we let's make a change to the code and use the BufferedReader. Comment out the second try-catch block lines 18-29. Add the following code after line 29:

```
try(BufferedReader brIn = new BufferedReader(new
FileReader("c:\\java\\test6.txt"))){
    String myBuf;
    while((myBuf = brIn.readLine()) != null){
        System.out.println(myBuf);
    }
}
catch(IOException ex){
    System.out.println("Read IO error" + ex);
}
```

Run the program again. The BufferedReader uses the FileReader as the input stream. Rather than reading individual characters, the readLine() method handles the reading in of individual characters into a buffer and then returns a string. If there are no more characters to read the loop terminates.

12.7.2 Computer Activity 12.7 - A Basic GUI Text Editor

Now that we have covered different file I/O operations, this last Computer Activity will bring the open and save operations into a GUI application. The application we will create is basic GUI text editor using Swing. The application will have a text area to write text into, it will handle multiple lines of text, and it will have a menu bar that will have items to open, save, and close a file. The application's GUI will look like Figure 12.9.

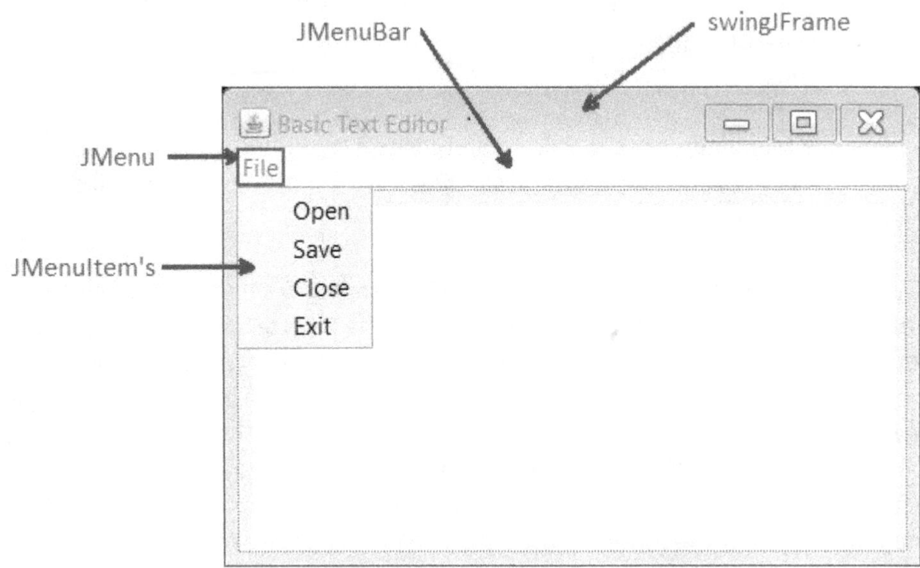

Figure 12.9 Basic Text Editor GUI

It is worth your while to learn how to build a GUI like the one we will be using for this Computer Activity. Most GUI's that have a basic frame with a title bar, maximize, minimize, exit controls, and drop-down menus are built like this GUI. We will start with the swingJFrame that is built for us when we create a new WindowBuilder Application Window project. Once we have this, we will add the JMenuBar to the top of the frame under the title bar. Then we will add a JMenu to the title bar, and finally, the JMenuItem's under the JMenu. Let's get started.

In Eclipse, create a new Java project called "CH12CA12.7-GUITextEditor". In the new project, right-click and choose New->Other from the context menu. Under WindowBuilder->Swing Designer, select Application Window and click next. Make the package name "jae.guitexteditor" and make the name "GUITextEditor". Click Finish, and Eclipse will generate the Swing project with the swingJFrame. Click on the "Design" tab, and you will see the basic frame in the designer area, click on the title bar of the JFrame to select it, and in the Properties pane change the title to "Basic Text Editor".

In the Palette, expand layouts. Click on the "Absolute layout", and click on the middle of the JFrame in the designer. Then click outside of the JFrame to deselect it. In the Palette, expand Menu. Click on the "JMenubar" and move the mouse over the JFrame. Note the orange box that says: "(Add items here)", the horizontal and vertical blue alignment lines, and the position indicator for the upper-right corner of the JMenuBar control. Move the mouse to the upper left corner of the inside of the frame, and when the position indicator says: 0x0, click the mouse. With the new JMenuBar still selected, move the mouse over the right side of the JMenuBar until the mouse cursor changes to the resizer. Click and drag the right side of the JMenuBar to the far right side of the frame. This will resize the JMenuBar so it spans the total width of the frame. Keep the default properties for the JMenuBar.

Now, go back to the Menu items in the Palette and click on the JMenu and then click inside of the JMenuBar. This places a JMenu item in the JMenuBar. With the JMenu item still selected, go to the properties and change the text to "File".

Now, we need to add the menu selections. We will be adding 4 selections to the File menu for Open, Save, Close, and Exit. Back in the Menu section of the Palette, click on JMenuItem and click in the box under the File Jmenu that says: "(Add items here)". With the name highlighted in the editor pane, type in "Open" and hit return and the text property will be changed to "Open". Add 3 more JMenuItems to the File menu item. With each one, click on the JMenuItem in the Palette and then move the mouse under the JMenuItem in the design window that was added before it. When the red alignment line shows just under the item before it, click the mouse. This will add each JMenuItem one under the other. As you add each one, change each name to "Save", "Close", and "Exit" respectively. Finally, under Components in the Palette, click on JTextArea and click in the middle of the window. Expand the box so that it fills the remaining portion of the window under the menu bar. Be sure to save the file. We will keep the default variable properties for each item added as shown in Table 12.13. Check each of the variables to make sure that they match the table, and subsequently will match the code.

GUI Item	Variable
JTextArea	textArea
File	mnFile
Open	mntmOpen
Save	mntnSave
Close	mntmClose
Exit	mntmExit

Table 12.13 Basic Text Editor GUI Variable Naming

Now, we will add some actions behind the menu items. In the last chapter, buttons had click events. For menu items, these are press events. Right-click on the "Open" menu item in the designer, and select Add Event Handler->mouse->mousePressed. The addMouseListener with mousePressed() method will be added to the code. Click back on the Design tab and repeat the same steps to add mouse pressed event handlers for the “Save”, “Close”, and “Exit” menu items. Each time you add an event handler, you will have to click on the Design tab to go back to the Designer. Save all files when finished adding the event handlers.

Click on the Source tab, and add the following imports:

```
import javax.swing.JFileChooser;
import javax.swing.filechooser.FileFilter;
import javax.swing.filechooser.FileNameExtensionFilter;
import java.io.*;
```

These imports add access to the classes needed to open and save the text document. Scroll down the source code to the mousePressed() method under the “Open” menu item, and fill in the following code:

```
JMenuItem mntmOpen = new JMenuItem("Open");
mntmOpen.addMouseListener(new MouseAdapter() {
     @Override
     public void mousePressed(MouseEvent e) {
          JFileChooser openFile = new JFileChooser();
          FileFilter typeTxt = new FileNameExtensionFilter("Text File
(.txt)", "txt");
          openFile.addChoosableFileFilter(typeTxt);
          openFile.setFileFilter(typeTxt);
          int filereturnVal = openFile.showOpenDialog(null);
          File file = openFile.getSelectedFile();
          BufferedReader reader = null;
          if(filereturnVal == JFileChooser.APPROVE_OPTION){
               try{
                    reader = new BufferedReader(new
FileReader(file.getPath()));
                    String s = "";
                    String finalString = "";
                    while((s = reader.readLine()) != null ){
                         finalString+= (s + "\n");
                    }
                    textArea.setText(finalString);
                    reader.close();
               }
               catch(IOException ex){
                    JOptionPane.showMessageDialog(null, "Error opening
file", "Open Failed", JOptionPane.ERROR_MESSAGE);
```

```
                }
            }
        }
    });
```

When the user selects the "Open" menu item, an open dialog appears allowing the user to navigate to the location in the files system where the file is located. The JFileChooser provides the open dialog. An instance of JFileChooser is created. A FileFilter is used to set the default extension, ".txt", in the open dialog and the filter is added to the JFileChooser instance and set as default. An instance of the opened file is created. Inside the If-statement, the BufferedReader tries to open the file based on the full path to the file. If the file is able to be opened, each line in the file is read into a string and then that string is written to the textArea. Save the project.

In the mousePressed() method under the "Save" menu item, fill in the following code:

```
 JMenuItem mntmSave = new JMenuItem("Save");
 mntmSave.addMouseListener(new MouseAdapter() {

     @Override
     public void mousePressed(MouseEvent e) {
         JFileChooser saveFile = new JFileChooser();
         FileFilter typeTxt = new FileNameExtensionFilter("Text File
(.txt)", "txt");
         saveFile.addChoosableFileFilter(typeTxt);
         saveFile.setFileFilter(typeTxt);
         int filereturnVal = saveFile.showSaveDialog(null);
         File file = saveFile.getSelectedFile();
         BufferedWriter writer = null;
         if(filereturnVal == JFileChooser.APPROVE_OPTION){

             try{
                 writer = new BufferedWriter(new
FileWriter(file.getPath()));
                 writer.write(textArea.getText());
                 writer.close();
                 JOptionPane.showMessageDialog(null, "File saved", "Save
Succedded", JOptionPane.INFORMATION_MESSAGE);

             }
```

```
                catch(IOException ex){
                    JOptionPane.showMessageDialog(null, "Error saving
file", "Save Failed", JOptionPane.ERROR_MESSAGE);
                }

            }

        }
    });
```

The JFileChoose is used to open a save dialog to allow the user to save the file in a specified location. The FileFilter is used again to set the default file extension to ".txt". Once the user has entered a name and selected a location, the contents of the text area are written to the file using a BufferedWriter. In the mousePressed() method under the "Exit" menu item, fill in the following code:

```
JMenuItem mntmExit = new JMenuItem("Exit");
mntmExit.addMouseListener(new MouseAdapter() {
    @Override
    public void mousePressed(MouseEvent e) {
        System.exit(0);
    }
});
```

In the mousePressed() method under the "Close" menu item, fill in the following code:

```
JMenuItem mntmClose = new JMenuItem("Close");
mntmClose.addMouseListener(new MouseAdapter() {
    @Override
    public void mousePressed(MouseEvent e) {
        textArea.setText("");
    }
});
```

These last two menu items simply exit the application and clear the text area. Save the project and run the program. Enter some text and save the file. Close the file, and then open the file.

12.8 Summary and Homework Assignments

We save files all the time, and never think about the details behind the save button. As we have explored, there is a little more complexity in saving data than you might think. Different data types can be saved in different ways. Java provides different file I/O solutions to meet different program requirements. How the data is structured in the file for efficient processing is an important part of the design process. The next chapter provides a look into other data structures. Before we move on, here are some questions and programming projects.

12.8.1 Questions

1. For Computer Activity 12.1, what happens if the c:\java folder is not present in the system?

2. For Computer Activity 12.1, the FileInputStream and FileOutputStream read and write bytes to and from the file. Why do int read() and void write(int b) use integers rather than bytes?

3. For Computer Activity 12.1, if we change `fosFileOut = new FileOutputStream("c:\\java\\test.bin")` to `fosFileOut = new FileOutputStream("test.bin")` where does the file get written to?

4. For Computer Activity 12.2, what can be added to the code so that the -1 doesn't print out?

5. In Computer Activity 12.5, what happens if the seek to read a value in line 25 is changed from `rafIO.seek(8)` to `rafIO.seek(7)`?

12.8.2 Programming Projects

1. Modify Computer Activity 12.1 to use the read() method in a loop to read in all the characters from the file.

2. For Computer Activity 12.6, add a second string "Now we can write and save strings", and use the BufferedWriter to write out each string in a different line in the file. Hint: use the BufferedWriter's newLine() method.

3. Recreate the GUI Text Editor application in JavaFX.

4. For the new GUI Text Editor Application created with JavaFX, add a menu item to print the open file.

5. Chapter 11 had you create the GUI coin flip game. Add an auto-save of the win/loss record after each press of a button. Have the win/loss record automatically restarted on the start of the application.

6. For the Yahtzee game created as a GUI in Chapter 11 program projects 5 and 6, add the ability to save the score to a file, to open the score file, and to allow the user to set the name of the file but with the mandatory extension of .ytz.

13 Introduction to Data Structures: the Collections Framework

"I suppose it is tempting, if the only tool you have is a hammer, to treat everything as if it were a nail."
-attributed to Abraham Maslow, 1966.

Since Chapter 5, arrays have been used to demonstrate various computer science concepts. Arrays are nice, primitive data types that help with learning, but per the chapter lead-in quote, arrays cannot be used for everything. An address book application that lists the names, phone numbers, addresses, and e-mail addresses can grow and shrink over time, and a different type of data structure is required to manage a dynamic collection of data. To manage larger complex collections of data, different types of data structures are needed. The ArrayList was also introduced in Chapter 5 to demonstrate a different data structure solution. Where arrays are fixed in size, ArrayLists can grow and shrink. The ArrayList class is part of the Collections Framework that includes a number of other data structure solutions. A collection is a single object that contains multiple objects. Data structure is a big topic that can be discussed in a book unto itself. Various universities have a data structure course or two that deep dives into the math and science of data structures and their associated algorithms, which includes a deep dive on the Big-O notation. This short chapter will provide a high-level overview of the Collections Framework with a few examples.

13.1 The Collections Framework

The first Java library release contained a few ad hoc data structure classes such as Hashtable, Stack Dictionary, and Vector. The classes were useful, but there was no way to extend them. The Collections Framework was introduced in J2SE 1.2 in 1999. The Collection Framework consists of a number of interfaces, Figure 13.1, that are a starting point for implementing different types of collection solutions. The top-level interfaces are List, Set, Queue, and Map, and there are interfaces for navigating through a collection with the Iterators and Spliterators, Figure 13.2.

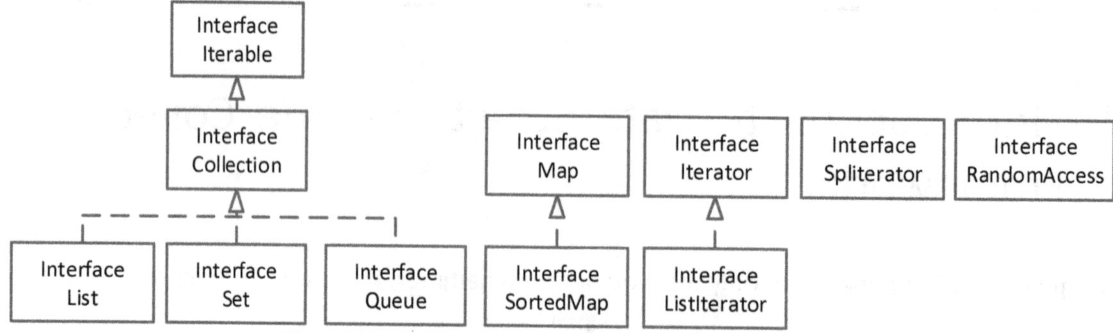

Figure 13.1 Collections Framework Interfaces

Built on the interfaces are a number of abstract classes that implement some of the capabilities defined in the interfaces. Finally, there are concrete classes (in bold) that provide complete collection implementations, Figure 13.2. Not all the classes are in the diagram.

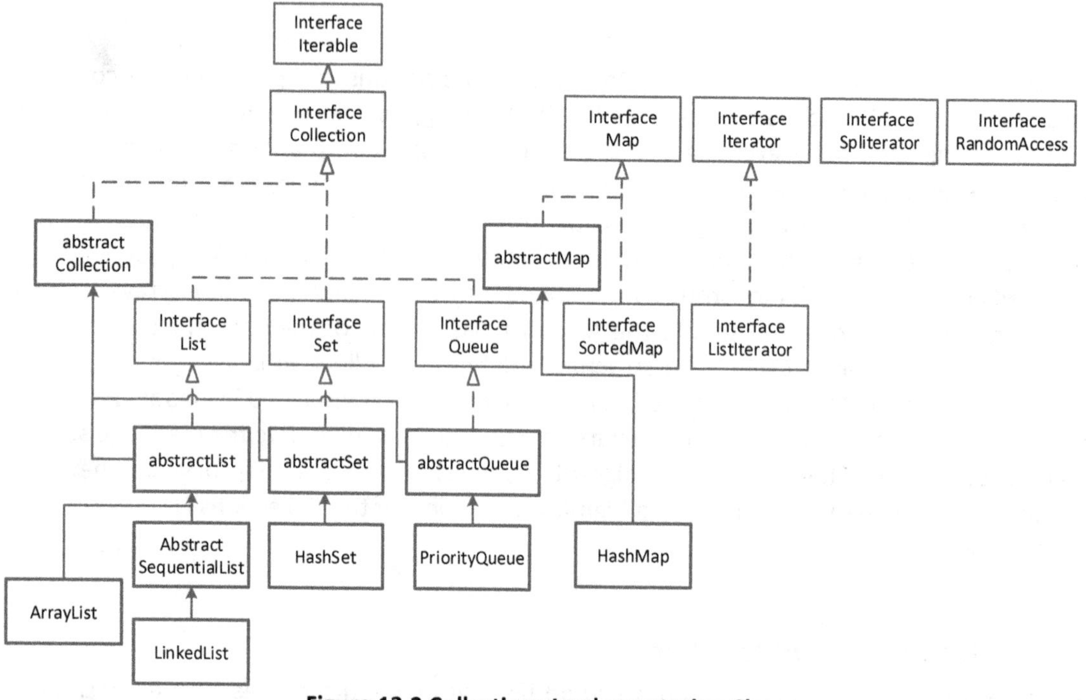

Figure 13.2 Collections Implementation Classes

The combination of interfaces, abstract classes, and concrete classes provides flexibility to expand on the collection framework. Now let's look at the 4 main interfaces and some of the concrete class implementations.

13.2 List Interface

The List Interface defines an ordered collection of elements. An index is used to access different elements in the collection. Data can be added to the end of the collection or inserted anywhere in the collection as long as you know the index. Retrieving data can be performed on the whole list, or you can get a specific element if you know the index. Duplicate items are allowed. The concrete classes in the library that implement the List interface are ArrayList, CopyOnWriteArrayList, LinkedList, Stack, and Vector.

13.2.1 Computer Activity 13.1 - LinkList Example

Chapter 5 covered the ArrayList. In this exercise, we will recreate the first ArrayList example, but this time we will use a LinkedList. Create a new Java project in Eclipse called "CH13CA13.1-LinkedListTest". In the project, create a new package called "jae.linkedlisttest". Then, create a new class under the packages called "LinkedListTest" with a main() method; and fill in the code with Code Listing 13.1:

```
Package jae.linkedlisttest;

import java.util.LinkedList;

public class LinkendListTest {

    public static void main(String[] args) {
        // TODO Auto-generated method stub

        LinkedList<String> llfruit = new LinkedList<String>();

        llfruit.add("apple");
        llfruit.add("banana");
        llfruit.add("orange");

        System.out.println("List items:");
        for(String fruit : llfruit ){
            System.out.println("Item # " + llfruit.indexOf(fruit) +
" is " + fruit);
        }

```

```
        System.out.println("\n Add Item:");
        llfruit.add(1, "lemon");
        for(String fruit : llfruit ){
            System.out.println("Item # " + llfruit.indexOf(fruit) +
" is " + fruit);
        }

        System.out.println("\n Remove Item:");
        llfruit.remove(3);
        for(String fruit : llfruit ){
            System.out.println("Item # " + llfruit.indexOf(fruit) +
" is " + fruit);
        }

        System.out.println("\n Change Item:");
        llfruit.set(0, "pear");
        for(String fruit : llfruit ){
            System.out.println("Item # " + llfruit.indexOf(fruit) +
" is " + fruit);
        }

        System.out.println("\n Add Item:");
        llfruit.add("pear");
        for(String fruit : llfruit ){
            System.out.println("Item # " + llfruit.indexOf(fruit) +
" is " + fruit);
        }
    }
}
```

Code Listing 13.1 LinkedListTest Code Listing

Run the program, and you should get the same output as the first ArrayList Computer Activity in Chapter 5.

```
List items:
Item # 0 is apple
Item # 1 is banana
Item # 2 is orange

 Add Item:
Item # 0 is apple
Item # 1 is lemon
Item # 2 is banana
Item # 3 is orange
```

```
 Remove Item:
Item # 0 is apple
Item # 1 is lemon
Item # 2 is banana

 Change Item:
Item # 0 is pear
Item # 1 is lemon
Item # 2 is banana

 Add Item:
Item # 0 is pear
Item # 1 is lemon
Item # 2 is banana
Item # 0 is pear
```

13.2.2 ArrayList versus LinkedList

The obvious question to ask is "what is the difference between the two?" From the programmer perspective, both lists appear to be the same. A collection is created that can be accessed using an index, Figure 13.3.

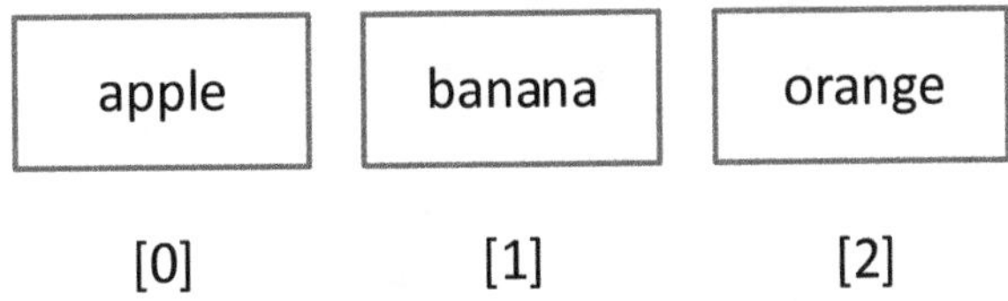

Figure 13.3 Indexed Collection

The difference is in the underlying implementation that only the developer of the class knows about. For an ArrayList, each index points to an object, Figure 13.4.

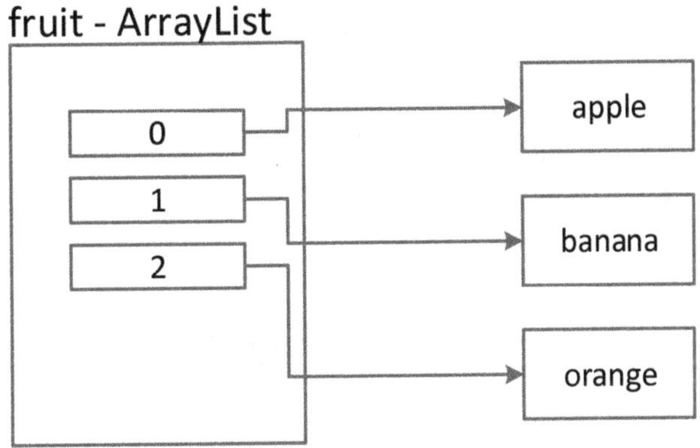

Figure 13.4 ArrayList Architecture

The LinkedList in java.util is a doubly-linked list implementation. Each object is tied to a node. Each node has a link to the node of the object after it and a link to the node of the object before it, Figure 13.5. The Computer Activity used the For-each-loop to access the collection.

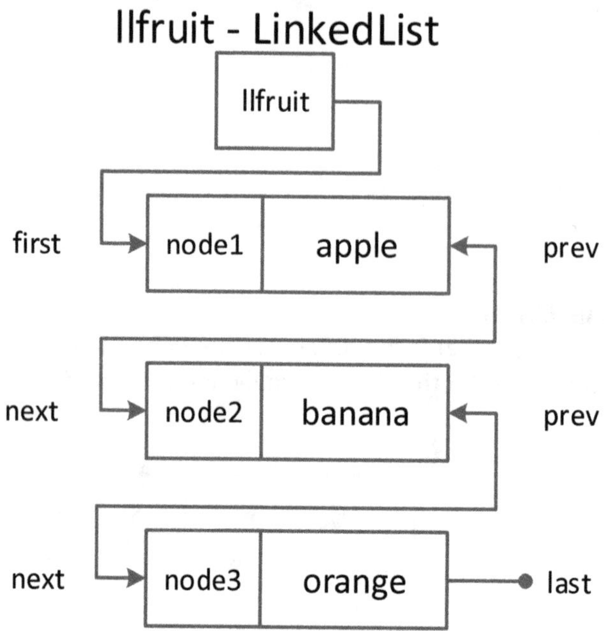

Figure 13.5 llfruit LinkedList Doubly-Linked List

Set a breakpoint at line12 and run the program in the debugger. The llfruit LinkedList starts out unpopulated, Figure 13.6. You may or may not have noticed that an ArrayList starts out with 10 items set to null.

(x)= Variables | Breakpoints

Name	Value
args	String[0] (id=16)
llfruit	LinkedList<E> (id=18)
first	null
last	null
modCount	0
size	0

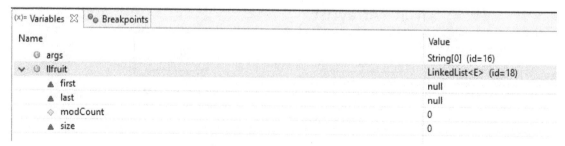

Figure 13.6 Empty LinkedList

Single-step through the code a few times, and the llfruit LinkedList fills with data. Each element added to llfruit has a node number associated with it. There is a reference to the previous node and the next node in the list. The debugger shows the node id values, Figure 13.7.

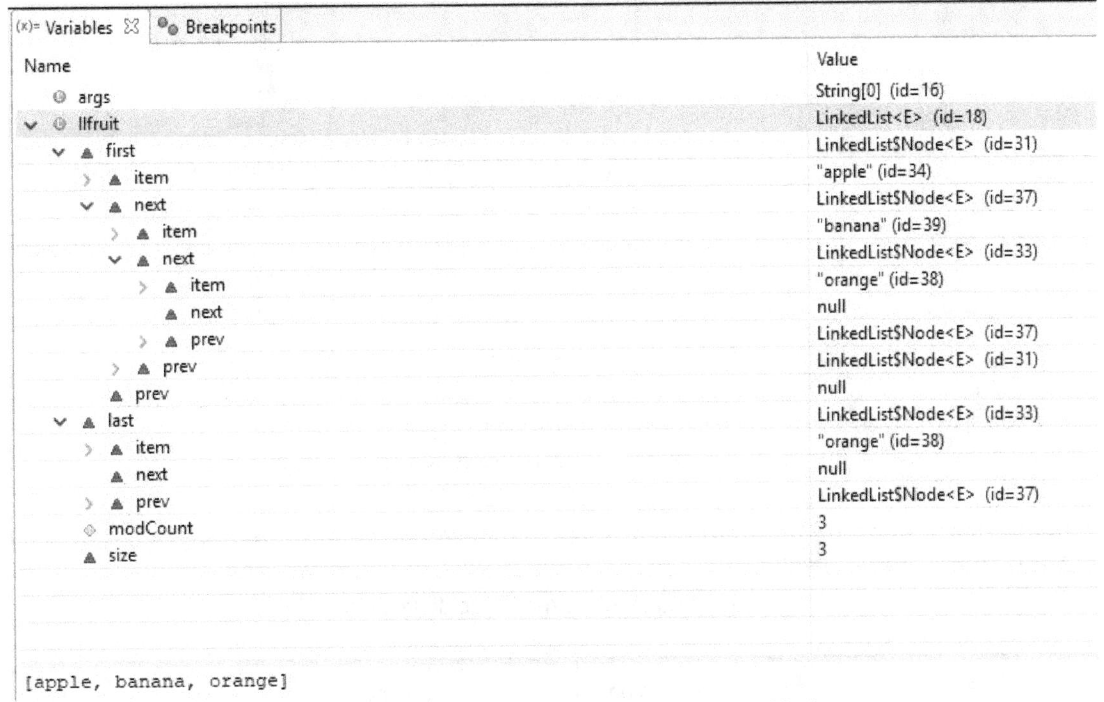

Figure 13.7 llfruit LinkedList with Objects Added

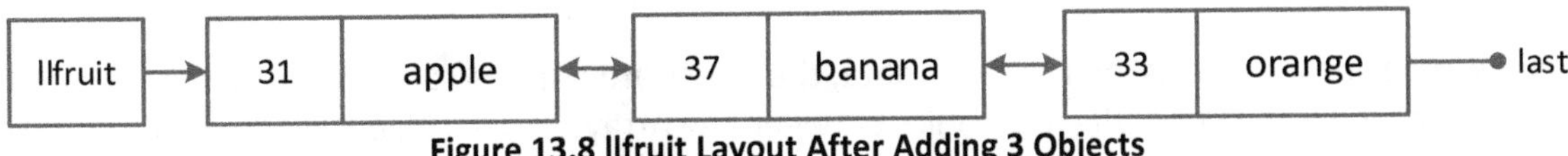

Figure 13.8 llfruit Layout After Adding 3 Objects

Line 22 inserts a new data object into index location 1 and all of the other items after index location 1 gets shifted down, Figure 13.10. Under the hood, a node value is assigned and the next and previous links are updated with the new node values, Figure 13.9. The LinkedList has two pointers for each node, thus the insertion simply changes the pointer values.

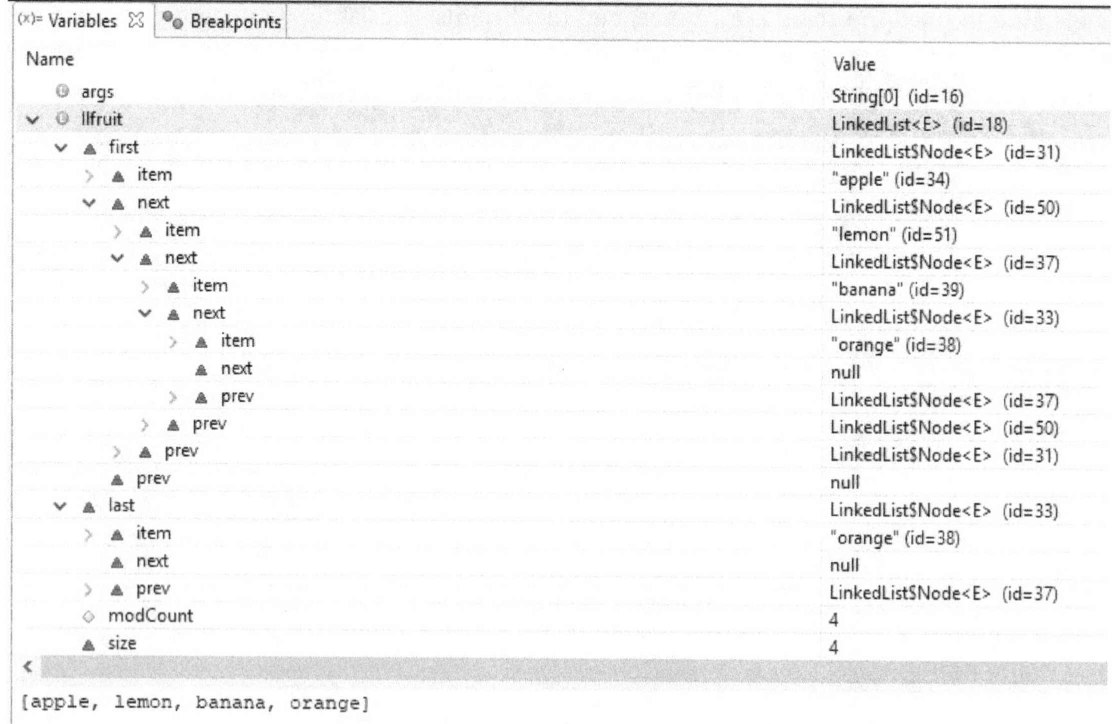

Figure 13.9 llfruit After Object Insertion

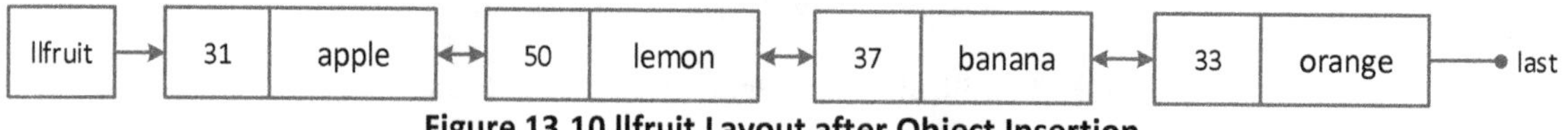

Figure 13.10 llfruit Layout after Object Insertion

As the code adds, removes, and changes data, the nodes are adjusted accordingly. As we pointed out above, under the hood, the mechanics between the ArrayList and LinkedList implementations are different. As the programmer using the classes, you don't need to know the underlying mechanics of the data structure. How the programmer sees and uses the data structure is abstracted from the actual implementations. A term used in computer science is called abstract data type.

Definition: *Abstract Data Type (ADT)* is a mathematical model for data types, or how data is stored and what functions access the data versus the actual implementation underneath.

The LinkedList, ArrayList, and the other data structures in the Collection Framework are examples of ADT. The real difference comes in performance and memory usage. The Big-O notation for searching in an ArrayList is O(1), where a LinkedList is O(n). For insert and remove operations, ArrayList is O(n) worst case, where a LinkedList is O(1). Changing the node pointer values in a

LinkedList is faster than shifting the whole collection in an ArrayList. For memory usage, the LinkedList takes up more memory since each node includes the previous and next node link values.

13.3 Set Interface

A Set is a collection that doesn't allow for duplicate elements. If you try to add an element that is already in the list, the element will not be added. If you remember the mathematical concept of sets, the Set interface models the mathematical set abstraction. A good example of a Set is a deck of cards. The concrete classes in the library that implement the Set interface are ConcurrentSkipListSet, CopyOnWriteArraySet, EnumSet, HashSet, JobStateReasons, LinkedHashSet, and TreeSet.

13.3.1 Computer Activity 13.2 - HashSet Example

Hashing is simply creating a hash code for a class object, which is a 32-bit signed integer and can be used as an index for storage and retrieval. Every class in Java provides a hashCode() method, which boils down the bit pattern of a class object into a 32-bit signed integer hash code.

A HashSet is a collection of objects that uses a HashMap to organize the storage of the objects. There are no duplicate objects in a HashMap. As objects are added to the collection, a hash code is generated and the element is placed in one of several buckets. When a HashSet is created, there are several HashSet constructors that determine the HashSet's characteristics. One constructor allows you to set the capacity (available buckets), but there is not a 1-to-1 relationship between the number of buckets in the HashSet and the number of objects that can be stored. Multiple objects can be stored in the same bucket. The objects could have different hash codes or they could have identical hash codes. Because of the nature of hashing algorithms, there is no "perfect hash", i.e., objects that are not equal can have identical hash codes. A simple LinkedList implementation is used to organize objects within each bucket. In this Computer Activity, we will implement a simple HashSet example, and investigate how it works. Create a new project in Eclipse called "CH13CA13.2-HashSetTest". In the project, create a new package called "jae.hashsettest", and then create a new class under the packages called "HashSetTest" with a main() method. Fill in Code Listing 13.2 to create the HashSetTest class:

```
package jae.hashsettest;

import java.util.HashSet;

public class HashSetTest {

```

```
    public static void main(String[] args) {
        // TODO Auto-generated method stub

        HashSet<String> hsfruit = new HashSet<String>();

        hsfruit.add("cherry");
        hsfruit.add("grapefruit");
        hsfruit.add("lemon");
        hsfruit.add("pear");

        System.out.println("First List:");
        for(String fruit : hsfruit){
            System.out.println(fruit);
        }

        hsfruit.add("apple");
        hsfruit.add("orange");
        hsfruit.remove("pear");
        hsfruit.add("lemon");

        System.out.println("\nSecond List:");
        for(String fruit : hsfruit){
            System.out.println(fruit);
        }
    }
}
```

Code Listing 13.2 HashSetTest Class

Run the program and the output will vary:

```
First List:
cherry
lemon
pear
grapefruit

Second List:
orange
cherry
apple
lemon
grapefruit
```

Notice that the output order is not the same order as the elements that were added to the HashSet. Since hashing is being used to generate a key and store the elements into different buckets, the storage and retrieval are ordered by the hash codes of the objects, not by the order that the objects were added. Adding the string value "lemon" a second time doesn't result in a second lemon object being added to the HashSet. There are no duplicate objects in a HashSet. Put a breakpoint at line 12 and run the debugger. As you step through the code, you will see the HashMap filled in with the hash value and the actual object, Figure 13.11. The HashSet uses the default capacity of 16, but only 3 buckets are used. When the String "pear" is added, the string object is placed in the second bucket with "lemon" as the next item in the iteration. The placing of objects in the buckets is controlled by the internals of the HashSet class. This can vary for different releases of the Java language and runtime environment.

(x)= Variables | Breakpoints

Name	Value
args	String[0] (id=16)
hsfruit	HashSet<E> (id=18)
map	HashMap<K,V> (id=28)
entrySet	null
keySet	null
loadFactor	0.75
modCount	4
size	4
table	HashMap$Node<K,V>[16] (id=32)
[1]	HashMap$Node<K,V> (id=35)
hash	-1361552575
key	"cherry" (id=39)
next	null
value	Object (id=42)
[2]	HashMap$Node<K,V> (id=36)
hash	102857938
key	"lemon" (id=43)
next	HashMap$Node<K,V> (id=44)
hash	3436754
key	"pear" (id=46)
next	null
value	Object (id=42)
value	Object (id=42)
[7]	HashMap$Node<K,V> (id=37)
hash	-2093036905
key	"grapefruit" (id=45)
next	null
value	Object (id=42)
threshold	12
values	null

```
[cherry, lemon, pear, grapefruit]
```

Figure 13.11 Debugger View of the HashMap for the HashSet

The output order matches the order of the data stored in the HashSet. A HastSet's Big-O notation for the basic operations of both the add and the remove is O(1).

13.4 Queue Interface

The final Collection interface implementation is the Queue interface. A Queue collection is designed to hold data for processing. An example would be a printer queue in an operating system, which holds a number of print jobs to be printed in the order that they were received. There are several concrete classes that implement the Queue interface, one of which we already covered: ArrayBlockingQueue, ArrayDeque, ConçurrentLinkedDeque, ConcurrentLinkedQueue, DelayQueue, LinkedBlockingDeque, LinkedBlockingQueue, LinkedList, LinkedTransferQueue, PriorityBlockingQueue, PriorityQueue, and SynchronousQueue. The Queue interface typically orders items in a first-in-first-out (FIFO) order, but not always. The lone class that doesn't follow the FIFO order is the PriorityQueue. A PriorityQueue will order the data either in a natural ordering or using a comparator.

13.4.1 Computer Activity 13.3 - PriorityQueue Example

In this Computer Activity, we will look at the Priority Queue. The Priority Queue provides the basic add() and remove() methods that we have seen in the other data structure classes. Priority Queue has different implementations for these methods. The offer() method is the same as the add() method to add data. The poll() method returns the top item in the queue and then removes it from the queue. The peak() method shows what the top item in the queue is but doesn't remove the item. Create a new project in Eclipse called "CH13CA13.3-PriorityQueueTest". In the project, create a new package called "jae.priorityqueuetest", and then create a new class under the packages called "PriorityQueueTest" with a main() method. Fill in Code Listing 13.3 for the PriorityQueueTest class:

```
package jae.priorityqueuetest;

import java.util.Iterator;
import java.util.PriorityQueue;

public class PriorityQueueTest {

    public static void main(String[] args) {
        // TODO Auto-generated method stub

        PriorityQueue<Integer> pqnumbers = new
    PriorityQueue<Integer>();
        int[] mynumbers = {5,7,29,8,1,7,0,15};
        for( int x : mynumbers){
            pqnumbers.offer(x);
        }

        System.out.println("Initial storage:");
```

```
18.         for(int y : pqnumbers){
19.             System.out.println(y);
20.         }
21.         System.out.println("\nThe head of the queue is " +
   pqnumbers.peek());
22.
23.         System.out.println("\nThe final output:");
24.         Iterator<Integer> myIterator = pqnumbers.iterator();
25.         while( myIterator.hasNext() ){
26.             //removing each item from priority queue
27.             System.out.println(pqnumbers.poll());
28.         }
29.     }
30. }
```

Code Listing 13.3 PriorityQueueTest Class

Run the application and you will get the following output:

```
Initial storage:
0
5
1
8
7
29
7
15

The head of the queue is 0

The final output:
0
1
5
7
7
8
15
29
```

Lines 11-15 set up a Priority Queue with data from an array. The offer() method is used to add items to the queue. Lines 17-20 display the elements as they are stored in the queue. The ordering is a bit scrambled and not the natural order as one expects. Re-ordering can be seen using the debugger. Initially, when all items are in the data structure they appear out of order except the value 0, see Figure 13.12.

(x)= Variables | Breakpoints

Name	Value
args	String[0] (id=16)
pqnumbers	PriorityQueue<E> (id=19)
comparator	null
modCount	8
queue	Object[11] (id=29)
[0]	Integer (id=31)
value	0
[1]	Integer (id=32)
value	5
[2]	Integer (id=33)
value	1
[3]	Integer (id=34)
value	8
[4]	Integer (id=35)
value	7
[5]	Integer (id=36)
value	29
[6]	Integer (id=35)
value	7
[7]	Integer (id=37)
value	15
size	8
mynumbers	(id=27)

```
[0, 5, 1, 8, 7, 29, 7, 15]
```

Figure 13.12 Queue After Loading The Integer Array

Line 21 shows that the topmost item in the queue is the integer '0'. Line 24 sets up an iterator as a check for when the queue is empty. The poll() method is used in line 27 to remove and print each item in the queue. When there are no items left in the queue, the while-loop can exit. As you step through the final while-loop, the data is getting re-ordered into the natural order, Figure 13.13.

(x)= Variables | Breakpoints

Name	Value
args	String[0] (id=16)
pqnumbers	PriorityQueue<E> (id=19)
comparator	null
modCount	9
queue	Object[11] (id=29)
[0]	Integer (id=33)
value	1
[1]	Integer (id=32)
value	5
[2]	Integer (id=35)
value	7
[3]	Integer (id=34)
value	8
[4]	Integer (id=35)
value	7
[5]	Integer (id=36)
value	29
[6]	Integer (id=37)
value	15
size	7
mynumbers	(id=27)
myIterator	PriorityQueue$Itr (id=62)

```
[1, 5, 7, 8, 7, 29, 15]
```

Figure 13.13 Queue Data Reordering

Another step and the remaining items are in the natural order, Figure 13.14. This operation takes place in the background and is not seen by the programmer.

(x)= Variables | Breakpoints

Name	Value
args	String[0] (id=16)
pqnumbers	PriorityQueue<E> (id=19)
comparator	null
modCount	10
queue	Object[11] (id=29)
[0]	Integer (id=32)
value	5
[1]	Integer (id=35)
value	7
[2]	Integer (id=35)
value	7
[3]	Integer (id=34)
value	8
[4]	Integer (id=37)
value	15
[5]	Integer (id=36)
value	29
size	6
mynumbers	(id=27)
myIterator	PriorityQueue$Itr (id=62)

Figure 13.14 Queue Data Reordering On Data Removal

Eventually, all the data in the queue is popped out in the natural order. A Priority Queue allows data to be added in any order, but when items are removed from the top of the queue, they are output in a natural order in this example.

13.5 Map Interface

The final data structure is the Map interface. The Map interface is not part of the Collection Interface. The Map has its own data structure that simply maps a key to a value. Each key has to be unique, since the key is used to retrieve the data. The value can have duplicates. The classic usage for a map is a dictionary for a word processing application, where each word in the dictionary has a unique key. Another example is the student database, where the student id is the key and the student information is the value. The put() method is used to add data to the data structure, and the get() method is used to retrieve data from the data structure. The replace() method can replace an element if you know the key. Maps don't implement the Iterable interface, thus the For-each-loop cannot be used directly. Instead, special methods provided a view into the Map data structure. The entrySet() method returns a Set that contains the elements in the map. The keySet() map returns the keys that are in the map. The value() method returns a collection of values that are in the map. The concrete classes that implement the Map interface are EnumMap, HashMap, TreeMap, WeakHashMap, LinkedHashMap, and IdentityHashMap.

13.5.1 Computer Activity 13.4 - HashMap Example

A HashSet was covered earlier in the chapter. A HashSet uses a HashMap in the background to store data using a hashing algorithm. The HashSet didn't allow for duplicate data in the set. HashMap allows for duplicate data, but the key associated with each entry must be unique. In this Computer Activity, we will implement a HashMap application for employee names and IDs. Create a new project in Eclipse called "CH13CA13.4-HashMapTest". In the project, create a new package called "jae.hashmaptest", and then create a new class under the packages called "HashMapTest" with a main() method. Fill in Code Listing 13.4 for the HashMapTest class:

```
package jae.hashmaptest;

import java.util.*;

public class HashMapTest {

    public static void main(String[] args) {
        // TODO Auto-generated method stub

        HashMap<Integer, String> hsmpEmployees = new HashMap<Integer, String>();

        hsmpEmployees.put(100, "Sally");
        hsmpEmployees.put(163, "Leon");
        hsmpEmployees.put(56, "Bob");
        hsmpEmployees.put(4, "Jen");
        hsmpEmployees.put(7, "Luke");
        hsmpEmployees.put(1, "Lisa");
        hsmpEmployees.put(8, "Ben");
        hsmpEmployees.put(3, "Tiffany");

        Set<Map.Entry<Integer, String>> myMapSet = hsmpEmployees.entrySet();

```

```
23.         for(Map.Entry<Integer, String> employee : myMapSet){
24.             System.out.println("Employee Number: " +
    employee.getKey() + "\t Name: " + employee.getValue());
25.         }
26.     }
27. }
```

Code Listing 13.4 HashMapTest Class

Run the application and the output will look similar to the following:

```
Employee Number: 1          Name: Lisa
Employee Number: 163        Name: Leon
Employee Number: 3          Name: Tiffany
Employee Number: 100        Name: Sally
Employee Number: 4          Name: Jen
Employee Number: 7          Name: Luke
Employee Number: 56         Name: Bob
Employee Number: 8          Name: Ben
```

Since items are stored in different buckets in the data structure, how the elements are added is not going to be consistent with an iterative output. Line 10 instantiates the HashMap. Two object types are used: one for the key (Integer), and the other for the value (String). In lines 12 – 19, add the elements to the HashMap. Since there is no iteration available, we take advantage of the enterySet() method to retrieve a Set from the HashMap in Line 21. Finally, lines 23-24 use the Set of all the elements in the HashMap to retrieve and print them out in the for-loop. The debugger shows that each entry is added to different buckets in the data structure, Figure 13.15.

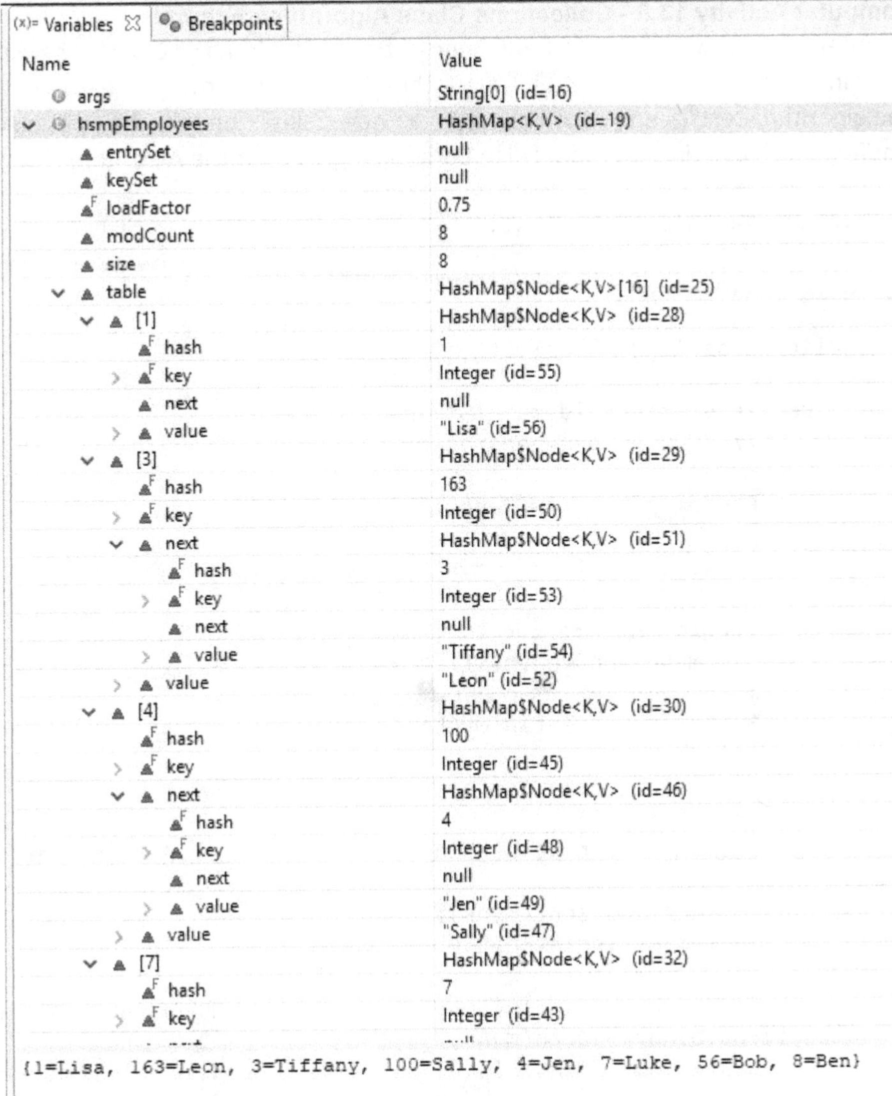

Figure 13.15 Debugger View of the HashMap

13.6 Collections Class Algorithms

The Collections Framework includes a set of algorithms in the Collections class. The algorithms are static and polymorphic so they can be applied to collections and maps. These algorithms include binarysearch(), sort(), min(), max(), shuffle(), and many more.

13.6.1 Computer Activity 13.5 - Collections Class Algorithms Example

In this Computer Activity, we will implement some of the methods in the Collections class. Create a new project in Eclipse called "CH13CA13.4-AlgorithmsTest". In the project, create a new package called "jae.algorithmstest", and then create a new class under the packages called "AlgorithmsTest" with a main() method. Fill in Code Listing 13.5 for the AlgorithmsTest Class:

```
package jae.algorithmstest;

import java.util.*;

public class AlgorithmsTest {

    public static void main(String[] args) {
        // TODO Auto-generated method stub

        Random gen = new Random();

        ArrayList<Integer> myAL = new ArrayList<Integer>();

        for(int x = 0; x < 25 ; x++){
            myAL.add(gen.nextInt(20));
        }
        System.out.println(myAL);

        System.out.println("\nMax Value is " + Collections.max(myAL));
        System.out.println("Min value is " + Collections.min(myAL));

        Collections.sort(myAL);
        System.out.println("\n" + myAL);

        System.out.println("\n The value 9 is found at position " + Collections.binarySearch(myAL, 9));
        System.out.println("\n The value 9 is found this many times in the list " + Collections.frequency(myAL, 9));
    }
}
```

Code Listing 13.5 AlgorithmsTest Class

Run the program a few times. The output will look something like the following (your random values will be different):

```
[14, 1, 8, 8, 18, 4, 16, 2, 7, 12, 9, 5, 9, 8, 8, 18, 16, 5, 15, 12, 11, 6, 4,
14, 15]

Max Value is 18
Min value is 1

[1, 2, 4, 4, 5, 5, 6, 7, 8, 8, 8, 8, 9, 9, 11, 12, 12, 14, 14, 15, 15, 16, 16,
18, 18]

The value 9 is found at position 12

The value 9 is found this many times in the list 2
```

Lines 12-17 set up the ArrayList and print out the values in the list. Lines 19-20 display the max and min values in the list. Line 22-23 sorts the array and displays the new sorted array. Lines 25-26 search for the number 9 in the list, how many times 9 is found in the list, and prints out the results.

13.7 Putting it all Together: Data Structures and File I/O

Creating the data structure and using the data structure methods helps us manage data, but if the program closes, all data is lost. Now we need to combine what was covered in the last chapter with what has been introduced in this chapter, so we can save the collection to a file. In the last chapter, the ObjectOutputStream and ObjectInputStream classes were used to save objects to a file. Iteration was used to write out and read in each object individually. The iteration process can be very time consuming and takes several lines of code. Since data structures group multiple objects into a single object, all that has to be done is to write out and read in as a single data structure object.

13.7.1 Computer Activity 13.6 - Saving and Retrieving an ArrayList of Inventory Objects

In this Computer Activity, we will implement an inventory application. Using a file, the application will save and restore a single ArrayList that contains several inventory objects. After writing the inventory objects to the file, the application will then be able to read the single object back and list all the contents in the ArrayList. Create a new project in Eclipse called "CH13CA13.6-DataStructuretoFile". In the project, create a new package called "jae.datastructuretofile", and then create a new class under the packages called "SupplyInventory". Fill in Code Listing 13.6 for the SupplyInventory class:

```
package jae.datastructuretofile;

import java.io.Serializable;

public class SupplyInventory implements Serializable {

    /**
     *
     */
    private static final long serialVersionUID =
4821886434972799187L;
    private String item;
    private int quantity;

    public SupplyInventory(String item, int quantity) {

        this.item = item;
        this.quantity = quantity;
    }

    public String getItem() {
        return item;
    }

    public void setItem(String item) {
        this.item = item;
    }

    public int getQuantity() {
        return quantity;
    }

    public void setQuantity(int quantity) {
        this.quantity = quantity;
    }
}
```

Code Listing 13.6 SupplyInventory Class

The SupplyInventory class stores the name of the item and the quantity in inventory. The constructor provides the means to quickly create objects with data during instantiation, and the access methods provide the means to retrieve and change the data. The class implements the Serializable interface since the data will be saved to a file.

Add a new class called "InventoryApp" with a main() method. Fill in Code Listing 13.7, and we will cover the warning that appears in a moment:

```
package jae.datastructuretofile;

import java.util.*;
import java.io.*;

public class InventoryApp {

    @SuppressWarnings("unchecked")
    public static void main(String[] args) {
        // TODO Auto-generated method stub

        ArrayList<SupplyInventory> myInventory = new ArrayList<SupplyInventory>();

        myInventory.add(new SupplyInventory("Pens", 15));
        myInventory.add(new SupplyInventory("Paper", 30));
        myInventory.add(new SupplyInventory("Staples", 150));
        myInventory.add(new SupplyInventory("Ink", 5));

        System.out.println("Added to the array list");
        for(SupplyInventory myL : myInventory){
            System.out.println("Item: " + myL.getItem() + "\t Quantity: " + myL.getQuantity()  );
        }

        try(ObjectOutputStream oOut = new ObjectOutputStream(new FileOutputStream("c:\\java\\inventory.ser"))){
            //Save the one object; no iteration
            oOut.writeObject(myInventory);
        } catch (FileNotFoundException e) {
            // TODO Auto-generated catch block
            e.printStackTrace();
        } catch (IOException e) {
            // TODO Auto-generated catch block
            e.printStackTrace();
        }

        //Clear the ArrayList
        myInventory.clear();
        System.out.println("\nCheck the Array is clear");
        for(SupplyInventory myL : myInventory){
            System.out.println("Item" + myL.getItem() + "\t Quantity: " + myL.getQuantity()  );
        }

```

```
        //Open the file and read the data back into the array list
        try(ObjectInputStream oIn = new ObjectInputStream(new FileInputStream("c:\\java\\inventory.ser"))){

            //Retrieve one object; no iteration
            //myInventory.addAll((Collection<? extends SupplyInventory>) oIn.readObject());
            myInventory = (ArrayList<SupplyInventory>) oIn.readObject();
            //All ArrayLists methods are still available for the collection
            myInventory.add(new SupplyInventory("Binders", 50));

        } catch (FileNotFoundException e) {
            // TODO Auto-generated catch block
            e.printStackTrace();
        } catch (IOException e) {
            // TODO Auto-generated catch block
            e.printStackTrace();
        } catch (ClassNotFoundException e) {
            // TODO Auto-generated catch block
            e.printStackTrace();
        }

        System.out.println("\nFinal List");
        for(SupplyInventory myL : myInventory){
            System.out.println("Item: " + myL.getItem() + "\t Quantity: " + myL.getQuantity()  );
        }
    }
}
```

Code Listing 13.7 InventoryApp Class

Run the application and the output will look like the following:

```
Added to the array list
Item: Pens    Quantity: 15
Item: Paper   Quantity: 30
Item: Staples Quantity: 150
Item: Ink     Quantity: 5

Check the Array is clear

Final List
Item: Pens    Quantity: 15
Item: Paper   Quantity: 30
Item: Staples Quantity: 150
Item: Ink     Quantity: 5
Item: Binders Quantity: 50
```

In lines 12 – 22, of Code Listing 13.7, the ArrayList is created using the SupplyInventory as the type and several SupplyInventory objects are added to the ArrayList. The contents of the ArrayList are then displayed to the terminal. In lines 24-33, the ArrayList is saved to a file. Only one call to writeObject() method is needed. In lines 36-40, the list is cleared and checked to prove that the ArrayList is empty. Reading the object back into the ArrayList requires some casting and a type suppression warning. There are two solutions for reading the data from the file. Line 46 is commented out, but it uses the addAll() method to add the collection to the ArrayList. Line 47 simply assigns the output from the oIn.readObject() method. Both solutions implement different casting on the oIn.readObject() to read in a SupplyInventory object. Since it might be possible to read in an incorrect object or bad data, for type safety, Eclipse and the Java compiler would issue a warning about a possible unchecked cast, Figure 13.16.

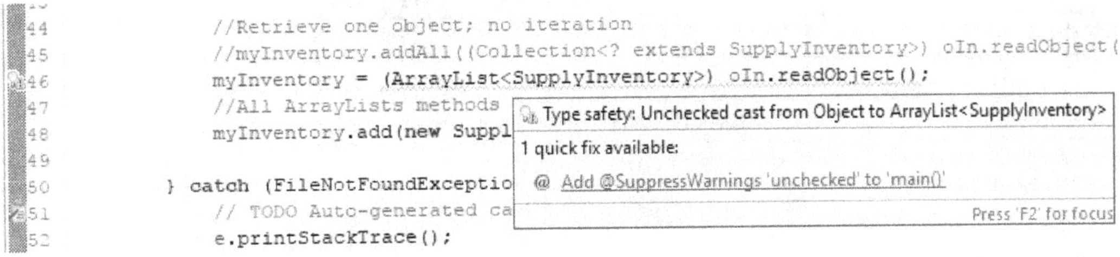

```
44            //Retrieve one object; no iteration
45            //myInventory.addAll((Collection<? extends SupplyInventory>) oIn.readObject());
46            myInventory = (ArrayList<SupplyInventory>) oIn.readObject();
47            //All ArrayLists methods
48            myInventory.add(new Suppl
49
50        } catch (FileNotFoundExceptio
51            // TODO Auto-generated ca
52            e.printStackTrace();
```

Type safety: Unchecked cast from Object to ArrayList<SupplyInventory>
1 quick fix available:
@ Add @SuppressWarnings 'unchecked' to 'main()'
Press 'F2' for focus

Figure 13.16 Type Safety Warning

To get around the warning, line 8 adds an annotation to suppress the unchecked cast. Once the data has been loaded into the ArrayList, another item is added in line 49. The final inventory list is printed out at the end. The inventory.ser file has one ArrayList object that contains multiple SupplyInventory objects, Figure 13.17.

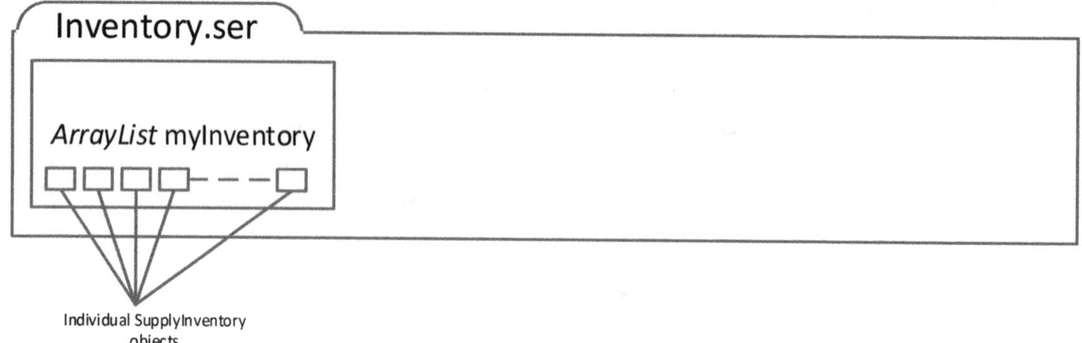

Figure 13.17 Inventory.ser File Structure

With the file that is able to save objects, it is possible to save different object types into a single file. Careful file architectural planning is important so as not to open the wrong object.

13.8 Computer Activity 13.7 – JavaFX ListView and ComboBox Controls

The architecture of the Collections Framework allows for expansion. JavaFX builds on the Collections Framework with a set of data structures that work in conjunction with a couple of JavaFX controls. These collections are defined in the javafx.collections package, which consists of a set of Interfaces and Classes. Here are the interfaces, Table 13.1, and some of the more frequently used classes, Table 13.2:

Interfaces	Description
ObservableList	Enables listeners to track changes when they occur
ListChangeListener	Receives notifications of changes to an ObservableList
ObservableMap	Enables observers to track changes when they occur
MapChangeListener	Receives notifications of changes to an ObservableMap

Table 13.1 JavaFX Collections Interfaces

Classes	Description
FXCollections	Consists of static methods that are one-to-one copies of java.util.Collections methods
ListChangeListener.Change	Represents a change made to an ObservableList
MapChangeListener.Change	Represents a change made to an ObservableMap

Table 13.2 JavaFX Collections Classes

The ObservableList extends List Interface and ObservableMap extends Map Interface. Both extend javafx.beans.Observable. In this Computer Activity, we will use ObservableList with the JavaFX ListView and ComboBox Controls. The application will look like Figure 13.18:

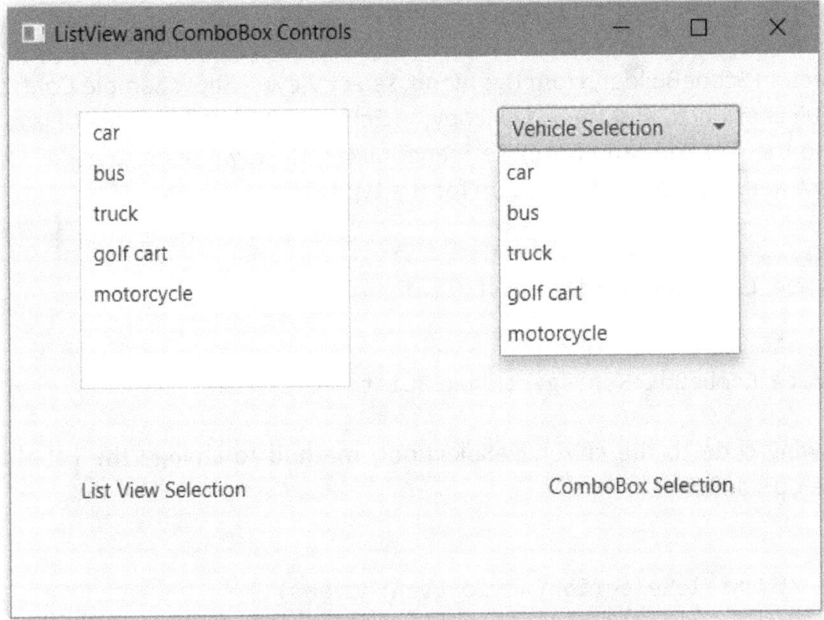

Figure 13.18 Computer Activity 13.7 GUI

Create a new JavaFX project called "CH13CA13.7-JavaFXViewCollections". Create a FXML file called "viewcollection.fxml". Open the FXML file in SceneBuilder. Remove any pre-populated containers. Add the AnchorPane container. Add the following controls:

1. ListView
   a. Change fx:id to lstView1
2. Label
   a. Change Text to "List View Selection"
   b. Change fx:id to lblListViewSelection
3. ComboBox
   a. Change Prompt Text to "Vehicle Selection"
   b. Change fx:id to cmboxCBList
   c. Set On Action to cbVehicleSelection
4. Label:
   a. Change Text to "ComboBox Selection"
   b. Change fx:id to lblComboBoxSelection

Save the file. Back in Eclipse, create a new Java class file called "ListViewControl". Now let's associate the FXML with the new class. Open viewcollection.fxml and add the following to the end to the <AnchorPane…> tag:

```
fx:controller="application.ListViewControl"
```

Save the project. In SceneBuilder, from the menu, select View-> Show Sample Controller Section. Click on the Full check box, and then click copy. In Eclipse with ListViewControl.java open, paste the contents to the file. You can now close SceneBuilder. Now, we need to make some changes. Set the ListView and ComboBox declaration for the type String:

```
@FXML
private ListView<String> lstView1;

@FXML
private ComboBox<String> cmboxCBList;
```

Add the following code to the cbVehicleSelection() method to change the Label to the value selected in the ComboBox.

```
@FXML
void cbVehicleSelection(ActionEvent event) {
    lblComboBoxSelection.setText(cmboxCBList.getValue());
}
```

Now, we will fill in the remaining code. For explanation purposes, Code Listing 13.8 shows the full code listing for the class. Add the missing imports and fill in the missing code for the initialize() method.

```
package application;

import java.net.URL;
import java.util.ResourceBundle;
import javafx.fxml.FXML;
import javafx.scene.control.ComboBox;
import javafx.scene.control.Label;
import javafx.scene.control.ListView;
import javafx.scene.control.MultipleSelectionModel;
import javafx.collections.*;
import javafx.event.ActionEvent;
import javafx.beans.value.ChangeListener;
import javafx.beans.value.ObservableValue;

public class ListViewControl {

    @FXML
    private ResourceBundle resources;
```

```

    @FXML
    private URL location;

    @FXML
    private ListView<String> lstView1;

    @FXML
    private Label lblListViewSelection;

    @FXML
    private ComboBox<String> cmboxCBList;

    @FXML
    private Label lblComboBoxSelection;

    @FXML
    void cbVehicleSelection(ActionEvent event) {
        lblComboBoxSelection.setText(cmboxCBList.getValue());
    }

    @FXML
    void initialize() {
        assert lstView1 != null : "fx:id=\"lstView1\" was not injected: check your FXML file 'viewcollection.fxml'.";
        assert lblListViewSelection != null : "fx:id=\"lblListViewSelection\" was not injected: check your FXML file 'viewcollection.fxml'.";
        assert cmboxCBList != null : "fx:id=\"cmboxCBList\" was not injected: check your FXML file 'viewcollection.fxml'.";
        assert lblComboBoxSelection != null : "fx:id=\"lblComboBoxSelection\" was not injected: check your FXML file 'viewcollection.fxml'.";

        ObservableList<String> vehicles = FXCollections.observableArrayList("car","bus","truck","golf cart","motorcycle");

        lstView1.setItems(vehicles);
        cmboxCBList.setItems(vehicles);

        MultipleSelectionModel<String> lvSelVehicles = lstView1.getSelectionModel();
```

```
53.         lvSelVehicles.selectedItemProperty().addListener(new
   ChangeListener<String>(){
54.
55.             @Override
56.             public void changed(ObservableValue<? extends String>
   observable, String oldValue, String newValue) {
57.                 // TODO Auto-generated method stub
58.                 lblListViewSelection.setText(newValue);
59.             }
60.
61.         });
62.     }
63. }
```

Code Listing 13.8 Computer Activity 13.7 Complete Code Listing

The same ObservableList is used for both JavaFX controls. In Line 47, the ObservableList is instantiated as a collection of Strings, and it is pre-populated with some strings consisting of vehicle types. The list is set up by both JavaFX controls in lines 49 and 50. The ComboBox event was simple to set up by just implementing a method. The ListView requires a little more work to check for events. When the user clicks in the list box, the change is stored in a model. Line 52 instantiates the selection model for the ListView instance. Lines 53-62 set up the Listener and implement an anonymous ChangeListener instance with an override for the changed() method. The changed() method override detects the user selecting a new item in the list, and then sets the label to the new value. Save the project and run the project. You should be able to select from either list and watch the labels change. Like any collection, items can be added to or removed from the list. You can also add other controls to add and remove items from the list.

13.9 Summary and Homework Assignments

Not every problem is a nail, and not all data can be handled with the same data structure. The Collection Framework has multiple concrete data structure classes to address a wide variety of programming problems. The framework allows a programmer to expand on the provided interfaces and classes to create a solution that meets the needs of a program. This chapter provided a brief coverage of data structures. Whole books and multiple classes dig deeper into the mathematics and science behind different data structures and how best to use them. The previous section tied how the data structure can be saved to a file. Now that you know how to structure and save data, you can start creating more real-world projects. Before we move on to the next chapter, here are a few questions and programming projects.

13.9.1 Questions

1. The diagrams for the Collections Framework were set up to show how the abstract and concrete classes plug into the framework. There are 4 interfaces not shown. What are they? Update the diagram with these interfaces.

2. Below is a list of concrete data structure classes. What is the abstract class that gets extended and what interfaces are implemented for each class?

   For example: ArrayList

   Extends: java.util.AbstractList
   Implements: java.util.List, java.util.RandomAccess, java.lang.Cloneable, java.io.Serializable

   ArrayBlockingQueue
   ArrayDeque
   ConcurrentLinkedDeque
   ConcurrentLinkedQueue
   ConcurrentSkipListSet
   CopyOnWriteArrayList
   CopyOnWriteArraySet
   DelayQueue
   EnumMap
   EnumSet
   HashMap
   HashSet
   IdentityHashMap
   JobStateReasons
   LinkedBlockingDeque
   LinkedBlockingQueue
   LinkedHashMap
   LinkedHashSet
   LinkedList
   LinkedTransferQueue
   PriorityBlockingQueue
   PriorityQueue
   Stack
   SynchronousQueue
   TreeMap
   TreeSet
   Vector
   WeakHashMap

3. For Computer Activity 13.2, what happens when you change HashSet to TreeSet?

4. For Computer Activity 13.4, what happens when you change HashMap to TreeMap?

5. Using the SupplyInventory class from Computer Activity 13.6, what is the output of the following code:

```
package jae.datastructuretofile;

import java.util.*;

public class InventoryTest {

    public static void main(String[] args) {
        // TODO Auto-generated method stub

        HashMap<Integer, SupplyInventory> myList = new HashMap<Integer, SupplyInventory>();

        myList.put(101, new SupplyInventory("Paper", 60));
        myList.put(130, new SupplyInventory("Pens", 50));
        myList.put(201, new SupplyInventory("Binders", 25));
        myList.put(201, new SupplyInventory("Paper Clips", 25));

        Set<Map.Entry<Integer, SupplyInventory>> myMapSet = myList.entrySet();

        for(Map.Entry<Integer, SupplyInventory> myInventory : myMapSet){
            System.out.println("Item: " + myInventory.getValue().getItem() + " Quantity " + myInventory.getValue().getQuantity());
        }
    }
}
```

13.9.2 Programming Projects

1. Modify Computer Activity 13.7, by allowing the user to add and remove items from the ObservableList vehicles. Use a text box so that the user can add items, and two buttons, one that performs the add operation and the other that performs the remove operation.

2. A contact address book application was first introduced in Chapter 6 Programming Project 10 and expanded upon in Chapter 8. Create a contact address book application in JavaFX. The data to be stored will be the following: First Name, Last Name, Street Address, City, State, Zip code, Telephone number, and e-mail address. The application will show only one contact in the GUI and have forward and backward buttons to browse through the list. The contact can be edited while in view. The program will allow for creating new contacts and saving the data to a file. When the application first opens, it will open the file to read in the data and fill in the fields with the first contact. Use an ArrayList to store each data record.

3. Chapter 6 Programming Project 7 had you create a golf handicap program. Create a golf handicap program in JavaFX. A user can open, edit, close, and save his own individual file with his scores. Upon opening his file, the handicap will be calculated and shown on the left side. Only the best 10 scores from the last 20 rounds of golf are used to create the handicap. A listing of the last 20 rounds is shown on the right-hand side with the following data: date, course name, course rating value, slope value, and 18-hole score value. Once the user has entered a new score, the oldest score can be removed from the list. Use a data structure to save each round record.

14 JavaFX 2D Games

"That's good. You've taken your first step into a larger world."
- Obi-Wan Kenobi, from *Star Wars: Episode IV - A New Hope*, A Lucasfilm Limited Production, 1977

Each chapter in this book was designed to build upon the previous to lay a foundation for your understanding of computer science and develop your computer programming skills. Rather than building a single application or focusing on a single programming subject, the various computer activities and programming assignments have covered a wide range of subjects, such as finance, games, sports, databases, and science. As you progressed through each chapter, some of these projects were expanded to add new features as new topics were introduced. There are many more computer science topics, projects, and Java features that remain to be discussed. If you have gone through each chapter and performed all of the different activities and exercises, then you have taken your first step into a larger world, the world of computer programming.

For our final chapter, we will focus on creating games using JavaFX. We have created a few games throughout the book, but in this chapter, we will create games that have graphics, sound, and animation. Certainly, there are other types of applications to develop. Different markets like agriculture, medical, security, industrial controls, home automation, etc. require programming to a variety of hardware platforms, which is not readily available on the budgets schools have, today. Creating video games is a fun way to expand your new programming skills using the PC platform you already have. It will also allow you to exercise many of the different subjects you have learned. Before we just dive into creating video games, we have a few more JavaFX features to cover before we put everything together.

14.1 JavaFX Multimedia and Game Engines

Video games would not be video games without the graphics, animation, video, and sound. To help create applications with rich media content, multimedia support was built into JavaFX and continues to be expanded upon. JavaFX 8 supports the following:

- Playback controls (Play, Pause, Stop, Volume, Mute, Balance, Equalizer)
- Animation timers and controls
- Seeking
- Image manipulation, transitions, and transforms
- Buffer progress
- Progressive download
- HTTP, FILE protocol support
- Audio: MP3; AIFF containing uncompressed PCM; WAV containing uncompressed PCM; MPEG-4 multimedia container with Advanced Audio Coding (AAC) audio
- Video: FLV containing VP6 video and MP3 audio; MPEG-4 multimedia container with H.264/AVC (Advanced Video Coding) video compression
- Support for 3D Graphics

Multimedia support is dependent on the JVM and native operating system. The JVM has to be ported to the operating system and processor. You can check the support requirements on the Java SE download site. Creating a JavaFX game for one platform is a bit limiting. More advanced game engines and libraries offer better 3D and multimedia support, as well as the ability to cross target different platforms. There are different game engines and library support for the various programming languages. The following table lists the available game engines and libraries for Java. Please note that the links and game solution do change over time. Using one of these game engines/libraries takes time and effort to understand all the features and capabilities they offer. For this chapter, we will stick with what JavaFX provides to create a couple of 2D Games.

Game Engine / Library	Website
Clyde	github.com/threerings/clyde
FXGL	almasb.github.io/FXGL/
JMonkeyEngine 3.0	jmonkeyengine.org
jPCT	jpct.net
LibGDX	libgdx.badlogicgames.com
Lightweight Java Game Library (LWJGL)	lwjgl.org
Ogre4J	ogre4j.sourceforge.net
Xith3D	xith.org

Table 14.1 Game Engines / Libraries

14.2 Media Content Production Software

A lot of artistic creativity and development goes into video games. Art designers create landscapes, 3D mesh models, and textures to create depth and realism in the game world. High-end video games have movie cutscenes between levels where actors and voiceover artists add their contributions. Creating media content that gets built into the code requires specialized tools. As you build up the tools to work with Eclipse, there are many tools to develop sounds, graphics, and 3D models. Many of the multimedia tools are free, and some you have to pay for. The following tables list some of the different multimedia tools that can be used to create content for games:

3D Modeling Tools	Website
Autodesk	autodesk.com
Blender	blender.org
Daz3D	daz3d.com
Lightwave 3D	lightwave3d.com
Sketchup	sketchup.com
Wings3D	wings3d.com

Table 14.2 3D Modeling Tools

Illustration Tools	Website
GIMP	www.gimp.org
Inkscape	inkscape.org
Terragen	planetside.co.uk

Table 14.3 Illustration Tools

Audio / Sound Tools	Website
Audacity	audacityteam.org/home/
Qtractor	qtractor.sourceforge.io/qtractor-index.html
Rosegarden Music	rosegardenmusic.com

Table 14.4 Audio and Sound Tools

Video Tools	Website
Lightworks	lwks.com

Table 14.5 Video Tools

Creating video games is a big hobby. There are a number of websites that offer royalty-free pre-built artwork and sounds. Table 14.6 below, is a table for some of these websites. Just make sure that you follow the usage and copyright rules and give credit to the artist.

Name	Website
Classic Gaming	classicgaming.cc
Free Sound	freesound.org
Free Sound Effects	freesoundeffects.com
Open Game Art	opengameart.org
Shutter Stock	shutterstock.com
Textures	textures.com
VG Resource	vg-resource.com

Table 14.6 Royalty-Free Gaming Resources

14.3 JavaFX Drawing, Import Graphics, and Text

In Chapter 11, there was a basic drawing Computer Activity for Swing. We didn't do the same for JavaFX since we wanted to save this until now. The following and the next three computer activities will demonstrate some basic features of JavaFX before we create a full game. Like Swing, JavaFX allows you to draw shapes, images, and text in a GUI application. JavaFX has packages and classes for each:

javafx.scene.shape
javafx.scene.image.Image
javafx.scene.text

The Shape package includes the basic 2D shapes of boxes, lines, circles, ellipses, etc. There are also Shape3D classes and meshes to make 3D designs. For our games, we will stick with 2D shapes.

14.3.1 Computer Activity 14.1 - Drawing, Graphics, Text

In this Computer Activity, we will create a circle, a rectangle, and some text on a Pane container. The circle will be filled with an image, the rectangle will just have a solid color, and the text will use a font. In a paint program create an image and save it as a .png file. As an example, the "Have A Nice Day" or "happy face" emoji, Figure 14.1, will be used to fill in the circle. You can download the image from the Internet if you like.

Figure 14.1 Happy Face Emoji

In Eclipse, create a new JavaFX project called "CH14CA14.1-DrawingGraphicsText". Right-click on the application packages and select "Import" from the context menu. Select File System and click next. Click on the Browse button, and locate the folder with the image. Open the folder and you will see the file listed in the right pane. Click the checkbox next to the file and click "Finish". The file will show up under the application package, Figure 14.2.

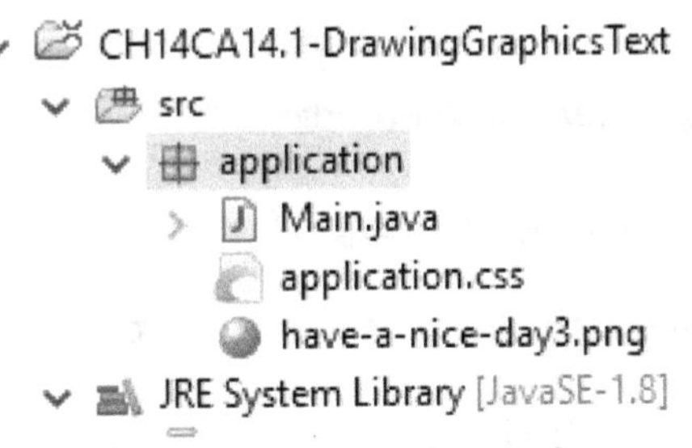

Figure 14.2 Application Package

Open Main.java file and add the following imports:

```
import javafx.application.Application;
import javafx.stage.Stage;
import javafx.scene.Scene;
import javafx.scene.layout.Pane;
import javafx.scene.paint.Color;
import javafx.scene.shape.*;
import javafx.scene.text.*;
import javafx.scene.image.Image;
import javafx.scene.paint.ImagePattern;
```

After the main() method, create a new method called "createApp(Stage myStage)":

```
public void createApp(Stage myStage){

}
```

Edit the start() method and remove the default setup in the try-block for a BorderPane, and replace it with a call to the createApp() method:

```
public void start(Stage primaryStage) {
    try {
        createApp(primaryStage);
    } catch(Exception e) {
        e.printStackTrace();
    }
}
```

Fill in Code Listing 14.1 for the createApp() method:

```
public void createApp(Stage myStage){

    //Set up the Pane and add the Pane to the Scene with a size of 800 x
600 pixels
    Pane root = new Pane();
    Scene scene = new Scene(root, 800, 600);

    //Create a purple rectangle that is placed in the middle of the pane
    Rectangle rect1 = new Rectangle(50, 70);
    rect1.setFill(Color.PURPLE);
    rect1.setTranslateX(375);
    rect1.setTranslateY(275);

    //Create a circle that is filled with the imported image,
    //and place the circle in the top left portion of the pane.
    Circle circle1 = new Circle();
    circle1.setTranslateX(50);
    circle1.setTranslateY(40);
    circle1.setRadius(50);
    Image happyday = new Image(getClass().getResourceAsStream("have-a-
nice-day3.png"));
    circle1.setFill(new ImagePattern(happyday));

    //Add some text to the  pane and place the text in teh bottom right
    Text mytext = new Text("Basic Drawing, Text, Images");
    mytext.setTranslateX(500);
    mytext.setTranslateY(500);
    mytext.setFont(Font.font("Verdana", 15));
    mytext.setFill(Color.BLUE);

    //add all nodes to the pane
    root.getChildren().addAll(rect1,circle1,mytext);
```

```
    //add the scene to the stage and show the stage.
    myStage.setScene(scene);
    myStage.show();
}
```

Code Listing 14.1 createApp Method

The pane is set up as 800 pixels wide and 600 pixels tall. The top left is coordinate (0, 0), and the bottom right is (800, 600). The Rectangle gets set with 50 pixels wide and 70 pixels high. The setTranslateX() and setTranslateY() methods place the rectangle about in the middle of the Pane. The Circle is placed in the top left and is filled with the image. Since the image is embedded into the project, the getClass().getResourceAsStream() method is used to get the local image resource in the project. Using the getClass().getResourceAsStream() method is recommended over trying to include an absolute path to the file. The Text is created with some default text in the lower right-hand side of the Pane. The Verdana font with a size of 15 is used to display the text. All three nodes are added to the Pane. Run the application and you should get something similar to Figure 14.3:

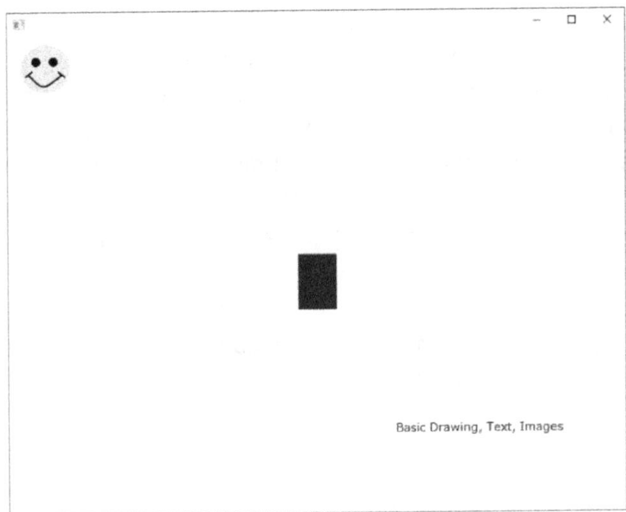

Figure 14.3 Basic GUI Rendering

Of course, SceneBuilder also has shapes available to add to an FXML file, Figure 14.4, but we are going to stick to using the code approach for the games.

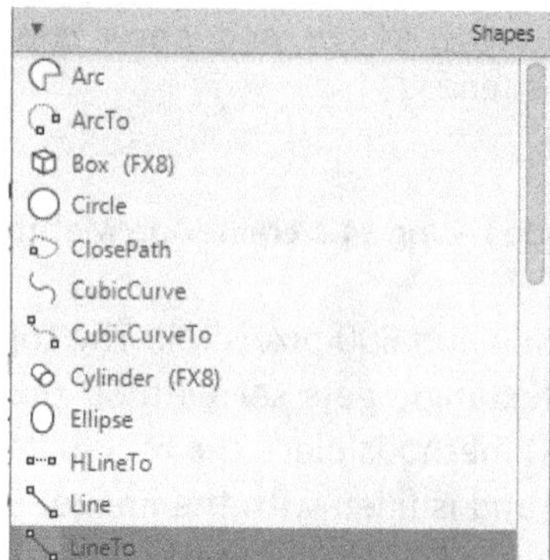

Figure 14.4 SceneBuilder Shapes

14.4 Animation and the Game Loop

JavaFX adds an Animation package to provide motion and movement to nodes in a container. The Animation support can be broken down into three features. The first Animation feature is a standard set of transition classes and methods that are predefined animations covering appearance effects, filling, rotating, and movement. The classes are FadeTransition, FillTransition, ParallelTransition, PathTransition, PauseTransition, RotateTransition, ScaleTransition, SequentialTransition, StrokeTransition, and TranslateTransition. Each of the transition classes includes the basic start(), stop(), and pause() methods to control the animation. The second Animation feature is using Timeline and Keyframe classes so that you can create your own custom animation solution. The final Animation feature is the AnimationTimer class that runs in a loop at about 60 frames per second (fps). The AnimationTimer class has 3 methods: handle(), start(), and stop(). The abstract handle() method is called by a timer so that anything in the method gets updates at a rate of 60 fps. You will have to fill in the code to override the handle() method with your graphical content. The start() and stop() methods provide the basic controls to start and stop the timer.

14.4.1 Computer Activity 14.2 - Transitions and Timer

This Computer Activity builds on the previous activity and is broken into two parts. The first part will demonstrate the different Transition classes. The second will demonstrate the AnimationTimer class. In Eclipse, open the previous Computer Activity project add the following imports:

```
import javafx.animation.*;
import javafx.util.Duration;
```

Add Code Listing 14.2 after myStage.show() method:

```
RotateTransition myRotate = new RotateTransition(new Duration(5000),
circle1);
myRotate.setAutoReverse(true);
myRotate.setCycleCount(4);
myRotate.setByAngle(360);

ScaleTransition myScale = new ScaleTransition(new Duration(5000),
circle1);
myScale.setAutoReverse(true);
myScale.setCycleCount(4);
myScale.setByX(1.2);
myScale.setByY(1.2);

TranslateTransition myTranslate = new TranslateTransition(new
Duration(5000), circle1);
myTranslate.setAutoReverse(true);
myTranslate.setCycleCount(4);
myTranslate.setByX(100);
myTranslate.setByY(100);

FadeTransition myFade = new FadeTransition(Duration.millis(5000),
mytext);
myFade.setFromValue(1.0);
myFade.setToValue(0.0);
myFade.setCycleCount(4);
myFade.setAutoReverse(true);


myRotate.play();
myScale.play();
myTranslate.play();
myFade.play();

//ParallelTransition myParallel = new
ParallelTransition(myRotate,myScale,myTranslate,myFade);
//myParallel.play();

//SequentialTransition mySequence = new
SequentialTransition(myRotate,myScale,myTranslate,myFade);
//mySequence.play();
```

Code Listing 14.2 myStage.show() Method

Run the application and you will notice the happy face moving, rotating, and growing and shrinking in size. The text also fades in and out. Each transition is set up to run for 5 seconds (5000 milliseconds). Each transition will reverse itself so that the image returns back to the original state. Each transition will also cycle 4 times: two forwards and two in reverse. The rotation spins the image 360 degrees. The scale will increase the image size 1.2 times the size in two directions. The transition moves the image to pixel coordinates (100, 100) in the Pane container. The text fades out to nothing and then back. All four transitions run simultaneously. The better alternative is to use the ParallelTransition class to run all 4 at the same time. Comment out the 4 transition play calls, uncomment the two ParallelTransition lines, and run the application. You should see the same effect. Now comment out the two ParallelTransition lines, uncomment the two SequentialTransition lines, and run the application. This time each transition runs in an ordered sequence. Now we will demonstrate the AnimationTimer. Comment out all the code we just added to demonstrate the transition classes. Add Code Listing 14.3 after the animation transition code:

```
AnimationTimer mytimer = new AnimationTimer(){

    Boolean xForward = true;
    Boolean yForward = true;

    @Override
    public void handle(long now) {
        // TODO Auto-generated method stub

        if(xForward == true){
            circle1.setTranslateX(circle1.getTranslateX() + 5);
        }
        else
        {
            circle1.setTranslateX(circle1.getTranslateX() - 7);
        }
        if(yForward == true){
            circle1.setTranslateY(circle1.getTranslateY() + 5);
        }
        else
        {
            circle1.setTranslateY(circle1.getTranslateY() - 7);
        }
```

```
            if(circle1.getTranslateX() < 0){
                xForward = true;
                circle1.setTranslateX(circle1.getTranslateX() +
(Math.random()*8));

            }
            if(circle1.getTranslateY() < 0 ){
                yForward = true;
                circle1.setTranslateY(circle1.getTranslateY() +
(Math.random()*15));
            }
            if(circle1.getTranslateX() > 800){
                xForward = false;
                circle1.setTranslateX(circle1.getTranslateX() -
(Math.random()*12));
            }
            if(circle1.getTranslateY() > 600 ){
                 yForward = false;
               circle1.setTranslateY(circle1.getTranslateY() -
(Math.random()*7));
            }

        }

  };
  mytimer.start();
```

Code Listing 14.3 AnimationTimer Method

Run the project and you should see the happy face image bouncing around the inside of the scene. Creating the new AnimationTimer instance requires that you implement the override for the abstract handle() method, thus the {} brackets hold the override. Alternatively, you could create a separate class that extends the AnimationTimer. The handle() method is the timer handler that is called on each pulse. The parameter "now" is the current system time passed to the method. You can use the time for higher level time interpolation. In the handler, there are some conditions that direct how the image moves about the pane. The first two if-else-statements move the image in a diagonal X-Y direction. The next 4 if-statements check to see if the image has reached the boundary. If the boundary has been reached, then the reverse action away from the boundary will be started, and the forward direction will be set to true or false. The use of the Math.random() method forces the image to move around a little randomly rather than a set direction. The animation will continue to run until you close the program.

14.4.2 Game Loop and Animation Timer

With the Animation Class, we can make our application look more dynamic and interesting. How does this help with creating a video game? Previous games for egg hunt and Yahtzee had you implement a simple game loop by asking the user to play again. For video games, the game engine is the heart and soul of the game. The game engine provides a game loop, Figure 14.5, that keeps everything moving until the user or an artificial intelligence (AI) provides input that changes the actions on the screen. The game logic makes the changes, and the updated images are rendered to the screen. The loop continues until the game ends.

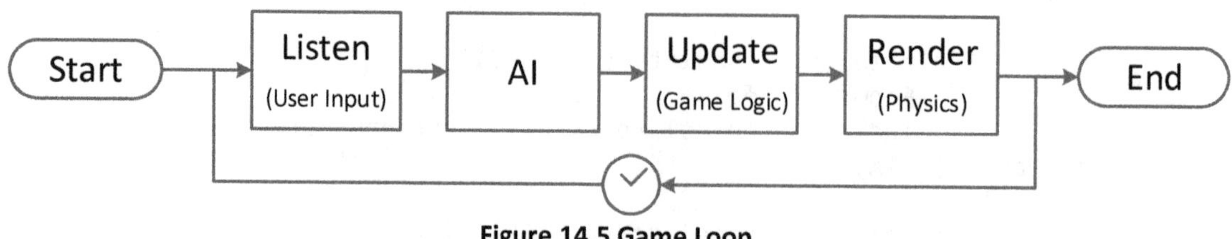

Figure 14.5 Game Loop

With a frame rate of 60 fps, the AnimationTimer can be used as a simple game loop to keep things moving on the screen. As you saw in the last Computer Activity, the image appeared to move smoothly across the screen, but add more graphics and the scene can get a little choppy. A game engine that implements interpolation can help smooth out the scene.

Definition: *Interpolation* – a method to construct new data points based on the current set of data points

There is an Interpolator class that can help with creating a more sophisticated game engine. The game engines and libraries listed earlier include this capability. For our purposes in this book, we will just use the AnimationTimer class as is.

14.4.3 Sprites and Animation

Today's high-end 3D video games provide the ability to immerse the player into a whole new world. The early video games of the '80s and '90s were simple 2D games. The movement of characters was accomplished using old movie and cartoon animation tricks. In cartoons, several pages of a drawn character have a slight change to provide movement. Flip through the pages and the characters look like they were moving. For video games, the term Sprite was eventually coined to describe this technique.

Definition: *Sprite* - a computer graphic object drawn either directly on the screen or to the graphics display buffer that may be moved on-screen and otherwise manipulated as a single entity.

Pac Man and Super Mario are examples of sprites. Some sprites move and others are just background for the game. The early video games used sprites combined together to make a scene. Some of the game sites that include artwork have sprite sheets available to use in games. We will use a couple of sprite sheets for our games. For 3D games, the character rendering gets a little more complex as 3D tools are used to create shapes.

14.4.4 Computer Activity 14.3 - Animation

For 2D video games, Sprite sheets are created that have drawings of all of the graphical elements on the screen. For characters that move, there are several iterations of the character on the sprite sheet. In this Computer Activity, we will create a JavaFX application that will animate the frog from the video game Frogger. A Frogger Sprite sheet by GaryCXJk can be found on one of the game hobby sites: https://www.spriters-resource.com/arcade/frogger/sheet/11067/. Download the sprite sheet and use an image or paint program to cut out and create three PNG files of the green frog in different positions, Figure 14.6 – frog1.png, frog2.png, and frog 3. png:

Figure 14.6 Frogger Sprites

In Eclipse, create a new JavaFX project called "CH14CA14.3-Animation". Now let's add our 3 frog images. Right-click on the application packages and select "Import" from the context menu. Select File System and click Next. Click on the Browse button, and locate the folder with the images. Open the folder and you will see the file listed in the right pane. Click the checkboxes next to each frogger png sprite file and click "Finish". Create a new Java class file called "ImageFactory" with no main() method. Add Code Listing 14.4 to the ImageFactory.java file:

```
package application;

import javafx.scene.image.Image;


public class ImageFactory {

	public Image frog1 =
new Image(getClass().getResourceAsStream("frog1.png"));
	public Image frog2 =
new Image(getClass().getResourceAsStream("frog2.png"));
	public Image frog3 =
new Image(getClass().getResourceAsStream("frog3.png"));
}
```

Code Listing 14.4 ImageFactory Class

In the Main.java file add the following imports:

```
import javafx.application.Application;
import javafx.stage.Stage;
import javafx.scene.Scene;
import javafx.scene.layout.Pane;
import javafx.scene.paint.ImagePattern;
import javafx.scene.shape.Rectangle;
import javafx.animation.AnimationTimer;
```

After the main() method, create a new method called "createApp(Stage myStage)":

```
public void createApp(Stage myStage){

}
```

Edit the start() method and remove the default setup in the try-block for a BorderPane, and replace it with a call to the createApp() method:

```
public void start(Stage primaryStage) {
    try {
        createApp(primaryStage);
    } catch(Exception e) {
        e.printStackTrace();
    }
}
```

Before the start() method, add the following:

```
private ImageFactory myImages = new ImageFactory();
private int x = 1;
private int timerTck = 0;
```

The first line adds an instance of the ImageFactory, so we can access the images. The two integers will be used for controlling the image displayed and the speed at which it is displayed. Add the following code to the creatApp() method:

```
public void createApp(Stage myStage){
    Pane root = new Pane();
    Scene scene = new Scene(root, 400, 400);

    Rectangle rect = new Rectangle(60, 60);
    rect.setFill(new ImagePattern(myImages.frog1));
    root.getChildren().add(rect);

    AnimationTimer myTimer = new AnimationTimer(){

        @Override
        public void handle(long now) {
            // TODO Auto-generated method stub

            switch(x){
            case 1:
                rect.setFill(new ImagePattern(myImages.frog3));
                break;
            case 2:
                rect.setFill(new ImagePattern(myImages.frog1));
                break;
            case 3:
                rect.setFill(new ImagePattern(myImages.frog2));
                break;
            case 4:
                rect.setFill(new ImagePattern(myImages.frog1));
                break;
            }
            //control animation speed
            timerTck++;
            if(timerTck >= 10){
                x++;
                if(x > 4){
                    x = 1;
                }
                timerTck = 0;
            }
        }
    };
    myTimer.start();
    myStage.setScene(scene);
    myStage.show();
}
```

First, a Pane is set up to hold the image and is added to the Scene. A rectangle instance is created with one of the frog images and added to the Pane. The AnimationTimer is the heart of the application. AnimationTimer timer runs at 60 frames per second. This might be a little too fast to see the frog moving. The timerTck integer is used to control the speed and change which frog image is shown in the rectangle. The switch case is used to select from 1 of 4 cases. Each case refills the rectangle with a new image and then cycles over and over through the 3 images. The last three lines of the method start the timer, adds the scene to the stage, and shows the stage. Run the application and you can see the image cycling through the sprite images.

14.5 Keyboard and Mouse Controls / Input Events

The next step is to add user input. Early video game consoles and arcade games featured a wide range of game controllers: keyboard, mouse, buttons, flying yokes, steering wheels, trackballs, paddles, foot pedals, gamepads, motion capture, throttles, touch screen, light guns, rhythm controllers, and the always popular joystick. As the PC games evolved, the keyboard and mouse have become the defacto input devices. The touchscreen is the main controller for tablet and smartphones. We will use a keyboard and mouse for our simple 2D games.

14.5.1 Computer Activity 14.4 - Controlling and Collision detection

We will build on the Computer Activity 14.1 and Computer Activity 14.2 to control the rectangle using a keyboard and mouse. Some new text fields will be added to display mouse position and click events. Finally, we will detect when the rectangle and the circle cross boundaries between two nodes. In Eclipse, for the last Computer Activity, comment out the code for the animation timer. If you run the application, there should be no animation running. The application should just be a static app like Computer Activity 14.1. Add the following imports:

```
import javafx.event.EventHandler;
import javafx.scene.input.MouseEvent;
import javafx.scene.input.KeyEvent;
import javafx.scene.input.MouseButton;
```

The common keyboard keys for controlling a game character are W A S D. W is up, S is down, A is left, and D is right. We will use these keys to move the rectangle around the app. After the commented-out Animation timer code block, add the following:

```
scene.setOnKeyPressed(new EventHandler<KeyEvent>(){

 @Override
 public void handle(KeyEvent event) {
    // TODO Auto-generated method stub
```

```
        switch (event.getCode()) {

        case W:
            rect1.setTranslateY(rect1.getTranslateY() - 40);
            break;
        case S:
            rect1.setTranslateY(rect1.getTranslateY() + 40);
            break;
        case A:
            rect1.setTranslateX(rect1.getTranslateX() - 40);
            break;

        case D:
            rect1.setTranslateX(rect1.getTranslateX() + 40);
            break;

        default:
            break;
        }
    }

});
```

Run the application and use the WASD keys to move the rectangle around the scene. The event handle is set up to detect when a key on the keyboard is pressed. The Switch-case determines which key is pressed and runs a method to move the rectangle in the detected direction by 40 pixels. The rectangle can be moved off the scene, as there are no boundary checks set up. Close the application if it is running. Now add the following code after the keyboard event handler to add mouse support and mouse pointer location information:

```
Text mouseXtext = new Text("MouseX: ");
mouseXtext.setTranslateX(10);
mouseXtext.setTranslateY(500);
root.getChildren().add(mouseXtext);
Text mouseYtext = new Text("MouseY: ");
mouseYtext.setTranslateX(10);
mouseYtext.setTranslateY(515);
root.getChildren().add(mouseYtext);
Text mouseRclick = new Text("Right Click ");
mouseRclick.setTranslateX(10);
mouseRclick.setTranslateY(530);
root.getChildren().add(mouseRclick);
Text mouseLclick = new Text("Left Click ");
mouseLclick.setTranslateX(10);
mouseLclick.setTranslateY(545);
```

```
root.getChildren().add(mouseLclick);


    scene.setOnMouseMoved( new EventHandler<MouseEvent>(){

     @Override
     public void handle(MouseEvent event) {
         // TODO Auto-generated method stub
         rect1.setTranslateX(event.getX());
         mouseXtext.setText("MouseX: " + event.getX());
         rect1.setTranslateY(event.getY());
         mouseYtext.setText("MouseY: " + event.getY());
     }

    });

scene.setOnMouseClicked(new EventHandler<MouseEvent>(){

     @Override
     public void handle(MouseEvent event) {
         // TODO Auto-generated method stub
         if(event.getButton() == MouseButton.PRIMARY){
             mouseLclick.setText("Left Click is clicked");
         }
         else
         {
             mouseLclick.setText("Left Click ");
         }
         if(event.getButton()== MouseButton.SECONDARY){
             mouseRclick.setText("Right Click is clicked");
         }
         else
         {
             mouseRclick.setText("Right Click ");
         }
     }

});
```

Run the application and you should be able to move the rectangle around the scene using the mouse. The text for X-Y coordinates will change on mouse movement. Click on either the left or right mouse button, and the two text fields will indicate which button was pressed, Figure 14.7.

Figure 14.7 The Game Scene

The last step is to detect when two nodes come in contact with each other. We will use a second animation timer (the first should still be commented out) to check when the rectangle and the circle are in contact. When there is a collision the text in the low right indicates the collision. Add the following code after the last mouse handler code:

```
AnimationTimer mytimer2 = new AnimationTimer(){

  @Override
  public void handle(long now) {
    // TODO Auto-generated method stub
    if(circle1.getBoundsInParent().intersects(rect1.
getBoundsInParent())){
        mytext.setText("Collision");
    }
    else
    {
        mytext.setText("No Collision");
    }
  }

};
mytimer2.start();
```

Run the application, and move the rectangle using either the keyboard or the mouse over the circle graphic. The collision should be detected, Figure 14.8.

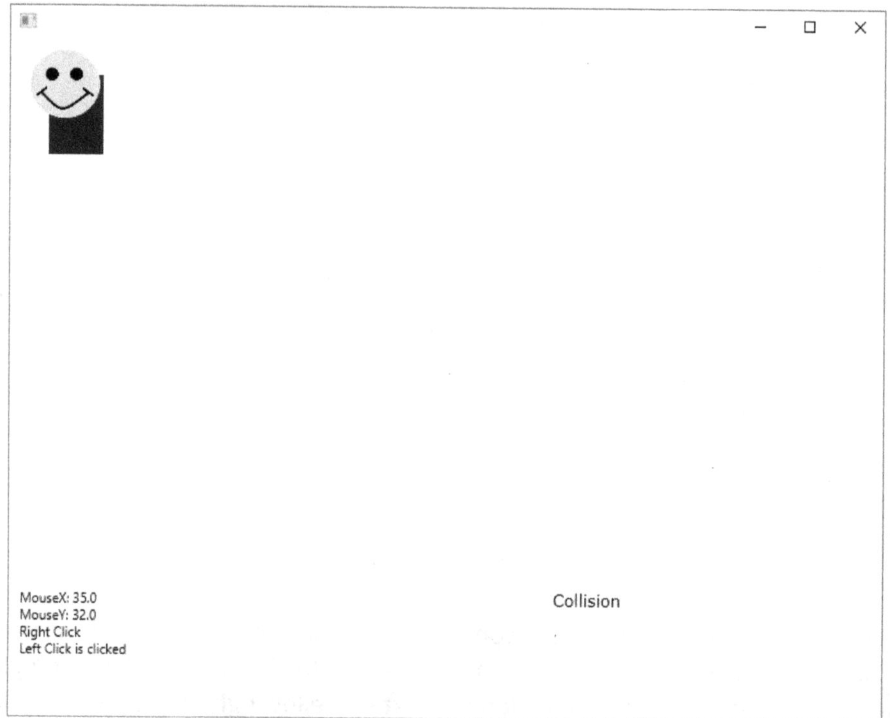

Figure 14.8 Collision Detection

14.6 Sound and Music Playback

A video game is not complete without sound or music, and JavaFX has built-in media and sound players under the javafx.scene.media package. There are the standard methods for Play(), Pause(), Stop() as well as volume and left/right balance support. You can set how many times the sound or song repeats.

14.6.1 Computer Activity 14.5 - Sound and Music

In this Computer Activity, we will create a simple JavaFX media player with buttons for play, pause, and stop, Figure 14.9. When the user clicks on a button, a sound from a WAV file will play, and then a sound from an MP3 file will play. Both the WAV and MP3 files will be embedded into the application.

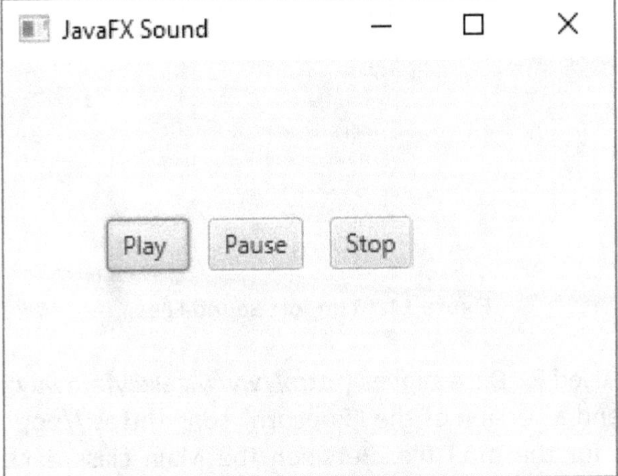

Figure 14.9 JavaFX Media Player

In Eclipse, create a new JavaFX project called "CH14CA14.5-Sound". Open the Main.java file, and add the following imports:

```
import javafx.scene.layout.Pane;
import javafx.scene.media.*;
import javafx.event.EventHandler;
import javafx.scene.input.MouseEvent;
```

Create a new method after main() called "createApp(Stage myStage)".

```
public void createApp(Stage myStage){

}
```

Edit the start() method, and remove the default setup in the try-block for a BorderPane. Replace it with a call to the createApp() method.

```
public void start(Stage primaryStage) {
    try {
        createApp(primaryStage);
    } catch(Exception e) {
        e.printStackTrace();
    }
}
```

Locate a WAV file or two, and an mp3 file. Import the files into the project, Figure 14.10:

CH14CA14.4-Sound
src
application
Main.java
application.css
boston-pops-Popcorn.mp3
R2D2b.wav
R2D2d.wav
R2D2e.wav
JRE System Library [JavaSE-1.8]

Figure 14.10 Import Sound Files

For the code listing, we used R2 D2 wav files (http://www.galaxyfaraway.com/gfa/1998/12/star-wars-sounds-archive/) and a version of the "Popcorn" song (https://popcorn-song.com/) by the Boston Pops Orchestra for the mp3 file. Between the Main class declaration and the start() method, add the following:

```
private AudioClip r2d2 = new
AudioClip(getClass().getResource("R2D2d.wav").toString());
private Media myMedia = new Media(getClass().getResource("boston-pops-
Popcorn.mp3").toString());
private MediaPlayer myPlayer = new MediaPlayer(myMedia);
```

You can replace the wav and mp3 files with your wav and mp3 files. The first line sets up an audio clip instance. The next two lines set up the media file and then the media player to play the media file. In the createApp() method add the following:

```
Pane root = new Pane();
Scene scene = new Scene(root,300,200);
Button bPlay = new Button("Play ");
bPlay.setTranslateX(50);
bPlay.setTranslateY(75);
root.getChildren().add(bPlay);
bPlay.setOnMouseClicked(new EventHandler<MouseEvent>(){

    @Override
    public void handle(MouseEvent event) {
        // TODO Auto-generated method stub
        r2d2.play();
        myPlayer.play();
    }


});
Button bPause = new Button("Pause");
bPause.setTranslateX(100);
```

```
bPause.setTranslateY(75);
root.getChildren().add(bPause);
bPause.setOnMouseClicked(new EventHandler<MouseEvent>(){

    @Override
    public void handle(MouseEvent event) {
        // TODO Auto-generated method stub
        r2d2.play();
        myPlayer.pause();
}

});
Button bStop = new Button("Stop");
bStop.setTranslateX(160);
bStop.setTranslateY(75);
root.getChildren().add(bStop);
bStop.setOnMouseClicked(new EventHandler<MouseEvent>(){

    @Override
    public void handle(MouseEvent event) {
        // TODO Auto-generated method stub
        r2d2.play();
        myPlayer.stop();
    }

});
myStage.setTitle("JavaFX Sound");
myStage.setScene(scene);
myStage.show();
```

The code simply sets up three buttons. When a mouse click event occurs, the audio clip plays and then the MediaPlayer method is called. Run the application and click the play button. The audio clip should play, and then the mp3 starts to play. You can then click the pause or stop button and the mp3 will pause or stop.

14.7 Computer Activity 14.6 - Street Frog

We now have all of the elements to put a JavaFX 2D game together. The first game we are going to create is a version of the classic arcade game Frogger that we will call Street Frog. Frogger was developed in 1981 by Konami and was released on several gaming platforms. Examples of the original game are found online. The gamer controls a frog that starts at the bottom of the screen. The frog must cross a busy street and then across a river to get to 1 of 5 slots at the top of the screen. Cars and trucks run in different directions and can squash the frog. The river has logs, turtles, and alligators. The frog must not hit the water or be eaten by an alligator. There is a time limit to make it across.

For our game, there will only be a street with a random number of cars and trucks moving in the same direction, left to right. The frog will start in the bottom left corner. The gamer will use the WASD keys to move the frog to the top of the screen without getting hit by a vehicle or having time run out. There are three frog lives in total. 100 points are awarded each time the frog makes it to the other side. The code for this game is based on the Frogger game developed by Almas Baimagambetov that was uploaded to his GIT hub account: github.com/AlmasB/FXTutorials/blob/master/src/com/almasb/frogger/ FroggerApp.java. He also has a video on his YouTube channel that walks you through the project, and he has several other classic arcade and board-game examples written in JavaFX. The first step is to gather the media content. If you have not done so already, download the Frogger Sprite Sheet by GaryCXJk from https://www.spriters-resource.com/arcade/frogger/sheet/11067/. Download the PNG file. Using a paint or image program to open the image, and cut out the car, truck, and a frog in the rest position and save them as separate .PNG files. You may have to rotate the truck around 180 degrees, Figure 14.11.

Figure 14.11 Street Frog Sprites

Go to the site: http://www.classicgaming.cc/classics/frogger/. Download the "Frogger hop" and squashed" wave files. As another reminder, be careful of the copyright for images and sounds files. You can create your own image files and sounds if you prefer. In Eclipse, create a new JavaFX project called "CH14CA14.6-StreetFrog". Import the .PNG and .wav files into the project, Figure 14.12:

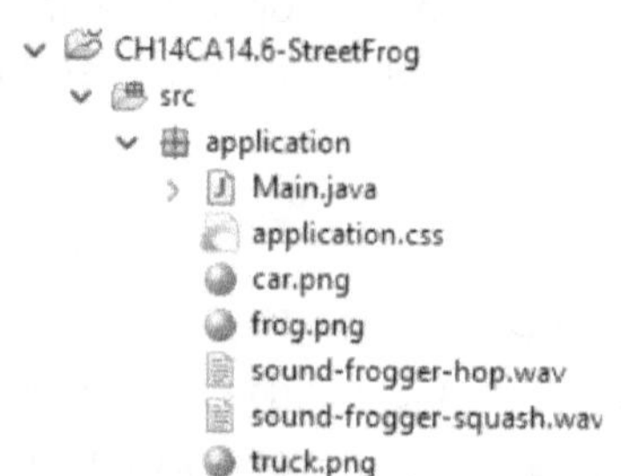

Figure 14.12 Import Street Frog Sounds

The next step is to break up the code into different Java class files. First, create a new class called "ImageFactory" with no main() method, add Code Listing 14.5:

```
package application;

import javafx.scene.image.Image;

public class ImageFactory {

    public Image frogimage =
new Image(getClass().getResourceAsStream("frog.png"));
    public Image carimage =
new Image(getClass().getResourceAsStream("car.png"));
    public Image truckimage =
new Image(getClass().getResourceAsStream("truck.png"));

}
```

Code Listing 14.5 Street Frog ImageFactory Class

The images for the game will be accessible from an instance of this class. Next, create a new class called "SoundFactory" with no main() method, add Code Listing 14.6:

```
package application;

import javafx.scene.media.AudioClip;

public class SoundFactory {

    public AudioClip frogjumpsound =
new AudioClip(getClass().getResource("sound-frogger-
hop.wav").toString());
    public AudioClip frogsplatsound = new
AudioClip(getClass().getResource("sound-frogger-
squash.wav").toString());
}
```

Code Listing 14.6 Street Frog SoundFactory Class

The sounds for the game will be accessible from an instance of this class. Finally, create a new class called "SpriteFactory" with no main() method, add Code Listing 14.7:

```
package application;

import javafx.scene.paint.ImagePattern;
import javafx.scene.shape.Rectangle;

public class SpriteFactory {

    private ImageFactory myImages = new ImageFactory();
```

```

    public Rectangle spawnCar() {

        Rectangle rect = new Rectangle(40, 40);
        rect.setFill(new ImagePattern(myImages.carimage));
        // y = from 0 to 560 (14*40) - leaving 40 pixels for the frog at the bottom
        rect.setTranslateY((int) (Math.random() * 14) * 40);
        return rect;
    }

    public Rectangle spawnTruck() {

        Rectangle rect = new Rectangle(93, 40);
        rect.setFill(new ImagePattern(myImages.truckimage));
        // y = from 0 to 560 (14*40) - leaving 40 pixels for the frog at the bottom
        rect.setTranslateY((int) (Math.random() * 14) * 40);
        return rect;
    }
}
```

Code Listing 14.7 Street Frog SpriteFactory Class

Having a separate SpriteFactory class allows us to enhance the application in the future. For example, maybe we want to add other vehicle types from the Sprite Sheet. The two methods create a rectangle and fill the rectangle with an image. Each vehicle is randomly placed in along the Y-axis at 40 pixels apart, thus the vehicles appear to be going down individual lanes. The bottom 40-pixel lane is only for the frog to start. We have already walked through a couple of JavaFX applications in this chapter. For the Main.java, use the same steps that we have used previously to set up and call a createApp() method. Fill in Code Listing 14.8 for the Main.java file:

```
//Released under the MIT License (MIT)
//Copyright © 2015 Almas Baimagambetov
//Adapted from @author Almas Baimagambetov (almaslvl@gmail.com)
//github.com/AlmasB/FXTutorials/blob/master/src/com/almasb/frogger/FroggerApp.java
//www.youtube.com/watch?v=K7Ll-dRydrQ
//Sound from: http://www.classicgaming.cc/classics/frogger/sounds
//Sprites by: GaryCXJk from: https://www.spriters-resource.com/arcade/frogger/sheet/11067/

package application;

import javafx.animation.AnimationTimer;
import javafx.animation.FadeTransition;
```

```
import javafx.application.Application;
import javafx.scene.Scene;
import javafx.scene.input.KeyEvent;
import javafx.scene.layout.HBox;
import javafx.scene.layout.Pane;
import javafx.scene.paint.Color;
import javafx.scene.paint.ImagePattern;
import javafx.scene.shape.Rectangle;
import javafx.scene.text.Font;
import javafx.scene.text.Text;
import javafx.stage.Stage;
import javafx.util.Duration;
import java.util.ArrayList;
import javafx.event.EventHandler;

public class Main extends Application {

    //several items need to be made available to the different classes
    private AnimationTimer gameloop;
    private Pane root;
    private ArrayList<Rectangle> vehicles = new ArrayList<>();
    private Rectangle frog;
    private int score = 0;
    private Text tscore = new Text("Score: " + Integer.toString(score));
    private int froglives = 3;
    private Text tlives = new Text("Lives: " + Integer.toString(froglives));
    private int countdown = 30;
    private int timertick = 0;
    private Text tcountdown = new Text("Time: " + countdown);
    private SoundFactory mySounds = new SoundFactory();
    private ImageFactory myImages = new ImageFactory();
    private SpriteFactory mySprites = new SpriteFactory();
    private Boolean froghit = false;

    @Override
    public void start(Stage primaryStage) {
        try {
            createApp(primaryStage);
        } catch (Exception e) {
            e.printStackTrace();
        }
    }

```

```
    public static void main(String[] args) {
        launch(args);
    }

    public void createApp(Stage myStage) {

        root = new Pane();
        root.setStyle("-fx-background-color: black;");
        Scene scene = new Scene(root, 800, 600);

        // Add the frog
        Rectangle rect = new Rectangle(38, 38);
        rect.setFill(new ImagePattern(myImages.frogimage));
        rect.setTranslateY(600 - 39);
        frog = rect;
        root.getChildren().add(frog);

        // Set up the score
        tscore.setTranslateX(700);
        tscore.setTranslateY(590);
        tscore.setFont(Font.font(14));
        tscore.setFill(Color.WHITE);
        root.getChildren().add(tscore);

        // Set up the frog lives count down
        tlives.setTranslateX(625);
        tlives.setTranslateY(590);
        tlives.setFont(Font.font(14));
        tlives.setFill(Color.WHITE);
        root.getChildren().add(tlives);

        tcountdown.setTranslateX(550);
        tcountdown.setTranslateY(590);
        tcountdown.setFont(Font.font(14));
        tcountdown.setFill(Color.WHITE);
        root.getChildren().add(tcountdown);


        //Game loop
        gameloop = new AnimationTimer() {

            @Override
            public void handle(long now) {

```

```
                // Move all vehicles forward, speed can be adjusted
                for (Rectangle vehicle : vehicles) {
                    vehicle.setTranslateX(vehicle.getTranslateX() + Math.random() * 10);
                }
                // adds more cars
                if (Math.random() < 0.075) {
                    Rectangle carSprite = mySprites.spawnCar();
                    vehicles.add(carSprite);
                    root.getChildren().add(carSprite);
                }
                // add more trucks
                if (Math.random() < 0.020) {
                    Rectangle truickSprite = mySprites.spawnTruck();
                    vehicles.add(truickSprite);
                    root.getChildren().add(truickSprite);
                }
                //increment the tick, when it reaches 60 decrement the countdown by 1 and reset
                timertick++;
                if (timertick == 60){
                    countdown--;
                    timertick = 0;
                    tcountdown.setText("Time: " + countdown);
                }
                //Check to see if the frog has been hit by a vehicle
                //if a hit, reduce the number of lives and move the frog back to the start
                //if frog lives is 0, end the game
                for (Rectangle vehicle : vehicles) {
                    if (vehicle.getBoundsInParent().intersects(frog.getBoundsInParent()) || countdown == 0) {
                        frog.setTranslateX(0);
                        frog.setTranslateY(600 - 39);
                        froglives--;
```

```
                        mySounds.frogsplatsound.play();
                        froghit = true;
                        countdown = 30;

                        tlives.setText("Lives: " + Integer.toString(froglives));

                        if (froglives == 0) {
                            gameloop.stop();
                            gameOver();
                        }
                    }
                }
                //Since vehicles are still moving off the scene
                //Clear the vehicles array and all elements if the frog is hit
                //don't want to run out of memory
                if(froghit == true){
                    for (Rectangle carclear : vehicles) {
                        root.getChildren().remove(carclear);
                    }
                    vehicles.clear();
                    froghit = false;
                }
                //if frog reaches the other side, increase the score
                //and move the frog back to the starting point
                if (frog.getTranslateY() <= 0) {
                    score += 100;
                    countdown = 30;
                    timertick = 0;
                    tcountdown.setText("Time: " + countdown);
                    tscore.setText("Score: " + Integer.toString(score));
                    frog.setTranslateX(0);
                    frog.setTranslateY(600 - 39);
                }
            }
        };

        gameloop.start();

        //set up the event handle to control the frog with the WASD keys.
        scene.setOnKeyPressed(new EventHandler<KeyEvent>() {

```

```
            @Override
            public void handle(KeyEvent event) {
                // If the frog live are greater than 0, the user can move the frog.
                //A boundary check is added to make sure the frog doesn't go off the scene
                if (froglives > 0) {
                    switch (event.getCode()) {

                    case W:
                        frog.setTranslateY(frog.getTranslateY() - 40);
                        mySounds.frogjumpsound.play();
                        break;
                    case S:
                        if (frog.getTranslateY() < 561) {
                            frog.setTranslateY(frog.getTranslateY() + 40);
                            mySounds.frogjumpsound.play();
                        }
                        break;
                    case A:
                        if (frog.getTranslateX() > 0) {
                            frog.setTranslateX(frog.getTranslateX() - 40);
                            mySounds.frogjumpsound.play();
                        }
                        break;

                    case D:
                        if (frog.getTranslateX() < 759) {
                            frog.setTranslateX(frog.getTranslateX() + 40);
                            mySounds.frogjumpsound.play();
                        }
                        break;

                    default:
                        break;
                    }
                }
            }

        });

```

```
219.            myStage.getIcons().add(myImages.frogimage);
220.            myStage.setTitle("Street Frog");
221.            myStage.setScene(scene);
222.            myStage.show();
223.        }
224.
225.        //Display an message that the game is over
226.        private void gameOver() {
227.
228.            String gameend = "Game Over";
229.            HBox hBox = new HBox();
230.            hBox.setTranslateX(280);
231.            hBox.setTranslateY(250);
232.            root.getChildren().add(hBox);
233.            for (int i = 0; i < gameend.toCharArray().length; i++) {
234.
235.                char letter = gameend.charAt(i);
236.                Text gameendtext = new Text(String.valueOf(letter));
237.                gameendtext.setFont(Font.font(48));
238.                gameendtext.setOpacity(0);
239.                gameendtext.setFill(Color.WHITE);
240.                hBox.getChildren().add(gameendtext);
241.                FadeTransition ft = new
    FadeTransition(Duration.seconds(0.66), gameendtext);
242.                ft.setToValue(1);
243.                ft.setDelay(Duration.seconds(i * 0.15));
244.                ft.play();
245.            }
246.        }
247.}
```

Code Listing 14.8 Street Frog Main Application Class

Strip away the images and sound, and the game is simply a bunch of rectangles moving across the screen, and the frog rectangle is moved with the WASD keys. If the frog rectangle intersects a vehicle rectangle, a hit is made, the lives are reduced, and the frog resets to the starting position. If the frog rectangle makes it to the other side, the score is increased, the frog resets to the starting position, and the vehicles are reset. A countdown timer forces the gamer to move the frog to the other side or a life will be lost.

The Main() and Start() methods perform the same operations as the other JavaFX programs that we have created. The createApp() method performs all the work, but there are two methods to create vehicles. As a result, lines 29 through 43 define the Pane, frog sprite, score, and frog lives. Instances for the vehicle sprites, audio and images are instantiated. Within the CreateApp() method, lines 60 – 89 perform the basic setup. The Pane container is instantiated and added to the scene. The scene is set up with the Pane container for 800x600 with a black background. The frog sprite is created and placed in the lower left corner. The score, countdown timer, and lives count are set up and placed in the lower right corner.

The game loop starts at line 93. The key to this solution is that all the vehicle rectangles are stored in an ArrayList. The first for-each loop moves all the vehicles sprites 10 pixels to the right during each pulse of the Animation Timer. Next, more cars and trucks are randomly created on the left. The spawnCar() and SpanTruck() methods are called to create each new car or truck sprite. These new rectangles are added to the Vehicle ArrayList and to the Pane container. Line 119 increments a timer tick. Since the Animation timer is running at 60 fps, when the timer tick reaches 60, 1 second is removed from the countdown timer. Line 132 performs the operation to check for collision status with each vehicle node. Line 132 checks to see if the frog and a vehicle have collided or if the countdown timer has timed out. If there is a collision, the number of frog lives is reduced by 1, the lives texts is updated, the frog splat sound is played, and the frog is moved back to start. If there are no more lives, the game ends, the timer is stopped, and the gameover() method is called to display the "Game Over" message. Line 152 checks for a hit toggle. There is an issue with this implementation of the game. Vehicles will continuously be created and added to the ArrayList as rectangles on the Pane. Since computers have finite memory, the frog hit will give a chance to reset the ArrayList and remove all the rectangles. If there is no hit, line 161 checks to see if the frog has reached the other side. If it has reset the frog sprite to the start point, the score is incremented, and the countdown timer is reset. The game loop repeats all of these steps until the game is over.

After the game loop, starting with line 176, the event handler for the keyboard input checks for the WASD keys. The event handler has the same implementation as Computer Activity 14.3, but some additional code has been added to make sure that the user doesn't move the frog beyond the bottom, left, or right sides of the Pane. Also, if the game is over, the controls should be disabled. Run the game and use the WASD keys to move the frog to the other side of the street, Figure 14.13.

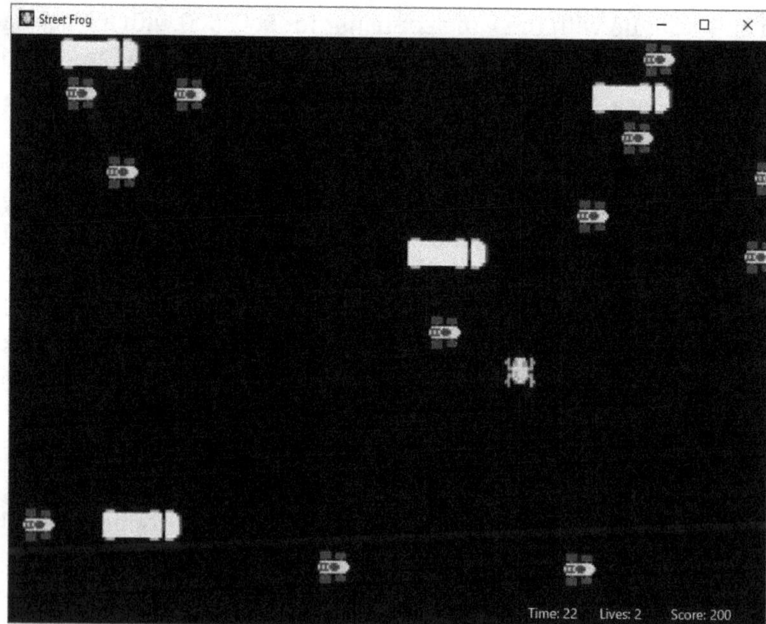

Figure 14.13 Street Frog in Action

If you decide to share your project source code, you will want to put a license text file for the license the project falls under. In this case, the original author chose MIT license. You will also want to add a readme text file that explains how to rebuild the code. There are improvements that can be made. For example, the street can be split in two and have cars go in two directions. Frog jump animation could be added. A high score and the ability to recover the high score can be added. Another idea is to add a river with frogs, turtles, and alligators like the original game. A final idea would be to create levels where the timer is shortened or the vehicles are moving faster.

14.8 Computer Activity 14.7 - Tie Attack!

In the spirit of the lead-in quote, the second game is a Star Wars™ themed game called "Tie Attack!" In the arcade, there is the game with a mallet called Whack-A-Mole. The mallet is used to hit down toy moles that pop up randomly from holes in the cabinet. The Tie Attack! game is similar in structure but has an outer space theme, rather than the farming theme of Whack-A-Mole. In this game, Tie Fighters will appear randomly on the screen. The player will use a mouse to fire at and destroy the Tie Fighters before they fly away (disappear from the screen). The Tie Fighters can fire back and reduce your shields. The game is over when the shields strength reaches 0. Points are gained with each Tie Fighter destroyed and points are lost when Tie Fighters disappear.

There are a number of visual and sound elements to this game. The first two items will be something you have to create using a drawing/image program like GIMP (https://www.gimp.org/). The first image to create is a targeting guide PNG file. The targeting guide will be the mouse cursor. The targeting guide is a circle with a dot in the center. The 25x25 pixel background must be clear so that the player can see the circle and the dot superimposed on the background image, Figure 14.14.

Figure 14.14 Targeting Guide Image

The second image is an 800 pixel x600 pixel background that contains some stars and/or planets. What it looks like is up to you and your imagination. This will be the background of space that the Tie Fighters will fly across, Figure 14.15.

Figure 14.15 Space Background Image

The rest of the media items are to be downloaded from different websites. The first items to download are the fonts. There are two fonts for the game: Aurebesh, which is a symbol replacement for each letter of the alphabet, and *Star Wars* Special Edition font. There are a number of places to download the Aurebesh font. Here is one location that has a solid implementation: http://davidocchino.com/portfolio/typography/aurebesh.html. The Special Edition font can be downloaded from here: http://www.fontspace.com/boba-fonts/starjedi-special-edition.

Next, we need a Tie Fighter image. A Tie Fighter sprite sheet can be downloaded from here: https://www.spriters-resource.com/pc_computer/starwarsgalacticbattlegrounds/sheet/65222/.

Using an image/drawing program, cut out the end Tie Fighter and clear the background so that only the Tie Fighter remains, Figure 14.16. Like the targeting guide, we want to see through to the background.

Figure 14.16 Tie Fighter Image

The last media items to download are Tie Fighter sounds. A set of Tie Fighter sounds can be downloaded from here: https://www.sounds-resource.com/pc_computer/starwarstiefighter/sound/3358/. The zip file contains a number of WAV files. The following 6 files are needed: CANNON-1.WAV, HT-SHD-4.WAV, EX-MED-6.WAV, EX-BIG-2.WAV, DANGER-2.WAV, and TI-LR-1.WAV.

In Eclipse, create a new JavaFX project called "CH14CA14.7-TieAttack". Create three Java class files with no main() method: ImageFactory.java, SoundFactory.java, and TieFactory.java. Import the .PNG and .WAV files into the project, Figure 14.17:

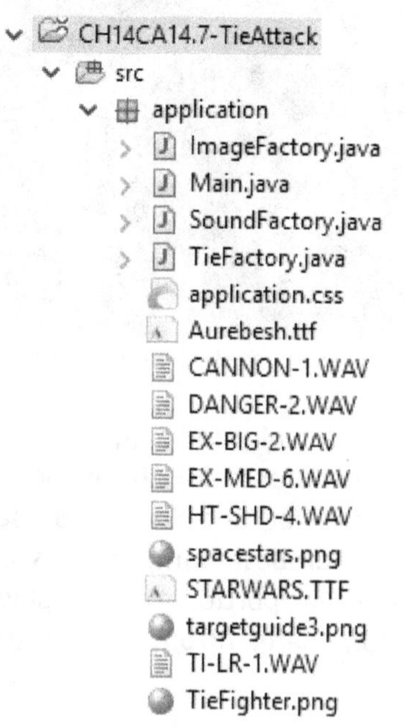

Figure 14.17 Create Tie ttack! Project

In the ImageFactory.java add Code Listing 14.9:

```
package application;

import javafx.scene.image.Image;
import javafx.scene.layout.BackgroundImage;
import javafx.scene.text.Font;

public class ImageFactory {

    public Image targetIcon =
new Image(getClass().getResourceAsStream("targetguide3.png"));
    public Image tiefighterImage =
new Image(getClass().getResourceAsStream("TieFighter.png"));
    public BackgroundImage gameBackGround = new BackgroundImage(new
Image(getClass().getResourceAsStream("spacestars.png")), null, null,
null, null);
    public Font aurebesh =
Font.loadFont(getClass().getResourceAsStream("Aurebesh.ttf"), 12);
    public Font startwars77 =
Font.loadFont(getClass().getResourceAsStream("STARWARS.TTF"), 42);

}
```

Code Listing 14.9 Tie Fighter Attack! ImageFactory Class

The images and fonts for the game will be accessible from an instance of this class. In the SoundFactory.java file, add Code Listing 14.10:

```
package application;

import javafx.scene.media.AudioClip;

```

```
public class SoundFactory {

    public AudioClip cannon =
new AudioClip(getClass().getResource("CANNON-1.WAV").toString());
    public AudioClip shieldhit =
new AudioClip(getClass().getResource("HT-SHD-4.WAV").toString());
    public AudioClip tieexplode =
new AudioClip(getClass().getResource("EX-MED-6.WAV").toString());
    public AudioClip gameoverfinal =
new AudioClip(getClass().getResource("EX-BIG-2.WAV").toString());
    public AudioClip shielddanger =
new AudioClip(getClass().getResource("DANGER-2.WAV").toString());
    public AudioClip tieflyin =
new AudioClip(getClass().getResource("TI-LR-1.WAV").toString());

}
```

Code Listing 14.10 Tie Fighter Attack! SoundFactory Class

The sounds for the game will be accessible from an instance of this class. In the TieFactory.java file, add Code Listing 14.11:

```
package application;

import javafx.scene.image.Image;
import javafx.scene.paint.ImagePattern;
import javafx.scene.shape.Rectangle;

public class TieFactory {

    public int tietimertick = 0;

    public Rectangle tiefighter;

    TieFactory(Image tieimage){

        this.tiefighter = spawnTieFighter(tieimage);
    }

```

```
    public Rectangle spawnTieFighter(Image tieimage){

        Rectangle rect = new Rectangle(60, 60);
        rect.setFill(new ImagePattern(tieimage));
        rect.setTranslateX((int) (40 + 700 *Math.random()));
        rect.setTranslateY((int) (26 + 500 *Math.random()));
        return rect;
    }
}
```

Code Listing 14.11 Tie Fighter Attack! TieFactory Class

Each Tie Fighter instance consists of a rectangle and an integer. The constructor is called for each new instance, which calls the spawnTieFighter() method to create the rectangle and fill in the image. The image reference is passed in so you have some flexibility with this class. The tietimertick integer starts with 0, will be increased every second, and the instance will disappear after a set amount of time. We have already walked through a couple of JavaFX applications in this chapter. For the Main.java, use the same steps that we have used previously to set up and call a createApp() method. Fill in Code Listing 14.12 for the Main.java file:

```
//Tie Attack! - Developed by Annabooks, LLC.
//Background and target guide by Annabooks LLC.
//Aurebesh font by David Occhino -
http://davidocchino.com/portfolio/typography/aurebesh.html
//Start Wars Special Edition Font by Boba Fonts -
http://www.fontspace.com/boba-fonts/starjedi-special-edition
//Tie Fighter Image - https://www.spriters-
resource.com/pc_computer/starwarsgalacticbattlegrounds/sheet/65222/
//Tie Fighter Sounds - https://www.sounds-
resource.com/pc_computer/starwarstiefighter/sound/3358/


package application;

import java.io.DataInputStream;
import java.io.DataOutputStream;
import java.io.FileInputStream;
import java.io.FileOutputStream;
import java.io.IOException;
import java.text.DecimalFormat;
import java.util.ArrayList;
import javafx.animation.AnimationTimer;
import javafx.animation.ScaleTransition;
import javafx.application.Application;
import javafx.stage.Stage;
import javafx.util.Duration;
```

```
import javafx.scene.ImageCursor;
import javafx.scene.Scene;
import javafx.scene.layout.Background;
import javafx.scene.layout.Pane;
import javafx.scene.paint.Color;
import javafx.scene.text.Text;
import javafx.event.EventHandler;
import javafx.scene.input.MouseEvent;
import javafx.event.ActionEvent;

public class Main extends Application {

    private Pane root;
    private AnimationTimer gameloop;
    private ArrayList<TieFactory> tiefighters = new ArrayList<>();
    private SoundFactory mySounds = new SoundFactory();
    private ImageFactory myImages = new ImageFactory();
    private TieFactory mytiefighter;
    private int score = 0;
    private Text scoretext = new Text("Score: " + score);
    private int highscore = 0;
    private Text highscoretext = new Text("High Score: " + highscore);
    private int shield = 100;
    private Text shieldtext = new Text("Shield Strenght: " + shield);
    private int hits = 0;
    private int shots = 0;
    private Text accuracytext = new Text("Accuracy: " + hits + " / " + shots);
    private int tieescaped =0;
    private Text tieescapedtext = new Text("Escaped: " + tieescaped);
    private DecimalFormat df = new DecimalFormat("###.##");
    private int timerTck = 0;

    @Override
    public void start(Stage primaryStage) {
        try {
            createApp(primaryStage);
        } catch (Exception e) {
            e.printStackTrace();
        }
    }

    public static void main(String[] args) {
```

```
        launch(args);
    }

    public void createApp(Stage myStage){

        root = new Pane();
        root.setBackground(new Background(myImages.gameBackGround));
        Scene scene = new Scene(root, 800, 600);
        scene.setCursor(new ImageCursor(myImages.targetIcon));

        //Main Title
        Text mainTitle = new Text("Tie Attack!");
        mainTitle.setFont(myImages.startwars77);
        mainTitle.setFill(Color.WHITE);
        mainTitle.setTranslateX(175);
        mainTitle.setTranslateY(250);
        ScaleTransition myTitleScale = new ScaleTransition(new
    Duration(4000),mainTitle);
        myTitleScale.setFromX(1.0);
        myTitleScale.setFromY(1.0);
        myTitleScale.setToX(0.0);
        myTitleScale.setToY(0.0);
        myTitleScale.setOnFinished(new EventHandler<ActionEvent>(){

            @Override
            public void handle(ActionEvent event) {
                // TODO Auto-generated method stub
                root.getChildren().remove(mainTitle);
            }
        });

        scoretext.setTranslateX(600);
        scoretext.setTranslateY(40);
        scoretext.setFont(myImages.aurebesh);
        scoretext.setFill(Color.WHITE);

        highscoretext.setTranslateX(600);
        highscoretext.setTranslateY(25);
        highscoretext.setFont(myImages.aurebesh);
        highscoretext.setFill(Color.WHITE);

        shieldtext.setTranslateX(300);
        shieldtext.setTranslateY(25);
        shieldtext.setFont(myImages.aurebesh);
        shieldtext.setFill(Color.WHITE);

```

```
        Text mouseXtext = new Text("MouseX: ");
        mouseXtext.setTranslateX(10);
        mouseXtext.setTranslateY(25);
        mouseXtext.setFont(myImages.aurebesh);
        mouseXtext.setFill(Color.WHITE);

        Text mouseYtext = new Text("MouseY: ");
        mouseYtext.setTranslateX(10);
        mouseYtext.setTranslateY(40);
        mouseYtext.setFont(myImages.aurebesh);
        mouseYtext.setFill(Color.WHITE);

        accuracytext.setTranslateX(10);
        accuracytext.setTranslateY(55);
        accuracytext.setFont(myImages.aurebesh);
        accuracytext.setFill(Color.WHITE);

        tieescapedtext.setTranslateX(10);
        tieescapedtext.setTranslateY(70);
        tieescapedtext.setFont(myImages.aurebesh);
        tieescapedtext.setFill(Color.WHITE);

        root.getChildren().addAll(scoretext, highscoretext,
   mouseXtext,mouseYtext, shieldtext, mainTitle, accuracytext,
   tieescapedtext);

        myTitleScale.play();

        try(DataInputStream dIn = new DataInputStream(new
   FileInputStream("TFAHIGHSCORE.bin"))){
            highscore = dIn.readInt();
            highscoretext.setText("High Score: " + highscore);
            dIn.close();
        }
        catch(IOException ex)
        {
            System.out.println("Read IO error" + ex);
        }

        gameloop = new AnimationTimer(){

            @Override
            public void handle(long now) {

                if (Math.random() < 0.010) {

```

```
                mytiefighter = new TieFactory(myImages.tiefighterImage);
                tiefighters.add(mytiefighter);
                root.getChildren().add(mytiefighter.tiefighter);
                mySounds.tieflyin.play();
            }
            //Tie fighters fire back
            for(TieFactory tie : tiefighters){
                if(Math.random() < 0.01){
                    mySounds.shieldhit.play();
                    shield--;
                    shieldtext.setText("Shield Strenght: " + shield);
                }
                if(shield == 0){
                    gameloop.stop();
                    gameOver();
                }
                //tie fighter flies away after 3 seconds
                tie.tietimertick++;
            }
            //tie fighter flies away after 3 seconds or more
            for(TieFactory tie: tiefighters){
                if(tie.tietimertick  >= 180){
                    score -= 50;
                    tiefighters.remove(tie);
                    root.getChildren().remove(tie.tiefighter);
                    tieescaped++;
                    tieescapedtext.setText("Escaped: " + tieescaped);
                    return;
                }
            }

            //Signal that shield strength is getting low
            if(shield <= 25){
                timerTck++;
                if(timerTck == 180){
                    mySounds.shielddanger.play();
                    timerTck = 0;
                    shieldtext.setFill(Color.RED);
                }
            }
```

```

                accuracytext.setText("Accuracy: " + hits + " / " + shots);
            }
        };
        gameloop.start();

        scene.setOnMousePressed(new EventHandler<MouseEvent>(){

            @Override
            public void handle(MouseEvent event) {

                if(shield > 0){
                    shots++;
                    mySounds.cannon.play();
                    for(TieFactory tie : tiefighters){
                        if(event.getTarget() == tie.tiefighter){
                            mySounds.tieexplode.play();
                            score +=100;
                            if( score > highscore){
                                highscore = score;
                                highscoretext.setFill(Color.GREEN);
                                highscoretext.setText("High Score: " + highscore);
                            }
                            scoretext.setText("Score: " + score);
                            hits++;
                            root.getChildren().remove(tie.tiefighter);
                            tiefighters.remove(tie);
                            return;
                        }
                    }
                }
            }
        });

        scene.setOnMouseMoved( new EventHandler<MouseEvent>(){

            @Override
            public void handle(MouseEvent event) {

                mouseXtext.setText("MouseX: " + df.format(event.getX()));
                mouseYtext.setText("MouseY: " + df.format(event.getY()));
```

```
236.            }
237.        });
238.
239.        myStage.getIcons().add(myImages.tiefighterImage);
240.        myStage.setTitle("Tie Fighter Attack!");
241.        myStage.setScene(scene);
242.        myStage.show();
243.    }
244.
245.    public void gameOver(){
246.
247.        try(DataOutputStream dOut = new DataOutputStream(new
    FileOutputStream("TFAHIGHSCORE.bin"))){
248.            dOut.writeInt(highscore);
249.            dOut.close();
250.        }
251.        catch(IOException ex)
252.        {
253.            System.out.println("Write IO error" + ex);
254.        }
255.
256.        mySounds.gameoverfinal.play();
257.        Text gameover = new Text("Game Over");
258.        gameover.setFont(myImages.startwars77);
259.        gameover.setFill(Color.WHITE);
260.        gameover.setTranslateX(280);
261.        gameover.setTranslateY(300);
262.        root.getChildren().add(gameover);
263.    }
264.}
```

Code Listing 14.12 Tie Attack Main Application Class

Lines 35-53 set up instances for the other Java class files, the text to be displayed on the screen, and the integers for scoring, shot efficiency, and mouse X-Y values. Lines 57-66 are the basic JavaFX main() and start() methods that set up the JavaFX application and call the createApp() method. Lines 70-73 set up the root Pane with the starfield background. The Pane is added to the Scene with a size of 800 pixels x 600 pixels. Finally, the mouse cursor is changed to use the targeting guide.

Lines 75-93 use animation on the “Tie Attack!” to scale from normal to 0 so that it looks like it is disappearing into space in true *Star Wars* style. The special edition font is used for the text field. Lines 86-93 remove the text field from the Pane completely when the animation is finished. Lines 95-132 set up the text fields for score, high score, shield strength, mouse X-Y coordinates, shot accuracy, and how many tie fighters escaped. Each text field is placed in a specific location at the top of the Pane. All of the text fields use the Aurebesh font. Line 134 starts the main title animation.

Lines 136-144 attempt to open any previously saved high score file to retrieve the previous high score value and display it at the top of the screen.

Lines 146-199 is the game loop. Lines 151-15, randomly generate tiefighter instances and show them in the Pane. Each instance is saved to an ArrayList, and the fly-in sound is played. Lines 158-173 cycle through each tiefighter instance in the ArrayList; and randomly lets the tie fighter fire back, which decrements the shield strength. If the shield strength reaches 0, the gameOver() method is called. Each tiefighter instance has its tietimertick incremented. Lines 174-184 check each tiefighter instance in the ArrayList to see if the tietimertick has reached 180 (3 seconds, 60fps x 3 = 180). If the instance has reached 180, the instance is removed from the pane and ArrayList. The score is decremented by 50 and the tieescaped count is incremented. Lines 186-194 will play a warning sound when the shield reaches 25 or less. Line 196 updates the shots accuracy information. Line 199 starts the animation timer.

Lines 201-227 are the event handler for the mouse right-click event. As long as the shield strength is greater than 0, each time the player clicks the right mouse button, a shot is fired, the cannon sound plays, and the location of the mouse X-Y coordinates are checked against all tiefighter instances. If there is an overlap, the tiefighter instance is removed from the Pane and ArrayList, the score is increased by 100, the tieexplode sound plays, and shot accuracy values are incremented. Lines 229-237 are the event handler for the mouse moving. The mouse X-Y coordinates are changed on the screen, which gives a dynamic feel to the game even though it doesn't really do anything.

Lines 239-242 complete the createApp() method by setting up the stage with a title and icon. The scene is added to the stage and the stage is shown. The gameOver() method is listed in lines 245-264. The high score is saved to a file, and the "Game Over" text is displayed. Run the game and use the mouse to hit each tie fighter as they appear on the screen, Figure 14.18.

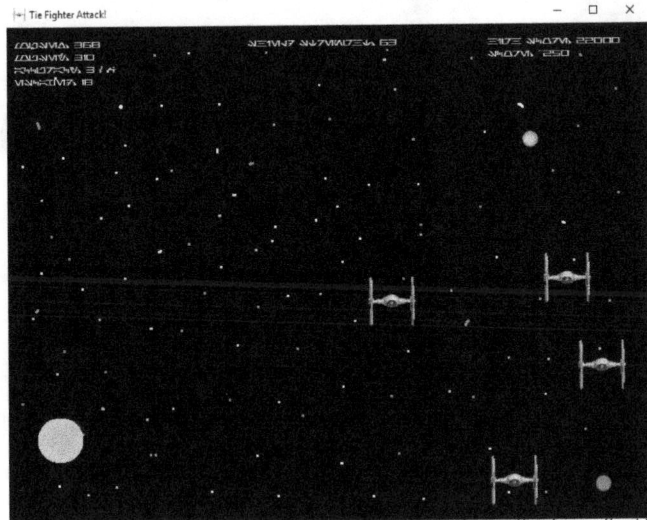

Figure 14.18 Tie Attack! In Action

There are areas for improvement. For example, each time the tie fighter is destroyed, the image could change to a destroyed tie fighter before disappearing from the screen. Another idea is to have the tie fighters move across the screen. They can also be at different levels where the shield strength is increased based on shot accuracy, and the frequency of tie fighters appearing could be increased.

14.9 Eclipse Feature: Export Runnable JAR File

Running the game from Eclipse is fine for development, but at some point, you will want to share the game. In Eclipse, you can export the project as a runnable JAR file.

1. In Package Explorer, right-click on the project and select Export from the context menu.
2. In the Select dialog, under Java click on Runnable JAR File, Figure 14.19, click Next.

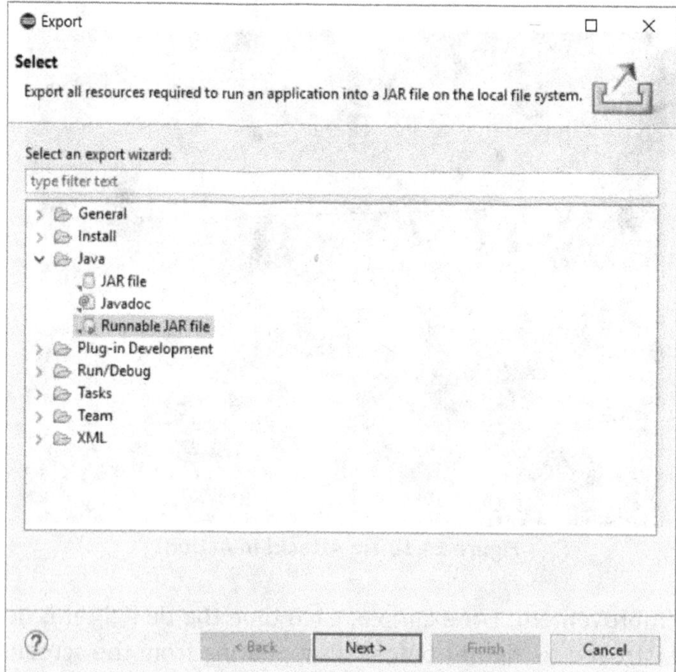

Figure 14.19 Export Runnable JAR File

3. In the Launch configuration, click the drop-down and select the Main from the CH14CA14.7-TieFigherAttack project. In the Export destination, select the path and name of the JAR file, Figure 14.20. Click Finish.

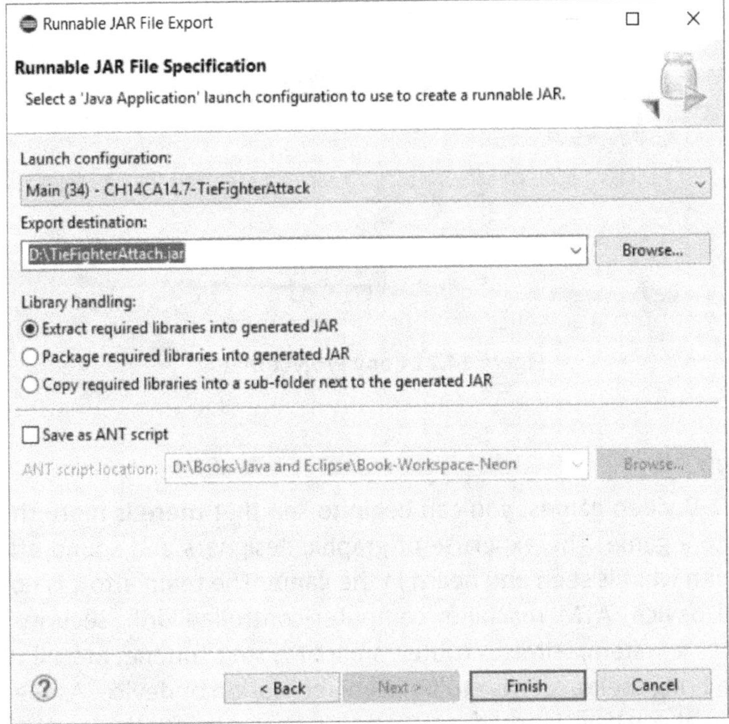

Figure 14.20 Select Launch Configuration and Export Destination

The final JAR file will be in the export destination location. You should be able to double-click on the JAR file and run the game. You can share the JAR file with others so that they can play the game. Of course, they will need to have the Java runtime installed on their system.

14.10 Eclipse Feature: Clone a Project for a New Version

If you want to improve the game over time, it is best to make a copy of the project first and edit the copy as a new version of the game.

1. In Package Explorer, right-click on the project and select Copy from the context menu.
2. In Package Explorer, right-click anywhere and select Paste. The Copy Project dialog appears, Figure 14.21.
3. Give the project a new name with version and click OK. The project will be copied and you can get started on the new version.

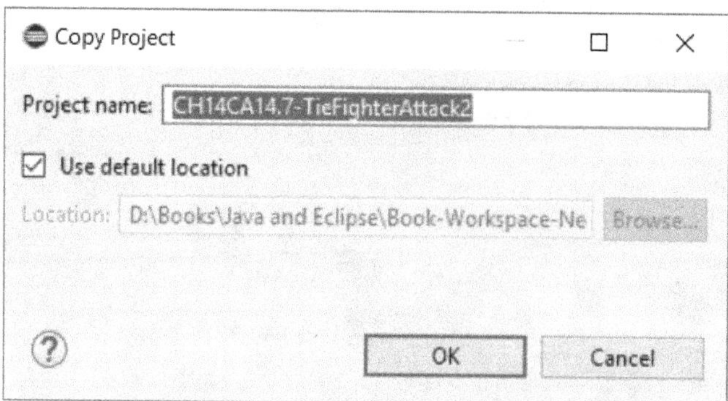

Figure 14.21 Copy Project Dialog

14.11 Summary

After a couple of 2-D video games, you can begin to see that there is more than just computer code that goes into a game. The expertise of graphic designers and sound effects creators are required to help with what is seen and heard in the game. The team effort is not limited to video games. A medical device, ATM machine, computer-controlled drill, security system, vending machine, point of sale system, wireless router, smart TV, smartphone, etc. all require a different group of people to bring their expertise to build an application or device. As the lead-in quote for the chapter says, what you have learned in this book is a big step into the larger world of computer programming.

It is the end of this book, and we hope a beginning of a wondrous journey into computer science and programming. The book has covered the basics of computer science, the features and capabilities of Eclipse, and introduced some of the topics to be discussed in other computer science classes. There are many other subjects to cover like multi-threaded applications, Lambda expressions, and network programming. The only homework assignment is to build on what you have learned and let your imagination create the next great application or device.

A Bibliography

"The Truth is Out There"
-Open message from ***The X-Files***, 20th Century Fox Studios, 1993

An old joke: if you get 10 teachers in a room and ask them how to teach a subject, you will get 20 answers. Each teacher presents a subject from their point of view and background. We are not the first to write about Computer Science, Java, or Eclipse, and we will not be the last. What we have done is brought all three together and included insights to provide a foundation for a programming job in industry. We have been programming for some time but writing to cover a specific curriculum is a different story altogether. This text took several years to develop with writes and rewrites, lots of research, and double-checking to make sure that we covered the curriculum for the AP® Computer Science test and beyond. Like the 10 teachers in a room, our approach to present and explain the subject is from our point of view, having gone through school and spent many years in the industry.

Most of the information on Computer Science, Java, or Eclipse can be found in some form or another on the Internet. Many of our searches led us back to 3 sites:

- oracle.com
- eclipse.org
- wikipedia.org

Below are many books, articles, online videos, and forums that we reviewed to make sure we covered the material. To spin the opening quote a bit, the answers are out there. Since the book is presented from our point of view, we recommend reviewing these other books, articles, online videos, and forums to get different points of view. For those taking the AP® Computer Science test, we strongly suggest the study guides from Skylight Publishing and others that include practice exams.

A.1 Books

AP® Computer Science A, 5th Edition, Roselyn Teukolsky, Barron's Educational Series, Inc. 2010, ISBN: 978-0-7641-4373-1.

Beginning Java 8 Games Development, Wallace Jackson, Apress, 2014, 978-1-4842-0416-0.

***Be Prepared for the AP® Computer Science Exam in Java,* 4th Edition**, Maria Litvin and Gary Litvin, Skylight Publishing, 2009, ISBN: 978-0-9824775-0-2.

***Be Prepared for the AP® Computer Science Exam in Java,* 6th Edition**, Maria Litvin and Gary Litvin, Skylight Publishing, 2014, ISBN: 978-0-9824775-3-3

Cracking the AP® Computer Science A Exam, 2017 Edition, Matt Gironda, et al. The Princeton Review, Penguin Random House, 2016, ISBN: 978-1-101-91988-0.

Data Structures and Algorithms Made Easy in Java, Narasimha Karumanchi, CareerMonk Publications, 2017, ISBN: 978-1-468-10127-0.

Eclipse Starter Guide for AP® Computer Science, Sean D. Liming and John R. Malin, Annabooks, 2013, ISBN: 978-0-9911887-0-3.

Fundamentals of Java, 3rd Edition, Kenneth Lambert and Martin Osborne, Thomson Course Technology – Thomas Learning, Inc., 2007, ISBN: 0-619-26723-2.

Introducing JavaFX 8 Programming, Herbert Schildt, Oracle Press, The McGraw Hill Companies, Inc., 2015, ISBN: 978-0-07-184255-6.

Java A Beginner's Guide, 5th Edition, Herbert Schildt, Oracle Press, The McGraw Hill Companies, Inc., 2012, ISBN: 978-0-07-160632-5.

Java for AP® Computer Science, Tom West and Christine Stephenson, Holt Software Associates, Inc., 2003, ISBN: 0-921598-51-3.

Java The Complete Reference, 9th Edition, Herbert Schildt, Oracle Press, The McGraw Hill Companies, Inc., 2014, ISBN: 978-0-07-180855-2.

Java Programming, Poornachandra Sarang, Oracle Press, The McGraw Hill Companies, Inc., 2012, ISBN: 978-0-07-163360-4.

Java Concepts, 6th Edition, Cay Horstmann, John Wiley & Sons, Inc. 2010, ISBN: 978-0-470-50947-0.

Java Programming, Gary B. Shelly, Thomas J. Cashman, Joy L. Starks, Michael I. Mick, Thomson Course Technology – Thomas Learning, Inc. 2004, ISBN: 0-619-20142-8.

Java Programming, 3rd Edition, Gary B. Shelly, Thomas J. Cashman, Joy L. Starks, Michael I. Mick, Thomson Course Technology – Thomas Learning, Inc. 2006, ISBN: 978-1-4188-5985-5.

A.2 Articles

"A Large Scale Blended and Flipped Class: Class Design and Investigation of Factors Influencing Students' Intention to Learn", Yulei Zhang, Yan Dang, and Beverly Amer, IEEE Transaction on Education, Volume 59, Number 4, November 2016, ISSN: 0018-9359.

"AP® Computer Science A Course Overview", The College Board AP, 2016.

"AP® Computer Science A Course Overview", The College Board AP, 2017.

"AP® Computer Science A Course Principles, Course and Exam Description", The College Board AP, 2016.

"AP® Computer Science Teacher's Guide", Deborah Power Carter, The College Board AP, 2007.

"Computer Science A Course Description", The College Board, 2014.

"Exam Appendix - Java Quick Reference", The College Board, 2014.

"More Time or Better Tools? A Large-Scale Retrospective Comparison of Pedagogical Approaches to Teach Programming", Gabriela Silva-Maceda, P. David Arjona-Villicana, F. Edgar Castillo-Barrera, IEEE Transaction on Education, Volume 59, Number 4, November 2016, ISSN: 0018-9359.

A.3 Internet – Websites, Articles, Blogs, Forums, and Videos

The various Internet sites have been broken down into the chapters that used the reference.

Syntax Highlight Code In Word Documents – Site used to convert the code to be formatted for text - http://www.planetb.ca/syntax-highlight-word

Chapter 1

"***History of computer science***", https://en.wikipedia.org/wiki/History_of_computer_science

"***History of Computers***", https://en.wikipedia.org/wiki/History_of_computing

Chapter 2

"***What Is the Java Virtual Machine & How Does it Work?",*** Simon Slangen, http://www.makeuseof.com/tag/java-virtual-machine-work-makeuseof-explains/, April 2, 2012

"***How the Java Virtual Machine (JVM) Works***", Bikash Shaw, https://www.codeproject.com/Articles/30422/How-the-Java-Virtual-Machine-JVM-Works, November 25, 2008

"***Understanding JVM Internals, from Basic Structure to Java SE 7 Features***", Esen Sagynov, https://dzone.com/articles/understanding-jvm-internals, October 19, 2012.

"***A Guide to Free java Integrated Development Environments (IDEs)",*** Priya Viswanathan, https://www.lifewire.com/best-free-ideas-for-java-developers-2373185, December 2, 2017.

“***InfoWorld review: Top Java programming tools***”, Andrew Binstock, InfoWorld, https://www.infoworld.com/article/2683534/development-environments/infoworld-review--top-java-programming-tools.html, September 22, 2010.

Chapter 3

Operators- Operator Precedence, The Java™ Tutorials, https://docs.oracle.com/javase/tutorial/java/nutsandbolts/operators.html

Unicode Character Table - https://unicode-table.com/en/

Chapter 4

“***Java-Exceptions***”, Learn Java Programming, Tutorialspoint, https://www.tutorialspoint.com/java/java_exceptions.htm

“***Class Exception***”, Java Platform Standard Edition 7, https://docs.oracle.com/javase/7/docs/api/java/lang/Exception.html

“***The catch Blocks***”, The Java™ Tutorials, https://docs.oracle.com/javase/tutorial/essential/exceptions/catch.html

“***Conditional Expressions***”, Dr. H. James de St. Germain, Jim's CS Topics, https://www.cs.utah.edu/~germain/PPS/Topics/index.html

Chapter 5

“***Tutorial: Objects and Classes in Python and Sage***”, Florent Hivert, http://doc.sagemath.org/html/en/thematic_tutorials/tutorial-objects-and-classes.html

“***Class ArrayList<E>”,*** Java Platform Standard Edition 7, https://docs.oracle.com/javase/7/docs/api/java/util/ArrayList.html

“***Wrapper Classes***”, Way2Java, https://way2java.com/java-lang/wrapper-classes/

"***Bingo (U.S.)***", https://en.wikipedia.org/wiki/Bingo_(U.S.)

Chapter 6

"***Array of Objects***", Java With Us, http://www.javawithus.com/tutorial/array-of-objects

"***Java ArrayList of Object Sort Example (Comparable And Comparator)***", Chaitanya Singh, https://beginnersbook.com/2013/12/java-arraylist-of-object-sort-example-comparable-and-comparator/

"***JAR file (Java Archive)***", Margaret Rouse, http://www.theserverside.com/definition/JAR-file-Java-ARchive

"***45+ Most Useful Java Libraries***", Sachin, http://www.fromdev.com/2014/10/most-widely-used-java-libraries.html, October 8, 2014.

"***Polymorphism in Java with example***", Chaitanya Singh, https://beginnersbook.com/2013/03/polymorphism-in-java/

"***Java Polymorphism with Example***", Lokesh Gupta, https://howtodoinjava.com/object-oriented/what-is-polymorphism-in-java/, July 15, 2013.

"***Declaring Member Variables***", The Java™ Tutorials, https://docs.oracle.com/javase/tutorial/java/javaOO/variables.html

"***Encapsulation (computer programming)***", https://en.wikipedia.org/wiki/Encapsulation_(computer_programming)

"***Instance (computer science)***", https://en.wikipedia.org/wiki/Instance_(computer_science)

"***Instance Variable vs Local Variable in java example***", VK. Jegan, http://javaonlineguide.net/2014/05/instance-variable-vs-local-variable-in.html

"***Class vs. Instance***", The Anatomy of a Java Application, The Java Tutorial!, Mary Campione and Kathy Walrath, http://www.cs.princeton.edu/courses/archive/spr96/cs333/java/tutorial/java/anatomy/static.html

“***Difference between instance class and local variables in Java***“,Javin Paul, http://javarevisited.blogspot.com/2012/02/difference-between-instance-class-and.html

Chapter 7

“***Abstract Class***”, https://www.techopedia.com/definition/17408/abstract-class

“***Generate class constructors in Eclipse based on fields or superclass constructors***”, Byron, http://www.eclipseonetips.com/2010/03/08/generate-class-constructors-in-eclipse-based-on-fields-or-superclass-constructors/

“***Generic Types***”, The Java™ Tutorials, https://docs.oracle.com/javase/tutorial/java/generics/types.html

Java source code Websites:

http://grepcode.com/
http://www.docjar.com/

“***Java – Polymorphism***”, Learn Java Programming, Tutorialspoint, https://www.tutorialspoint.com/java/java_polymorphism.htm

“***Java Access Modifiers - Public, Private, Protected***”, Alberto Pareja-Lecaros, java-made-easy.com, https://www.java-made-easy.com/java-access-modifiers.html

“***UML Class Diagrams***”, The University of Wisconsin Madison http://pages.cs.wisc.edu/~hasti/cs302/examples/UMLdiagram.html

"***All the UML you need to know***”, Paul Gestwicki, Ball State University, http://www.cs.bsu.edu/~pvg/misc/uml/

ObjectAid - http://www.objectaid.com/installation

Achitexa - http://www.architexa.com/learn-more/download

Violet UML Editor - http://alexdp.free.fr/violetumleditor/page.php

Eclipse Papyrus Documentation - https://www.eclipse.org/papyrus/documentation.html

"***Java reverse engineering***", Abel Hegedus, Andy Halper and Ansgar Radermacher, Shuai Li, et al. https://wiki.eclipse.org/Java_reverse_engineering

"***Class Diagram***", https://en.wikipedia.org/wiki/Class_diagram

"***UML, Abstract Classes and Methods, and Interfaces***", The Oxford Math Center, http://www.oxfordmathcenter.com/drupal7/node/35

"***The class diagram - An introduction to structure diagrams in UML 2***", Donald Bell, IBM, https://www.ibm.com/developerworks/rational/library/content/RationalEdge/sep04/bell/index.html, September 15, 2004.

Math Formulas: http://www.math.com/tables/geometry/volumes.htm and http://www.math.com/tables/geometry/surfareas.htm

__Chapter 8__

"***Capability Maturity Model (CMM)***" - https://en.wikipedia.org/wiki/Capability_Maturity_Model

"***Things every Java developer must know about Exception handling***", Umer Mansoor, https://10kloc.wordpress.com/2013/03/09/runtimeexceptions-try-catch-or-not-to-catch/ March 9, 2013

"***Checked vs Unchecked Exceptions in Java***", GeeksforGeeks.com, https://www.geeksforgeeks.org/checked-vs-unchecked-exceptions-in-java/

"***Checked versus unchecked exceptions***", Javapractices.com, http://www.javapractices.com/topic/TopicAction.do?Id=129

"***Lesson: Exceptions***", The Java™ Tutorials, https://docs.oracle.com/javase/tutorial/essential/exceptions/index.html

Java Exception Diagram - http://www.falkhausen.de/Java-8/java.lang/Exceptions.html

"***Java Custom Exception Example***", Chandan Singh, JavaCodeGeeks.com, https://examples.javacodegeeks.com/java-basics/exceptions/java-custom-exception-example/, November 3, 2014.

"***A Java Programmer's Guide to Assembler Language***", Stephan Rauh, BeyondJava.net, https://www.beyondjava.net/blog/java-programmers-guide-assembler-language/, January 17, 2015.

"***[JVM] How to see Assembly code for your Java Program***", Ashish Paliwal, https://www.ashishpaliwal.com/blog/2013/05/jvm-how-to-see-assembly-code-for-your-java-program/, May 7, 2013.

"***Experimentation Notes: Java Print Assembly***", http://psy-lob-saw.blogspot.in/2013/01/java-print-assembly.html

"***From Java to Assembly: Down the Rabbit Hole: An adventure in JVM Wonderland***", Charles Oliver Nutter, https://www.youtube.com/watch?v=7p1_S-6bWhk

"***Refactor Actions***", http://help.eclipse.org/luna/index.jsp?topic=%2Forg.eclipse.jdt.doc.user%2Freference%2Fref-menu-refactor.htm

"***Explore refactoring functions in Eclipse JDT***", Prashant Deva, IBM, https://www.ibm.com/developerworks/library/os-eclipse-refactoring/, November 24, 2009.

"***Refactoring for everyone***", David Gallardo, IBM, https://www.ibm.com/developerworks/library/os-ecref/, September 9, 2003.

"***Code Refactoring***", https://en.wikipedia.org/wiki/Code_refactoring

"***VisualVM for Java Development***", Eric Bruno, Dr. Dobb's, http://www.drdobbs.com/jvm/visualvm-for-java-development/229403052?cid=DDJ_nl_cpp_2013-03-21_h&elq=699f427baa0d4c3b8bfad2cffdef3efa
May 09, 2011.

Chapter 9

"***Recursion (computer science)***", https://en.wikipedia.org/wiki/Recursion_(computer_science)

"***What is recursion and when should I use it?***", https://stackoverflow.com/questions/3021/what-is-recursion-and-when-should-i-use-it

"***Mastering recursive programming***", Jonathan Bartlett, IBM, https://www.ibm.com/developerworks/library/l-recurs/ , June 16, 2005.

"***Understanding Tail Recursion***", Chris Smith, Microsoft, https://blogs.msdn.microsoft.com/chrsmith/2008/08/07/understanding-tail-recursion/, August 7, 2008.

"***What is tail recursion?***", https://cs.stackexchange.com/questions/6230/what-is-tail-recursion

"***Tail Recursion***", http://wiki.c2.com/?TailRecursion%20=%20this%20was%20used%20for

"Threads, Call Stack, Stepping",
https://www.dvteclipse.com/documentation/e/Threads.2C_Call_Stack.2C_Stepping.html

The site for integer sequences – http://oeis.org

"***Hofstadter sequence***", https://en.wikipedia.org/wiki/Hofstadter_sequence

Chapter 10

"***A beginner's guide to Big O notation***", Rob Bell, https://rob-bell.net/2009/06/a-beginners-guide-to-big-o-notation/

"***Big O Notations***", Derek Banas, https://www.youtube.com/watch?v=V6mKVRU1evU&=&list=PLGLfVvz_LVvReUrWr94U-ZMgjYTQ538nT&=&index=9

"***Big O Notations***", Derek Banas, http://www.newthinktank.com/2013/03/big-o-notations/, March 18, 2013

"***Big O notation***", https://en.wikipedia.org/wiki/Big_O_notation

Big-O Cheat Sheet - http://bigocheatsheet.com/

"***Analysis of algorithms***", https://en.wikipedia.org/wiki/Analysis_of_algorithms

"***What is the big O notation and how do I calculate it? Will you give me examples of code and their corresponding representations in O notation?***", Gayle Laakmann McDowell, https://www.quora.com/What-is-the-big-O-notation-and-how-do-I-calculate-it-Will-you-give-me-examples-of-code-and-their-corresponding-representations-in-O-notation, September 17, 2013

"***Algorithms Lesson 6: Big O, Big Omega, and Big Theta Notation***", XoaX.net https://www.youtube.com/watch?v=6Ol2JbwoJp0, February 19, 2010

"***Big O Notation***", Andrew Ellinor, Ivan Koswara, Agnishom Chattopadhyay,et al., brilliant.org. https://brilliant.org/wiki/big-o-notation/

"***How to calculate binary search complexity***", https://stackoverflow.com/questions/8185079/how-to-calculate-binary-search-complexity

"***Mergesort in java***", https://stackoverflow.com/questions/13727030/mergesort-in-java

"***Program: Implement merge sort in java***", Nataraja Gootooru, Java2novice.com, http://www.java2novice.com/java-sorting-algorithms/merge-sort/

"***Merge Sort Java Example***", Lokesh Gupta, HowToDoInJava.com, https://howtodoinjava.com/algorithm/merge-sort-java-example/, October 23, 2015.

"***Merge Sort using Java with program code***", Code2Learn.com, http://www.code2learn.com/2011/07/merge-sort-using-java.html

"***Merge Sort: Java Sorting Program Code along with Example***", Subham Mittal, http://javahungry.blogspot.com/2013/06/java-sorting-program-code-merge-sort.html

"***Analysis of merge sort***", Thomas Cormen and Devin Balkcom, Khan Academy, https://www.khanacademy.org/computing/computer-science/algorithms/merge-sort/a/analysis-of-merge-sort

"***Analysis of MergeSort and QuickSort***", Lydia Sinapova, Simpson College, http://faculty.simpson.edu/lydia.sinapova/www/cmsc250/LN250_Tremblay/L08-AnalysisMergeSort.htm,

"***Java Program to Implement Merge Sort***", Manish Bhojasia, http://www.sanfoundry.com/java-program-implement-merge-sort/

"***QuickSort Java Example***", Lokesh Gupta, HowToDoInJava.com, https://howtodoinjava.com/algorithm/quicksort-java-example/, October 28, 2015.

"***QuickSort Sorting Algorithm in Java***", Javin Paul, Javarevisited.com, http://javarevisited.blogspot.com/2014/08/quicksort-sorting-algorithm-in-java-in-place-example.html

"***QuickSort***", https://en.wikipedia.org/wiki/Quicksort

"***Overview of quicksort***", Thomas Cormen and Devin Balkcom, Khan Academy, https://www.khanacademy.org/computing/computer-science/algorithms/quick-sort/a/overview-of-quicksort

"***Analysis of quicksort***", Thomas Cormen and Devin Balkcom, Khan Academy, https://www.khanacademy.org/computing/computer-science/algorithms/quick-sort/a/analysis-of-quicksort

Chapter 11

"***Event-driven programming***", https://en.wikipedia.org/wiki/Event-driven_programming

"***Creating Javafx Project in Eclipse***", Pranish Shrestha, https://www.youtube.com/watch?v=s7fUJKt9PkU, April 10, 2014.

"***Bye Bye JavaFX Scene Builder, Welcome Gluon Scene Builder 8.0.0***", Bennet Schulz, DZone.com, https://dzone.com/articles/bye-bye-javafx-scene-builder, March 14, 2015

"***What Is JavaFX?***", Monica Pawlan, Oracle, https://docs.oracle.com/javafx/2/overview/jfxpub-overview.htm, April 2013.

"***JavaFX - The Rich Client Platform***", http://www.oracle.com/technetwork/java/javase/overview/javafx-overview-2158620.html

"***Learning JavaFX GUI Development***", Peggy Fisher, Lynda.com, https://www.lynda.com/Java-tutorials/JavaFX-GUI-Development/466182-2.html, May 26, 2016.

"***Using Scene Builder with Eclipse IDE***", Jerome Cambon and Cindy Castillo, Oracle, https://docs.oracle.com/javafx/scenebuilder/1/use_java_ides/sb-with-eclipse.htm, October 2013.

E(fx)clipse - http://www.eclipse.org/efxclipse/install.html

"***Swing (Java)***", https://en.wikipedia.org/wiki/Swing_(Java)

"***WindowBuilder - is a powerful and easy to use bi-directional Java GUI designer***", https://eclipse.org/windowbuilder/

"***Standard Widget Toolkit***", https://en.wikipedia.org/wiki/Standard_Widget_Toolkit

"***Why is Swing Called Swing?"***, https://blogs.oracle.com/thejavatutorials/why-is-swing-called-swing

"***A Visual Guide to Layout Managers"***, The Java™ Tutorials, https://docs.oracle.com/javase/tutorial/uiswing/layout/visual.html

Chapter 12

"***JavaFX 8 Tutorial***", Marco Jakob, code.makery.ch, http://code.makery.ch/library/javafx-8-tutorial/, April 19, 2014.

"***Byte stream and Character stream***", https://stackoverflow.com/questions/3013996/byte-stream-and-character-stream

"***Character Stream Vs Byte Stream in Java***", Mohit Gupta, GeeksforGeeks.com, https://www.geeksforgeeks.org/character-stream-vs-byte-stream-java/

"***Introduction to I/O STREAMS in JAVA***", Hitesh Garg, Codinggeek.com, https://www.codingeek.com/java/io/introduction-to-io-streams-in-java/, October 14, 2014.

"***Java.io.ObjectInputStream.readObject() Method***", Learn Java Programming, Tutorialspoint, http://www.tutorialspoint.com/java/io/objectinputstream_readobject.htm

"***Java – Serialization***", Learn Java Programming, Tutorialspoint, http://www.tutorialspoint.com/java/java_serialization.htm

"***Java IO Overview***", Jakob Jenkov, http://tutorials.jenkov.com/java-io/overview.html, October 7, 2014.

"***How to Print Text***", The Java™ Tutorials, https://docs.oracle.com/javase/tutorial/uiswing/misc/printtext.html

"***Printing for JavaFX***", https://wiki.openjdk.java.net/display/OpenJFX/Printing+for+JavaFX

"***JavaFX How to - Print Text out***",.java2s.com, http://www.java2s.com/Tutorials/Java/JavaFX_How_to/Print/Print_Text_out.htm

"***Introduction by Example: JavaFX 8 Printing***", Carl Dea, Dzone.com, https://dzone.com/articles/introduction-example-javafx-8, July 17, 2013.

"***How to Save from JTextArea using JFileChooser as a TXT file***", Sultan Altoobi, coderanch.com, https://coderanch.com/t/561950/java/Save-JTextArea-JFileChooser-TXT-file

"***Customizing a JFileChooser : File Chooser « Swing JFC « Java***", java2s.com, http://www.java2s.com/Code/Java/Swing-JFC/CustomizingaJFileChooser.htm

Chapter 13

"***Abstract data type***", https://en.wikipedia.org/wiki/Abstract_data_type

"***Java Programming Examples on Data-Structures***", Manish Bhojasia, , http://www.sanfoundry.com/java-programming-examples-data-structures/

"***Algorithms and Data Structures***", Introduction to Programming in Java, Robert Sedgewick and Kevin Wayne, https://introcs.cs.princeton.edu/java/home/ October 20, 2017.

"***Collections Framework Overview***", https://docs.oracle.com/javase/8/docs/technotes/guides/collections/overview.html

Java Collections Cheat Sheet - http://files.zeroturnaround.com/pdf/zt_java_collections_cheat_sheet.pdf

"***Collection Classes Summary Table***", programcreek.com , https://www.programcreek.com/2009/02/collection-interface-concrete-implementation-classes-summary-and-some-examples/

"***Annotated Outline of Collections Framework***", https://docs.oracle.com/javase/6/docs/technotes/guides/collections/reference.html

"***Collections Overview***", Fred Swartz, https://www.leepoint.net/data/collections/06overview.html

"***Big-O summary for Java Collections Framework implementations?***", https://stackoverflow.com/questions/559839/big-o-summary-for-java-collections-framework-implementations

"***Difference between ArrayList and LinkedList in Java***", Chaitanya Singh, https://beginnersbook.com/2013/12/difference-between-arraylist-and-linkedlist-in-java/,

"***5 Difference between ArrayList and LinkedList in Java with Example***", Subham Mittal, http://javahungry.blogspot.com/2015/04/difference-between-arraylist-and-linkedlist-in-java-example.html

"***Using JavaFX Collections***", Scott Hommel, Oracle, https://docs.oracle.com/javafx/2/collections/jfxpub-collections.htm, April 2013.

"***JavaFX Collection's ObservableList and ObservableMap***", DZone.com, https://dzone.com/articles/javafx-collections-observablelist-and-observablema

"***Trail: Collections***", The Java™ Tutorials, https://docs.oracle.com/javase/tutorial/collections/index.html

Chapter 14

"***Tutorial : How To Change The Cursor in JavaFX***", Nathan Howard , IDR Solutions, https://blog.idrsolutions.com/2014/05/tutorial-change-default-cursor-javafx/

"***Class ImageCursor***", https://docs.oracle.com/javafx/2/api/javafx/scene/ImageCursor.html

"***Using Text in JavaFX***", JavaFX: Working with JavaFX UI Components, https://docs.oracle.com/javase/8/javafx/user-interface-tutorial/text-settings.htm

"***FXGL — a JavaFX library for game developers***", Almas Baimagambetov, JaxEnter.com, https://jaxenter.com/fxgl-a-javafx-library-for-game-developers-127807.html, July 19, 2016.

"***List of game engines***", https://en.wikipedia.org/wiki/List_of_game_engines

"***Game Loops!***", Eli Delventhal, Java-Gaming.org, http://www.java-gaming.org/index.php?topic=24220.0

"***Using the JavaFX AnimationTimer***", Michael, https://netopyr.com/2012/06/14/using-the-javafx-animationtimer/, June 14, 2012

"***Game loops Applying the theory to JavaFX***", Steven Van Impe, http://svanimpe.be/blog/game-loops-fx

"***Animation Basics***", Dmitry Kostovarov and Andrey Nazarov, Oracle, https://docs.oracle.com/javafx/2/animations/basics.htm

"***Using Transitions to Simplify JavaFX Animations***", Jeff Friesen, informit.com, http://www.informit.com/articles/article.aspx?p=2359759, July 2, 2015.

"***Introduction to JavaFX for Game Development***", Lee Stemkoski, https://gamedevelopment.tutsplus.com/tutorials/introduction-to-javafx-for-game-development--cms-23835 May 19, 2015

"***JavaFX 2 GameTutorial***", Carl Dea, https://carlfx.wordpress.com/2012/03/29/javafx-2-gametutorial-part-1/

"***Space Invaders FX***", The Techno Lark, http://technolark.blogspot.com/, January 10, 2013.

"***Introduction to JavaFX Media***", Cindy Castillo, Oracle, https://docs.oracle.com/javafx/2/media/overview.htm, April 2013.

"***Introduction to JavaFX Media***", https://docs.oracle.com/javase/8/javafx/media-tutorial/overview.htm

"***JavaFX 8 Event Handling Examples***", Marco Jakob , http://code.makery.ch/blog/javafx-8-event-handling-examples/ , May 03, 2014

"***Getting Started with JavaFX Game Programming***", http://www.java-gaming.org/topics/getting-started-with-javafx-game-programming-for-java-programmers/37201/view.html

Almas Baimagambetov's JavaFX and FXGL Game Videos:
https://www.youtube.com/channel/UCmjXvUa36DjqCJ1zktXVbUA

FXTutorials, Almas Baimagambetov, https://github.com/AlmasB/FXTutorials

"***Sprite***", TechTerms, https://techterms.com/definition/sprite

"***Sprite (computer graphics)***", https://en.wikipedia.org/wiki/Sprite_(computer_graphics)

B Table of Code Listings

C Index

D

E

F

G

H

I

J

K

L

M

O

P

Q

R

S

T

U

V

W

X

Y

CPSIA information can be obtained
at www.ICGtesting.com
Printed in the USA
BVHW050541280820
587361BV00003B/32

9 780991 188734